HARLEM'S RATTLERS AND THE GREAT WAR

# Modern War Studies

# Harlem's Rattlers
## and the
# Great War

The Undaunted 369th Regiment

& the African American Quest

for Equality

JEFFREY T. SAMMONS AND
JOHN H. MORROW, JR.

University Press of Kansas

Published by the University Press of Kansas (Lawrence, Kansas 66045), which was organized
by the Kansas Board of Regents and is operated and funded by Emporia State University,
Fort Hays State University, Kansas State University, Pittsburg State University, the University
of Kansas, and Wichita State University

Library of Congress Cataloging-in-Publication Data
Sammons, Jeffrey T. (Jeffrey Thomas), 1949–
    Harlem's Rattlers and the Great War : the undaunted 369th Regiment and the African
American quest for equality / Jeffrey T. Sammons and John H. Morrow, Jr.
        pages cm. — (Modern war studies)
    Includes bibliographical references and index.
    ISBN 978-0-7006-1957-3 (cloth)
1. United States. Army. Infantry Regiment, 369th. 2. World War, 1914–1918—Regimental
histories—United States. 3. World War, 1914–1918—Participation, African American.
4. World War, 1914–1918—Campaigns—Western Front. 5. United States. Army. American
Expeditionary Forces—African American troops. 6. France. Armée—African American
troops—History—20th century. 7. African American soldiers—History—20th century.
8. African Americans—Social conditions—To 1964. I. Morrow, John Howard, 1944–
II. Title.
    D570.33369th .S25    2014
    940.4'1273—dc23
                                                                                          2014001451

British Library Cataloguing-in-Publication Data is available.

Printed in the United States of America
10  9  8  7  6  5  4  3  2  1

The paper used in this publication is recycled and contains 30 percent postconsumer waste.
It is acid free and meets the minimum requirements of the American National Standard for
Permanence of Paper for Printed Library Materials Z39.48-1992.

Dedicated to the men of the 15th/369th
who served and sacrificed
and to all who supported them

CONTENTS

Acknowledgments, *ix*

Introduction, *1*

1 "He HAS a Flag": The Relationship of the Military to
Black Identity, Community, and Citizenship and the
Origins of the Black Regiment Movement, *22*

2 "Positions of Honor and Trust": Charles Ward Fillmore,
the Equity Congress, and the Byzantine Politics of the
Black Regiment Movement, *41*

3 "Second Only to . . . the Emancipation Proclamation":
The Trying Campaign from Authorization to Formation, *69*

4 "Mulligan's Guards": The (Re)-Birth and Growing Pains
of the 15th New York National Guard, *94*

5 War and Expediency: The Politics of Federal Recognition,
Regimental Training, and the President's Call to Service, *119*

6 Race War at Home or Combat Abroad? Tested in the
White-Hot Crucible of Camp Life, *156*

7 "Over There": The 15th New York/369th Regiment
in France: From the AEF to the French Army,
January–April 1918, *189*

8 Trial by Fire: In Combat with the French 16th Infantry
Division, Mid-April to June 1918, *217*

9 "The Battle of Henry Johnson" and Neadom Roberts:
The Night Two Ordinary Men Became War Heroes and
Race Symbols, *265*

10 A Midsummer's Nightmare: Race Swirls above the 369th, May–August 1918, *296*

11 The Big Push: Offensives in Champagne/Meuse-Argonne and the Capture of Séchault, September 7–October 4, 1918, *327*

12 War's End: Final Campaign, First to the Rhine, Occupation, and Hasty Departure, *357*

13 "War Crossed Abroad and Double Crossed at Home": Triumphant Heroes, Objects of Ridicule, or Fearsome Trained Killers?, *381*

14 Your Services Are No Longer Needed: The War Department's Postwar Decimation and Denigration of Black Soldiers and the 369th's Fight for Survival and Recognition, *399*

15 Winning the Battle and Losing the War: The Renewed Fight for a Black Commander and the Disfiguring Transformations of the 369th, *422*

Conclusion: Henry Johnson and Neadom Roberts: Cautionary Tales, *447*

Epilogue: A Brief Look at the Postwar Careers and Lives of a Few Outstanding Black and White Officers and Men, *476*

Appendix: Deaths in the 369th Infantry during Service with the 93rd Division, AEF, *491*

List of Acronyms, *499*

Notes, *501*

Bibliography, *585*

Index, *597*

*An illustration gallery follows page 242.*

I thank Harold Rabinowitz of Reference Works for approaching me to write a book on the 369th. Although our differing visions led to an eventual separation, I doubt that I would have ever pursued this project without his encouragement. As testament to his foresight and the project's worth, grant proposals led to essential support from the National Endowment for the Humanities in the form of a year-long fellowship for university professors and a scholar-in-residence award for six months at the Schomburg Center for Research in Black Culture. There, I benefited from the support of the center's former director, Howard Dodson; its former director of the Scholars' Program, Colin Palmer; and Diana Lachatanere, its former curator. I also thank my fellow scholars, especially Barbara Savage, who alerted me to the critical connection of the 369th to *Stormy Weather*. Film scholar Annette Brauerhoch of the University of Paderborn helped me interrogate it and provided valuable insights into European repositories as well as battlefields and cemeteries from the Rhine to the Rhone to the Meuse-Argonne and beyond.

Early in the process, I realized that my expertise in African American social and cultural history would be inadequate to do justice to either the foreign or the military experience of the Regiment. Without hesitation, I enlisted the partnership of my friend John Morrow, a leading military historian of World War I with fluency in French and German and, by fortunate circumstance, great familiarity with the French records of the 369th. This book would be very different and far less complete without his invaluable input and perspective. The collaboration was far greater than the sum of its parts. Enduring countless setbacks along the way that could have led to resignation or surrender, we drew upon deep reserves of resolve and persevered, in the process strengthening a partnership that would have made the ultimate partners, James Reese Europe and Noble Sissle, proud.

Of course, a work so steeped in primary sources owes much to the largely unsung heroes of history—archivists and librarians. First among them is Dr. James Folts of the New York State Archives. Dr. Folts facilitated the microfilming of the abstracts and muster rolls of the 15th/369th and thereby made easy access to those records possible for me as well as other scholars. As a result of his support, I also received a grant from the Larry J. Hackman Research Residency Program. As I am fond of saying, with any research project all roads lead to Washington, DC, and invariably the National Archives and Library of Congress. Mitchell Yockelson, at the former, proved invaluable in sharing his encyclopedic knowledge of the World War I records at the National Archives and Records Administration. No single repository has provided more primary material to this book than the National Archives. At the latter (LOC), I am indebted to Adrienne Cannon, who directed me to and through the NAACP Papers as well as those of William Howard Taft. Another important destination is the Moorland-Spingarn Research Center, where, with the help of curator Joellen ElBashir, I pored through the papers of Joel Spingarn, Walter Loving, and the Washington Conservatory of Music. Ann Distell of the Federal Bureau of Prisons, Tim Rives formerly of the National Archives–Central Plains Region, and Greg McCrory of the National Archives of Canada made telling the still unfinished story of Valdo B. Schita possible.

There are so many others at collections, from the New York Historical Society to Cornell to Yale to West Point to the Army War College and more, who contributed to this project. Please forgive me for not mentioning all of you by name.

Not to be forgotten are the friends of the Regiment, starting with former commanders Maj. Gen. Nathaniel James and Maj. Gen. Stephen Seiter, both of whom provided vital information and access. Included in that category is Michael Aikey, former director of the New York State Military History Museum. Few know the history of this Regiment as well as he and what kind of book will do it justice. We hope that he will be pleased with what he reads here. Perhaps no greater friend of the Regiment ever lived than Vietnam War veteran John Howe, who fought tirelessly to see Henry Johnson receive the recognition he so justly deserves. John and I became friends over the years, and I am sad to say that he passed before the completion of this book. To honor his memory, we will continue his unfinished mission to have Henry receive the Medal of Honor.

I am most grateful to the invaluable research assistance provided by Brian Purnell, Shobana Shankar, and Rebecca Welch. Without their fine work, the story in this book never could have been so deeply told or richly documented. I also thank my friend and former colleague Walter Johnson for his encouragement. Last, let me thank my wife, Mariam, whose patience has been severely tested by a seemingly never-ending project with far too many twists and turns and ups and downs to instill confidence in a happy resolution.

My son Adam, now a young adult, was in middle school when the project began. I do not know whether he learned a lesson about procrastination or perseverance from his vantage point. I only hope that my ailing mother, Agnes Greene, will be as proud of this book as she was of my first, oh so many years ago.

*Jeffrey T. Sammons*
New York University

I thank my colleague and friend Jeff Sammons, professor of history at New York University, for inviting me to join him in writing the history of the 15th/369th Regiment. The book has certainly benefited from our complementary research foci in African American and military history and our consequent exchange of ideas. Jeff essentially did most of the research for the book based on sources in American archives, whereas I added the research in French archives. The result is a study of the famed Regiment that is based on more extensive archival research in the United States and France than previous histories of the 15th/369th.

I am also indebted to Brig. Gen. (ret.) Robert A. Doughty, former professor and head of the Department of History at the US Military Academy (USMA), West Point, the leading American authority on the French army in World War I. Through his auspices, I was a visiting professor of history at USMA in 2005, an unforgettable experience that proved most beneficial to my research. Bob introduced me to the helpful staff of the library, who made the papers and diary of John Wesley Castles available to me. He then wrote me a personal introduction to his friend Col. Frédéric Guelton, directeur des recherches (director of research) at the Service Historique de l'Armée de Terre (Army Historical Service) in Vincennes, who graciously offered his advice and then opened the archives to me.

Jeff and I have appreciated the enthusiastic reception and continued support that Mike Briggs, editor in chief of the University Press of Kansas, has extended to our work, as well as the detailed assessment and recommendations of reader Chad L. Williams and the strong endorsement of reader Bob Doughty. Finally, my Franklin Professorship at the University of Georgia enabled me to do the research and visit the battlefields in France and to pay for the rights to some of the photographs in the book.

My family members—in particular my wife, Diane Batts Morrow, a noted historian in her own right—have always provided me with support and inspiration. The war veterans of the Batts Morrow family remained foremost in my mind throughout the project: my great-uncle on my mother's side, Thomas Davis of the 368th Regiment, 92nd Division, who was awarded the Distinguished Service Cross and the Croix de Guerre for his exploits at Binarville, France, on October 30, 1918; my father-in-law, Dr.

James A. Batts, Jr., awarded a Bronze Star for his service as a regimental surgeon in the 92nd Division in northern Italy, 1944–1945; my uncle, Lt. William Morrow, an infantry officer who served in the North African and Italian campaigns, 1942–1945; and our son, SFC Evan Batts Morrow, who was awarded the Bronze Star for his service in Iraq during deployments that lasted from 2005 to 2010. May my contribution to this important work serve as a tribute not only to the men of the 15th/369th but also to those family members who have served the country overseas in time of war.

*John H. Morrow, Jr.*
Franklin Professor of History
The University of Georgia

HARLEM'S RATTLERS AND THE GREAT WAR

# Introduction

It is only fitting that this book begins and essentially ends with the first combat hero of the 369th Regiment, Henry Johnson, for no single member is more closely identified with its history and reputation and also its mythology. Shortly after the war, a reporter for the *New York Age* asked the little sergeant to describe the events of May 15, 1918, in which he and Neadom Roberts repelled an attack by a German raiding party.[1] According to the article, Johnson recalled that a French lieutenant had warned him to move back from his outpost because of a possible enemy raid. In response, he proclaimed, "I'm an American, and I never retreat." These words bear a striking similarity to those attributed earlier to Col. William Hayward, the Regiment's first commander, a white man. As reported by the same paper, when ordered to retreat by a French general during an assault, Hayward instead led a charge and defiantly replied, "My men never retire. They go forward or they die."[2]

Whether either man really said what has been ascribed to him can never be known for sure. In Johnson's case, the *Age* more than likely embellished or fabricated a story and unquestionably intended to contribute to the race's newest and perhaps greatest icon by representing him as a quintessential lone hero. Yet, by appropriating the pithy retort of his white leader and by fixing his identity as "American," the paper used Johnson to signify black leadership of the Regiment, in deed if not in rank, as yet more justification for black people's claim to martial valor as a prerequisite to full and unqualified citizenship.[3] For better or worse and certainly beyond Johnson's control, serving as an instrument for others' voices and purposes became the ultimate statement of this seemingly reticent man's life and death.

However, the usefulness of these utterances and the identity of their sources transcend concerns with factual accuracy. These mythic pronouncements reportedly out of those heroic mouths speak to a larger representation of a Regiment that by most accounts never lost a man to capture or a foot of ground that it had taken. Its adopted symbol, the rattlesnake, reinforced that record and simultaneously reflected and contributed to the standard the Regiment set for undaunted courage and tenacity. "The Rattlers" was the appellation the men gave themselves and embraced. The rattlesnake identified these citizen-soldiers with a Revolutionary War icon of indigenous power, defiance, and independence frequently associated with Benjamin Franklin's attacks on the Crown and indelibly captured in the motto of the Gadsden flag, "Don't Tread on Me." No one could provoke it with impunity: "Nemo me impune lacesset." The men clearly adopted the meaning and power of the symbol and understood its relation to their self-identification and role. By appropriating *the* American snake, they indicated their readiness to fight battles against internal as well as external foes.

Thus, joining the Regiment did not signal loyalty to country as much as it served as a means to an end, namely, full citizenship for self and, by extension, the "race." These men did not fight the war to make the world safe for democracy; instead, they fought to convince America to live up to its democratic promise. The nickname that endures, however, is "Harlem Hellfighters," probably because it was alliterative, more sensational, otherworldly, and assigned from without, not by the French or Germans but most likely by the American press. Still, like most myths, ideas that stand over facts, the name survives as the result of its racial value and its frequent reinforcement by scholars, popularizers, politicians, and especially those associated with the Regiment today. The absence of this nickname in this book's title signals our commitment to telling the story right even at the risk of alienating those who have embraced the term and associated the Regiment with it as part of a mythmaking and / or tradition-preserving practice. Our purpose is not to invoke the familiar or to confirm conventional wisdom and certainly not to perpetuate and reinforce myths.

Moreover, the book's subtitle gestures to far more than the Regiment's combat experience because the word *undaunted* conveys the idea of moving forward and never giving up, thereby capturing the essence of the organization's protracted and difficult struggle for recognition and survival. Before the end of the nineteenth century, New York's citizens had initiated and pressed the fight for an all-black National Guard infantry unit. Against overwhelming odds, they succeeded. Even in its long gestation period, the 15th/369th Regiment had been nourished and tempered by the fierce determination of its proponents to secure an institution that would counter the horrendous stereotypes of blacks, especially men, as indolent, ignorant, immoral, violent, and cowardly "coons" and instead signify them as ready for and deserving of full and equal citizenship. Thus, a never say die/never give up spirit and record have always marked the Regiment and its first real hero, Charles Ward Fillmore, who overcame personal disgrace, internecine power struggles, and fierce external opposition to keep the regiment campaign alive for six long and torturous years, from his initial involvement in 1910 to official authorization in 1916.

The history of the 15th New York National Guard/369th Regiment in the pages that follow is largely a World War I–era narrative. Yet, as will become clear, this Regiment's story begins well before the war, and its influence and impact continue to resonate, albeit in modulated tones, to this very day. A ride up the Harlem River Drive reveals a relatively new exit sign at 135th and Madison reading "369th Harlem Hellfighters' Drive," courtesy of a New York State Department of Transportation ceremonial redesignation of the parkway stretching from 131st Street north to 145th Street. A few blocks west at Fifth Avenue and 142nd and 143rd Streets stands the massive 369th Armory, a stunning, living monument to the men and women who campaigned for an all-black National Guard regiment and to those who fought and died in the service of their country. The armory, built in stages between 1921 and 1933, houses a hall of fame dedicated to the history of this proud unit.[4] The centerpiece of that hall is a replica of the monument erected in 1997 in Séchault, France, honoring the Regiment's successful assault on the German stronghold in that tiny village in the Champagne region.

Each year in May, the 369th Veterans Association marches up Fifth Avenue to honor the memory of the Regiment and to remind the community of the treasure it helped to supply and support.[5] This lasting significance has found added reinforcement in a recent spate of books, essays, documentaries, and Internet representations as well as in the activities of the 369th Historical Society and in ongoing efforts to secure the Medal of Honor for Henry Johnson. Perhaps no finer tribute to the Regiment's lasting significance could be given than that by Toni Morrison in her 1992 novel *Jazz*, in which the homecoming parade of the fighting "three six nine" filled protagonist Joe Trace with so much pride that it "split his heart in two."[6]

Possibly the most revealing measure of the Old 15th's lasting appeal and value, however, can be found in its symbolic call to service in 1943. Almost twenty-five years after the Regiment triumphantly returned home and marched up Fifth Avenue and at the same time that its successor, the 369th, returned from action in the Pacific theater of war, Hollywood released *Stormy Weather*, a film that reprised some of that notable occasion for the ostensible viewing pleasure of thousands. The Regiment's role in the film may have done more to etch the 15th/369th in popular memory than any other treatment. Yet, even that seemingly innocuous portrayal almost failed to materialize, as social and political turmoil gave pause to Hollywood executives and federal officials.[7] Sad to say, had the decision to withhold release prevailed, the memory of the Regiment might have been the better for it. Despite much contemporary and more recent critical commentary about the film, short shrift has been given to the film's (mis)treatment of the 15th/369th Infantry and how it failed to do justice to a deserving organization and, by extension, to all blacks. The film trivialized the performance and role of the individual soldier of the 15th, and it almost certainly contributed to a distorted history of the Regiment that has influenced significantly many subsequent treatments of it to this day. There can be little doubt that it and other war films of the time were meant to correspond to the War Department's visions of and policies toward black combatants. World War II for blacks, irrespective of the Double V campaign, was like déjà vu, which points to how connected these events were and how significant the first was to all that followed as part of the long freedom struggle. Only recently has World War I received historical justice and an effective counternarrative emerged, yet it resides most forcefully and successfully in works that address the broader context of blacks in the Great War, as will be discussed.

The summer of 1943 was an extraordinarily troubled time in America. While United States and its Allies battled the Axis powers for world dominance and perhaps humanity's future, palpable racial tension threatened to tear the nation apart from within. For example, the national defense industry's discrimination against blacks provoked a march on Washington movement in the middle of a war campaign that targeted fascism and nazism. Some suggested, in jest, that Adolf Hitler was giving racism a bad name and making Americans look like hypocrites. Race riots erupted in Detroit, Harlem, and Los Angeles, but they were only the most visible expressions of smoldering discontent on the part of blacks, who responded forcefully to the massive oppression and repression meted out by white individuals and government authorities.

The domestic press reported racially inflected and motivated lynchings, shootings, and labor disputes throughout the country. Black soldiers occupied the center of many such encounters—mostly as victims, sometimes as defenders, and rarely as aggressors. Civil rights activists protested Jim Crow policies and conditions within the nation's military bases. In fact,

Robert Weaver, one member of Franklin Roosevelt's so-called black cabinet, concluded that resentment toward discrimination in the armed services was the "primary, fundamental cause" of the Harlem riot.[8] Ironically, not long before that event, the 369th, according to political scientist Daniel Kryder, contributed to the Camp Stewart, Georgia, incident on June 9 in which black soldiers ambushed white military police (MPs), killing one and wounding four, in response to horrible physical conditions, the segregation of the unit's officers, and military police brutality.[9]

In the midst of these threats to "national unity," executives at 20th Century Fox apparently agonized over a decision to release the all-black musical *Stormy Weather* in part because of a clash between zoot-suit-wearing Mexican youths and American sailors that exploded into a full-fledged battle as young black males, who also sported the contraband fashion, joined the fight. The large-scale violence that followed in Los Angeles became known as the Zoot Suit Riot, named for a signifier of disloyal and disruptive excess, the zoot suit, when the national mood and government authorities and their deputies demanded blind obedience and severe material sacrifice. This particular event most certainly alarmed studio executives, who saw the potential for subversion in the scenes featuring a zoot-suited and jive-talking Cab Calloway, a personification of that transgressive style. They may even have feared that this intended tribute to William "Bojangles" Robinson, known most for his safe on-screen appearances with Shirley Temple, and the showcasing of the greatest black talent in a patriotic salute might be received unfavorably by a seemingly restless and volatile black population, demanding changes to the status quo.[10]

Yet, black leaders, especially Walter White of the National Association for the Advancement of Colored People (NAACP), had been pressuring Hollywood and the government to employ more blacks in the movie industry and give them more "dignified," even "human," roles. Despite his opposition to the musical as the appropriate genre for properly changing the image of blacks in film and, by extension, in the larger society, White, as well as blacks from all political sectors, praised the studio for resisting pressure to withdraw the film. Wanting better from motion picture executives in the future, White curried favor with the image makers by claiming that such conflicts required "affirmative prevention" and not the elimination of blacks from the screen to avoid giving offense. Unfortunately, only the film's beginning and end seemed to have held much promise for contributing to the improvement of the black image and then ever so briefly.[11]

The film opens with its view of adoring and lovable children dancing with an avuncular black man on the porch of a spacious and supposedly charming country home. Everything about the imagery, from the bucolic setting to the neatly dressed and coiffed children to the debonair yet kindly "Uncle Bill" (Bojangles Robinson), is intended to suggest material and transcendent success. The man and the children seem to embody the availability of the American dream for all even amid rigid racial segregation. The children are not just willing and attentive listeners to a revered man's tales, they also play a pivotal role in the film's message. They represent the future, they validate the film as family entertainment, and their presence underscores the absence of Bill's own children. The time is the early 1940s, and the scene implies that the only missing piece to complete this utopian and perhaps unintentionally artificial existence is not an integrated society but a female companion for Uncle Bill.[12]

As the children clamor for the popular and respected uncle figure to regale them with tales of his life, we soon learn why such an attractive and well-to-do man lives alone. Nonetheless, it is what that man was and did some quarter century before that supposedly has profound historical significance for the children and untold observers. That story unfolds through the pages of a magazine recognizing "the magnificent contribution of the colored race to the entertainment of the world." Numerous dedications grace the publication, one of which reads: "'Jim Europe would have been proud of you.' Signed: Noble Sissle, Ex-Drum Major."[13]

Predictably, the children want to know about Jim Europe, whose untimely death shortly after the war goes unmentioned. Uncle Bill tells them that Jim led the greatest band in the greatest regiment in the world. As proof of the latter's greatness, he cites the 191 days the Regiment served "under fire" and the regimental Croix de Guerre it earned. As Uncle Bill nostalgically recalls the cheering crowds and waving flags during the victory parade in 1918 (the year of the parade was incorrectly cited), a flashback, the objectified memory of the man filtered through the children's mind's eye, transports the film audience to the awe-inspiring event in which hundreds of armed men march, in tight formation and lockstep, up Fifth Avenue in New York City. This impressive scene comes from actual footage of the unprecedented and historic victory parade of February 17, 1919, by the 369th Regimental Infantry United States—the moment that, David Levering Lewis maintains, heralded the start of the Harlem Renaissance.[14] Suddenly, this magnificent sight gives way to jarring cuts in visuals and mood from a panoramic documentary cinematography to studio-shot images of the band, especially two drummers, Bill Williamson (an imperceptibly younger Uncle Bill) and his "promoting" friend Gabriel Tucker (Dooley Wilson). During a break in marching, Gabe casts aside military discipline and plans postparade activities by searching through an address book for contact information on desirable women he should invite to and impress at the gala dance later that night. The huge drum, which requires two men to carry it and which seems more appropriate for a circus than a military band, reads: "Jim Europe's 15th New York Infantry Band." Among other things, it marks Bill and Gabe, central figures of the film, as noncombat soldiers.[15]

The next scene cuts to the site of the evening's festivities, where a large banner on a public hall announces, "Welcome Home 15th Regiment." A chauffeur-driven limousine arrives and catches the attention of two young black male onlookers. Obviously impressed by the style and class of such an entrance, one of them speculates that "it must be General Pershing." The other replies, "Can't be; General Pershing is a blond." Then, Bill Williamson and his "running buddy" from the band, Gabriel Tucker, exit the car. The veiled racial reference to Pershing is as close as the film comes to showing or mentioning whiteness in this all-black pseudofantasy.[16]

Inside, Lt. Jim Europe (Ernest Whitman) leads a dance band as soldiers and their awestruck dates "cut the rug." When Selina Rogers (Lena Horne) greets Lieutenant Europe and asks to meet her brother's friend, Bill Williamson, Europe quickly locates him and calls his subordinate to attention; he introduces Bill to Selina, the sister of his war-hero buddy Clem Rogers, who is the conveniently missing member of the "Three Musketeers of the AEF." Bill presents Selina with a Croix de Guerre that Clem was awarded for "bravery"—something he wanted her to have. Before he can explain its meaning, the scene quickly shifts to the comic relief and distraction provided by the trivial interplay of Gabe with his date. When the scene returns to Bill and Selina, she thanks him for telling her about Clem. Effortlessly, this seemingly lighthearted musical reveals nothing about how Clem fought and presumably died.

Selina then pins the medal to her dress, just above the heart, and wears it while dancing with Bill and then singing "No Two Ways about Love." Had the medal been American, its wearing by Selina would have been a violation of military regulations. Instead, her action, which seemingly honors the award, actually undermines its value.[17] First, it transforms or reduces a medal for bravery into a shining symbol of sibling bonding. Second, it shows how a foreign medal can have different treatment and consequently different meaning and worth than an American equivalent. Moreover, the decision to display the medal on a black woman's chest suggests an intentional displacement of ownership out of a black male frame. Last, Selina's unselfconscious wearing of the medal, which most "respectable" women would have considered inappropriate and presumptuous, possibly marks her as a usurper of masculine prerogatives—a transgression that requires eventual correction.

Meanwhile, Gabe, who has barely more than $5 to his name, tries to impress the film's obligatory Sapphire figure—an overweight, opportunistic, gaudy, garrulous, shallow, and overbearing female character—with his pseudocosmopolitanism and affected savoir faire, which he supposedly acquired in France. The transforming effect of foreign service for him entails a fondness for the finest French champagne, big cigars, and excessive pretense—none of which he can sustain adequately as a bootblack (his not yet revealed occupation). Yet, the film's blatant misogyny and play to black female stereotypes even elevates Gabe, a lovable rogue, above a female character who manages to reveal him for what he is but who cannot discern what she has uncovered through her incredible denseness, gullibility, and loquacity.

The much more reserved, modest, and unambitious Bill, instantly smitten and inspired by Selina, has only two desires: to make this nubile beauty his wife and to achieve money and fame as a dancer. He vows not to return to New York until "he gets to be somebody," which, in the film's logic, suggests his service with the 15th counted for nothing more than the "three square meals a day" it afforded him. All of this imagery and representation appears unmistakably similar to the white press's coverage of the real parade and the subsequent festivities, as will be detailed in chapter 13.

Bill returns to his native South, where he bales cotton, works and dances on riverboats, and plays any role he can, from dancer to waiter to cook to bartender, in a small Memphis nightclub while looking for the big break. After much spatial, comedic, dramatic, romantic, and aesthetic movement, Bill, in a happy-ever-after ending, becomes an international stage and screen star and eventually wins back his distant, strong-willed, fiercely independent, hard-to-keep woman, who—after taking the "city of sin" by storm, à la Josephine Baker, and retracing Bill's steps in France—finally realizes that without her man, "there is no sun up in the sky," only *Stormy Weather*. In one fell swoop, the film has the distant, urbane, and career-oriented Selina realize her errant ways and apparently agree to accept the rightful place of a woman as helpmate to the man and mother of his children in the comfort of a country/suburban dream house. The film's ending suggests that, together, they will perpetuate both the cult of domesticity and the antebellum idyllic that Bill, the ideal black man, personifies. Thus, the film deftly steers the audience from the rightful place of blacks to that of women.

This bewildering and bothering, if not bewitching, thinly veiled biopic of Robinson and backstage musical more than anything reveals Hollywood's conflicted efforts to respond to pressures from blacks, especially the NAACP, as well as the Office of War Information to represent black actors and entertainers more favorably. That these pressures peaked at the start of World War II explains, in part, the film's multiple and fragmented plotting, to say nothing, according to cinema scholar Thomas Cripps, of the incompatibility of the propagandists' visions in Washington and Hollywood with those of black leadership.[18]

Nonetheless, most black contemporary critics welcomed the film. A headline in the *Amsterdam News* read 'STORMY WEATHER' SIGNALS NEW ERA. The paper touted the movie as proof that nothing was wrong "with Negro pictures or Negroes in pictures that money can't cure."[19] Ted Yates, entertainment writer for the *New York Age,* called *Stormy Weather* "S" for superb and "a crowning success" for the cinema capital. Still, even one of the film's biggest supporters had to admit that it "positively does not offer an exhibition of great acting, not even good acting."[20] Despite these shortcomings, the film's superior production quality and huge entertainment value recommended it as a popular attraction. The production's showcasing of the greatest black talents, including Horne, Robinson, Fats Waller, Ada Mae Brown, Katherine Dunham and the incomparable Nicholas Brothers, certainly made for spectacular entertainment. The black embrace of the film, however, could only be truly understood in the context of films that preceded it. Yates, from a typically masculine perspective, explained that the black man "has been depicted as a clown, a servant, or minstrel man. He has almost never existed on the script except to provoke laughter. Yes Siree, it is about time Uncle Tom gave way to a genuine portrayal of the Negro, showing him as he really is—a human being."[21] Unfortunately, that human being, except for soldiering, serving, and bailing cotton, is limited to the role of entertainer.[22]

When *Stormy Weather* is compared to *This Is the Army,* whose black production number featured zoot-suited black soldiers made up for a minstrel show and singing "That's What the Well-Dressed Man in Harlem Will Wear," one can better understand the views of contemporary black critics. According to film scholar Cripps, this scene and others featuring soldiers often "revealed the tension between old and new black imagery." Other scholars have concluded more critically that "the movie's racial themes were a throwback to the painful era of the first war" with white soldiers in black face and drag, to say nothing of a half-naked, crossed-dressed black man who evokes images of natives in Tarzan movies.[23]

Even in relative terms, *Stormy Weather* did not escape harsh appraisal from white film critics. A review in *Time* concluded that the film only showed how Hollywood apparently regarded black performers "less as artists (despite their very high potential of artistry) than as picturesque, Sambo-style performers." Denis Preston, a well-known British radio writer and producer, called it a hodgepodge "of comico-pathetic 'nigger characterisation,'" presenting the "vital functional art" of blacks "in its most debased form." African American composer William Grant Still, who quit the movie because of film executives' assumptions about his musical capacity and assaults on his work as not authentically black, must have agreed with these characterizations.[24]

Without the lived experience, emotional investment, and practical concerns of contemporary observers, current scholars of black film, being more critically distant, have been far less kind to *Stormy Weather*. To Donald Bogle, it "represented wartime escapist entertainment at its peak" and was "no major departure from past movie depictions of African Americans as gentle folks."[25] Like Al Jolson's "My Mammy," it pretended to the absence of conflict between blacks and whites. Others have criticized the film for its miscasting of Horne and Robinson as love interests, its shameless illogicality, and its devolution into outright minstrelsy.[26]

*Stormy Weather* represents just one of Hollywood's many missed opportunities to give black soldiers proper credit where due, in the interest of playing it safe at best. Even the serious, contemporary war films—such as *Bataan, Sahara, Crash Dive,* and *Lifeboat,* which included a black soldier as a central character—"used the war to thrust a black figure into a small white circle" and in the end, according to Thomas Cripps, reassured whites that they had nothing to fear from "an enhanced black status."[27] Thus, the mere referencing of the 15th Regiment did not necessarily serve a positive purpose. In fact, the content and context of that representation appear regressive and disabling.

Perhaps fearing a negative reaction by veterans and soldiers, 20th Century Fox, the movie theater where *Stormy Weather* was to debut, and the Interstate United Newspapers acted preemptively and extended a formal invitation to the executive staff and other officers of the 15th New York Guard to attend the film's premier at the Roxy on Broadway. Such an association lent considerable authenticity and legitimacy to the film's military message, positively identified it with the Regiment, and facilitated invaluable photo opportunities for the promoters. That the organization had no official relationship to the Old 15th or its successor, the 369th, did not seem to matter. Even the black press downplayed the fact that these men were home guard replacements for those serving overseas. That the event took place at the Roxy and not the Alhambra in Harlem suggests that the promoters sought a maximum return on their investment while advancing some form of materialist interracialism for an all-black film that avoided any serious engagement with race relations and integration.[28]

This tactical move could not, though, hide the fact that the production, like so many media and official representations, merely sought to ensure black loyalty while protecting the racial status quo. In other words, even black soldiers could be represented only to the extent that they did not seriously threaten the prescribed roles for blacks as contented, fun-loving, and musically talented folks. As Cripps astutely observes, *Stormy Weather* "brought into play the tension between integration and cultural uniqueness and produced in the minds of black activists no end to anxiety over the implied retreat from integration."[29]

No doubt, the film foregrounds some of the Regiment's important achievements, such as the regimental citation and its record length of service on the front. Such revelations, however, leave unanswered questions as to why the unit received a French award and not an American honor. Moreover, the film associates the award with only 1 of 171 individual recipients, and he is conveniently "absent" and presumably dead, so as not to complicate or impede the film's rapid departure from the merest mention of bravery in combat to its exclusive treatment of the black soldier as entertainer. The absence of explicit death in the film avoids tragedy and also clearly subverts the combat experiences (hence potential violence against whites) of the soldiers. Consequently, the only actual member referenced, other than Noble Sissle, is James Reese Europe in his position as bandleader, and there is absolutely no hint that he served in the Regiment's machine-gun company and took great pride in his combat role, albeit a brief one. The film seems to have accepted the commonly held notion that black officers were much too threatening and problematic to highlight and justified such avoidance and devaluing as respect for the Negro masses' putative rejection of condescending and elitist black men with commissions.[30] Europe as a bandleader does not challenge prevailing assumptions about black officers despite the acknowledgment of his rank in the film by Selina and Bill, whom he addressed as private and called to attention. The stand-in for the black officer is Bill's foil, the light-skinned, arrogant, and controlling impresario and romantic rival Chick Bailey.

Not only does the film undermine and trivialize the black military experience, it also produces endless confusion in distinguishing between the real and the imagined, as film images of actual events, for instance, merge with the imaginary. The actual scenes occupy a very prominent place but quickly vanish, thus creating an interesting tension between "the known" and "the staged." As such, the staging attempts to confine or displace "the real," of which we catch a brief but revealing glimpse. Likewise, a few actors play themselves, others have roles closely based on self, and some represent characters likely to be taken as real. To this day, many sources, some official, insist that Bojangles Robinson, whose generosity earned him the ceremonial title "Mayor of Harlem," served as the Regiment's drum major. Remarkably, Rudi Williams of the American Forces Press Service, a publication arm of the Department of Defense, wrote in 2002 that James Reese Europe "recruited the best drum major he could find—Harlem dancer Bill 'Bojangles' Robinson." In actuality, Noble Sissle performed that function until being replaced by Sgt. Gillard Thompson. Robinson never even served in the Regiment.[31] The fact that his funeral in 1949 was held in the 369th Armory certainly has contributed to his association with the unit.[32]

To grasp the extent, duration, and resilience of the film's factual inaccuracies and conflations, even contemporary cinema scholar Paula Massood refers to the 15th as "Jim Europe's . . . (African American) Regiment." Thus, the bandleader, as a result of the film's confusing representation, the author's academic shorthand, inattention to detail, or some combination thereof, becomes the signifier of not just the band but also the whole Regiment.[33]

The fact that the film refers to the Regiment as the 15th and not the 369th also raises significant questions. Without doubt, the 15th was the name of choice for most members of the Regiment who went to Europe under that designation. Influenced by pride of ownership and the need for exclusivity, the local community embraced the appellation and the institution it identified long after the war. These realities notwithstanding, even at the time of the parade the designation was inaccurate. Preferences and sentiments aside, many of the soldiers who marched that glorious day in February 1919 never ever belonged to the Old 15th New York National Guard. More than half were replacements who joined the outfit in France, many long after the change in designation. Although the War Department forced that unwanted and inappropriate number on the Regiment, for reasons that will be detailed subsequently, the war actually transformed the unit in size and composition and also in character and experience. Indeed, the transformation began long before the Regiment arrived in France.

Regrettably, by using the original designation of the Regiment, the film simultaneously distances itself from the present (and an existing 369th) and avoids difficult and complicated questions about the change in name and its significance. This strategy by the filmmakers enables a return to a less troubled time and fixes the Regiment forever in a romanticized past. It carefully avoids the transforming effects of war and the individual's role as an agent of social transformation. However, the real members of the Regiment were men who learned French, saw the world, fought and died in trenches, and experienced freedom and enjoyed respect as never before. The resultant changes in them raised frightening and threatening questions in others who expected the men to remain the same or at least accept the status quo ante.

When Bill Williamson tells the children that the Regiment marched in 1918, the scriptwriters probably made no simple dating error. More than likely, the intent was to have the film avoid the mere mention of another troubled time in the recent past—1919, the year of the Red Summer and Red Scare when race riots broke out across the nation and the Bolshevik threat loomed large in people's minds, if not on the ground. Likewise, the only reference to the current war comes during a United Service Organization (USO) show in which the Cab Calloway, Jr., character emerges backstage in an officer's uniform and meets Bill Williamson. Thus, Cab Calloway, the zoot-wearing, jive-talking hepcat, affirms his patriotism vicariously through his "son" and also states that he wishes to join him. The film stays as far away as it can from the current reality of racial strife within the military and a larger black seething over "Jim Crow blood-banks, discrimination in industry and housing, and the circumscribed role for blacks in the war."[34] Instead, it ends with tens of black officers contentedly dancing with their proud dates.

Therefore, one must not casually dismiss the film's abbreviated and light-hearted, comedic and musical portrayal of the Regiment as insignificant or harmless. Even its omissions speak volumes. One should not lose sight of the fact that Bill and Gabe, though sans uniform after the opening scenes, are forever veterans of the 15th. Thus, *Stormy Weather* is both a complex and a highly flawed representation.

Unfortunately, no other single source of information about the Regiment was likely to have reached more people in 1943 (and for many years to come) than *Stormy Weather*. Although not a great box office success, it drew audiences three times larger than *Cabin in the Sky* did and found a niche.[35] Lena Horne noted that the film's all-black cast allowed for wide distribution, including in the South and on military bases. As such, it helped make her a star and a black sex symbol.[36]

Before the film, most treatments of the 15th/369th were limited to newspapers, public speeches, and word-of-mouth accounts, as well as in the few contemporary publications on black soldiers during the war written by Emmett J. Scott (1919), W. Allison Sweeney (1919), Madame Touissant Welcome (1919), and Charles H. Williams (1923).[37] None of these, however, would ever find an audience the size of *Stormy Weather* or reach people in the same way.

Additional evidence of how *Stormy Weather* carried on a tradition, rather than breaking from past representations of blacks, can be found in Irvin Cobb's *Glory of the Coming: What Mine Eyes Have Seen of Americans in Action in This Year of Grace and Allied Endeavor* (1918), as well as in subsequent, less flattering treatments of black soldiers. Cobb's racist reputation had long preceded him, and a chapter titled "Young Black Joe," dedicated to the black soldier in the aforementioned book, probably did little to enhance his standing with blacks but certainly honored the style of his times. As an "embedded" journalist with the 369th, Cobb witnessed firsthand the performance of the black soldier and gained a favorable impression.

In his works, Cobb touts the exploits of Henry Johnson and Needham (Neadom) Roberts, the Regiment's first two heroes, and confesses that the black soldier had made him reconsider his racist southern ways. Yet, Cobb's treatment still reeks of paternalism and stereotype and features the N word despite his admission that no matter its context or meaning, the term "never fell on black ears" without leaving behind "a sting for the heart." That consideration notwithstanding, Cobb confidently predicts that the black soldier would give that word new meaning, for "hereafter n-i-g-g-e-r will merely be another way of spelling the word American."[38]

Only two dedicated treatments of the Regiment existed before *Stormy Weather*—a 1920 documentary film entitled *From Harlem to the Rhine* and a book of the same name by Arthur W. Little, published in 1936. The first was a motion picture and slide show "depicting the old Fifteenth Regiment 'over here' and 'over there.'" Accompanied by vaudeville acts, the multimedia presentation reportedly was "a big screen hit," playing to capacity crowds at the Lafayette Theatre in Harlem. According to *New York Age* entertainment critic Lester Walton, the "colored public is hungry for moving pictures in which race soldiers appear on the screen in a favorable and complimentary light." The production consisted of five reels of film and over fifty slides, including images of Bert Williams in uniform, soldiers training at Peekskill and on the front lines in France, the triumphal march into Germany, Jim Europe's band entertaining Teutonic civilians, and the march up Fifth Avenue. The show particularly impressed the *Age* because it featured the colored soldier in the world war "without attempt to disparage." For that result, Walton reminded the public that it owed a debt of gratitude to William Hayward, the Regiment's first commander.[39]

The extent of the production's reach and influence cannot be measured accurately. Although organizers scheduled a screening in Brooklyn, the *Age* ominously suggested that it was a film for the veterans and their friends and relatives.[40] Perhaps cost and limited entertainment value, not level of interest, militated against the show's appeal to larger audiences. In any event, the *Age*'s measured endorsement unwittingly raised doubts about the extent of the hunger of blacks for the subject, at least as conveyed in its current vehicle.

Eight years before Little's book-length treatment appeared in print, the story of the Regiment found condensed and embellished expression and wide circulation in *Rank and File: True Stories of the Great War,* by Theodore Roosevelt, Jr. (1928). Roosevelt, son of the former president, borrowing heavily from Little's unpublished manuscript, immortalized the incident involving Johnson and Roberts in a chapter titled "The Battle of Henry Johnson." Although error ridden and melodramatic, the chapter prominently covered the history of the Regiment from its inception in 1916. Reflective of his time, Roosevelt, sometimes channeling Little, revealed how even the most well meaning and supportive whites could not avoid racial essentialism in their explanations and observations of black character and behavior, as he reminded readers that "colored People are emotional under any circumstances, and the strain and excitement of war did not lessen this trait. In many ways these days in New York suggested a revivalist meeting rather than a military mobilization." When it came to narrating Johnson's feat, Roosevelt resorted to the worst of essentialist tendencies in describing how the black hero responded to the jamming of his gun and the simultaneous charge of a German soldier with pistol in hand: "The colored boy's fighting blood was up. The spirit of ancestors who fought to the death in the tribal wars of the forest-choked Congo surged up in him."[41]

In 1936, Little, who had led the 1st Battalion during the war and commanded the entire Regiment from 1921 to 1925, finally published *From Harlem to the Rhine,* a book based on many official documents, contemporary notes, and firsthand observations. Although he was once considered a great friend of the Regiment, Little seemed completely comfortable with racialist assumptions of his time. He naturalized Negro dialect and darky humor in his self-professed sympathetic but full treatment of these men, whom he had seen transformed by their experiences, turning from boys to soldiers. Although told mostly from his personal vantage point as a regimental adjutant and officer in the Brooklyn battalion before the war and the 1st Battalion during the war, Little's account remains invaluable, and it stood alone until Reid Badger's fine biography (1995) of James Reese Europe.[42] Unfortunately, Noble Sissle's rather hagiographic but nonetheless revealing firsthand account of Europe and the Regiment (1942) has never been published. Arthur W. Davis, brother of Sgt. Hannibal "Spats" Davis, contributed a short account in 1979, *Here and There with the Rattlers,* based on his own brief experience with the 15th and what he learned in interviews with and letters from his combat-experienced brother.[43]

Not even those works, including Badger's, could possibly rival the reach and influence of *Stormy Weather.* Only William Miles's *Men of Bronze,* through public screenings, video rentals and sales, and school and library adoption, has found a comparable audience. This 1977 documentary features extensive film footage of the soldiers—their weaponless exercises in Harlem, their combat and occupation experiences in Europe, the concerts performed by the great band, and their triumphal march and overwhelming reception in New York. Moreover, the film has the benefit of first-person accounts from three veterans: Hamilton Fish, Frederick Williams, and Melville Miller. The last, Miller, was a marvelous raconteur and quintessential New York character, somewhat in the manner and style of Congressman Charles Rangel. In sum, *Men of Bronze* rescues a largely lost or forgotten history and frames it in a tale of triumph over adversity and a lesson in the value of interracial cooperation and open-mindedness. A 1998 History Channel documentary, *Harlem Hellfighters,* which, among other things, addresses some of the postwar adjustment problems for the men, repeats some of Miles's treatment but at the same time pales in comparison to the original in visual and narrative effect.[44]

None of these works, however, discusses the pre-1916 history of the Regiment and its context. The first study to explore the unit prior to 1916 is Charles Johnson's 1976 dissertation on blacks and the National Guard, published in 1992 as *African American Soldiers in the National Guard.* Johnson's pathbreaking scholarship makes us all indebted to its insights and discoveries. Stephen Harris's *Harlem's Hell Fighters* (2003) also treats the pre-1916 history of the Regiment and links it to Charles Fillmore but even more to James Reese Europe, his Clef Club Orchestra, and eventually the regimental band.[45] Yet, Harris, even with the best of intentions, might not have heeded the criticisms of contemporaries concerning the "undue prominence given the jazz band." Instead, they wished for the men of the unit to be remembered as they were described by Colonel Hayward: "They are American men. They fought for their country. They did not know how to quit. Not one was taken prisoner. That tells it to those who ask." To Hayward's call, a black woman, reportedly voicing Harlem's sentiment with homage to Julius Caesar's "veni, vidi, vici," responded: "They have been; they done it, they've come back."[46] Nonetheless, Stephen Harris's work is a significant improvement upon William Harris's *The Hellfighters of Har-*

*lem* (2002) and holds up well against Peter Nelson's *A More Unbending Battle* (2009).[47] Still, none of these works makes much, if any, use of French military sources, and the latter three works lack sufficient historical context beyond the unit. The most sophisticated and engaging treatment thus far is Richard Slotkin's far-reaching and imaginative *Lost Battalions* (2005), which compares the experiences of the 308th and the 369th Regiments of infantry, the former as part of the "Melting Pot" 77th Division. Both units, according to Slotkin, symbolize the unresolved dilemma of the actual purpose of the war to make the world safe for democracy or to determine who counts as American and what civil rights citizenship guarantees. Slotkin's basis for comparison is that both were lost in the war and in history, and his mission is to recover and relate them in collective memory.[48] *Lost Battalions* is beautifully written, wonderfully crafted, and seriously contextualized in its treatment of politics and myth and popular culture. Yet, for all its contribution to our understanding of the 369th and its larger significance on and off the battlefield, the work has divided loyalties and still begs the question of a dedicated treatment of the 15th/369th that shows the Regiment standing alone, as it most characteristically was.

*Harlem's Rattlers and the Great War* departs from all of the works mentioned here in its insistence that the subject of this narrative be represented in at least four critical dimensions. First, this volume ensures that the prehistory of the Regiment is carefully and fully explored in order to demonstrate the unit's significance to larger issues, including its prominent role in city, state, and even national politics. Previous treatments have paid far too little attention to the prolonged and complex struggle of black New Yorkers to force the state to authorize and recognize a black National Guard unit, which had deep and widespread implications for manhood, community, and citizenship. Yet, serving was one thing, leading another. Thus, continuous demands for black officers, even black leadership, spoke to the need of blacks to demonstrate "manly" capacity in perhaps the nation's most critical mission of all—its own defense.

Second, this book explores how, from the beginning, those associated with the campaign insisted on being a combat regiment of infantry. They knew the history of the black soldier and had every intention of upholding that proud tradition. Although there was some minimal backing off from that demand in the interest of survival, no one publicly expressed such a sentiment, perhaps in fear of the terrible consequences befalling anyone identified with such betrayal. Consequently, *Harlem's Rattlers* attributes far less importance to James Reese Europe and the band in the Regiment's birth and development than do Little, Badger, Harris, or Miles. Access to and careful exploration of French as well as American military documents distinguish this book from all others in its attention to the details of everyday life and the heat and fog of battle on the front. At the same time, that emphasis on the foreign experience has allowed us to heed historian Thomas Holt's injunction "to elaborate the nexus between the remote or global levels of that experience and its immediate or micro-local expressions."[49] The men's reaction to and characterization of African colonial troops is a classic case in point. So is the soldier who wrote home that "these French people don't bother with no color-line business. They treat us so good that the only time I ever knows I'm colored is when I looks in the glass."[50]

Third, *Harlem's Rattlers* strives to capture the complexity of a regiment campaign and its resultant organization as shaped by all the vagaries of human nature and interaction. One should keep in mind that the 15th/369th came into being under the most tangled of circumstances. The very organization that championed the cause of a black regiment, the Equity Congress, was made up of black Republicans and Democrats. More frequently than not, partisan politics and personal differences influenced the pace and shape of progress. This is to say nothing of the ultraconservative, elitist, and exclusionary leadership of the National Guard, which fancied itself a social club as much as a military organization and did all that it could to defeat efforts for an all-black regiment. In time of war, the Guard's reputation preceded it and provoked nothing but contempt and ridicule from the regular army. Thus, black National Guard troops suffered compound stigmatization as "weekend warriors" and as members of a despised and devalued "race."

Yet, the internal dynamics of the 15th/369th demand as much attention as any external ones. The presence of black and white officers in the Regiment was extremely rare, and it created a special internal environment. Indeed, two murders in the Regiment, one committed by a black sergeant and the other by a white officer, exposed not only interracial tensions within but also intraracial conflicts between old-timers and newcomers, between officers and men, and between northern- and southern-born men of color. Like no other treatment, however, *Harlem's Rattlers* reveals the strained relations among white officers, many of whom put personal advancement ahead of institutional loyalty. They understood better than most the lowly position on the totem pole of a predominantly black National Guard unit with a mixed officer corps, and some, including Hamilton Fish, did all that they could to extricate themselves from that predicament.

Fourth, informed by recent feminist scholarship on war, *Harlem's Rattlers* attempts to complicate the role of gender in the story and contribute to the ongoing revision of the widely held view that military matters are strictly masculine. Indeed, James Reese Europe was far from alone in characterizing the Regiment as an instrument in developing the "moral and physical negro manhood of Harlem."[51] Such a sentiment makes clear, as the editors of *Behind the Lines* have argued, that "war must be understood as a gendering activity itself, which ritually marks the gender of all members of society."[52] Black women recognized this fact all too well and strived to play their part and to shape the discourse of participation. Thus, members of the Women's Auxiliary of the 15th/369th defined themselves, through word and deed, as more than aides to the Regiment: they were partners in a struggle for full citizenship.

In the end, *Harlem's Rattlers* attempts to show the Regiment, for better or worse, in all its manifestations and implications. We have tried to avoid the easy and inaccurate binaries that have so often marked studies of black institutions. This book is not simply about victimization, agency, and heroism. It seeks to do justice to the well-known fact that individuals embody a range of characteristics that emerge in relation to impulses and circumstances. We hope to avoid contributing to the production and reinforcement of underdeveloped and unsatisfying one-dimensional characters who often reside at the center of disabling myths.

Yet, no matter how much one might try to exercise caution in representing the Regiment, its connection to so many important individuals, institutions, events, and issues of the day resists the best attempts to moderate its significance. The list of individuals with ties to the Regiment or the movement to establish it includes, to name a few: President William Howard Taft, Henry L. Stimson, Newton D. Baker, W. E. B. Du Bois, Booker T. Washington, Col. Charles Young, Charles W. Anderson, William H. Lewis, Oswald Garrison Villard, Joel Spingarn, Edward M. House, Madam C. J. Walker, Hamilton Fish, and Egbert "Bert" Williams. The growth and development of Harlem, the rise of the NAACP, the colored officer training camps, the riots of Houston and East St. Louis, the debates about black officers, the suitability of blacks as combatants, black soldiers in southern camps, concerns about patriotism and loyalty, the role of the black press, military justice, and notions of respectable black manhood and womanhood all involve or relate to the Regiment.

What we have discovered about the Regiment is this: the more one finds, the more one becomes convinced that the full story of the 369th has only begun to be told. Indeed, the certainty with which someone knows the Regiment is more than likely directly proportional to his or her ignorance of it. With respect to an individual such as Henry Johnson, the more we have learned about him as a person, the less we really know. Johnson has become, more than anything, the projection of others' desires, hopes, and aspirations. In fact, as a former officer in the Regiment, W. O. Waters, once wrote: "The story of the regiment is such a strange epic—so fantastic, comic, absurd, heroic, tragic and sentimental—that I once believed that all its essential elements never could be adequately put between the cover of several volumes." Although Waters implied that Little's *From Harlem to the Rhine* had proved him wrong, we beg to disagree with that assessment and hope that what follows contributes to a fuller and richer telling of the truly epic tale of this Regiment.[53]

Above all else, we can arrive at but one overriding conclusion about this story—to ignore the relationship of blacks to the military is to deny one-self a vital perspective on understanding the black experience in America in all its richness and complexity. By exploring a discrete but representative subject in intense and exact detail in *Harlem's Rattlers*, we hope to establish that scholarly concern with the franchise, education, the church, and even civil rights broadly defined must be joined with a careful consideration and inclusion of blacks and the military, for without that, the others cannot be truly understood nor can there be a full appreciation of the black experience.

Although the notion of going forward and persevering tenaciously characterizes the Regiment and speaks to its history explicitly, it also captures the essence of a larger mood and spirit among black people—an understanding that they too could not go back to the days and ways before the Great War. Far from a lost cause in which blacks blindly and mindlessly embraced patriotism, the war, together with their support for it and service in it, allowed them to distinguish themselves individually and collectively. The repression and violence and the denigration and disparagement, official and unofficial, that followed the war certainly caused much harm. What mattered more, however, was that blacks had internalized the positive values gained from the war, and no amount of persecution, discrimination, and disparagement could erase them.

What the war made clear to all, especially blacks, was that "character is more fundamental than reputation," and the character of black Americans, according to contemporary scholar and activist William Pickens, shone clearly "in the light of war" caused by "the all-exposing fires of a burning world." Suddenly, "the most undesirable element in the United States" became "the most reliable element," as symbolized and recognized by the calling out of black National Guard troops to protect the White House. That the war had allowed blacks from Africa and America the opportunity to make their "first great record as a modern international factor and a positive world influence" was a lesson never to be lost on blacks.[54] World War I helped to produce a self-confident New Negro, and all change that came later owes much to the forward-looking and forward-moving people of the time.

In the end, we hope that *Harlem's Rattlers* will be the in-depth institutional study that starts inward and looks outward, complementing and reinforcing the more recent macrolevel studies of the black experience in World War I that have addressed its scholarly neglect or elision and established its continuing significance. Among these fine works are Mark Whalan's *The Great War and the Culture of the New Negro* (2008), Adriane Lentz-Smith's *Freedom Struggles* (2009), Chad Williams's *Torchbearers of Democracy* (2010), and Nina Mjagkij's *Loyalty in Time of Trial* (2011). Unlike these works, however, *Harlem's Rattlers* tells a story not only *through* war but also *of* war, paying near-equal attention and consideration to both perspectives.[55]

# I

## "He HAS a Flag"

### The Relationship of the Military to Black Identity, Community, and Citizenship and the Origins of the Black Regiment Movement

*In the early days you scorned them. . . .*
*Then distress fell on the nation,*
*And the flag was drooping low;*
*Should the dust pollute your banner?*
*No! the nation shouted, No!*
*So when War, in savage triumph,*
*Spread abroad his funeral pall*
*Then you called the colored soldiers,*
*And they answered to your call.*
    Paul Lawrence Dunbar, "The Colored Soldiers"

Important institutions and organizations cannot be considered or understood properly in isolation. The greater their significance, the more they must be situated in larger social, political, cultural, and economic contexts. The historic magnitude and complexity of the 15th/369th Regiment demand not only that it be placed in a context of black survival, protest, and advancement strategies and tactics but also that it be removed from the margins and allowed to take its place among the central and fundamental instrumentalities in the black freedom struggle.

Although some blacks long have argued over whether inclusion in American society or separation from it represented the best path to self-liberation and realization, most have debated strategies and tactics to claim their birthright within the nation and not outside it. Rarely countenancing rebellion, let alone revolution, even when pushed to the wall, blacks have almost always tried to persuade authorities to remove policies and practices that violate avowed national principles and ideals. African Americans have not sought to destroy the nation's legitimate institutions; they have petitioned and fought for inclusion in them. Nothing could be more closely identified with America's existence than the military, which won the nation's independence, ostensibly ensures its survival, and putatively protects its freedoms. Consequently, blacks have long understood that no institution connects to nation and citizenship so fundamentally as does soldiering. Indeed, one can legitimately argue that no single national institution has meant more to African Americans than the military.

Yet, military service offered no panacea. It often presented blacks with the damnable dilemma—"damned if you do and damned if you don't." Rather than debunk stereotype, military service frequently reinforced it. Far too commonly, white officers during the Civil War and after brought low expectations and long-standing prejudices to their relations with black troops, leading to assessments that these victims of slavery "had no independence, no self-reliance, not a thought except for the present, and were filled with superstition."[1] Despite rendering heroic service in the Civil War and on the western frontier, blacks could not change negative opinions within the military. Alabama native and West Point graduate Capt. Robert Lee Bullard, who eventually became one of the most powerful and influential critics of black soldiers during and after World War I, consistently demonstrated in his words and deeds that familiarity often bred contempt. His experience as commander of the "colored" 3rd Alabama Volunteers during the Spanish-American War had inspired him to write that the Negro had to be treated as a different species, requiring special methods of instruction and discipline to deal with the vast differences in nature and evolution. In Bullard's rendering, only under genteel white patriarchal authority would blacks respond effectively as soldiers. Otherwise, they would simply revert to the carefree and lazy types they were by nature.[2]

Even more disturbing were the attitudes of so-called friends of blacks such as Oswald Garrison Villard. Even their praise resonated with stereotypical characterizations of the black men's "astonishing sociability," cleanliness, "pride in their uniforms," and tendency to "tell stories and crack jokes" rather than sleep, "no matter how hard the day has been." Villard, whose words and views were sometimes hard to distinguish from those of unreconstructed southerners, also reported "dark sides" in which black soldiers turned "merited punishment into martyrdom," gambled "almost beyond control," habitually and incurably carried "concealed weapons," and allowed minor quarrels "to cause scuffling and fighting." Playing upon old stereotypes of weak black men and lascivious black Jezebels, Villard warned that for soldiers unable to control their sexual appetites, women represented "at all times a potent temptation to misconduct and neglect of duty."[3]

Despite such damaging characterizations and vicious treatment and rejection at the hands of the military, blacks saw no alternative. They could only, as Villard also pointed out, let their "sterling characteristics," "loyalty to the service," and "splendid" record help make their case for better treatment, greater recognition, and larger representation. With limited opportunities for advancement elsewhere and with unparalleled meaning attached to military service, blacks continued to value and embrace it as an instrument of liberation, empowerment, and not least reputation, especially as men. In the end, blacks held firmly to the notion that "in a fight, the color of a man's face cuts no figure, so long as it be not pale." These words—from such an unlikely source, another white native Alabaman and West Point graduate named Capt. Matthew Steele—offered considerable hope.[4]

Black Americans have long known that in the master narrative of the nation, manhood finds no better place for demonstration than war, and Americanism finds no better representative than the citizen-soldier, who initially had secured the nation's defense as a member of the militia. The fact that the nation's first president, George Washington, was also its first great military hero did not escape black people, including those of the World War I generation. Successors from Andrew Jackson to Ulysses Grant to Theodore Roosevelt had followed the same path, evolving from leaders of men on the battlefield to heads of state.

Moreover, military service sometimes connected directly to emancipation. During the Revolutionary War, blacks offered their services in exchange for freedom. They adopted names, such as Jupiter Free and Ned Liberty, that reflected their expectations of personal independence. Despite the almost exclusive association of men with war, black women also understood the liberating potential of military service and numbered among the captured slaves responding to Lord Dunmore's promise of freedom in exchange for service to the British. Deborah Gannett took a different route to liberation and enlisted in the 4th Massachusetts Regiment under the name Robert Shurtliff and performed the duties of a "faithful, gallant soldier." The most famous female poet of her era, Phillis Wheatley apotheosized George Washington in verse and befriended the great naval hero John Paul Jones and in the process demonstrated a keen respect for and understanding of the relationship between military rank and political power.[5]

Identification with military service reached unprecedented heights with Frederick Douglass's famous 1863 broadside "Men of Color: To Arms! To

Arms!," in which Douglass presented participation in the Civil War as the last chance to save the race from doom: "We must rise up in the dignity of our manhood, and show by our own right arms that we are worthy to be freemen." Even if they fell short of victory on the battlefield, fighting black men would, according to Douglass, belie the belief "that we are craven cowards, without soul, without manhood, without the spirit of soldiers." Douglass's call also reflected personal desperation to protect a reputation at risk because earlier he had cajoled authorities into accepting black soldiers with a claim that "[we were] striking the guilty rebels with our soft, white hand, when we should be striking with the iron hand of the black man." Thousands of black men answered Douglass's call to fight and die in the Civil War. Of 178,975 black soldiers, 37,847 died, many as cannon fodder, in the struggle to "prove ourselves men."[6]

Dutiful and often heroic service did help blacks earn their freedom, but it did less to secure their equality, even in the military. An 1866 law, purportedly intended to protect the rights and privileges of the newly enfranchised citizens, provided for their inclusion in "the ranks of the regular army" but actually ensured their exclusion from all but four regiments. Sections 1,104 and 1,108 of the *Revised Statutes of the United States* required that the enlisted men (not officers) of the 9th and 10th Regiments of cavalry and the 24th and 25th Regiments of infantry be "colored." The same Captain Steele who had offered those hopeful words condemned the law as "the only one upon the statute-books of the national government which treats the negro citizens as a class apart—which sets up a 'Jim Crow car' for them, as it were, and requires them to ride in it or none." To him, "no more exclusive law can be found in the codes of Alabama or Mississippi."[7] Considering his provenance, Steele's claim could not be dismissed easily, for he knew firsthand of that which he spoke.

Consequently, at the start of the Spanish-American War, exclusion from the National Guard relegated most black men to the sidelines of military service. Congress responded to black outrage by authorizing ten black regiments, but it stipulated that black members could not attain a rank higher than second lieutenant. Most such volunteers, resentful of their exclusion, answered the calls of eight states that had no such restriction. Yet, many of these soldiers would find themselves caring for the victims of yellow fever and malaria rather than charging up San Juan Hill. Despite the ravaging effects of tropical diseases on these men, such clear evidence did nothing to alter assumptions about their resistance or immunity to these pathogens. As a result, black soldiers earned the right to serve as part of an occupation force in the Philippines, where, with few exceptions, they helped to suppress, with extreme brutality, an indigenous war for independence in 1899. One military man and author, Chaplain James M. Guthrie, used the occasion to demonstrate that blacks had not only sought their own freedom through soldiering but also contributed mightily to the cause of American democracy at home and abroad in the process. The title of his book alone makes clear his intent: *Camp-Fires of the Afro-American, or The Colored Man as Patriot, Soldier, Sailor, and Hero in the Cause of Free America*. On a practical level, none of the officers given commissions with volunteer forces in the Filipino wars found a place as an officer in the regular army.[8] Once again, blacks paid a great moral price for seemingly very little material gain.

Then, in 1906, President Theodore Roosevelt authored the supreme injustice to African American soldiers and their supporters in his heavy-handed and grossly unfair dismissal of black soldiers for rioting in Brownsville, Texas. Roosevelt already had denigrated the character and performance of the "smoked Yankees" in the Spanish-American War in the process of exaggerating the role of the Rough Riders at San Juan Hill.[9] Despite a dearth of evidence linking the soldiers of the 25th Regiment to the disturbance, neither Roosevelt's mind nor his decision changed. The stench of the (mis) handled event lasted for years. These numerous setbacks in the military, combined with the outrageous racism of the Wilson administration on the eve of World War I, forced blacks into a compensatory and celebratory and sometimes angry mood regarding their role in and contributions to the nation's military history and operations.

Then, unstinting praise for the "glorious record" the sable soldiers had made contrasted with unsparing condemnation for the injustices of the government.[10] Black people even heard this message in an institution where, at first glance, it might be least expected—the church, far and away black America's most influential, respected, and very often conservative institution. The representative words of African Methodist Episcopal (AME) minister and soldier W. Spencer Carpenter in 1913 certainly resonated deeply and widely:

> As a soldier, the American Negro equals any soldier in the world, and this fact will be admitted by any unbiased historian or student of this world's events in time of peace or of war. . . . As a race we have every reason to be proud of our contribution to this government in its times of war; but above that we can boast that among our troops not in a single case is there on record any knowledge of cowardice nor one case in which a Negro soldier failed to do his full duty. Yet, in spite of these facts, in spite of the glorious record of our troops in every

American war, there are those who insist that the Negro has no flag. He HAS a flag. He fought for it in 1775, in 1812, in 1863 and in 1898. He who says we have no flag denies the valor and patriotism of thousands of Negroes who on hundreds of battlefields have proved their worth as soldiers and as men.[11]

Then, Carpenter angrily denounced the sins of the great white fathers. He warned that blacks had grown weary from coping "with those who have his neck under their heels, and whose power is exerted to keep him where he stands, burdened with the contempt and loathing put upon his race." Not unlike Jeremiah, Carpenter predicted, "the same undaunted spirit which led him to offer his body as a target for the enemy's bullet will lead him to declare that he has suffered long enough, and then—well, the seat of oppression will be the scene of a bloody uprising unparalleled in the history of the world."[12] The summer of 1919 came frighteningly close to a prophecy fulfilled as Chicago, Washington, and Omaha, along with some twenty-one other cities and towns, erupted in racial violence, resulting in the loss of hundreds of lives.

Black New Yorkers had a long and mixed military history that included triumph and tragedy, notably the deadly and destructive draft riot of 1863 in which Irish immigrants used the draft and looming emancipation as a pretext to scapegoat blacks for their economic woes and social degradation. The rioting lasted for five days and resulted in the deaths of approximately 1,200 to 1,500 white rioters and untold numbers of blacks. Between 1860 and 1865, the black population of New York decreased by 3,000.[13]

The event demonstrated to the many blacks who escaped the carnage and chose to stay just how vulnerable they were. Rather than cower, significant numbers of New York's black citizens gained a greater appreciation for preparedness and added incentive to fight back against those who would deny their freedom, destroy their property, and take their lives. To that end, black citizens of the Empire State continued to desire, pursue, and embrace service to the country, state, and locality. Despite the fact that government and military officials as well as a significant portion of the population opposed black military organizations, New York State blacks throughout the nineteenth century actively fought to establish their very own martial institutions. Whether in the cause of self-defense in the instance of the Fugitive Slave Act of 1850 or in the fight for life and freedom in the Civil War, New York's blacks, as well as their brethren throughout the land, considered an investment in military service worth the risk of injury, death, and continued indignity.[14]

Angered and dismayed by official inaction or even complicity in the activities of Southern slave catchers in Northern states, some blacks considered emigration; others decided that the only solution lay in forming their own militias. For that purpose, a group of black citizens met in New York in April 1851 and resolved to impress upon the young men of Brooklyn and Williamsburg the necessity of organizing militia companies. William J. Wilson and Henry M. Johnson urged their communities to introduce military science tactics as a part of the educational process both for their own defense and for the nation's as well. By August 1, New York had a company of cadets, soon to be followed by the Hannibal Guards, the Free Soil Guards, and the Attucks Guards. The units caught the attention of the *New York Tribune,* which commented on the soldierly conduct of the men while questioning whether they "would fight like men" when the need arose.[15]

Following the passage of the General Militia Act of July 17, 1862, the Association for Promoting Colored Volunteers organized the 1st Brigade of the New York State Colored Volunteers. With permission from the secretary of war and the assistance of the newly formed Union League Club in 1863, this military organization grew to include the 20th, 26th, and 31st Regiments. Even then, Democratic governor Horatio Seymour excluded the men of the units from the state quota—not unlike the famous three-fifths clause of the Constitution, which counted a slave as less than a whole person. In a scenario that would be repeated, these soldiers served not as regular army troops but as members of the US Bureau of Colored Troops. When the next opportunity for service came during the Spanish-American War, the Republican governor, Frank S. Black, rebuffed the offer of prominent New York citizens, including *New York Age* publisher T. Thomas Fortune, to raise a black regiment. From that point on, black New Yorkers determined to secure a regiment in the state's National Guard. Governor Black's rejection and the circumstances of the Spanish-American War set the stage for the organized and unrelenting efforts that crystallized in 1910–1911.[16]

Despite rampant racism, both institutional and individual, blacks in New York had managed to make significant gains under the law, if not in practice. In 1895, Governor Levi P. Morton signed into law a civil rights bill that entitled blacks to full access to public accommodations, from restaurants to theaters to transportation. Many condemned the measure as the worst kind of government intervention in "social relations" and "higher law." In the minds of most whites perhaps, such a law would increase tensions between the races and produce economic hardships. Even worse, it could only contribute to the development of "lazier and more untrustworthy" Negroes. Nothing, however, could have been further from the intent of the legislation's supporters, including Charles W. Anderson, who saw it as a necessary step on the road to full equality.[17]

This law made the exclusion of blacks from the state militia even more galling. The painful effects of that condition became intolerably acute with the war against Spain and the call-up of National Guard regiments, including many from New York. Adding insult to injury, New York blacks also watched helplessly as their brethren from other states answered the call. Even more, some entered national service as officers.[18]

The New York press gave frequent and extended coverage to the mobilization, which included five of New York's twelve National Guard regiments. At the same time, it condemned those who refused to enlist and condoned the behavior of people who "hooted," "hissed," and "pelted" the slackers with eggs. On May 17, the *Times* reported that Governor Roger Wolcott of Massachusetts had signed the commissions of Capt. William J. Williams and Lt. William Hubert Jackson, among others, for the 6th Massachusetts US Volunteers. As such, they became the first black officers from the ranks of the militia or National Guard to serve with the US Army in war. The company itself was the first black unit mustered into service for the war and the only one attached to a white regiment.[19] A month later, a former slave, John R. Marshall, enjoyed the distinction of being the first black colonel to serve with the US Army as commander of the newly federalized 8th Illinois Volunteer Regiment. Marshall had received his first military training in 1874 at age fifteen from a school in Alexandria, Virginia. Later, he studied military science at Hampton Institute.[20]

Since April of that year, perhaps earlier, a former soldier had been enrolling black New Yorkers for service in the war. A West Point graduate on sick leave from the army drilled them every night. These earnest preparations, however, led to no positive action on the part of authorities. At the same time, reports of southern governors in Virginia and North Carolina sending volunteers to President William McKinley further frustrated and enraged New York's black citizens and spurred them to action. With a list of 400 men, the Committee on Organization of Afro-American Volunteers, headed by T. McCants Stewart, a prominent black lawyer, requested that Governor Black accept the provisional regiment into the state's National Guard. The committee called the governor's attention to the sterling record of blacks in past wars, especially the record compiled by three New York regiments in the Civil War. Despite opposition to the "separation of the races in organizations under the control of the state," the committee understood that integration of established National Guard units in New York would not happen before war's end, and thus, the only hope rested with a separate unit.[21]

Governor Black hid behind President McKinley's decision to rely exclusively on the existing National Guard in meeting his call. Despite his professed disagreement with the order, Black found the state's Guard "more than sufficient" to meet the need. When told that blacks had suffered nothing but rejection in applications to join the Guard, Black expressed regret. Nonetheless, he refused to use his discretionary powers to enlarge the Guard, citing fiscal restraints. The governor's rejection provoked anger and resentment as well as forceful action, despite assurances from Adjutant General C. Whitney Tillinghast that nothing in the law prevented black enlistment in the National Guard and that the governor would give equal consideration to all citizens, no matter their race or color. [22]

On June 22, one of the largest mass meetings of black citizens "in recent memory" took place at St. Mark's Methodist Episcopal Church. Nearly 1,000 people, including 200 fully uniformed and armed volunteers, had gathered in a show of force and determination to become members of the New York National Guard. Speaker after speaker aroused the crowd with stirring messages, none more so than the Reverend Dr. J. M. Henderson, pastor of Bethel Methodist Episcopal Church. Henderson said that the heart of the Afro-American and the white American beat as one "in this hour of war." Blacks, he noted, "were as anxious to die on the battlefield as our white brethren," even more anxious than some. Although Henderson could accept inclusion on an individual basis, he really "wanted an Afro-American regiment to make history for the race." Leaving no doubt as to the significance of the regiment, he concluded, "It is our right."[23]

Keenly aware that agitation had brought about the integration of public schools and equal access legislation recently, organizers intended to fight just as fiercely on this matter. Leaders of the movement understood that the problem could not be solved in New York alone, as evidenced by McKinley's alleged pursuit of "a policy of exclusion against all Afro-Americans as commissioned officers." They vowed to take the fight to Washington and resolved:

That this meeting deplores the refusal of Gov. Black to afford relief to the Afro-American citizens of New York upon the untenable ground that he is controlled by the War Department on the one hand, and that the taxpayers of the State would not justify him in making the expenditure necessary to furnish the desired relief on the other, when the taxpayers have placed the matter in his discretion and have never required a close-fisted parsimony in defraying the expense of furnishing troops for the common defense, and would in no wise do so when a flagrant injustice was possible to be done a large and patriotic section of the tax-paying citizenship of the State.[24]

At war's end, blacks found themselves on the outside of the New York National Guard, both as individuals and as a regiment. However, they did not give up the fight. Among the members of the Committee on Organization of Afro-American Volunteers were the Reverend William H. Brooks and James D. Carr. Brooks continued to speak out on matters involving the military, giving a devastating indictment of President Roosevelt's handling of the Brownsville tragedy. Both he and Carr remained committed to the regiment movement until it succeeded. Brooks eventually and briefly served as the Old 15th's chaplain. Although their patience and resolve must have been sorely tested, these pioneers of the regiment movement did not just wait for another opportunity; rather, they purposefully positioned themselves and others to take advantage of any favorable circumstance that might arise when a highly developed and forceful black political organization could give the will a way.[25]

By the turn of the twentieth century, the growing numbers of black residents and the contest for their votes meant that a political calculus became part of decisions affecting them. In 1900, over 60,000 black people lived in New York, more than half of them born outside the city and increasingly outside the country. Blacks had lived in Harlem since the eighteenth century and occupied blocks and tenements in the late nineteenth century that earned names such as Nigger Row and Darktown. Nonetheless, the turn of the century marked the beginning of a movement to Harlem from overcrowded communities to the south. Philip Payton, a black realtor, broke through the racial barriers in Harlem, and the IRT Lenox Avenue subway line facilitated access uptown when it was completed in 1904. Race riots in 1900 and 1905 led blacks to seek safety in critical masses within protected racial enclaves.[26]

By 1911, using liberal boundaries, the *New York Age* estimated that some 50,000 of the city's 100,000 blacks lived in Harlem. With its "safe" location and superior housing stock, Harlem also attracted a new black elite. W. E. B. Du Bois arrived in Harlem in 1910 as editor of *The Crisis*. James Weldon Johnson, compeer of the Harlem Renaissance, permanently settled in New York in 1914 after residing there off and on since 1900. Poet Claude McKay took up residence the same year. Madam C. J. Walker moved her business and residence to New York in 1916. Marcus Garvey and Amy Ashwood, cofounders of the Universal Negro Improvement Association, settled in Harlem in 1918, just one year after Hubert Harrison left New Jersey and the Socialist Party in the state to establish the Colored Liberty League and its organ, the *Voice*.[27]

Other prominent blacks associated with prewar Harlem included many of the future members of the yet-to-be formed 15th New York National Guard, among them James Reese Europe, bandleader for dancers Vernon and Irene Castle and director of the Clef Club Orchestra; Noble Sissle, Europe's business partner and a future collaborator with Eubie Blake on many classic musical and theatrical productions; Egbert Williams, vaudeville star; Vertner Tandy, black architect; and Napoleon Bonaparte Marshall, Harvard track star, lawyer, and counsel in the Brownsville court-martial.[28]

Yet, few black residents of New York enjoyed such privilege or fame. Most labored in unskilled jobs, and many lived in dire poverty. With the dramatic increase in population came the need for services and organizations to accommodate the many requirements of the population, especially those of women and youngsters. Prostitution and street gangs ranked high among the many concerns of reformers. Health, however, became the most pressing issue. The high mortality rate for blacks in the city indicated the impoverished population's difficult plight. Astonishingly, between 1895 and 1915, the death rate for black New Yorkers exceeded the birthrate.[29]

The black churches, the backbone of the African American community, influenced and responded to the shifting demographic patterns and relocated northward. They included three of the oldest black churches in the city—Bethel African Methodist Episcopal, Mother African Methodist Episcopal Zion, and St. Philip's Protestant Episcopal Church. Despite his involvement in Harlem, Adam Clayton Powell could not convince his congregation at Abyssinian Baptist Church to move from the Tenderloin district (West Fortieth Street) until 1923.[30]

According to contemporary scholar and community activist George Edmund Haynes, the Negro church was "the most resourceful and the most characteristic organized force in the life of the Northern cities." More than anything, Haynes noted, these institutions had in their "organization, support, and operation become largely independent of white people." As such, they provided black people with "valuable experience and group training in standing upon their own legs and in going forward to achieve ends mapped out by themselves." Harlem, perhaps better than any other place, illustrated the "independent, voluntary character of the Negro church." Churches not only ministered to the spiritual needs of their congregants, they also played key roles in caring for the material and health concerns of their communities. Even more, these churches stood as "visible evidence of the struggle of an aspiring people to express the best of life within them."[31]

Although New York's black citizens gained valuable lessons and support from the church and its leaders ("fellows with followers"), they could not fulfill their aspirations or solve their many problems through religious institutions alone. They desperately needed political organization and influence. The *Age* decried the sorry state of affairs:

> No other race in the great city is so deficient as ours in civic virtue and organization. The Italians, Japanese, Chinese, and what not, all have organizations backed with civic pride to protect the interests they have and to promote other interests they want. They are represented in all of the civic movements and life of New York City; while the Afro-American is represented in none of it. We have social, secret, beneficial, fraternal and religious organizations galore to promote the lighter and gayer side of life, to care for the sick and bury the dead and to lay up enough treasure in heaven to keep us out of hell, but as to the matters of citizenship and civic well-doing, upon which all of the others depend, we are as naked of preparations as a new-born baby. It is scandalous; it is criminal.[32]

The black press—unquestionably the most visible and maybe the most far-reaching community institution—often served as a bully pulpit against external and internal enemies. Led by Frederick R. Moore's *New York Age,* black newspapers played an important role in creating a sense of local community and connecting New York's blacks to a larger national collectivity. These papers featured black achievements, advertised significant events and meetings, and reported local news; they also served as an instrument of grievance, protest, and introspection locally, regionally, and nationally. The New York that appears in the pages of the black press is often troubling and troubled. Reports of discrimination and exclusion, racial incidents, and police brutality abound despite laws that forbade such practices. Sadly, hostile reactions often followed attempts to secure the rights and privileges the laws afforded. This is to say nothing of the damaging assault on black character resulting from widespread dissemination of the "coon" image through song, literature, theater, and the press. The contented, happy-go-lucky, harmless, and comical minstrel stereotype of the antebellum plantation had given way to the lazy, scheming, unreliable, immoral, and ultimately violent urban black male and the oversexed, domineering, and emasculating black woman. Even the white *New York World* held the opinion that "New York has never been a city over friendly to the Negro."[33]

At the same time, the black press urged self-help and racial solidarity in the economic arena. Pointing to successful businessmen of the race and the need for patronage by black residents, the *Age* simultaneously acknowledged and promoted a "hire black/buy black philosophy" and appealed to black pride before that term found currency: "Every Negro who can so spend a dollar with a Negro thereby serves not only his race but himself at the same time. The race should have long since passed its silly period of jealousy and white skin preference and patronage."[34]

Stories of black military achievement and disappointment often dominated the front pages of the *Age*. The amount of prominent space dedicated to the subject suggests a directly proportional relationship between the status of blacks in the military and the society at large. Nothing could do more to counter the prevailing stereotypes of black men as female-dominated, laughable buffoons and out-of-control beasts than upright, disciplined, and proud soldiers marching in military formation. COLOR LINE IS FORGOTTEN, read the lead to a July 29, 1909, article about the 10th Cavalry, famous, ironically, for its service against Native Americans and Filipinos. The article described the reception that New Yorkers of all races gave the parading unit. Community pride and optimism suffused the piece, as it criticized Vermonters who had reservations about the unit's marching there and who had thwarted attempts to form black military organizations in the past. At the same time, the article suggested that symbolic gestures of inclusion should not replace real efforts to address racial bias in the city's courts, segregated hospitals, and unfair police examinations. The *Age* expressed confidence in the new administration of William J. Gaynor to continue the successes of Democratic mayor George B. McClellan, Jr., son of the infamous Civil War general, and avoid the waste and corruption that inhered in machine politics.[35] Support for a black National Guard unit would constitute one critical indicator of his commitment to black progress.

The issue of a "colored regiment" had implications far beyond New York City and even the state. Only four years earlier, the Brownsville incident had cast a huge shadow over the future of blacks in the military and, by extension, over their future as citizens. Their discipline, integrity, character, intelligence, and morals all came into question as a result of that signal moment when gunfire erupted on the streets of a racially tense Brownsville, Texas, on August 14, 1906, killing one civilian and wounding two others.[36] The alleged precipitating incident involved the pistol-whipping of a black soldier by a white official for his refusal to give way to a white woman on a sidewalk. The white man punctuated the beating with a cautionary message: "I'll learn you to get off the sidewalk when there is a party of ladies on the walk." This reported encounter, with its obvious appeal to the frightening specter of black power and vulnerable white womanhood in public space, provided an eminently believable motive for black revenge and plausible deniability for white culpability. Thus, despite reports of marauding bands of armed whites and a lack of concrete evidence linking the newly arrived 1st Battalion of the 25th Infantry to the event, these soldiers stood accused. When they denied any involvement in the incident, President Theodore Roosevelt saw a "conspiracy of silence," rushed to judgment, and dishonorably discharged all who might have been involved. Roosevelt's actions also did irreparable harm to an already strained relationship between the Grand Old Party (GOP) and black people.[37]

A minority report authored by Senator Joseph B. Foraker of Ohio both reassured and incensed blacks even more, as it virtually shattered the official account and revealed that some of Brownsville's citizens had likely framed the black soldiers. Foraker, a bitter foe of Roosevelt, instantly became a hero to black people, a serious presidential candidate, and a marked man in his own party.[38] Furthermore, direct links existed between Brownsville and the creation of a black New York National Guard organization. New York's Gilchrist Stewart, a black politician and lawyer, conducted his own investigation of the Brownsville incident and sided with Foraker against Secretary of War William Howard Taft and Roosevelt. Stewart, who would play a prominent role in the creation of the Old 15th, consequently lost his seat on the Republican County Committee. Napoleon B. Marshall, who seemingly was already an ardent Democrat, served as a counsel for the defendants at the court-martial and would become an officer in the 15th. Even more, the regiment issue eventually ensnared the man who would succeed Roosevelt as president, William Howard Taft.[39]

Until the Houston Riot of 1917, Brownsville stood as the signal event in shaping discussions, perceptions, and policies relating to blacks and the military. Despite ceaseless appeals and sustained pressure, the federal government did not exonerate the soldiers until 1972, when only one victim of the injustice, Dorsie Willis, remained alive to see it undone.[40]

At the time, however, the Brownsville "catastrophe" did not so much dampen the black spirit as steel an aggrieved people's determination to right its wrongs by heroic and loyal service, if not direct vindication. The soldiers of the 25th Regiment, in their refusal to implicate each other, taught blacks of all persuasions a valuable lesson in solidarity. The influential moderate leader Mary Church Terrell believed that nothing had so hindered the race as a "lack of unity in everything." Brownsville suddenly changed that reality for her and "10,000,000 colored people of this country" whose hearts "beat as one." Brownsville had united the race "for a time at least" and stood "as an evil out of which good will eventually come."[41]

The black press played a pivotal role in promoting Brownsville as an empowering event, by linking military service directly to citizenship. The publication in March 1909 of William B. Sapp's urgent plea to push for the enlistment of more "colored" troops to supplement the US Army's meager four regiments of infantry and cavalry represented one of many examples. Sapp, a veteran of the 9th Cavalry, and the press agreed that military service "not only makes men of many, who today walk the streets and are of no earthly use to the country, but awakens us to the fact that we, too, must assist in maintaining and preserving our great republic." Attesting to the power of the press and even more to the absence of forceful and effective leadership to champion such causes, Sapp reasoned that the paper would bring the issue to the attention of leaders and at the same time not allow their support for the cause "to flag."[42]

Whether by coincidence or design, the most promising response to Sapp's plea came from abroad. NEGROES FOR FRENCH ARMY, read the lead to a long front-page story in the *Age* four months later. As Ida B. Wells had shown and other black leaders knew, the United States often responded best when addressed by European mediators. The *Age* exploited the proposal of Col. Charles E. M. Mangin, the French organizer of African colonial troops, to maximum effect. Through Mangin, the *Age* rendered images of a color-blind French society that respected men for their value and not their color. The paper gushed over the revelation that the French would rescue black men "from neglect" or "inhuman distinctions" at the hands of their own government. The *Age,* tactically and tactfully, ignored the biases inherent in Mangin's reference to the black man's "peculiar abilities," which included "a special love for show and a melodramatic desire to figure amid moving surroundings." At least Mangin would not allow his perception of blacks' excessive flashiness, self-importance, and love of action to deny them "an adequate living" and "great chances for the future."[43]

Soon after Mangin's appeal, reports on the experiences and future of black soldiers reflected a miraculous shift in the national mind-set. Discussions of Brownsville were "attended by a fresh compliment for some one of the four Negro regiments in the regular army." From West Point, Sacketts Harbor, and the Philippines came stories praising black troops. Even in the face of southern press reports about more damaging evidence in the Brownsville affair, the *Age* noted that the *Spokane Forum* had only praise for the deportment of the troops of the 25th Regiment, stationed at neighboring Fort Wright. The *Age* attributed these positive reports to a recognition that a "higher type of colored than white men go into the regular army." It maintained that "racial pride of uniform, eagerness for army experience and untoward industrial conditions make army life much more attractive for the ambitious athletic Negro youth." These men were "the cream of the physical manhood of the race."[44] That "cream" would rise to the top in Spokane, a site of radical labor protests, around January 1910 when the 25th supported a police action against "recent disturbances in the city." A most grateful city council issued a formal proclamation, thanking "the federal troops . . . [who] by their soldierly bearing and correct deportment, their sympathy and moral support in the maintenance of good order, and by their constant example of orderly, law-abiding, sober and gentlemanly conduct at all times, greatly contributed to the aid of our police officers in handling a most serious situation, involving in large degree the great principle of law enforcement."[45]

The commandant of the fort maintained that such an action by a city council was a first for any northern city. Speaking for his men, he asserted that they "feel a helping hand has been extended to them, and, through them, to their race." One sergeant saw the proclamation as "the first ray of hope from white men in his twenty-eight years of service."[46] Unfortunately, if they had acted, as the commendation suggests, to quell labor unrest, the act demonstrated that the price of recognition was often extremely high.

Still another factor coupled civic development to military organization—local pride. At the time, neither Harlem nor black New York writ large could lay claim to being America's black capital. Chicago contested vigorously with New York for the title "Black Metropolis." In the first two decades of the twentieth century, black New Yorkers often pointed to Chicago's institutions with envy and ambition. Despite the fact that W. E. B. Du Bois considered New York to be the "greatest single center of modern civilization in America," black New Yorkers gave frequent indications that black Chicago had much to teach them and much they could emulate.[47]

In 1907, New York, for example, had no equivalent to Chicago's Pekin Stock Company, leading Lester Walton, entertainment writer of the *Age,* to ask: "If Chicago can support a theater and an all-colored cast, why not New York?" Walton rejected tired excuses about different conditions and predicted that a "colored playhouse would be one of the most unique and attractive amusement places in the metropolis."[48] Far more important to New Yorkers' sense of inferiority, black Chicagoans understood and took advantage of party politics far better than did numerically superior New Yorkers. Black Chicagoans had registered extraordinary achievements in the city's electoral politics. In 1906 alone, Ferdinand L. Barnett, Oscar DePriest, and Edward Green had become their party's nominee for city judge, county commissioner, and state legislator, respectively. Neither population size nor district concentrations explained why New York lagged so far behind. According to a *New York Age* editorial, "The Chicago Afro-American plays the game of politics with consummate shrewdness and dexterity. He belongs . . . to his ward clubs . . . and makes himself one of the inmost cogs of the machine." New Yorkers, by contrast, fought among themselves too much and devalued local politics.[49]

Without that local clout, one of black Chicago's most honored, envied, and coveted institutions might never have become a reality—the 8th Illinois Regiment. The origins of the regiment can be traced to 1878, when the 16th Battalion became part of the Illinois State Militia, the result of the political will and determination of black Chicagoans who supposedly elected a representative dedicated to the formation of a black military unit. The 16th became the 9th Infantry Battalion as a result of reorganization in 1890 and 1895.[50]

Before long, the Spanish-American War created the first real opportunity for the unit to see combat. The serious disappointment of the battalion's omission in the first call of troops from Illinois led to protests and petitions to Governor John R. Tanner. The governor promised Col. John R. Marshall and supporters that if a second call came, the 9th would go to war, provided it could increase in size to regimental strength. Despite pessimistic predictions, Marshall led a feverish recruitment campaign, which included the services of Ida B. Wells-Barnett, the Reverend Reverdy C. Ransom, and Cook County commissioner Edward H. Wright. With a 9th Regiment (white) already in existence, Governor Tanner, on June 18, 1898, redesignated the 9th Battalion as the 8th Illinois Infantry Regiment and appointed John Marshall its commander, despite pressure from "the very doors of the White House, advising me not to officer this regiment with colored men."[51]

Although called up and sent to Cuba, the 8th did not see combat there; instead, it performed provost guard and service duties. Some ten years later, typical of the reluctance of authorities to recognize blacks as combat troops or peacekeepers, Governor Charles Deneen refused to involve the 8th Illinois in one of the most important events in the history of race relations—the Springfield Riot of 1908. White troops drank outside town and let black citizens die and homes and businesses burn, and observers asserted that had the governor called the 8th Illinois, it would have responded without delay and effected a very different outcome.[52]

So large loomed the reputation of the all-black 8th Illinois that even New Yorkers saw it as a worthy model and called upon its leaders for advice in the creation of its own National Guard unit, without which black New York, as they saw it, would remain underdeveloped. As the history of the 8th Illinois demonstrates, creating a military organization transcended local boundaries and politics. It reverberated nationally in almost every sphere of life. Brownsville and other such miscarriages of justice seriously affected black attitudes toward government leaders, especially Republicans. The riot in Springfield also produced unintended consequences, namely, the formation in 1909 of the organization that would become the NAACP. Based in New York, this fledgling institution changed the racial and political dynamic of the nation by demanding political and social equality, foregoing patience, and calling international attention to the black plight just as Ida B. Wells had done more than a decade earlier in her lonesome crusade against lynching.

In an open letter to the European community, W. E. B. Du Bois, seemingly in the name of the NAACP, unleashed the first international salvo in "their crusade for the recognition of manhood despite differences in race." Furthermore, the stunning document openly expressed discontent with the race's top-ranked leader and his methods. In an (un)civil declaration of war, the letter accused Booker T. Washington of being the purveyor of misleading information about the plight and condition of blacks:

> The undersigned Negroes have heard with great regret, the recent attempt to assure England and Europe that their condition in America is satisfactory. They sincerely wish that such were the case, but it becomes their plain duty to say that Booker T. Washington or any other person giving the impression abroad that the Negro problem in America is in process of satisfactory solution, he is giving an impression which is not true.[53]

The letter listed and described the manifold, systemic racist practices oppressing blacks, from disrespect, forced illiteracy, and disfranchisement to rape and lynching. It concluded by calling Washington and others like him prevaricators: "It is one thing to be optimistic, self-forgetful and forgiving, but it is quite a different thing, consciously or unconsciously, to misrepresent the truth."[54] In one bold stroke, Du Bois assuaged internal and external concerns that Washington might use his friends among the leadership of the NAACP, especially Villard, to control its activities.

Although the letter did not specifically refer to military participation, at least two of its signatories had close associations with the military—Maj. Allen A. Wesley, M.D., surgeon, 8th Illinois, and Napoleon Bonaparte

Marshall. With a few years of time and a sea change in conditions, the NAACP—through its board chairman, Joel Spingarn, and organ editor, W. E. B. Du Bois—would take a very active role in military affairs. Although the majority of the board maintained its pacifist stance, Spingarn would join the Military Intelligence Branch of the army and promote the establishment of colored officer training camps in direct violation of the NAACP's opposition to segregated institutions. Yet, before the exigencies and expediencies of war, the NAACP did very little publicly to advance the cause of a black regiment for New Yorkers. The pacifist tendencies of key members such as Villard, Mary White Ovington, Jane Addams, and Lillian Wald, among others, probably contributed to the apparent disinterest, but so did the identification of the regiment movement with party politics. Even more, some of those most directly involved in the fight for a black regiment had, as will become clear, close ties to Booker T. Washington, namely, Charles W. Anderson, Fred Moore, and by association Charles W. Fillmore. Most of all, the black regiment movement eventually conflicted directly with Joel Spingarn's vision for black officer training camps. However, as will be shown, Du Bois and Villard worked quite hard behind the scene to influence the leadership of the Regiment and use it for the association's purposes. Competing interests and strategic choices, more than anything else, determined the nature of the organization's involvement.[55]

Nonetheless, the formation of the NAACP and the "open letter" served notice that a new era in race relations and black activism had arrived. That announcement and subsequent activity alone helped to create a climate conducive to establishing a black National Guard regiment in New York. The NAACP's emergence and the altered battle lines that resulted probably strengthened the bargaining position of those who had cautioned patience or sought change through electoral and party politics. Concessions by authorities to more moderate individuals and organizations not only rewarded those who cooperated with the powers that be, they also often obscured and weakened the influence of more militant elements. The rise of the NAACP and the development of black electoral politics and civic organizations in New York City frequently acted in synergy. Such an enhanced combination of forces helped facilitate the movement to establish a black regiment.

# "Positions of Honor and Trust"

*Charles Ward Fillmore, the Equity Congress,*
*and the Byzantine Politics of the*
*Black Regiment Movement*

Despite its auspicious start and high profile, the NAACP, located at 20 Vesey Street and later at 69 Fifth Avenue, was not a Harlem institution. More than geographic placement distanced the organization from the community. Its national interests and largely white leadership cadre would not allow it to address, let alone solve, many local problems or help fill the black institutional void. The apparent inattention of the NAACP to the early regiment movement is a case in point. The fledgling organization openly directed its energies to Booker T. Washington, on the one hand, and lynching, segregation, and other obstacles to black dignity, safety, and progress, on the other. When, how, and to what extent the organization supported the regiment movement almost always reflected self-interest and power relations and not so much a spirit of community betterment and pride. Thus, its objectives often did not coincide with those of many black New Yorkers who decried and regretted the city's lack of indigenous black civic and political organizations.

In the forefront of this critical assessment of the community stood Frederick Randolph Moore, editor of the *New York Age*. In October 1910, an *Age* editorial posed the rhetorical question: "What's ailing Harlem?" Despite its claim to primacy—"First in population, first in money, and first in glory"—Harlem had not become a unified, solidified, and purposeful community. It stood like the gangly, awkward youth not able to handle a sudden growth spurt. Perhaps its critics expected too much of it, considering its young age and the significant forces aligned against its progress. Nonetheless, Moore, like other community critics, could not understand why Harlem, with all of its advantage as the "center of the business activities of a race and the home of the best housed Negroes in the world," failed to live up to its promise.[1]

The root of the problem, in the minds of many, lay in political ineptness and selfish leadership. Said to possess "more political 'leaders' than any three cities could conveniently use," Harlem could not claim tangible results: no representative on the board of aldermen, no member of the state assembly, and hardly any representation in the political organizations of the city. Not even the "hard, untiring, unselfish work" of Charles William Anderson, the so-called model leader, appeared to make a significant difference. As his admirers implied, he had to fight far too many pretenders bent on "empty praise and glory for themselves than on any purpose to aid the people to win from hostile hands what ought cheerfully to be given without a contest."[2] Still, no matter how much Anderson's supporters might have blamed others, they failed to realize that his unflagging and largely unrewarding allegiance to the Republican Party made him and them a part of the problem. Described as an almost "religious devotion" by historian Gilbert Osofsky, this commitment to an institution that took black support for granted only exacerbated the already weak position of black citizens.[3]

Yet, as early as 1892, cracks appeared in the wall of black solidarity with the Republican Party, which had, since the inauguration of Rutherford B. Hayes in 1877, largely abandoned its commitment to blacks—a commitment initiated and sustained by Radical Republicanism. Democrats in New York recognized the rapidly growing black population as a potential source of electoral power and moved to exploit the complacency of their opponents.

In 1892, Tammany Hall leader Richard Croker had funded the travel of a delegation of representatives to a black Democratic convention in Albany. Hugh McLaughlin, leader of Kings County Democrats, did the same. Two years later, the Parqueto Club, led by R. F. MacIntyre and Charles E. Brown, issued a call for another black statewide Democratic convention in Syracuse for the purpose of "broadening the healthful democratic spirit already infusing itself among our race." That convention chose delegates for the National Colored Democratic Convention scheduled for Indianapolis in August of that same year. These black Democrats claimed to have influenced the outcome of the vote in favor of Grover Cleveland for president and Roswell Flower for governor, even though neither man was a friend of Tammany Hall.[4]

In 1896, the erosion of the relationship between blacks and the Grand Old Party continued, as the next call for a black Democratic convention urged black voters "to get away from the past, from its prejudices and impediments; its treachery and hypocrisy, and to look to other ways of growth, advancement, and development." This time, spokesmen offered evidence that the Democratic Party represented the future. Charles Brown noted that President Cleveland had appointed blacks to high positions and that state Democrats had nominated and elected a black to an important county office. Brown then castigated the Republican Party for using blacks "as political slaves" only to be recognized "at election time."[5]

Nevertheless, criticizing the Republican Party carried great material and personal risks. James Ross, a city employee in the Republican administration of William Strong, found himself under attack from the Colored Republican Association of New York State, and his job was threatened for his association with black Democrats. These black critics wrote Strong and demanded that he forbid servants of his "administration to put forward any unnecessary efforts to stir up a feeling against McKinley, sound money, reciprocity, and protection."[6] McKinley, however, had done little to deserve such loyalty, as he and his party rejected any responsibility to protect the rights of blacks and aligned themselves "with the forces of racial proscription in the name of national unity." During his second inaugural address, the president did not even mention lynching, disfranchisement, or any other serious issue confronting blacks at the time. Instead, he directed his attention externally to Cuba and the Philippines. The move toward lily-white Republicanism had begun in earnest. The trend continued with McKinley's successor, Theodore Roosevelt, who, with few exceptions, put his own and the party's interests far above racial justice.[7]

As abuse of loyalists inside the GOP threatened to exceed that awaiting anyone who switched sides, more and more prominent blacks dared to join the Democratic Party. James D. Carr, a highly educated black lawyer, had been denied a position as assistant district attorney by the Republicans, and Edward E. Lee, a politically astute bellman, led the rapidly accelerating movement. Already concerned about the party's treatment of them personally, they soon learned that all blacks in New York could expect little for their continued support of the Republicans. Lemuel Eli Quigg, Republican county leader, drove this disturbing message home with a public boast that "you couldn't drive them (blacks) out of the Republican Party with a sledgehammer."[8]

Incensed with Quigg and what he represented, Carr, Lee, and other witnesses of the outrage vowed to break with a party that personally insulted them and no longer championed black interests or those of the working class. They reached an agreement with Tammany Hall leader Richard Croker, who promised patronage in exchange for black votes. As a result, these "defectors" backed the Tammany (regular Democratic) candidate for mayor, Robert Van Wyck, in 1897 and received official sanction from Tammany for their United Colored Democracy (UCD) in January 1898. Although Lee and Carr benefited directly from the alliance—Tammany made Lee a sheriff and appointed Carr assistant district attorney—both became the objects of black criticism, if not scorn. Moreover, the deal they cut did not lead to the modest gains that even they had expected. In New York, political power and representation emanated from the precinct and district levels. Unlike most Tammany Hall affiliates, the citywide UCD had no effective political base in any particular voting precinct. Consequently, it lacked the clout to reward the rank and file with jobs in Harlem or any other community for that matter.[9]

Though GOP loyalists condemned the so-called traitors, they probably owed the UCD a debt of gratitude. Republican power brokers such as Charles Anderson must have understood that the UCD allowed them to make the case to party leadership that the Democrats now posed a potential threat to the once-solid Republican black constituency. A major objective in this public scramble for perquisites would be a black National Guard regiment.

The Spanish-American War had made many black New Yorkers keenly aware of the status attached to National Guard units and their real and symbolic connection to nation and citizenship. In 1905, the *New York Age,* for instance, condemned the disbanding of black military organizations in Georgia as a deprivation of "the prerogative of bearing arms" for the nation. The action amounted to "de-citizenization," by which a state used federal funds to provide for only one part of its population at the expense of another. Even more blacks lamented the loss of these "ancient" and "honorable" organizations that could no longer "thrill the breasts of the admiring Afro-American populace." These voluntary organizations, which emerged all across the South after the Civil War, represented black solidarity, resistance, and collective power. The assault upon them contributed to and signified inferior status. Diminishing access to the National Guard elsewhere strengthened the resolve of black New Yorkers to secure their rightful place within the ranks of citizen-soldiers. Now, they believed that their growing numbers and increasing political organization and influence effectively positioned them to forge a change in a regressive development. They correctly understood the symbolic and real value of these organizations.[10]

By the second decade of the twentieth century, New York blacks, who had created black military organizations in the past only to see them disbanded or rejected, determined to change that sorry history. The story of the sustained and protracted effort by blacks to become an integral part of the New York National Guard is complex, tortuous, and often infuriating. In a more lighthearted vein, it might be called "the tale of the four Charlies"—Anderson, Fillmore, Young, and Whitman. Yet, in the early stages of the formal movement, two of the Charlies dominated—the well-known, politically connected, and influential Charles Anderson and the opportunistic outsider Charles Ward Fillmore.

Anderson, called Charlie by his friends, was a self-educated and self-made man. Born in rural Ohio in 1866, he, like so many others, left the hinterland, in 1886, for the potential rewards of New York City. Immediately, he became a player in Republican politics, stumping for candidates in black wards. In 1890, Anderson won the presidency of the Young Men's Colored Republican Club of New York County and received a low-level patronage position as a gauger in a district office of the Internal Revenue Service. From there, he rose through the ranks of government service on the basis of his political skills, mental acuity, and the approval of Booker T. Washington, who admitted that Anderson's drive and competence impressed him greatly. The "strong," "sturdy," and "aggressive" Anderson remained a loyal ally of Washington's, and both men influenced black political appointments in New York for many years.[11]

In 1911, twenty-five years after Anderson, another staunchly Republican black Ohioan made his way to New York—the ambitious and determined Charles Fillmore. Circumstantial evidence suggests a possible personal link between Anderson and Fillmore. Only three years Anderson's junior, Fillmore hailed from Springfield, studied law, and was a staff member in the Department of State in Ohio. As a veteran of the Ohio militia, he rose from the rank of private to major. Even more, he apparently used his connections in the Republican Party to secure a commission as a first lieutenant in the 9th Volunteer Infantry. Known as the "Colored Immunes," the 9th was recruited particularly for service in the Spanish-American War because of blacks' putative resistance to tropical diseases such as malaria and yellow fever. The cost of such pseudoscientific, racialist assumptions proved high, as many black soldiers died while caring for white soldiers. Fillmore himself contracted yellow fever, received an honorable discharge, and took a year to recover. He left Ohio shortly after the war and secured a position in the Treasury Department's Bureau of Public Health and Marine-Hospital Service in Washington.[12]

While in Washington, Fillmore somehow became interested in the affairs of New Yorkers, especially concerning the creation of a black regiment. In the absence of hard evidence, one can only speculate that Anderson played a role in Fillmore's involvement in New York. For months,

Fillmore shuttled between Washington and New York, advising proponents of the regiment movement on strategy and tactics. Those advocates had coalesced in an uneasy alliance of Republicans and Democrats dedicated to fighting housing discrimination, promoting the patronage of black businesses, and securing representation of blacks in municipal government, especially the police and fire departments. Last but not least, that alliance led the struggle to establish a black regiment. The organization called itself the Equity Congress of Greater New York.[13]

Based loosely on the structure of the federal government, the self-proclaimed nonpartisan and nonsectarian organization included executive and legislative branches. Belying its lofty name, the Equity Congress denied females representation, even though the organization relied on women for support. Henrietta Vinton Davis, for example, staged the play *Christophe* for the benefit of the organization. At the same meeting in which she made a presentation about her efforts, the congress voted to prevent nonmembers from voting on questions before the membership. That measure seemingly targeted Davis and perhaps women generally.[14] Who else would attend these meetings and not be allowed membership? The unjust exclusion of women from black political and civic organizations, especially one with *equity* in its title, reinforced and underscored male dominance and the tendency of black men to accept and perpetuate existing gender relations and roles.

Despite its claims of nonpartisanship, the organization might be better described as multiparty. James C. Thomas, a prosperous mortician and real estate tycoon, cofounded the organization along with prominent criminal lawyer J. Frank Wheaton and Egbert Austin Williams, better known as Bert, star of the Ziegfeld Follies and a former officer in the California National Guard.[15] The founders clearly understood that blacks had to apply outside pressure to both major political parties and elected officials in order to be effective change agents. The congress's founding and purpose seemed to be a direct, albeit delayed, response to the call of the *New York Age* for an effective civic organization. The Equity Congress certainly caught the attention of Charles Anderson, who warned President Taft that the Democratic faction of the organization was using the campaign for a black National Guard regiment to advance the cause of Democrats in New York and beyond. Although various sources claimed that organized efforts and protests for a black militia unit might have started as early as 1885, the sustained, institutionally based, and unremitting push seems to have begun with the formation of the Equity Congress on January 22, 1910.[16]

On May 5, 1911, Anderson alerted Taft's secretary, Charles D. Hilles, to the fact that J. Frank Wheaton, James Thomas, and D. E. Tobias, three leaders of the Equity Congress whom he labeled Democrats, had asked him for a letter of introduction to the president. Although Wheaton had excellent Republican credentials in the recent past, he and Tobias actually gained access to the secretary of war through Democratic assemblyman Louis Culliver. For the uncompromising Anderson, this association might have been enough to deny the men access to the president. Nonetheless, they found another route to Taft through William H. Lewis, an assistant attorney general and the highest-ranking black in the federal government. Perhaps Lewis, less familiar and concerned with party politics than Anderson, recognized the quality of the men and considered them worthy.[17]

The outcome of the meeting and the representation of it by Anderson gave Lewis a quick and painful political lesson. After the meeting with the president, Wheaton, Thomas, and Tobias, according to Anderson, went to the press with claims that he approved of their plan to form a black regiment. TAFT IS IN FAVOR: PRESIDENT HEARTILY APPROVES COLORED REGIMENT PLAN, read a newspaper headline shortly after their visit. The men allegedly reported not only that the president openly embraced the cause but that the secretary of war did as well; indeed, according to them, Secretary Jacob M. Dickinson of Tennessee praised the efficiency of the black soldier and promised to do all he could on the matter if it ever came to him. It never did. In a strange twist of fate, Henry Stimson replaced Dickinson as secretary of war only two weeks later. If the committee had a friend in Dickinson, it would not have one in the person who really mattered now, Stimson.[18]

The delegation from the Equity Congress—escorted by Lewis and James C. Napier, a close friend of Booker T. Washington's and register of the Treasury—also called upon James Hay, Democrat from Virginia and chairman of the Military Affairs Committee, in addition to former senator Charles Dick of Ohio, the so-called father of the modern National Guard. Dick's legislative initiatives strengthened the fiscal and supervisory relationship between the federal government and state militia units, facilitating, in part, the eventual transformation of these organizations from social clubs with military trappings into serious martial institutions.[19]

Notwithstanding the involvement of Lewis, Napier, and prominent white Republican officials, Anderson feared that the Democratic governor of New York, John A. Dix, would get credit if the regiment effort succeeded. Anderson cited Democratic campaign literature enticing the black vote with promises of representation on the police force and the authorization of a black regiment. As a result, he claimed, many blacks voted Democratic, and he believed that the party leaders should make good on their promises or admit that they were fraudulent.[20]

Was Anderson's reaction all about protection of the president and Republican interests? Or was it a matter of personal politics and territorial sovereignty? Lewis thought the latter and let Hilles, who had passed on Anderson's letter to him, know that he had merely introduced three old friends to the president so that they could make their case for a worthy cause. In a tongue-in-cheek tone, Lewis promised Anderson that in the future, he would "not undertake a personally conducted tour of any of the 'brethren' from his bailiwick without his consent and approval." Lewis also assured him that he would not involve the president in matters of "local personal politics," a pointed comment about Anderson's imperial style that hit a sore spot.[21]

Anderson veiled his true reaction by praising Lewis's character and ability and attributing the unfortunate characterization as "a mere verbal infelicity" and not an attempt to impugn his motives. In muted tones, Anderson explained that Lewis was wrong in downplaying the blame the Republicans might receive if the regiment movement failed and how they were unlikely to gain if it succeeded. Press reports support Anderson's account and provide evidence that the regiment issue had influenced black Republican leaders to leave the party, as Governor Dix and even Charles Murphy, the leader of Tammany Hall, apparently gave their consent for a black regiment. The postelection comments of the *Age* definitely support Anderson's assertions: "Now that John A. Dix is elected governor, we shall look forward to that Negro regiment of the National Guard, and an armory for it that will repay for all the inglorious defeats of former years."[22]

Anderson tried to let the "facts" speak for themselves as he provided Hilles a brief history of the movement. According to Anderson, about two years earlier a group of blacks had applied to the Republican governor, Charles Evans Hughes, for a black regiment. The governor had denied the application on the ground that the Constitution only provided for a maximum number of 18,000 National Guardsmen. Despite the fact that only 15,000 men belonged to the Guard at the time, the governor had claimed to need the vacancies for undermanned units to reach full strength. All involved knew that Hughes was using a mere technicality to thwart the movement and to protect his and the party's interests, for the prospect of a black regiment did not please many constituents, especially Guardsmen. Furthermore, Adjutant General Nelson Herrick Henry, who served at the pleasure of the governor as an appointed member of his staff, had persuaded his superior to oppose the measure.[23]

The Democrats had seized upon the issue in the 1910 election and had used it to demonstrate Republican insensitivity to black concerns. Ander-

son believed that the gubernatorial candidacy of Henry L. Stimson had suffered badly from the Democratic politicization of the regiment issue. Stimson had lost by more than 100,000 votes in New York City. The state went
Democratic, and beyond that, Anderson maintained that every Republican
district containing a large black base had gone Democratic by a larger plu-
rality than any others. One Republican congressman who had won by 8,000
votes in the previous election had lost badly in a district of 20,000 blacks.
Anderson said that the regiment question, more than anything else, had
turned blacks against the party.[24] This issue would dog the Republicans for
some time to come, as matters grew steadily stranger.

Not long after taking office in 1911, Governor Dix had met with a group
of black Democrats, including Robert N. Wood of the United Colored Democracy, who had asked him to fulfill the party's campaign promises of a
regiment. By all accounts, Dix had responded favorably, but another Republican, Adjutant General William Verbeck, ostensibly had disapproved on
the same grounds that Hughes and Henry had. The real reason lay in the
opposition coming from Guardsmen who objected to camping, training,
or socializing with black troops. Nonetheless, a Democratic assemblyman,
Louis Culliver of New York City's Thirtieth District, sponsored a regiment
bill in return for black votes. Passage, according to Anderson, would not
redound to the benefit of Republicans because a Democratically controlled
assembly and senate and a Democratic governor would then get credit for a
measure opposed by a Republican adjutant general. To Anderson, this was
the real significance of the regiment movement, not "personal politics" as
Lewis had suggested.[25]

On May 19, a gleefully vindicated Anderson wrote Hilles with news that
the assembly had killed the regiment bill by a vote of 68 to 25. It showed,
in his mind, "the insincerity of the [D]emocrats on the proposition." Nonetheless, Republicans still could not escape blame for the defeat of the measure, as the testimony of Adjutant General Verbeck, a Republican, that the
regiment would cost $50,000 to equip and $20,000 a year to support and
would be racially divisive and provocative probably raised serious doubts
in the minds of those inclined to support the measure and hardened the
conviction of those already in opposition. The strength and determination
of the National Guard lobby had proved decisive for the moment.[26]

Charles W. Fillmore soon emerged from his outsider status to bear
the standard for the regiment movement. And what a standard-bearer he
would prove to be—dauntless and resilient. First, however, he needed to
become a New Yorker, and only a new job could make such a move possible. His efforts in securing worthy federal office revealed the traits that

made him so effective as a campaigner for the regiment and so annoying as a person. Fillmore contacted Hilles on July 7, 1911, and echoed Anderson in urging the president to act quickly to prevent the Democrats from endearing themselves to black New Yorkers through the passage of the regiment bill.[27] Fillmore's timing appeared impeccable, as Taft longed to do something to restore his flagging reputation among blacks. He had spoken in favor of improved education for blacks, made a few black appointments, and publicly condemned the violent physical assault on Booker T. Washington by a white man in March 1911.[28]

Yet, Taft could not overcome his own past on issues affecting blacks, namely, the Brownsville incident in which he, as secretary of war, supported President Roosevelt's heavy-handed dismissal of many apparently innocent black soldiers from military service on the flimsiest of evidence. Nor could he escape blame for the current virtual inaction against lynching and the advancement of lily-white Republicanism. W. E. B. Du Bois had already begun to question the degree to which the president and his party deserved black support. He urged blacks to consider alternatives to a party that lived on past glory.[29] Du Bois's criticisms paled in comparison to those of *New York Age* editor Fred Moore, who relentlessly attacked Taft for removing able men from office, for refusing to appoint black Republicans to southern positions, and for failing "to crush the lily white serpent that poisons the bosom of the party."[30] Moore and many others believed that Taft needed to earn the respect of blacks.

The leaders of the regiment movement refused to accept the defeat of the first Culliver bill. Instead, *The Crisis* reported, "they aroused sentiment, saw the governor and other prominent Democrats, and the Assembly reconsidered the vote passing the bill unanimously." In a follow-up letter of July 27, 1911, Fillmore cited passage of the bill by the senate and assured Hilles that the bill's enactment was now a foregone conclusion. Consequently, the only way to prevent Tammany control of the regiment was to appoint a loyal Republican as colonel. Fillmore convinced Hilles that his sage advice and extensive military experience had so impressed the leaders of the regiment movement that they asked him to become commanding officer. What Fillmore did not tell Hilles was that the upstart *Amsterdam News* had credited passage of the Culliver bill to the efforts of Robert N. Wood, heir apparent to Chief Lee as head of the United Colored Democracy. The issue heightened tensions between Democrats and Republicans within the Equity Congress and nearly destroyed it. When Assemblyman Culliver addressed the group later and blamed Republicans for the defeat, two members of the congress tried to settle the dispute on the street.[31]

In the meantime, Hilles went to work on securing a transfer for Fillmore, who desired to be a special agent in the Treasury Department. Hilles referred the matter to Secretary of the Treasury Franklin MacVeagh for consideration. On July 29, Anderson wrote a letter requesting that Fillmore be made a gauger in his office. Accordingly, Fillmore would become Anderson's subordinate, and he would also occupy the very entry-level position in which Anderson began his own federal career. MacVeagh approved the transfer on July 31. Fillmore complained ceaselessly about the position being beneath his station, but he accepted it and moved to New York without delay. By day, he would inspect bulk goods and assess their value. At night, he would serve as a high-ranking member of the Equity Congress and the "rightful" leader of the regiment movement.[32]

Optimism soon turned to disappointment and frustration as Governor Dix, apparently responding to pressure from his own adjutant general and the state's militia council, refused to sign the bill. Instead of vetoing it and taking direct blame for the betrayal, he cleverly persuaded Culliver to ask for a return of the bill to his committee, where it died. Some had already complained about the shoddiness of the legislation, which would surely disappoint "the high hopes entertained by colored men whose political influence won votes for it." Moreover, the *Times* openly campaigned against a measure that it cynically maintained would further the exclusionary practices of the National Guard. In the end, the *Times* argued that the issue needed serious consideration because it was a social, not a political, matter, and concern over the black vote should not be a factor. Perhaps such public questioning of the wisdom of the legislation provided a cover to Culliver to commit an act of legislative infanticide. The legislature voted down Dean Nelson's repeated attempts to revive the legislation.[33] The Irish-controlled Tammany Hall was not ready to take on the New York National Guard over a black regiment.

In the absence of favorable signs for the legislation, the Equity Congress decided to take matters into its own hands by organizing a regiment and seeking National Guard approval for inclusion into its ranks. With the amendment of the Militia Law in 1862, all able-bodied males between the ages of eighteen and forty-five were members of the unorganized, or reserve, militia. The law excluded from service only "idiots, lunatics, paupers, vagabonds, drunkards, and persons convicted of infamous crimes." Fillmore and others behind the movement seized upon the absence of a racial clause and confidently dismissed the exclusions as serious obstacles, but they failed to understand the complex relationship between the legal and the practical, especially where race reared its ugly head. Under normal circumstances, their approach should have led to success, as the provisional regiment would establish undeniable proof of interest and support among black New Yorkers for the regiment and would provide indisputable evidence of the ability of its promoters to organize and lead. Moreover, an actual regiment would put authorities in a position of having to undo something that already existed. Full of optimism and confidence, Fillmore and his allies anticipated an easy progression from provisional to official status.[34]

On October 2, 1911, the *Globe and Commercial Advertiser* reported that blacks were determined to have a regiment and had already equipped and uniformed a battalion led by Maj. E. L. Reed. The Equity Congress planned to present to the state a fully formed regiment with a band of forty pieces. Fillmore, who held the rank of colonel and commanding officer of the provisional regiment, announced that he was acting "upon the approval of the Equity Congress to organize a provisional regiment in keeping with the spirit of the Congress and the demand of the colored people of the state of New York." The original field officers, in addition to Reed and Fillmore, were Lt. Col. J. Frank Wheaton; Maj. Herbert Jackson; Maj. Hamilton Herman Blunt; and Capt. J. A. Jaxson, adjutant (head administrator and record keeper).[35]

At the same time, black Democrats, up in arms over the inaction and the apparent defeat of the bill, pressured Dix and the legislature to make amends. Governor Dix, however, had concluded that his future and that of Democrats in the state were best served by responding to the desires and needs of white constituents. Whites in the Guard, especially officers, did not want a black regiment, and he could not ignore their will, let alone their power.[36]

The provisional regiment encountered difficulty from the very start. Fillmore knew that arms would be necessary for recruiting and training the men, but the state of New York and the War Department refused to supply an "independent military organization." Without the arms, recognition was remote. Consequently, the provisional regiment found itself in a vicious and perpetual cycle of rejection and neglect.[37]

Then, reports quickly surfaced that the organizers of the regiment were assembling it in the wrong manner by appointing officers without securing sufficient numbers of enlisted men, especially privates. The press attributed these and other criticisms to no less an authority than Col. John R. Marshall of the 8th Illinois. While on an unofficial inspection of black military outfits in the Northeast, Marshall reportedly expressed great skepticism about the prospects for a successful effort to establish a black regiment in New York. He predicted that the regiment's top-heavy organizational structure, the

National Guard's higher examination standards, and increased expenses in arming and equipping the men posed serious difficulties. This assessment said nothing of the capital requirements of an armory. According to the *Age,* Marshall even cautioned the organizers that their number for company size did not meet the minimum.[38] The reports painted a bleak picture of ineptness and, even worse, cronyism.

More bad news followed. Some of the men appointed as officers had no military experience whatsoever. Among them were Frank Wheaton, who held the rank of lieutenant colonel, and J. A. Jaxson, captain and adjutant. Further, reports from Ohio suggested that Fillmore was unfit to be the commanding officer of the regiment. Clearly stunned by these revelations, Fillmore and the Equity Congress fought back publicly. They maintained that Marshall expressed no such reservations to them and blamed the reporter for misconstruing the colonel's assessment. Contrary to the impassioned response, the details of the story seem to suggest that Marshall actually did offer such criticisms.[39]

Even the Equity Congress's leaders had to admit that they made exceptions to the rule on past military service as a qualification for a commission. The claim that they granted exemptions "to men very useful to the body by virtue of their intense interest and unselfish labor, or some particular value or connection that will facilitate our organization" did not satisfy critics, and it embarrassed many supporters. To some observers, the Equity Congress appeared fixated on an outdated vision of the Guard, when it existed largely for "social purposes, punctuated with elaborate ceremonies and parades" featuring a "gorgeous soldiery" in red jackets and bearskins. Black New York did not need a social club with "military trappings"; it required a serious martial institution. To counter the claim about top-heaviness, the Equity Congress pointed out that it had recruited 510 privates and disproportionately few officers. Still, the troubling question that the *Age* had asked a year before became all the more relevant and embarrassing: "Where are the privates and the non-commissioned officers? We know about the high officers; they are everywhere." Taking the offensive, the leaders of the regiment accused the *Age* of sabotage and warned its editor, Fred Moore, that pessimistic stories on the movement "would injure the whole cause rather than any of these temporary officers."[40]

Public defenses in the press did not suffice to stop the bleeding. On or around November 13, the *Amsterdam News,* an upstart weekly once considered the personal organ of the Equity Congress, reported that the prestigious Mu-So-Lit Club (Musical, Social, and Literary Club) of Washington, DC, had dropped Fillmore from its membership. The article stated that

Washington was "agog with gossip and speculation" over Fillmore's dismissal. Ironically, the club admitted William H. Lewis at the same meeting. Fillmore demanded a public explanation and apology to clear his name. Immediately, the club president, Dr. Arthur S. Gray, obliged, citing a constitutional provision that prevented nonresidents from holding membership as the sole reason for the dismissal.[41]

Fillmore, however, saw sinister forces at work among various individuals attempting to minimize his efforts. His detractors included some "busy-bodies" in Washington, Fred Moore of the *Age,* and other unnamed parties who were perhaps suggesting that Fillmore was merely a Republican lackey.[42] No amount of denial, however, could hide a disgraceful episode in Fillmore's past in Ohio that had come back to haunt him.

In 1897, a black man, Click Mitchell, had been lynched by a mob in Urbana, Ohio. Governor Asa W. Bushnell, though aware of threats on the man's life from an angry crowd, failed to take decisive action to avoid the tragedy. The *Cleveland Gazette* excoriated Bushnell not only for his failure to act but also for his "cowardly, hedging talk after the tragedy." Despite predictions to the contrary, his bungling of the tragic situation did not prevent Bushnell's reelection. Fillmore—described as "a good-natured, easy harmless sort of fellow with about as much backbone as a fly"—nonetheless knew who signed his paycheck and offered his 9th Battalion as an escort in the inaugural ceremony. The governor accepted the offer, and Fillmore faced charges by blacks of having "disgraced and insulted his troops by tendering their services to a man who is smeared all over with the Urbana lynching."[43]

When Bushnell, a Foraker man, sought the defeat of Mark Hanna for the Senate, Fillmore chose to side with the McKinley faction and withdrew his offer to the governor. Bushnell denied Fillmore's retraction, and the battalion marched without its commander. A disgraced Fillmore lost dignity and a commission, which a vengeful Bushnell had revoked. The *Gazette* showed absolutely no sympathy and wished him "good riddance" and hoped that his rapid exit would serve as a lesson to "all such weak-kneed, backboneless, time-serving, white politicians' toadies," who "serve at the expense of principles of vital interest and concern for the race."[44]

Ironically, a regular army lieutenant by the name of Charles Young, who had helped train the unit, eventually replaced Fillmore as commander of the battalion and held a temporary rank as major from May 14, 1898, to January 28, 1899. Young's move to the Ohio National Guard left the army with no black line officers. Even more, his volunteering for such duty foretold a continuing interest in National Guard service and field command, which cast Young's ever-growing shadow over Fillmore for many years to come. Despite Young's outstanding leadership and the battalion's reputation as the "best drilled organization" at Camp Alger, the 9th Ohio Battalion never stood a chance of receiving the call to war because it belonged to no regiment in its own state. Before the end of the conflict, Young returned to regular army duty and served with the 9th Cavalry in Cuba.[45]

Although Fillmore never seemed to obtain exactly what he wanted, he had an uncanny knack for almost always getting what he needed. In this instance, his dismissal proved a blessing in disguise, as it afforded him the opportunity to volunteer for service in the war against Spain. His participation in the war proved to be the first step on his long road to personal redemption and military honor.

One thing that Fillmore apparently did not volunteer to officials in Washington was information about his troubles in Ohio. In the face of withering criticism, he simply told his patrons that he was doing his best "to organize a colored regiment that will be friendly to the President and his administration."[46]

Undaunted, Fillmore stepped up recruiting efforts by circulating a broadside to "Colored Men" between the age of eighteen and forty-five to join the "First Colored Provisional Regiment of Infantry." The advertisement offered as enticements the chance to have a "line Armory and everything that goes with a Regiment," including "Colored Officers." All of this would be achieved through "intelligent organization."[47] Fillmore's best was not good enough for many, including Oswald Garrison Villard, grandson of William Lloyd Garrison, newspaper publisher, and cofounder of the NAACP.

Although a pacifist, Villard had a long-standing interest in blacks and the military. In August 1901, the *Nation* published "The Negro as Soldier and Officer," and two years later, a greatly expanded and updated version appeared in the *Atlantic Monthly* as "The Negro in the Regular Army." Although full of stereotypical characterizations, as we know, both pieces expressed Villard's favorable view of blacks not only as soldiers but also as officers. Charles Young, "a captain and a most efficient one," found the most favor with Villard and stood as the shining example of what a black officer could and should be. Villard believed the army was wasting Young's considerable talents by employing him as an instructor of military science at Wilberforce University. Villard continued to advocate for Young whenever he could.[48]

As Young's career developed, his value to the race increased. In 1903, the army sent Young to the West, where he served as acting superintendent of Sequoia National Park in California. Before the creation of the National

Parks Service, Young and his buffalo soldiers protected the park. In short order, Young's proficiency in languages, including Latin, Greek, Spanish, French, and German, made him an invaluable asset abroad, especially in nonwhite countries. From 1904 to 1907, Young served as military attaché to the American legation in Port-au-Prince, Haiti, where he studied the local military and mapped the terrain. Upon his return from Haiti, the War Department assigned him to the 2nd Division of the General Staff, the forerunner of the Military Intelligence Division (MID). In 1908, the army sent him to the Philippines, where he commanded two black companies.[49] These assignments also reflected the army's extreme care in placing black officers where they would be least threatening to the racial order within and without the military. By 1911, the multitalented Young stood as an iconic figure in black America and a self-proclaimed race man. He also had become a pawn in the struggle between the NAACP and the Tuskegee Machine of Booker T. Washington.

In November 1911, a written exchange between Young and Washington suggested the officer's place in the middle of the expanding tug-of-war between the NAACP and the Bookerites. Reed Paige Clark, the recently appointed receiver of customs for Liberia, admired Young for his "considerable tact and great executive ability" and asked Booker T. Washington "to enlist his active interest in Liberia." Within a week, Washington wrote Young. The ever-dutiful Young replied, "I am always willing to aid in any work for the good of our country in general and of our race in particular, whether that race be found in Africa or in the United States." Yet, Young's letter revealed more than a little hesitation. With a wife and small children, he must have considered an assignment so far away and in difficult tropical conditions not particularly inviting, even less so than his current post at Fort D. A. Russell in Wyoming. What really appealed to Young was "the organization of a Negro Regiment in connection with the New York National Guard."[50]

Young revealed that "sometime ago," Oswald Garrison Villard had asked him to consider the formation and command of this regiment and Young consented, "not knowing that I would be wanted for the 'homeland' detail." Regretfully, the refusal of state officials to authorize the regiment made the point moot for the time being. Young demurred: "Now if you and the War Department think I can be of more good to the country and our people on the African detail . . . I am perfectly willing to go, and shall render . . . faithful and loyal service." Washington replied, "You will have a splendid opportunity I think, to render service in a particular [way] most needed in that important field."[51]

Washington might have had his own reservations about the assignment, but he did not want to disappoint potential benefactors. Moreover, he did not want Young to strengthen the hand of his enemies in New York. Young went to Liberia in 1912, came down with blackwater fever (an often fatal complication of malaria named for its symptomatic dark-colored urine), and was never the same again. Yet, his chance to command the regiment had not ended entirely.[52]

In early December 1911, Fillmore reported confidently to Hilles that the provisional regiment would number more than a thousand men by the middle of the month, thus completing the recruitment process. With impressive press clippings to attest to his effectiveness, Fillmore bragged, "I have accomplished more in the three months since I have been here than has been accomplished for more than ten years in the efforts of prominent colored men of this city to recruit even a battalion." He predicted that when completed, the regiment "will be a larger and a more potential political factor than any other organization of color in the state." Fillmore naively assured Hilles that the regiment bill would pass in the next session of the General Assembly "without a dissenting vote."[53]

For his contribution to the cause of party, Fillmore once again requested reassignment so that he might "not be embarrassed in my efforts to serve the President and his Administration." Hilles did pass Fillmore's umpteenth request on to MacVeagh, but he also warned Fillmore that his requests for help from the assistant secretary of the Treasury and claims that "the Administration does not appreciate what I am doing" both annoyed and embarrassed him. An increasingly desperate Fillmore indicated that he could not adequately provide for his family on the gauger's salary.[54]

The unpredictable internal and external dynamics of the regiment movement seriously threatened its chances for success. Fillmore seemed unable to understand that a guarantee meant nothing in New York politics. On December 29, 1911, he requested that Governor Dix grant recognition to the provisional regiment. Dix did not oblige. Once again, according to Charles Anderson, the Democrats found a way to shift the blame. In a January 23 letter to Hilles, Anderson, with evidence supplied by Fillmore, informed the president's secretary that Adjutant General William Verbeck refused to accept the provisional regiment into the National Guard. Verbeck blamed Secretary of War Stimson for the failure.

According to Verbeck, Stimson opposed any new appropriations for equipment and would look upon "the creation of new Organizations . . . with extreme disfavor." Anderson claimed he "anticipated that our democratic state government would kill this proposition, and would in some way try to unload the responsibility on the national administration." Attempting to vindicate his earlier interventions seemingly against the regiment, Anderson attributed his advice of "caution in dealing with the committee, which called on the President and the Secretary of War last year" to such foreboding. To him, the Republicans were victim of "the old democratic trick"—bait and switch.[55]

Hilles clearly understood the gravity of the matter and relayed letters from Anderson and Fillmore to Stimson, whom he asked to communicate with the president. Was Stimson truly agonizing over the regiment issue? Or was he exacting some measure of revenge on those he associated with a movement that possibly helped cost him an election in New York? Stimson's response to Anderson had the ring of disingenuousness and evasion. The secretary of war denied any opposition in principle to a black National Guard regiment. He maintained that "there is no color line recognized by the war department in respect to the National Guard any more than in respect to the regular army." To reinforce his position, Stimson pointed to the highly regarded black battalion in the nation's capital as "one of the most satisfactory National Guard organizations that I know of." At a minimum, he seemed to be drawing a tortured distinction between exclusion and discrimination or segregation.[56]

How Stimson thought anyone would accept this flimsy excuse defies credulity and reveals his cynicism. The army's record clearly indicated a pattern of differential treatment of blacks as well as an explicit policy of racial segregation. Stimson then explained that New York authorities had reached the limit of their allotted funds and did not qualify for emergency aid. Shamelessly, he maintained that records did not show that the application was made for the benefit of a black regiment. Yet, before Stimson could respond to Anderson, Robert Shaw Oliver, acting in his stead, had informed Charles Fillmore that until the cavalry and artillery of the New York National Guard reached "the necessary numerical strength," the War Department would "defer any further allotments for the purpose of equipping additional infantry." Insincerely, Secretary Stimson assured Anderson that the War Department had done nothing to prevent the state of New York from "organizing a regiment of colored infantry . . . provided it has the necessary funds to equip the same and in future years, such a regiment, if it satisfactorily meets the regular inspection, will be recognized by the War Department as part of the New York National Guard."[57]

Had Stimson truly supported the regiment proposition, he would have impressed its urgency on Taft and sought some solution. Yet, there is no available evidence that he ever communicated with the president pursuant to Hilles's request. Moreover, Fillmore called the War Department's bluff. Bypassing the New York State authorities, he offered "to have this regiment designated as one of cavalry or artillery." The Taft administration did nothing. Stimson did not want to give the impression that his party opposed the regiment, but he also did not want to hand a victory to the Democrats. In a tactfully conciliatory letter to Hilles, Fillmore let the president's secretary know that the "response" of the War Department had done much to mollify the antipathy toward the administration. Fillmore once again stressed his value to the president and the party by alluding to his role in the defeat of an Equity Congress–led attempt to run blacks for office. And of course, he asked Hilles to get him a promotion.[58]

Fillmore's investment in the success of the regiment movement and his unyielding loyalty to the Taft administration drove him to take stands that alienated some members of the rapidly expanding Equity Congress, which numbered more than a thousand. By early 1912, a significant number of Equity Congress representatives believed the organization should flex its growing political muscle and run black candidates for the state assembly. A resolution proposing such action narrowly failed passage at the fifty-second meeting of the organization. Congressman Charles Fillmore led the opposition to the measure and "blocked it at every angle."[59] Even the support of the resolution by Second Vice President I. B. Allen could not overcome the argument that pushing black candidates would threaten the regiment movement by offending officeholding supporters of the initiative and by hurting other candidates, especially white Republicans. The resolution fight opened old partisan wounds in the Equity Congress that severely harmed Fillmore and the organization.[60]

Nonetheless, Fillmore continued to pursue a partisan agenda. Two months later, he informed Hilles that he had tabled a motion to endorse Theodore Roosevelt for president. Taft's tenuous position became increasingly clear. In addition to the Democratic threat, he faced a more formidable one from within. Now, his former ally and mentor had mounted a third-party run for the presidency after the defeat of Progressive Republican candidate Robert M. La Follette at the Republican convention. The entry of Roosevelt in the race spelled disaster for Taft and the Republicans in the 1912 election. Nonetheless, Fillmore believed his action proved his loyalty, if nothing else, and deserved reward. Once again, he asked Hilles to secure him "a more desirable place."[61]

The impatient and persistent Fillmore circumvented Hilles and contacted another secretary of the president, Carmi Thompson, about a promotion. More important, Fillmore reported that "conditions are changing in our favor in New York." Whether "our" meant the Republicans or supporters of the regiment movement was not clear. On either count, Fillmore was wrong, especially regarding the party. In addition to the challenge from Roosevelt, the Democrats mounted a significant bid for the black vote, including support for the National Colored Democratic League, touted by its leadership as "the first bona fide national political organization of Colored men ever formed in this country."[62]

Taft came in third in New York State and third in the general election. He lost by almost 200,000 votes in New York City alone. Teddy Roosevelt certainly siphoned off some of the black vote, and the National Colored Democratic League's motto "Make the Negro Vote a Factor" and endorsements for Democrats from the likes of W. E. B. Du Bois suggest erosion from outside the party ranks as well. After all, one source reported that the Democratic gubernatorial candidate, William Sulzer, received 50 percent of the black vote in New York State.[63]

The last communication on record between Hilles and Fillmore came after the election. In it, Fillmore wrote, "Now that the smoke of the battle is over I presume there is a chance for a few of the faithful to be rewarded before the end of Mr. Taft's Administration." The content reveals much about Fillmore's personality, his self-importance, his persistence, his naiveté, his tenuous economic position, and, most important, his struggle for dignity through a job commensurate with his leadership aspirations. Most of all, it shows how Republicans treated even the most loyal black supporters. The failure to do better by Fillmore, although attributed to his lack of qualifications and the scarcity of positions he sought, demonstrated the plight of the few blacks in federal service. Even those in higher positions than Fillmore occupied remained marginal. A provocatively titled cartoon, "'Mr. Lewis gets his!'" in the April 1911 issue of *The Crisis* made the point painfully clear. In it, President Taft, dressed as a chef, gives a squatting Assistant Attorney General Lewis a taste from the "political pot stew" with a long-handled spoon that extended across the "color line," while white federal officials scooped freely from the kettle labeled "white help only."[64]

Growing dissatisfaction with the Republicans locally and nationally led many blacks to throw their votes to the party commonly identified with the Old South. Supporters for change pointed to the record of the Democratic Congress of 1912, which reported no anti-Negro bills out of committee. They also trusted Woodrow Wilson. The National Colored Democratic League, led by Bishop Alexander Walters of the African Methodist Episcopal Church, even went so far as to adopt the claim by John B. Syphax, scion of a prominent black family from Arlington, that "there never was a gentleman born in Virginia who was an enemy of the Negro."[65] President Wilson took little time to disappoint, embarrass, and anger black supporters. Despite candidate Wilson's mild overtures to Du Bois and other black leaders, his subsequent actions rendered meaningless his conciliatory and reassuring words that, if elected, he intended "to be a President of the whole nation—to know no white or black, no North, South, East, or West and no home-born or foreign-born." Beyond avowing adherence to these broad principles, Wilson made specific pledges to veto discriminatory legislation and to provide for blacks as well as the Republicans had—a troubling prospect in and of itself.[66] In spite of these inadequate assurances, Wilson did what some could not imagine: he treated blacks worse than the Republicans had.

In one of the first acts of his new administration, he removed black officeholders in Washington, DC, the South, and everywhere, including William H. Lewis and Charles W. Anderson. So devastating was Wilson's "Jim Crow by executive order" that even the restrained, optimistic, and forgiving Booker T. Washington applauded *Evening Post* publisher and Wilson supporter Oswald Garrison Villard for his paper's editorials attacking racial discrimination in the federal government. Nonetheless, in his typically appeasing fashion, Washington proclaimed his faith in Wilson and hoped that he would "realize to what extent a lot of narrow little people in Washington are taking advantage of these orders and are overriding and persecuting the colored people in ways that the President does not know about."[67]

Washington lived long enough to witness the truly bigoted spirit of Wilson, but his death in 1915 mercifully limited his personal exposure to its effects. According to historian John Hope Franklin, the first Congress of Wilson's administration received the greatest flood of bills proposing discriminatory legislation against blacks that had ever been introduced into that body. Although most of the legislation failed to pass, Wilson used his presidential authority to segregate black and white employees and to phase most blacks out of civil service. Even more, by denying discriminatory intent in his actions and in those of people around him, Wilson sent a terrible signal that whites could violate black rights, interests, and even lives with impunity. Not surprisingly, lynchings and other forms of violence increased during the Wilson administration. This hostile and condescending treatment of people of color extended beyond the nation's border as well, with American troops in the name of democracy occupying Haiti and "invading" Mexico, disregarding the sovereignty of both nations while threatening the existence of many of their citizens.[68]

With Wilson's victory, black leaders of the regiment campaign could no longer expect to call upon the president or his cabinet for an audience, let alone support. Perhaps the removal of the Republicans was a blessing in disguise for the initiative, given that Hughes as governor had refused support and that the Taft administration seemed ambivalent at best. Now, Democrats stood to get full credit or blame on the issue. Moreover, the leaders of the movement could now focus their energies on state authorities and no longer had to worry about pleasing a Republican administration. Reports that William Sulzer, the Democratic candidate for governor, had promised support for a black regiment circulated widely before the election, leading some to believe that their efforts to secure a regiment would yield dividends at last. Optimism turned quickly to doubt and disappointment as Sulzer, soon after taking office, denied making any such promise.[69]

Beyond that, the most powerful figure in the New York National Guard, Maj. Gen. John F. O'Ryan, its commander, openly opposed a black infantry regiment. O'Ryan, a Dix appointee, was a friend of Tammany leader Charles Murphy and was most likely responsive to his patron's opinions and directives and probably in agreement with them. The *Age* surmised that the "social equality" bugaboo was behind O'Ryan's opposition and astutely concluded that the National Guard saw itself as a "social, instead of a military organization, which makes it possible for them to shine at pink teas in gold braid, etc." O'Ryan, who controlled commissions and field operations, certainly took the military functions of the Guard seriously, but he also understood the socioeconomic status implications of black membership and intended for blacks to play servile roles at best. Numerous assurances from blacks that such a regiment would be a fighting outfit and not a social one fell on deaf ears as so-called fears of "friction between white and black officers dulled the senses."[70]

In a meeting with Fillmore, O'Ryan extended an invitation for him and his men to affiliate with the Quartermaster's Corps, the Ambulance Corps, and the Sanitary Corps—all of which involved, to a greater or lesser degree, laborious, distasteful, and/or degrading jobs that white men avoided. When Fillmore rejected the offer, O'Ryan appealed to putative black pretentiousness and vanity by informing him that the men would wear fancy uniforms. Fillmore reportedly countered, "Colored men were looking for more than pretty suits; they were desirous of positions of honor and trust."[71]

Certainly aware of the prevalent imagery of blacks as worthless, shiftless, and even violent inferiors, Fillmore saw the Guard as an instrument of advancement, not further degradation. He valued the Guard not just for its military capacity but also as a "great educational institution," which purportedly produced a better class of citizen through an insistence on rigid discipline, the development of mind and body, and the precise and orderly performance of duties. The resulting traits—"sobriety, energy, initiative, neatness, order, punctuality, good health, and habits of concentration and application"—not only marked good soldiers and citizens but also identified good employees. Fillmore clearly understood the direct link between National Guard membership and employment opportunity. Unfortunately, this connection caught blacks in a vicious cycle in which exclusion from the Guard denied men the opportunity to be better employees and vice versa.[72]

Despite his secret offer to the War Department, Fillmore openly insisted that New York State recognize the regiment as an infantry unit—the "great standby and backbone of an army." The infantry represented a miniature army in itself, with detachments of mounted scouts and orderlies and a machine-gun company. Moreover, the infantry provided the frontline troops— those men who were mostly likely to die first in modern warfare but who also stood first in line for glory and individual heroism. The infantry offered the best opportunity for blacks to prove their capacity as warriors. In keeping with past traditions and enhancing them, they could hardly afford to accept anything less.[73]

With the unceremonious departure of Adjutant General Verbeck, for reasons that will be discussed, the leaders of the regiment campaign held high hopes for success. Yet, the new adjutant general, Henry De Witt Hamilton, a direct descendant of Miles Standish, and the commander, O'Ryan, already seemed hell bent on dashing these hopes. Signals from Washington that army officials proposed to eliminate the black man as an American soldier caused more alarm, for such an action threatened not just the regiment movement in New York but also the status of blacks as soldiers anywhere in the US military and, by extension, as full citizens. The editorial in the *Age* reflected widespread sentiment: "Our fatherland . . . has entered upon a career of race persecution and restrictions, dating from 1870, which threatens in the end to make the United States as uncomfortable a place of residence as England, France, and Germany used to be and Austria and Russia are now for the Jews."[74]

On April 11, 1913, New York offered hope against this terrible trend as it strengthened an existing civil rights law by making it a crime to advertise racial or religious discrimination by signs or other printed matter. Although the law had come about as a result of Jewish initiative and pressure since 1907 against "Christian Only" notices and practices, its benefits, blacks believed, would redound to them. The *Age* astutely suggested, "The wise thing for the Negro to do is to form as close an alliance with the Jew as is possible so that the latter in fighting for his own rights will, in some degree, fight for ours also." Du Bois biographer David Levering Lewis notes that "after 1910, philanthropy and civil rights in Afro-America attracted sustained Jewish attention." Blacks would need all the help they could get at the state and local levels, as the Supreme Court a month later declared the federal civil rights law of 1875 to be completely null and void.[75]

Just as promising was a flurry of legislative activity in support of the regiment issue that began immediately after the 1912 election. Regrettably, the disparate sources of support and competing proposals troubled leaders of the movement, who wondered whether the issue would again fall prey to partisan and racial politics. Progressive Henry Salant of the Nineteenth Senatorial District introduced legislation for a black battalion at the same time Democrat Thomas Kane of Manhattan's Twenty-First Assembly District introduced similar legislation for a regiment. The Equity Congress endorsed the Kane bill and avoided a tough political fight when Senator George W. Simpson replaced Salant and made a strong and forceful argument for the Kane bill. His contention that the National Guard barred blacks only because of race prejudice put the legislature on the spot. Furthermore, he cited the valor of black troops during the Civil War and the Spanish-American War as evidence of black capacity and worthiness. Finally, black leaders petitioned the legislature, asserting that membership in the National Guard "would improve the morals and physique of the young men of the race in New York by taking them off the street and giving them the many advantages of an armory, including athletic games and a library."[76]

On May 2, 1913, the Kane bill passed both houses of the New York legislature with little opposition. Almost immediately, the Equity Congress sent a delegation to Governor Sulzer to urge him to fulfill his oft-professed commitment to racial justice by signing the legislation, regardless of whether he had pledged support for the measure in his campaign. Meanwhile, optimistic press reports gave the impression that only the governor's signature stood in the way of the realization of a community's dreams. With 832 members of the provisional regiment in place and the assurance by Comptroller William A. Prendergast that a vacant armory at Sixty-Eighth and Columbus could be made available at no additional cost to the city, there seemed to be cause for optimism. However, appearances proved misleading. The deadly combination of race and politics could easily turn victory into defeat and deny justice no matter how much it might be deserved. Even Sulzer's signing (like so much of the history of this struggle) did not lack drama.[77]

Governor Sulzer gave no immediate indication of what he would do with the legislation. His National Guard commander, O'Ryan, opposed the establishment of the regiment, and so did the newly appointed adjutant general, Henry De Witt Hamilton. Sulzer had dismissed a plea from his predecessor, John Dix, to uphold his removal of O'Ryan and appoint Verbeck as commander. Dix had come under heavy fire for his attempts to oust the insubordinate O'Ryan and reorganize the New York National Guard (NYNG) so that the commander would be more responsible to the governor. To that end, he created a new position of chief of staff and named Verbeck to it. The gambit failed, and Dix and Verbeck paid a heavy price, as both lost their jobs. The O'Ryan episode was undoubtedly one of the many reasons the ineffective Dix lost Tammany support. Recognizing the popularity and political clout of O'Ryan, Sulzer, in his first official act as governor, had fired Verbeck, replaced him with Hamilton, and strengthened the authority of O'Ryan, who he knew would rid the Guard of "petticoat rule" and make the officers something more than "ballroom heroes." Sulzer was unlikely to repeat the mistakes of Dix by opposing the advice or desires of O'Ryan or his Tammany backers, despite his characteristically self-important claim that he stood "as firm as a rock in a tempestuous sea for civil and religious liberty; for equality before the law; for equal rights to all, and special privileges to none."[78]

With little other recourse, prominent blacks appealed to Sulzer's apparent sense of fairness in revealingly divergent ways. Eugene Kinckle Jones, assistant director of the National League on Urban Conditions among Negroes, contended that "military training and discipline will serve to produce added strength of character and respect for citizenship among the colored men of State." Others curried favor with the governor against rivals while at the same time seeking support for the regiment. Many used the opportunity to support Charles Fillmore for commander and promote the cause of all-black leadership. Some placed the regiment bill in a larger context of progressive racial legislation, including an appropriation for celebrating the fiftieth anniversary of black emancipation and the antidiscrimination law. [79]

James Thomas, Jr., of the Equity Congress, stressing respectable black manhood, sought to convince the governor that the regiment could alleviate idleness among young black men who loitered on street corners or wasted money, time, and their lives in poolrooms or other places of vice, "where there is no chance for them to build up their bodies, and make men of themselves that the community in which they live will be proud of them." Thomas also struck the themes of red-blooded Americanism, citizenship, and the franchise in his appeal. Sulzer acknowledged Thomas's letter and told him he "noticed all he had to say relative to the establishment of a colored regiment." Yet, Sulzer offered no clues as to his intentions and seemed more interested in the support Thomas promised for the passage of the direct primary bill.[80]

The impending approval of the regiment bill rekindled the hopes of Oswald Garrison Villard to have Maj. Charles Young organize, train, and command the regiment. Villard reportedly had the support of Robert N. Wood of the United Colored Democracy. More important, "private assurances" from Maj. Gen. O'Ryan that Young was "his first, second, and third choice" made Villard confident that the decision rested with Young. O'Ryan, however, seems to have been very careful to avoid expressing such views in writing—a possible warning sign that Villard missed.[81]

Nonetheless, Villard urged Du Bois to convince Young to meet with Lt. Col. Romulus Foster Walton, a member of O'Ryan's staff, an 1898 graduate of West Point, and "a former southern regular army officer with a very high opinion of Young," who was "eager to co-operate with him." Villard naively informed Du Bois that Walton had promised to make the regiment a success and believed that with Young at the helm, the unit "will make almost every other regiment in New York sit up and take notice." Having witnessed so many false starts and disappointments, Du Bois waited until Governor Sulzer's decision was made before approaching Young, as he called him.[82]

On May 31, only two days before the deadline for signing the legislation, an "exceedingly anxious" Robert N. Wood, leader of the Tammany Hall United Colored Democracy (UCD), contacted Sulzer's secretary, Chester C. Platt, to ask whether Sulzer had signed the bill. In the event that the governor had not signed, Wood requested an appointment for a "delegation of Colored men" to meet with Sulzer on Monday, June 2—the last day before the bill's expiration. Unfortunately, the UCD was not on the best of terms with the reform-minded Sulzer, who was now at war with Tammany Hall. The Reverend J. H. McMullen, pastor of Rush Memorial AME Zion Church, had reminded Sulzer not long before the communication from Wood that "colored Tammanyites" were his "most violent critics on account of the Primary Bill." Platt telegrammed Wood on June 2 with bad news: "Bill not yet acted on by Governor."[83] The hopes of the black people of New York hung on a three-letter adverb that signified possibility for or against.

Sulzer had waited until that same day to send a copy of the bill, for advice, to Mayor William Jay Gaynor. In a somewhat confusing and ambiguous response, reflecting fuzzy jurisdictional boundaries and the need for plausible deniability, Gaynor opposed the governor's approval of the legislation by claiming that the city could not afford to "have any further obligations put upon it." "For that reason alone," Gaynor told the governor, "I think that I should have to disapprove it if it were before me."[84] The mayor, however, was not sure that he had authority—and for good reason.

Under state law, applications for an armory in New York City could only come from commanding officers of a military unit, including the major general and the commanding officer of the naval militia. These applications had to be made to an armory board composed of "the mayor, the comptroller, the president of the board of aldermen, the two senior ranking officers of or below the grade of brigadier-general, in command of troops of the national guard quartered in said city, the commanding officer of the naval militia and the president of the department of taxes and assessments." Should the Armory Board approve such an application, it had to "make its recommendation to the commissioners of the sinking fund." Final authority for funding rested with the Sinking Fund Commission, which could approve or reject the recommendation.[85]

Unfortunately, nothing about the black regiment seemed to follow the existing guidelines. In fact, the legislation authorizing the establishment of a "colored regiment" created a whole new set of circumstances. First, no other regiment required a state law to authorize its formation. So long as the number of active Guardsmen fell between 10,000 and 18,000, the governor of the state had almost absolute authority under the law "to alter, divide, annex, consolidate, disband or reorganize any organization or corps and create new organizations," when such changes "will increase the efficiency of the state forces." Second, the authorizing legislation presented a dilemma in its requirement that the "armory board of the city of New York shall provide quarters for such a regiment."[86]

Mayor Gaynor correctly regarded the provision as an unfunded mandate. More than economics influenced Gaynor's opposition, however, as he reportedly admitted he "did not think much of the colored regiment idea." He had high-level state support for his position. John H. Delaney, the commissioner of the newly created Department of Efficiency and Economy, fearing that the governor would seek state funding for the armory, painted a bleak fiscal picture in which the costs associated with a new armory would threaten the well-being of existing vital institutions such as state hospitals. He too recommended that the governor "disapprove the bill to further enlarge the National Guard this year."[87]

As the deadline approached, the "delegation of colored men," which included members of the United Colored Democracy and the Equity Congress, raced to Albany and urged Sulzer to sign. Sulzer signed the bill into law only twenty minutes before the midnight deadline, claiming that his simple sense of justice prevailed against the advice of friends. Disapproval of the bill "would have belied all that I have been talking about and doing for the past quarter of a century"—acting on the principle that there should be "no discrimination against citizens in matters of race, creed, or color." The act read:

> Within three months after this section takes effect, the adjutant-general shall organize and equip a colored regiment of infantry in the city of New York. Such regiment when organized and equipped shall become a part of the national guard of the state of New York, and subject to all the statutes, rules, and regulations governing such national guard. The officers of such regiment shall be commissioned by the governor, subject to the provisions of this chapter, in relation to eligibility and examination. The armory board of the city of New York shall provide quarters for such regiment.[88]

At last, the long and hard political fight for a regiment had been won. Organizers and supporters prepared to celebrate this sweet legislative victory, but developments in Albany would soon dampen the mood of jubilation and reveal that the real battle had just begun. Few understood that the military politics were every bit as difficult as the electoral variety. Now, the regiment movement found itself in the hostile theater of combat controlled by the New York National Guard and the War Department of the United States. They proved to be formidable, almost deadly opponents.

# 3

## "Second Only to . . . the Emancipation Proclamation"

### The Trying Campaign from Authorization to Formation

Despite the order calling for the authorizing act to take effect immediately, Governor Sulzer and Adjutant General Henry De Witt Hamilton, in less time than the ink could dry, violated the provisions of the law by deciding to muster in only one company and not the whole regiment, by the end of the ninety-day period. The results of this "experiment" would determine whether to continue or terminate the process. One can only surmise that Sulzer struck a deal with the state National Guard leaders in deference to their misgivings and in anticipation of a hostile reaction by officers of other regiments. The *Albany Times Union* reported that many officers of the Brooklyn regiments had declared their intention to resign as soon as they learned that the governor had signed the bill. None of these officers, however, gave permission for his name to be used, an indication of intent to posture and intimidate but not to surrender a valuable commission and all that went with it. When questioned about the threat, Major General O'Ryan shamelessly said he knew nothing about the organization of the regiment and doubted it would cause the resignation of any white officers. Sulzer, the self-proclaimed champion of civil rights, conceded that the new regiment would have black officers but that they would not come into contact with whites.[1]

Thus, the arrangement of mustering in by company could have been, at best, a way to assure the soundness of this "risky" initiative by forcing the regiment to prove itself on a probationary basis. At worst, the plan might have served to complicate the process and frustrate black aspirations, without giving the appearance of real opposition. Sulzer, the consummate politician, found himself in a delicate balancing act involving white officers, black constituents, Mayor Gaynor, and the state legislature. Sulzer could ill afford to alienate further a legislature whose support he needed for important reform initiatives. A pocket veto of the bill would have caused even more harm to an increasingly tenuous relationship with his party. In fact, the *New York Sun* questioned Sulzer's professed altruism and credited the measure to the legislature, in which "there was no opposition at all to the proposal." Adding to questions of Sulzer's sincerity was the establishment of temporary quarters for drilling purposes, when permanent facilities apparently existed. The action strongly suggested official intent to marginalize the regiment and demoralize its leaders and supporters.[2]

Despite the dampening effects of "the experiment," supporters of the regiment campaign gave every public indication of victory and openly rejoiced. They shrugged off the obstacles placed before them now as only minor impediments on the path to full and speedy recognition. In appreciation of the efforts of Governor Sulzer and Assemblyman Kane, the Equity Congress held a "big jollification meeting" to thank the two men for their work and to pledge support for both of them. The *Age* also credited Dr. V. T. Thomas for his efforts to broker an alliance between Fillmore, of the Equity Congress, and Robert N. Wood, leader of the United Colored Democracy. Without their cooperative strength and united front, the paper reported, the regiment effort could not have succeeded.[3] The Democrats clearly had scored a major victory with the blacks of New York City. The *New York Age* condemned the Republican Party as strongly as it praised the Democrats for the apparently successful outcome, while giving itself more credit than it probably deserved. WE HAVE THE REGIMENT! exclaimed the *Age*:

> Governor William Sulzer, a Democrat in a truer sense than any of his Republican predecessors in office, has signed the act authorizing the mustering in of the regiment. This is a great victory for the *Age* and all the other agencies that have contended for twenty-five years that the Negroes of the State should have representation in the National Guard. All the previous governors from New York who have passed upon the question, from Frank S. Black down, mostly Republicans, have been too weak to overcome the objections, mostly on the social features of the service, of their Adjutant-Generals and staffs, against the authorization of the Negro regiment. Gov. Sulzer had the same objections to overcome, and overcame them, brushing them aside as a strong man should, as having nothing to do with the merits of the case. That is the sort of Governor the State of New York should have

all of the time; a Governor disposed to treat all the elements of the citizenship by the same rule of justice and fair play.[4]

Wanting to do nothing to jeopardize the prospects for the regiment, organizers prepared in earnest to comply with official orders no matter how unjust. Before they could act, however, the *Albany Argus* reported that Sulzer had tapped Capt. Louis F. Jackson to head the new regiment. The announcement must have affronted those who had waged the long and hard fight to create the unit. Jackson, described as a former member of the regular army, had no apparent connection to the regiment struggle. Who he was and how he even came to Sulzer's attention was not clear. Sulzer simply called Jackson a soldier of note and cited his experience on the firing line in Cuba, the Philippines, and the American West during the "Indian uprisings."[5] The man's name quickly and mysteriously disappeared from view.

Charles Fillmore did not let the announcement discourage or sidetrack him. Certain that no one else could rightfully claim or deserve command of the regiment, he assumed the role of leader and wrote Adjutant General Hamilton on June 5 with plans to expedite the timetable for recognition. Fillmore wanted Hamilton to equip and authorize the first company as soon as possible, as he envisaged a unit of men with the capacity to be officers and leaders to help train the rest. Fillmore further worried that he would lose many of the nearly 1,000 men in the provisional regiment, who had trained at their own expense, if they were prevented from becoming official members of the organization. He offered, "We are prepared to give instruction to all of these men in order to facilitate the work of preparing the full regiment." He assured Hamilton that the process would not "interfere with the regular work of the first authorized company."[6]

Fillmore conceded defeat on the issue of an armory and displayed a resourceful and cooperative spirit by requesting temporary quarters in Harlem and suggesting Van Cortlandt Park as a summer training venue. In a gentle prod, he advised Hamilton that the regiment "upon short notice" could "produce full regimental strength." Clearly, Fillmore had begun to regret his acceptance of "the understanding that only one company be organized at a time."[7]

Behind-the-scenes moves to obtain the services of Maj. Charles Young, the highest-ranking black officer in the US Army, also threatened Fillmore's leadership. With Young reportedly on leave from the military for three months, W. E. B. Du Bois decided the moment was right to press his case to the War Department. Presumptuously acting in the interests of the "colored people of the state" who were "anxious to have this regiment of the highest proficiency," Du Bois, on official stationery of *The Crisis,* requested Secretary of War Lindley L. Garrison "to put [Young] at its head at least during its formative period." To add legitimacy to his request, Du Bois informed Garrison that Major General O'Ryan enthusiastically supported Young. Du Bois also sought Garrison's advice about procedure and solicited his "good offices."[8]

Rather injudiciously and prematurely, he contacted Young before receiving Garrison's reply. Although he asked for Young's advice as to how to proceed, he had already written the secretary of war. Du Bois held nothing back in trying to convince Young of the importance of his making himself available for what was "the biggest and best chance for us." Then, Du Bois, while obviously exaggerating, placed the regiment in the middle of a monumental internecine contest, remarking, "We have got some other big things on foot in New York and with you at the head of the regiment we will put this state at the head of the Negro race in the place of Alabama."[9] Young and the regiment were to be powerful weapons in the black civil war, pitting the NAACP (North) against Booker T. Washington's Tuskegee Machine (South).

A dismissive Garrison informed Du Bois that New York State had filed no record with the War Department or stated any intention to form such a regiment. This inaction constituted further evidence of ill will on the part of Adjutant General Hamilton and Major General O'Ryan, if not the governor. In any event, Garrison apprised Du Bois that a request for the services of Major Young "should be made by the Governor." Contrary to Villard's assertion that Young was on leave and headed home, Garrison apparently rendered the issue moot, however, as he concluded "that the services of Major Young are not available, he being on detail as military attaché in the State of Liberia."[10]

Issues of leadership and commitment aside, the grand gesture sparked great public and private praise for Sulzer. Robert Wood congratulated the governor for rejecting "the petty spirit of race prejudice" and demonstrating continued "devotion to the principles of democracy" by abolishing "one of the most unjust practices that ever disgraced the fair name of the State." Wood astutely pointed out that to exclude the state's 200,000 black citizens from representation in the National Guard amounted to taxation without representation. James Anderson, president of the *Amsterdam News,* called Sulzer the "idol of the colored people in the Empire State, to say nothing of the United States."[11]

Although Anderson's effusive praise might have overstated the perception among blacks of Sulzer, it did not exaggerate the significance of the legislation outside the state. In response to inquiries from black southern newspaper editors about the regiment, Sulzer's secretary, Chester Platt, sent copies of the legislation as well as an editorial from the *Argus,* which bragged that Sulzer had again proven that "he can rise above race prejudice and religious bigotry, and do justice to man on account of man—regardless of race or religion." The editorial also praised Sulzer's role in passing the civil rights law and supporting a celebration of the fiftieth anniversary of the Emancipation Proclamation.[12] Platt and Sulzer clearly took great pleasure in presenting themselves as friends of the race. Yet, the real measure of Sulzer's sincerity would be in the implementation and enforcement, not the signing, of the legislation. How he handled opponents of the black regiment within his very office would provide a greater measure of the man's commitment—or lack thereof—to racial justice.

Here as in so many instances, blacks represented a special case and test. The difference in the governor's handling of discrimination against Jews in the National Guard and that of blacks is telling. Only four days after Sulzer's historic act, Samuel Littman, a sergeant in Company D of Brooklyn's 47th Regiment, publicly charged that he had been denied a commission on the basis of his Jewish identity. The timing was not a coincidence, as the "success" of blacks created a wave that Jews sought to ride. Immediately, Sulzer ordered Attorney General Thomas Carmody to investigate. Judge Leon Sanders, a municipal court justice and grand master of the B'rith Abraham, brought the charges to the governor's attention only after Adjutant General Hamilton appeared ready to sweep the matter under the rug. This high-level intervention indicated the seriousness of the issue and the power that could be brought to bear upon it. On June 10, Sulzer announced a public hearing and vowed he would "give this case the attention it deserves." Though promising not to act hastily, Sulzer acknowledged that "some of the most distinguished citizens" of the state had leveled these charges of the "gravest importance."[13]

Sulzer, who had represented the Lower East Side of Manhattan in Congress for eighteen years and risen from that district as assemblyman, owed much to his Jewish constituents. He himself was of German and Scottish-Irish descent, but he had worked closely with Louis Marshall of the American Jewish Committee on many issues affecting the lives of this politically and economically powerful yet much-persecuted group. Marshall had been pushing since 1907 for legislation to prevent the posting of "Christian Only" signs on business establishments and discrimination against Jews at resorts and hotels. Not one to miss an opportunity to demonstrate his bona fides as an enemy of bigotry and a champion of fairness, Sulzer relentlessly pressed for truth and justice in the Littman case as well as evidence that the state's Guard acted more like a social club than an efficient and effective military organization.[14]

Sulzer, aware that a standard investigation would yield little, appointed a special board of inquiry headed by Lt. Col. Herman Bendell. After over a month of public hearings and extensive press coverage, the dirty little secrets of the National Guard emerged in clear public view. Surely, the problem extended far beyond Sergeant Littman and Company D. First, although Company D was 30 to 40 percent Jewish, no Jews held commissions. Other units had higher percentages of Jews in their ranks but no Jewish commissioned officers. Littman, who had earned a law degree from New York University, had entered the National Guard in 1904 and by all accounts was well qualified to be a second lieutenant.[15]

Col. Henry C. Barthman, commander of the 47th Regiment, admitted he had told Littman that he "would find it unpleasant to be the only Jew in the Council of Officers." On July 9, the governor's board of inquiry ruled that Sergeant Littman had been the victim of "gross discrimination." It censured Barthman and ordered the regiment to reconsider Littman's candidacy on the merits or face dissolution or reorganization. On July 13, Sulzer endorsed the report, made it public, and warned all concerned that "there must be no discrimination in the National Guard on account of race, religion or previous condition."[16]

Littman, who had resigned in protest earlier, refused the offer to reenlist out of concern for the best interests of the regiment and its worthy men. However, he vowed to continue his "struggle to strike down the barriers of religious intolerance in the National Guard so that Americans, regardless of race or creed, might have the opportunity to give themselves up in military service to the state." Sulzer declared victory: "As Col. Henry C. Barthman has been censured, the recommendations of Col. Herman Bendell have been carried out in letter and spirit. This practically ends the case." Unfortunately, the end of that case did not end the problem. Continuing instances of discrimination and exclusion necessitated many more investigations. Samuel Littman kept his promise and participated in the continuing struggle for equitable treatment of Jewish Guardsman.[17]

The Littman case goes only so far in helping to understand the plight of blacks. Discrimination against Jews was widespread but not total. No black at that time could expect to belong to a white National Guard unit, not even as a member of an auxiliary or service unit. Furthermore, the case of Sergeant Littman demonstrates the political power that Jews could muster in their own defense, as well as its limitations. Last, it represents the tension in American society and within the Jewish communities—especially among elite German Jews—about assimilation and accommodation. Some Gentiles asserted that it was neither religion nor race but attitude that caused discrimination against Jews. A high-ranking NYNG officer claimed that many Jews were too sensitive, too quick to see "an order brusquely given as a personal insult on account of his race." To him, the problem was not a matter of religion but one of "individuals who have . . . made themselves unpleasant." By contrast, the officers pointed to Jews who "because of their pleasant personalities had made themselves most popular commanders."[18] In the manner and substance of this denial, the officer revealed the insidious nature of American anti-Semitism in the early twentieth century.

Blacks, for better of worse, received virtually no such mixed messages about race and behavior. Neither class nor character could outweigh the burden of blackness and its stigmatizing effects. As such, assimilation was not a viable option for them. Indeed, such attempts among race leaders to distinguish between different classes of blacks increasingly degraded less fortunate blacks and did nothing to improve the position of those who maligned their poorer, uneducated, and less cultured sisters and brothers. Color and historical position ("previous condition"), coupled with a contingent political impotence and economic weakness, hindered racial pride and contributed to sanctioned and systematic exclusion.[19]

Nonetheless, blacks grew more and more bold in pressing for equal access to public accommodations, as NAACP vigilance committees frontally attacked discriminatory establishments. Black New Yorkers understood, however, that the National Guard acted like a private club and that their only hope of respectable inclusion in it was as a separate unit. To that end, they formed the first company in early July, with John L. Waller as its captain. Most of these men, already members of the provisional regiment, drilled and trained in preparation for the mental and physical tests required by military law and so impressed their officers that the latter began organizing a second company. Shrewdly, the Equity Congress played to the ego of the governor, showering him with official praise in the form of a resolution that ranked his support of the regiment movement "second only to the signing of the Emancipation Proclamation."[20]

Yet, internal power plays threatened the progress of the enterprise. According to the *Age,* local black Democrats attempted to put through a resolution that would have changed the membership criteria of the Equity Congress. The proposal stipulated that in the future, any member holding a federal, state, county, or municipal office would be ineligible to hold office in the organization. Such a regulation would affect the leadership of the regiment as well, since the provisional regiment was so closely tied to the Equity Congress. The initiative clearly targeted Fillmore, who, as the organization's first vice president, quickly ruled the motion out of order. He referred the membership to the preamble of the organization's constitution, which stated that the Equity Congress came into existence "to promote the interest of men holding political positions."[21]

In the meantime, Charles Young had returned from his difficult assignment in Liberia more than ready to take command of the regiment. He had written Du Bois on the first of July, which evidently prompted Du Bois to contact General Hamilton about Young's interest. The adjutant general agreed to a meeting on July 14 at 3:00 P.M. in his Broadway office. Whether this or a subsequently scheduled meeting near the end of July actually took place is unsubstantiated.[22] More certain was a growing sense of frustration and desperation on the part of all who supported the regiment. Villard was chief among them and told Young: "After a great show of fuss and feathers last year . . . enough physically capable men have not been discovered to fill a company." He worried about the impact on blacks "in this town and elsewhere" should the organizers "fall down as badly" as the signs indicated. Perhaps mistaken about the source of the problem, Villard tried to convince Young that only he could save the day. The recent assignment of a regular army officer to command an Oregon National Guard regiment lifted his hopes that the War Department would release Young.[23]

Yet, the troubled political fortunes of the governor would make the Young issue moot for the time being. Whether Sulzer was ever committed to the regiment at the time would never be known, for on August 15, 1913, the state assembly adopted a resolution of impeachment citing Sulzer for "willful and corrupt conduct in office and for high crimes and misdemeanors." After running roughshod over the legislature and Tammany Hall, Sulzer had his effective political career come to a screeching halt on October 17, 1913, when a high court of impeachment found him guilty, mostly on the grounds of fiscal malfeasance. He had brazenly affronted Tammany Hall, employed heavy-handed tactics in pushing his radical direct primary initiative, displayed almost no political loyalty, and taken every opportunity to embarrass his opponents.[24]

Furthermore, his extremely affected behavior and appearance, characterized by overblown rhetoric, pompous gestures, and a conscious Henry Clay look, endeared him to few. Many saw these as visible signs of a shallow, opportunistic, and disingenuous individual—a man who would authorize and press investigations of graft while using campaign funds for personal reasons and investing in Wall Street firms he condemned. Although his backers argued that he had been victimized by a Tammany witch hunt, they could not explain why he did not testify in his own behalf. The opposition could: "If Sulzer doesn't go on the stand, his failure will be interpreted as a confession; if he does go on, it will be suicide."[25]

Even before he left office, Sulzer seemed to have abandoned the regiment campaign and its supporters. A telling moment occurred on August 25 when Charles Fillmore sent a desperate telegram to the governor, informing him that a battalion was ready for muster under his command. With only six days before the ninety-day period expired, Fillmore and a "committee of colored citizens" sought a meeting the next day with the adjutant general, who, unbeknownst to them, was in Ohio. The response from the governor's office was cold and curt: "The whole matter mentioned in your telegram is under control of the Adjutant General. Advise with him about everything." Sulzer had washed his hands of the regiment, as he now directed all of his energies into saving his political life.[26]

In March 1925, nearly twelve years after his impeachment, a still politically ambitious Sulzer seemed haunted by the role he had played in office and desperate to clear his name; he was also committed to embarrassing his long-standing political enemy Governor Alfred Smith, the unquestioned boss of the new Tammany Hall. Before a crowd of more than 4,500 mostly black citizens gathered to promote the campaign for an all-black officer corps for the regiment, Sulzer maintained that he had not only supported the original authorizing legislation but had also written and introduced it in both branches of the legislature. Moreover, he had signed the bill in the face of vast opposition, which included his own adjutant general, who threatened to resign and take the staff with him if the bill became law. Sulzer then proudly boasted, "But I signed the bill and it became a law, and this man whom I appointed head of the National Guard, instead of doing as I told him to do, helped to do me." The organizers and audience, either in denial or ignorant of the truth, applauded the persuasive ex-governor tumultuously. Spurred on by cheers that he was a "second Lincoln," Sulzer told his rapt listeners that the movement and the legislation had intended that the regiment should be black from the colonel down. He urged them to petition Governor Smith to issue an order directing the Regiment to be officered by blacks only.[27]

Whatever Sulzer might have claimed for his role and intentions twelve years later, he had failed to give his support at the critical moment. Louis Stotesbury, a member of an examination board in 1913, admitted twenty-three years later that the original act of the legislature authorizing a black regiment "was hardly treated with sincerity."[28] Even before the governor's removal, Fillmore and supporters of the regiment learned that they could no longer expect help from the commander in chief. Sulzer's successor, Lieutenant Governor Martin H. Glynn, who filled the vacancy and by some accounts performed admirably, did nothing to advance the regiment issue.

If nothing else, Charles Fillmore was a fighter and a survivor, a man who refused to surrender. Ever resourceful, he tried to acquire more suitable headquarters for the unit in mid-October 1913. This space would suffice until the mustering, when he hoped an armory would be made available. Fillmore even planned a café and pool tables to help defray expenses and meet obligations.[29]

The National Guard leadership was not impressed. Instead of encouraging Fillmore's initiatives, O'Ryan and Hamilton sent the strongest signal yet that they intended to kill the regiment. The adjutant general, as chief administrative and financial officer of the state's National Guard, appointed a board of examiners to determine the eligibility of the applicants for commissions. Just as Colonel Marshall had predicted upon his inspection two years earlier, the board established tough standards, including a requirement that all applicants for field officer had to have served from two to three years as commissioned officers in the New York National Guard. Observers pointed out that if officials applied this rule strictly, only white men would qualify as colonels and majors.[30]

If supporters thought that the rule might mean no regiment at all, they did not utter this possibility publicly, for fear of fostering a sense of resignation and despair. Instead, the *Age* urged "colored citizens" of the state to show their "resentment in no uncertain terms" to the use of white officers. Although Fillmore was reluctant to speculate on the motives in order not to jeopardize the cause, even he had to admit that his prospects for commanding the regiment appeared to be evaporating. One telltale sign was the unconventional method of selection employed by Col. Nathaniel Thurston, chairman of the examination board. Instead of examining from the top down, the board summoned second lieutenants first, the lowest-ranking and least qualified commissioned officers. Thurston maintained that he reversed the standard practice in order to give field officers a longer time to study. It was a sham, as Stotesbury also revealed to Little in 1936, "I recall that before I became Adjutant General . . . the Act had been treated as a dead letter." Regiment supporters had no illusions at the time and condemned the unjust scheme and threatened to petition Attorney General Carmody for relief. Despite his membership on the examining board that went through "the form of an examination" and that saw only one applicant, the chaplain, pass in his account, Stotesbury still found a way to take credit. In his capacity as adjutant general, he claimed to have "advised Governor Whitman that the Act should either be repealed, or that there should be an appropriation for making it effective." With the governor's approval to "go ahead," he "selected the designation, '15th Infantry' . . . with the result with which you are familiar."[31]

As concerns about racism in the New York National Guard heightened, treatment of the black soldiers in the Philippines demonstrated the depth and breadth of the problem throughout the military. Members of the 24th Infantry complained to Secretary of War Lindley M. Garrison that white officers treated them worse than the prisoners they guarded. Their officers assigned them excessive labor duty, denied privileges afforded other soldiers, and verbally and physically abused them.[32] However, none of this news deterred the leaders of the regiment effort from their objective.

In early January 1914, Fillmore, as chair of the Military Affairs Committee of the Equity Congress, released an urgent report on the operations of the Congress and the state of the regiment. The message was sobering. Of twenty-two men called for examination, only eleven appeared. The rigidity of the process discouraged the others. Apart from the physical and mental tests, applicants had to furnish three letters vouching for their "moral and intellectual status, sobriety, and financial standing." The third requirement here proved devastating, as most of these young men held menial, low-paying jobs. National Guard officers had opposed having blacks in their ranks because many of these candidates were beneath their station socially, economically, and professionally. Regrettably, Fillmore had never used this argument explicitly and clearly in his many requests for promotion or transfer earlier. This circumstance reveals the dire predicament faced by Fillmore, as well as many young men who were far worse off, as economics and racism conspired to limit black access to commissions. Yet, the resilience and determination Fillmore possessed in personal matters found application to the plight of the regiment. He and his supporters formed an officers' instruction school to assist men in preparing for the exams. He also acquired more suitable facilities for the soldiers, both officers and enlisted men, to train under noted architect Vertner W. Tandy, Max Green, and Sgt. Henry Cole, US Army (ret.).[33]

At the same time, Assemblyman Culliver tried his best to overcome the opposition and stonewalling of the state Guard leadership by appealing directly to Washington. On May 4, 1914, Culliver asked Brig. Gen. A. L. Mills, head of the Division of Militia Affairs, "to cause" the New York National Guard to recognize the provisional regiment of infantry. Culliver gave four reasons for his support. First, the adjutant general had been authorized by law to establish the regiment. Second, able men, mostly "honorably discharged soldiers of the 10th Cavalry, 23rd and 28th Infantry," comprised the regiment. Third, these very soldiers had proven by previous service in Cuba that they were ideal for service on the Mexican border because "colored" men could "endure the climate and hardships more so than the white man." Most important, the federal government had an obligation to see that its appropriations were properly used in the best interests of the US Reserve Army to which the Organized State Militia belonged. Mills, without dignifying Culliver's obvious lack of military knowledge as signified by citing the white 23rd and 28th Regiments as sources of men, tersely replied that it was "a matter over which the War Department can exercise no control whatever." Culliver's fight was at home and alone.[34]

Just as the men and officers appeared to be making good progress, C. Franklin Carr, adjutant of the unit, publicly challenged the authority, integrity, and competence of his commander, Charles W. Fillmore. Carr, whom Fillmore handpicked to be adjutant and treasurer of the officer training school, released a letter, dated May 9, 1914, from the office of Adjutant General Hamilton that ordered a "temporary" postponement in the organization of the regiment because an insufficient number of officer candidates had passed the exam. In unauthorized communications with Hamilton, Carr had maintained that Fillmore had unduly revised the list of men scheduled to take the exam. He alleged that although "Fillmore styled himself as the Colonel of the New York provisional regiment of infantry, he is supported by a few who are impressed with the idea that he, Mr. Fillmore, is the choice of the colored citizens at large as the most fit person to head this regiment." Then Carr, in defiance of all that the Equity Congress and the leaders of the regiment movement had advocated, dared to suggest that white officers would be acceptable if the choice was between having them or having no regiment at all.[35]

With the 8th Illinois as its shining symbol of an all-black unit, the regiment campaign leaders wanted to show that the "Pride of Chicago" was not an anomaly, not an exception to the rule that black soldiers were only effective if led by white officers. Without black leadership, the regiment would not be a truly black institution capable of challenging vicious racial stereotypes and fighting the battle for full citizenship. Not only could blacks serve and fight, the regiment campaigners insisted, they could also lead.

Fillmore moved swiftly against Carr by publicly denying all of the man's allegations and by removing him for dereliction of duty as adjutant of the regiment and as treasurer of the training school. He also denied that the officers had failed, asserting incorrectly, however, that many had done well.

T. Henry Karney became adjutant, and Lee A. Pollard, the author and expert on chauffeuring, replaced Carr as treasurer. In late June, wanting no future internal threats, Fillmore dissolved the old board and appointed an administrative council to monitor the affairs of the regiment. The new council members were: Charles Toney, chairman; Philip A. Payton, Jr.; Richard C. McPherson; Samuel A. Duncan; and Conrad Norman, recorder.[36]

In mid-July, C. Franklin Carr sued Fillmore and an unidentified local paper, probably the *Amsterdam News,* for libel. Reportedly, the unnamed paper had explicitly denounced Carr's actions as traitorous and self-interested. Carr had championed the candidacy of the wealthy and powerful Cornelius Vanderbilt, a friend of General O'Ryan and inspector general of the NYNG, for colonel of the regiment. Knowledgeable observers maintained that such an appointment would have benefited Carr personally. Carr insisted, however, that he had acted for the good of the regiment, knowing that Hamilton and O'Ryan would never settle for a black colonel or an all-black officer corps. He might have been right, but Fillmore and the others were not willing to concede and accept a compromise that many believed amounted to defeat. So they continued to march, train, and prove themselves capable of leadership.[37]

The continued lack of progress virtually eroded Villard's optimism. In September 1914, he revealed to Young his long-standing misgivings about the adjutant general, whom he accused of "trying to block the whole scheme by letting it die of inanition." Villard had urged Governor Glynn in June to redress the problem by applying to the War Department for Young's services. Glynn agreed to take up the matter, but after three months, Villard had heard nothing more from him and saw no evidence of forward movement. Villard asked Robert Wood and Du Bois to impress upon the governor that if he cared at all about black support, "he must state definitely what he proposes to do about this regiment."[38] Instead, Glynn apparently accepted the restrictions his predecessor put in place and allowed the National Guard leadership to determine the fate of the regiment.

Soon, the National Guard of the state dealt the regiment movement a devastating blow. Opponents of the campaign proved stronger than the laws they were sworn to obey and uphold. Adjutant General Hamilton, in his official report for the year 1914, announced the end of the "regiment experiment." His language revealed the old prejudices that damned not only black soldiers but also the entire black race as unable to become leaders of men. The adjutant general allowed that capable enlisted men "would not be so hard to get" but added, "under inexperienced or incompetent officers, however, the bravest and best soldiers would be of little value to the taxpayers, who have rights not to be ignored."[39]

Hamilton claimed to have devised a fair and equitable system to select those "qualified by fitness and merit to serve as officers." Of the fifty-seven men called, only two, according to Hamilton, passed the exam. Out of those two, only one really passed "because he possessed the basic education necessary to a commissioned officer." The other, a candidate for chaplain, passed because he needed only to "show that he was a duly ordained minister of some regularly organized religious denomination." The exams replicated those given to white candidates, Hamilton stated, with one exception—the presence of a stenographer "to settle questions of fact or fairness which might be raised."[40]

Hamilton seems to have missed some of the many implications inherent in the stenographer's presence. Certainly, the use of a stenographer anticipated accusations of unfairness because of the history of his office in this matter. Yet, the absence of stenographers in the exams of white officer candidates could have been equally suspect. Indeed, stenographers might discourage favoritism as well as prejudice. Even more telling was his summary judgment that "the result was so disappointing as to make it obviously improper to expend public funds any further in the attempt to comply with the act."[41]

The regiment movement had taken a powerful and perhaps lethal blow. So dim were the prospects for success that for the next year and a half, the issue virtually disappeared from the pages of the *New York Age*. Now, the front page of the *Age* turned to other subjects—Booker T. Washington, the economic state of Harlem, racial violence across the nation, and the continuing segregationist practices of the Democrats. The *Age* even featured black women, previously absent from front pages. The paper suddenly took note of their potential in terms of spiritual uplift and racial pride, as well as expanded readership and increased revenues.

To these ends, the *Age* held a serial beauty competition to determine the race's ideal type. Although seemingly trivial and self-serving, the contest also reflected concerns about the negative image of black women, whom the white media and, especially, coon songs stereotyped as "babies, honeys, and mercenary wenches"—everything that a proper lady was not. Thus, photos of largely light-skinned, straight-haired black women graced the front pages of the paper weekly as counters to these vicious stereotypes, while at the same time appealing to captivated and excited readers, who contributed opinions ranging from the voyeuristic to the "scientific." Not until late 1915 did the treatment of women expand beyond attention to ideal physical types, when the paper sympathetically covered the women's suffrage movement and featured Madam C. J. Walker as the employer of

10,000 blacks. Still, the *Age* represented a man's world and worldview that valued politics and war, and both those subjects largely excluded or marginalized women.[42]

Now, national and international developments in the political and military spheres certainly gave blacks much to observe and discuss. Before the outbreak of World War I, blacks focused considerable attention on American policy and practices toward Mexico. Many questioned the legality and morality of the siege of Vera Cruz, provoked ostensibly by the Mexican detention of US Marines but in reality by US opposition to Mexican president Victoriano Huerta.

As the United States found a new target in the Mexican general and revolutionary Francisco "Pancho" Villa, race certainly was a factor in black press opinion. Some press reports claimed that Villa was black and hailed from Baltimore. Others identified him as George Goldsby of Vinita, Oklahoma, a part-Cherokee freedman who had served in the 10th US Cavalry. Even those who dismissed stories of Villa's black heritage still considered him nonwhite, perhaps a "half-breed," the offspring of a union between a Spanish man and a Native American woman, who struck out against the dominant Spanish ruling elite. In Villa, blacks saw themselves as the "half-breed" sons denied "a fair part in the inheritance of the common father." They were "outcasts in the citizenship and manhood of the country," and they warned that unless the United States changed its ways, it would "reap the whirlwind of what it had sown" just as the Spanish had in Mexico.[43]

Nonetheless, the tensions with Mexico and the likelihood of larger military operations put many blacks in a difficult position, for war had always offered black men a means of distinguishing themselves even when fighting people of similar status and condition, namely, Native Americans. Mexico proved no different, as black soldiers performed border duty as early as 1914. Within two years, black soldiers would be leading the charge against Pancho Villa.

Then, on August 1, 1914, the event that many anticipated with dread arrived—the outbreak of World War I. Despite Wilson's pledge of neutrality on August 4, many blacks wondered what the war would mean for them and watched events across the ocean intently. As early as 1911, the brilliant James Weldon Johnson, writing from his diplomatic post in Corinto, Nicaragua, had warned, in a perceptive and prophetic essay called "Excess Patriotism," of the dangers of nationalism, especially "the Red Hot brand." It was "the air in which was germinated and nourished the war code between nations, just as, once, the foolish, unreasonable pride of individuals kept alive the code duello." Johnson knew all too well the "blind, stubborn spirit, which makes a nation provincial, intolerant, narrow, and hidebound." He offered a solution in "the spirit of Cosmopolitanism: the spirit, which is ready to see and acknowledge excellences in others, and as quick to imitate them, is what makes a nation really great."[44] In late 1915, Johnson found public outlet for that still-poignant essay from his influential position as contributing editor of the *Age*.

In the meantime, blacks expecting American involvement asked: "Why fight for a flag whose folds do not protect?" In the *Chicago Defender*, Ralph Tyler voiced the sentiments of many black people who questioned what incentive they had "to take up arms in defense of the United States when the government will allow mobs to burn and lynch innocent citizens, but will go to trouble and expense when Mexican bandits kill an Englishman." Tyler and other African Americans anticipated a war in alliance with England against people of color in Mexico and Japan, a prospect that gave black citizens little inspiration to embrace a "do-not-fear-to-die" spirit in support of the nation.[45]

Members of the Equity Congress and the provisional regiment paid careful attention to the war, as it might have proved the one event capable of reversing the movement's bad fortunes. Very soon after the declaration of war in Europe, Lt. Gen. Nelson A. Miles, Civil War hero and ranking officer US Army (ret.), addressed a packed house of the Equity Congress. He praised the bravery and heroism of black soldiers in the Civil War and proudly recounted the men who had volunteered for service on the untested *Monitor*. He heralded the men of the 24th Regiment who had sacrificed themselves to care for the victims of yellow fever in the Spanish-American War. Miles acknowledged that "rarely has such courage and character been exhibited," and he encouraged men already eager to show their potential value in the service of the state and the nation.[46]

Then, Miles expressed relief at the present fortune of American young men, who, unlike European boys and men, would not have "to face long lines of entrenched infantry, and field artillery, to be torn to pieces and to be buried where they fall." He concluded that the war was "less called for than any conflict" and potentially the most destructive in human history. Although some in that room may have been silently praying for the chance to fight that the war offered, many blacks shared Miles's sentiment, with one important exception. They perceived the war as evidence of the destructiveness of racism and tribalism and, before long, condemned Germany for its assault on the colored peoples of Asia and Africa and for its attacks on France for employing colonial troops in the war. African American sympathies toward France would only grow.[47]

Something more immediate and tangible than war in Europe occupied the thoughts and actions of many blacks—the upcoming midterm election. Perhaps no such election ever symbolized so much. Blacks regarded it as a referendum on the terrible two-year reign of the Wilsonian Democrats in Washington. Many black New Yorkers found that as bad as the Republicans had been, the Democrats had proved far worse. Even though an old friend, Joseph Foraker, suffered defeat in the Ohio Republican primary, blacks did all that they could to defeat Democrats wherever they ran. Booker T. Washington urged a new policy for the race based on an "aggressive and constructive progressive policy in business industry, education, moral and religious life," but many, especially northern, urban blacks, could not accept the absence of political activity in that "new" program. News that Charles Seymour Whitman, New York City's district attorney, had won the Republican primary for governor boosted the hopes of many.[48]

Whitman, who had appointed African American Cornelius W. McDougald to the post of assistant district attorney and had prosecuted police for brutality against black citizens, had a reputation for honesty, fairness, and racial progressivism. Expectations that he would serve the interests of the race reenergized the black Republicans in the city and state. Moreover, his opponent, Martin Glynn, had done virtually nothing to endear himself to blacks. The *Age* initially expressed some skepticism about Whitman, but within a week the paper had nothing but praise for him, in part because of his record but even more because of his upholding of the values they associated with the party of Lincoln: "Charles Whitman . . . is a Republican of republican ancestry. It is a sad thought that the term Republican has lost some of its ancient magical charm; nevertheless, it is still prima facie evidence of good will toward us."[49]

James Weldon Johnson's very first editorial put his unequivocal stamp on the *Age*. He clearly intended to return the paper to its Republican roots and take his readers and others there too in the process. As he saw it, support for Democrats in New York or anywhere else merely endorsed and strengthened Democratic practices in Mississippi, the symbol of racist excess. Johnson charged that the national Democratic Party stood for keeping the Negro in "his place." To vote for it, he argued, "is nothing less than to barter our weapons of defense for a bauble, nothing less than to sell our brethren into bondage." Many influential black ministers seconded Johnson's sentiments, including Adam Clayton Powell, Sr., of Abyssinian Baptist; R. M. Bolden of First Emmanuel; and J. W. Brown of Mother Zion, AME.[50]

The urgency and importance of politics and war and the likely confluence of the two brought the regiment movement out of obscurity. First, an anonymous "Negro Soldier" submitted to the press a lengthy and well-conceived plan for strengthening the army. Might the author have been Maj. Charles Young, the ranking black officer in the regular army and soon-to-be commander of the 2nd Squadron of the 10th Cavalry on the Mexican border? Or could it have been Benjamin O. Davis, Sr., officer instructor in the military science program at Wilberforce University? Whoever he was, this soldier knew well the history of the military, its officer training system, and current conditions. Since blacks had little chance to receive commissions in the regular army, the writer recommended the formation of a black national militia. The "humiliating" failure of the black militia movements in Pennsylvania and New York convinced him of the intransigence of local political and National Guard opponents. Moreover, he had no faith in the effectiveness of the current militia system, for modern warfare necessitated modern training methods. He conceded, however, that a national black militia had no chance of passage at present, but an inevitable American involvement in the war and changing political circumstances would create a need for black soldiers led by black officers.[51]

Shortly thereafter, the United Colored Democracy endorsed the candidacy of Glynn, while condemning Wilson, and listed examples of the support that blacks had received from state Democrats, including the black regiment. James Weldon Johnson knew that the war had diverted attention from the moral and other failures of the Democratic Party, but as contributing editor of the *Age,* he determined not to let that happen in New York. Johnson reminded the UDC and readers that "the disposition of State officials with regard to this matter [the regiment campaign] has been as effectively adverse as a veto of the original bill had been." Johnson opened fire with a deft martial metaphor: "The political ammunition in the Negro Regiment Bill is about exhausted, and it can't be replenished until the regiment is one in fact, and not on paper."[52]

One week before the election, the *Age* questioned the sincerity of Governor Glynn and the Democrats on the regiment issue. Inadequate funding did not excuse inaction, the paper argued, for examining boards needed no special appropriation. Not only did the board examine the least qualified first, it contravened the custom "to set up the regiment, drill and train the men, and then appoint or select the officers."[53] The regiment issue would test the next governor's commitment to the race, although none of the candidates had made any campaign promises to take up the matter.

Despite the distracting effects of war, domestic concerns prevailed, and Republicans made big gains in the East and West. In a rebuke of the Wilson administration, nearly 150 Democrats lost seats in the House, squandering the large majority there. Democratic control of the Senate was equally tenuous. The Progressive Party made a miserable showing and signaled the extinguishing of Theodore Roosevelt's political star. Blacks played no mean role in the outcome, as they returned to the "Party of Lincoln" in large numbers, perhaps influencing the outcome of many congressional races.[54]

Blacks merely had chosen between the lesser of two evils. With the familiar Charles D. Hilles as chair of the Republican National Committee (RNC), the party's leadership prior to the election had ratified a plan to reduce the number of southern delegates to the national convention in 1916. The policy would make the Republican Party in the South "respectable," a euphemism for lily white, and by 1916, only thirty-two black delegates—compared to sixty-two in 1912—came from the South. The reduction in black political power strengthened the enemies of blacks and left blacks even more vulnerable.[55]

The Republicans scored especially big victories in New York State. Whitman won the governor's race by more than 150,000 votes over Glynn. Although Whitman lost in New York City, he received large Republican majorities in both houses of the state legislature. The Age reminded Whitman and the party that overwhelming support in the so-called colored districts had given him his victory. The election of Whitman rebuked Tammany and the Wilson administration. The election results also hit local black Democrats hard, exposing them as losers with little more to show than mismanagement, corruption, greed, and internal squabbling. The United Colored Democracy could not even deliver petty patronage, for Tammany had bragged that it did not even need to pay black Democrats for their votes. Tammany's leaders accorded them no more respect than they once showed their newspaper's stereotypical black mascot, the Reverend Jim Crow.[56]

Despite Whitman's victory, the regiment issue all but disappeared again from the pages of the press for more than a year. The Age reported military developments at home and abroad, praising the 9th and 10th Cavalries and the 25th Infantry, but wrote nothing about the provisional regiment. On November 5, two days after the election, the paper ran a story from the New York Times, not known for its racial enlightenment, praising the ability of African and East Indian colonial troops. The article offered their example as evidence that "dark folk" did not need white instruction and leadership to make them "good" soldiers anymore than white troops did. The Times argued that the "often-demonstrated superiority of white armies to those, black, red, or yellow seems to be more largely a matter of weapons than of courage or natural military ability." Ironically, now long-standing Negrophobes believed that blacks could be effectively deployed, if only as cannon fodder, in a war that meant little to America.[57]

A few months later, in March 1915, the *World* framed the regiment campaign as an act of selfless patriotism and a lesson in the "principles of America First" from people who needed no special instruction. Citing the deracination of black Americans as an advantage over other immigrant Americans, the *World* argued that blacks had "no distinctive language, literature, manner, or customs that they are entreated to preserve." Blacks were, in the *World*'s view, along with American Indians, "plain Americans," and "hyphens in their cases are unnecessary." In a calculated expression of the value of "Negroes," the *World* admitted that blacks, like all other Americans, were immigrants. Unlike other immigrants, however, they were "wholly native in every sentiment and interest" because they really knew no other home than America.[58]

The *World* also lauded the African American record as a "fighting race," distinguishing itself from Fort Pillow to San Juan Hill. The paper concluded with a powerful endorsement of a black regiment: "The enrollment of Negroes in New York for national defense is natural and commendable, but the best feature of it is that it will proceed without a single mental reservation as to the foe, whoever he may be." Although the editorial was a gross oversimplification of black loyalty, a blatant insult to many loyal European Americans, and a deliberate attempt to pit blacks against more recent immigrants, it still spoke for blacks in ways that most white publications did not. In using the uppercase *N* in *Negro,* the *World* distinguished itself even from Oswald Garrison Villard's *Evening Post.*[59]

Meanwhile, Whitman and his adjutant general, Louis Stotesbury, quietly wrestled with the regiment dilemma. The new governor had three options: repeal the law, disregard its provisions, or attempt compliance. The state's militia council recommended repeal of the law. It cited, among other things, "the attitude of the Federal Government" on the excessive size of the extant infantry in the state. Stotesbury asked Gen. A. L. Mills, chief of militia affairs, for an official opinion from the army. Although admitting that the state possessed the ultimate authority, Mills pointed to Circular no. 19 of 1914, which confirmed the militia council's finding of superfluous infantry regiments. Then, Mills explicitly stated that a conversion of "unutilized infantry" into "auxiliary units" would serve "Federal needs." He informed Stotesbury that the racial makeup of the regiment was inconsequential because "the organizational plans of the War Department made no distinction between white and colored troops."[60] The NYNG would not look favorably upon any plan to make room for a black regiment by converting white ones into auxiliary units. The safest move for Governor Whitman at that point was to wait.

Unaware of the secret maneuvers, the black press focused intensely on the continuance of the disgraceful racist practices and policies of the Democrats in Washington, including legislation to prevent black immigration and interracial marriage. James Weldon Johnson neatly summarized the first two years of the Wilson presidency as the first in which a president "has openly and officially endorsed discrimination between citizens on account of race." Furthermore, Wilson had made his administration entirely partisan and sectional.[61] The antiblack epic film by D. W. Griffin, *The Birth of a Nation,* clearly demonstrated the implications of this national disorder.

Blacks everywhere protested the film as a denigration of the "race" and a provocation for racial animosity or even race war. The futile attempts of New Yorkers to ban the film locally revealed much about the racial atmosphere of the great metropolis and the political weakness of its black citizens. Black leaders and the press called upon "fusion" mayor John Purroy Mitchel, who many believed owed his nomination to black support, to remove the film from the Liberty Theatre. Mitchel first ignored the demands and then sent staffers to see it, but he did nothing. An angry Lester Walton, entertainment and sports editor of the *Age,* also blamed blacks for the situation because of "their refusal to properly organize for their own good." Soon thereafter, a large multiracial delegation of concerned citizens, led by the NAACP, pleaded its case to Mayor Mitchel, who announced that producers had agreed to cut the "more objectionable" parts of the film. Thousands lined up for tickets. According to David Levering Lewis, the attendant publicity helped the film—but it *made* the NAACP. The *Age* reported a different outcome in Illinois, where a black representative in the legislature sponsored a bill that banned the screening of *The Nigger* and *The Birth of a Nation.* New York could only hope for such a force that could secure for them what it had "secured for the race in Chicago."[62]

As the off-year election of 1915 approached, the *Age* began to assess the records of Mitchel and Whitman. Mitchel had not appointed a single black to his administration. The hiring, however, of another black to the police force created considerable interest and hope. Samuel J. Battle had broken the blue color line in 1911. Now, the press encouraged qualified black men "to bring the number up to 25 then 50 then 100." Police conduct in Harlem significantly affected the condition of blacks, for "law enforcers" frequently brutalized blacks and refused to protect them. Moreover, the police of Harlem purposefully "worked to ensure that Harlem became Manhattan's vice and crime headquarters," contributing in no small way to the area's eventual decline as a viable and vibrant community.[63]

Whitman, for all of his association with blacks and his professions of empathy, had not appointed any blacks to his staff or state office. His words did not match his actions. What the *Age* opined about the Republican Party applied to Whitman: "[It] is not so warm in our defense or so active in our interests as it ought to be." Like most politicians, Whitman would do what was expedient, and even his conservative supporters saw him as "a rank opportunist."[64] Neither mayor nor governor appeared to be interested in the regiment question. Even more disturbing, many in the black community seemed not to care either.

Up to that point, the NAACP had shown very little public interest in the regiment, as the few relevant blurbs in *The Crisis* simply reported but never advocated.[65] Disinterest in the military does not explain this virtual neglect. Even though disfranchisement and lynching occupied much of the interest of the NAACP and space in *The Crisis,* the military also figured prominently. Perhaps a commitment to integration made the organization uneasy with an all-black institution. Just as likely, it wished to protect its reputation as a national organization and avoid the appearance of provincialism. Yet, two of its most powerful officials had no qualms about working behind the scenes to put a man who shared their interests in charge of the regiment.

Even the *Age,* which had staunchly supported the regiment and took much credit for the apparent victory during the Sulzer administration in 1913, seemed to adopt another cause, a black Young Men's Christian Association (YMCA), as an answer to some of Harlem's institutional and social problems. Speaking for the black people of Harlem and New York City as a whole, the *Age* maintained that the YMCA could provide for the "thousands of colored young men, lacking in the right sort of moral and social environment and influences." With great fanfare, it announced the approval by YMCA officials of a "Colored Branch of the YMCA" on 135th Street just west of Lenox. Its location, near the Harlem branch of the New York Public Library, would, in the minds of backers, "create a new atmosphere and better conditions in making this one of the best residential blocks in the city."[66]

John E. Nail of Nail and Parker Realtors negotiated the deal. The firm's deft handling of the property transaction inspired confidence that black architects would design the structure. The opportunities that developments such as the YMCA offered black entrepreneurs were, however, often outweighed by the devastating consequences of forced segregation. The so-called Colored YMCA not only symbolized a desperate need of black

Harlemites for social and communal institutions tending to the needs of a woefully underemployed, oft-maligned, and largely mistreated population, it also revealed that New York was becoming, antidiscrimination laws notwithstanding, an increasingly segregated city. Even integrated churches in Harlem urged black parishioners to leave. Soon, the churches themselves would vacate, as did many of Harlem's white citizens.[67]

Despite the lack of media coverage and apparent inaction on the part of officials, the regiment issue still had a pulse, albeit a weak one. Escalating tensions with the Germans and heightened concerns about preparedness brought new life. On March 30, 1916, the front page of the *Age* reported that Harlem's black regiment would have white officers. The news brought no elation. Charles Fillmore received word of the plan directly from Gen. Louis Stotesbury, who informed Fillmore that the regiment would receive no state or federal money until it demonstrated its efficiency and completed its organization. Major General O'Ryan had apparently convinced Stotesbury that only white officers could affect this end and satisfy the War Department. The plan called for the mustering of one company at a time, just as Hamilton had authorized three years earlier.[68]

Stotesbury, concluding that Fillmore would oppose the plan, directed Lee A. Pollard, a board member of the provisional regiment, to organize the first company and carry out the arrangement. Fillmore finally realized that he would never command the regiment he had struggled to create and sustain through the most trying of times. Nonetheless, he refused to accept an all-white officer corps for the regiment. He led drills once a week, while Pollard, Julius Watson, A. B. Roberts, James C. Thomas, and the Reverend Isaac B. Allen "took charge" of the formation of the regiment. These men, sensing that the moment all had worked so hard for was near, submitted an application to the "Preparedness Day Parade" Committee and hoped to have 1,500 men ready to march. These hopes were soon dashed, as the military law of the state permitted only recognized units to parade.[69]

In the meantime, events beyond the state would change the internal dynamics of the regiment question. The activities on the Mexican border intensified with Pancho Villa's raid into New Mexico, and war in Europe moved closer to the United States with the sinking of the British channel steamer the *Sussex* by a German U-boat. Powerful proponents for readiness pushed plans for a significantly larger standing army and a 400,000-man reserve force. In order to forestall this threat to its existence, the National Guard would have to prove its relevance. The National Guard Association had already agreed to increased federal control, a measure it had opposed vigorously in the past. With legislation pending in Congress to make the

Guard a much more viable instrument of national security, it did all that it could to signal its worthiness for this new role.[70]

Partisan politics also intervened, as Republicans tried to gain advantage by being the party of preparedness. In no state was "martial spirit" stronger than in New York, which "boasted the headquarters of the chauvinistic National Security League, supplied the Navy League with a large membership, and introduced . . . the 'Plattsburg' plan for summer military camps."[71]

On May 1, heavy artillery fire sounded in a crowded downtown New York at the noon hour, launching a campaign to raise the strength of the New York City commands by 3,000 men. Under the slogan "3,000 men in thirty days," General O'Ryan vowed to have the Guard up to full war strength for maneuvers at camps in the summer. By May 23, only 1,400 men had enlisted, and O'Ryan raised the possibility of a draft, although he considered it was probably unnecessary. Was O'Ryan ready to accept the hundreds of black men who yearned to belong to the Guard? Or had he, by raising the specter of a draft, given an opening to the governor? Preparedness was one thing; a peacetime draft entirely another.[72]

On May 25, 1916, less than two days after O'Ryan's startling proposal, Governor Whitman, the principal speaker at a Booker T. Washington memorial meeting of 2,000 blacks, made the stunning announcement that he "had issued an order authorizing the organization of a negro regiment of the National Guard." As a sign of his commitment, Whitman had already appointed three doctors to examine candidates for the new organization. According to the *Times,* the attendees leaped out of their seats and gave the governor a standing ovation. Whitman told the jubilant and proud audience, "This negro regiment will serve the interest of the state in times of peace and in times of war. We need a negro regiment. History shows that our negro soldiers have always rendered distinguished service to the country."[73]

Why then? Why there? The heroic acts of black soldiers on the Mexican border and the tragic ambush of the 10th Cavalry at Carrizal, Mexico, had fired black ardor for service. No doubt, the approach of war and the election motivated Whitman, as Republicans used war preparedness to appeal to a patriotic electorate and certain large business interests. Moreover, talk of a draft brought the injustice to the black citizens of New York into bold relief. It suggested that anything but a black regiment would do. Last, the president had already called out the National Guards of Texas, Arizona, and New Mexico on May 9 for service on the Mexican border. New York's call would soon follow and, with it, a manpower shortage in the National Guard. Whitman seized the moment and the occasion, knowing the effect that the context would give the announcement. He had set his sights on a larger prize, the presidency, and this action made him a governor whose commitment to preparedness and racial justice resonated nationally.[74] The supporters of the regiment also owed a debt of gratitude to Pancho Villa, a contributing factor to the president's call.[75]

The *Age* remained strangely silent on the matter. Perhaps the problems of the past, even with gubernatorial authorization, recommended caution and skepticism. Further, the announcement left unanswered many important questions. Would the adjutant general or major general find ways of undermining the process? Who would command the unit, and would it be all black from the top down? These questions concerned both black and white observers. In an editorial on May 27, the *Times* pounced on the term *exclusively negro* in the official announcement of the regiment. The *Times* considered the possible deployment of an all-black officer cadre as well as black enlisted men in riots or strikes as "an experiment likely to excite some apprehension." It warned that "coercive measures used by such a regiment" in these matters "would be more hotly resented and resisted than like actions on the part of white soldiers, and thus the disorders would be aggravated."[76]

The *Times* almost invariably commented negatively on black citizens and their aspirations, but it did publish letters from two Civil War officers who wholeheartedly lauded the record of black soldiers and endorsed their membership in the National Guard. The *World,* by contrast, had nothing but praise for the record of black troops in the nation's past wars and the current crisis in Mexico. It quoted Abraham Lincoln on the black soldier: "And then there will be some black men who can remember that with silent tongue and clenched teeth and steady eye and well-poised bayonet they have helped mankind on to this great consummation." The *World* proclaimed that Lincoln's words "summed up the patriotic desire of the colored people of the State to be represented by a regiment of the National Guard."[77]

The answer to many of the questions came on June 25, when Whitman announced that William Hayward, public service commissioner, would command the regiment, which had neither designation nor home. Dreams of an all-black regiment for New York vaporized. Charles W. Fillmore, for all of his efforts, would have to play a subordinate role, if any at all. The man who had fought so hard for the regiment would receive very little credit for its creation. Most accounts date the history of the regiment from 1916 and name Whitman and Hayward as its fathers. Yet, without Fillmore and other African Americans who never quit the fight for a black regiment, Whitman certainly would have had far less and perhaps no reason at all to act.[78]

# 4

## "Mulligan's Guards"

*The (Re)-Birth and Growing Pains of
the 15th New York National Guard*

The decision by Governor Whitman to effect the legislation of 1913 returned the regiment issue to the front pages of the city's press and likely to the center of the community's attention. Harlemites sorely needed an institution that they could identify as uniquely their own. The YMCA, although many saw it as the center of intellectual and social life of New York's black population in the first decade of the twentieth century, did not yet have a Harlem identity, for the Harlem branch did not open until 1919. The YWCA established on West 132nd Street in 1913 provided invaluable educational, social, employment, and moral services, but it never received the credit it so richly deserved for contributing to the uplift of the entire community through its work with young women. Black men competed directly with black women in the YWCA forums and other outlets for control over the public and even the private construction of African American identities.[1] A black regiment would give black males a highly masculine space primarily dedicated to furthering the interests and values of black men, whose strengthening would putatively benefit the race. As such, the quest for the black regiment was as much gendered as racial.

Few black men could see any other way to proceed. They had to fight the race war mainly on masculine terms, through manly institutions and with men in the lead. To them, the authorization of the regiment was perhaps the most positive accomplishment the beleaguered and politically weak community could claim to date. Without elected officials and with limited employment in the city's public service sector, black men primarily made the regiment a symbol of their fledgling influence. Furthermore, they would use the regiment against those who viewed African Americans as incapable and immoral, as contaminants to be confined in space and limited in numbers and influence. In the hotly contested streets of Harlem, the regiment, like the YMCA, could serve as a potent institution in shaping power relations. However, racist white landlords and property associations, intent on maintaining the status quo, characterized such organizations as threats to the stability and purity of the community.[2]

The economic sphere proved no less hostile an environment. The *Age* reported that of 130 stores on Fifth Avenue between 131st and 138th Streets, only 16 had black owners. Even more, whites only employed twenty-eight blacks in 114 establishments. Although black businesses fared better on 135th Street, where they operated 65 of 117 establishments, they still faced discriminatory practices, especially high rents and bad service, at the hands of hostile landlords. Nothing symbolized the plight of Harlem as an exploited colony more than the white-owned saloons with their infamous "back rooms," which irate black leaders condemned as harmful to "legitimate" black operations and destructive of the morals and health of the community's young people.[3]

No matter how bad it seemed, though, Harlem's suburban atmosphere appeared beautiful, if not idyllic, to those who had left behind the railroad flats, outdoor toilets, and racial violence of lower Manhattan. Harlem offered at least prime housing stock, grand churches, and spectacular nightlife, alongside police repression, street crime, and increasingly squalid conditions. In the words of one resident, "Life in Harlem had much to offer, yet a lot of courage and stamina was still required to exist."[4]

As war approached, the urgency and import of the black regiment became increasingly clear to Harlem's leaders. Yet, of the many issues concerning the regiment, one preoccupied them most—the appointment of a white man, William Hayward, to lead it. The son of a US senator, Monroe L. Hayward of Nebraska, the younger Hayward had been a lawyer, a judge, and the head of the western headquarters of the Republican National Committee. Hayward's military aspirations reportedly began at the age of fourteen, when he attempted to enlist in the Nebraska militia as a drummer. Rejected because of his age, Hayward, after attending school in Munich, Germany, tried again at age eighteen and rose quickly from private to sergeant. He enrolled in the Cadet Battalion at the University of Nebraska and studied military science under the tutelage of none other than future commander of the American Expeditionary Forces (AEF), Lt. John J. Pershing of the 10th Cavalry. A year prior to the war with Spain, Hayward became a captain and commanded Company C, 2nd Nebraska

National Guard. The entire regiment was mustered into service, and Hayward served slightly less than a year.[5]

After the war, he returned to the Nebraska National Guard as a major. Within a year, he rose to colonel and commander of the 2nd Regiment, remaining in that position for three years. Soon after, Governor Ezra P. Savage appointed him adjutant general of the Nebraska National Guard, but Hayward, who had been elected a county judge, declined in favor of a political career. He then retired from active military service and served on the military board of the state.[6]

In 1910, Hayward lost a race for the US House of Representatives. Devastated by the defeat, he left Nebraska forever and moved to New York with his wife, Sarah, and young son, Leland, and joined the law firm of Wing & Russell. Three years later, he became an assistant in the office of Manhattan's district attorney, Charles Seymour Whitman, and subsequently managed Whitman's successful gubernatorial campaigns in 1914 and 1916. Hayward served briefly as Whitman's counsel before the governor rewarded him with the office of public service commissioner in 1915. Hayward also held the rank of colonel in the New York Militia Reserve.[7]

William "Big Bill" Hayward, president of his senior class and a star football and baseball player at Nebraska, was a commanding figure—tall, dark, and handsome—and exceedingly well suited for the role he was to play in qualifications and temperament.[8] Whitman had selected Hayward for political, practical, and racial reasons. Without white command, the regiment stood little chance of receiving Maj. Gen. John O'Ryan's blessing or support. Hayward had to overcome the resentment and suspicions not only of many blacks who felt betrayed by his appointment but also of many whites who believed the regiment owed its existence and he, his command, to rank party politics. Indeed, critics often characterized the regiment as having been "conceived in politics, born in ridicule, and reared in opposition." Whitman undoubtedly believed that he had picked the ideal white man to organize and lead a black regiment while navigating the treacherous shoals of racial and political resentment. The colonel did not shy away from the awesome responsibility.[9]

Hayward maintained that his sincerity and sensitivity prepared him to face and overcome the difficult challenges ahead. He likened himself to Whitman, a man "sincere in his feeling that the great colored population of New York ought to be given an opportunity to shine in the National Guard without prejudice." The colonel often told anyone who would listen that he accepted the opportunity to serve with complete seriousness and in full appreciation of the difficulties inherent in the assignment. Rarely accused of modesty, he often jokingly claimed that he commanded a regiment of one. He was only technically correct.[10] What the regiment lacked in facilities and equipment, it more than compensated for in an anxious and willing reserve of men and a reservoir of community interest and support. Hayward and the Guard's leadership needed to do only one thing to preserve and enhance that goodwill—fill its officer ranks with blacks.

In early June, black New Yorkers heard news that indicated the regiment so long in gestation would soon materialize. The adjutant general, Louis Stotesbury, issued orders to prospective members of the still unnamed "Negro regiment" to appear for physical examinations on June 17 and 19 in preparation for mustering. In Manhattan, Colonel Hayward recruited a friend, Dr. George Bolling Lee, grandson of Robert E. Lee, to administer the medical examinations.[11]

The ease of recruiting "enlisted" men starkly contrasted with the problems of finding black officers. Vertner F. Tandy, the well-known and highly regarded architect and community leader, passed the mental and physical examinations and became the first black commissioned officer in the New York National Guard. Hayward then appointed Tandy, a first lieutenant, to lead the recruitment efforts. Observers, however, did not necessarily view Tandy's appointment as evidence that other blacks would follow his path into the officer ranks. The *Age* tentatively informed its readers that authorities had assured that "there will be no strings attached to any commissions, and there will be no favoritism shown."[12]

On June 29, the first day of enrollment, scores of willing, eager, and able young men rushed to join "the pride of Harlem" at its makeshift headquarters on 2217 Seventh Avenue, an old cigar store that the colonel had secured with the assistance of Mayor John Puroy Mitchel and Lawrence Meehan, superintendent of the Armory Board. Hayward "recalled" that William Bunting came through the door first. Bunting, twenty-four years old and single, was born in Washington, DC, and lived at 144 West 136th Street, in the center of a rapidly expanding Harlem. He typified the young men who initially joined the Regiment. Many, if not most, had roots in the South. A large percentage came from Virginia and North Carolina, with South Carolina and Georgia not far behind. Many of them listed seaport or industrial cities as their places of birth, suggesting that the northbound migration did not follow a straight line from rural farm life to urban industrial and commercial life. Many listed no relatives in the city, and some even gave out-of-state addresses for relatives, indicating that they had migrated to New York very recently, perhaps specifically to join the Regiment. Though a large percentage of the men had been born in the South, almost every state in the

Union could claim members of the 15th. These men participated in a large prewar migration that made black New York a city of migrants.[13]

The reach of the 15th did not stop at the nation's borders. The British West Indies provided its fair share of men, although even more of them tried to form a volunteer regiment of their own and others preferred enlistment in the British armed services. After all, 40,000 West Indians settled in New York between 1900 and 1930.[14] Some volunteers listed foreign countries as their places of residence. Contrary to popular belief, only the intent to become a citizen, not citizenship, qualified a man for service in the US military. In fact, service itself often provided easier access to citizenship. Men born in Cuba, Canada, Panama, and the Dutch West Indies also joined the Regiment. Joe Ally listed "Palestine, Turkey" as his place of birth, which might have qualified him for the distance record.[15]

Although the Regiment might have owed its conception and locus to Harlem, it could not claim exclusive rights to the unit's soul—the rank and file. In fact, many of the New York natives did not list Harlem residences. Black New Yorkers still lived throughout the city, from the Village to the Tenderloin to San Juan Hill, and the rolls of the Regiment reflected the legacy of old residential patterns. Brooklyn, because of the headquarters there, contributed large numbers of men to the Regiment, enough to form a second battalion commanded by Arthur W. Little. Unlike Manhattan's recruits, many of the young men from Brooklyn were natives, a fact that reflected the low rate of migration to the borough before 1910. As the Regiment expanded its recruiting centers and efforts, more and more of the men listed addresses outside New York City, among them Yonkers, New Rochelle, Mount Vernon, White Plains, Flushing, Glen Cove, Goshen, and Haverstraw. Albany, in part because of the attention the Regiment received in the press of the state's capital and the recruiting efforts of Lorillard Spencer, sent at least thirty-two young men to the outfit, including a man of destiny, the diminutive manual laborer Henry Johnson. Sizable contingents also came from the neighboring states of Connecticut, New Jersey, and Pennsylvania.[16]

July 1, 1916, marked a historic date for Harlem, New York City, New York State, and, even the nation as the first company of the 15th Regiment was mustered into the New York State National Guard. Company A, led by Vertner Tandy, became the nucleus of the first state-authorized black regiment in New York history. The Empire State had never officially recognized previous black volunteer regiments raised there. An already euphoric mood in the community soared even higher amid reports that Governor Whitman had requested the War Department to assign Maj. Charles Young, commander of the 2nd Battalion, 10th US Cavalry, as inspector-instructor to the

Regiment. Unfortunately, the War Department had no intention of placing Young in a position that might lead to the recruitment of black officers for the Regiment or to his permanent association with it.[17]

Despite a lack of proper facilities, equipment, and uniforms, the ranks of the 15th grew rapidly. By the second week of July, four more companies were mustered in, adding some 173 men to the 53 already enlisted. These men immediately received instruction in physical fitness, duties and responsibilities as enlisted men, and the handling of service rifles. Men who had recently trained with sticks now used weapons that Gen. Leonard Wood had made available for civilian shooting clubs. One such club coincidentally occupied the same address as Hayward's Public Service Commission offices.[18]

Pleasantly surprised by the success of the Brooklyn recruiting office, Hayward opened another in the Bronx. Joining the Regiment soon became the thing to do for young black men. According to Hayward, some were overwhelmed by being asked to join anything; others joined out of a sense of patriotism; and most, he believed, "were at heart adventurers" who "wanted to see the big show, to move about to be doing something different from what they had been doing." This last characterization reminds one of Colonel Mangin's interpretation of black men's motivations for service. Yet, Arthur P. Davis, one of four Davis brothers to join, captured the essence best: "To be somebody you had to belong to the 15th Infantry or jealously look at them in uniform." The fact that many young ladies seemed to prefer men in uniform added to the Regiment's allure.[19]

Regrettably, lingering questions about black officers dampened enthusiasm and affected recruitment. Tandy remained the only black officer, and white officers provided almost all of the instruction. Within two and a half weeks, the Regiment numbered 425 men, about one-third of the 1,400 men needed for a peace-strength regiment. A week later, more than 500 men had joined. An anxious moment approached as Charles W. Fillmore, Virgil H. Parks, and John A. McCoy stood before the examining board.[20] On July 18, Fillmore, the man most responsible for keeping the regiment movement alive, passed the officer's examination and earned the rank of captain. Parks followed him as a first lieutenant. What happened to McCoy is not clear, but James Hovey Wyatt passed the exam as a second lieutenant. With only four black officers, three of them lieutenants, prospects for significant black leadership appeared bleak. Even more, no one could guarantee how long these few men would remain with the unit.[21]

The recruitment efforts to increase the numbers of those characterized as "the cleanest cut men in the National Guard" took Hayward and his assistant, Lorillard Spencer, directly into the snake pit of black politics in Harlem. Dispatched by Governor Whitman to a meeting of the Equity Congress, Hayward and Spencer received a lesson about the almost sacred meaning of the Regiment to black leadership in the community and the viciousness of local black politics—a condition often afflicting those who lack the power to fight external enemies and thus turn on themselves.[22]

Charles W. Anderson, in his role as leader of black Republicans in New York City, took it upon himself to call the meeting of the Equity Congress to order, evidently for the purpose of introducing the governor's men. Whatever Anderson's intent, his presumptuousness did not impress the members, who immediately demanded he relinquish the chair to Fillmore, once Anderson's subordinate but now president of the Equity Congress and the clearly recognized champion of the regiment campaign. Congress members believed Anderson had long opposed the plan for a regiment, and they relished the opportunity to embarrass him publicly, especially in front of the governor's emissaries. It was also a devastating rebuke of Anderson for his apparent failure to support movements to improve Harlem, for his opposition to black candidates for office, and for his inability or unwillingness to secure representative political positions for others.[23]

Supporters of the regiment movement saw Anderson's "sudden change of heart in favor of a colored military organization . . . as a plot to gain personal political prestige." Perhaps they assessed Anderson too harshly, for he never really opposed the regiment movement in principle but as a matter of politics. He always believed that the Democrats had used the movement for political gain, and in three successive state and citywide campaigns, they had promised a regiment and never really delivered. Anderson always put party before race. After the Whitman decision for a regiment, Democrats had accused Republicans of political opportunism. The charge apparently had some influence with the NAACP, and Anderson felt a compelling need to defend the Grand Old Party in a letter to Progressive Joel Elias Spingarn, chairman of the board of the NAACP. Evidently, Spingarn or the organization had questioned the legitimacy of the Regiment and the governor's motives in authorizing it. In fact, Anderson promised to "donate $100.00 to the Society for the Advancement of Colored People (NAACP) if a single piece of republican campaign literature can be produced in which any promise of a regiment has been made or implied for the sake of getting votes."[24]

Certainly concerned about his own reputation, Anderson also understood that NAACP support of the Regiment and recruitment efforts might be critical to the success of the project. Hayward and others involved agreed. Spingarn apparently had reached out numerous times to Hayward only to sidestep any commitment to helping the Regiment meet its quota and fulfill its promise. Two plausible explanations might clarify Spingarn's ambivalence. Although the Columbia professor had attended military camps in the summer of 1915 and 1916, he might not have reconciled fully questions of military participation and racial justice. According to military intelligence reports, Spingarn, at the time of the Regiment's organization, had told recruits that in light of Jim Crow laws and the humiliation they suffered at home because of their race, "there was no reason for blacks to fight, because they had nothing to fight for."[25] By contrast, his experiences at these camps might have suggested better ways to represent blacks in the regular army, especially as officers.

Desperate for high-level support, Hayward invited Spingarn to his office on June 27, 1916, to discuss the role that the NAACP chairman had offered to play. Hayward followed up on the request a week later, citing the accomplishments of the organizing effort while admitting that accusations of party politics had hurt the process. The colonel assured an apparently skeptical Spingarn that he personally did not care about a man's politics, for "no party adherence can make a soldier." He sought efficiency and loyalty and nothing else. Hayward maintained that Whitman had chosen him because the governor had confidence in his "ability to make a success of it and deal fairly with the men." The commissioning of Napoleon B. Marshall, a leading black Democrat, supported his assertion. Then, in an obvious appeal to Spingarn's ego and military interests, Hayward said that he knew of "no one who could head such a movement better than yourself."[26]

The tactic appeared to work. On July 31, Gilchrist Stewart, a prominent black lawyer and regimental supporter, responded to a Spingarn proposal to host an event in the interest of the 15th Regiment combined with an appreciation of the 10th Cavalry. Stewart praised Spingarn's timing because "everybody is talking about the regiment." Stewart wanted to hold the meeting in the Lafayette Theatre and suggested that they invite Capt. Benjamin O. Davis, then an instructor of military science at Wilberforce College, to speak. He urged a meeting with Hayward to discuss this plan and another unnamed matter that he was sure would interest Spingarn. The latter possibly concerned the still-troubling question of officers. Stewart told Spingarn that they must not only appeal for soldiers but also strive "to list the activities of all of those who had sufficient military experience to serve as officers." Stewart also revealed the fear that consumed the minds of black supporters of the movement: "I am afraid that we may get up against a stone wall in that an attempt may be made to put in white officers 'temporarily' and you and I know what temporarily would mean."[27]

In any case, Spingarn postponed the plan to hold a big recruitment meeting for the 15th until after the Amenia Conference, an event designed to facilitate a rapprochement between the Bookerites and the NAACP for the purpose of forming a united front among blacks and their allies "to meet the problems of the world."[28] Hayward accepted an invitation to the conference, and the influential black businessman John Nail asked that Vertner Tandy be invited, citing Tandy's prominence as an architect and his lieutenancy in the 15th NYNG. These men, along with Stewart, Charles Anderson, and Governor Whitman, would attend the conference and guarantee that the 15th was well represented.[29]

Up until the conference, Spingarn continued to demonstrate some interest in leading the recruitment and fund-raising campaigns. Stewart not only encouraged Spingarn to lead, he also welcomed full NAACP backing of the enterprise, unless ethical concerns might preclude such an arrangement. Stewart held Spingarn and the NAACP in such high esteem that he proposed a secondary role for the Citizens Committee of One Hundred, which he had formed for the purposes of assisting Hayward with the Regiment. By mid-August, however, evidence of Spingarn's interest in the Regiment virtually disappeared. The big event to benefit the unit apparently did not happen. When Capt. Hamilton Fish, III, turned to Spingarn, out of desperation, for recruitment help in early May 1917, he approached him because of Spingarn's membership on the Dutchess County Defense Committee and not as a close supporter of the Regiment. In fact, the letter's details reveal no meaningful prior connection between Spingarn and recruiting efforts.[30] The reasons for Spingarn's sudden loss of interest soon would become crystal clear.

Largely without the NAACP, the regiment-building process proceeded. In early August, Hayward secured, through the Sinking Fund Commission of New York City, a lease of the third floor and basement of Lafayette Hall, at the corner of 132nd Street and Seventh Avenue—a space that could not accommodate "more than a single company at a time." The Armory Board maintained that the small size of the Regiment precluded the unit from securing permanent space, although Hayward had applied for the erection of a large facility at an estimated price of $1 to $2 million, exclusive of real estate costs. The serious matter of inadequate space stood as one of many issues threatening the success of this "street urchin of a regiment."[31]

Recruitment did not proceed as fast as expected, and the *Age* and the community often seemed more concerned with the 10th Cavalry and the battle of Carrizal, Mexico, than they did with their own 15th. Salem Methodist Church in Harlem hosted a memorial service for those killed in the battle. Its victims had become martyrs, as many blacks simply craved heroes. They grew impatient with the pace of the Regiment's development and wondered if it would ever be in a position to fight and give New York heroes of its own. It had already missed one opportunity when units from the New York National Guard received orders to patrol the border in the "police" action against Pancho Villa.[32]

Yet, if those interested in the Regiment wanted heroes, they wanted heroic leaders even more. Once again, attention turned to Lieutenant Colonel Young, the most famous black soldier in America and the man many black New Yorkers had hoped would lead their 15th. Young symbolized the potential and the problems of black officers. The *Age* warned the supporters of the Regiment and the community in general against an unthinking racialist approach to the matter. Citing the compulsory dismissals of two high-ranking officers in the 69th Regiment, the *Age* argued against a false and counterproductive belief in the omnipotence of white skin privilege and political influence. It supported "all colored regiments officered by Negroes from colonel down" but insisted that merit and fitness precede partisan sentiment. All would benefit, the *Age* concluded, if black people sought "fair play," not "charitable consideration."[33]

Of course, the *Age* understood that both "a white face" and "political pull" often meant the difference between success or failure in American society. What it failed to acknowledge was that no amount of positive thinking or individual capacity could overcome the effects of long-standing structural impediments to progress. Charles Young's own difficult experience, for example, was a success story compared to the plight of other blacks who tried to make the grade as officers. Upon his graduation in 1889, Young, forty-ninth in a class of forty-nine, had been only the third of nine blacks admitted to the US Military Academy at West Point to earn a degree since its founding in 1803. Called a "load of coal" by his peers, Young endured merciless hazing and total social isolation, a combination that few could have withstood. This inhuman treatment and his difficulties with mathematics, not questions of his intelligence, contributed more directly to his low academic standing. Official discouragement and the poisonous racial culture meant that the academy had graduated only two more blacks, John Hanks Alexander and Young, since Henry O. Flipper broke into "the long gray line" in 1877.[34]

Though Young's West Point experience symbolized the problem at its highest level, it did not begin to reveal its scope and depth. George J. Austin, major and commander of cadets at St. Paul Normal and Industrial School in Lawrenceville, Virginia, brilliantly analyzed the circumstances. Austin had carefully followed the "colored" regiment campaign and pinpointed the source of its long and painful gestation—the inability to find "efficient officers who could pass muster both in education and professional training as a soldier and also in experience." Whites did not face such a problem because "crack military schools" throughout the Northeast afforded white boys expert military training at a tender age. Even the South, not known for its educational institutions, had made progress in this area. The enormous stakes, Austin maintained, involved definitions of character and citizenship and the opportunity to achieve at the highest level:

> Achievement is all there is to any individual, nation, or race. Character sprouts, grows, and fructifies through achievement. In the military world the officers give character to a command, no matter who the men are, the achievements of a body of troops are generally accredited to the race to whom the officers of the command belong. As a race it behooves us to achieve in a military sense . . . , but I warn you that future achievement and victories directed by black brains in black officers will be infinitely more glorious in the national history and will precipitate greater character to [the] race itself.[35]

Austin admitted that few blacks knew much about the art of war and that only a handful could be entrusted with commands or young men's lives. Before war erupted with Mexico or the United States entered the conflict in Europe, Austin urged black men of all ages and professions to rush to military training camps to be trained in the practical duties of soldiering as a step toward developing "a goodly number of young reserve officers for volunteer troops."[36] The military Preparedness Movement of Gen. Leonard Wood and Theodore Roosevelt, among others, had spawned these training camps.

Stemming from concerns over uncontrolled material progress, social disintegration, and individual immorality, the Preparedness Movement was intended to reform America's collective morality through a chosen few while preserving through these same young men the sources of the nation's wealth and power. The first of these so-called businessmen or executive training camps emerged in Plattsburg, New York, in the spring of 1914, creating what became known as the Plattsburg Movement. The founders sought young business executives and recent college graduates who already possessed the social and intellectual qualities normally associated with leaders. Emmett Scott later referred to Plattsburg as "almost a social camp" that, in the American tradition, excluded blacks. These young men with the right pedigree only needed military training to help them "realize leadership in its highest, most exalted, and disinterested sense." At first glance, Austin's call appears naive, but a closer analysis suggests a method to his apparent madness. More than likely, he urged blacks to seek entry into the camps as a demonstration of interest and a way of exposing the exclusionary policies and practices of the camps, their backers, and ultimately the War Department.[37]

Perhaps no one understood the situation better than Joel Spingarn, who had attended the Plattsburg Camp. Honest self-reflection on his experience could not have inspired any hope for the prospects of integrated camps. Even before the release of Austin's letter, Richetta J. Randolph, assistant to NAACP secretary Roy Nash and wife of A. Phillip Randolph, had floated the idea of separate training camps to executive committee member and W. E. B. Du Bois's close friend Butler Wilson. Wilson took Mrs. Randolph's suggestion very seriously and promised to raise it before the executive committee at its next meeting, despite his opposition "to giving countenance to segregation by accepting its benefits, which are in the long run, always more expensive than beneficial." Whether the outspoken Randolph was acting on her own or serving as a conduit for Spingarn or Nash is not entirely clear. In any event, the separate training camp proposal would test the very principles upon which the organization stood.[38]

The Democratic Congress and administration as well as the military did not make matters easy for the NAACP. Not only did they oppose integrated camps and black officers, some within these ranks argued that blacks had no place in the American military at all. The prospects of arming blacks alarmed many whites. The fear that the transforming effects of military service and war might make blacks question their place and challenge white authority disturbed them even more. Thus, as war approached, Congressman Thaddeus Horatius Caraway of Arkansas introduced legislation, on July 27, 1916, calling for a ban on the enlistment or reenlistment of "any person of the Negro or colored race" in the military service of the United States. To his credit, Secretary of War Newton Baker opposed the measure and praised black soldiers: "Those familiar with the history of our country from the armies of George Washington . . . down to the present day, know that brave and often conspicuously gallant service has been rendered by colored troops. In the most recent instance, at Carrizal, in Mexico, these colored troops conducted themselves with the greatest intrepidity, and reflected nothing but honor upon the uniform they wore."[39] Actions spoke louder than words, however, as the War Department announced that it had no intention of increasing the number of black regular army units. These machinations in Washington must have sent mixed messages to the black faithful, testing their patience and resolve.

Rather than become discouraged, the organizers of the 15th realized that time was of the essence. An order to disband the Regiment or a declaration of war might occur at any moment. In preparation for their call into active service, the partially formed Regiment drilled regularly and performed the very formal, rigid, and (when well executed) impressive ceremony of guard mount at Olympic Field in Harlem. The exercise had practical and symbolic value. It served as a much-needed recruitment tool, but it also had direct application to the job of soldiering.

Other than training, a soldier's most time-consuming activity in the field or garrison was guard duty. Yet on Sunday, September 24, the guard mount assumed special significance, as the Regiment, under the direction of the officer of the day, Capt. Charles W. Fillmore, drilled one last time before its public debut. The presentation of colors at the Union League Club of New York, with Governor Whitman presiding, would be the biggest moment in the history of the fledgling outfit. Nothing could demonstrate the men's "military bearing" better than a precise execution of the guard mount or changing of the guard.[40]

On Sunday, October 1, the 900 or so men of the 15th Regiment, led by the band of Egbert E. Thompson, made their way from Columbus Circle to the Union League Club at Fifth Avenue and Thirty-Ninth Street. Thousands of cheering spectators lined the route, proudly recognizing these young men who represented *the* first black National Guard regiment in the state's history. The event could not have occurred under more fitting and noble auspices than offered by the Union League Club, which maintained its Civil War traditions in this ceremony. The club had recruited and equipped regiments of black soldiers in New York during the Civil War. These units, which were not permitted to be part of the state's militia, served as separate "Colored" troops. The club had direct contemporary connections to the Regiment as well. Whitman and Hayward held membership in the Union League Club, as did some of the unit's future white officers.

As evidence of the importance of this event, tens of dignitaries filled the reviewing stand, including Adjutant General Louis Stotesbury and Charles W. Anderson. The NYNG commander, O'Ryan, missed the event because of his service on the Mexican border. After the Regiment reached parade rest, Governor Whitman delivered a stirring and respectful address appropriate for the occasion of "committing a sacred trust" in the presentation of the regimental colors of the 15th Infantry, the standard of the state of

New York, and the Stars and Stripes—"the flag of the free hearts hope and home." Whitman first appealed to the men's sense of honor and duty:

> There can be no more honorable service than that upon which you are entering—the protection of the Commonwealth, and should occasion require, the defense of your native land. . . . The honor of the state is involved in your daily conduct an in your every act, not only when you are wearing the uniform and following these colors, but wherever you are and in whatever activity you may be engaged, and the people of the State are going to judge your Regiment by the conduct of its men wherever they are and in whatever activity they are engaged.[41]

He then appealed to the soldiers' pride by placing them in the context of a long and distinguished tradition of military service:

> The record of the colored soldier in the armies of this land has been an honorable record, and all who have been interested in the recruiting of the 15th Infantry, National Guard of New York, are confident that the men who have volunteered so willingly and so gladly will be true to the record made by the many of your race who have worn the Army blue, who in the hour of danger were never found wanting in courage and in devotion.[42]

Last, he appealed to their sense of duty: "These colors are yours. Guard them as a sacred possession; protect them, as I know you will, should the necessity arise, even with your lives. God grant that you may never be called upon to make the sacrifice offered by those who have gone before you that the freedom and the civilization and the enlightenment, which the flag embodies and represents may abide and remain forever."[43]

No amount of "military bearing," solemnity, or honor, however, could satisfy the rabidly antiblack *New York Times*. What others reported as an impressive martial ceremony, the *Times* turned into a minstrel show featuring Bert Williams on horseback. Relegated to page twenty-two, the story began: EMOTIONAL HORSE OF CAPTAIN BERT WILLIAMS BECOMES HYSTERICAL AS THE BAND PLAYS. The content only enhanced the distasteful, sensational disparagement suggested in the lead. The majority white crowd reported by the *Age* became in the *Times*'s version "thousands of negroes" witnessing the "darky" comedian's "impromptu equestrian act." Williams, "borrowed" by

Hayward to be inspector of small arms and a member of his staff, rode directly behind the colonel and ahead of the men, and things went bad from the start, according to the *Times:*

> Bert's horse, a light gray charger, began to waltz about the street the moment the Captain-comedian got into the saddle. Colonel Hayward gave the command to march. The band struck up "Onward Christian Soldiers." The long column moved—and Williams's horse, ears straight back, tail out, and feet flying, dashed ahead. The rider was taken by surprise, but clung to his saddle and succeeded in stopping his charger. . . . In front of the Union League Club . . . Captain Bert's temperamental mount once more abandoned the parade. Down the avenue the animal rushed, Bert staying in his seat, but apparently his self-confidence had been left with the regiment.[44]

The *Times* continued its detailed description of the "comic" event and ended the farce with Williams's being rescued by a policeman, at which time Williams decided not "to continue his act any longer." Instead, he "slid from his saddle to the ground and planted the well-known feet on the pavement with more emphasis than he ever waved them over the footlights." Blacks and their feet, as Booker T. Washington knew all too well, supplied the platform of black stereotypes and the vehicle for so many "darky" jokes. The *Times* devoted only the following three sentences to serious coverage: "Governor Whitman, in presenting the colors to the regiment, spoke to the men on their duty as members of the National Guard. The regiment was authorized by recent legislation. Most of its staff officers are white men, but its line officers are Negroes."[45]

Hayward, who appreciated showmanship and had recruited Williams because of his fame and stature, could not have seen anything funny in the *Times*'s coverage. The colonel wanted nothing to detract from the perception that the Regiment was a serious organization worthy of federal recognition under the new National Defense Act of 1916, which greatly strengthened the federal authority over the National Guard. Already known as a glorified version of "Mulligan's Guards" because the unit trained without proper weapons and in ill-fitting, incomplete uniforms, the 15th could not afford such coverage. Unfortunately, that very article found its way to the top of the Militia Bureau in Washington and did not make a good impression.[46]

On October 3, 1916, only two days after the parade, the Militia Bureau rejected the request for federal recognition made by Adjutant General Stotesbury on September 18. Until New York added more auxiliary arms to support "higher tactical organizations," no increase in infantry units would be approved. The fact that no "colored regiments" existed in the state "did not enter into the consideration," as a "colored regiment will form part of a tactical brigade exactly the same as any other regiment, and will be on an identical basis." Favorable consideration would "be given to the organization of field artillery, cavalry, engineers, signal, and sanitary troops."[47] Despite appeals to respect the "patriotic spirit of our colored citizens"—from public officials, concerned individuals, and even Colonel Hayward, in addition to black organizations—the War Department refused to budge. A direct appeal from Governor Whitman to Secretary of War Baker elicited the same response about the necessity of a balanced force.[48] As usual, the government claimed color blindness whenever that was convenient.

The *Times*'s reportage, however damaging, did not represent the entire white press of New York. The *Evening Globe,* in a serious and respectful tone, reinforced much of what Whitman said about the men and the Regiment. Instead of ridicule, the paper extended a welcome to the men, from Bert Williams to the common laborer, because they had volunteered to serve the state and the nation should it need them. This recurrent reference to volunteering signified the distinction between the regular army soldier and the Guardsman: "The one does his work for a stipulated compensation, as a matter of business; the other as an act of good citizenship." Yet, the *Evening Globe*'s motives were not entirely altruistic. In its praise of blacks, it implicitly questioned the loyalty of so-called hyphenated Americans: "The Afro-American is no hyphenate. Made a slave for 250 years and discriminated against for half a century, he does not lose faith in Americanism." This xenophobic theme of loyal native blacks recurred in many forms and found considerable currency among black commentators as well.[49]

Despite the Williams incident and the federal rejection, the event paid large dividends at the state and local levels. Questions about Whitman's commitment to the race virtually disappeared in the *Age* and perhaps the community at large as a result of his attendance at black functions, his hiring of blacks, his removal of the ban against "mixed" boxing matches, and his "broad views on race question," including an unqualified declaration at the Amenia Conference that blacks should receive equal rights. These accomplishments compared to Mayor Mitchel's refusal to speak before black gatherings made black support for Whitman entirely understandable. Of all the measures blacks believed defined Whitman's commitment to their cause, none loomed larger than his authorization of the 15th Regiment.[50]

The Regiment offered material as well as symbolic benefits to the black community. The state National Guard compensated men for drilling. In addition, the 15th provided four men with steady and well-paid jobs at the "armory." The Brooklyn facility, "a dilapidated old dance hall and beer garden," would provide similar employment opportunities. The Regiment also established an employment bureau "to secure good positions for members of the organization in commercial houses and other business institutions." Some fourteen men found jobs paying $2 to $3 per day. Although the number of jobs appears insignificant, they meant much to an economically distressed and depressed community. The $1,400 per year salary for each of the four armory employees was much more than most blacks could expect at the time.[51]

In two of the few occupations available to black men—as janitors and elevator operators—they earned a maximum of $31 monthly. As late as the 1920s, the average Harlem family earned $1,300 annually. Often, women were the primary breadwinners, a factor that Colonel Hayward viewed as a recruitment advantage. The sociologically astute commander reported to a federal inspector that "members of the colored families in this city are mutually inter-dependent, and there are many fewer cases where any one male member is the sole provider." The women's jobs as domestics, laundresses, and nannies made them "to a great extent independent of the male members of the family." One recruit, William Bonaparte, supposedly admitted to superiors that his wife earned more in a week as a washerwoman than he earned in a year. Thus, military service for him and others in similar situations was more than a job; it was a means to dignity and strong manhood. Indeed, many women encouraged their significant others to join for the purpose of making "men" of them.[52]

The combination of unemployment, menial labor, low wages, and high rents forced many black Harlemites into a life of poverty and emotional despair. Authorities in Canada recognized the plight of the city's blacks and recruited heavily in New York for the services of young black men with promises of good pay, fair play, and steady employment in the Canadian army. As a result, the *Age* found itself in the difficult position of supporting a foreign competitor at the expense of a valued local institution. Without a hint of guilt, however, the paper ran advertisements and feature stories for the Canadians, while simultaneously urging more able-bodied young men to enlist in the 15th. It further pleaded for capable young men to volunteer to become officers.[53]

As the Regiment ranks filled, anxiety over the composition of the officer corps grew. Even outsiders voiced their concerns about the paucity of officers. Only twelve out of fifty officers' positions had been filled as late as November. Like Austin, others closely associated with the military watched the New York situation intently. Clearly, who held commissions in the 15th had implications far beyond New York and even the military, as officers not only led men in war and peace but also symbolized the qualities and capabilities whites denied blacks.[54]

A letter to the *Age* from Quartermaster-Sergeant Presly Holliday, stationed in Arizona, revealed the stakes. The inability to enforce discipline upon their own kind, Holliday observed, was "one of the common weaknesses" white officers attributed to blacks. Holliday blamed educated blacks for the poor showing and wondered why all of the doctors, lawyers, merchants, and other "ambitious Negroes" had not fallen "over each other to get commissions" in the Regiment. Among these men, Holliday argued, should be those "so accustomed to being deferred to that it will be natural for them to enforce discipline." Holliday also laid to rest the faint hope that Lt. Col. Charles Young would accept a commission in the Regiment because a regular army officer would expect advancement of several grades to serve in a National Guard unit. The most the Regiment could hope for from Young, which it did not receive, was six months of instruction. Last, Holliday warned that the worst thing that could happen to the unit was inferior leadership.[55]

The *Age* apprehended Holliday's concern and launched a scathing attack against the city's young black elite: "Where are those who have been clamoring for years for a colored regiment; and where are the ambitious, intelligent, progressive young men who believe in race recognition?" As far as the *Age* could discern, the rigorous but fair standards applied to all applicants had "killed the ambition of many who previously spoke with no little enthusiasm of becoming officers." Yet the *Age* had to admit that more than mental and physical tests presented stumbling blocks. Finances also played a role. Rumors suggested that some of the present officers could not afford the uniforms and equipment required of their rank. If these reports proved true, then these men would undoubtedly face a host of embarrassing predicaments in both public and private National Guard affairs.[56]

In fact, the *Age* regarded the whole recruitment and organization situation as embarrassing: "We want a colored regiment and we have one. But so far we have not shown sufficient mental, physical, and financial capacity to maintain one." The newspaper emphasized that the 15th had to have black officers or risk shutting the door of opportunity for black men to lead any black military unit in the future. At stake lay the reputation of the race: "Should we fail, our white friends would be impelled to point out that here was another case of the colored man being too ambitious to have something for which he was not yet ready."[57] For now, the 15th had only one white officer—its commander, Col. William Hayward. That situation would not last long.

The cause of black officers would soon suffer serious blows from within and without and from friend and foe alike. Although Joel Spingarn received almost all the credit or blame for the separate training camp idea, he actually might have followed the lead and advice of a black military man. George Austin, who had written the *Age* concerning the training of black officers, now served as acting private secretary to James Reese Europe and reportedly as a captain in the 15th. Near the end of 1916, Austin met with Spingarn about a preparedness camp for a black battalion. Austin had contacted Gen. Leonard Wood about the concept and had even secured applicants for such a camp, which Wood thought might be best located in Norfolk, Virginia, considering the origins of the applicants. Around the same time, Spingarn had contacted Delancey Jay, executive secretary of the Military Training Camps Association, to gain support for black training camps. Jay informed Spingarn that the association would be glad to support any project that General Wood approved and administered, but the association could not and would not "recruit for colored camps."[58]

In the meantime, Austin wrote Spingarn to inform him of his conviction about the necessity of a training camp. Leading young "men of color will be poorly provided for next spring and summer unless that campaign of education and arousement is carried on now." Although Austin considered himself the foremost expert on "the situation among our colored youths," he believed that influential whites, such as Spingarn, had to take the lead in convincing other white leaders that such a measure represented "the only possible chance for the educated and deserving Negroes who might have the capacity for leadership, to learn in an intensely brief way the science and art of war enough to ever hope to be in line for volunteer officership."[59]

Austin's persistence worked, and Spingarn responded immediately and favorably, urging Austin "to interest as many friends as possible." Austin agreed, "even at a fearful cost" to himself. Although that cost remained unspecified, he willingly "sacrificed" self for the cause and volunteered to disseminate Spingarn's letter. Not ready to go public, Spingarn forbade Austin to use his name in connection with the effort. Spingarn continued to work behind the scenes until the moment appeared right. As preparedness assumed new urgency and America's entry into the conflict grew nearer, Spingarn negotiated a plan with Maj. Gen. Leonard Wood, commander of the Department of the East, to "organize and maintain a military training camp for colored men." Wood set the bar for success high by requiring 200 applications from qualified men. On February 15, 1917, the same day

General Wood announced that the army would sponsor a citizens' training camp in Plattsburg, Joel Spingarn not coincidentally released an open letter "to the educated colored men of the United States" to take advantage of the opportunity "to become leaders and officers instead of followers and privates." Spingarn knew the risks inherent in a call that promoted segregation but felt that "the crisis is too near at hand to discuss principles and opinions." Simply put, he believed that with war on the horizon, a segregated training camp was better than none at all.[60]

Spingarn's open letter, issued with little consultation from his own board, produced much tension within the NAACP and created a firestorm of controversy without. Black newspapers across the country condemned the plan as a backward step, if not a betrayal of the race. The *New York News* accused the NAACP of being "the first to lose its head in the national excitement and [going] blindly, bag and baggage, into the camp of the enemy." To Spingarn's argument about lost opportunity, the *News* replied: "Better the opportunity lost forever than that colored men should themselves set up a national military Jim Crow training camp." Some reduced the idea to one word—"monstrous."[61]

Even Charles Young agonized over the issue, but he ultimately agreed with Spingarn that "we must all in actual practice at times stoop to conquer—not cringing, but with our eyes upon a star." A somewhat reluctant Du Bois eventually supported his chairman and took much criticism for his "capitulation." Within the vocal and visible black leadership, the very few supporters of Spingarn's plan constituted, according to David Levering Lewis, a small minority who believed they were "laying firm ground" for the future achievement of integration "by accepting a demeaning expediency."[62]

Aware that he had stirred a hornet's nest in and outside the organization, Spingarn tried to control the damage in two important ways. First, he attempted to distance the NAACP from the training camp debate and to find a prominent black citizen to lead the campaign. He employed denial as the primary strategy to defend against attacks on the NAACP. As late as April 25, 1917, Spingarn told irate supporters of the association that it "had nothing whatever to do with the Camp for Colored Officers, which I have inaugurated. The Association should neither be praised nor blamed for it."[63] Try as he might, Spingarn could not convince observers that his actions on the camp matter had nothing to do with the NAACP. Du Bois's "Give Us the Camp" editorial in *The Crisis* belied Spingarn's claims, as would subsequent actions.[64]

Spingarn's second step directly affected the Regiment. He attempted to enlist John Nail, the father-in-law of James Weldon Johnson, as the point man for the training camp initiative. By putting a prominent black New

York businessman into the leadership position in the campaign, Spingarn believed he could simultaneously reduce charges of white paternalism and relieve pressure on the NAACP. Nail informed Spingarn privately of his support for the idea and his willingness to help recruit and stand behind Spingarn at a public meeting at Bethel Church, but pressing business matters prevented him from taking the lead. Nail further told Spingarn that he could not do "the sort of justice to this end that you can." Whatever credit (responsibility) was due, Nail offered, should go to Spingarn.[65]

Although Nail, like Gilchrist Stewart, saw no conflict of interest between the colored officer training camp and the recruitment of officers for the Regiment, other observers found the two totally incompatible. The *Age,* which only a few months before had attacked blacks for failing to make themselves available for officer candidacy, redirected its attention and blame toward Spingarn, the NAACP, and the training camp. The paper's editors believed that the supporters of the separate camp movement promoted "voluntary segregation" and that they were also threatening the black leadership of "colored volunteer regiments." This strong observation clearly referred to the fledgling 15th. Then, in a simultaneous lapse of memory and logic, the *Age* maintained that a deep pool of black officer candidates rendered officer training camps for blacks unnecessary and that the government would not be "so indiscreet as to advocate the appointment of white officers in colored volunteer regiments." Despite this misplaced faith, the *Age*'s argument made sense in terms of principle and emotion. Like so many others, the paper refused to contribute further to segregation and wanted "no 'Jim Crow' training camp!"[66]

Charles Fillmore brought the relationship between the training camps and the Regiment into even sharper focus. He had opposed the separate training camp concept from the start because of its potential to compete with the 15th for officers. By mid-March, the deleterious effects on recruitment had become all too clear. Fillmore did not, however, oppose the movement per se and recognized its potential outside New York City. He encouraged Spingarn to persuade the type of men he sought for the camps to join the 15th, where they would get the "best training" and commissions. He hoped that Spingarn would not be influenced by those more intent on questioning his military record than in lending assistance.[67] Spingarn's camp and "Fillmore's Regiment" competed directly. Each man continued to do what he thought best for his own cause; unfortunately, one would prevail and at considerable expense to the other.

The promotion of an all-black volunteer regiment and the rejection of an all-black officer training camp struck many as paradoxical. No such contradition, however, seemed to exist for the supporters of the Regiment. Not only did they rely on history and tradition to justify their position, they also had current examples of ethnically homogeneous units, to say nothing of the 8th Illinois. Even more, blacks could accept separation if they initiated the process and owned the results. The black church had proven that parallel institutions of their own making could provide distinct advantages to its members and the larger community. Moreover, many viewed separation and in-group development as necessary precursors to full inclusion. To have a Wilson-led administration set up a segregated officer training camp represented nothing more than forced exclusion and a reinforcement of continued subordination.

The lack of officers was not the only problem the 15th faced. By late March 1917, it had yet to reach full regimental strength. Until the Regiment reached that goal, it stood little chance of gaining federal recognition in time to ready it for the rapidly approaching war. In a desperate race against the clock, Hayward met with "prominent colored men of Greater New York" in a conference to formulate and execute an effective recruitment plan. Among those in attendance were James C. Thomas of the Equity Congress, the Reverend Adam Clayton Powell of Abyssinian Baptist Church, Charles W. Anderson, James Weldon Johnson, John E. Nail, and Fred Moore of the *Age*. Those present pledged to support Hayward in any way possible, including conducting meetings on street corners and participating in parades with the troops.[68]

The failure to recruit a sufficient number of officers and soldiers did not indicate simple apathy or indifference. As the war approached and the national Democrats continued their assault on black citizens, blacks in turn questioned the value and appropriateness of loyalty to the 15th Regiment and, by extension, to the nation. The question of whether blacks should serve or fight preoccupied many prominent blacks. Although some observers have suggested that most blacks cared less about the war than about their everyday lives, others believed the two concerns were inseparable.

The *Age* used the attitude of a potential recruit to indicate the mood of the rank and file. The thrilling sight of "colored men marching with the easy swing of veteran soldiers to the music of their magnificent band," with regimental and national colors fluttering above them on a perfect spring day, did not impress all. According to the *Age*, "the spell was broken by a young man" who said, "They'll not take me out to make a target of me and bring me back to 'Jim Crow' me." Anticipating readers' questions, the paper agreed that blacks had fought and died willingly for the country on many other occasions, but now the federal government under Wilson abused blacks in its pursuit of total segregation. Even post offices in the South had separate windows for black and white patrons—a stark example of federal complicity in American apartheid. Unwillingness to fight now showed no disloyalty to the nation, only resentment of the Wilson administration. In the end, the *Age* argued against the young man's outlook only because "the Negro" could not "afford to be rated as a disloyal element in the nation." Even more, "he should not do anything to mar his splendid record from the Boston Massacre to the slaughter of Carrizal."[69]

On April 1, 1917, just five days before the official declaration of war, Governor Whitman reviewed the Regiment one last time before its impending federalization. A host of dignitaries witnessed the event, including the chairman of the Public Service Commission, Oscar Strauss; the adjutant general, Louis W. Stotesbury; and Capt. Joseph L. Gilbreth, an inspector for the War Department who would determine the Regiment's readiness for federal recognition. Even Major General O'Ryan appeared, and seeing the Regiment for the first time, he offered high praise to the outfit on its appearance and efficiency. Now numbering 1,100 men, the Regiment needed 300 more men to reach the peacetime strength required by the US Army. But the *Chicago Defender* gloated that all was not well with the Regiment because it "was made up of members of the Race but led by a white man."[70]

Moreover, the numbers of white officers below the rank of colonel continued to grow and fill the commanding positions, but many did not distinguish themselves or the Regiment. Lt. Col. Lorillard Spencer commanded the 1st Battalion, Maj. Monson Morris the 2nd, and Capt. George Hinton, whom Maj. Edwin Dayton would replace within a week, the 3rd. Capt. Hamilton Fish served as regimental adjutant.[71] Their record was at best mixed. A similar record among black officers would have been treated far more critically and attributed to racial incapacity, not individual failings.

Spencer, who had been Whitman's military secretary before his promotion, would be dogged by charges of incompetence during his entire service. Yet, despite questions about his ability, he would prove himself in the crucible of battle, suffering serious wounds and earning the Croix de Guerre and Distinguished Service Cross. Monson Morris would fail miserably as a leader of men and become known as the hard-drinking, cigar-smoking, do-nothing major who eventually lost his command. Hinton, fifty-four years old at the time, would command a supply company during the war, with no apparent distinction. Dayton, with twenty-six years of National Guard experience, would chafe under Hayward's leadership and receive a transfer during service in France. Fish, who earned a Croix de Guerre and a Silver Star, would spend much of the war in officer school and/or at headquarters while seeking transfers and promotion. To his credit, Fish, later an eleven-term member of Congress, faithfully represented the interests of the Regiment and its men long after the war.[72]

The black officers—Vertner Tandy, Charles Fillmore, Virgil Parks, Napoleon Bonaparte Marshall, James Reese Europe, and George Lacy—commanded the smallest units, the companies. Bert Williams was simply a figurehead with no possibility of real service or leadership. White officers commanded the remaining companies and already outnumbered blacks. Their numbers continued to grow.[73]

On April 6, 1917, Congress approved US entry into a world war against Germany. Long portrayed as the ruthless aggressor in this conflict, Germany, through its use of unrestricted submarine warfare and attacks on civilian vessels, offended many neutral nations, lost the propaganda war, and offered a much-needed pretext for American intervention. The release of the so-called Zimmerman note to the American public on March 1 had stirred passions against the kaiser even more. Sent in January by the German foreign secretary, Alfred Zimmerman, to the German liaison with Mexico, the note, decoded and verified in late February, proposed a German defensive alliance with Mexico in case of war between the United States and Germany. In return, Germany promised to help Mexico regain lost territories.[74]

Suddenly, the war no longer seemed so far removed and of so little threat to national security. Coupled with the continued sinking of numerous merchant marine vessels by German submarines, this note pushed a reluctant Woodrow Wilson to act. Despite the protests of pacifists and antiwar socialists as well as isolationists from the American mainstream, the president, already involved in plans for a postwar world, understood that if his vision for that world had any chance of success, America had to play a role in the present conflict. He issued his war message on April 2 and declared that the United States had to fight "for the ultimate peace of the world and the liberation of its people." He ended with his immortal and pretentious mandate. "The world must be made safe for democracy." Three days later, the Senate endorsed the president's call by a vote of 82 to 6, and the following day, the House affirmed it by a vote of 373 to 50.[75]

If most blacks had been preoccupied with their own conditions before, many of them now paid close attention to the rapidly unfolding events at home and abroad, with all their global implications. Although some might have seen a more pressing need to make America safe for democracy and realized that the war was largely about empire, especially Africa, even these skeptics understood that combat presented a rare opportunity for advancement, both personal and collective. Others saw the potential for economic opportunity, given the demands of war mobilization and a possible reduction in immigration after the war. Most observers focused on the potential benefits of participation in and support for the war in the quest for full and equal citizenship. Despite attempts by some whites to link blacks with the enemy, most black Americans did not identify favorably with Germany, if they thought about the matter at all.

Black opinion makers went out of their way to criticize not just Germany but German Americans as well. After the sinking of the *Lusitania* in May 1915, James Weldon Johnson had raised serious questions about the reaction of German Americans, who seemed more concerned with the lack of support by the US government for the German position on the incident than with the act or its consequences. If they reacted in that way then, Johnson had asked, what would they do "if this country were actually at war with their beloved Fatherland?" Then, Johnson showed how high the stakes were in the race for survival and advancement. He played the "nativist card" and pointed out that because of their numbers and under the circumstances, German Americans, some 20 million strong, constituted a far greater danger to the nation than the so-called Negro problem. Whatever problems blacks represented, Johnson maintained that disloyalty and treason were not among them.[76]

Two years later, he argued for black participation in the war despite the fact that many black Americans were asking why they should fight for a country that kept them "from the ballot box, disfranchised, segregated, discriminated against, lynched, burned at the stake, Jim Crowed, and disarmed." Johnson answered unambiguously that a failure on the part of blacks to claim all of the "rights of American citizenship will be equal to a surrender of those rights." This opinion was not confined to black leaders. The Sunday after the declaration of war, Bethel Church in Chicago rocked with patriotic fervor as the audience enthusiastically applauded and endorsed speeches calling for black support of the war effort. The *Defender* reported that the men "stood as one" with the "government in this crisis, forgetting all the injustice for the time being." The *Baltimore Afro-American* endorsed the sentiment but added, with an allusion to the Fourteenth Amendment of the Constitution, that in war, "all should be on the same footing, and no distinctions made as to race, color or previous condition."[77] The 15th itself and the community embrace of it best expressed most black New Yorkers' view of the war and the role of African Americans in it.

# 5

## War and Expediency

### The Politics of Federal Recognition, Regimental Training, and the President's Call to Service

At that point, the struggle shifted to securing federal recognition. On March 23, 1917, Adjutant General Stotesbury again had requested recognition through telegram and letter. This time, the effort would succeed as Major General O'Ryan had convinced Gen. William A. Mann, chief of the Militia Bureau, that white officers exclusively would command the Regiment. O'Ryan had been in contact with Mann about this matter since February and actually initiated the discussion about white officers. Out of conviction and in an attempt to curry favor with the War Department, he had revealed that he and "most other officers of the National Guard regarded this movement for a negro regiment as a political movement." For that reason, he and others in the Guard had "discouraged the movement in every proper way." O'Ryan had predicted that the six black officers still with the Regiment would fail the federally administered examination. Moreover, his repeated claim that all of the men exceeded the age limit for their grade suggested other potential grounds for disqualification if necessary.

O'Ryan nonetheless had urged the War Department to take advantage of the "large number of fine physical specimens among the large negro population of the city." With morale problems and manpower shortages caused by the lengthy deployment of the New York National Guard on the Mexican border and the attendant economic hardships on families and businesses, O'Ryan's views on black citizen-soldiers had shifted suddenly and dramatically. Clearly, he had no problems with a regiment of black men led by capable white officers, but he shared the common perception that the failures of black soldiers lay with black officers, "who had neither the capacity nor the professional ability to satisfactorily perform their functions."[1]

Mann had kept his promise to O'Ryan that "any application made now for recognition will be favorably considered." And he had expected O'Ryan to uphold his end of the bargain. On March 28, 1917, Mann had ordered Capt. Joseph L. Gilbreth to inspect the Regiment. In the meantime, Colonel Hayward, fearing that the lack of an adequate armory might hurt chances for federal recognition, had sought and received assurances from Mayor Mitchel and the secretary of the Armory Board, C. D. Rhinehart, that the Regiment would be adequately housed after federal recognition as he had requested. On April 8, Gilbreth inspected the Regiment and "strongly" recommended "that this regiment be accepted as a unit of the National Guard of the State of New York." He cited the qualifications of the men and officers, the financial assurances of the city, and the "great interest" taken "by the best class of citizens both white and colored in the neighborhood" for his recommendation. His only reservations applied to the inadequate facilities and to officers commissioned prior to the National Defense Act of June 3, 1916, who were possibly subject to reexamination. Gilbreth expected both issues to be addressed with federal recognition.[2]

On April 19, the *Age* prematurely announced that the War Department had officially recognized the Regiment. As of April 18, however, the department had extended recognition to only the Headquarters, Machine Gun, and Supply Companies. As late as May 5, Secretary of War Baker, seemingly unaware of this development, reported to US representative Murray Hulbert that General Mann had advised him "there is no need of additional infantry regiments in the National Guard of New York at the present time." As a result, he could give no assurance of recognition. Nonetheless, the 15th Regiment proceeded as if it had earned full recognition and all that came with it—added prestige, the credentials to receive the president's call when needed, and entitlement to federal logistical and material support.[3]

Yet, every time the unit reached one benchmark, it immediately had to prepare for the next. With only 1,346 men, the unit was more than 600 recruits short of the 2,002 required for full war strength. Thus, the recruitment efforts continued at a frenetic pace, facilitated by double-deck buses equipped with bands and megaphones. Moreover, the lack of black officers continued to cause concern, if not alarm. The *Age* assigned a reporter to approach the commander for answers.[4]

The *Age* and other supporters of the Regiment had resigned themselves to Hayward's leadership. Because of his friendship with the governor, Hayward, many believed, thus far had succeeded "when others would have met with rank failure." Even more, blacks appreciated Hayward's "engaging manner," his "directness," and the lack of a "patronizing air" so common in politicians. Most of all, they respected his "conviction," as he was prepared to relinquish a prominent position on the Public Service Commission to accept a two-thirds pay cut in order "to serve his country as head of a colored regiment at an annual salary of $5,000." The *Age* went so far as to say that without Hayward and his special traits, "there would be no Fifteenth Regiment today." Other sources concurred. John Wesley Castles, Jr., a young white lieutenant with no particular fondness for Hayward, observed that as the only "colored regiment in the state," the 15th had many "enemies among the other Guardsmen, but Colonel William Hayward, backed by Governor Whitman, has put it over in grand shape and beaten every obstacle." The *Age* did not doubt Hayward's integrity, but it believed the lack of black officers gave the appearance of impropriety.[5]

In a remarkably honest public explanation, Hayward told his side of the story. First, the colonel admitted that the recruitment of officers was the most difficult of the many obstacles he had to overcome in organizing the Regiment. He had to find "enough colored men to pass the mental and physical tests" required, and beyond that, he had to identify and win over those "who possessed sufficient means to maintain the dignity of their position." The former proved relatively easy, but the latter resulted in "refusal after refusal." Some prospects told Hayward that Regiment members, who wanted no "highbrows," had discouraged them. Whether that particular charge had merit cannot be proven, but Hayward revealed that leaders of the community and officers within the Regiment opposed his proposal to expand the search for officers beyond New York. Despite his warnings about this counterproductive parochialism, Hayward claimed that he found no constructive support among blacks in this matter.[6]

Only when the War Department summoned him to Washington and asked if his unit was ready to receive federal supervision did he decide to meet the minimum requirement of thirty-six officers by recruiting white acquaintances in other Guard regiments. With fewer than twelve black commissioned officers at the time, Hayward recognized that he had to "either nominate experienced white men for commissions or be left out of the service." He emphatically denied any responsibility for the small number of black officers and said he had done all possible to advance the cause, challenging anyone to refute his claim that at no time had he "refused to nominate a member of the regiment for a commission or promotion upon being asked to do so." He pointed out that three of the five captains he had nominated were black, some of whom led companies with white commissioned subordinates. This progressive practice seriously challenged the conventional wisdom, which maintained that having both black and white officers in a regiment would cause friction. Hayward did not foresee a problem because he insisted that those white officers who sought membership already knew the situation and would see black officers only as soldiers who had to be treated "according to their rank." The reality, however, would fall somewhat short of that ideal.[7]

Last, he addressed the troubling question of the fairness of examinations. Hayward saw no justification for questioning the process and found not "an iota of truth in such a charge." If anything, he angrily replied, black candidates had an advantage over whites by receiving a preliminary exam and instructions before the final test. The colonel apparently did not know or had forgotten that a similar arrangement existed when fifty-five out of fifty-seven applicants failed the test during the Sulzer and Glynn administrations. Hayward also pointed out that twenty-six white applicants had failed to meet the requirements. At the time of federal recognition, some twenty vacancies still existed. Now, the federal authorities controlled the examination process, and despite Hayward's assurances about its fairness, only one more black joined the officer ranks—Dennis Lincoln Reid, a native of Virginia and a Harlem resident, as a second lieutenant. Even worse, the number would fall to five by the time the Regiment departed for Europe. Nonetheless, the issue, perhaps because of resignation, virtually dropped from sight.[8]

Was Hayward revealing all that he knew, or was he uninformed? Although the evidence reveals a far less fair process than he indicated, that in no way implicates him in the machinations. The same cannot be said for Major General O'Ryan, who concerned himself more with the plight of a cadre of white, college-trained young men with National Guard experience who could not find places in the established regiments. Unimpressed with the quality of black officers in the 15th, O'Ryan believed that the development of the regiment "under the competent leadership of white officers" would serve the best interests of the New York National Guard and the US Army. O'Ryan already had struck a secret deal with the chief of the Militia Bureau to eliminate or cap the number of black officers in the Regiment.[9] The evidence indicates that by the time Hayward got the call from Washington, O'Ryan's maneuvering had already tied his hands. Thus, the timing of the federal authorities' rapid acceptance of the Regiment seemed as much a measure to preclude more black officers as one to prepare for war. What appeared an honorable action on the surface had perhaps far more sinister motives and implications beneath. The white supremacist administration would do anything to deny black men the opportunity to prove their capacity to lead, especially in battle.

With the officer question largely behind him, Hayward focused on bringing the Regiment to full war strength. Members of the unit recruited on street corners, in churches, and even in theaters. According to Capt. Napoleon Bonaparte Marshall, not all of these efforts struck a responsive chord. One evening in early May 1917, he appeared at the Lafayette Theatre to appeal for recruits. He claimed that the audience first applauded him when he emerged in uniform but then jeered him when he called for volunteers. The crowd apparently respected his identification with the 15th but did not appreciate his support of the Wilson government. Someone shouted, "What has that uniform ever got you?" Marshall allegedly replied that any man not willing to fight for his country was not worthy to be one of its citizens. He claimed that newspapers ran a story of the incident and called him a "patriot." Whether the incident is true is not as important as what it says about a man who had defended the accused soldiers at Brownsville in 1906, who had become a prominent figure in black Democratic politics, and who would suffer injustice during and after his military career. The final indignity would come after the war, when military authorities declared Marshall 29 percent disabled from his service on the western front, whereas the threshold for disability compensation was 30 percent. Despite this, he would remain loyal to the end.[10]

Recruitment efforts went into high gear along numerous fronts outside the city. Hamilton Fish took a recruiting party of men to Newburgh, Peekskill, and other river towns in Duchess, Putnam, and Orange Counties. Other men led similar efforts in Yonkers and New Rochelle. In the windows of homes throughout the city, placards announced, "One boy from this home is serving his country in the 15th N.Y. Infantry." Numerous sets of siblings—including the four Davis brothers; the four Alstons from Charleston, South Carolina; the four Brewsters of Roslyn, New York; and, amazingly, the seven Fowlers from Glen Cove, Long Island—joined the 15th. Federal recognition and supervision also boosted the enlistment process, as it gave needy young men an important fiscal incentive to belong. The pay for drilling, approximately one-fourth of the salary for a soldier in the regular army, could make a measurable improvement in their quality of life.[11]

The Regiment also found support among the black women of the city. Apparently less ambivalent about backing the war than some of their white counterparts, many black women willingly assumed roles that they believed would increase their standing as citizens and respectable ladies. In the process, they had to navigate the dangerous straits between resistance and cooperation. The first could bring the wrath of the government and its numerous and powerful supporters down on them, and the second might reinforce the narrow constructions of maternalism often imposed upon women. As Alice Dunbar-Nelson put it, "Into this maelstrom of war activity the women of the Negro race hurled themselves jealously." Still, these women had to be aware of the "firm hand of repression" that Wilson warned awaited those who did not support the war. For instance, mothers who did not encourage and permit their sons to become soldiers could be censured for undermining the national security. Nonetheless, a few elite black women, such as M. Cravath Simpson of the Northeast Federation of Women's Clubs, resisted the demand for blind loyalty, argued that a tainted nation could not win a pure and clean victory, and warned that God might intervene to "adjust" the wrongs.[12] Most elite black women, like black men, knew, however, that the low status of blacks in the American order required them to accept roles and positions that were often at odds with their principles and consciences. Some, more than not, would try to exploit this opportunity to their minimum disadvantage; the most they could hope for was something that did not hurt them too much.

The 15th benefited directly from this practical mind-set and political reality. A call by the National League for Women's Service to help the nation in its moment of crisis prompted "a few thoughtful women of the race" to cooperate with the Woman's Loyal Union of Greater New York to coordinate the response. They immediately directed their efforts to the Regiment, which they knew meant so much to the community, and adopted it as an instrument of their aspirations. Led by Susan Elizabeth Frazier, president of the Women's Loyal Union, the delegation—which included Elizabeth and Helen Mae Fillmore, the wife and daughter, respectively, of Capt. Charles Fillmore—presented its plans for assisting the Regiment to Fillmore. He then introduced them to Hayward, who outlined the "urgent needs of the regiment."[13]

From that meeting emerged the Woman's Auxiliary, 15th Regiment NY Infantry, NG of Greater New York, with headquarters at 2217 Seventh Avenue. Its officers were Susan Elizabeth Frazier, president; Maria C. Lawton, first vice president; Eva Bowles, second vice president; Charlotte Bell, chair of the executive board; Helen Mae Fillmore, recording secretary; Rose E. Harper, corresponding secretary; Emma Fox Fin, secretary; and E. Montgomery Jones, treasurer. Hayward granted official recognition to the organization on May 9 and urged that other women interested in helping the Regiment follow this fine example.[14]

Seemingly consistent with the roles women were expected to play, the members of the auxiliary provided food, clothing, and money to dependent families. Although often modest, their assistance frequently determined whether a soldier's family had a roof over their heads or a meal on the table. Their valuable support and effective performance engendered Hayward's respect and appreciation even when his officers seemed to take them for granted. On learning that the auxiliary's request for the names of needy families had been ignored, Hayward made clear to his officers that "these ladies have been indefatigable in their efforts to serve the members of this regiment and a prompt and full response to their appeal for information should be evidence of our appreciation." No doubt, Frazier's reputation commanded some of this respect. A graduate of Hunter College, she had engaged the school board in a protracted legal battle to become, in 1895, the first black teacher employed at a predominantly white school in the city.[15] She would bring that same determination to her leadership of the auxiliary, challenging the boundaries of women's places and roles in wartime and demanding equal inclusion in the society that war would purportedly transform.

Despite the widespread recruitment efforts and the much-needed assistance from the Women's Auxiliary, Hayward remained dissatisfied with the pace and quality of the Regiment's development. Numerical strength would not suffice; he desired distinction for his Regiment. In his quest to build "the crack regiment" in the state, he turned to James Reese Europe, who had joined the unit on September 19, 1916, as a sergeant. Europe, born in Mobile, Alabama, on February 22, 1882, had moved with his family to Washington, DC, as a youth. An accomplished pianist and violinist and a member of his high school cadet corps, Europe left the family in 1899 upon the death of his father to seek fame and fortune as a musician in New York. After struggling to survive financially, he organized a quartet of instrumentalists and vocalists in 1903 and became the official musician of the Wanamaker family of Philadelphia. From there, Europe's success grew, and he organized the famous Clef Club, which performed in 1911 at Carnegie Hall. He played and composed for the famous dance team of Irene and Vernon Castle and gave the world the slow tempo dance called the fox-trot, known by some as the fish walk.[16]

Europe had joined the Regiment because he respected its purpose and saw it as an opportunity to associate with the finest citizens of Harlem. Furthermore, close friends Bert Williams and Lester Walton had recommended he join. According to Noble Sissle, Europe announced the news like an exuberant child: "I'm in it now! I did it! I'm real stuff now!" When Sissle, an accomplished musician, close friend, and business partner, inquired why Europe would abandon their thriving musical projects, Europe replied, "Don't worry, you're going to join too." Sissle protested vigorously but in vain, as his friend had already enlisted him. Europe took his service seriously and desired to ascend to the officer ranks. He passed the officer's examination and earned the rank of first lieutenant.[17]

Colonel Hayward appreciated Europe for his leadership as a soldier but even more for his talents as a musician, composer, and conductor. Nevertheless, he could not employ him as band director until E. E. Thompson vacated the position. Thompson's inability or unwillingness to recruit band members for the Regiment not only frustrated Hayward but also proved costly, as he had to pay many of the musicians' professional rates.[18]

By early April, Hayward secured Thompson's resignation and approached Europe with an offer to become band director. Sissle described Europe's reaction: "I will never forget the worried expression on Jim's face that night as I met him coming out of the colonel's office." A reluctant and shocked Europe shrank from the opportunity. According to his biographer, Reid Badger, the musician did not particularly like the brassy sound of military orchestras. Furthermore, he wanted to command fighting soldiers, not lead a band. In fact, his rank would create issues down the road, issues that Hayward had to circumvent. After contemplating the matter, Europe presented to Hayward an extreme set of demands that were likely to encounter rejection. He would need support to make the band first rate so as not to injure his professional reputation. The support would entail money being set aside for the band members, a practice in violation of army rules. Further, Europe wanted far more than the twenty-eight pieces specified in army tables of organization. In his opinion, the band could have no fewer than forty-four pieces and preferably sixty or more. Last, he insisted that he be allowed to recruit musicians outside New York.[19]

To Europe's surprise and dismay, Hayward, who believed the great success of the 8th Illinois came in no small part from its band, would do anything to create the best military band in the land. To that end, he approached a rich and powerful friend, Daniel G. Reid, a director of US Steel Corporation and American Can Company, to help him reach out to donors. Reid simply donated $10,000 and allowed Hayward to call Europe's bluff. A rueful Europe had no choice but to accept. Looking on the bright side, he speculated that if he created a truly great military band, he might realize his dream of a forging a national negro orchestra. Sissle and he set up offices at regimental headquarters and immediately advertised for "Crack Colored Musicians" in the city's black papers.[20]

Frank de Broit, the great cornet player from Chicago, became the band's first big-name recruit. His prominent mustache and eccentric behavior often put Europe in the position of defending the man, for de Broit's flamboyancy was off-putting to some, though no one could deny his musical genius. Even more important to the band's success was the enlistment of Francis Eugene Mikell, a South Carolina native and very experienced musician who had taught at a host of black colleges and headed many fine orchestras, including the one at the world-famous Pekin Theatre in Chicago. Europe made Mikell assistant conductor and bandmaster. Yet, a key piece of the puzzle remained missing. For proper balance and a mellower sound, Europe sought reed musicians, who were in short supply in the States. The ever-resourceful bandleader found these musicians in Puerto Rico.[21] Their musical talents made the band unique, and their presence as exotic others provided much ethnic "humor" for the Regiment's black soldiers.

Amid all of this positive activity, rumors out of Washington cast a dark shadow over the role black men would play in the war effort. Joel Spingarn had published information indicating that the General Staff of the army had decided to reduce the number of men in its training program as a way of eliminating blacks from the plan. The Spingarn circular alleged that

> the South does not want colored men to get any kind of military training; nothing frightens it more than the thought of millions of colored men with discipline, organizing power, and a dangerous effectiveness. That is why [Senator] Vardaman is so bitterly opposed to universal military training. That is why the General Staff of the Army has decided to exclude colored men from the training and has reduced its original estimate of 900,000 to 500,000. That is why the colored man who refuses to take advantage of this hard-won chance for a camp is biting off his nose to spite his face.[22]

Spingarn's circular, dated March 8, clearly demonstrated the aggressiveness with which its author pursued his mission. With only seventy-two applicants nearly a month after his initial call, Spingarn hoped to arouse blacks behind his cause as well as put the War Department on the defensive. The strategy seemed to have worked. By the end of March, Spingarn boasted that he had "a good many more [applicants] than the required 250." What he might not have expected was that Fred Moore of the *Age* would take his charges directly to Secretary of War Baker, who issued a prompt, unequivocal denial. Baker referred Moore to section 4 of the General Staff Universal Military Training and Service Bill, which provided that "white and colored enlisted or enrolled men shall not be organized in or assigned to the same company, battalion, or regiment." Although this confirmation that rigid segregation existed and would continue to exist in the army did not refute Spingarn's charges, it seemed to satisfy Moore, who published an author's note that concluded the rumors in circulation "seem to have been without foundation."[23]

Despite the government's inaction, the movement gained in strength as students, administrators, and faculty on black college campuses organized for purposes of recruitment and agitation. On April 27, Spingarn led a delegation to meet with Secretary Baker. The group included Moorfield Storey of Boston, Archibald Grimke, Professors George Cook and Montgomery Gregory, and Dean Kelly Miller of Howard University along with Whitfield McKinley, James W. Robinson, and Roy Nash. Armed with a list of more than 350 applicants, "nearly everyone of them representing the type best fitted for leadership in war," Spingarn "asked" that Baker "immediately authorize General Wood to invite three hundred colored men to enter Plattsburg or any other of the regular training camps." Baker said that he could not act immediately but remained committed to the plan to train "colored officers for colored regiments." He added that he had not decided whether to place black battalions in regular camps or to establish a separate and distinct camp. In the end, he would choose "'whichever was least offensive to the colored people.'"[24]

Spingarn circulated an account of the meeting and charged that War Department inaction would not have occurred if "the whole colored world had risen up and demanded such training." To avoid even more delay and possible rejection, he urged "all men, white and black, to start an organized campaign to see that the Secretary of War does not forget his promise." Students at Howard University led the way by setting up the Central Committee of Negro College Men, and within ten days, the group had collected the names of 1,500 black collegians who desired to become military officers.[25]

On May 12, 1917, Stephen M. Newman, president of Howard University, received official notification from Baker's private secretary that the department had approved a "training camp for Colored men" at an undetermined location. Howard University had hoped its campus would be the site. The War Department had decided that the camp would last for three months instead of one and result in a commission of no less than second lieutenant, at an annual salary of $1,700. Spingarn warned that the camp offered the only chance to avoid being conscripted as privates. He also touted the historic quality of the camps and what they would mean to posterity.[26]

Yet, all was not as it seemed. The War Department reset the age range for recruits, making it from twenty-five to forty, and thus virtually eliminated all of the college applicants. It rejected Howard's proposal to host the camp and instead located it in Des Moines, Iowa, in part because of that city's purported "racial safeness" and remote setting. Even worse, high-ranking military officers set out to diminish the impact of what they saw as a political concession to black pressure and the fear of disaffection among such a large minority. Army leaders insisted upon the following restrictions, according to military historians Arthur Barbeau and Florette Henri:

1) that no more than 2 percent of officer candidates should be black;
2) that few colored officers would ever be utilized;
3) that these few should be washed out as quickly as they could be charged with incompetence; and
4) that there should be no black officers of field rank (major and up).[27]

Although 693 men out of the original 1,250 received commissions, the military succeeded in limiting the roles and effectiveness of these graduates. First, by changing the age requirements, the War Department purposely eliminated the best and the brightest, those who stood the greatest chance of advancing in the military. This obstructionist pattern continued after graduation in the form of assignments largely unrelated to the graduates' training. This is to say nothing of the dangerous or fatiguing duties these officers had to perform. All too frequently, commanding officers declared the men lacking and asked for their dismissal or reduction in rank. The graduates faced discourteous and even abusive treatment at the hands of some officers and endured deplorable conditions in places such as Fort Sill. The army replaced almost all of the black captains, which produced a self-fulfilling prophecy "that blacks did not have the makings of company commanders."[28]

Although Hayward never connected Spingarn's movement to his difficulties in recruiting regimental officers, he would soon feel its direct impact. Shortly after the announcement about the approval of the training camp, the *Age* reported that the War Department had asked Hayward to nominate candidates for the officer training camp at Plattsburg and then listed the twenty-five he selected. The location listed in the paper, which seemed at odds with reports on the program, could have been a sign of the confusion about the matter within the War Department, a simple case of miscommunication, or bad reporting by the *Age*. In any case, the *Age* corrected the story a month later and reported that the men would report to Fort Des Moines. Yet the correction seemed to produce another discrepancy, for four new names replaced those of four men on the original list. Two of the men omitted, Ira Aldridge and Archie McLee, would later appear on a roster of graduates of the officer training camp at Fort Des Moines. Two of the replacements also appeared on the list of graduates, Homer Butler and Edward Rudd.[29]

If the record is accurate, at least nine men from the 15th would receive commissions through the separate training camp. More significant, however, not one of these nine officers served overseas with the Regiment. By the time they emerged from what became a four-month-long training camp, the 15th had filled its officer ranks. Moreover, the army had no intention of delivering these men to units with white officers of equal or lesser rank. Thus, those who argued that the training camps would not benefit the Regiment had been vindicated.

There were deeper implications as well. Another ten men from New York City, apparently unattached to the Regiment, also graduated from Fort Des Moines. The success of the nineteen men in negotiating a four-month officer training program under the demanding general Charles Ballou raises serious questions about previous explanations for the lack of black officers in the Regiment and reinforces the evidence that the actions of certain officials contributed significantly to the low numbers. The results also suggest that the Spingarn movement did have some siphoning effect on the Regiment. Even worse, the Regiment lost some of its best noncommissioned officers to the camp. As will become evident, their importance to the unit's success cannot be overstated. The camps did not prove to be a boon to many of them either, as they would have been better off going abroad with the Regiment, securing opportunities to earn commissions overseas. Henry Plummer Cheatham, for example, departed as a sergeant in the 15th, attended officer school in France, became a lieutenant, received a mandatory transfer to the 370th Regiment, and won a Croix de Guerre.[30]

For the time being, the Regiment and the community behind it had other matters to occupy their attention. The men would undergo their first real training in small-arms practice and field exercise. They were about to take the first major step, as Hayward put it, in the transformation from "colored boys . . . chauffeurs, preachers, cooks, barbers, waiters, street sweepers, porters, bell hops, white washers, 'Pride of San Juan Hill,' carpet cleaners, ash cart drivers, bartenders" to "MEN, real men." On May 13, 1917, the Guardsmen departed for training camp near Peekskill, New York. Jim Europe's band led the way to the tune of "Onward Christian Soldiers." Noble Sissle recalled it as a disastrous debut in which the drummers set three different marching tempos, the buglers did not play when they should have and continued playing when they should not, and the Puerto Ricans could not take their eyes off the crowds and the buildings. In contrast, Capt.

Arthur Little, not at all averse to making jokes at the expense of his men, characterized the event as transformative. It made him forget all about the ragtag outfit, the weaknesses of their command, and even the disparaging words some had hurled at them. For that moment, they "were Christian and American soldiers marching on to war."[31]

As unprepared as the men of the 15th were to fight a war, the nation itself was hardly ready to engage in a large, modern conflict. Geographic isolation and a mistaken belief in America's exceptionalism had fostered a false sense of national security. However, rapid technological developments in transportation and warfare had reduced the oceans as natural barriers to invasion and also made them "easy avenues of approach" for the disruption of trade and travel. The United States could no longer hide in splendid physical isolation or pretend to be above and beyond the nationalist and imperialist ways of Europe.[32]

At the time the Congress declared war, the regular army consisted of a mere 5,791 officers and 121,797 enlisted men. Approximately 168,000 men composed the National Guard, but only 67,000 Guardsmen were in federal service, most of them serving on the Mexican border. The rest remained in units under state control, none of which possessed the equipment or skill to fight a modern war. The lack of American readiness shocked European political and military leaders. By June, an official American report to the British government revealed that the United States could have 120,000 to 150,000 men in France by January 1, 1918, and 500,000 by the end of 1918. Allies had expected at least 1 million US troops by the first of the year.[33]

Numbers revealed only a part of the abysmal situation. The French army's representatives in Washington found the entire American military establishment in a state of disarray. During the summer of 1917, the French military mission in the United States, under the direction of Commandant Edouard Réquin, criticized the condition of the US Army, from the General Staff down to training methods. French officers encountered "a state of non-organization that is difficult to imagine." Only a continual exchange of information between Paris and Washington, he asserted, could remedy such basic deficiencies, as the US Army lacked experienced and competent instructors.[34]

American plans to instruct officers appeared "defective and narrow." The training measures they anticipated for staff and artillery officers would be inadequate for warfare in Europe. The US General Staff's penchant for excessive deliberations killed the spirit of decisions and prevented their immediate realization. American military leaders, in Colonel Réquin's opinion, were simply not "desirous of taking initiatives and accepting responsibilities."

American military training consequently proceeded with no competent superior direction of the regular army or National Guard divisions.

The shortage of instructors ensured that training would differ from division to division and be "quite mediocre on the whole." The US Army War College lacked the authority to enact its recommendations and programs, and the officers in the US War Department lacked the qualifications to exercise its control profitably. Ultimately, generals without adequate preparation for their roles would have to organize, train, and command divisions where everything—organization, arms, and combat—was new.[35] Although the US Army was requesting more French instructors and wanted to send officers to France, Réquin nevertheless noted, "It is difficult not to be too unpleasantly impressed by the slowness of the American military administration and by the retrograde state of mind of some of its chiefs." At least some American officers advocated more rapid measures, but Réquin feared that the US Army would not be ready for the western front in time to meet the anticipated German offensive in the spring of 1918.[36]

At Christmas 1917, Réquin assessed the comparative condition of American divisions. Poorly trained, politically appointed officer cadres and vicious methods of recruitment in some states plagued National Guard divisions. The regular army divisions appeared substantially better, and Réquin concluded that training National Guard with regular army divisions would rectify the inadequacies of the Guard units.[37] Such assessments of the US Army by the representative of the French army, which would train and equip most of the American Expeditionary Forces, provided the context for the early evolution of the 15th New York National Guard Regiment.

An American army division contained 979 officers and 27,082 men. A division comprised two infantry brigades, which in turn each comprised two regiments. The four regiments of some 3,720 men (up from the prewar organizational table quota of 2,002) each formed the basic units of a military division. Regiments were subdivided into battalions of more than 1,000 men, battalions into companies of over 250 men, and companies into platoons of roughly 50 men. An American division also included three field artillery regiments, one engineer regiment, a machine-gun and signals battalion, and supply and sanitary troops. The total was actually 40,000 all told, with support troops included. The shortage of trained officers in the US Army necessitated the increase in regimental strength and the large size of the division, and large divisions might also better absorb the high losses of attrition warfare.[38]

An American division had more than twice the number of men of a French or German division, which had only 10,000 to 14,000 soldiers in 1917.

A European division consisted of three regiments, each containing some 2,500 to 3,000 men; the regiments had three battalions of 800 to 1,000 soldiers. Whereas the American division formed a "square" in its organization, the European division had become "triangular" during the course of three years of warfare. The smaller size enabled a greater measure of control suited to positional warfare in the confines of the western front. The European divisions also had far greater destructive capacity in artillery and machine guns, for harsh experience had proven that in a war of position and attrition, tremendous firepower was required to support infantry in offense or defense.[39]

Now, President Wilson had to appoint a commander to transform chaos into order and weakness into strength. Most observers assumed he would choose the army's senior-ranking officer, Maj. Gen. Leonard Wood. However, the hawkish and opinionated Wood had attacked the president's cautiousness and, worse, hitched his star to Theodore Roosevelt, thereby earning a reputation as the "most insubordinate general in the entire army." Wilson instead turned to Maj. Gen. John J. "Black Jack" Pershing, who had amassed a stellar record as a leader from his days at West Point through his service in the Spanish-American War and the Philippines Insurrection. More recently, Wilson had charged Pershing with the capture of Pancho Villa. A lack of cooperation by the government of Mexico and restraints from Washington hampered Pershing's attempts to capture the man, but his efforts did reduce the capacity of Villa's forces to launch effective offensives across the border. Despite the mixed results, Pershing benefited from his outstanding reputation, loyalty to superiors, dedication to duty, and political ties.[40]

Two days after being assigned to command a division, Pershing became the commander of the entire AEF. He sailed for Britain and France on May 28, 1917. Once in Europe, however, his leadership caused grave concern to the Allies and eventually to American officials. By May 1918, the British had suggested that Pershing be relieved of his command. Consequently, some powerful figures in the government became convinced that he was incapable of handling his vast responsibilities. On June 3, 1918, Col. Edward House advised the president to relieve Pershing "from all responsibility except the training and fighting of our troops." But Pershing convinced the president that any division of responsibility could prove disastrous, and then he reorganized his operation and retained full authority.[41]

Starting in June 1917, the first four American divisions sailed for France—the regular army's 1st and 2nd Divisions and the National Guard's 26th (Yankee) and 42nd (Rainbow) Divisions. The 2nd Division included a brigade of two marine regiments, the 5th and 6th Marines. The 42nd Division, which included the 69th New York Infantry, had rejected the application of the 15th New York for membership in its ranks with the flippant reply, "Black is not a color of the Rainbow."[42] Neither is white, of course, but the 42nd's answer racialized a geographic designation and made brutally clear that the so-called American melting pot did not include African Americans. Not even the crucible of war could break down the nation's solid racial barriers.[43]

Although the nation mobilized the manpower rapidly through conscription, it did not have sufficient arms, equipment, or organization to train the men properly or adequate vessels to transport them quickly and safely.[44] As a result, only these four divisions would spend the winter of 1917—1918 in France, while the rest of the army formed in the United States. When the men of the 15th made their way to Camp Peekskill, New York, no one in the Regiment knew if or when this raw, neglected group would depart for service overseas.

After a joyous and tearful send-off, characterized by a combination of good wishes and desperate pleas, the 15th arrived at the camp just outside Peekskill at 3:00 P.M. on Sunday, May 13, 1917. What they found surprised and dismayed them. Hungry and tired, the men soon learned that the Regiment had to prepare its own meals in a facility built for an outside caterer. With no equipment of their own for messing, unit leaders made an urgent plea to state authorities for tin plates and utensils. Preparing a meal for over 1,300 men took until 10:00 that night. As the scent of food replaced the mess call and "the rule of first come first served" supplanted military order, many men went to bed hungry and angry.[45]

After the chaos of the first night, officers insisted on discipline and imposed a strict military schedule, with lights out at 9:30 P.M. and reveille at 4:45 A.M.—when the bugle sounded and the rooster crowed. Nothing could have been further removed from Harlem time. The men soon learned that the sound of taps, signaling lights out, was their friend. Good sleep proved essential to withstanding the rigorous and demanding daily schedule that awaited the raw recruits, for, as Capt. Arthur Little remarked, for eighteen days "they drilled and shot, rain or shine."[46]

Despite the rigid discipline, most men adapted remarkably well to their new and very different circumstances. Peekskill borough president Leverett F. Crumb praised them for their deportment and informed Colonel Hayward that they had given local authorities far less trouble than any of the other NYNG outfits. Not one complaint had been registered against them. The Regiment so greatly impressed Crumb that he sent letters to Governor Whitman and General O'Ryan. Although proud of the compliments, the men also understood them as signs of intense and constant scrutiny. They were keenly aware that any missteps reflected badly on the unit and, by extension, their "race." No one recognized these circumstances better than their moral and spiritual leader, Capt. William H. Brooks, the chaplain. In a sermon entitled "As a Man Thinketh So He Is," Chaplain Brooks reportedly moved men to tears with his warnings about bad women, unclean thoughts, gambling, and offensive language, in that order. However, he emphasized that he served all of the men, and he let the white officers know that they had to speak respectfully of the enlisted men and not refer to or call them "niggers."[47] His message was undoubtedly both preventive and corrective.[48]

On that second Sunday at Camp Peekskill, the weather provided an ideal opportunity for families and loved ones to visit. Spiritual nourishment alone could not compensate for the camp food and homesickness. The more fortunate soldiers "gorged themselves on delicacies such as spring chicken, cake, and pie." Wanting no man to be denied a special treat after a week of hard duty, Lt. Col. Lorillard Spencer saw to it that each soldier received a box of candy. Yet in accounting for the welfare of these men, one must not overlook the invaluable service of the Women's Auxiliary. Its most notable contribution came in the form of comfort bags, whose contents indicated the extent to which the Regiment was left to its own devices and how little support it received from state or federal sources. In addition to insufficient weapons and munitions, the men lacked the most basic items, such as collapsible aluminum drinking cups, soap, facecloths, handkerchiefs, toothbrushes, hair brushes, and foot salve or powder. The comfort bags also contained pads, pencils, envelopes, thread, needles, thimbles, safety pins, scissors, and luxury items such as tobacco and cigarettes.[49] That most of these items were not standard issue seems inconceivable today but characterized the US Army at the time.

The Peekskill experience was a major milestone for the Regiment. It revealed the worthiness and commitment of many recruits, despite incidents of misbehavior—mostly curfew violations and some defections. Here, the men found their way as soldiers. The most detailed description of this experience comes from Arthur W. Little's firsthand account, *From Harlem to the Rhine.* Full of "military absurdities"—humorous anecdotes about the performance, mannerisms, and speech of the men—it portrays men who know nothing about guard duty, military formations, or the proper mode of salute. This purportedly positive history, however, reveals as much about Little as a man of his times as about the black men it describes. Noble Sissle credited Little and many other white officers for their "sincere democratic treatment of the soldiers." Yet, Little sometimes appealed to the basest stereotypes about black women and African American gender relations and showed particular contempt for timid soldiers, who "let their women folks do the talking" and hid behind their skirts: "'Mah man is mah on'y suppo't. Ef yoo all takes him erway, me and mah fo' chillen will stave, cuz I cain't do no washin' now 'till after mah bebby is bone." Despite this damaging imagery, preserved for posterity, Little claimed that he had no intent to hold "the individuals concerned or the organization up to ridicule." His purpose was to "complete the development picture of this famous American volunteer regiment."[50] *From Harlem to the Rhine,* as the view of the friend of the Regiment and of blacks, clearly demonstrates the difficulties these men faced as soldiers and as humans. A contemporary and somewhat sardonic review by Walter Wilson in the *New Republic* favored other accounts of blacks in the war that were "free from the 'understanding and respect' shown by Colonel Little for the Negro."[51]

Many readers believed, however, that Little "rescued the battered reputation of Negro soldiery from its defamers," but even some of them regretted that he undercut it with excessive use of dialect and exploitation of black humor. The book, like so many of its kind, is a tale of redemption, promise, and transformation. As such, it relies on dramatic contrasts to trace the rise of men from the lowest depths of society to top billing on an international stage. In its pages, we see the "Saluting Fifteenth" and the "15th Heavy Foot" become the "Rattlers," the "Fighting Fifteenth," and the "Harlem Hellfighters." The Peekskill experience accelerated the transformation process, and Little credited

> the officers of the 15th New York [who] did wonderful things during those eighteen days at Peekskill. Our men, by the time we returned to our city, could drill as well as any regiment in the New York Guard. They knew the important names of the many parts of the service rifle. They knew the function of those parts. They could take their rifles apart and put them together again. They knew the duty of the sentinel . . . and could perform such duty in most exacting fashion. Every man had shot for the standard qualification score of the U.S. Rifle Association over every range from 100 to 600 yards, including both deliberate and rapid fire.[52]

Certainly, as Noble Sissle noted, the predominantly white officer cadre—especially Colonel Hayward, his adjutant Arthur Little, Hamilton Fish, Lorillard Spencer, David L'Esperance, and Edwin Dayton—contributed much to the Regiment's progress. But so did black officers Napoleon Marshall,

Charles Fillmore, George Lacy, and Dennis Reid, whom Sissle complimented for their "splendid examples of Negro soldiery." The unsung heroes of the Regiment's early stages, however, were the noncommissioned officers. Their role would only grow larger and more important in the course of time and events. These men, whom Sissle considered "brilliant," included Regimental Sgt. Maj. Charles Conick and four battalion sergeant majors, Chauncey Hooper, William Chisum, Henry Plummer Cheatham, and Warrick Cheesman.[53]

Early in the morning on Memorial Day, May 30, 1917, the Regiment broke camp, and each enlisted man received $22.50 in cash, which, according to Captain Little, "meant the difference between hunger and food." Richer for the experience, the men boarded a train for New York City, where they would join other NYNG organizations for a march up Riverside Drive. Captain Little recalled the wild reception New York gave the Regiment that day as the men marched "beautifully." The *New York World* confirmed Little's account and exceeded it:

> On Memorial Day they paraded along Riverside Drive in a manner
> that put the marching itch in the feet of every colored elevator chap-
> erone that saw them. That parade made it easy for the regiment to
> make its quota, and it is said that the colored man who doesn't sport
> a soldier's uniform these days and can't give some good excuse might
> as well forget he ever had a girl.[54]

Despite the irresistible urge to embrace racial humor, the *World*'s treatment of the Regiment could have not been more laudatory. It compared the unit favorably to the 7th Regiment, perhaps "the best drilled regiment outside of West Point"; to the 69th, with a "fighting record that looks like a chronology of the Civil War"; and to the 71st, which exhibited a "devotion and patience in service that would crush the spirit of less patriotic men." Yet, the "most interesting organization in the State" was the 15th, "the first of the infantry regiments to attain full war strength, and the first to begin the enrollment of reserves." Even more, the *World* reported, the Regiment attracted "favorable comment wherever its men appear" and allayed any fears that the "uniform has spoiled them."[55]

Maj. Edwin Dayton, a seasoned military veteran, concurred: "The enlisted men represent the very best class of our colored citizens, the orderly, thrifty class of educated men who have seized the opportunity to prove afresh that there is no braver nor more reliable soldier than the North American negro, that is when he is properly trained and competently led by the right officers." In a dramatic departure from the conventional wisdom of the day, Dayton considered black officers among the "right." Of "singular significance," he noted, "is the fact that Fifteenth is officered by men . . . who bear some of the best known names in New York City's social, military, professional, and business circles." They included the six black officers, among them Capt. Napoleon Bonaparte Marshall, who was the son of well-to-do parents, a graduate of Phillips Andover Preparatory School, an "erstwhile Harvard football star and champion quarter miler," and the husband of Washington Conservatory of Music founder Harriet Gibbs-Marshall, the daughter of Judge Mifflin Wistar Gibbs and Marie A. Alexander.[56]

Among the white officers was Lorillard Spencer, Jr., son of the wealthy publisher of the same name. Spencer's mother, the former Caroline Suydam, was an international philanthropist and introduced the Boy Scouts to the Philippines, carrying forth an interest of her son, one of the founders of the Boy Scouts in the United States. Perhaps the richest of the white officers was Richardson Pratt, whose grandfather helped John D. Rockefeller create Standard Oil. Some of that wealth contributed to the founding of Pratt Institute. As Arthur Little recalls, most of these officers were graduates of the finest universities and members of the most prestigious clubs, including the Knickerbocker, the Metropolitan, and the Union League. These were men who had the "easiest way" open to them but who, according to Little, felt a deep obligation to the upper-class tradition of noblesse oblige.[57] Not all within the Regiment looked so favorably upon these sons of the elite, and some found them personally snobbish and ambitious. Many of them would be known as members of "the club," and they could even turn on their own should one not live up to the expectations of his class.

Eric Winston possessed all the credentials for membership in the club—the grandson of Frederick Winston, first president of the Mutual Life Insurance Company; captain of the Harvard squash team; and three-time national amateur squash champion. Winston married Maud Arden Kennedy of the Van Rensselaer family. Despite his solemn marriage vows, Winston, while a lieutenant in the 15th NYNG, allegedly "became infatuated" with a Brooklyn woman known in the record as "Miss X." Some of Lieutenant Winston's fellow officers testified against him for his misconduct in a boardinghouse in the appropriately named town of Stormville, in Duchess County. Mrs. Winston filed for divorce and won back her maiden (good) name and the right to remarry. Yet, because adultery was the only ground for divorce at the time and the state did not want to encourage divorce, the penalty for the perpetrator was a life sentence: for as long as Miss Kennedy lived, the divorce decree forbade Eric Winston from marrying again—an act that not only denied him his "freedom" but also presumably prevented him from having a legitimate heir and perpetuating his bloodline.[58] Winston eventually rose to the rank of captain but seemingly remained estranged from that group to which he "naturally" belonged.

Among the forty-eight white officers, perhaps the best pedigree belonged to Hamilton Fish of Company K, the scion of a prominent New York family that traced its roots back to Peter Stuyvesant, the last governor of New Amsterdam, and Lewis Morris, a signer of the Declaration of Independence. Fish's great-grandfather had served as a colonel and confidant of George Washington in the Revolutionary War. His grandfather, named for Alexander Hamilton, had been a congressman, senator, and governor of New York as well as secretary of state in the Grant administration. Fish's father and namesake had served as congressman and speaker of the New York State Assembly.[59]

Fish, born December 7, 1888, in Garrison, New York, had attended Saint Mark's School in Southborough, Massachusetts. He had played football—all-American tackle and team captain—at Harvard, where he distinguished himself by graduating cum laude in three years. A follower of Teddy Roosevelt, he had served from 1913 to 1916 as a Progressive Party member of the New York State Assembly. In 1915–1916, Fish had attended the training camp at Plattsburg established by the former president and Gen. Leonard Wood, the driving forces behind the Preparedness Movement. To his credit, Fish bristled at the elitism of such camps and argued that they should not be "confined to the sons of people of means." With virtually no military experience, he joined the 15th after a hostile examining officer ostensibly failed him for a lack of cooking knowledge.[60]

Arthur West Little, president of Pearson Publishing Company (a subsidiary of J. J. Little) and publisher of *Pearson's Magazine,* although not an Ivy League man, had a proud heritage and considerable privilege. He was born in New York City on December 15, 1873, the son of Joseph J. Little, a member of the 52nd Congress and longtime president of the New York City Board of Education, and Josephine Robinson Little. Arthur Little attended private schools in New York City and a business college. He began his National Guard service at age eighteen as a private in the 7th Regiment. He later served as an officer in the 71st and 171st Regiments before his tenure on the General Staff as inspector general with the rank of major from 1910 until his resignation in 1912. Little actively participated in New York and national politics and cultivated invaluable high-level contacts in the process, including Col. Edward House, an influential presidential adviser and statesman. As friends, the two men corresponded frequently on a variety of matters.

Their early correspondence focused on New York state and city politics, but as war approached, the subject shifted to questions of preparedness and presidential strategy.[61]

In October 1916, Little, as long-term member of the Guard, had expressed serious reservations about its use on border duty and recommended to House that the War Department deploy special volunteers as it had done in the Philippines in 1899 and 1900. Little had also worked closely with House in repairing damage between the Wilson administration and German Americans, who believed that the president was unjustly anti-German. By February 1917, Little had begun his quest to serve as an officer in the volunteer army should one materialize. When the Congress and the administration agreed to a strengthening of the National Guard in lieu of forming a volunteer army, Little had tried to raise his own regiment with House's help. Frustrated by the difficulty he had in obtaining "permission to die for one's country," he finally got his chance when General O'Ryan, possibly as part of his scheme to ensure a predominantly white officer corps for the Regiment, assigned him in April to the 15th while he was still on the reserve list.[62]

Little now used his friendship with House to benefit the Regiment. During the Peekskill experience, Colonel Hayward worried that with only two weeks of training, the Regiment would regress without proper facilities, such as an armory. Little arranged for Hayward to communicate his concerns to Colonel House in late May. House immediately informed Acting Secretary of State Frank L. Polk that the Regiment could not afford to wait until July for the president's call. An extension of the troops' training at Peekskill or assignment to the proposed camp at Syracuse would prevent the unit from falling apart and having to start all over. On May 27, only three days after House had contacted Polk, Secretary of War Baker regretfully informed House that an "embarrassing" lack of supplies obliged him "to decline to call out any regiment until it was actually needed for training in the Federal service." Furthermore, he could not privilege the 15th over regiments in other states that sought federal duty as a means to address unemployment. The 15th would have to simply "await its call in order." Around the first of June 1917, House showed Little the letter from Secretary Baker and an enclosure from Gen. William Mann with the disappointing news. Even House's power had limits, and he might have overplayed his hand by going around Baker to his "dear friend" Polk. In any event, Little let House know that his "prompt effort in behalf of the 15th N.Y. Infantry was greatly appreciated."[63]

Little shared the documents with Colonel Hayward. Both understood the urgency of continued training and recruitment. Little stepped up his enlistment efforts and prepared for the officer's examination. With no assurances that he would become a permanent member of the Regiment and that the 15th would be called into federal service, he hedged his bet on a volunteer regiment and asked for and received from Colonel House an introduction to the secretary of war.[64]

Reading the Baker response as both a setback and an opportunity, Hayward and his officers had to do everything in their power to keep the Regiment largely intact. They accelerated the training program and urged forbearance on the part of the men—above all else, they had to be ready when "the call" came. In preparation for that call, Lt. Col. Lorillard Spencer impressed upon his men the seriousness of the process and the high expectations he had of them. His instructions to the troops, as he prepared them for the transition from National Guard to US soldiers, offer a revealing glimpse into the strict hierarchy of military organizations and the highly formalized social relations among soldiers.[65]

Spencer informed new recruits and enlisted men that "the army is built on a system of responsibility," discipline, and order. The chain of command ensured the proper functioning of the military organization. Privates, the lowest-ranking members in the military personnel structure, could do virtually nothing without consulting a corporal. If the corporal could not address the issue, he referred the matter to a first sergeant, who either submitted it to a company commander or gave permission to the soldier to approach that officer directly. Under no circumstances, except in the line of duty, was an enlisted man to address an officer without the permission of the first sergeant, who had to use discretion and judgment in giving such permission. No enlisted man had the authority to address a field-grade or staff officer. Only the company commander could approach officers of field-grade or staff rank. These rules and orders had to be obeyed cheerfully, and excuses were not tolerated.[66]

Spencer stressed that the Regiment was only as strong as its weakest link. Failure on the part of one affected the whole. Punctuality was a hallmark of soldierly behavior. Lateness was hardly better than absence and might be counted as such, and absence could be very costly. Under army regulations, the federal government paid one-fourth of regular army pay to enlisted men of the National Guard when they were not on an active duty, provided that more than 60 percent of the members of a company participated in forty-eight drill periods during the year. No one could deny

Spencer's argument that the "shirker from drills steals money out of the pocket of those who do their full duty."[67]

Things went well for the Regiment. Praise flowed from every direction, and the unit took advantage of its popularity by hosting public events, including a big fund-raiser for the band on June 22 at the Manhattan Casino. Soon thereafter, noncommissioned officers sponsored a reception for the purpose of introducing enlisted men to some prominent military officers of the Allied forces as well as veterans of the four black regular army regiments. The noncoms expected that the event would entice enlisted men to aspire to join their ranks.[68]

Yet, a prophetic cartoon appeared on the front page of the *Age* that day. It featured a black soldier pointing Uncle Sam to a placard that read: "All we ask is a square deal." The illustration would presage one of the most devastating blows to the hopes of black soldiers and to the African American community at large. No doubt, the unfolding drama reverberated through the ranks of the 15th, which some had thought would be an ideal command for Lt. Col. Charles Young, the nation's highest-ranking black officer. At that very moment, certain individuals within the army had been pressing for the creation of a small, basically equipped, single black division. Young seemed the likely candidate to head it, but powerful forces within Congress and the military opposed such a development. Nonetheless, Young's selection board recommended him for promotion.[69]

As was standard procedure, the army ordered Young to undergo medical tests, which were administered at Letterman General Hospital in San Francisco on May 23, 1917. Doctors diagnosed "nephritis, high blood pressure, sclerotic arteries," and enlargement of the left ventricle. Young acknowledged suffering from high blood pressure but attributed it to his service in Africa and Haiti. No evidence indicated that any permanent medical condition had impaired his performance. By all appearances, he was a robust and fit forty-nine-year-old man. Secretary of War Baker, the most liberal member of Wilson's cabinet and very protective of Young for his value as a symbol of minority excellence, ordered the General Staff to hold Young's case "in suspense."[70]

Baker's boss, President Wilson, had other ideas and soon got the pretext he needed to accelerate the process of Young's removal. Lt. Albert Dockery, a white Mississippian, vehemently expressed his refusal to serve under a black officer to Mississippi senator John Sharp Williams. Williams appealed on Dockery's behalf to the president. In a June 29 communication, Wilson, almost a month before the final medical report reached Baker's desk, had assured Williams that Young "will not in fact have command because he is in ill health and likely when he gets better himself to be transferred to some other service."[71]

Wilson won the battle, and on July 30, the president ordered Young promoted to full colonel and retired him from the active list, assigning him to the General Staff of the Ohio National Guard. Young vigorously protested the order and rode his horse from Ohio to Washington, DC, to prove his fitness. The act of uncharacteristic defiance proved futile because the army held firm, and some joked that all he proved was that his horse was hardy. A forlorn Young considered himself "jobless" in light of the fact that the militia of the state had been mustered into the federal service. Moreover, the War Department rejected a recommendation from the Militia Bureau that Young command a regiment of "colored drafted troops in Ohio" for service in France because "it was against policy to have a retired officer command" in war. Instead, the War Department ordered Young to assist and advise the governor and adjutant general of Ohio "in matters connected with colored troops from that state." Young, still the good soldier, respectfully commented on his fate: "It seems regrettable for both the country and our people, for I have done good work for both, but as the President willed it and ordered it, I submit cheerfully, like a soldier."[72]

Needless to say, African Americans viewed Young's "retirement" as a "racial calamity." The black public rejected the basis for his forced retirement. To these people, Young was a victim of racial bias and the pawn in a conspiracy against black achievement. The timing and method of the decision to retire Young revealed duplicity. The simple fact of his removal from active service and placement on active duty to "advise" and "assist" on matters relating to troops who would not see combat made no practical sense. A close friend of Young's called it, ironically, "a dirty black trick," designed not only to keep Young out of command but also in his existing rank, as military regulations required that an "officer retired from active duty with the regular army and put on duty during the war will not receive a higher grade or promotion than he had when appointed."[73] Interestingly, historian David Levering Lewis uncovered information revealing that Young had been a marked man, considered by two examining officers "a very intelligent colored officer, hampered with characteristic racial trait of losing his head in sudden emergencies."[74]

The resentment caused by Young's removal lingered throughout the war. As late as May 1918, *The Crisis* spoke for some "twelve million Negroes" who "demand[ed] that Colonel Young be restored to 'active service.'" Meanwhile, Young remained a virtual prisoner in Ohio. Requests for his services as a speaker met with the following response from Washington:

"The policy of the War Department is not to divert officers from their military duties for the purpose of making addresses, and it is not considered desirable to make an exception in the case of Colonel Young." A nation expecting and demanding loyalty from blacks could not have acted with more insensitivity and hostility.[75]

Even after the war, supporters of Young, both black and white, made numerous attempts to secure his reinstatement to active service. Some concluded that the logical place for him was in command of the 15th Infantry New York National Guard. Congressman Jerome F. Donovan made a request to that effect on April 24, 1919. Gen. Peyton March, army chief of staff, replied that the War Department had no objection to the appointment as long as Governor Smith desired to make it and Young to accept it. Yet, in late October, Young still remained inactive. Once again, his dear friend W. E. B. Du Bois requested that Young be put in command of the 15th. The response Du Bois received from the War Department amounted to a declaration of Young's death sentence: "Colonel Young . . . has just been called back into active service and ordered to Liberia for certain duty under the Department of State and his services cannot be spared at the present time." Young died a little more than two years later, on January 8, 1922, in Lagos, Nigeria. Reflecting the anger and dismay of African Americans and their friends across the nation, *The Crisis* bitterly and rhetorically asked:

> If Charles Young's blood pressure was too high for him to go France, why was it not too high for him to be sent to the even more arduous duty in the swamps of West Africa? . . . And the real reason he did not go to France was neither his age, his blood pressure, nor his ability— it was simply that the General Staff did not want a black General in the United States Army. They knew that there was not a single white officer at the front who was Young's superior as a military man, and very few his peers. They knew what Young could have made of the 92nd Division.[76]

And if the treatment of Colonel Young did not suffice to shake the confidence of black Americans in their government, events in East St. Louis, Illinois, from July 1 to July 5 gave them even more pause about their personal and collective safety. The sudden and marked increase in the black population of East St. Louis, some 2,400 since 1916, had added political and economic tensions to a volatile racial climate. On May 29 and 30, whites shot at black residents, but the National Guard prevented a crisis. A month later, blacks fired on what they believed to be white marauders and provoked violent retaliation. By the morning of July 2, whites went on a deadly rampage through the city, burning black homes and shooting blacks indiscriminately. Some 6,000 people lost their homes. By July 5, thirty-nine black and eight white people had died in the "riot." Property damage totaled almost $400,000. Indeed, as William English Walling had predicted in 1908 after the Springfield riot, the race war had been transported to the North. Questioning the value of loyalty in the face of such an assault, blacks asked mockingly, "Mr. President, why not make America safe for Democracy?" [77]

According to David Levering Lewis, "Black Americans began, as never before, to fear that they were an endangered species." Direct appeals to the White House produced no appreciable response. Wilson even turned away a delegation of prominent blacks from Baltimore. William H. Brooks, pastor of St. Mark's Episcopal Church and chaplain of the 15th Regiment, led his congregation in the drafting of a resolution calling upon President Wilson "to put forth every effort to bring the murderers to justice." One of the strongest condemnations came from former president Theodore Roosevelt, who missed no opportunity to chastise his bitter rival, Woodrow Wilson. Roosevelt scored the appalling brutality of the event, which stained "the name of America," and demanded that government officials "use with ruthless sternness every instrumentality at their command to punish murder, whether committed by whites against blacks or blacks against whites." [78]

In Roosevelt, blacks found a powerful voice for their cause. They seemingly had forgiven him for his transgressions of the past, for they embraced as friends all those who defended them. Chaplain Brooks's congregation expressed its gratitude in a resolution that praised the "world's greatest living statesmen" as "a pillar steadfast in the storm, whenever and wherever the lives or the rights of the humblest in the land are assailed." Although no such public expression came from the Regiment itself, the Women's Auxiliary of the 15th Regiment spoke for it in tones full of "indignation" against wrongdoing "heaped upon a race always prayerful, long suffering, truly American, ever patriotic, and loyal to the interests of our country." Determined to see justice done to the perpetrators, the women appealed to the nation's conscience and connected America's welfare to the protection of all its citizens: "We know this Nation can never become a power until every citizen, regardless of race, color, or creed, enjoys the life, liberty, and pursuit of happiness that is his God given right." [79]

The statement masterfully framed the issue in terms of the nation's ideals and promises, its demands for "universal human rights." Though never explicitly making a demand for gender equality, the statement expressly represented the sentiment of "375 thoughtful colored women banded together to serve the Nation in its crisis." Even more, the women took advantage of their attachment to a proven instrument of citizenship and made their case for the granting of "universal human rights" that the "Nation is demanding." Largely avoiding specific references to blacks or women, the statement brilliantly employed prevailing official discourse about the purpose of the war and implicitly argued for black women's proper place in the world that the great conflict would transform.[80]

While the men of the 15th trained at Camp Whitman for war abroad, the women of the 15th Auxiliary continued their crusading role by marching for peace at home in the Silent Protest Parade of July 28, 1917. Wilson's refusal to meet blacks or issue a sympathetic response led Oswald Garrison Villard to suggest a march in New York City to get the president's attention. James Weldon Johnson and W. E. B. Du Bois organized the event with the help of some of New York's leading black citizens, including John Nail; Fred Moore; Madam C. J. Walker; and M. C. Lawton, first vice president of the Women's Auxiliary of the 15th NYNG. Some 8,000 to 10,000 neatly attired and disciplined black children, women, and men marched down Fifth Avenue. The sign in front of the women's division clearly linked military service to citizenship and equal protection, reading: "The first blood for American independence was shed by a Negro Crispus Attucks." New York City had never witnessed such an event, as muffled drum rolls and countless banners proclaimed louder than human voices ever could that America's "hands were full of blood" and that the nation should be made "safe for democracy."[81]

Without fanfare, social distinction, or the usual visual and aural effects, the parade created and depended upon a shared "spiritual atmosphere" between participants and observers. The march placed an entire community in a public space in ways that had been denied its members. According to historian Alexandra Lorini, the parade expressed itself in the language of utopia and countered the "dehumanizing, grotesque caricatures of *The Birth of a Nation*" and so many other popular representations of blacks, from stage to the press to serious literature. On that day, New York's black citizens played "the symbolic role of moral witness to the nation's Bastille of prejudice."[82]

Despite the parade's obvious power, organizers feared that the march alone would not yield the desired results. Thus, the leaders petitioned President Wilson to do what the states could not or would not do—"put down lynching and mob violence." They appealed to Wilson's sense of justice and also to his sense of morality by linking the ideals of the war with the reality at home, as "no nation that seeks to fight the battles of civilization can afford to march in blood-smeared garments." M. C. Lawton's signature, as well as Madam C. J. Walker's, appears on the document.[83]

What blacks did not realize at the time was that the East St. Louis "riot" and the reaction to it contributed to a strong governmental response of a kind they neither wanted nor expected. The fear of growing black hostility to the government and the war effort, combined with rumors of German money flowing freely through Harlem and the anticipated outbreak of racial violence in Houston, convinced the director of the Military Intelligence Branch, Col. Ralph Van Deman, that combating so-called Negro subversion should be an essential component of military counterintelligence. By early September 1917, no longer content to allow the Bureau of Investigation to "handle the question of African-American loyalty," Van Deman saw the need to recruit experts for this important matter. The practical effect would be that black agents and informants would spy on, report, and influence the expressions and actions of other blacks. As a result, trust became the most precious of commodities, for no one knew who might be working for the government, including women such as Hallie E. Queen.[84]

At the very moment of the East St. Louis conflagration, however, New York City nearly had one of its own, involving some members of the 15th. On Tuesday, July 3, about twenty-five uniformed men of the regiment stood at Sixty-First Street and Amsterdam Avenue when a Patrolman named Henson ordered them to move. Most obeyed the order to avoid trouble, but Pvt. Lawrence Joaquin, of 51 West Ninety-Ninth Street, protested. Henson arrested him, and a fight broke out between whites and blacks. Officials charged Joaquin with disorderly conduct, and the court sentenced him and a civilian, Vernon Cox of 225 West Forty-Sixth Street, to ten days of imprisonment on Blackwell's Island. Another civilian participant, Isaac Brown, faced more serious charges of attacking a police officer with a knife and was held on $1,000 bail.[85]

Keenly aware of the long-standing tensions between blacks and New York City police and protective of the reputations of the men of the 15th, Fred Moore of the *Age* and Pastor George H. Sims of Union Baptist Church promised an investigation of the incident. To their relief, Colonel Hayward had "taken up the matter" already and apparently resolved it to the satisfaction of all concerned. No such incidents occurred again in the city, and Joaquin remained a member of the Regiment, although no stranger to trouble, until his honorable discharge in 1919. More important, the 15th maintained its reputation as "a picked regiment, composed of the very best, self-respecting law-abiding Negroes in New York."[86]

Despite the difficulties, the 15th remained intact and, in fact, made simply astounding progress. The usual suspects were trumpeting its development as an efficient military organization, and so did an unlikely source—the state's assistant adjutant general, Lt. Col. Edward V. Howard. In a letter to General Stotesbury dated July 10, Howard reported on the performance of the noncommissioned officers and admitted that he was "astonished at the intelligence displayed by these men and the rapidity with which they grasped details of the work." He opined that "most of the men would have no difficulty in holding their own in any company." He also found the rolls and financial ledgers to be "models of accuracy and neatness," which reflected "credit upon the organization." As a result of the firm hand and industriousness of its leadership, which permeated the ranks, the Regiment, Howard predicted, would reach "a high state of efficiency within a very short time." Needless to say, the first sergeants and regimental clerks delighted in the praise of their performance. Once again, they proved the value of the noncoms to the well-being of the unit. That the letter of praise and the accelerated deployment to Camp Whitman came at the same time was more than coincidental.[87]

On July 16, William Hayward's "Fighting 15th" became the first regiment of the New York National Guard to respond to President Wilson's call into United States service. At 7:00 A.M. that Monday, the band proceeded to the station, playing the stirring and melodic strains of "Billy Boy," a popular tune dedicated to Colonel Hayward. The members of the 15th fell in line and marched to West 128th Street, where they entrained for Camp Whitman. An estimated 4,000 "mothers, wives, sweethearts, sisters, and fathers" gave "kisses," shed "tears," and made "promises." Despite the uncertain future that awaited them, the men enthused over the prospect of seeing active service.[88]

Capt. Vertner Tandy, the first black officer commissioned in the state, did not accompany the Regiment to Camp Whitman. Hayward placed him in charge of organizing a "home depot" to serve as a state guard in the absence of the newly federalized 15th. That home depot would form the basis for the 15th NYG, soon to be known as "the New 15th." The already thin black officer corps consequently suffered another great loss. Not long before, during the exercises at Peekskill, Capt. Vergil Parks, who had served with the 10th Cavalry during the Spanish-American War, left the Regiment over a dispute about absence without permission. He had been with the 15th since August 17, 1916. Now, only three black captains remained with the Regiment, and Brooks, the fifty-eight-year-old chaplain, would fail the physical examination and receive his honorable discharge on July 23, 1917. Like so many others discharged from the unit, Brooks soon found a place with the home guard. The reduced standards, the total acceptance of married men, the domestic service, and the overlapping associations would make the New 15th a poor cousin of the original unit and would create endless confusion and debate, if not resentment, among the men of the Old 15th.[89]

The disorganization that Little had described upon arrival at Peekskill did not recur at Whitman. In the week preceding the opening of the camp, the command had secured cooks, waiters, janitors, and other necessary employees and readied the barracks and requisitioned supplies. Advance notice, adequate preparation time, and past experience ensured that Camp Whitman ran like a "well-oiled machine."[90]

Nonetheless, problems of another sort surfaced and remained with the unit throughout its federal service. Lt. John Wesley Castles, Jr., a wealthy New Jerseyan with no prior military service, resented and disagreed with the leadership of Colonel Hayward and became part of a clique that groused, sniped, and threatened the commander's authority and even his job. Castles's "War Diary" provides rare insight into the behind-the-scenes personality disputes and power struggles of a unique military organization. Events at Camp Whitman disillusioned the ambitious and opinionated Castles, who recorded that company officers' attempts "to instill discipline among the men" elicited tirades from Hayward about "my boys"—the men of the Regiment—and threats to break officers "he had made." Castles concluded that the Regiment was "purely a political game."[91] The young lieutenant fervently believed that Hayward owed his position to his close relationship with Governor Whitman and not to military experience or expertise.

Despite Castles's gloomy assessment, the open-air life and regular habits reportedly worked wonders on the men of the 15th. Robert Russa Moton visited the camp and brought five singers from Tuskegee to entertain the men. Visitors from nearby towns supplied tobacco and cigarettes. According to the *Age,* most men shunned a local burlesque show in favor of religious meetings at the YMCA tent. The band, although missing its hospitalized leader, Jim Europe, continued to grow and improve and never failed to entertain the men, as did Noble Sissle's singing. The men particularly enjoyed "stunt nights" in which "brave" soldiers displayed their musical, comedic, and dancing talents.[92]

For those unaccustomed to camp life, the YMCA seemed indispensable, as the prayer of one man suggested: "O God, bless the YMCA and those who made it possible for them to be here, because Thou, O God, knoweth that this would be an awful place for us if it were not for the YMCA." Sometimes, the camp proved too much of a good thing and Hayward had to assert his authority. Stores set up operations to exploit the men by offering items that "appealed to their fancy rather than their judgment." When soldiers started falling out from overeating and excessive sugar intake, Hayward closed these stores and opened a post exchange, which stocked more healthful products.[93]

Despite such lapses, the *Age's* special correspondent, Thomas E. Taylor, was impressed by the men's esprit de corps and the pride in uniform. During dress parade in front of 10,000 spectators, each company vied against the others "for the best company line." Taylor found a great respect among the men for their officers and the officers for the men. Almost every man appreciated the "courtly manner" and "fatherly advice" of Chaplain Brooks, whose services they were about to lose. Yet, Taylor gave his highest compliments to the regular army veteran noncommissioned officer cadre, the Regiment's cornerstone. These men had to be "at all times living examples of the highest standards of soldierly deportment, discipline, and honor." Spread evenly throughout the Regiment, the regular noncoms worked "zealously in session and out of session in imparting the thousand details of a soldier's life and duties that can only be learned by experience." Although the camp occasionally had serious trouble in the ranks, Thomas reported that the process eliminated many "misfits."[94]

The stricter standards of the US Army physical examination significantly contributed to the elimination process. Author Theodore Roosevelt, Jr., claimed nearly half of the men failed the examination and received their discharge papers. Fortunately, the Regiment had reserves from which it could draw. The lax standards associated with the initial entrance exam no longer applied, as the army held the doctors who made mistakes responsible for the money spent on recruits whose subsequent physical and mental deficits suggested they should never have passed the physical examination. The army considered the appearance of the men, their fitness, and the absence of disease serious matters. A limp could throw a soldier out of step. The weight of equipment required a considerable amount of strength. Men could not be objectionable to their tent mates, and thus, skin diseases, even if harmless, disqualified applicants. Doctors paid close attention to eyes, ears, and even teeth, as dental problems often led to more serious medical complications, to say nothing of the fact that chewing the hard tack and other tough war rations required healthy dentition. Weight, height, mobility, and the relation among them also determined suitability. Last, the doctor assessed mental health and capacity. A soldier had to demonstrate a reasonable command of English in order to understand and carry out orders. In the end, the physician had to determine if the soldier could meet this key standard: "Has he sufficient physical endurance to carry out the daily routine of a soldier, and has he, or can he develop sufficient reserve force to stand up under the strain of unusual physical exertion?"[95]

Despite the disciplinary problems and the loss of many good men to disability, Captain Little recalled the time at Whitman fondly. The men swam and bathed in a beautiful stream that they had dammed to make a swimming pool. Companies ambushed one another as they marched through the woods to swim. Drill sergeants trained new recruits as rapidly as possible to catch them up with their platoons, although one sergeant complained to Little that a certain new recruit was "so dumb that to be any dumber he'd have to be bigger." The sergeants, disregarding regulations prohibiting certain disciplinary actions, also meted out corporal punishment to wayward members of their platoons.[96]

The men did have to learn to contend with lice, the bane of the infantryman's existence, particularly in the trenches, in World War I. Initially, for men who took great pride in their cleanliness to be called "lousy" sufficed to cause a fight; in one case, it even led one youth to draw his knife on a sergeant who had referred to him as "you lousy kid." As the soldiers had only one uniform each and lacked the facilities to boil their clothes, they had to wash their uniforms, bedding, and themselves in a combination of gasoline and hot, soapy water. While they waited for everything to dry, they played baseball or boxed, in the nude.[97]

Just as in the Peekskill experience, life at Camp Whitman gave Little the opportunity to ridicule his black subordinates. As regimental adjutant, he had to protect large sums of cash when any army quartermaster left it with him overnight. Little selected three sergeants to guard him and the money, armed them with pistols, and went to sleep. His choices—Sgts. Edward Giles, Abraham Gilliard, and Bayard—had records "out of the ordinary." Instead of relieving one another in shifts, the three sergeants remained awake the entire night. The next morning, when Little inquired if they had experienced any problems, Giles lamented: "Nobody trahed enythin'. We shore ded hav' bad luck!"[98]

On July 25, in the middle of this month-long experience, the 15th Regiment, New York National Guard, was mustered into the federal service. The men read the order as the government's acceptance of them as a fighting-trim outfit. They could not wait to do their part; when and with whom, however, remained in doubt. Unbeknownst to them, the 15th did not belong to the 6th Division (soon to become the 27th Division) of the New York National Guard. Instead, at the time of mustering, the 15th became "a component of Provisional Brigade (4th) of New York Infantry, additional organizations not included in the 6th Division." It would not be the last time that the men of the 15th would find themselves a part of a provisional organization. They were "mavericks" with no apparent place among "the fighting forces of the country."[99]

On its departure from Camp Whitman, the Regiment received orders for guard duty from the army. Some interpreted the assignment as a sign that the War Department was reluctant to accept the Regiment as a combat unit. Others believed that it simply reflected army disorganization and indecision. Only A. Phillip Randolph and Chandler Owens's radical publication the *Messenger* publicly supported the deployment. The editors argued that "only the Negro leaders will object to their absence from the bloody fields of France." Declaring the "terminals . . . safer than the trenches," the *Messenger* suggested "Du Bois, Kelley, Miller, Pickens, Grimke, etc. volunteer to go to France, if they are so eager to fight to make the world safe for democracy." In this respect, black leaders resembled white leaders who "want[ed] war" if "'George'" would fight it. Randolph and Owens preferred to "make Georgia safe for the Negro" first.[100]

Seemingly oblivious to the debates surrounding them, the men approached their new duties with characteristic zeal. The 3rd Battalion, under the command of Maj. Edwin W. Dayton, undertook construction and guard duty at the National Army Camp at Camp Dix, New Jersey. The band joined the 3rd Battalion at Camp Dix, where a recovered Jim Europe returned to the Regiment. At the request of the general commanding the camp, every evening the band, accompanied by Hamilton Fish's Company K quartet, played concerts for the entire cantonment. The army assigned the 2nd Battalion, under Maj. Monson Morris, to help build and guard Camp Upton on Long Island. Finally, the 1st Battalion, commanded by the recently demoted major Lorillard Spencer, divided into some forty to fifty units as small as squads of twelve men to guard public works, factories, navy yards and ammunition stores, railroad lines, tunnels, and bridges throughout the Northeast, in the Erie Basin, in Brooklyn, in Red Bank (New Jersey), in Easton (Pennsylvania), in Poughkeepsie, and in Albany.[101]

Interestingly, the men were now doing the kind of duty about which the *New York Times* had expressed grave reservations. Although not deployed to quell civil disturbances, the men of the 15th now found themselves in situations where they not only guarded against domestic and external threats but also performed police duties. Their blackness, however, made them more acceptable for these roles than were so-called hyphenated Americans, whose "broken English" could raise suspicions of disloyalty. For that very reason, President Wilson had called out the 1st Separate Battalion District of Columbia National Guard to protect the nation's capital on March 25, 1917. According to Emmett Scott, the blacks of Washington, DC, and the nation regarded such an assignment as the equivalent of those awarded "guard regiments in England where men of undoubted loyalty and integrity are given the sacred obligation of protecting . . . the places that stand nearest to the welfare and dignity of the British crown."[102] Once again, limited and symbolic black gains came with xenophobic costs. The *Baltimore Afro-American* understood the high price and made the case for more benefits in exchange for such service and sacrifice:

> For loyalty of this kind our country ought to be willing to pay something. It ought to be willing to pay the price of having its loyal colored men educated for commissioned officers in the very best schools in the nation; it ought to be willing to pay the price of having these citizens enjoy every right and privilege that German-Americans or any others enjoy; it ought even to be willing to have trustworthy colored officers command regiments of white men, which may not be regarded as quite so trustworthy.

The *Afro-American* urged its readers to pressure a government that would only respond "if the Negro will regard his loyalty as an asset, to be sold at the price of Citizenship."[103]

Some of the men of the 15th undoubtedly understood the larger implications and significance of their guard duties, but most had to concern themselves with properly executing these serious responsibilities. Too often, fellow citizens and even soldiers failed to share the minimal confidence in the men that the government had displayed. Consequently, the men of the 15th doing guard duty fought a daily battle for respect and would have to let their example speak to larger issues.

On August 23, 1917, Pvt. Eugene J. Besner of Company B, 10th Infantry New York Guard (home depot unit), Albany, faced court-martial for allegedly attacking two members of the 15th Infantry New York National Guard in violation of Articles of War nos. 61, 93, and 96. The court accused Besner of committing "felonious assault" on and intending to do "bodily harm" to Pvt. Samuel Jones, who had been performing his duties as a sentry on a bridge in Cohoes, New York. It also charged that he had done the same to Cpl. Lawrence Joaquin, who had "escorted" Besner to the local jail. Joaquin, all too familiar with racial conflict, this time found himself on the opposite side of the law but on the same side of color bias. Besner allegedly hurled "loud, vulgar, insulting, and abusive language" as well as fists at the men and also earned charges of disorderly conduct and threatening the peace.[104]

Besner faced a total of five criminal charges. The military court found him guilty of three: assault on Corporal Joaquin, disorderly conduct and breach of peace in his conduct toward Jones, and the same with relation to Joaquin. The court ruled Besner not guilty on the more serious charges of "felonious assault" and "intent to do bodily harm" and dropped charges of verbal abuse. The conviction on the three counts still seemed to have constituted a serious breach of military law. Nonetheless, the court fined Besner $20 and ordered a reprimand. The incredibly light penalty would not deter further incidents and must have added insult to the injuries of Jones and Joaquin.[105]

Not long after the incident in Cohoes, a more troubling and potentially bloody situation emerged at Camp Upton in Yaphank, Long Island. The 2nd Battalion, stationed at the camp for nearly a month, had avoided significant problems. Then in mid-September, the proprietor of a Sayville hotel ejected two black members of the 15th from his establishment. The men claimed that the proprietor refused them food service, and the owner claimed that the soldiers had become unruly when he told them he did not serve liquor to men in uniform.[106]

Tensions between the soldiers and locals thus far had been held in check, but the experience at the hotel revealed underlying resentments that could have erupted into conflict at any moment. The men of the 15th had arrested nearly 300 camp employees for various and sundry offenses. They were responsible for weeding out "the undesirable element among thousands of workmen engaged in erecting barracks," whom the *Age* characterized as "drug peddlers, yegg men (safecrackers), stick-up men, and plain thieves." The workers resented showing identification to the black soldiers and, even more, being searched for weapons and alcohol.[107]

On the morning of September 13, a fight between a mess attendant and a soldier occurred. A special police officer clubbed a corporal to the ground, and some noncoms came to the corporal's defense. More special policemen joined the row, and a guard fired his revolver into the air, causing an officer of the 15th to respond with armed troops. The shots aroused workmen and other members of the 15th, who readied themselves for a fight against the civilians. More "officers appeared" on the scene and ordered the soldiers back to their barracks. The incident ended with "one or two broken heads and four prisoners" surrounded by "barbed wire and four canines."[108]

Both men and officers knew that continued skirmishes at home threatened to upset their chances of seeing combat overseas. On September 25,

1917, Captain Little informed his friend Colonel House that the Regiment would soon end its guard duty after two months at Dix and Upton. He did not know what duty awaited them but he noted that "almost every man in the regiment, from Colonel Hayward down to the newest recruit hoped that that duty may be in France." Seeking glory for himself and the Regiment, Little told the colonel that "France is the place where military distinction has got to be won and I want to win some." Given the fact that the 15th's fine service had earned it many official friends, Little asked House to deliver a "personal word of friendliness to our hopes" in the direction of the decision makers. Little's confidence that a "word" from House would be the "deciding factor" was well placed.[109] Within a matter of days, the War Department would make a decision that forever changed the lives of these men and the history of the African American soldier.

# 6

## Race War at Home or Combat Abroad?

### Tested in the White-Hot Crucible of Camp Life

Notwithstanding their rapid progress, the men of the 15th needed far more training to prepare them for war in Europe. Besides, the War Department had not decided important questions of deployment and affiliation. Organization of the Provisional Division (Colored, 93rd) to which the Regiment eventually belonged would not begin until December 1917.[1] For the time being, the men would confront not the conflagration overseas in Europe but white-hot southern racism in Spartanburg, South Carolina.

Back in July, the War Department had announced that a large contingent of the New York National Guard would be stationed at Camp Wadsworth near Spartanburg. Anticipating the economic benefits to the community a military camp afforded, the leaders and residents of Spartanburg did all they could to convince New York and federal officials of their good intentions. In fact, the mild reaction to the naming of the camp after the New York native Gen. James Wadsworth, a Union commander at the battle of Gettysburg, reflected the readiness of the community to "embrace" the symbol of its defeat and subsequent "oppression" for the sake of economic gain.[2]

The enthusiastic attitude came in no small measure from assurances to US representative and Military Affairs Committee member Samuel J. Nicholls that no black soldiers would be sent there. Nicholls, who had championed the camp cause, had much to lose politically and economically from an unstable business and racial environment.[3] Soon, reports indicating a change in policy on the stationing of black troops shook his confidence and revealed how fresh the Civil War and Reconstruction remained in the southern white psyche, especially in South Carolina where the sheer size of the black population threatened many whites. Now, however, reports of racial subversion by German agents heightened these fears and prejudices and produced an upsurge of white chauvinism and a determination to defend the status quo. Consequently, public officials and journalists alike warned that sending northern black and Puerto Rican soldiers—dangerous aliens to southern culture, mores, and traditions—would be "exactly like flaunting a red rag at a bull."[4]

On August 21, 1917, a deeply concerned Nicholls wrote Gen. William A. Mann, chief of the Militia Bureau, for clarification. He simultaneously cautioned Secretary of War Newton Baker against taking such a reckless step, which might "cause friction between the races" and "would in great measure kill the war spirit" there. Nicholls did not tell the secretary that such measures might upset his grand scheme for banks, hotels, theaters, and railway stations on his property adjoining the camp.[5] Race and economics were entangled as usual.

General Mann straightforwardly informed Nicholls by telegram that one "colored" company of the Tennessee National Guard had been ordered to neighboring Greenville, South Carolina, with other troops of the 30th National Guard Division. Effective and efficient training took precedence over such racial concerns as the War Department discounted southern objections and decided to assign one "Negro regiment at every National Army cantonment." The recent riots in the North had convinced the army that concentrating black troops there offered potentially more dangers than doing the same in the South. It decided that black soldiers, whenever possible, would be stationed in the states from which they came as long as their numbers did not exceed one-third of the total number of soldiers in a camp.[6] Despite War Department explanations and assurances, the prospect of black and white troops in the same cantonment at roughly the same time as racial conflagrations in East St. Louis (Illinois), Chester (Pennsylvania), and Houston (Texas) raised the anxiety level of Nicholls and his constituents even more. The last incident proved especially troubling, as it involved soldiers of the 24th Infantry Regiment, combat troops who had fought bravely in the Philippines and on the Mexican border. A Spartanburg paper portrayed the 24th as "vicious" Negro soldiers who had killed "officers, citizens, and women."[7]

Ever since their arrival in Houston as guards at Camp Logan, the men of the 24th Regiment's 3rd Battalion had endured racial insults, discriminatory treatment, blatant disrespect, and a removal of their weapons by military authorities in order to reduce the chances of violence. Tensions between the soldiers and the citizens and especially the police force of Houston had reached a breaking point when, on August 23, a black soldier intervened to stop the abuse of a black woman by two white policemen. The police pistol-whipped and arrested the soldier. Later, a black corporal inquiring about the incident received the same treatment at the hands of the police. Back at Camp Logan, rumors spread of a black soldier's lynching and a white mob's imminent attack on the camp. Fearing the fate that blacks across the nation had suffered at the hands of whites, these soldiers armed themselves and marched to town, where they encountered police and a posse. After a violent exchange of gunfire, sixteen whites, including four policemen and one white military officer, lay dead. The soldiers returned to camp, having lost four of their own.[8]

Military officials disarmed the entire battalion and sent them to New Mexico. In October and November, the army court-martialed sixty-five soldiers at Fort Sam Houston for murder and mutiny. It then hanged thirteen soldiers secretly, without review by the War Department or the president. Forty-two soldiers received life sentences. Two further trials condemned sixteen more men to death and another twelve to life sentences. Black organizations such as the NAACP, reflecting the fury of African Americans at the summary executions, petitioned President Wilson for clemency. After reviewing the trial record, Wilson commuted ten of the death sentences to life imprisonment. In 1921, after receiving a further petition, President Warren Harding reduced the prison sentences of the remaining soldiers, most of whom were freed by 1924. The last soldier was released in 1938. The case led Congress to pass a law providing for War Department review of all military death sentences.[9] At the time, however, the tragedy sent a chilling signal to whites who would violate the rights and dignity of black soldiers and an even more cautionary message to black soldiers who would dare defend themselves against white civilians.

On August 30, only days after the tragic event in Houston, a reporter from the *New York Times* announced in Spartanburg that the 15th New York National Guard would join the rest of the New York troops at Camp Wadsworth. Spartanburg's white citizens were about to realize their worst nightmare. Immediately, the city officially protested to the War Department. Spartanburg's mayor, J. F. Floyd, anticipated that "trouble might result if the Fifteenth refused to accept the limited liberties accorded to the city's colored population." "Northern ideas about race equality" would prompt the soldiers to "expect to be treated as white men," and whites in Spartanburg planned to treat them like their "resident negroes." The Spartanburg Chamber of Commerce, which had promoted a camp at Spartanburg for its potential revenue, could tolerate "Southern negroes" with whom they had mutual understanding—that is, the Negroes who knew their place. The chamber warned that they had no intention of changing their customs. No Negro could drink from the same glass that a white man might use. If African American soldiers entered a soda store and requested service, someone would knock them down and throw bottles at them. The city did permit integrated chain gangs, but one of its newspapers even objected to the practice of blacks and whites working "with elbows touching everyday."[10]

Spartanburg officials and the local press had a quick change of heart. Perhaps they realized that further protests would jeopardize the camp experiment and impede the progress of the self-anointed "City of Success." Watson Bell, editor of the more hostile *Journal,* urged his readers and Spartanburg officials "to make the best of a bad situation." He placed the burden of racial peace upon whites, who had to ensure that "hot-headed" members of the race "do not precipitate the trouble." Charles Hearon, editor of the more moderate *Herald,* did not discount the potential for trouble and urged the community to treat these soldiers "rationally and sensibly." Like Bell, Hearon believed that "the burden is still the white man's."[11]

That the apparent change in attitude coincided with the imminent arrival of General O'Ryan was no accident. The press vowed that the city would support his command as a service to the country and praised his troops as the finest body of soldiers in the armed services. Even more, the "Spartans" claimed O'Ryan as a kindred spirit: "From his public utterances Spartanburg people have conceived the idea . . . that they are going to find his ideas and their ideas coinciding in many particulars." Perhaps they understood O'Ryan's attitude toward and treatment of the Regiment, which he had never accepted as an organic part of the New York National Guard. Moreover, O'Ryan argued for the deployment of black soldiers, especially those from the South, as laborers, stevedores, waiters, cooks, orderlies, and personal servants. To show the state's commitment to supporting the newly created 27th Division, Governor Richard I. Manning officially welcomed General O'Ryan and pledged to cooperate "at all times" during the division's stay. O'Ryan compared the tone of the governor's greeting to the fine spirit shown each of his soldiers. Even more, local papers touted the planned visits of Governor Whitman and Mayor Mitchel.[12]

On October 8, 1917, with little fanfare and a few well-wishers, the 2nd and 3rd Battalions of the 15th NYNG departed for Camp Wadsworth to the familiar tune "Billy Boy." The 1st Battalion, reflecting further official ambivalence about use of the Regiment, remained on guard duty in New York City. Despite the conciliatory gestures from Spartanburg, the officers and men of the 15th had grave doubts about the potential dangers awaiting them. At least one officer, Hamilton Fish, had tried to convince military authorities to revise the order. On the morning of October 4, a worried Fish wired his friend, Assistant Secretary of the Navy Franklin Delano Roosevelt, as follows:

> My brother officers believe with me that sending northern volunteer negro troops south would cause recurrence of race troubles. [T]his battalion (3rd) could render immediate valuable service in France on line of communications where there is great present need to relieve French troops. [W]hy not solve difficult southern problem by letting these northern negro soldiers go where they can be of immediate use and train for firing line quicker than in the south[?][13]

Roosevelt quickly passed on Fish's telegram to Gen. Tasker Bliss, army chief of staff, apparently without comment. Bliss expressed regrets about disagreeing with Captain Fish but assumed that Roosevelt understood the situation. He shared with Roosevelt a letter to US senator William Musgrave Caulder of New York; Caulder's concerns echoed and reinforced Fish's. Inaccurately and perhaps disingenuously, Bliss informed Caulder that the 15th was an integral part of the 27th Division. As such, it should be with the division in camp. Moreover, he was convinced that fears of unrest were unfounded because these men, like other soldiers, would "adapt themselves to local conditions." If that were not convincing enough, Bliss argued that service overseas was "the very greatest reward . . . for good conduct and efficiency." To send the 15th to France as a way of avoiding trouble would create resentment and envy among "the other organizations of General O'Ryan's Division."[14]

For better or worse, the 15th would go to Spartanburg. Lieutenant Castles observed, "We were not crazy at all about taking colored troops to South Carolina, but orders are orders."[15] The soldiers were not the only ones worried about potential problems, nor were the southerners the only cause for concern. The *Age* accused the New York press of undermining good feelings between the 15th and the white New York regiments by stirring up "racial frictions" in the interest of "sensations." Good reason for such concern existed, as the *Evening Sun* ran a provocative story under the sensational headline DIXIEITES FORECAST CLASH: "Some folks of marked Dixie ideas have not tried to mask their feelings in matter and are forecasting all sorts of catastrophes. Though admitting the dark skinned fighters are men of mettle, the populace . . . threaten to put the 'bar sinister' on all members of this famed outfit who undertake to touch elbows with the rest of the boys in the pursuit of happiness."[16]

To its credit, the article struck a conciliatory note in reporting that the officers of the 27th Division stood in solidarity with the men of the 15th, refused to "side with the natives," and "pooh pooh[ed] the suggestion that anything but regular Carolina hospitality will be dealt out to the boys of the Fifteenth." Nonetheless, Fred Moore, editor of the *Age,* saw no redeeming value in the piece and asked Emmett J. Scott to appeal to Secretary Baker to censor "news stories calculated to provoke racial strife in the army."[17]

Colonel Hayward and four officers, including Captain Little, arrived in Spartanburg a few days before the Regiment in order to prepare for the arrival of their men. The trains bearing the two battalions and the band of the 15th New York reached Spartanburg during the night and morning of October 10–11. The men detrained, marched to the training area, and found a semicantonment in which mess halls, bathhouses, administration quarters, hospitals, storage houses, and remount stations were constructed of wood. Not long before the arrival of the 15th, men had slept in tents on bare floors, but the War Department responded to wet conditions and the oncoming winter by ordering that sleeping quarters be floored and walled. The men of the 15th quickly brought their site up to the standards of neighboring ones by draining a marsh and erecting new buildings, stables, roads, and bridges.[18]

Camp life was difficult, but Spartanburg would prove even worse. Racist and fundamentalist and called "a Methodist Rome," the city was "bone dry" and largely devoid of "entertainment." Moreover, its "Jim Crow" shops and restaurants were "dingy," "poorly stocked," and generally unsatisfactory. On top of this, military officials found some Spartanburg businesses guilty of price gouging, a practice all too common in military towns.[19]

On October 12, Hayward spoke to the Regiment about the circumstances and encouraged the men not to sink to the level of Mayor Floyd and the whites of Spartanburg, to forbear even if struck, and to promise to refrain from violence. The colonel knew that Spartanburg represented the biggest test yet and emphasized its significance to the men: "You are in a section hostile to colored people. I am depending on you to act like the good soldiers you have always been and break the ice in this country for your entire race." Hayward knew that he could rely on his men to show restraint, but he decided to institute safeguards to reduce the potential for confrontations. These measures included strict adherence, by the men, to southern Jim Crow laws: "I want you to stay away from places where you are not wanted." He specifically ruled the mills off-limits because of the "decidedly hostile" actions and attitudes of the workers there. Perhaps most difficult for the men to accept was Hayward's order that they must keep their tempers if they heard the word *nigger.* Despite the concessions and their attendant humiliation and degradation, the men understood the stakes, pledged their allegiance, and cheered their commander.[20]

Within minutes of the colonel's speech, some soldiers of the 15th faced their first challenge. Anxious to see the town and enjoy themselves, at around 10:00 P.M. on Thursday, October 11, four black soldiers and four white comrades were walking arm in arm along the main thoroughfare to Spartanburg, when a gang of young residents "made insulting remarks." The white soldiers took umbrage at the affront and retaliated against the youths with their fists. In the nick of time for the locals, military police arrived, scattered the crowd, and made no arrests. The black soldiers dutifully followed Colonel Hayward's orders and "kept out of the fracas." Nonetheless, "news of the disorder spread like wild fire, adding fuel to the already hot resentment against the so-called intrusion of the dusky-skinned soldiers." Authorities expected more trouble and placed the military police on a high state of alert.[21]

A white soldier's letter to his parents and brother clearly revealed the intensity and depth of the resentment and hostility: "The 15th N.Y. Infantry which is composed of nigers arrived here the day before yesterday. And those black boys are right there. The Southern People hate a negro worse than a snake."[22] Despite the incident, Little recalled that no soldiers were "better behaved" than the men of the 15th when they went to town on pass. Jim Europe's band played a concert their first Saturday in Spartanburg that Little claimed reduced the grumbling of the crowd to silence. The *Brooklyn Eagle* supported Little's assessment and praised the 2nd and 3rd Battalions for their impressive maneuvers, resulting from "careful training" received before their arrival at Camp Wadsworth.[23]

After the concert, a committee of businessmen met with Hayward to tell him they deplored their own mayor's rash and provocative statements but regretted the War Department's decision nonetheless. As a gesture of solidarity, they invited the regimental officers to become honorary members of the country club and the band to play at the club's upcoming dance. Obviously, the entrepreneurs did not know that the commissioned officer ranks of the 15th included five African Americans, whom they most certainly would not have welcomed at the country club.[24]

In fact, not long after the Regiment arrived, white residents of Spartanburg had insulted Captain Marshall, a Harvard graduate and lawyer, and ordered him off a streetcar after he had paid his fare. Marshall, having promised with the others to avoid any altercation, acquiesced and exited. Noble

Sissle observed that the white soldiers of the 12th Regiment, which was encamped next to the 15th at Wadsworth and located at Sixty-Sixth Street and Broadway in New York, knew a number of the black soldiers of the 15th who came from the San Juan Hill section of the city. The white New Yorkers had received treatment Sissle termed "none too cordial," sympathized with their black comrades in arms, and awaited an excuse "to blow up the town."[25] White soldiers of the 71st and 12th Regiments of the New York 27th Division asked the proprietors of soda shops near the camp if they would serve the colored soldiers. The proprietors emphatically and abusively replied in the negative. The white soldiers retorted that they had better close their shops because they themselves would not patronize men who treated the Negro soldiers unfairly. The "colored soldiers were all right," were "their buddies," and were fighting with them "for our country."[26]

Later, when two town toughs attacked a black soldier without provocation and threw him off the sidewalk into the gutter, the soldier, according to Sissle, walked away, explaining to the gathering crowd that he had promised his colonel not to strike back. Two white soldiers from the 7th Regiment intervened, declaring that they had promised *their* colonel nothing, and then knocked the toughs into the gutter.[27]

Despite these purported, individual examples of solidarity, one should not draw conclusions that the white soldiers of New York and the people of Spartanburg differed so greatly on race. Perhaps the sentiment of these white northerners was as much antisouthern as it was problack. The very neighborhoods that Noble Sissle named as common ground were also battlefields between whites and blacks, as the recent incident in San Juan Hill involving Private Joaquin indicated. The apparently sympathetic letter from John to his parents in its conflicted language—"nigers" and "negro"— revealed some of the complexities of race relations among New Yorkers. The men of the 15th were "our Niggers," not the South's.[28]

Even more telling, the official publication of the 27th Division, the *Wadsworth Gas Attack and Rio Grande Rattler*, frequently played to racial stereotypes, especially that of the lazy, easily frightened, and generally ignorant black as embodied in Sam (short for Sambo), the bellhop and elevator operator. In one cartoon, Sam met a rotund military officer, who asked him, "Why don't you enlist?" Sam responded, "Captain, I'd like to, 'deed I would. But then they might make me wear spiral puttees and I'd ketch the disease." "What disease?" the officer asked. "Spiral meningitis!" Sam exclaimed.

General O'Ryan topped the list of the publication's honorary editors. The 27th would transport that same minstrel mentality and tradition to Europe, where Al Van Zandt impersonated Bert Williams in Oudezeele,

France.[29] A northern black soldier could easily lose sight of the differences with and distance from his white New Yorker comrades in such an alien and hostile environment.

Always vigilant, officers of the 15th Regiment walked the streets of the city every evening until the men had returned to camp from passes, but the provocations continued. According to Little, during the Regiment's second week in Spartanburg, a local white man told some soldiers that the police had arrested and hanged two of their number. Two soldiers who had gone on pass the night before had missed roll call. The promise to Colonel Hayward did not apply in this situation—a potential replay of the Houston disaster. Hayward and Captain Little were out in the field when Sgt. Harry Leonard found Hayward. According to Little, Hayward and Leonard took off at a run, despite Hayward's lame heel, before roaring off in the colonel's car. Leonard had reported that half a company of men, armed and dangerous, had set out to shoot up Spartanburg. The car careened down the road between camp and town, as Hayward cursed at his driver, Reese, to go faster and at MPs who tried to stop them to get out of the way.[30]

Hayward arrived at the edge of Spartanburg to find some forty-five men standing at ease in a column of squads. They snapped to attention; their leader saluted the colonel. When Hayward demanded an explanation, the soldier explained they had heard about the rumored lynching and had come to shoot the police and anyone else who attempted to interfere. He further reported that they had marched in perfect discipline, saluting officers in automobiles that they passed on the road. The leader had detailed two men to inquire at the police station.

Hayward left Sergeant Leonard with the men and drove to the police station. There, Little recalled, Hayward found the two soldiers, standing at attention, inquiring about the missing soldiers. The colonel calculated that the local law enforcement thought that they were military police or provost guards. His men saluted him and, in Hayward's words, "permitted me to do the talking." The police said that no men of the 15th had gotten into trouble. They then showed Hayward the police blotter and allowed him and the two soldiers to inspect the jail to confirm that no soldier of the 15th was there.[31]

Hayward and his two soldiers departed and drove back to the detachment, which stood in perfect order where he had left the men but now in the midst of a crowd of civilians. Hayward stepped from the car, called the detachment to attention, and ordered them back to camp. He commented later how smartly the men "swung off" and "snapped their rifles to right shoulder," all to the applause of the crowd of spectators, who had no idea what had just happened and, more significantly, what had not. In the back seat of the car, which slowly followed the men, Hayward "almost had hysterics." The two missing men reported back to the Regiment shortly after the detachment returned.[32] Hayward, according to Little, ensured that the incident remained a secret—so secret, in fact, that Little's description in 1936 was the first published record of the event.

Little observed that the businessmen of Spartanburg arranged dances for the men to which "the best class of civilian colored population was invited," and these families began to invite the men to church and Sunday dinner. It appeared that the 15th and Spartanburg might reach a modus vivendi, especially since the Regiment seemed likely to winter in Spartanburg. Yet, Hayward and Gen. Charles L. Phillips, acting commander of the 27th Division, understood that they had narrowly averted disaster.[33]

The Regiment had benefited from the absence of General O'Ryan, who was on assignment in Europe, assessing the organization of Allied forces. Phillips, who, unlike his commander, lacked a long and adversarial relationship with the Regiment, judged it favorably and found its discipline and successful avoidance of trouble impressive. Consequently, he deemed the "disciplined" Regiment fit to represent the United States abroad and deserving of a place in France, where supposedly no color line existed, to complete its training. He recommended to the War Department that the 15th New York be sent "at once to France." He then arranged for Hayward to meet the chief of staff of the army and the secretary of war, Newton Baker. On October 21, Hayward boarded the next express train for Washington.[34]

Two evenings after Hayward's departure, Maj. Monson Morris and Captain Little, who had agreed to remain in town and in constant communication with the police, learned at 8:30 P.M. of a riot in progress at a nearby hotel. They arrived to find no riot but a crowd of soldiers and civilians, black and white. Morris and Little assembled all the men on pass from the 15th and had them march back to camp.[35] The two officers' further inquiries elicited an account of the preceding events, which Noble Sissle recalled later in an unpublished memoir.

Jim Europe and Sissle were walking past the hotel when Europe had inquired where he could purchase a New York paper. According to Morris and Little, a white waiter from the hotel answered; according to Sissle, it was "a local gentleman of color." All agreed, however, that the individual showed Europe the newsstand in the lobby, and when he asked further if a colored man could enter, the man answered in the affirmative. In the account of the white officers, Sissle offered to buy the paper; Sissle recounted that Europe had asked him to go and that he did so reluctantly.[36]

Sissle entered the hotel lobby, purchased a paper, and was crossing the lobby to return when a white man—the hotel proprietor—rushed, cursing, at Sissle and hit him in the head, knocking off his hat. Sissle did not retaliate and stooped to pick up the hat. The man then kicked him to the floor and proceeded to follow the retreating Sissle until he had kicked him onto the sidewalk.[37]

Some forty white soldiers lounging about the hotel lobby witnessed the incident, and one yelled to "kill" the proprietor and pull his hotel "down around his ears." A Jewish soldier from New York ran out to corral the black soldiers in the street. As some hundred black and white soldiers prepared to rush the proprietor, Lieutenant Europe entered and ordered them to get their hats and coats and leave quietly. The soldiers obeyed instinctively, but white and black faces glowered angrily through the window at the proprietor inside.[38]

Then, the proprietor proceeded to curse his "savior," Lieutenant Europe, when the military police arrived. The proprietor accused Sissle of not taking off his hat when he had entered, although all the white soldiers inside were wearing their garrison caps. White officers who had remained in the hotel complimented Europe on his cool conduct and assured them that Sissle had done nothing wrong. Europe turned and departed, dispersed the crowd, and reminded the black soldiers of their promise to Colonel Hayward. All returned to camp.[39]

Morris and Little reported the incident to General Phillips and swore the newspapermen in town to silence.[40] Lieutenant Castles confided in his war diary, "But, of course, the inevitable occurred. Some 'cracker' assaulted and 'beat up' one of our sergeants for venturing into a hotel to buy a paper. At once the racial feeling flamed into white heat, and we had to hold the men very close in hand, in practical confinement, in fact."[41] 1st Lt. Lewis Shaw, adjutant of the 2nd Battalion who had served five months on the Mexican border with a machine–gun troop of the New York Cavalry in 1916 and joined the 15th on April 12, wrote to his mother shortly after the incident, "We are all straining every nerve to prevent race troubles and our men so far in spite of every insult and provocation have shown wonderful control." He explained that the proprietor "of a dump of a hotel here" had assaulted Sissle, whom he described "as one of our most inoffensive and harmless noncoms." "We are now determined," he continued, "to prosecute the dog for contempt of the U.S. uniform."[42] Officers and men of the 15th Regiment wanted to bring charges against the proprietor, but Major Morris demurred, and they decided to wait for Colonel Hayward.[43]

The colonel returned to the camp with a visitor, Emmett J. Scott, the recently appointed "advisor to the War Department" on Negro affairs. Scott, the longtime private secretary of the late Booker T. Washington and secretary of Tuskegee Institute, was responsible for "matters affecting the interests of the 10,000,000 Negroes of the United States, and the part they are to play in connection with the present war." Secretary of War Baker assigned Scott, in attendance at the meeting with Hayward and Phillips, to investigate the conditions and report back. The situation was dire, and, as Noble Sissle opined, "the honor and glory of the 15th almost went up in smoke."[44]

Hayward called a meeting of all officers with and without commissions. Then, he withdrew all of the commissioned officers and gave Scott a private audience with the noncoms, "the backbone of a regiment," as Scott pointed out. Scott appealed to the men "to do nothing that would dishonor or stain the regiment." He remembered vividly how these men "with tears streaming down their faces voiced how bitterly they felt in the face of the insults which had been heaped upon them" but listened "to the counsel of patience for the Great Cause, even in the face of studied insult and maltreatment." The War Department had three options according to Scott:

> It could keep the regiment at Camp Wadsworth and face an eruption, and possibly further anger the white citizens who were opposing the retention of the regiment there, while at the same time inflaming the men of the regiment and many of the white New York guardsmen who were restive under the treatment accorded the colored soldiers, or the regiment could be removed to another camp and thereby convey the intimation that whenever any community put forward sufficient pressure, the War Department would respond thereto and remove soldiers from such location, whether they had given provocation for such demand or not. As a third alternative the Department could order the regiment overseas. The latter [last] alternative was decided upon.[45]

Two mornings after the incident, the 15th New York received orders to prepare to move in two days. A mere two weeks after its arrival, the Regiment readied to leave Spartanburg. Ironically, the *Spartanburg Journal* had suggested before the troops arrived that they be trained in France. Relieved by the 15th's sudden and welcome departure, the paper told its readers that the Regiment presented "a splendid appearance" at its final review. Early in the morning of October 24, the 15th New York broke camp and marched in review for General Phillips. As the men passed through the camp of the

New York 27th Division, thousands of the white soldiers gathered to sing them on their way with "Over There." The white division had not included the 15th New York in its farewell parade in New York, when it had departed for Spartanburg. Yet, the young men of the division, who had been quick to defend and retaliate on behalf of their black comrades in arms in Spartanburg, now spontaneously cheered the men of the 15th, who had arrived after them and were now departing before them.[46]

Hamilton "Ham" Fish wrote his father on October 23 in strictest confidence that they had just received orders from Washington. The 15th would sail from Hoboken, New Jersey, on Saturday, October 27, for France. This "bombshell" of an order delighted all the officers. He continued:

> The situation between our soldiers and the poor whites of Spartanburg has been most critical since we arrived owing to the disgusting treatment our men received. Several serious race riots have just been prevented in nick of time and all of us knew that it was only a question of time before our men would retaliate and shoot up or burn up the town. The War Dept. realizing the menacing situation ordered us to embark Sat. for Europe. Of course we are all glad to go.[47]

Fish reassured his father not to worry, as he anticipated they would spend four months training before being sent to the front. Furthermore, he firmly believed that his command—K Company of 3rd Battalion—the company "largest in numbers" and "the best in esprit," was the "best in the regt. and that they would follow" him anywhere. As for their coming departure, Fish ventured that every regiment in the country would be envious. He closed by asking his father not to pay his dues to his various elite social clubs and to write them that he was serving with troops in Europe.[48]

However, not all the men shared Fish's enthusiasm about the sudden departure. The news made "a sort of cold chill" run up Noble Sissle's spine, accompanied by a "sinking feeling." One soldier regretted not telling "my folks good-bye." Another asked what kind of army would force him "to leave that brown-skinned gal of mine without a last good-bye," to which a "hard-hearted" fellow soldier called out, "Sing them blues, brother."[49] Sgt. Maj. Chauncey Hooper sought good luck to carry him through and acted on a hunch by requesting a transfer to Company B because: "It's a case of 'B' here when you go and 'B' here when you come back."[50]

Noble Sissle failed to see any humor in the prospects of a "single regiment as part of no division . . . denied the right to train in camps in our own country" being sent to France ahead of the 27th Division. He had a point:

after all, fewer than 50,000 American troops had gone to Europe by then. Even Jim Europe could not console his extremely distraught friend. According to Sissle, after the Regiment had left Spartanburg, Europe apologized for asking him to secure a paper and jokingly added, "The man has kicked us right to France." An angry Sissle still felt the sting of humiliation and questioned fighting for a democracy where he had to "stand for somebody to kick you about like any dog and not [be] allowed to fight back."[51]

The trains full of soldiers sped north, stopping early in the morning on October 25 for the men to eat and exercise and again at midnight in Washington, DC. Colonel Hayward took the express train in order to arrive early at the Port of Embarkation in Hoboken, New Jersey. The next morning, October 26, the men arrived at 9:00 A.M. at Camp Mills, near Garden City, Long Island. Captain Little, in command of the troop trains, learned that the ship on which they had been scheduled to sail could not depart, so they would remain in camp until the next convoy.[52]

Instead of giving the men an opportunity to see loved ones, the delay mostly set up more possibilities for racial conflict. Clashes between black and white soldiers in stateside training camps occurred all too frequently during the war. The 15th New York now seemed unable to escape white southerners. At Camp Mills, men of the Regiment confronted members of the 167th Alabama Infantry. The southern officers admitted that their men "*might* [italics added]" have done "a little kidding," but they "claimed they respected the uniform, regardless of the wearer."[53]

The sorry past of these southern soldiers was no laughing matter. Not long before the arrival of the 15th at Camp Mills, members of this southern component of the Rainbow Division reportedly attacked Charles Farrar, a fifty-two-year-old black porter who had stumbled upon some seventy-five of their ranks on a Long Island Railroad train car. Claiming that he did not move fast enough when ordered to leave, the soldiers kicked, punched, and stabbed the helpless man before throwing him off the train. He lost an eye in the brutal assault, yet no one made a complaint to the police. The railroad company lodged a complaint with General Mills and the commander of the Alabama troops. The authorities seemed to have exacted little or no punishment and even allowed the Alabamans to remain as military police.[54]

The white southerners' claim of having respect for the uniform seems highly dubious given the constancy of their racist behavior, but officers of both regiments minimized the significance of the clash, not wishing to jeopardize the deployment of the Regiment. The *Chicago Defender,* however, contradicted Captain Little's representation that the "trouble was greatly exaggerated and amounted to little more than threats from the southerners to get rid of the men of the Fifteenth."[55] Its headline on the incident read FIFTEENTH NEW YORK AND SOUTHERNERS IN FIGHT: FIGHT LANDS TWO IN HOSPI-TAL. The *Defender* took great pleasure in a group of black men standing up to southern whites and getting the better of them, a situation rarely seen outside of a boxing ring.

Not only did the "Alabamans get worst" of the last "mixup," they reportedly came up short in some twenty-five encounters. George "Kid" Cotton, a professional boxer of some repute and the sparring partner of the famous former heavyweight champion Jack Johnson, took credit for two knockouts and "regretted having to leave the territory . . . when plenty of action was on the program." Cotton seems to have learned more than boxing from the flashy former heavyweight champion. Not to be outdone, rhetorically at least, the patrician Hamilton Fish sanitized John L. Sullivan's famous challenge of licking any "son of a bitch in the house" and volunteered to take on "any five southerners, either officers or men." In a somewhat contested and contradictory account with a healthy measure of hyperbole, Fish bragged that no one accepted. What seems indisputable is that whatever happened, Fish's standing with the men grew as a result. Only the removal of weapons from the Alabamans prevented a deadly encounter, as they had angered troops from Ohio as well as the 69th NYNG, both of whom were prepared to shoot it out with them.[56] The camp commander finally released the Alabamans from MP duty, and all seemed forgotten. In fact, no sooner had the 15th departed than the *Brooklyn Eagle* praised the troops of the 167th for their "warm hearts" and generosity to the other members of the Rainbow Division.[57]

After only two nights at Camp Mills, the 15th, to the cheers and best wishes of all but the Alabamans, moved to New York City, where the men stayed in four city armories. Their unit acquired a new nickname, the "Moving Regiment." Upon returning to New York City, Colonel Hayward established headquarters at the old armory of the 8th Coast Defense Command on Ninety-Fourth Street and Park Avenue and continued the serious training of the Regiment. The reinforced headquarters company, the supply company, and the band joined Hayward at the armory. The 2nd Battalion, commanded by Maj. Monson Morris, established camp at Van Cortlandt Park. Maj. Edwin Dayton installed the 3rd Battalion in the 2nd Field Artillery Armory in the Bronx. The 1st Battalion, under the command of Maj. Lorillard Spencer, remained at the 8th Coast Defense Armory, where it had been since August.[58]

During the next two weeks, the 15th prepared for departure and reequipped. The men's gear had shipped on the convoy of October 26, and all knew they would never be able to find it in France. Their personal baggage, shipped in advance, awaited them at their newly designated ship at Hoboken. On November 8, the 15th paraded to the tunes of the band in Central Park before the commanding general of the Eastern Department of the United States. The band then presented a concert in the park. On November 11, the separate battalions marched to the pier at Ninety-Sixth Street and the East River to board the excursion steamer *Grand Republic.* The steamer descended the East River, rounded the Battery, and ascended the Hudson River to the Hamburg-America Line piers at Hoboken. There, the men transferred to their transport, the *Pocahontas.* That night, the blacked-out ship, with the men of the 15th New York Infantry Regiment on board, departed for France.[59]

The next morning, the convoy had sailed beyond sight of the American coast. A fine day on a calm ocean beckoned. Yet, early that afternoon, without warning, the *Pocahontas* left the convoy to return to New York. About 150 miles out, an engine piston rod had broken, disabling one screw. The ship could not keep pace with the convoy and had to limp home on its other screw. As the *Pocahontas* turned about, Capt. Seth B. McClinton had observed Colonel Hayward, standing on the bridge of the ship, in tears at the prospect of returning. By midnight, they had berthed again at the Hamburg-America pier in Hoboken. The 15th received orders to report by train to Camp Merritt, near Tenafly and Englewood, New Jersey.[60]

When the 15th New York arrived at Camp Merritt, southern white officers' horror at sharing a barracks with black officers nearly caused another melee.[61] According to Lt. John Castles, one of the white officers of a black stevedore regiment from Louisiana "called one of our men 'a son of a bitch of a nigger' and drew a pistol on him because he failed to move out of his way fast enough. A small riot almost developed." Capt. "Ham" Fish and he managed to avert serious trouble, "but it was like walking on thin ice from then on."[62]

The Military Intelligence Bureau's Morale Section invariably attributed such encounters between blacks and whites to black soldiers "deliberately seeking confrontation" rather than to the race prejudice of whites, despite the implausibility of such an interpretation in the midst of lynching and race riots around the country. Maj. L. B. Dunham, a northerner and an intelligence officer at the Hoboken port, noted that no black officers should have had to endure such "insult and humiliation."[63]

The 15th remained at Camp Merritt, which was still under construction, during three weeks of abysmally cold weather. They anticipated imminent departure and consequently unpacked the bare minimum of their gear. After a few days, some 850 men were absent without leave (AWOL), and some of the families and friends of the other 1,150 were visiting their loved ones at Camp Merritt. As Captain Little noted, the men did not intend to desert; they merely wanted to see their families. The Regiment sent military police ranging about northeast New Jersey, Manhattan, and Brooklyn to recover wayward men. Soldiers awaiting summary court trials filled the guardhouse.

According to Little, a penniless private managed to visit his mother, who lived near Pittsburgh, by train-hopping. He rode local passenger trains until the conductors discovered and removed him, only to board the next train. A sergeant traveled to Pittsburgh at company expense to retrieve him. One day, regimental headquarters received a telegram from the police of a nearby city informing them that a dozen AWOL soldiers were being held in the city jail. Headquarters informed the police that they had dispatched a guard. When the guard arrived, the men had long since departed. A corporal had overheard the exchange and, realizing that a friend was among the group, had taken an army truck, masqueraded as the guard, and freed them. All thirteen escaped detection and punishment.[64]

With each passing day, the morale of officers and men plummeted. Lieutenant Castles complained that the officers had to spend five hours a day listening to the lectures of former marine officer Lt. Col. Woodell A. Pickering while the men ran wild. Colonel Hayward, who was often absent, "gave every evidence of not giving a damn what happened now that we were sure of going abroad." Castles feared the "break-up" of the Regiment, as Hayward openly insulted Maj. Edwin Dayton and called him "a liar in front of all the officers in the regiment." Hayward considered Dayton's 3rd Battalion officers, many of whom came from Ivy League schools, too "clubby," and friction between him and Dayton occurred frequently. Dayton, as an "old soldier," may also have posed a challenge to Hayward's authority. Castles thought that all his battalion's officers would have resigned had they not been scheduled for imminent departure.[65]

Inadequate and cramped facilities limited exercise to road marches. The mess arrangements were the worst the Regiment had ever experienced. Under such conditions, one could expect the worst, and the worst happened when a gambling dispute led to homicide. According to Little, the perpetrator, "a full blooded Zulu by birth . . . picked up his service rifle, loaded it, took deliberate aim at his victim and fired."[66] Little's description of the tragedy as "the most cold-blooded murder in all the history of the regiment" is expectedly sensational and disappointingly incomplete, even excluding many important details such as the names of victim(s) and assailant. Moreover, it fails to convey the significance of the event and its complex meanings, especially in regard to the internal dynamics of the Regiment, involving a purportedly destructive tension between racial solidarity/consciousness and healthy military culture. All of it indicates how little was known about recent recruits and how there was no time to find out who they were and what they were about.

The "Zulu" was a man who called himself Valdo B. Schita. He mustered into the 15th on August 14, 1917, at the relatively advanced age, especially for a private, of thirty and a half years. He listed Calcyetta (an unknown town), South Africa, as his place of birth and Buffalo, New York, as his home. Later, he would claim "Uganda, Zulu Land, British East Africa" and other variants of it, including Basoutuland, as his native country—perhaps evidence of foolish inconsistency or an ingenious stratagem for covering tracks.[67] Nonetheless, Schita's story proved so intriguing that, according to writer Stephen Harris, the *Brooklyn Daily Eagle* took notice of this man who apparently had served twelve years in the British army, fighting in the Second Boer War (1899–1902) and later on the western front. Even more, Schita reportedly had distinguished himself in more than 200 bayonet encounters with the Germans and had "scars all over his body to show for his prowess with the cold steel." Of course, skill with blade was no match for modern western technology, and as the story goes, a gas bomb disabled Schita, forced him out of the service, and led him rather inexplicably to the United States. Anyone doing the math would certainly have questions about his age during the Boer War in relation to that given at the time of enlistment. That notwithstanding, as soon as authorities "verified" Schita's fantastic story, they promoted him to sergeant.[68] Schita was no doubt an unreliable narrator, but he seemed to have accomplices in spinning such tales, including the press and perhaps members of the Regiment. In fact, Schita told a different, but no less fascinating, story of his life in numerous official documents and court testimony.

His tale began with his "adoption" by a white man at age twelve. The putative relationship prefaced Schita's inconsistently crafted narrative of his affection for and deference to whites—an understandable and perhaps necessary coping strategy in colonial Africa or possibly the American South. By age sixteen, he supposedly joined the Native Constabulary, a paramilitary force designed to keep order among the "subjects" not only in his own country but also in other British colonies, including Kenya and the Sudan. At twenty-two, Schita said he left the constabulary and made his way to Cardiff, England (actually Wales), and learned to fire boilers. While assiduously avoiding dates of any kind in his tale(s), Schita conveyed a sense of longing for foreign travel, adventure, and most of all military service, which he allegedly found in the Lincolnshire Regiment or the Lancashire Fusiliers or the Middlesex Rifles. (He provided conflicting testimony on these affiliations.) Schita once again placed himself in a position of quelling native unrest, this time as a foreign legionnaire in Egypt and the Sudan.[69]

After nearly two years of service, Schita reportedly went to South Africa, "not home but in the neighborhood," where he enviously witnessed two sisters leave the country to attend "Dr. Booker T. Washington's school in the South." Although he did not "have exactly the qualification that they [Tuskegee] wanted," he determined to follow his sisters to the United States. First, the story went, he sailed to Callao, Peru, as a heaver on the *Victoria* out of Cape Town. From there, he reportedly made his way to Newport News, Virginia, where he worked as a fireman in the navy yard and reestablished a tenuous connection to the military. Schita placed his arrival around 1910. After nine months, weary of the heat and "various things," he left the navy yard and worked odd jobs before heading to Canada and traveling to and working in Wellington, St. Catherines, and Hamilton. Before long, however, he returned to the United States and claimed to have worked foundry jobs in Buffalo and Elmira, New York.[70] Schita represented travel as a way of passing time and surviving as he awaited another opportunity to return to his true calling—military service. His story, seemingly by design, portrayed a man with no real identity, family, or life outside a uniform. Yet, the possibility exists that the only military uniform he ever wore was in his head, at least until November 1916. Although his restless spirit and "foreign" identity could have been motivated by concerns about status, employment, and discrimination, they might have been driven by a desire to hide and run from a past that required spatial mobility, temporal vagueness, factual remoteness, and familial estrangement.

As Schita told it, when war in Europe broke out he quickly seized the opportunity to serve his king and answer his calling again. The war in Europe began in 1914, but official records indicate that Schita first volunteered for service in 1916. To that end, Schita claimed to have visited the British vice consul in Buffalo, who immediately asked, "Are you a British subject?" Schita answered, "I will leave that for you to decide." Schita's accent, perhaps southern, apparently confused the official. Schita explained that he had sisters in the South and had been "working backwards and forwards different places." According to him, the vice consul then told him that the country needed him and that he would do all that he could to help. The British Royal Army generally did not accept black subjects as soldiers, but the Canadian Overseas Expeditionary Force did. Schita departed for Hamilton, where he "seen the sign out and went in."[71]

Although one might envisage a large and imposing man from the reports, Schita stood only 5'6" or 5'7", weighed 141 pounds and, contrary to the *Eagle* story, had one 4-inch scar on the back of his neck. Under oath, Schita listed his place of birth as South Africa; subsequently, he listed Johannesburg as his birthplace. He gave his date of birth as February 27, 1888, making his age twenty-eight years and ten months. He claimed his father as next of kin and identified him as Belonda Schita of Johannesburg. His mother's name appeared as Pesyondias on another Canadian document. He answered no to the question of marriage and yes to being a Presbyterian, an appropriately British denomination of Protestantism. Then, Schita provided information that conflicted directly with the record he gave to officers of the 15th upon enlistment and in subsequent testimony and documents related to his court-martial. This pattern of conflicting and contradictory biographical reporting would continue until his death.[72]

Schita did not deny past military service, but when asked to "state particulars," he claimed service with the "U.S.A. Army" for "6 years."[73] One can only speculate that he either had no service in the British armed forces or wished to hide something in that record, which the Canadians might suspect and discover. They were far less likely to check on American service, and perhaps they lacked the will or the means to investigate such. After all, the Canadians long had been recruiting in America for black soldiers and offered them better pay and treatment. In this regard, they were competitors. Moreover, if Schita's description of the encounter with the vice consul is credible, he appeared fully Americanized, and his claims of American military service and cultural immersion made far more sense than some recent attachment to British institutions. His use of *seen* in the past tense, instead of *saw*, seems typically American. Last, Schita also understood that claiming American military service might impress the Canadians and lead to elevated rank, status, conditions, and compensation. Clearly, the American authorities did not conduct serious background checks on recruits and asked far fewer questions of its candidates than did the Canadians. In times of war, the modus operandi was "sign them up and let the wash bring things out."

Declared fit, Schita went to Camp Borden for training. From there, the story became more convoluted, as Schita purportedly traveled from "one place to another" before his assignment to a black battalion as an instructor. His cross-country travels supposedly resumed as a recruiter.[74] The Canadian file simply listed him as a private in Construction Battalion no. 2 of Nova Scotia, and his mobility seemed to have resulted from a bad case of hemorrhoids, for which he received treatment in London, Ontario.[75]

On March 21, 1917, the Canadian army discharged Schita for "violation of immigration laws" and directed that he be treated as "Alien," which certainly included deportation even though service records listed his conduct and character while in the service as "very good."[76] The timing and nature of Schita's discharge, however, raise serious questions about the cause. Canadians actively recruited black Americans for service and did not disqualify them because of national origin. Furthermore, the Canadian army did not require a declaration of citizenship, although Schita's claim of South African nativity and six years of service in the US military might have opened him up to suspicion and provided the technical grounds to release him. Interestingly, Schita's battalion departed for France only five days after his discharge, which suggests that officers found reason to doubt his worth to them overseas. As later evidence and events suggest, Schita might have purposefully provoked authorities to release him so as to avoid the possible hell that awaited the unit—and him—in Europe.

Schita reportedly returned to Buffalo and found work at the Lackawanna Steel Company. When the United States entered the war, he "volunteered." He claimed that his first attempt to enlist in Buffalo ended with the words "Glad to use you, but can't do it." Perhaps the recruiters directed him to the busy eastern recruiting station of Fort Slocum on western Long Island Sound, where—despite his age, nationality, and recent discharge from the Canadian army—authorities assigned him, possibly by choice, to the 15th.[77] Schita testified under oath that he informed American officials that his release from service in Canada resulted from illness. As proof, he produced a "last pay certificate," which listed him as a casualty who had been "struck off strength," or removed from duty with his outfit. As other documents—apparently withheld by Schita—demonstrate, his casualty status had nothing to do with injury or illness. Nonetheless, he maintained that his placement on the list entitled him to casualty relief and the opportunity to recover at home in Buffalo. When his health did not improve rapidly enough, the Canadian authorities discharged him by mail. In actuality, the lag between removal and official discharge resulted from procedural requirements, including a review of the charges and the processing of his severance pay.[78]

Although Schita's "extensive" foreign service record seemingly mattered little upon enlistment, it and his purported reverence for the military and commitment to discipline soon paid dividends. Schita claimed that while at Camp Dix in Wrightstown, New Jersey, Lieutenants Siegel and Wilder (possibly Edward Siedle and Edward A. Walton of Company I) "kind of favored" him and presented him to Captain Napoleon Bonaparte Marshall for promotion to sergeant.[79] A black soldier, Warren B. Green, took credit, or possibly blame, for introducing Schita to Marshall and vouching for his general intelligence and particular insights about "the modern war." When Schita first arrived at Camp Dix, he bunked with Green, whom he apparently mesmerized with his conversation. Schita told Green that he had been a "Regimental Sergeant Major in the English Army." That revelation convinced Green that Schita "would be some benefit to the Captain [and] to his company."[80]

Green's apparent role in his promotion did not advance Schita's narrative of white paternalism and black resentment, and predictably, Schita never acknowledged the man's instrumentality in his promotion. His narrative instead conveyed his gratitude toward whites for their confidence in him and his determination to fulfill their expectations. In reality, the Regiment most likely had promoted a "con man," who probably understood that he had to compensate for his lack of qualifications or raise suspicion. Though the real motivation for all of his actions might have been in the service of self, he portrayed his mission as one to prove that the type of man he claimed to be was best qualified to effect change in a culture of theft, profanity, and disrespect for authority, which he attributed to dangerous "race consciousness." Indeed, Schita maintained that all his troubles began when he told the men that he believed "the white officer got the best results out of them."[81] The comment supposedly marked him as an Uncle Tom or an enemy of the race. Schita, of course, made no mention of the fact that he had once threatened a fellow soldier with a gun and might have carried out the threat were it not for the timely intervention of others. That act no doubt caused both resentment and fear of him among the men.[82]

Schita wanted the court to believe that the men resented him because he was a newcomer to the Regiment, a self-proclaimed foreigner, and a lackey to whites. Even worse, in his role of enforcer of military discipline and order, Schita "admitted" to many negative encounters with soldiers and created ill will in the process. He also maintained that Captain Marshall undermined his own authority by playing favorites with men who had been with the Regiment in the early days of its existence. One of the men was Benjamin F. Alston of New York City, by way of Charleston, South Carolina. Alston had joined the Regiment in August 1916 as an eighteen-year-old. Although Alston, in a strange twist of fate, would eventually earn the Croix de Guerre, he was, in Schita's opinion, a scoundrel protected by Marshall. When Schita reported Alston to Marshall for disobeying an order, he said his captain and company commander responded: "Alston, you was with me in the old days of overalls, galluses, and [when we] only had one shoe on. You [We] always have been good friends. You stood by me, and I will stick by you."[83]

Considering the vast difference in age and social standing between the two men, to say nothing of Marshall's well-known erudition, the quote is more likely the product of a desperate man's mind and perhaps a court reporter's ear rather than an accurate representation of Marshall's voice. To Schita's credit, Alston verified the incident, if not Marshall's purported response. Marshall and Alston probably did have a close relationship forged through their relatively long membership in the Regiment. Any such relationship, however, would have operated more along the lines of father/son and mentor/student, if not officer/soldier. Schita dismissed the last possibility because the men showed no deference to Marshall and often addressed him as "Cap" without saluting or standing at attention.[84]

Worse, Schita claimed they even defied the captain. One soldier by the name of Paul Golden said that he would do nothing the "son of a bitch said to him." The exchange, according to Schita, led a witness, Capt. Hamilton Fish, to ask Marshall, "What [Why], [do] you allow your men to talk that way for?" Schita believed that the black officer got what he deserved by showing favoritism to his "friends" and "picks." He painted an ugly picture of race loyalty run amok, even alleging that Marshall refused to collect fines from soldiers because the money would only go into the hands of whites. He also blamed Marshall and race fanaticism indirectly for the homicide he committed. After all, it was Marshall, according to Schita, who vowed never "to let his men be without ammunition" and vulnerable to attack by hostile white soldiers.[85] Schita had twisted a justified measure of self-preservation into mindless attachment to race loyalty.

On Sunday, November 25, with so much time on their hands and little to do, the men amused themselves by playing blackjack, pinochle, poker, and "coon-can" and, of course, shooting craps. Although betting was not permitted, even the "disciplinarian" Schita indulged. Gambling, for some, was not only a way of passing time but also a way of earning a few precious dollars to make the short trip to New York City, where many men had family, friends, and lovers or sought to take advantage of Gotham's many attractions. On this day, the shortage of money and the denial of passes added to the already tense environment of close confinement and inactivity. Schita, who had "suffered" a severe back injury on board the *Pocahontas*, claimed virtual immobility. His condition, he maintained, led many soldiers to take advantage of him. For example, no one would escort him to the latrine without compensation. As Schita told it, they all wanted his money any way they could get it. Perhaps they suspected him of malingering and wanted to exact a price from him for it.[86]

Despite the less than cordial relations between Alston and Schita, they, along with Erasmus Carr, began playing blackjack, also known as twenty-one, for pennies. Before long, Pvt. Joseph Fagan of Harlem entered the barracks, saw the card game, and told Schita, "Deal me some, too."[87] Fagan, twenty-nine and a newcomer, had joined the Regiment on November 9, only a few days before it first departed for France. Although all of the witnesses to the event admitted that he owed Schita some amount between $1 and $2, not one of them impugned his character. Yet, no one seemed to know the man very well, as evidenced by references to him as "John" and "Fergins."[88] On the record, Fagan came across as brash, cocky, and injudicious.

Schita claimed that he tried to discourage Fagan from playing because "they were trying to break Carr." In other words, it was a game among friends, and he did not belong. The dispute began when Schita claimed that Fagan had bet and lost $1.45 and Fagan claimed that he had only bet and lost $1.00. When Schita handed Fagan $.55, Fagan tossed the change back at him and demanded a dollar. When Schita refused, Fagan took a $2 bill from the pot and announced that he would get change.[89]

When Fagan returned to the barracks, he immediately entered a crap game and ignored Schita. Angered by Fagan's impudence and disrespect, Schita seethed and plotted his revenge against someone who would take money from him "just because I was sick in bed." Sensing imminent danger in Schita's mood and words, Pvt. Robert Foxworth counseled restraint: "I thought you was too much of a gentleman to get into any trouble over any money." The appeal to the scorned man's apparent sense of decency failed, as Schita reportedly threatened to "get him [Fagan] before the day is gone."[90] Eventually, he took up his rifle, found or was given ammunition, loaded the weapon, crawled from his bed to a position close to Fagan, announced to the men "look out," and shot Fagan in the forehead, killing him instantly. The bullet exited the "intended" victim's skull and hit Pvt. Eugene Hines, who screamed that he had been shot before jumping out the window, only to be followed by a host of comrades as pandemonium erupted in the barracks.[91]

A few composed soldiers overpowered Schita, removed the gun, and reported that he yelled, "I would kill any son of a bitch [or any God damn nigger] that takes his money." When the smoke had cleared, the men found Fagan on the floor, wearing his cap; his head was turned to the side in a pool of blood, and he had a die in one hand and his winnings in the other.[92] Life proved as ephemeral and unpredictable as luck in a game of chance.

Now, Schita had to fight for his life, if not his honor, before an army court-martial, beginning on November 28, only three days after the tragic event. In a case too complex and lengthy to treat fully here, he maintained that all the witnesses were lying and out to get him. What they characterized as malicious and intentional Schita maintained was an accident. He had no intention of shooting anyone, only a desire to bring order to a chaotic barracks in which men were stealing from him and out of control. He claimed that he summoned Captain Marshall, who did not respond. When his calls for help failed, he resorted to a tried and tested method of restoring order—loading a gun and pointing it.[93]

The defense called no witnesses and tried to show that Schita's physical condition, his actual position in relation to the victim, the configuration of the room, the placement of objects in it, and the numbers of men there made an accidental shooting more likely. His counsel dismissed the evidence of intent as simply the product of his enemies. Yet Schita's own words during the initial interrogation came back to haunt him. When asked what he had said before the shooting, Schita replied, "I pointed the gun at him and said 'You give me my money.'"[94] Nonetheless, Schita still swore that nerves, not intent, produced the deadly outcome. In the face of such damaging evidence, the counsel, Martin W. Littleton, a famous Democratic politician, orator, and one of New York's finest criminal lawyers but a self-confessed novice to military trials, relied almost exclusively on his client's testimony about his background and experience, the atmosphere in the barracks, and the manner of the shooting to argue for Schita's virtue in the face of a virtually lawless mob.[95]

Showing disdain for the Regiment and little knowledge of it or of the human nature of black people, for that matter, Littleton argued that there could have been no premeditation and not even passion because these men had no relationship of any kind that would engender any real feelings, negative or positive, toward one another: "They were a flock of men, an assemblage of men now in a new adventure for some of them." He described the scene as a virtual bacchanalia populated by the dregs of society: "Here is a great barracks, untrained, uncontrollable men, rebellious, disobedient, and dissatisfied men, gathered together during the war; gathered from the elevator shafts and porters' places, and from every place where men can enlist." He called them "a mob instead of a regiment," without "a good soldier in the whole barracks" except for Schita—"the object of their oaths and imprecations" but "the only serious, determined man in the whole place." Littleton conveniently overlooked his client's participation in "an orgy of gambling on every side" and "the perfect holocaust."[96]

Schita's lawyer achieved the seemingly impossible. He gave a summation even more fantastical and illogical than that of his client. Perhaps both realized that logic had no value, given the facts. Instead, they chose a visceral strategy with but one end—to convince the tribunal that Schita was a white man's Negro, like the invoked Booker T. Washington, and that even in killing a fellow soldier, he represented a far less dangerous threat than those arrayed against him. Littleton, a southerner by birth and upbringing, played the race card in reverse and found an ace in Schita's self-proclaimed foreignness: "He had come from far-off Uganda; he was not one of the negroes of the South, far from it." Despite the fact that he "had lived on the very firing line of civilization," he had distinguished himself more than those who "had lived in the bosom of at least the most domestic civilization of the world."[97] Schita and Littleton sought to deflect attention from the perpetrator and exploit an obvious sore point within and without the military—black men as soldiers, especially officers. They had put the Regiment on trial.

Littleton's strategy and possibly Schita's was to avoid the death penalty. In that, they succeeded. The court found Schita guilty of a violation of the 92nd Article of War for maliciously, premeditatedly, "willfully, deliberately, feloniously, [and] unlawfully" killing Private Joseph Fagan. It also found him guilty of "felonious assault" on Pvt. Eugene Hines. Yet, the court spared Schita's life. His sentence read: "To be dishonorably discharged [from] the service, to forfeit all pay and allowances due and to become due, and to be confined at hard labor at such place as the reviewing authority may direct for the term of his natural life."[98]

All ten members of the court, however, recommended Schita "to the clemency of the reviewing authority on the ground that the lamentable absence of discipline in the command to which the accused belonged may have caused extreme aggravation in his mind." The reviewing authority approved the court's sentence and designated the US Penitentiary in Atlanta, Georgia, as his "place of confinement."[99] Littleton and Schita clearly succeeded in convicting the Regiment. Of all the incidents involving the Regiment, the Schita court-martial had to be the greatest threat to its reputation and existence. There can be no doubt that it left a blot that could never be erased. Perhaps only the desperate situation in Europe, the tenuous political conditions at home together with a fear of upsetting blacks, and the nearly exemplary record of the Regiment prior to the incident saved it. Just a month before the tragic events of November 25, a letter from L. V. Meehan, superintendent of construction, repairs, and supplies for the Armory Board of New York City, to its secretary, C. D. Rhinehart, had revealed the esteem in which at least one high-ranking public official held the Regiment:

It is with the greatest pleasure that I report that the old Eighth Armory
. . . occupied for several weeks by a portion of the Fifteenth Infantry,
were left in very much better condition than when they entered them.
It is hard to believe that the number of men who were quartered in
this building during that period of time would be so thoroughly careful and leave no trace of their extended occupancy.[100]

Even more, Meehan had reported, Upper East Side residents had "nothing but favorable comments of the action of the men outside of the armory." Although extremely flattering, the report also underscored the constant scrutiny the unit endured. One misstep could confirm commonly held
prejudgments and relegate the men to labor duty or worse. Even Meehan
had admitted he placed less reliance than he should have in Captain Little's
assurance that the men would leave the armory in better condition than they
found it.[101] Irrespective of such high praise, if General Pershing and his staff
needed an excuse to remove black officers from the Regiment eventually and
deny it and its men the recognition they deserved, they now had one.

Although Schita and his lawyer resorted to exaggeration, distortion, and
misstatement to argue their case, both did point to real problems in the
Regiment. Even Arthur Little's account makes abundantly clear that the
stay at Camp Merrit was the worst moment in the unit's history. Yet, Little
blamed circumstances more than intrinsic problems with leadership or race
fanaticism. Moreover, neither Schita nor his counsel compared the 15th to
other regiments, which had their share of unrest and disorder. For proof,
one need not look further than the 167th from Alabama. There is no denying that men such as Fagan lacked adequate training and acculturation.
He was a body filling a quota, just like so many white soldiers. His late
enlistment and that of many others point to the fact that even before the
Regiment went to Europe, the necessity of adding largely untrained and
unacculturated men, or "replacements," had altered the chemistry of the
Regiment. Some men, such as Capt. Charles Fillmore, Sgt. Maj. Charles
E. Conick, Jr., Pvt. George W. Brown, and Pvt. Richard Banks, to name a
few, had been with the Regiment since its provisional incarnation in 1911.
Many others joined in the summer of 1916 and saw themselves as char-
ter members of the club.[102] They had drilled and trained in Harlem in the
Regiment's infancy and had military and community ties that bound them.
Many others joined the Regiment in June and July 1917 and experienced
Camps Wadsworth and Dix, guard duty, and Spartanburg as crucibles of
indoctrination, acculturation, and cohesion. Men like Fagan and, in many
respects, Schita were outsiders. The mixing of old and new, trained and un-

trained, northern and southern, and educated and uneducated was bound to cause problems. Under the circumstances of Camp Merrit, these problems became volatile.

Federal prison authorities in August 1939 would declare Schita insane and secure his transfer from Atlanta to Springfield.[103] Originally known as the US Hospital for Federal Delinquents, the facility "treated" men suffering from "the most serious physical, mental, and nervous disorders," ranging from diabetes to "passive homosexuality" to "psychopathic personality." In Springfield, Schita would continue his sociopathic behavior and clever manipulation and reveal his homosexuality openly. His confinement there raises more questions about his discharge from the Canadian army, about whether the basis might have been sexually related, and about whether it and the injury aboard the *Pocahontas* might have been ploys to keep the "great warrior" from actually seeing combat. The shooting of a fellow soldier was a sure way of escaping combat. Perhaps he made a complex calculation between the risks of execution by court-martial and death at the hands of the Huns.

In the end, the vexing question remains—who was Valdo B. Schita? It must have been a question that men of the Regiment asked themselves over and over. Much of the man seems to have been an invention, beginning with his name. Neither Valdo nor Schita was or is a Zulu name. Valdo or Waldo were and are common European names. Schita, as a surname, belongs to Romanians, Croatians, and Russians in Ellis Island records. It means "sketch" or "brief history" in Romanian. "Schita" is also a transliteration of the Hebrew term for ritual slaughter, most commonly represented as "Shechita." When, how, and where the subject acquired the name may never be known. Could it have been given to him by the white man he claimed adopted him?[104] If nothing else, he was a consummate con artist. Almost all that he was seemed to be an act, including his persona as a "white man's Negro." Schita cared only about himself and resorted to any device or disguise to serve his self-interest. His seemingly invented adventurism and questionable foreign identity placed him within a long tradition of African American self-creation. His penchant for violence probably set him apart. Nonetheless, like many others of this type, he eventually became native to the place that best suited his interests at any particular moment.

Whoever the man was, he managed to find legal immortality and name recognition. In the late 1930s and early 1940s, he filed numerous appeals for release from prison and actually won the right to a new trial in federal court, which resulted in a confirmation of the original verdict and sentence. He successfully appealed the verdict and received a second federal trial, which confirmed the original verdict again. He appealed once more and lost, whereupon he petitioned the Supreme Court, which denied him a hearing. An unsuccessful appeal to the War Department in 1944 ended his legal fight and perhaps his will to live. Valdo B. Schita died on January 26, 1945, at the Medical Center for Federal Prisoners in Springfield, Missouri. Nonetheless, he lives on through his determined litigation in *Schita v. King* and *Schita v. Cox,* both of which established legal precedents for civil jurisdiction in military trials and expanded the boundaries of habeas corpus protections.[105]

The 15th New York boarded the *Pocahontas* for the second time on December 2, only to watch their convoy depart without them again one day later. This time, coal at the bottom of the ship's bunkers had spontaneously combusted, necessitating emptying, cooling, and repainting the bunkers before coaling the ship again. Wretched frustration reigned as the Regiment remained aboard ship for the next eleven days.[106]

Finally, on the afternoon of December 12, the *Pocahontas* departed the pier to anchor off the coast of New Jersey and await another convoy. Late the next afternoon, a storm broke, and that night at 8:45, the ship left in darkness, buffeted by blizzard and gale. Shortly thereafter, with the depth of the water decreasing, the *Pocahontas* dropped anchor off Sandy Hook, New Jersey. Early the next day, about 3:00 A.M., a British oil tanker drifted into the *Pocahontas,* its bow tearing three or four metal plates away from the main deck on the starboard side.

The ship's captain initially believed that they should return to port for repairs, although the damage affected only the ship's superstructure. The ship lacked appropriate tools, particularly steel drills, to repair the plates. Fortunately, the Regiment's transportation company included skilled tradesmen equipped with the latest machine-shop equipment, including steel drills, thanks to the persistence of their company commander. Directed by the ship's carpenter, the ship's crew and the Regiment's soldiers set to work in shifts. Little recalled their hanging in slings on the side of the ship in the ten-degree weather. By order of the convoy flag officer, the *Pocahontas* could sail only if they completed repairing and painting the panels by dusk. At 6:20 P.M., the crew pulled the last frozen painter on deck, and the engines started five minutes later. They sailed with the convoy.[107]

At least good weather attended their voyage, as the convoy took a southern route to Europe. During the very short days, from 7:30 A.M. to 4:15 P.M., the officers spent their time studying military subjects in the morning and taking examinations during the afternoon. One day, they took nine examinations, and Ham Fish boasted to his father that his average of 87 placed him fifth out of fifty officers and ahead of all the majors and that his company officers maintained the highest average in the Regiment. They break-fasted at 8:00 A.M., inspected quarters at 10:30 A.M., lunched at 12:00 noon, took examinations from 1:15 to 3:15 P.M., and dined at 3:30 P.M. No lights, no smoking, and no diversions disrupted the long and tedious nights. At least, they saw no submarines, which Fish hoped were home for Christmas.[108]

Castles, undoubtedly sick of examinations, wrote that the convoy comprised the *Pocahontas, Susquehanna, President Lincoln, President Grant,* several merchant ships, the battleship USS *North Carolina,* and the converted cruiser *De Kalb.* The last was the former German raider *Prince Eitel Friedrich,* interned at Newport News, Virginia, the previous year. Castles also noted that Colonel Hayward dispersed the officers of Major Dayton's battalion among the other battalions, as a way of breaking up "the club." The fact that Arthur Little subsequently took command of the 1st Battalion as a result of Dayton's transfer indicates that Hayward possibly switched the commands of Maj. Lorillard Spencer and Dayton, giving Spencer command of the 3rd Battalion and Dayton command of the 1st.[109]

Four officers crowded into a stateroom meant for one passenger. With nothing to do after dark, Jim Europe would play a piano they had found in one of the passageways as long as anyone desired. Castles observed, "Jim's repertoire was practically without limit and he was as familiar with Wagner and Beethoven as he was with ragtime." The K Company quartet and then Sissle as a soloist sometimes accompanied Europe; occasionally, all the officers sang along. Abovedeck, the officers' choices of songs reflected their "loneliness," and only requests for a lively song from an old soldier such as Maj. Edwin Dayton, alert to morale, broke the spell of loneliness.[110]

In the tropical weather a week into the trip, Castles often escaped from the rest by spending evenings in a lifeboat suspended from the boat deck, watching the black shapes of the other ships and the black water crested with whitecaps and wakes. He would drift off to the roar of wind and waves, watching the stars and moon, forgetting the war, until a voice in the dark or a lurch of the ship reminded him "there was no future as long as the war lasted."[111]

Seasickness and measles plagued the Regiment, and the men of the 15th were crowded below in even more uncomfortable conditions than the officers. In their cramped quarters, many of the men "rolled in agony from seasickness." Noncommissioned officers would command, "Fall Out!" A soldier would reply, "Can't make it, Sergeant, I'm dying." The response was quick, "Die and prove it. Fall out!"[112]

The men followed a daily regimen of making up bunks, eating breakfast, and then exercising on deck until dinner hour at noon. In the afternoon, the band played on deck, and the men finished eating by 4:00 P.M. so that the crew could clear everything during daylight, as only little blue lights near the floor of the passageways shone at night. Noble Sissle recalled that during the "blue hazy nights," soldiers crowded the decks, some walking arm in arm around the ship, some just lounging about leaning against the lifeboats. The day's program sustained the men's spirits, but the night seemed to drain them of their hilarity, as no one spoke above a whisper. Belowdecks in the hold, men sang and prayed or moaned from motion sickness.[113]

One night, "a tremendous rattling and a thud that seemed to shake the ship from stem to stern" awakened and frightened some of the men. Believing that a submarine torpedo had struck the ship, they rushed to the captain, only to learn that a swell in the ocean had made the stern rise and the propellers leave the water, causing the resulting noise and vibration. Many of the soldiers had slept right through the incident, including Sergeant Major Cheatham, although Sissle claimed to have stepped right in Cheatham's stomach as he exited their stateroom.[114]

Beneath the humor of Sissle's account of lodging arrangements lay a telling fact about the limits of social relations between black and white officers as well as the leveling effects of race on rank. Although Sissle attributed the bunching of Captains Marshall and Fillmore and Lieutenants Europe and Lacy to happenstance, it had to be by design. Even more, Sissle revealed that he and Cheatham, by virtue of their friendship with the "colored officers in civilian life, "were allowed the privilege of bunking in their room."[115] Although the sleeping arrangements must have been in violation of military regulations, the black officers clearly saw some of these noncoms as their social and military equals. Only race prevented them from attaining the commissions they deserved. Where the fifth black officer, Lieutenant Reid, bunked is a mystery. One can safely assume that it was not with white officers.

On December 24, a squadron of ten to twelve destroyers arrived to shepherd them through the "Danger Zone," encircling the convoy at "bewildering speed." The battleship *North Carolina* turned back for home. In the danger zone, the men slept in their clothes and wore life vests at all times, and the soldiers joined the sailors in their watch for submarines. No one was allowed to sleep belowdecks. On Christmas Eve, the weather turned cold and blustery, depressing all. Castles and two friends took their last bottle of Scotch and descended ladders to the engine room, where they drank it. Soon, the heat and oil smell made them feel sick, so they went up on deck, walked, and went to bed, feeling happier than they had earlier.[116] Christmas Day, a few sprigs of holly appeared in the officers' mess, and all ate turkey and cranberries. That night, the *Pocahontas* ignored an SOS from a ship torpedoed forty miles south of them, reminding all of the possible fate that awaited them if they encountered a submarine. On December 31, "they sighted the French coast and by noon were lying safely in harbor."[117]

On January 1, Fish sent a "Dear Franklin" letter to Assistant Secretary of the Navy Franklin D. Roosevelt. He advised Roosevelt in confidence to "remedy a condition which in the near future will endanger the lives of thousands of American soldiers and concerning the delay in disembarkation of troops in French Ports which are under our control." Fish continued, "It was a great surprise to all of us to find that our convoy was not protected by destroyers until two days from the French coast." He professed to have reliable information that American destroyers were protecting English grain ships even as American merchant vessels were entering ports unprotected.

He complained, legitimately, that the harbor facilities were "utterly inadequate," which compelled ships to wait for weeks to disembark troops and freight. The loss of time and of use of ships, though important, paled before the ill effects on the men, "on account of the lack of space to exercise and the closeness of the quarters." He noted that epidemics of scarlet fever, mumps, and pneumonia filled port hospitals with soldiers and sailors, as twenty-five to thirty ships waited to unload. The 15th had been on board ship since December 2, and other ships had been waiting even longer.[118]

At last, on their third attempt, the 15th New York had reached the shore of France. By this time, strains among the white officers of the Regiment had surfaced, as Lt. John Castles's diary indicated. Castles had begun his tenure with the 15th in admiration of Colonel Hayward. However, when the Regiment landed in France, Castles had nothing favorable to say about Hayward or the Regiment's executive officer, Lieutenant Colonel Pickering. Capt. Ham Fish's comments about besting the Regiment's majors in examinations also indicated the potential for dissatisfaction, if such ambitious younger officers as Castles and Fish judged their elder superior officers wanting in ability.

The soldiers often disappeared from the accounts of their officers, who were preoccupied with their own affairs. Thus, the soldiers' indiscipline prior to sailing comes as no surprise. Transferred from camp to camp as a result of incidents with white southerners and northerners alike, unable to pursue their training because of unstable circumstances, and living under worse conditions and with fewer outlets than their officers, the soldiers naturally sought relief from their plight. Castles lamented the lapses in discipline, but his diary revealed that the officers' preoccupations and their own declining morale left them little or no time or energy to pay attention to the men.

When it counted, however, the men of the 15th rose to the challenge. The rapid repair of the *Pocahontas* under difficult conditions demonstrated their mettle. The 15th New York Regiment survived the transatlantic voyage in better condition than units in surrounding ships, and it had reached the French shore just happy "to see land again" and ready "to kiss the earth" after "rocking like a drunken man" for the better part of fourteen days, according to Cpl. Horace Pippin. Yet, Pippin recalled France as "that terrible ground of sorrow" that "brought out all of the art in me." He returned from France unable to "forget suffering" and "sunset" and "with all of it in my mind" painted from it till the end of his life.[119]

Spartanburg's response to the arrival of the 15th had demonstrated white southerners' overt determination to resist any importation of so-called northern mores of "racial equality." Racial equality, however, existed nowhere in the United States—or anywhere else, for that matter. Racial discrimination in the North, as blatant and serious as it might have been, appeared to be "equality" from the perspective of the extreme inequality that white southerners imposed and enforced upon the black population. Sadly, the transformation in attitudes that *Colliers* reporter and propagandist William Slavens McNutt found in his observations of white southern soldiers who were "done talking against niggers" was nowhere evident in the experience of the 15th.[120]

Instead, white southerners had no qualms about exporting their blatant and vicious discriminatory attitudes north and abroad. Southern soldiers stationed in New Jersey and New York openly, violently, and with impunity displayed their prejudice against African American soldiers who came from those very states. The authorities made every effort to cater to the southerner's bigotry at the expense of the black soldiers.

Perhaps the North had won the Civil War, but the South had certainly won the peace. As a consequence, white southerners through their representatives in the civilian government and in the military and in their travels north continued to determine the treatment of African Americans far into the twentieth century. Nonetheless, racism and racists prevailed everywhere in America in 1917, and African American soldiers preparing to fight for their country had to contend with this reprehensible reality everywhere they went in the United States. Only in France could the men of the 15th hope to escape prejudice and bigotry. Instead of defamation, derogation, and discrimination, they would face death.

# 7

## "Over There"

### The 15th New York/369th Regiment in France:
### From the AEF to the French Army, January–April 1918

As of January 1918, the French military mission in Washington, DC, had serious reservations about the state of the US Army. The US War Department lacked direction, interservice coordination, and an efficient division of labor. The secretary of war lacked the permanent civilian bureaucracy and competent military officers necessary for the efficient operation of his office. The coexistence at the top of the army of the adjutant general, the chief administrative office of the US Army, and the chief of the General Staff, the agency responsible for wartime plans and preparations, diminished the power of the latter, confused prerogatives, and slowed military decision making. The General Staff lacked coordination, continuity, and liaison with its subordinate agencies, whereas duplication of effort and indecision reigned. Just when preparation of the armed services for industrial warfare demanded colossal effort, no civilian or military chief commanded the bureaucracy needed to coordinate the mobilization as in France and England. Even the War Council that Woodrow Wilson formed on December 20, 1917, consisted of service chiefs who, relieved of their functions, lacked responsibility.[1]

The 15th New York had left this bureaucratic muddle in Washington far behind when it arrived in France in early January 1918, only to find itself in the chaos of the American Expeditionary Forces's buildup overseas. The Regiment disembarked in a country ravaged by three and a half years of war. The trench lines of the western front ran like bloody and suppurating wounds across some 475 miles of northeastern France and Belgium. The German invasion of August 1914 had occupied the ten northeastern departments of

France, where much of French industry and mining lay. The war had stalemated and both sides had become bogged down since October 1914. The trenches stretched north from the Franco-German-Swiss border through the Vosges and then through the heavily fortified regions of Alsace and Lorraine. They curved northeast of the fortress city of Verdun on the Meuse River, site of the lengthy Franco-German battle of 1916, then through the dark Argonne Forest and on to the northwest, through the regions of Champagne and Picardy, the latter the site of the bloody British offensive against the Germans along the Somme River in 1916. The lines stretched on through northwestern France into Belgium, where repeated British and German struggles at places such as Ypres and Passchendaele claimed the youth of those countries in 1915, 1916, and 1917.

The millions of soldiers concentrated on a front of fewer than 500 miles eliminated the possibility of maneuver and flank attacks. Both sides, reduced to head-on attacks in this war of attrition, steadily increased their firepower: heavy artillery that fired shells of more than 6 inches in diameter; rapid-firing cannon, with which skilled crews could unleash more than twelve 3-inch rounds a minute at the enemy; howitzers, whose high-trajectory fire sent shells containing more explosive than cannon into enemy ranks; mortars both monstrous and small that lobbed canisters of high explosive or shrapnel so slowly that targeted troops could see them coming; and machine guns whose skilled gunners could rake enemy lines directly and even arc indirect fire over hills to strike targets on the other side.

Great battles that consumed hundreds of thousands of men for the seizure of inconsequential amounts of territory punctuated a struggle in which thousands died daily. The key to success in offense and defense was the coordination of artillery and infantry and the incorporation of new weapons—aircraft for observation, bombing, and strafing and tanks to support infantry attacks—in a war of combined arms. After targeted artillery barrages of enemy lines, infantry troops followed directly behind the advancing shells of a moving barrage, reaching as far as possible toward enemy lines. They attacked in rushes, seeking cover where possible on cratered battlefields so that the men could provide covering fire for their comrades as they advanced toward enemy trench systems. The systems of defense in depth meant that the penetration of the first, usually sparsely held trench line was merely the prelude to a struggle to punch farther into heavily defended lines from which the enemy could launch counterattacks while shelling the enemy troops in their own lines. Between the great battles and on so-called quiet sectors of the front, bloody encounters in trench raids—where men clashed hand to hand with gun and blade, no quarter asked and none given, in a no-man's-land or in the confines of trenches—claimed their victims nightly.

Millions of men had fallen and millions more were maimed for life on the western front. By 1918, all the combatants were nearing exhaustion. Their populations, mobilized to continue this "total war," were reaching the end of their manpower and material resources. Compensating for having the smallest population of the western front powers, the French army already included elite North African colonial divisions in its ranks on the front at the outbreak of war. In 1915 and 1916, the army proceeded to draw upon increasing numbers of sub-Saharan or black African soldiers (*Tirailleurs Sénégalais*), as Gen. Charles Mangin had suggested in his prewar book entitled *La Force Noire* (1910).

Now, the American Expeditionary Forces offered new grist—the lives of American youth—for the blood mill of the western front. The prospect of an American army prompted the German High Command to prepare an offensive for March 1918 in an attempt to win the war before the United States could bring the weight of its manpower to bear. Everyone anticipated the great German offensive; the only questions that remained involved where, when, and whether the Allies could withstand the onslaught.

The 15th New York National Guard landed in Brest, France, on New Year's Day 1918, the climactic year of the Great War. The Regiment disembarked before a crowd of French soldiers and sailors, and the band immediately began to play the French national anthem, "The Marsellaise." French onlookers were accustomed to hearing their anthem played like a hymn, not in the rhythm and spirit that Jim Europe had arranged, but when the French recognized the music, it pleased and thrilled them.[2] Pvt. Horace Pippin recalled how happy the men were to "put foot on land" again; he wanted to kiss the earth "of that terrible ground of sorrow." As the Old 15th New York Infantry trod the troubled ground of France, Pippin observed that the French—the elderly, women, and children, since all the younger men were either dead or in uniform—were all glad to see them.[3]

The 15th departed at 10:30 A.M. by train from Brest, heading for St. Nazaire. The men squeezed into little French freight cars designed to transport either eight horses or forty men, thus their name *quarante/huit* (40/8). Trying to find sufficient space for themselves and their packs, the men asked jokingly, "Where in the hell are they going to put eight horses?"[4] Lacking sufficient room to lie down during the night, the men also endured the numbing cold, which easily penetrated their army overcoats. "We may as well have been on top of the car," Pippin lamented, and a number of men suffered frostbite.[5] When the Regiment arrived early the next morning at

St. Nazaire, some 2,000 nearly frozen men marched to their large camp 2 miles outside the city.[6]

The men's barracks consisted of flimsy shacks without floors, uncomfortable and inadequate quarters in any weather. The AEF command had assigned the 15th to duty as laborers to build a huge supply base at Montoir, 8 miles away. At 6:45 A.M., trucks arrived to take them to Montoir, and the men, armed with picks and shovels and wearing hip-length rubber boots, set about their work "enthusiastically."[7] Ham Fish wrote his father that they were building a dam, railroads, warehouses, and docks but added that they had no adequate provisions or fuel against the bitter cold of the first two weeks; the men's barracks were "not even rain proof."[8] The Regiment worked long days in the mud clearing a huge swamp, and the base hospital soon filled with soldiers felled by the mumps and influenza. Pippin recorded that some of the soldiers died of Spanish flu in the cold, rain, and wind of St. Nazaire, as they laid some 500 miles of track so that the United States could speedily unload cargo ships. During the short days of winter, the men rose in the dark, went to work to the light of the moon, and went to bed in the dark.[9] To maintain a spit-and-polish appearance, older officers offered prizes for the most snappily turned-out soldiers in their units, but maintaining a military appearance would become increasingly difficult if they were relegated to such duties for a long time.[10]

Capt. Napoleon B. Marshall commanded 400 men constructing the bed of a 3-mile-long railroad from the American debarkation docks to the American army storehouse at Montoir. During the transatlantic voyage, Marshall had requested release from his duties as judge advocate because he believed that the men needed a "defender rather than a prosecutor."[11] Other than Fish and Marshall, the officers seemed little concerned about the plight of the men and led quite comfortable lives. Fish spent the time reading and studying French and military tactics. He even secured a twenty-four-hour pass to visit some of the sights of the region and to dine at a world-class restaurant. Fish also served as president of the special court (that is, the court-martial) for two cases. Castles sat on the court for three weeks but found it "not much to my taste."[12]

On January 11, 1st Lt. Lewis E. Shaw noted that the officers lived comfortably and ate well, although the climate was "beastly." The only indications he saw of the "fearful struggle" consisted of German prisoners working around the camp who seemed "well satisfied with their lot" (in other words, happy to have their personal war over), a "great number of young widows," the "restrained and sombre attitude of everyone," and a peasantry that seemed "dazed by it all." He lamented that the French "certainly didn't bathe much" and that a public bath he had visited amounted to "an outhouse disguised as a bath," but he had heard that these circumstances were "a universal continental custom." As a universal alibi for all conditions the French offered, "C'est la guerre!" Shaw did plan "to take French lessons regularly in the evening from some attractive widow," ostensibly to improve his language skills.[13]

Officers had orderlies to care for them and prepare their meals and uniforms. They consequently had "a considerable amount of freedom" and lunched or dined in town three or four times a week. Castles "boss[ed] his gang" and studied French. For lunch, he would dine at the hotel in Montoir village, and in the evening, the officers would go to St. Nazaire for drinks and dinner. Castles and friends also took several trips to Nantes, where they "dined and wined extraordinarily well." Only after the Regiment had been in France for four months would any enlisted man receive a week's leave, but the officers easily obtained passes to go off base.[14]

Fish noted that his relations with Colonel Hayward remained pleasant "at present" and that he would wait before attempting a transfer. He predicted that neither Maj. Lorillard Spencer nor Maj. Monson Morris would ever reach the firing line, "as they are not qualified to take command of a Battalion in action at least that is the opinion of nearly all of our officers." At the time, Spencer was suffering from measles and bronchitis, leaving Fish in charge of the battalion.[15] The junior officers in the Regiment clearly lacked respect for the abilities of their superiors and were champing at the bit for a chance at command.

The commissioned officers endured a few onerous duties and regulations. They censored the letters their men sent home, a task they considered initially entertaining and then merely time-consuming. Two company officers read their 200 men's weekly output of some 400 letters, each about four pages long and written in pencil. Captain Little summarized one regulation that they had received at Brest in the following manner: "Officers are not permitted to be seen in public with women of bad reputation; and a woman of bad reputation, for the purposes of this order, will be considered to be, any woman who may be seen in public with an officer."[16] No women could enter the barracks of the camp at St. Nazaire. Consequently, distinguished female visitors from the United States stayed in the YMCA hut away from the camp, and French laundresses had to stand out in the wind, rain, and mud when they delivered the Regiment's clean clothing.[17]

An occasional death punctured this depressing and dull atmosphere. Bystanders along the road to the cemetery, including German prisoners in work gangs, all doffed their hats as the hearses passed. Fish described the typical funeral as "imposing," with the 15th's band playing and squads firing volleys into the air. At least in the rear area, the men had time to give their dead a decent burial.[18]

St. Nazaire rapidly wore thin with the 15th. Castles wrote, "After three or four weeks, St. Nazaire began to be very boring, and we began to lose patience. Ditto the men, who hated the labor work." After five weeks, he remarked on the officers' great discontent, the incompetence of some of his superiors and the resulting lack of discipline and organization in some companies, and Colonel Hayward's "utter disregard" for his officers' feelings and regimental affairs.[19]

In the third week in February, three companies of the 15th, including Castles's, traveled by train to work at the French base at Coëtquidan until March 12. The officers incurred only light duties. On base, they ate in the French officers' club, which offered them "all the liquor we wanted." Evenings were often spent wining and dining at a small restaurant run by two attractive French women, where the port, wine, and champagne flowed freely.[20] Castles never mentioned the men of the Regiment, who were left to live and work in atrocious conditions while the officers indulged themselves.

All the officers of the 15th worried that the war might end before they saw combat. In February, they speculated that the fighting would last from three months to three years longer. The French expected a major German offensive, but Capt. Ham Fish calculated that the Germans would "settle their eastern affairs"—finish the war on the eastern front against Russia—"before turning their attention to France." Although Hayward believed that the war would end by July 1, Fish hoped not, as the men of his unit wanted "a chance to show their prowess" and were "anxiously awaiting orders to go to training camp."[21] Fish would prove correct, as the Germans dictated a peace with the revolutionary Bolshevik regime in Russia and sent all divisions not needed to keep order in the east to bolster their forces for the attack on the western front that was planned for March.[22] The Regiment would have ample opportunity to prove its prowess.

Castles's perceptions of Hayward's "utter disregard" to the contrary, the colonel was preoccupied with getting his Regiment away from St. Nazaire and to the front. On February 1, Colonel Hayward wrote to the AEF commander, General Pershing, observing that the 15th had arrived in France as combat troops and desired to serve as originally intended. Hayward noted their accomplishments and emphasized, at Captain Little's suggestion, that the 15th Regiment had not experienced a case of venereal disease in three months. A venereal disease–free record was truly phenomenal, as St.

Nazaire's base commander, General Walsh, observed when he forwarded the letter to Pershing.[23]

From the start, the US Army command had railed against the perils of venereal disease and shut down red-light districts close to military bases in the United States. General Pershing, who enjoyed the attentions of a French mistress, vowed to keep the AEF free of venereal disease. Sixty percent of the orders the 15th received from AEF Headquarters concerned this subject.[24] Little, a magazine publisher and a pioneering crusader for sex hygiene, had insisted on strict enforcement of prophylactic treatment in the 15th starting in August 1917, and his efforts had paid dividends.[25]

Hayward and the Regiment did not know that at the level of the American and French High Commands, the 15th had been the subject of discussions between Pershing and Gen. Philippe Pétain since its arrival in France in early January. In fact, two sets of negotiations occurred, with Pershing at the center of both—the first between the French and American Allies, the second within the US Army between Pershing and the army chief of staff in Washington. The discussions internal to the US Army, which both preceded and followed Pershing's negotiations with Pétain, indicate substantial confusion, ambivalence, and disagreement existed regarding the use of African American troops in France.

Following US War Department orders of November 1917, the organization of a "Provisional Division (Colored)" had begun in December 1917. "National Guard Infantry (Colored)" from Connecticut, the District of Columbia, Illinois, Maryland, Massachusetts, New York, Ohio, and Tennessee, as well as South Carolina draftees, would form the nucleus of the division. On December 15, 1917, at Camp Stuart in Newport News, Virginia, Brig. Gen. Roy S. Hoffman assumed command of the division, whose infantry regiments were scattered all over the eastern and north-central states.[26]

Prior to the Franco-American negotiations concerning "colored soldiers," memoranda between Pershing and the chief of staff in Washington indicated that they planned to use the 15th New York, the 8th Illinois, and the two additional black regiments (the 371st and 372nd) as "infantry pioneers," not as combat soldiers but as supply troops and laborers building lines of communication. As late as January 5, the 15th New York, deemed to be only at two-thirds strength, would consequently serve behind the lines as pioneers or engineers.[27]

On January 6, Pershing offered the four regiments of the Provisional Division (Colored), now designated the 93rd Division (Provisional), for attachment to French divisions for an undetermined time for training and service. Pershing refused a definitive allocation of white American units to French divisions. On January 11, the French army's commander on the western front, General Pétain, willingly accepted the black regiments and offered to welcome any other units that Pershing could spare.[28]

Pétain requested information from Pershing on the value of the black troops two days later. In response, Pershing guaranteed the quality of two of the regiments—the 15th New York and the 8th Illinois—as both, he claimed, had served on the Mexican border, although they now incorporated a large proportion of recruits. He volunteered that the great majority of the regiments' officers were white and the noncommissioned officers black. Pershing's assertions diverged from actual conditions to varying degrees in a seemingly deliberate attempt to make the units more attractive to the French. Very few, if any, men of the 15th New York had served on the Mexican border, and the 8th Illinois maintained an entirely black commissioned officer corps. Pershing allowed that he had no precise information on the other two regiments.[29] On January 15, 1918, he verified to the chief of the French mission at the American HQ that Pétain had accepted the offer of two brigades of colored infantry.[30]

On January 11, Pétain had accepted the US Army's offer of the 185th Brigade, composed of the 369th (15th New York) and the 370th (8th Illinois) Regiments, as well as the future designated 186th Brigade of the 371st and 372nd Regiments. They learned that the 369th, then serving at St. Nazaire as labor troops, comprised 46 officers and 1,818 men and lacked two companies. The other three regiments would contain a full complement of 95 officers and 3,604 men when they arrived. Pershing's staff could not inform the French about the racial identity of the superior officers of the future regiments; all that was known was that the AEF had planned to use them as pioneer troops in a black division and would send them to the French as soon as possible. The French army agreed to supply them with French rifles and equipment.[31]

The US Army assigned numbers in the 300s to regiments of draftees. The AEF renumbered the African American National Guard volunteer regiments, the 15th New York and the 8th Illinois, as the 369th and the 370th US Infantry Regiments, respectively, to form the 185th Brigade. In the 186th Brigade, made up of the 371st and 372nd Regiments, the first regiment comprised draftees from the South, primarily North and South Carolina; the second comprised a variety of smaller black National Guard units from various states—battalions from Ohio and the District of Columbia and companies from Massachusetts, Connecticut, and Maryland. Brigaded together, the two formed the 93rd Division (Provisional).[32]

The 371st and 372nd Regiments would serve together in the French 157th Division, but the 369th and 370th served with different French divisions. The 93rd Division (Provisional) remained an artificial construct, never to be fully organized or to serve "assembled in one body."[33] The original officers and soldiers of the 15th/369th would continue to refer to the Regiment as the 15th during and after the war. Because they were volunteers, they resented the US Army's demeaning of their status to that of a draftee regiment simply to fit it into a division that existed only on paper. In fact, the men of the 15th New York would learn of their new designation only months later, much to their surprise, when the first French officers they met in March referred to them as the *trois cent soixante-neuvième,* or the 369th.[34] On January 22, the French military mission informed French General Headquarters that the 369th was at its disposal. The military mission anticipated that the other black regiments would arrive by late March, and it had requested two replacement regiments from the AEF to complete the ranks of and provide replacements for the two black brigades.

The assignment of the 93rd Division (Provisional) to the French army occasioned an illuminating exchange of cables between the AEF commander in chief, Pershing, and Maj. Gen. John Biddle, the army's acting chief of staff in Washington. On January 26, Pershing cabled Biddle that he required "two negro replacement regiments" for the 369th through 372nd Regiments in order "to conform to adopted plan of having replacements in France equal to 50 percent of the combatant forces." If possible, he wanted these two additional regiments shipped at the same time as the remaining black regiments.[35] Biddle answered Pershing on February 2, stating that the four regiments were National Guard regiments, "not part of any real division," and that "it is understood you are to use them as line of communication and not combatant troops."[36] Despite Pershing's clear intent to assign these regiments to the French army for combat, Biddle still maintained that the regiments of the 93rd Provisional Division were destined for labor duties, not combat.

On February 11, Pershing advised Biddle that the "confusion" and "misunderstanding" in Washington about "the employment for Negro regiments" must have stemmed from the "confidential character [of] preceding cables." He informed Biddle, "These regiments are not to be used as labor troops but to be placed at disposition of French for combat service in French divisions. This utilization of these regiments already approved by War Department." He insisted on the importance and necessity of the replacement regiments to keep such combat units up to strength. He queried "if it was now understood and [whether] these replacements [would] be sent" and desired "definite information" on their shipping.[37]

A recalcitrant Biddle answered Pershing on February 16: "Still considered undesirable to organize two new negro regiments here." He proposed to ship two regiments of the black 92nd Division for replacements and later, when the 92nd had arrived, to use the 369th through 372nd Regiments as replacements for the 92nd Division.[38] On February 21, Pershing pointed out that regiments "trained and accustomed to work in French divisions" could not have other regiments substitute for them. Furthermore, the French were pressing him for information on the arrival in France of the 370th through 372nd Regiments.[39] Biddle informed Pershing three days later, on February 24, that the 370th, 371st, and 372nd Regiments and one brigade (two regiments) of the 92nd Division would sail for France between March 10 and April 1. Yet, Biddle, believing that the French had only temporary use of black regiments, still thought that the 369th through 372nd Regiments would serve as replacements for the 92nd Division of African American soldiers when it arrived.[40]

This last letter from Biddle indicated the continued misunderstanding between the AEF commander in France and the acting chief of staff in Washington. Biddle initially understood that the black troops would not see combat, a belief consonant with the 15th's actual labor duties at the time and with the AEF's original intent to assign it to such duties permanently. He clearly had great difficulty comprehending the agreement Pershing and Pétain had struck for the black troops to serve as combat soldiers in French divisions.

The 15th New York Infantry would owe its service at the front to French leaders' insistence that the Americans provide them with some troops that they could train for combat. Pershing reluctantly (and only provisionally) released black troops for service with the French, out of the political and personal necessity to mollify French commander Pétain. Had the 15th suffered the misfortune of remaining within the AEF, it would have found itself relegated to labor and supply duties, despite the assurances of Secretary of War Newton Baker to African American notables that their soldiers would see combat.

Just as Biddle was proving to be a hindrance, Secretary of War Baker replaced him with Maj. Gen. Peyton Conway March. Biddle had become acting chief of staff upon Gen. Tasker Bliss's retirement on December 31, 1917. Yet, *before* Bliss retired, Secretary Baker had asked for General March—a ruthless, abrasive, but highly efficient artillery officer who had become Pershing's chief of artillery for the AEF—to return to the War Department as army chief of staff, replacing Bliss. Although March preferred to remain in France, on January 26 Baker insisted to Pershing that he required March's services. General March arrived in Washington to assume the duties of acting chief of staff on March 4, 1918.[41]

When he arrived, he found the War Department deserted in the evening, as no one worked past 5:00, and there were piles of unopened mail sacks. March was in his element, and with the full support of Secretary of War Baker, he set out to streamline the General Staff and reorganize it according to principles followed by the major armies of the world.[42]

When Pershing next wrote to Washington, on March 7, Peyton March answered promptly. Pershing noted that "under approved arrangements with [the] French," the 369th through 372nd Regiments would serve as combat units with French divisions and that the three regiments coming from the United States needed to be brought to combat strength before shipping and maintained at that level. He consequently requested 1,800 men immediately as "exceptional replacements" to raise the 369th Regiment, which had only 1,650 men, to full strength. He further requested automatic replacements for Negro infantry at the rate of 6 percent monthly.[43]

Since American regiments greatly exceeded the size of their French counterparts, Pershing would arrange for the French to place some 50 percent of a full-strength regiment in depot as replacements. This initial reserve and monthly replacements would maintain the black regiments at a manpower level appropriate to French needs. He consequently instructed the General Staff to ignore his previous request for two additional Negro regiments as replacements, since he considered it preferable to deem these regiments combat units and not replacements for the 92nd Division.[44]

March replied within the week that the three regiments, the 370th, 371st, and 372nd, were almost ready to sail. Although their strength varied from 2,500 to 3,500 men, he thought it wiser to send them at once and complete them later with replacements, as filling their ranks prior to sailing would cause delays. March assured Pershing that 1,800 "exceptional replacements" for the 369th would sail early in April, and the 6 percent automatic replacements would begin to arrive late in April. Pershing agreed with March on all points and approved his plan on March 16.[45] The exchange between Pershing and March concerning the size of the regiments indicates that the AEF had raised regimental war strength from the 2,000 men deemed appropriate in 1916–1917 to some 3,600 soldiers. This increase and the need for 50 percent ready replacements reflected realistically the manpower that was required for a regiment to absorb the high casualty rates and continue to function effectively on the western front. When Pershing insisted that the four regiments were not to be available for labor and were not to be confused with any pioneer regiments, March assured him that he would follow Pershing's wishes "as nearly as practicable" and that he would manage future phases of shipment better.[46] By late March, Pershing and General March had settled the status of the 369th Regiment and the other three regiments of the 93rd Division as combat units assigned to French divisions.

Yet, the arrival of a general and staff "as [an] advanced party of provisional 93d Division" at Pershing's headquarters, on March 4 and 12, 1918, respectively, surprised the AEF commander. He wrote March, "This is first information furnished us that those 4 negro regiments are organized as a division."[47] March advised Pershing four days later that the 93rd was a "provisional division for administrative purposes, consisting of Generals Hoffman, Harries, and Blanding, and staffs, and four infantry regiments. No other organizations to be assigned."[48] The three superfluous generals and their staffs thus commanded an administrative unit without a division.

Brigadier General Hoffman, whom Pershing ordered to Bar-sur-Seine to await the arrival of future regiments and assembly of the division, would wait in vain. As the regiments of black soldiers arrived, they went to the French army to be brigaded with French units, although Hoffman claimed that he "continued to exercise, in part, an administrative control." He anticipated that the AEF would soon obtain the release of the 93rd Division for assembly and "American training under its original commander and staff." He remained in denial as late as 1920, when he reported that the "division was never re-assembled, neither were orders disbanding" it "ever published." First, something never assembled could not be "re-assembled." In the end, even he admitted that "excepting headquarters, the history of this division in the A.E.F., therefore, resolves itself into the histories of the four regiments composing it."[49]

While Pershing went back and forth with Washington about the deployment and organization of the 93rd Division (Provisional), the French increased the pressure on him for the immediate attachment of the 15th/369th, the only black combat troops in France. On February 9, French headquarters had requested that the 369th move from St. Nazaire for assignment with the French army as quickly as possible. On February 11, Pershing's AEF chief of staff, Gen. James Harbord, explained to the chief of the French mission that the Americans had not understood the French desired the 369th immediately and that the AEF was using the regiment for labor to complete work of importance to both the French and the Americans. He suggested postponing the transfer of the 369th until the other three black regiments arrived, when the US Army would transfer them all at the same time. If the French insisted, the AEF would send the 369th immediately, but Harbord considered their services as labor troops of more value to the Allied cause than their assignment to the French in an incomplete state—ten companies of 1,818 men instead of twelve companies of 3,652 men.[50]

The French chief of staff answered the next day, insisting on obtaining the 369th as soon as possible. The Regiment did need to be complete, and on February 15, he inquired how the AEF planned to complete the 369th without further delay. AEF Headquarters replied that it had requested two replacement regiments to supplement the four colored regiments but had no information on them.[51]

On February 25, French headquarters assigned the 369th Regiment to the 8th Army Corps of the 4th Army. On March 4, AEF Headquarters informed the French that it would send the 369th anywhere they desired. The AEF planned to take the Regiment's weapons and personal equipment, since the French were willing to equip the Negro regiments. French headquarters suggested the 369th should keep its equipment other than rifles and bayonets, but the AEF insisted that the French should completely equip the black troops.[52]

By mid-March, the AEF informed the French verbally that the 370th, 371st, and 372nd Regiments would arrive by mid-April and that the US War Department would ship 1,800 additional Negro infantry to complete the 369th in April. The AEF promised an automatic replacement rate of 6 percent of the total complement of the four regiments, beginning in April. On April 1, the 369th received 419 additional soldiers.[53]

The French initially planned to station the black regiments south of Troyes, with their depot at St. Florentin on the right bank of the Armancon River. There, at the border of the French Zone of the Armies, they would be close to French training battalions and the American lines of communication. French General Headquarters (GQG, or Grand Quartier Général) planned to place the US general inspector of black troops and his French counterpart, the French inspector general, far away from the depot for black soldiers, so that the American officer would not be able to intrude on their organization and training.[54]

Pershing's very offer of the 369th Regiment and the three future regiments of the 93rd Provisional Division to the French proved highly significant. The British and French governments had been pressing the US government to assign American divisions to their armies for training and combat, in order to get them into combat as quickly as possible. Pershing, Secretary of War Newton Baker, and President Woodrow Wilson refused. They were determined to form an independent US Army or American expeditionary force and not squander their forces in the service of their Allies. American politicians, generals, and the public would not appreciate such permanent subordination to their European partners. Political reasons in particular dictated the formation of an American army—it would provide Wilson the necessary instrument to influence the course of future peace negotiations.

Pershing had essentially placated the Allied demands for American soldiers with the offer of the 93rd Division to the French. He would later offer the British the temporary services of the 92nd Division, but the British War Office "strongly" opposed "the attachment of any battalions of colored infantry for training," for the British would not even allow any "aboriginal" soldiers from their empire to serve in Europe except as laborers. Pershing informed the British foreign secretary that he could not "discriminate" against these black "American citizens" and hoped that he could overcome the objections of the British army.[55] In the British War Office, Pershing had discovered a source of prejudice against black people that enabled him, despite the bigotry of the American army, to seize the so-called moral high ground by refusing to discriminate against black citizen-soldiers. The British War Office never relented in its opposition to the use of African American combat troops, although the exigencies of war and pressure from black British subjects in the United States and the West Indies forced British authorities to accept their own black subjects into "combatant or other units of the British Army" on March 13, 1918. Referred to in official documents as "wooly headed niggers," refused posting to "white units," and relegated to "native units," Britain's black subjects now prepared to integrate existing units of the British military.[56]

The French harbored no such reservations because of their positive experience with North African soldiers as assault regiments on the western front starting in 1914 and their increasing use of sub-Saharan African troops in the same role starting in 1916. Pershing offered neither France nor Britain white American soldiers, although he would allow the 1st Division to bolster the British front at Cantigny during the great German offensive in late March and later detach the 27th and 30th Divisions for service with the British. The first African American soldiers of the US Army to see combat would consequently serve with the French army.

Colonel Hayward mistakenly believed that he had an "ace-in-the-hole" in his negotiations to get the 15th to the front, in the form of the regimental band. The AEF command did not want white American soldiers to spend their one-week leaves in the fleshpots of the great French cities, so it commissioned the YMCA to establish rest camps for soldiers on leave in small cities and towns. Most black soldiers would enjoy no such privilege until

December 1, 1918, after the signing of the Armistice. Winthrop Ames and Edward H. Sothern, the men in charge of organizing entertainment for the first camp, located at the resort town of Aix-les-Bains, had heard the 15th's band play at St. Nazaire. Ames declared, "It became obvious that we were not listening to the ordinary army band at all, but to an organization of the very highest quality, trained and led by a conductor of genius." Upon further inquiry, they were surprised to learn that James Reese Europe, "already famous in America," was now a soldier in France.[57] They immediately contacted General Pershing to have the band sent to Aix to open the rest camp. Hayward concurred with the request for the band's services because he believed in its potential value in securing their release from labor camp. Hayward in turn urged General Walsh to request personally that AEF Headquarters assign Lieutenant Europe, who was a machine-gun company officer, as band director, with Captain Little in overall command.[58]

On February 10, the Line of Communications Department, later renamed the Service of Supply (SOS), ordered the band of the 15th New York Infantry and a detachment of its Headquarters Company to report to the newly opened rest station for American troops at Aix-les-Bains by February 15. It would play at Aix for two weeks, until March 2. Lieutenant Europe and Captain Little traveled first-class on the train; the men traveled in specially reserved third-class coaches.[59]

The detachment stopped overnight at Nantes, where the band first played several pieces in the city plaza to an enthusiastic French audience. Then, in honor of Lincoln's birthday, it performed in a concert for a French charity at the Opera House to galleries packed with spectators in evening dress and to a full house as the doors opened to the public for general admission. After playing a French march, overtures and vocal selections by K Company's quartet, then John Philip Sousa's march "Stars and Stripes Forever" and southern or "plantation" melodies, the band's musicians concluded the performance with a mighty crash of cymbals, then relaxed, their eyes half closed, and launched into "The Memphis Blues." The syncopated rhythm proved infectious. The trombones had a "jazz spasm," and the audience caught the "jazz germ" and began to move to the beat along with the band. Musician Noble Sissle observed, "Colonel Hayward has brought his band over here and started ragtimitis in France."[60] The smiling faces and roaring laughter of the audience members documented their appreciation of this "new" music.[61] The concert brought down the house.

The next day, February 13, after playing a concert in the public square when the train stopped at Angers, the band members waited at Tours from 6:00 P.M. until the southbound express was scheduled to arrive at 3:18 A.M. to continue their journey south. A lieutenant colonel, the American assistant provost marshal (APM) or second in command of the military police, while stamping Little's orders, queried if the band with him was a good one. Little replied that it was the best in the army and offered to play a "surprise serenade" for the commanding general, Maj. Gen. Francis Kernan.

The APM agreed but warned Little that some of his young officers had returned from St. Nazaire two weeks before with reports of a "colored band" that was the "real thing in bands." The lieutenant colonel recalled that the leader, "a chap by the name of Europe," used to play dance music in New York for the famous dance team of Vernon and Irene Castle "when they were all the rage." When he asked Little if he had ever heard of the band, Little informed him that that was the very band in his barracks.[62] The surprise serenade, held at the general's headquarters in a chateau on a hill outside the city, so impressed Kernan that he complimented the band, predicted their tour would be a great success, and observed that they were not merely American musicians and soldiers but also representatives of their race and of the American nation: "The eyes of France would be upon them; and through the eyes of France, the eyes of the world."[63]

After playing at ten stops, the band arrived at Aix-les-Bains on February 15 and that afternoon led a parade formally opening the camp for the rest and recreation of American troops, with the first 3,000 American soldiers on leave marching snappily behind. By February 26, the band had proved so popular that the commanding general of the SOS extended its visit at Aix to a month. The band members would be the only black soldiers ever permitted to visit the resort at Aix, as AEF HQ granted leaves to members of the 92nd Division to lesser resort towns in the region in late October.[64]

Winthrop Ames observed the band's effect on French civilians and American soldiers alike. The musicians' rendering of "The Marseillaise," the French national anthem, "fairly swept them off their feet," and Ames reported that "an old man near me cried out: 'Mais, Mon Dieu, c'est magnifique!'" When Europe's band opened its concert for the doughboys in the casino with "Over There," Ames recounted, "It excited those tired boys as I have rarely seen any body of men excited. They climbed on tables and chairs; they waved caps and chocolate cups, they shouted: they demanded that it be played again and again, and again. No other form of entertainment appealed to them quite so much."[65]

Many years later, Sissle explained the band's magical hold on its listeners, including European musicians. First, he remembered that the American soldiers "would have none of the staid music of the French and English bands and orchestras. They clamored for the St. Louis Blues, as only Jim

Europe's boys could play it." Equally fascinated were English and French musicians, who were "astounded" to find that "none of the complicated riffs and breaks" the men played could be found in the written music. According to Sissle, one of the musicians bought him a drink and asked, "Now I can see how one man can make one of those mistakes . . . but how do all the others seem to know just when he will make the mistake and how to make just the right mistakes themselves?" Sissle explained improvisation, the essence of jazz, as music played from the heart in which written notes were only signposts for musicians who "shut their eyes, wandered up and down the chord, in and out of minors, and let the music in their hearts flow out of their instruments in easy rhythm."[66]

Amid the overwhelmingly positive reception of the band, occasional comments from white American observers often commingled admiration with racist resentment. Marian Baldwin, a canteen worker in Aix, observed: "These niggers play in a way that would lead the worst slacker to battle. There are about thirty of them and of course since they have been here they have been the wonder and admiration of the townsfolk. . . . This adulation has caused these ridiculous niggers to put on the most screaming airs and graces," as symbolized by the "Major Domo (drum major) puffing out his chest and waving a magnificent decorated stick!" Yet what seemed to offend Baldwin most was the pretensions of the bandleader, James Reese Europe, who was "arrayed in shoulder straps and the silver bars of a First Lieutenant!"[67] She did not know that Europe had earned his stripes as a machine-gun company officer. Unfortunately, her perception of Europe as undeserving of the rank due him represented a widely shared sentiment that led to the identification of the Regiment with the band and hence as noncombatants.

At Aix, the band rehearsed in the morning in the casino theater, then played afternoon concerts either in the park or the casino and major evening concerts as part of a vaudeville show. Europe accepted all French requests to play music and spent his nights arranging their orchestration, as they invariably honored a family member who was either fighting at the front or deceased. The band also played several concerts at Chambéry, a city with mineral baths, a small casino, and a famous cathedral that was not far from Aix but nowhere near it in class, size, or facilities and activities. AEF HQ eventually made Chambéry the rest area available to black soldiers.[68]

At one concert in Chambéry at the orphan asylum, one chubby child emulated bandmaster Europe's every motion. Europe gave the child his baton, brought him in front of the band (which he instructed to play a simple tune), and then walked over to Little. As the young French orphan led the band, the crowd "went crazy." Little, moved by the bandleader's "big-hearted" gesture, was convinced that with Jim Europe and his band as ambassadors, the Entente Cordiale between France and the United States was safe.[69] Noble Sissle jested that reporters had written so much about the band that "editors wondered who was winning the war, Pershing or Europe."[70] The band, its jazzy rhythms, Europe's masterful diplomacy— the sheer exoticism of the total impression they made—certainly swept the French civilians off their feet.

On March 14, orders arrived for the band to rejoin the Regiment. Two nights later, when the YMCA official in charge of entertainment announced that the band was leaving for the front, the audience rose en masse and interrupted him with cheers and whistles, as women burst into tears and people tore down flags hanging from the balcony and waved them. Little noted, "On the stage, the colored soldiers who had been spat upon in Spartanburg, rose and bowed and grinned."[71]

The mayor of Aix-les-Bains presented the band with a silver vase; the mayor of Chambéry gave a gilt laurel sheaf with streamers in the colors of France. The secretary of the YMCA thanked the band officially for its concerts on behalf of the American soldiers and for the citizens of Aix, which had "aided greatly in cementing the friendly relations between the two nationalities." The headquarters of the APM officially commended the band in its report of March 17, noting that "the conduct of the men of the Band has been of the very highest order and their work deserves high commendations."[72] On March 17, the band played its last afternoon concert, and that evening at 6:00, as Little and Europe struggled to complete the necessary champagne toasts and baby kisses, the band paraded to the station at Aix. The police escort proved totally ineffectual as the band marched through a throng of cheering and weeping elderly people, females, and children and played farewell as the train slowly departed.[73]

By the morning of the second day, the train entered the Marne region, where destroyed towns, ravaged countryside, and impromptu cemeteries filled with wooden crosses bore witness to the ferocity of the battles of 1914. Now, hospital trains of wounded and groaning soldiers passed by, the sights and sounds shocking the musicians. They continued on the overnight train to Givry-en-Argonne, near Verdun, where the 15th/369th had just begun its training for the front. [74] Sgt. Noble Sissle and half the band members, who were traveling in a different coach, awoke to find themselves not at Givry but near the front. They descended from the train to be greeted by German shellfire. Two days later, they rejoined the Regiment after their unexpected and frightening introduction to the front, the first members of the unit to experience enemy fire.[75] Now, all would prepare for their baptism of fire as a regiment on the western front.

The 369th US Infantry Regiment of the 93d Division, formerly the 15th New York National Guard, began its training with the French army in mid-March 1918. It wore the regimental insignia, as Capt. Napoleon Marshall noted, "of the Serpent: 'Don't Tread on Me.'"[76] From that insignia derived the soldiers' favorite nickname for themselves, "the Rattlers." They preferred the designation Old 15th and would refer to themselves either as the Old 15th or the Rattlers, never the 369th or some of the other sensationalist names (such as Hell Fighters) that others would later apply to them. The Regiment traveled northeast by rail through the valley of the Marne, scene of great battles in 1914, to the Argonne, where its troops lodged by battalion in three separate towns a few miles apart. Colonel Hayward and the rest of the 15th New York Regiment learned of their new designation as the US 369th Infantry Regiment only when, as noted earlier, the French staff officer meeting them upon their arrival greeted them as such.[77]

1st Lt. Lewis Shaw, who had now transferred from F Company to the machine-gun company, wrote to his mother on March 9 informing her of the Regiment's new numerical designation. Like many other officers, he had commissioned a watercolor portrait of himself by a "distinguished member of the French Academy" for $10, and he was sending the painting to her. He had survived a mild case of the mumps and was particularly pleased that his horse had arrived, since his new position entailed a mount. He further requested that "Dear Mumsie" send him cigars and have his Williams Club bills paid, a common concern among the graduates of the Ivy League and other elite northeastern schools.[78]

In a letter dated March 18, Hayward observed to Col. Reginald L. Foster, an old friend with the 27th Division, still in Spartanburg:

> There are no American troops anywhere near us, that I can find out, and we are "les enfants perdus," (the lost infants) and glad of it. Our great American general [Pershing] simply put the black orphan in a basket, set it on the doorstep of the French, pulled the bell, and went away. I said this to a French colonel with an "English spoken here" sign on him, and he said "Weelcome leetle black babbie."[79]

Hayward found the French "wonderful—wonderful—wonderful." He acknowledged that he would never get over his "disappointment and chagrin" about being excluded from the 27th Division, but he kept recalling the saying "And the stone which was rejected by the builder has become the corner stone of the temple."[80]

Although the AEF might have made the French custodians of the Regiment, it never relinquished visitation rights and the attendant potential interference. For a time, the Regiment even held on to the vain hope that it would become part of a 93rd Division. Hayward himself embraced the prospect and extended a cordial invitation to General Hoffman upon learning from a representative of the General Staff that the "commander" planned to visit.[81]

Every night, the troops could see the artillery flashes on the horizon and hear the distant thunder of the guns. Lt. John W. Castles of 3rd Battalion wrote his mother, "It takes this outfit to pull the unexpected & sensational, & once more we have done it." He complained about French cigarettes and the absence of chocolate but had no problem with the champagne and wine. He did request that she order him a new khaki uniform from Brooks Brothers and send it right away.[82] Captain Little observed that the men of 1st Battalion, "his boys," were itching for a fight and kept saying, "God damn, le[t']s go."[83] When the commander of the 1st Battalion, Maj. Edwin Dayton, transferred to another regiment, Capt. Arthur Little succeeded him as battalion commander on April 1 and served in that post for the duration of the war.

The men of the 369th exchanged their Springfield rifles with knife bayonet for French Lebel rifles with a long cruciform or rapier-like blade. The French often referred to *escrime à la baionette,* or fencing with the bayonet, and they meant exactly that. The men wore the American khaki uniform, the blue helmets of the French infantry, and French leather equipment. Although the future regiments of the 93rd Division wore the blue helmets of the French army, the 369th never fully accepted them. In fact, Col. H. B. Fiske, assistant chief of staff, AEF HQ, G-5, noted on March 18 that a "question has arisen as to helmets." "On account of morale and to distinguish" the men of the 369th "from French Colonial troops," Fiske considered "the American O.D. helmet desirable." Within a week, Col. W. D. Connor, assistant chief of staff, AEF, HQ, G-4, transmitted Pershing's order to the commanding general of the SOS "to take necessary action" to furnish American helmets to the 369th.[84] When the new headgear arrived cannot be determined precisely, but subsequent events indicate that the men wore olive drab helmets before and during the great offensive in September. The dispute over helmets notwithstanding, the 369th began training in camps in the towns of Herpont and Herpine in the French Advanced Zone of the Armies. Five French officers and interpreters joined regimental and battalion staffs; and five French sergeant or corporal drill instructors joined each company.[85]

On the way to Herpont, Horace Pippin actually greeted his first view of the trenches from earlier battles with ambivalence and some relief. They were not as bad as the worst rumors suggested, although life and work in them was wet and slow and the men went to bed wet, without fires to dry themselves and their clothes.[86] Pippin appreciated that Herpont, which he spelled "Hairpont," had once been a nicely laid out town, but now, he noted, few buildings remained standing and one could see through them. Old women and men greeted them with tears of joy. Pippin had never before seen a town in so much need. In 1916, German shells had wrecked the little homes so badly that the old people now used sheets and blankets to protect themselves from the cold. Pippin informed his "Dear Reder" that Americans did not know what cold was. His overcoat offered little protection, and the wind was so cold that it penetrated any clothing. "I felt for the old wimen and men," he concluded, "to think how they had to get along in that friendless and helpless town." In the next town, a church steeple and three houses remained standing, but the village itself was lifeless and uninhabited.[87]

General Le Gallais, commander of the French 16th Division, which incorporated the 369th, visited the day they arrived. At the end of his visit, Le Gallais asked whether he could count on the 369th if the German offensive, which began on March 21 against the British sector of the front, came toward his division in, say, four or five days (!). Hayward replied that the Regiment would do the best it could and that no man could do more. Le Gallais, satisfied, replied, "Bon!" Arthur Little recalled that as the French general and American colonel strode away, Dr. John Bradner, a lieutenant in the Medical Corps, cynically quipped that if the Germans came "piling through" that night, much less in four or five days, "the 369th could be counted upon—to spread the news—all—through—France."[88]

Hayward soon received a visit from Maj. Herman Harjes, a liaison officer on Pershing's staff and a wealthy banker in civilian life. Harjes reported that the 369th, shrouded in mystery, had become the talk of France. AEF HQ had received very complimentary reports about the Regiment. Now, Harjes could see for himself, and although what he reported is unknown, it likely confirmed earlier favorable assessments; harsh criticism would have benefited no one, least of all Pershing, had Harjes cast the consequences of the general's decision in an unfavorable light so soon.[89]

Lt. John Castles considered the 369th's assignment to the French "marvelous," for he "would much rather go in with the French than the Americans, as they are better trained, more experienced, and know trench warfare as the Americans cannot expect to for a long while. . . . We are only sixteen miles behind the lines now and hear the guns plainly. . . . We are the only Americans who have ever been in this sector and are quite curiosities." As African Americans, the troops of the Regiment undoubtedly intensified the curiosity of the French.

Castles and his good friend Lt. Comerford "Cub" McLaughlin secured comfortable billets in a farmhouse inhabited by a sixty-year-old French-woman with "a fine beard," along with her daughter, daughter-in-law, and grandson. Her son had been a prisoner of war in Germany for three years. The Germans had shelled the home, commandeered the livestock, and plunged the family into poverty, and the old woman, whom Castles found "the most perfect example of hatred incarnate" he had ever seen, cursed the "Boches" and wanted them "exterminated."[90]

Castles's dislike for Colonel Hayward increased. At regimental head-quarters in the presence of enlisted men, Hayward had launched into "the customary tirade," berating his officers and calling Capt. John Holley Clark "a boob." Castles remained concerned about the lack of discipline in the Regiment as a whole,[91] but he may have exaggerated the tirades, as Clark and Hayward became law partners after the war. In any event, Castles consequently found it a "relief" to leave for a "real 'military' atmosphere" when he became one of fourteen officers from the 369th who were de-tached to AEF 1st Corps officers training school at Gondrecourt. The offi-cers included Lieutenants McLoughlin and Shaw.[92]

Unfortunately, lectures, demonstrations, study, examinations, and in-spections at Gondrecourt smacked too much of college for Castles, the young lieutenant who had joined the army to escape law school. He rel-ished grenade throwing and target practice. The "theory," in his opinion, seemed always to degenerate into unfounded American and British criti-cism of the French army, and he considered 50 percent of his peers inade-quate. He therefore appreciated his return to the Regiment at the end of April, just in time to enter the trenches with his battalion.[93]

At the school, the officers invariably dined in the evening in French pen-sions—boardinghouses or small hotels—or with French families, and they enjoyed excellent food and "plenty of good French wine." Shaw found time to romance "the sweetest little French girl of eighteen" who was "a great comfort and pleasure" to him, particularly when "dear Mumsie" informed him that his friend Helen had taken up with another fellow.[94] Shaw, who was taking an advanced course in machine gunnery, likened the school experi-ence to "boarding school" with "strict discipline, inspections and lectures," and he was pleased with his progress in training. Shaw thought that within six months, he might return home as an instructor, since a few officers from each regiment secured such duty, and he believed that the 369th would "be detailed to train in turn the colored draft division" when it arrived.[95]

Shaw completed his advanced course in machine gunnery, placing third in a class where half of the students were majors and captains and half were first lieutenants. The use of machine guns for indirect and long-range fire, at which the Germans particularly excelled, meant that the guns operated like artillery. To hit targets out of sight on the reverse slopes of hills, machine gunners had to plot trajectories in the same manner as artillery gunners—hence, the difficult nature of the subject. Shaw also spent a week as an observer with French units on the relatively quiet front in Alsace.[96]

After seven weeks away from the 369th, he returned absolutely convinced that the unit would join "the colored division"—the 92nd—as instructors when it finally arrived. Shaw also found himself now in favor with Colonel Hayward, who disliked the "clubby third battalion" because its Ivy League junior officers, such as Castles and Fish, did not respect him. Shaw's transfer to Capt. John Clark's company in the 2nd Battalion and his excellent performance in that battalion and in officers' school had redeemed him in Hayward's eyes and made him a likely machine-gun company commander or attaché on the regimental staff.[97] Unlike Castles, Shaw returned unaware that the 369th was moving forward into the trenches.

On April 8, Ham Fish wrote his father of their preparations for the coming tour of duty in the trenches. He considered the 369th "the most envied regiment in France." As the only American regiment with the French army, the troops possessed the advantage of French training and experience. Fish stated proudly, "I am a great believer in the fighting quality of the educated American Negro, provided he is well led. If the regiment does not make a splendid record, it will be the fault of the officers." He ventured that if censorship were lifted, the 369th, the "American Foreign Legion of France," would become as famous as the Rough Riders in the Spanish-American War.[98]

On April 12, the French staff informed AEF Headquarters that the three battalions of the 369th had only one machine-gun company and noted that US regiments composed of only one machine-gun company for every twelve infantry companies sorely lacked the firepower necessary for the western front. Every French regiment had three machine-gun companies, so the French requested a machine-gun company for each battalion, or two more per regiment, from AEF Headquarters.[99] Later in April, AEF HQ declined the French officials' request and left them and the black regiments to their own devices.[100] By the time of the reply, the 369th had already reorganized like a French territorial regiment, with three battalions and three machine-gun companies totaling 68 officers and 2,498 men. On April 14, the French mission announced that the 185th Brigade, comprising the 369th and 370th Regiments, and the 186th Brigade, comprising the 371st and 372nd Regiments, formed the 93rd Provisional Division. The black units would have all French arms and equipment, as did the 369th. The AEF request that the units' training adhere as closely as possible to that of other American units caused the French mission no concern because the French were training the AEF.[101]

French battalion chief Bonnolte assessed that after a month of training, the 369th demonstrated "very satisfactory" performance,[102] under the tutelage of twenty-six instructors and seven interpreters. The men had learned the use of the rifle and bayonet: the names of the parts, assembly and disassembly, maintenance, functioning of the weapon, and carrying and firing it. They practiced handling and shooting their rifles, fencing and assault with the bayonet, and daily grenade throwing, as well as assembly and combat formations. The instructors departed at the end of March, leaving only interpreters, and American instructors trained by the French completed the training of specialists. Bonnolte had detached a captain instructor to coordinate efforts and perfect diverse formations in daily maneuvers, as the troops had made such rapid progress.[103]

The 369th, in Bonnolte's judgment, had displayed a good attitude when it approached the front to contact French line regiments on April 12. By that time, all the men had thrown live grenades without accident, and the specialists—machine gunners and grenadiers—had made "extraordinarily rapid" progress and begun firing their weapons. The grenadiers had undergone courses of grenade throwing from all positions. In technical training during the evening, they learned to use all types of French and German grenades, to fire grenade launchers, and to understand German military organization and combat maneuvers.[104]

Light machine gunners used the French Chauchat Model 1915 automatic rifle and spent mornings practicing physical exercises and the use of the weapon and evenings studying and practicing emplacement, firing, tactical offense and defense, and approach march and assault. The twenty-pound Chauchat, or "Sho-Sho" as the Americans referred to it, with its distinctive semicircular, or "half-moon," magazine of twenty 8-mm. Lebel rounds, developed an evil reputation among small-arms experts as a weapon plagued by poor manufacture, constant malfunction, and long recoil bolt action that impeded steady aim.[105] No record of complaints from gunners of the 369th exists, probably because the Chauchat was their first and only light automatic weapon and the gunners valued its firepower, regardless of its numerous imperfections.

Heavy machine gunners fired the Hotchkiss and spent their mornings learning the theory of the use of the gun, its assembly and disassembly, tactical use, flanking and surprise movement, and the limits of direct fire. In the afternoon, they executed firing exercises, practiced clearing blockages, and studied the use of different terrain and ideas of indirect fire. The Hotchkiss Model 1914 was the latest in the line of the French army's standard machine gun, first adopted in 1897. A gas-operated weapon, which relied on propellant gas to drive the mechanism rather than the barrel recoil of the Maxim and Browning machine gun, the Hotchkiss used a 250-round articulated belt of 3-round metallic strips linked together. The gas mechanism and the need to keep it from overheating gave the gun a distinctive appearance, with five large circular brass fins around the base of the barrel and a metal tube under the barrel that drove the gun's piston backwards. Although the 56-pound Hotchkiss was heavy compared to the German Maxim MG08 and MG08/15, at 31 pounds, and the British Vickers, at 40 pounds, it was reliable and found favor with its crews.[106]

The troops also trained in gas defense and in communications with telephone and telegraph. Capt. Napoleon Marshall, who commanded a machine-gun company, became the Regiment's first gas officer. In this position and accompanied by an orderly, he patrolled the forests close to the trenches to determine when to sound the gongs to alert the sleeping men to an imminent gas attack. He had to distinguish among gas shells, which made a wobbling sound as they spun on their axes traveling through the air, and solid shells that whistled. The gas officer had to judge carefully: too flighty judgments would keep the men awake all night, but failure would result in casualties and a court-martial for the officer. Every morning, the officer presided over gas instruction school for the noncommissioned officers, who often combed the forest for German shells and fragments with the different markings signifying different gases. They sent the shells to the division's Chemical Unit.[107] All units knew attack formations and bayonet assault, which they practiced with dummies in the morning. Bonnolte judged the overall results more than satisfactory.[108]

Certainly, one reason for the 369th's rapid progress lay in the fellowship that developed between the troops and the French at all levels, from commissioned and noncommissioned officers to men in the ranks. Noble Sissle observed that African American soldiers and French poilus "stroll[ed] down the road arm in arm, each hardly able to understand the other, as our boys' French was as bad as their English."[109]

Lewis Shaw commented, "Our boys are all very funny in their attempts to converse." Shaw's "faithful servitor" Ellis—every officer had a batman or servant to tend to his needs—could arrange or buy anything, including luxurious billets and breakfast in bed, until the Regiment disallowed such practices. Shaw could not understand how Ellis managed, as he used "words at random" and did not "bother about verbs," but when Ellis reported he had ordered "woofs" for Shaw for breakfast, "des oeufs" (or eggs) invariably appeared.[110] Soldiers from time immemorial have made themselves understood in foreign countries; the men of the 369th did the same.

Ham Fish observed that the men of the Regiment especially outshined the French at grenade throwing because of the baseball training that was common to all American soldiers. "Grenade throwing for distance, accuracy and speed," Fish explained, was "the war sport of France." Several of the men of the 369th could throw grenades 80 yards, 12 yards farther than the best French grenadiers.[111] Americans' penchant for boxing also helped them adjust quickly to the techniques of fighting with the rifle and bayonet. The 369th had trained hard for a month. Now, it would enter the trenches of the western front for its initiation to combat.

The AEF, which believed that most black men could not be combat soldiers, had initially intended to use the 15th/369th Regiment as either labor or pioneer troops: the former worked as the Regiment did for two months after landing at St. Nazaire, whereas the latter labored right behind the front lines and thus often under enemy fire. The great majority of African American soldiers—some 330,000 of 370,000 draftees—labored either in the United States or in the Services of Supply in France under the most atrocious and demeaning conditions in which they were harassed by their bosses (officers), white soldiers, and military police. Historian Chad Williams labeled the Regiment's initial "relegation to a glorified labor battalion" a "painful insult,"[112] especially for a unit of volunteers.

As previously mentioned, Hayward had erroneously believed the band to be his ace in the hole in the negotiations to send the 15th/369th to the front, but in fact, the French commander, Gen. Philippe Pétain, dealt the hand that determined the Regiment's fate. The Regiment had fortuitously arrived in France just as Pétain's request for combat soldiers from Pershing prompted the latter to give the French the only soldiers he was willing to spare—African Americans. Furthermore, there is no evidence to indicate that Pershing was responding to black pressure at home. Ironically, the band impressed the command of the future Services of Supply, the very organization the Regiment needed to escape in order to exchange its status as a labor unit for combat duty. Perhaps the Regiment's spotless record in terms of venereal disease impressed Pershing, but the bottom line was that

Pershing was already busy exaggerating the quality and composition of the Regiment to Pétain in order to assure its acceptance by the French.

Lieutenant Castles, for all his objections to Hayward's leadership, correctly acknowledged the advantages of training and entering the lines with the experienced French rather than the novice American army. In fact, the 15th's early departure from the States and its assignment to the French army rescued the men from initial training according to AEF commander Pershing's misguided emphasis on the rifle and bayonet and devaluation of heavier weapons such as machine guns, artillery, aircraft, and tanks. Historian Robert B. Bruce has condemned Pershing's approach as "hopelessly outdated and "completely unsuited" to the realities of the western front, where overwhelming firepower reigned supreme.[113] Hayward lamented that he would never get over his disappointment at the 27th Division's rejection of the 15th, but the 27th would not even arrive in France until May and would enter combat under British/Australian command in mid-August.[114]

The 15th/369th Regiment had experienced discrimination, denigration, and outright hostility at the hands of white American civilians and soldiers, but at least the black soldiers did enjoy the unequivocal support of their key officers, such as Hayward and Fish. Unlike white American soldiers, the French army instructors literally welcomed their African American trainees as comrades in arms, as French and African American soldiers walked about arm in arm, chatting animatedly in their own pidgin language. The regimental band may have aroused a sense of the exotic among French civilians, but to the pragmatic French army instructors, the soldiers were Americans, black Americans, to be trained for combat within their ranks. The trainees clearly excelled at their tasks.

In light of the desperate need for soldiers, one might ask whether the French rushed the 369th into combat based on their actual achievement or an underlying attitude that black Americans, like black Africans, would be ferocious and expendable warriors. Later, some of the 369th's officers would boast (and others complain) of what they viewed as the Regiment's short time in training. The French had taken a month to train the men—more time than they usually gave their own new regiments—to share the front with a French regiment. In comparison, the British took a month and a half to train two American divisions, the 27th and the 30th, to share trenches with their forces and two months for them to begin to move into the lines.[115] It was much easier to train and deploy a regiment than the much larger divisions, so to conclude that the French "rushed" the 369th to the front would be incorrect. Furthermore, as will become evident, the

French drew distinctions between the civilized urbanites of the 369th and their colonial soldiers from the sub-Saharan hinterland.

Like the French training detachment, American officers such as Hayward and Fish expected the black soldiers to succeed in combat. Fish's observation to his father that the fault would be the officers if the Regiment did not perform splendidly is scarcely imaginable coming from the mouths of other white commanders of black troops, as the experience of the 92nd Division amply demonstrated. In the States, its commanding general threatened the division with dissolution in case of racial problems, thereby devastating the morale of his soldiers. The commanders then assumed no responsibility for difficulties in combat, which they attributed to the race of their ill-trained black officers and men, and after the war, they further denigrated the performance of their black troops.[116]

Scholar Richard Slotkin has correctly labeled the Regiment's "transfer to the French" "a liberation rather than an exile."[117] Insulated from the direct impact of the racism of American society and the AEF and liberated from the demeaning travail of the SOS, the soldiers of the 369th Regiment were now free to shed their blood for the United States within the ranks of the French army on the western front.

# 8

## Trial by Fire

*In Combat with the French 16th Infantry Division,
Mid-April to June 1918*

On April 7, General Le Gallais, commander of the French 16th Division, informed his superior, the commanding general of the 8th Army Corps, of the following: "The 369th R.I.U.S.'s training is altogether very satisfactory. Starting on 9 April, one of this regiment's battalions will be permanently attached to one of our front-line reserve battalion's companies; they will later hold down a relatively calm sector, with our instructors along." He requested and received authorization to move the 369th forward toward the front.[1]

General Le Gallais also issued the following memorandum to the units of the 16th Division on the subject of the "369th R.I.U.S.'s Entry into Sector":

As the 369th R.I.U.S. comes to the front, the Commanding General of the 16th Inf. Div. wishes to bring the following points to the attention of the officers via their regimental commanders:

*I. Example.*

We officers and men must at all times set the example for American troops and especially for the 369th R.I.U.S., which is recruited among the blacks of New York.

The *example* of bravery under fire; of discipline, of dress—under fire or in camp, and this, in our twofold quality as French and white who have been at war for four years.

Let us not forget that the black American soldiers will have to fight with their eyes on our soldiers, and that the devotion, affection, and even respect of these brave men full of good will depend on our attitude.

*II. Delicacy of Sentiment.*

The Frenchman has a shortcoming; he is rebellious, mocking; we cannot hold our tongues and we must always find a nickname for those who serve us or lead us.

All the officers must convince their men that the blacks of the 369th are not unfortunate central African savages, but civilized men who live in one of the largest cities in the world, who are citizens of a country whose industrial enterprises of all kinds surpass all our conceptions.

It must not be forgotten that even though America entered the war to protect its own self-interest in preventing German world domination, it was guided above all by the very noble sentiment of high justice, affection for France, [and] contempt for the barbarity, bad faith and monstrous impudence of the Germans.

*III. Conclusion.*

Let us treat the men of the 369th as good comrades and facilitate their task. We will thus gain their affection, their respect, and let us not forget that we need American gold, steel, and blood to chase out the invader and regain our lost provinces.

The officers should communicate this memorandum to their men as soon as possible.

The Commanding General of the 16th I.D.

Le Gallais[2]

Le Gallais's communiqué to the officers of his division is instructive as an individual example of French views of the black American soldiers. He wanted his white French soldiers to secure "the devotion, affection, and even respect of these brave men full of good will" from New York. He emphasized that his officers had to convince their soldiers that the black soldiers of the 369th were civilized urbanites, not "unfortunate central African savages." He thus took pains to distinguish African Americans from sub-Saharan Africans, whom the French perceived as uncivilized inferiors, albeit supreme warriors, whom they brought from the colonies to fight for the France that had brought them "civilization." Ultimately, these black men were American citizens, and the French needed "American gold, steel, and blood" to drive out the Germans. Such admonitions clearly indicate that Le Gallais realized it was imperative the French not view their new charges as they viewed their African soldiers. His emphasis on the proper treatment of African American soldiers contrasts ironically with the increasing concerns of AEF HQ as the war continued that the French were treating their African American soldiers entirely too well for white America to tolerate.

On April 13, the 369th marched from its billets in Herpont and Herpine north to its new base, centered in the town of Maffrecourt. On the way, in the tiny town of Auwe, General Le Gallais and Colonel Hayward reviewed the troops as they marched by to the music of the band. Through interpreters, Le Gallais told the men of his joy at having them in his division and the great spirit they had injected into his depressed unit, in which, after four years of combat, few veterans of the first battle of the Marne and of the slaughter at Verdun remained. They and the men of the 369th were now equal on the battlefield, fighting for the Allied cause. Colonel Hayward in turn pledged General Le Gallais the undivided support of every soldier under his command, as no greater honor could have been extended to his Regiment than to become part of the great French army that had so bravely fought the terrible onslaughts of the kaiser's forces. The band played the "The Star Spangled Banner" and then "The Marseillaise."[3]

At the colonel's signal and to the notes of "The Stars and Stripes Forever," the band swung into line down the street and the 3rd Battalion shouldered arms. The command "Forward March" resonated through the ranks, and to the beat of drums and the blaring of horns, "the first detachment of American Negro soldiers started on their pilgrimage down into the perils of no-man's-land." Sissle recalled the death of Crispus Attucks,[4] which occurred at the beginning of the Revolutionary War, as well as the valiant charges of the 54 Massachusetts during the Civil War and of the 9th and 10th Cavalry Regiments at San Juan Hill. The men of the 369th, their "black, swarthy faces beneath the blue French helmets," now marched forth to continue this fine tradition of "courageous Negro soldiers."[5]

On the outskirts of the town, the band played the battalion on to the "ragtime syncopated strains of the jazzed up 'Army Blues,'" the favorite tune of the colonel and the Regiment. The men promptly shed their serious demeanor, smiled, and began to sing the words, while the remaining members of the battalion waved their helmets at their departing comrades. Long after the playing had stopped and the 3rd Battalion was beyond earshot, the band, the Regiment, and the villagers stood on the hill watching "the little army as it wended its way down the winding roads . . . some of them never to return."[6] The other battalions soon followed.

That afternoon, the 369th changed its marching formation to small groups at large intervals. A battalion of some 800 men covered 3 miles on the road, the men ready to don gas masks at a moment's notice. They had arrived within range of German shellfire. As they advanced, the sound of big shells bursting came closer. After they crested a hill, with the road stretching straight into the distance, they could feel the concussion of the exploding shells. Everyone concluded that the Germans were "sniping" with their artillery; no one considered that the French were also firing big guns and that they might be hearing French fire.[7] As the men marched through Maffrecourt to encamp beyond it, Pippin observed that the French themselves had shelled the town to drive the Germans out in 1915, and the few houses that still stood—and even the stables—remained uninhabitable.[8]

That night when the troops of the 369th encamped, the Germans were shelling the trenches in front of them and the towns behind them. They could hear the whine of the shells passing overhead. Pippin bunked in a dilapidated old building in a camp that he believed dated from Napoleon's time. He lay awake listening to the big guns, and the shells burst so frequently that he soon became used to them and fell asleep. In the morning at reveille, he could see his housing clearly for the first time. He had slept under a hole in the roof; consequently, he and his cot were wet from the rain, and the dirt floor had become a muddy mess. The men spent the day cleaning up.[9]

On April 14, they marched farther east to shelters for reserve troops. The men of Captain Little's 1st Battalion, for example, moved into barracks; the officers moved into huts built into the west, or reverse, side of a ravine nicknamed Death Valley, where the hill could protect them from German shelling. German artillery promptly lobbed some thirty shells into the camp in fifteen minutes to welcome the Americans. A French officer explained that the French and Germans knew everything about each other from spies and reconnaissance and that the Germans had not shelled the camp for months. Little noted that his men promptly and in good order moved under cover and greeted the shells with laughter and shouts. Two of his junior officers seemed more preoccupied with strolling coolly down the camp's central road than with seeking shelter, until Little yelled at them to stop showing off and take cover immediately. The morale and esprit de corps of the 1st Battalion were clearly evident.[10]

In K Company, 3rd Battalion, at 6:00 P.M. on April 14, Pippin was ordered to prepare his squad for guard duty that night. He took the 11:00 P.M. to 1:00 A.M. shift as corporal of the guard and was sitting in the guardhouse door when he heard a sound like a rifle crack to the right of the town. The few inhabitants of the town had been ordered not to move about after dark, so he was already advancing toward the sound when the sentries at the post near the crossroad outside town began to call for the corporal of the guard. When Pippin arrived, he saw two men in the grass approaching the village.

He ordered them to halt three times; one did, but the other continued, so Pippin shot him. He took his prisoner to the officer of the day, but under interrogation, the fugitive volunteered no answers and was taken away,[11] most likely to be executed as a spy.

The morning of April 15, the 1st Battalion broke camp and marched to the front, nearly 4 miles away, to subsector Afrique. French captains then took Captain Little forward on a mule-drawn flatcar to meet Lt. Col. Adam de Villiers, commander of the 131st Territorial Infantry Regiment and of subsector Afrique. After dining with de Villiers, Commandant Josse, the French officer directly responsible for the 369th, took Little on a tour of the trenches. They walked through the swampy woodland's irregular trenches on duckboards surrounded by barbed wire. Although they were only 440 yards from the German lines at the closest point, the taller Josse never stooped or ducked as they passed low points in full view of the German trenches. A slightly disconcerted Little followed suit, and when they reached the foremost point of the line, Josse asked him to fire the first American shot in the sector. After Little and then Josse fired, all the French and American officers present shook hands.[12]

The trenches ran in curves and angles, to prevent an enemy from firing the length of the trench if he entered at one end. Soldiers in squad or half-platoon strength (twelve to twenty-four men), armed with rifles and light machine guns, manned positions that were a quarter to a third of a mile apart but commanded clear and overlapping fields of fire. In front of these positions, often jutting into no-man's-land and connected to the stronger emplacements with shallow trenches, lay more lightly manned observation posts. Fields of barbed wire surrounded the positions, and behind them lay more fortified positions with heavy machine guns to protect them with covering fire.

Any potentially successful attack on these emplacements usually required an artillery barrage to sever them from their reinforcing positions prior to the assault. Under attack, the strongpoint would signal by flare to unleash an artillery barrage and machine-gun fusillades upon the enemy. If the enemy reached the fortified emplacement, hand-to-hand combat ensued, with combatants using pistols, blades, shovels, or anything else they could wield.[13]

On April 17, Squadron Chief Lobez characterized the relationships between French and American officers as perfect. The American officers of the 369th welcomed their French peers and yearned to fight, he observed, although they did not yet pay sufficient attention to administrative details. He described the men as "fine troops" (*une belle troupe*). They had already entered the support trenches for training in small groups interspersed with French soldiers.[14]

The night of April 17, C Company, 1st Battalion, in concert with the French, sent out a patrol to ambush any German units on the prowl. Earlier that day, by Little's account, the men had practiced by emulating a demonstrative French poilu who wore a patch over one eye. He crouched and crawled silently, threw a mock grenade, and then charged with bayonet fixed, emitting blood-curdling yells. The men thoroughly enjoyed the exercise. That night, as the patrol set out, some wag commented that second lieutenants were perfectly suited for such tasks because they were expendable. Their ambush snared no Germans, although down the line, Lt. Marshall Johnson of 2nd Battalion had already earned a recommendation for the Croix de Guerre for capturing a German during a raid. The next night, officers had to restrain small groups of soldiers from venturing into no-man's-land to duplicate Johnson's feat.[15]

On April 20, Little's 1st Battalion took sole control of the Malzicourt subsector of Afrique, next to Josse's Montplaisir, and became the first unit of the 369th to occupy a sector alone. The 1st Battalion would occupy subsectors Malzicourt or Montplaisir on a rotating basis with the other two battalions of the 369th for the next three months. Following standard procedure, 1st Battalion assigned two companies to the first line, holding the third in reserve, in the Malzicourt subsector.[16] During the rest of April, the 2nd and 3rd Battalions of the 369th changed cantons behind the lines. On May 1, the 3rd Battalion relieved the 1st, which marched to the regimental base at Maffrecourt, some 7 miles to the rear, for ten days' rest. The 1st Battalion's initial tour in the trenches had passed uneventfully.[17]

At the end of April, the troops, including a battalion of the 369th, were reviewed by Gen. Henri Gouraud, "the Lion of France" and commander of the French 4th Army; Gen. Helie d'Oiselle, commander of 8th Army Corps; and Gen. Le Gallais, commander of the 16th Division. The French troops always cheered Gouraud, a favorite of theirs who had lost his right arm at Gallipoli and limped from another wound. The three generals, facing the American flag, bowed very low. The American color-bearer, the muscular Sgt. William H. Cox, responded with a graceful low bow before the generals, dipping the flag. A color-bearer should never dip the flag, but Cox, witnessing the tears in Gouraud's eyes and the reverence of the three French generals, ignored regulations that day.[18]

The information officer of the US 3rd Division, Lieutenant Heinemann, reported on April 24 on the overall progress of the 369th based on his discussion with Capt. Fleury Herald.[19] Colonel Hayward and his officers believed that this regiment of volunteers would become an elite unit, and experience seemed to justify that prediction. By April 12, Heinemann reported, the entire Regiment was in the frontline area. They had pushed training as quickly as possible due to the cordial relations between French and American officers. The Regiment was still experiencing problems of liaison with the division, which would be solved by the permanent assignment of one or two French officers to the 369th as technical advisers.[20] Heinemann believed, as did all who had come in contact with the 369th, that the unit "can render the greatest services and can hold honorably its place at the side of the best French regiments." Its officers and men asked only one thing, and "that is to fight." They had stood up well under bombardment and already participated in several raids.[21]

As of May 1, the regimental headquarters of the 369th were located at Maffrecourt, west of Ste. Menehould, with the brigade headquarters, and the 369th Regiment took command of subsector Afrique, which now became subsector US. The French army referred to regiments and their battalions by the name of the commanding officer. Subsector command fell to Colonel Hayward, so Regiment "Hayward" now occupied subsector US. On May 2, the 3rd Battalion of the 369th relieved the 1st at Malzicourt, and the 1st moved to the rear at Maffrecourt.[22]

Ironically, rotation into the front lines alleviated the boredom that the men in the rear had suffered. With relatively little to do in reserve behind the front, soldiers in the rear battalions began to amuse themselves by roaming about the country as far as Chalons-sur-Marne and Ste. Menehould. General Le Gallais warned the Regiment that if its men did not remain in their assigned camps, he would relegate the unit to labor service. An officers' council of the Regiment elected Capt. Napoleon Marshall, now one of the regimental staff officers, as acting provost marshal (APM) when he missed their meeting. The APM faced the onerous task of keeping the men in camp. If he failed, the 369th would find itself humiliated in the rear; if he succeeded, the Regiment would remain a fighting unit at the front.[23] Responsibility for the future of the Regiment had descended on the broad shoulders of this Harvard athlete.

Marshall was assigned a "splendid chestnut sorrel standing sixteen hands high and very fleet footed" for his duty, and he received a roving commission to corral the AWOL men on the roads and in the towns. He succeeded in his task and observed that the men always obeyed him when he ordered them to report back to their commanding officers.[24] The soldiers had departed out of boredom—Marshall himself noted that life had become "humdrum"—and not with any intention to desert. The 369th remained in the line. In contrast, the AEF would experience very high rates of straggling and AWOLs during its time at the front in October 1918.[25]

Late in April, Capt. Hamilton Fish desired to join the staff of an American division whose general had offered him promotion to major. Although Fish enjoyed his position as commander of a line company, staff positions meant more prospects for advancement. Fish remained attached to K Company, but he was one of several white junior officers who realized that their chances for promotion in the 369th did not equal those of young officers in regular units of the AEF.[26]

Yet, only two days later, on May 1, Fish was enjoying "immensely" K Company's first tour in frontline trenches with the French. His men had lived up to "his highest expectations," and "their fearless conduct under heavy fire showed that they had the willingness and ability to fight." His men showed "aptitude for night work, especially reconnoitering," and they were "delighted with the cordial treatment of both the French officers and soldiers." Their condition and morale remained so "excellent" that they did not want to be relieved when the time came.[27] But they had experienced "a most unfortunate accident." Their first night in the trench, a French soldier had knocked a hand grenade down the steps of a dugout 30 feet deep in which three of Fish's men slept; the explosion badly wounded the three Americans. Fish termed the incident "one of the chances of war." Other than the cloudy and cold weather and "innumerable rats of all sizes," which ate through uniforms and bags and climbed over the men at night, he only regretted that gas shells had "completely knocked the sportiveness out of this war."[28]

On May 15, after another fifteen days in the front line, Fish found it "quite a relief" to clean up and take off his shoes at night. His men, though tired and dirty, were in good spirits. Even though he liked the excitement of the front, he now enjoyed a "respite from the worries and responsibilities." At least the weather had grown warmer.[29] Fish complimented the French, from the captain in command, who personally reviewed the menu, to the French officers and noncommissioned officers, who treated his men as comrades and supervised them in friendly fashion. His men had never enjoyed better or more regular meals. He considered the French splendid and brave soldiers. A French raiding party had suffered three killed and three wounded, and when the French lieutenant, wounded in the head at close range by a pistol shot, reported to the captain, he was more concerned about his men than about the bullet in his head.[30]

In Company K, Cpl. Horace Pippin awaited the rotation of 3rd Battalion to the front lines. Every night from the hill they occupied, they could see the fire from the big guns. They advanced into the muddy front trenches, where Pippin found a bunk in a dugout that was too damp and airless to sustain the light of a candle. He made do in the dark, washing his hands with the water that gathered in the moss on the beams and posts of the shelter. Initially, the constant drip of water kept him awake, but afterward, he was happy to have any place to sleep, even in mud, with only his helmet for a pillow during his first twenty-day rotation at the front.[31]

After two days in the trenches, Pippin's lieutenant entered the dugout in the morning and asked for volunteers for a patrol, or "scout trip," in no-man's-land that night. Everyone wanted to go, so the lieutenant left it to Pippin to choose his men and have them ready at the command post (CP) at midnight. That evening, after mess, the volunteers slept until the changing of the guard awoke Pippin at 11:00 P.M. He roused his men and led them to the CP by 11:30 P.M.; the lieutenant appeared at 11:45. The weather was cold and so rainy that the water flowed through the trenches like a river in some places, but out they ventured on their first patrol.[32]

As they started the patrol, German shellfire increased. Pippin claimed not to mind the shells but referred to no-man's-land as "that Hell." They encountered shells and gas, and at the end of the zigzag trench (fortified position), a shell landed so close to them that its concussion blew them off their feet as its shrapnel whistled by them. No one was hurt, and Pippin insisted that they remained unafraid. Penetrating the barbed wire entanglements took some time, after which they moved into the shell holes. The volume of small-arms fire about them increased, forcing them to take cover in a shell hole. They found the patrol "bad goeing" because they could not travel fast in the dark and rain, but they saw no one during the entire patrol,[33] then reentered their lines soaking wet from the constant rain. They dared not light a match, much less a fire, so they went to bed and awoke the next morning in wet clothes. At mail call, Pippin was pleasantly surprised to receive a very short letter from home, which he read repeatedly until he knew it by heart before he fell asleep.[34] He slept until mess time, awoke feeling good, and calculated they faced another midnight trip into no-man's-land. When they were ready to sortie this time, he recalled, *"The shells did not bother me any more I were youse [used] to them."* New soldiers would duck every time a shell came over and continued ducking "all day long" until they became accustomed to them.[35]

The next night, Pippin stood guard in the rain until midnight, when the Germans began to increase their shellfire, including gas shells. Anticipating a German raid, he woke his men, but all they received was gas, which forced them to wear their masks for three hours, from midnight to 3:00 A.M. By this time in the war, gas proved more an annoyance than a danger to trained soldiers, and it prevented the men who were not on guard duty from returning to the dugouts to sleep until daylight. The men, Pippin wrote, "shor did bless them Germans." Beyond the cursing, however, he noted that he had "never seen the time yet, that the 15th N.Y. inf were not ready. they were all ways ready to go and they did go to the last man."[36]

Pippin recalled his time at the front in separate accounts written at different times after the war, which led to certain minor discrepancies. The accounts are genuine—if telescoped and occasionally confused—recollections of Pippin's first tour in the front trenches. The intermittent confusion in official war records based upon on-the-spot accounts indicates the difficulty of precisely recalling events and their order even under the best of circumstances. Pippin revealed the life of a common soldier in the line, when the only clear demarcation of time was the rotation from the front to the rear after twenty days. His accounts bear witness to the abysmal weather and conditions encountered in the frontline trenches, the tedium and tension, the adjustment to life and death under constant fire, the importance of mail, and the readiness of the men of the 15th/369th to patrol and defend, if need be to the last man.

Lewis Shaw, a first lieutenant who was now commander of the 3rd Battalion Machine Gun Company, found it "very pleasant with Jim Europe," who served as his second in command, along with his other two lieutenants and the entire company, whose spirit he found "wonderful." He considered himself fortunate, as his work was primarily "administrative and tactical," and his company spent twenty days in the trenches for every ten days at rest in the rear. His orderly, Ellis, took care of him, and the company had retained "an excellent colored cook," as they entertained and "associated with the finest French officers."[37]

With the 3rd Battalion's arrival in the front lines, Lt. James Reese Europe undertook his first patrol, an experience recounted by his friend Noble Sissle.[38] Europe was drinking wine with French officers in the neighboring sector and listening to tales of their wartime exploits. Emboldened by the wine, he volunteered that he wanted to experience "the hair breath thrills of the modern warfare." The French cheerfully congratulated him and told him to get permission from his colonel to accompany them on a raid that night.

Europe hoped that Hayward would reject the idea, but the colonel approved. When night came, Europe donned a skullcap, for the French and Germans preferred skullcaps and soft round caps, respectively, for raids. He and his French comrades, the latter "as happy as larks," downed a bottle of wine and set off on their mission. The French officers gave Europe a small automatic pistol, which looked like a cap gun and left him wondering what use it might possibly have. Yet, his French colleagues all carried the same weapon, which was probably a Belgian-made Browning Model 1910 automatic pistol, a small (6 inch), light (1 pound, 5 ounces unloaded), and handy gun that officers often carried as a personal weapon.[39]

As the raiding party filed down the trench, Europe kept stumbling in the dark. His throat dry, he observed how starlit the night was, but an officer reassured him that brush in front of the trench obscured them from the Germans and the light would help them observe the enemy trenches. "Over the top" they crawled, past their barbed wire into no-man's-land. They reached a hole in the German wire that had been cut by a French patrol the previous night. One soldier crawled through with a ball of white tape to mark the shortest distance to the German trench and to guide them on their return.

French 75-mm cannon opened a two-minute barrage on the German trenches, as Europe hugged the ground for dear life. Suddenly, the lieutenant next to him fired a red flare into the air. The raiding party rose to a crouch, went through the hole in the wire, and formed a skirmish line on the other side. As the barrage crept forward toward the German trench, the Very, or flare, pistol cracked again, and they ran behind the barrage for the German position. Once in it, Europe and the French lieutenant halted, while the men followed the barrage as it swept the enemy trenches, shouting and bombarding the lines and dugouts with grenades. After three minutes of this marauding, the lieutenant fired a green flare. The men raced back, bringing papers and parts of uniforms but no prisoners with them. Stretcher-bearers carried a wounded French soldier.[40]

As they approached the French lines, German artillery began to bombard them. Europe observed, "Don't tell me Frenchmen can't run," as he dived into a dugout where he would remain for a quarter hour until the Germans stopped firing. When he returned to the officers' shelter, he learned that two of the four officers and two men had been seriously wounded during the raid. Europe declared that before he undertook another raid, "they will have to read orders to me with General Pershing's name signed and resigned to them."[41]

Colonel Hayward wrote immediately to Emmett Scott, the black special assistant to the secretary of war. He reported that the experience of the 369th in the trenches answered two questions "of the gravest importance to our country and to your race." The first question concerned how well American Negro soldiers and officers would get along with their French counterparts. Hayward reported proudly that the black officers, "of whom he still had five," and the soldiers had gotten along well with the French. "The French soldiers," he observed, "have not the slightest prejudice or feeling," and consequently, "the poilus and my boys are great chums." French officers had some concerns about Negro officers, based on "skepticism that a colored man (judging of course by those they have known) can have the technical education necessary to make an efficient officer." Yet, Capt. Napoleon Bonaparte Marshall and Lt. Dennis L. Reid were then living as "honored guests" at the French officers' mess at the division *Infanterie* (infantry) school.[42] Hayward's assertion about the French reception of the two officers Marshall and Reid (beyond General Le Gallais's welcome, which distinguished between African and African American soldiers) indicated that at least some Frenchmen were more capable of a flexible application of racial stereotypes than their white American Allies, who considered all black people inferior.

The second question Hayward referenced concerned the American Negro's ability to "stand up under the terrible shell fire of this war . . . and thus prove his superiority, spiritually and intellectually, to all the black men of Africa and Asia, who have failed under these conditions and whose use must be limited to attack or for shock troops." Hayward did not think it premature to report his soldiers had stood up well and proved both stoic and humorous under shellfire, to the extent that French officers had commented that his men were not as excitable as Africans and Indians under fire. Hayward explained that his "public school boys" were "wise" and "accustomed to the terrible noises of the subway, elevated and street traffic of New York City" and were "all Christians," so that they suffered from "no delusions about Boche shells coming from any heathen Gods."[43] Rumors that African soldiers saw heathen gods or Satan in gas clouds, believed by some to be evidence of their credulity, are no more outlandish than British soldiers' claim that they saw an angel at the battle of Mons in 1914. Hayward's claim about urban life preparing soldiers better for the western front did parallel European armies' realizations that the urbanization and industrialization of their societies rendered moot their prior primary reliance on peasant soldiers and that soldiers from cities may have adapted more easily to the huge masses of men encamped on and behind the front. In any case, shellfire was more likely to render soldiers catatonic rather than excitable.

Hayward was convinced that he knew more "about Negro soldiers and how to handle them, especially the problems of Negro and white officers, than any other man living today." He was "proud to think that our boys were the first Negro American soldiers in the trenches" and that "Jim Europe was certainly the first Negro officer" in what was a "tremendously important experiment, when one considers the host of colored men who must come after us."[44]

In fact, though the 369th certainly held the honor of being the first African American *unit* in the trenches, the *men* of the 369th were not the first African Americans to serve in the trenches of World War I, for a number of African Americans (including the world's first black combat aviator, Eugene Bullard) had served in the French Foreign Legion on the western front as early as 1915. Hayward's reference to living in New York as being good preparation for service in the front lines did demonstrate an awareness of the conditions on the western front, where huge camps behind the lines approximated small cities. Millions of troops equipped with rifles, grenades, machine guns, trench mortars, and tens of thousands of cannon crowded into a front of fewer than 500 miles. The western front consequently became the first battlefield in which soldiers from urban environments might feel as much at home as, if not more so than, their rural counterparts, whom armies had always valued as soldiers.

Hayward's allegation that African and Indian troops had not endured shellfire well reflected an oft-noted stereotype that the evidence does not substantiate. The British withdrew Indian infantry after they had been decimated on the western front in 1915, but individual units of Indian cavalry remained to the end of the war. The French imported increasing numbers of black African soldiers for use as assault or shock troops, in the conviction that though they might not be useful for holding trenches, particularly in the winter, they displayed unparalleled ardor in the offensive. Charlie Charles, a white machine gunner in the French Foreign Legion who hailed from Brooklyn, New York, noted in mid-1916 of the Africans: "It is said that the colored chaps are afraid of shell fire, but from personal observation I know it is not true"[45] The rumor that African and Indian—that is, colored—troops could not endure shellfire was obviously a canard. Soldiers of all nations and races endured shellfire with difficulty, as the rapidly increasing cases of shell shock in European armies indicated. Every soldier, regardless of race, training, or discipline, had his breaking point.

Although Hayward praised the men of the 369th, Lt. John Castles and Lt. Marshall Johnson grew increasingly dissatisfied, particularly with conditions among the officers in the Regiment. Castles referred to inefficiency and ego, clearly implicating Hayward, and he planned to apply for a transfer after his time in the trenches. Others were going to request transfer in hopes of causing a "row," as the Regiment had "escaped inspection to date & is still carrying a full quota of inefficients."[46] Lieutenant Johnson, whom Hayward had recommended for the Croix de Guerre, actually wrote a personal note to Brig. Gen. Walden S. Metcalf, commander of the 77th Infantry Brigade, about his two months in the 369th. Johnson complained of the lack of discipline, courtesy, collaboration, and support by superior officers, which made the life of junior officers discouraging and "unbearable." Indeed, 75 percent of the Regiment's officers, according to Johnson, were applying for transfers.[47] The dissatisfaction of the junior officers of the 369th coalesced in a core of Ivy Leaguers whose social connections extended into the US Army and who could circumvent the military chain of command to complain about the Regiment.

Castles and his cohort from Gondrecourt had returned to the Regiment to learn from Colonel Hayward that the 1st Battalion was already in the frontline trenches. That information, Castles reported, "knocked us dead . . . because we had a pretty good idea of how little they knew." Castles soon met his platoon, which included eight replacements "who did not even know how to load a rifle!"[48] The next day, they advanced to the frontline trenches with the 3rd Battalion for its eleven-day rotation. Castles found the trenches dilapidated and unsanitary, the typical state of affairs in the French lines and something that other American officers had taken in stride, setting their men to work to improve the positions. That first night, the company captain ordered Castles to lead a seven-man patrol along the wire. Their first patrol "crashed along in swampy ground like a circus parade" but drew no German fire. In the course of eleven days, Castles and his men went on five patrols. Twice, neighboring friendly units shot at them; once, the Germans did. When the Germans fired on his patrol, Castles felt fear for only "a fraction of a second . . . but during that fraction of a second, I just hurt physically all over, especially my mouth." The Germans shelled their positions twice. They suffered no casualties. He found the nights "awful," as the men fired at shadows and threw grenades at scuttling rats; the lieutenants did not sleep at night and spent most of their days reporting to the company command post. By the end of the eleven days, Castles was jumpy and exhausted.[49]

Back in rest billets in Maffrecourt for ten days, he visited with officers of the 7th Company of the French 27th Infantry. One of the French officers had participated in his eighty-seventh raid during his previous tour. After seeing the men of the company, Castles exclaimed, "And these small, dirty, bearded men had seen and done *some* fighting too!"[50] He applied for a transfer from the 369th while in rest camp at Maffrecourt, the day before his battalion returned to the trenches. His first tour in the frontline trenches had convinced him that he did not want to be responsible for leading such poorly trained men. He damned Hayward for cleverly convincing all concerned, the French included, that the Regiment was "thoroughly trained

. . . an exceptionally fine 'shooting regiment'" and well disciplined. Castles, in contrast, found the men "mere cannon fodder," "since they have not had training. They are brave and want to fight, but don't know how." Castles considered them "careless," with a tendency to fall asleep on guard duty and even while waiting in ambush. His men asked for bolo and trench knives and pistols for close combat, but he had none to distribute. That last day at Maffrecourt, Castles alleged, Hayward told him that he was nominating him for a captaincy, to which Castles replied that he was requesting a transfer to the Tank Corps. He calculated that as a captain in the 369th, he would have even less of a chance to transfer than he would as a lieutenant.[51] Hayward promised to endorse Castles's request.[52]

The 3rd Battalion rotated to frontline trenches in Malzicourt, which Castles once again found "in terrible shape." The troops lacked maps, intelligence reports, gas masks, and even flares to call in artillery support, all of which confirmed Castles in his decision to request a transfer. He spent the long night watches in his dugout "heart in mouth" and revolver cocked. The artillery barrages, machine-gun fire, and rockets made the nights "hideous." "The nervous strain of these nights is terrible and they are years long, especially the hours of dawn," he wrote. "During those hours of stand-to, I used to wander up and down the trenches, talking to the men and trying to instill a confidence that I did not have myself." One night, under machine-gun fire, eight of his men panicked and fled, while the other eight in his half section stood fast and fought in the dark. Castles stopped the fleeing men at pistol point, but the troops still in the line suffered three casualties, including one of Castles's sergeants, who died the next morning.[53]

As German bombardments and raids increased in frequency, Castles noted that "the usual luck of the Regiment" kept their casualties to a minimum. When the captain went on leave, he left Castles in charge of the company, and despite "several set-to's with Fritz . . . everything went O.K. during his absence." The day his battalion rotated to the rear, Castles received an order to return to his old company as it entered the trenches, so he began a second rotation at the front. Although exhausted, he willingly rejoined his friends. When his orders to report to the Tank Corps came through on his thirty-fourth day in the trenches, he left immediately, but the night prior to his departure, his last night with the 369th, proved to be "a hot one."[54]

The Germans boxed in his outpost and two others with a heavy barrage and raided in battalion strength. The 369th's two machine guns hidden in the front lines impeded the raid, and Castles's men beat back the Germans with grenades and pistols while the fire of flanking machine guns raked the enemy. Meanwhile, the Germans unleashed machine-gun fire and rifle grenades on his position for nearly an hour. The Germans took no prisoners; Castles noted they had yet to capture "one from us." The 369th suffered light casualties, "as the same luck stuck to us." A 77-mm shell penetrated the roof of a dugout and exploded, wounding one man in the hip and another in the arm, when it should have killed both merely from shell shock. Castles concluded, "The men I had fought like lions and deserve a lot of credit, considering the handicaps in the way of no training, etc. they were up against."[55] By the next night, he had departed the Regiment.

Castles's complaints about inefficiency in the 369th seem ironic, as he had already condemned the inadequacy of half the officer candidates at the AEF officers training school at Gondrecourt. Why would he hope that the AEF would inspect and weed out inefficiency in a black regiment that it had discarded? The AEF had more than enough inefficiency and indiscipline in its inexperienced white units to occupy it to the end of the war. Castles's constant refrains about the men's lack of training and discipline and his attribution of their low casualties to luck also prove problematic. His men's first tour in the trenches did not differ from the first experience of other units at the front. The jumpiness, panic, carelessness—all were normal phenomena among inexperienced soldiers. Replacements throughout the AEF often did not know how to use their weapons, so if Colonel Hayward exaggerated the preparedness of the 369th, Castles denigrated its readiness. As a novice himself, his awareness of his own inexperience, compounded by that of his men, weighed heavily upon him. He admitted to strain and fear during the "awful" nights, but he had no basis for comparison to indicate the experience would have been any better or the men any more prepared in another unit. The accounts of both Castles and Fish, junior officers of superior merit, clearly indicate the stress imposed by the "worries and responsibilities of command," for they had to master their own personal feelings while leading their units.

Hayward would have fully and proudly acknowledged Castles's accusations about his political machinations and his manipulation of the American press. But was the colonel so calloused and uncaring that he would send "his boys" to certain death as the untrained and undisciplined recruits Castles alleged? Castles was away at Gondrecourt during the month the French instructors trained the Regiment. The instructors could have rushed the African American soldiers to the front and waxed enthusiastic about them simply to secure more cannon fodder as quickly as possible. Yet, a disastrous performance by the 369th would have damaged all concerned, American and French. So it is more plausible that the French, like American Lieutenant Heinemann, found the performance of the 369th in training and in its first tour of duty at the front to be as promising as they stated. The unit's performance in the "quiet sector" corroborated the positive assessments of the French, of Heinemann, and of Hayward—not that of Castles.

The French postal service monitored French attitudes through its censorship of military correspondence. Its report of May 15 praised the African American troops' soldierly qualities, commenting, "They are considered well trained and well disciplined. They establish very good relations with our troops. The units charged with providing training for these new allies are struck by their 'good will' and their desire to do well. . . . They are above all very dedicated."[56] The African American soldiers appreciated the manner in which their French counterparts treated them, and many of them had begun to learn French.[57] The report reinforces the impression given by General Le Gallais in his introduction of the Regiment to his division to the effect that the French sought to distinguish clearly between African Americans and their sub-Saharan African colonial soldiers. The French were clearly concerned with and pleased that the relationships between French and black American Allies were "very good," a mutuality of sentiment that never entered French commanders' minds in regard to their black African charges.

On May 27, Captain Alcan of the French military mission to the AEF reported on his visits to the black regiments of the 93rd Provisional Division. As part of the French 16th Division, the 369th stationed two battalions in line, with two companies in the front line and a third in support, while the 3rd Battalion trained at Maffrecourt. The 369th comprised 2,501 men, and its officer cadre included 4 black lieutenants and 1 black captain. In comparison, the 370th Regiment had all black officers; the 371st had none and desired none; and the 372nd had 72 black officers, including several captains.[58]

Alcan's report merely recorded the racial composition of the regiments' officer corps. White officer observers of black regiments in the 93rd Division invariably predicated the efficiency of a unit on its proportion of white commissioned officers and denigrated the importance of black commissioned and noncommissioned officers. For instance, on June 24, 1918, Col. A. T. Ovenshine of the inspector general's staff ranked the regiments of the 93rd, listing the 371st first, the 369th second, the 372nd third, and the 370th last. After commenting that the entire 93rd should return to the AEF, Ovenshine pointed out that the best regiment, the 371st, had a regular army commander and no "colored" commissioned officers; the worst, the 370th, was all black in its composition.[59] The AEF consequently determined to segregate the officer corps of the four regiments of the 93rd Division and ensure white leadership at the top of each regiment in July and August.

In the meantime, Sgt. Hannibal Davis, company clerk at 1st Battalion, provided the only extant black soldier's opinion of the Regiment's officers. He considered the regiment "very fortunate" in its "quota of officers," "for practically without exception, they were as fine, brave, and intelligent men as you could find anywhere. The only trouble was, we never had all the officers we needed, and which we were entitled to."[60] Davis did not mention the tension that roiled relations among the white officers. Although Castles asserted that some confrontations occurred in front of the men, perhaps the soldiers who were present simply dismissed such incidents as normal. More likely, the separation between officers and enlisted men, which in this case may have been heightened by race, was so great that the men ignored the tense relations among the officers so long as they did not affect the officers' performance. Although the men must have discussed the officers among themselves, any observations or judgments they made did not seem to have affected regimental morale. Davis also found nothing appalling about exhausted men falling asleep while marching, standing sentry duty, or lying in wait during an ambush.[61]

Castles attributed too much to luck in assessing the performance of the 369th. His last encounter with the Germans, on the night before he departed, illustrated his penchant for attributing the success and survival of the men to luck and exaggerating their lack of training. His reference to "no training" simply did not apply, and his men, who "fought like lions," clearly knew what they were doing. They did not break under the German artillery and machine-gun barrages or the weight of an attack by a superior force, they lost no prisoners to the Germans, and they emerged with light casualties. A combination of training (however rudimentary), discipline, and courage—not luck—enabled these achievements. In fact, Castles acknowledged this circumstance in a letter to his mother. He noted that the men "have no fear whatsoever. Several have been wounded and they are the proudest ones in the world." In the major German raid, he observed, "the men did wonderfully, fighting like veterans." As for the war, it was "a great game and would be good sport if it were not for the gas."[62] The reference to "fighting like veterans" indicates Castles acknowledged that the soldiers of the 369th were no longer undisciplined recruits. He took his officer's duties seriously and felt the heavy weight of responsibility and the resulting "wear & tear on the nerves," but he believed that his regimental staff officers in the 369th took their responsibilities lightly.[63] His attitudes reflected the division evident in all armies between the staffs above and the company officers and their men in the trenches.

Cpl. Horace Pippin's recollection of these first months in the trenches not only provides an account of life in the 3rd Battalion—Castles's unit—from the perspective of the enlisted men but also suggests the men's rapid metamorphosis into hardened trench soldiers.[64] Enlisted men served twenty days in the front trenches and ten in the rear for rest, which they invariably spent drilling, sometimes for eight hours a day. Then, they would rotate to another sector of their front in the Argonne Forest. "In that black woods" the trees were so thick and dark that in the daytime, the men could only hear, not see, people approaching; at night, they could not see their hands in front of them.[65]

German artillery constantly shelled the woods, the highway to the front, and the rear areas. The shelling even smashed the track for the handcar that they used to bring provisions forward. If the Germans suspected that troops were rotating in or out, they would shell the woods extensively with gas, sometimes for two nights just in case the rotation changed slightly. Shells crashing into the forest snapped a tree "like a pipe-stem." They tore the top off a giant acorn tree next to Pippin's dugout, causing the soldier to lament, "We hardly knew what to do, for we could not fight shells. But we could fight Germans. We would rather for the Germans to come over the top then to have th[e]ir shells."[66]

The daily German shellfire gave them "a hard time" during their twenty days at the front in the forest, although they were fortunate to lose only five of their men as well as their kitchen. Pippin was convinced that the Germans would strike them when they rotated back for their ten days of rest. The afternoon of the rotation, he received orders to report to the lieutenant's dugout after dark for orders. With shells falling in the night sky, Pippin followed the handcar track a mile to the command post, where he received orders to guard the track that night until all of the men had left to start the 5-mile trek to the rear. By 5:30 A.M., the last man passed Pippin, who returned to the trench for his gear, slept, ate at the French kitchen, and then hiked the 5 miles himself.[67]

The days merged, separated only by rotation to and from the front lines either in Champagne or in the Argonne sector next to it. In both sectors, the German artillery plagued the infantry. "The Germans would shell one man," Pippin observed, "as well as they would one hundred"[68]—a reference to their noted tendency to "snipe" with cannon. The men drew their water at night from a French water tank hidden in a deep valley. The Germans never hit the tank but instead occasionally fired so much gas into the valley that a blue haze hung over it. The Americans would go without water until it cleared.[69]

On one occasion, when Pippin's unit was in reserve trenches behind the French front line, the Germans began to shell it, a sure indication of a coming attack. The unit's officers ordered them out of their dugouts, with shovels. Gas masks on, they started down the trench as the shells dropped around them, in places caving in the trench. When his men reached the end of their trench at the edge of their sector, they began to dig another one in case the Germans broke through the French lines. They remained there for three or four nights. Ultimately, the Germans proved to be bluffing, so the men of the unit rotated to the rear for their ten days of rest.[70]

One day in the rear, after drill, Pippin stretched out to take a nap under a tree. As he lay on his back, he looked at a sky that was empty except for clouds. Then, he heard an engine noise above; a German plane emerged from the clouds over their lines, heading right over him toward a hill. From the German's left, a French plane was in pursuit The Frenchman circled his diving and ascending prey, then opened fire. The German plane crashed in flames. Pippin approached the downed aircraft, which was in pieces, while its two airmen "looked like mush." The French plane circled its downed prey victoriously, "like a king over his great foe," and then swooped down to the cheers of the onlookers.[71]

That night, in retaliation, German planes raided across the lines, and the next day witnessed heated aerial combat in which Pippin saw three German planes and one French plane downed. Not a day passed without aerial combat. German planes strafed groups of men walking or working on the road or in the fields, "deel[ing] out death to them." One cloudy afternoon, as he was heading down a zigzag trench for mess, he heard a rush of air over him. He fell to one side of the trench just as the German aviator fired at him. He attributed the miss to his quickness, although he was very fortunate. When he told his comrades of his experience, one of them thought it was a joke.[72]

After mess, Pippin sat smoking a French cigarette in a corner of the dugout when the gas alarm sounded; the Germans had fired mustard gas shells. The soldiers went out into the trench, expecting a German attack. After a time, they returned to the dugout, and then the sergeant appeared and picked sixteen men, Pippin among them, for a patrol into no-man's-land. At least the rain ensured that their movement would cause no rustle of dry leaves or weeds.[73] The patrol descended the trench and entered no-man's-land, while German and American machine guns to their left swept the zone between the lines. Creeping as close to the ground as possible, they headed for the ruin of an old house, where they thought the German gunner was hiding. The German stopped firing as they moved toward the ruin. The patrol split to surround the house, the men silently crawling through the weeds. When they reached the back of the ruin, they rushed down the stairs to the cellar, only to find it full of everything except the German. They decided to ambush any German patrol and to lie motionless in shell holes in the heavy rain to keep the occasional German flare from giving away their position. They abandoned the ambush at 3:30 A.M. and returned to the trench by dawn, empty-handed and exhausted. They spent the rest of their time during that rotation at the front, working on their trenches.[74]

The unit spent its next stint in the frontline trenches next to Algerian[75] infantry troops on its right flank, whom Pippin labeled "a good lot of fellows." The Algerians did not like the French; every time a Frenchman passed, an Algerian would say, "Par [Pas] bon" (No good). What impressed Pippin most was that the Algerians "would not give a foe a chance": they often went over the top armed only with knives with 8-inch blades clenched in their teeth, and they never returned with any prisoners, just their knives with fresh blood on them. One dark night, French artillery opened fire on the German lines to their right at "zero hour," midnight, to sever the German frontline trenches from their support trenches. At the signal of a flare, the Algerians "broke the still air like a pack of mad men," tore off for the German trench, and "did their work fast and good."[76]

The Americans anticipated a retaliatory German raid. On the third night, a lone German soldier crept close to their line to spy on them, but he stayed too long and was caught in the breaking dawn. A sentry shot him twice. The next night, the men left the trench by squads as they rotated to the rear to Maffrecourt. As they climbed the last hill up to the road to town, incoming German shells nearly caught them in the open, but they ducked into trenches and dugouts until the shelling finally abated. At a distance of nearly 2 miles from the front, the shells were still bursting around them, shaking the ground thunderously. As they passed through the place they called Death Valley, Pippin felt better because they were 3 miles away from the front, although he knew that the Germans could still reach them at that distance. He thanked God that he survived the shellfire.[77]

In some parts of the line, German snipers made merely going to mess dangerous. Two men in a squad would bring rations up three times a day, but Pippin's squad received their rations irregularly because a German sniper picked off the ration detail or the men going to mess. The sentries could not locate the German, so their officer ordered Pippin and the other corporal in the dugout to find the sniper at any cost. Pippin considered German snipers the best on the front, so he knew that locating this one, who had to be on a hill across from them, would be like finding a needle in a haystack.[78]

The two corporals scanned the opposing lines all day and all night, Pippin so well that he would recognize any changes. Occasionally during the rainy night, he heard the report of the sniper's rifle, which did not sound like a standard-issue German rifle, and concluded that the German was not far away. As day broke, Pippin scanned the landscape with his binoculars, but he and his "buddy" could spot no telltale puff of smoke. Then, Pippin noticed a large tree in no-man's-land that they could not see clearly. He told the other corporal to cover him as he moved down the trench to a place in the area, where he would have a better view. Once in position, Pippin remained hidden until mess time, and he was about to crawl back to his lines when the sniper's rifle cracked. He saw the tree's leaves move and return to their original position, and although he had spotted no smoke, he carefully aimed at the place in tree where the firing originated. Just after Pippin's shot, his buddy crawled to him to tell him that the sniper had fallen from the other side of the tree.[79]

Pippin and his spotter reported the incident to the command post and returned to the dugout to find the squad busy bailing water. An exhausted Pippin fell sound asleep and did not awaken until roused for mess the next morning, to find the squad still bailing. After mess, they all wanted him to recount his experience, and they confirmed that the sniping had ceased.[80]

Pippin advised his men "to get what sleep they could" when they had time. He was pleased that the "Old 15th N.Y. Inf" never feared danger and that they always stood by one another. If one soldier looked downhearted, the others would cheer him. He checked the youth on sentry duty, then Pippin sat down on an old soup box, took a crumpled letter from home from his pocket, and read "that old letter" twice, as it reminded him of home and made him feel good; he replaced it carefully in his pocket and went to mess in the rain.[81] The Germans had been quiet all day, and then a runner from the command post arrived to inform the sergeant of a patrol that night. Pippin anticipated "a bad night on that job," so he rolled some cigarettes, sat back down "on that old box," and read "that old letter" once again. His sergeant approached Pippin and told him to select eight men and be ready at 9:00 P.M., when the sergeant would join them for the patrol. Headquarters anticipated a German patrol and wanted to give the enemy "a good time," so they were sending out patrols from K and L Companies. The Germans had dug a trench out into no-man's-land as cover for their patrols, and Pippin's men were to see to it that no Germans got in or came out of that trench. Pippin did not like the fact that they would be patrolling the trench line between the Germans and M Company's machine-gun position on their left, thereby placing his men in the middle of two lines of fire.[82]

Pippin's squad assembled at 9:00 P.M. and waited in silence; ambushing the Germans meant they had could not sortie until after the enemy did. At 11:00 P.M., Pippin rolled another cigarette and enjoyed "a good smoke," noting that all his men seemed to be watching him. He observed that he always tried to keep in good cheer in a dangerous situation and to look for the good in a bad situation. The corporal knew that his men took their cue from him, and he intended for them not to fear what lay ahead.[83]

Under shellfire, they moved toward the trench, but just as they took cover in the dugout, a German machine gun opened up and swept the top of the shelter. One of his men commented that "Mr. German" had gotten the "right dop[e] on us," and before the words escaped his lips, machine-gun bullets richocheted off the bank of the dugout, throwing dirt in their faces. They crawled out into no-man's-land one by one without losing a man. The night was so dark that they could not see one another. Pippin struggled through the barbed wire and then helped the others through it. Then, they crawled from one shell hole to another, one by one, keeping as low as possible and taking their time, as the German machine gunners, seemingly aware that something was up, kept firing in their direction every few minutes. Pippin's men waited for the lulls before moving on. Pippin and three of his men had gathered in a large hole, and just as he rose to move, he heard one of his men groan. Knowing the man was hit, Pippin rolled over to him but found he was already dead. Pippin reached the next hole, where the sergeant was, and reported the death. The sergeant replied, "That's three gone," for two men had been hit some time earlier. The sergeant feared that Pippin had been one of them. "Not yet," thought Pippin.[84]

The two men could discern a line of new dirt—they had found the German trench. They took up positions along the trench about 1:00 A.M. Pippin hoped they would lose no more men for if they did, they would be in "a bad fix" if they encountered a German patrol. The men were angry about their losses. The bullets were singing "their death song," humming like bees when they glanced off the barbed wire. Pippin, thinking every minute would be their last, listened for the telltale groan of another man hit. None came. A hand tapped him, then a low voice—"Germans." They could hear the sounds of the patrol amid the bullets. Every heart beat faster. They saw the Germans; a shot rang out, and the Americans, knives drawn, were on the enemy troops in a flash. There were no more shots, just groans, as they "cleened up" the German patrol and took one prisoner, sending him on ahead with one of their men. Pippin's men left the nine dead Germans—the only good German "in them dayes"—and then began to collect their own dead. Dragging a dead body from shell hole to shell hole over the rough ground of no-man's-land, while ducking German machine-gun fire, Pippin wrote, was the hardest job he ever had. Day was breaking as he helped pull the third man into the American trench. They were "all in," exhausted.[85]

Pippin recounted one other patrol, when a lieutenant picked eight of them and left Corporal Pippin to make certain that they were ready at midnight. Once again, the men prepared in silence. When the "looey" (lieutenant) returned, he briefed them that they were out to ambush any enemy patrol they encountered, even if they were outnumbered. This was a kill or be killed situation, as they were either to capture the Germans or to leave their bodies in no-man's-land.[86] As they entered the dark trench line in the rain, Pippin reflected that they had been in the trenches so long "that all of fear had gon from us."[87] From one shell hole to the next, through the barbed wire and thick grass they crept, until a German flare forced them to go to ground. Once they recovered their night vision, they lay in wait in a silence disturbed only by the sound of German artillery and shells soaring overhead to burst 5 miles in their rear. Then, a German machine gun opened fire, the sound and flash close to them. The looey ordered them to take the gun; they surrounded the German from his rear and closed in on him. The next thing the gunner knew, a rifle barrel nudged him in the head, at which point he threw up his hands without uttering a sound. One of the men took him back as prisoner.[88]

The rest crawled back on their hands and knees to resume their wait for a German patrol. Every minute seemed like an hour to Pippin, as the cold rain soaked him, the water dripping off his rifle. Just when it seemed they had waited in vain, he heard sounds that drew closer. It was too dark to see anything. The looey whispered to be ready for anything. Soon, they could hear disembodied voices in the darkness. They waited, unable to discern the strength of the German patrol. From the blackness came a sound like three hoots of an owl. An American answered with three hoots. Had he replied correctly? Yes. Nine German soldiers emerged from the darkness, to find themselves surrounded. "Hände hoch!" The Germans complied at once. The Americans crept back with their prisoners, keeping low as German machine guns opened fire, the bullets dancing off the barbed wire close to them with a sound like birds chirping.[89]

After a detail took the Germans to the command post and the men retired to their quarters, Pippin lay in his bunk and thought of home, wondering if he would ever see it again. He had received no letter from home in two months, but he shook off his disappointment and drifted off to sleep, awakening for mess feeling fine. That evening, before darkness fell, he sat on the dugout step and smoked his last cigarette, sharing it with five members of his squad who also had no more. He and his squad were so used to smoking that they had once barely managed for five or six days without cigarettes, he recalled. Initially, they could not stand the strong French tobacco, but Pippin was so desperate he could have smoked anything.[90] As he stood guard duty in the rain, at least he knew that early the next morning at 3:00 A.M., his squad would take the 5-mile hike for their ten days in the rear, where they could secure all the cigarettes they needed.[91]

When he finished his watch and descended into the dugout, his squad was asleep, wrapped in blankets to keep warm because they had no overcoats. No man, he later contemplated, no matter how good a soldier he was, could stand eight months in the frontline trenches; if he survived, he would not be able to return to the front again. He might have the will, but his body would not stand the stress.

The men never took off their shoes for twenty days or more until they returned to the rest area in the rear. Once, he wore his shoes for a month. At the time, however, he and his men never gave such limits a thought.[92]

Toward the end of this rotation, they experienced one of their worst nights in some time. "Altho it do rain in that country [France] all the time," Pippin observed, "but not like it did that night."[93] They lay on their bunks, smoking and telling stories. As Pippin watched his smoke curl toward the ceiling, he thought "of the good old U.S.A." and wondered "about Brodway."[94] Just as he imagined he could see the bright lights shining, one of the boys said that he wished he were home so that he could see his mother, whom he had not seen in a year or more. There was no one in France, Pippin replied, who would not give anything just to have one hour with his mother at home. The youth explained he had dreamed that he had had a fine time with his mother and started to go somewhere, when she asked him to come back to her. When he started to return, he woke up. "Go to bed!" someone shouted, and Pippin and the youth said no more, although the corporal could see that the boy took it hard. At that moment, a shell landed near the dugout, ending their reveries. As they made up their bunks the next morning, their sergeant appeared and informed them that they would stand guard duty at the command post. Pippin slept well that day, his squad stood guard that night, and they completed that tour in the trenches.[95]

Pippin's account of frontline service during the 369th's first months in the trenches provides a unique and detailed glimpse into the enlisted man's life in the trenches. Letters from home, tobacco and cigarettes, meals, sleep—all loomed large for men fighting in the depressingly rainy conditions of a northern European spring. C Company's 1st Sgt. M. Bridgett actually penned a poem, published after the war, entitled "Fags," an ode to the cigarette and its importance to soldiers.[96] Black Americans and Frenchmen got on well from the start, but the American soldiers took much longer to acquire a taste for the small, slender, but potent French cigarettes. Pippin's recollections particularly show the noncommissioned officer's crucial but often overlooked and unacknowledged role in preparing men for and leading them in combat and keeping up their morale under stress. Squad members undertook to bolster each other's spirits, and Pippin, as their leader, took pains to exhibit no fear and to take everything in stride in order to set the tone for his men. In the front lines, the corporals, soldiers of proven capabilities, took on the more difficult tasks, such as hunting German snipers. On trench raids and during withdrawals from the trenches to the rear, they were first in and last out, bringing in the last bodies after combat and standing guard to ensure that they lost no one during withdrawals. Pippin's account exemplifies how skillful the men of Lieutenant Castles's battalion had become at trench warfare during their relatively short time in combat. They were, in fact, accomplished veterans, survivors of mortal combat on the western front.

In June, Castles secured his transfer to the Tank Corps, where he joined a regular army unit with West Point officers. As an officer in Col. George Patton's Tank Corps in October 1918, Castles would win the Distinguished Service Cross and the Croix de Guerre in a disorganized and expensive attack and then spend six months in the hospital recovering from his wounds.[97] At his departure from the 369th, Castles reproached Hayward for using the band to advertise the Regiment "all over France" and for exploiting Henry Johnson's "fracas" to the fullest with the press. Castles's constant annoyance with Hayward culminated in his condemnation of the colonel's adept attempts to publicize the Regiment. His disdain may have stemmed from his awareness that regular army officers allegedly adhered to a code that avoided the mention of specific units to the press. Yet, skillful public relations and exploitation of the press brought fame to various units and branches of the armed forces, such as the Marine Corps at Belleau Wood. Henry Johnson's so-called fracas had occurred on May 15, the same day as the release of the favorable French report on African American soldiers and the official disbandment of the command of the 93rd Division (Provisional) and its brigades. Brig. Gen. Roy Hoffman, his two aides, and his chief of staff had received orders to join the 1st Division; the rest of his staff would join the 42nd Division. Johnson's exploit would prove to be the defining moment of the 369th Regiment and the signal exploit of African American soldiers in the Great War.

15th · NEW YORK · COLORED · INFANTRY
369th INFANTRY · U.S. · A.E.F.
369ème Regiment d'Infanterie R.I.U.S. · 16ème & 161ème Division
8ème Corps · · · · · · · · · · · · · · · · 4ème Armée Français

## FAMOUS · FIRSTS

Only Volunteer Regiment raised for the War which got to France

Embarked as part of First 100,000 of the A.E.F.

Shipwrecked Three Times en route to France

Only Regiment in history of U.S. to carry State Flag throughout War

First American Regiment in history of U.S. to serve as integral part of a Foreign Army

First American privates in Army of France to receive Croix de Guerre (Henry Johnson & Needham Roberts)

Regiment cited by French High Command (approved by American High Command) for Extraordinary Gallantry in Action and Colors decorated with Croix de Guerre

First Regiment of the Allies to reach the Rhine

Served 191 days in Action; longest of any American Regiment

Never lost a man by capture or a foot of ground

First Combat Regiment home and to march up Fifth Ave. under the Victory Arch

*Presented* to
Colonel Benjamin O. Davis
Commanding Officer 369th Infantry N.Y.N.G.
*by the*
Officers' Association 369th Infantry A.E.F.
23rd JUNE 1939

*Decorated by*
DOUGLAS H. HILLIKER
1st LIEUT. 369th INF.U.S.AEF.

Commemorative history and firsts of the 369th. Note the reference to the 15th Colored Infantry, indicating estrangement from the New York National Guard, as well as the rattlesnake as symbol with no reference to Hell Fighters.

Egbert "Bert" Austin Williams, singing a hymn at the first regimental open-air service for the 15th at Olympic Field, 1916. (Photo by Underwood & Underwood, Courtesy Library of Congress)

A prematurely aged and possibly demoralized Col. Charles Young in 1920, heading to his death in West Africa. (© Bettmann/Corbis)

Color-bearers of the 15th in prewar Harlem. (Courtesy Photographs and Prints Division, Schomburg Center for Research in Black Culture, New York Public Library, Astor, Lenox and Tilden Foundations)

Men of the 15th drilling in prewar Harlem. (Courtesy Photographs and Prints Division, Schomburg Center for Research in Black Culture, New York Public Library, Astor, Lenox and Tilden Foundations)

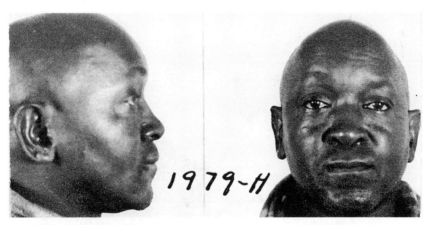

Prison photograph in 1943 of the man known as Valdo B. Schita, who gave his age as eighty. (Courtesy Federal Bureau of Prisons)

The 369th in the trenches in spring 1918. Note the men's French helmets and Lebel rifles with bayonets fixed and a grenade launcher on rifle in foreground. (© Bettmann/Corbis)

A stylized rendering of Henry Johnson and an image of a very young Neadom Roberts. (© Bettmann/Corbis)

Two unnamed soldiers, often misidentified as Henry Johnson and Neadom Roberts, in a characteristically staged VanDerZee studio session postwar. (Special Collections/Archives, John B. Coleman Library, Prairie View A&M University, Prairie View, TX)

"Our Colored Heroes": World War I poster featuring Henry Johnson in the foreground with a knife to the throat of an enemy soldier. Neadom, although also engaged with the enemy, is relegated to the background. Note Pershing communiqué documenting and validating the episode. (© Bettmann/Corbis)

James Reese Europe leads the band in France. (© Bettmann/Corbis)

Bugler Clarence Clarke, D Company, from New York City, the first of three
oil-on-canvas portraits of the men of the "15th New York Infantry" by
famed French war artist Raymond Desvarreux, himself a combat veteran.
Note the US Brodie helmets, which could suggest an end-of-war return to
the American models or a stylized artistic rendering. (Courtesy West Point
Museum Art Collection, US Military Academy, West Point, New York)

Cpl. Clarence L. Thompson, A Company, from New Jersey, born in Yonkers, New York. (Courtesy West Point Museum Art Collection, US Military Academy, West Point, New York)

Standard-bearer Sgt. William H. Cox, D Company, from Brooklyn, born in New Bern, North Carolina. (Courtesy West Point Museum Art Collection, US Military Academy, West Point, New York)

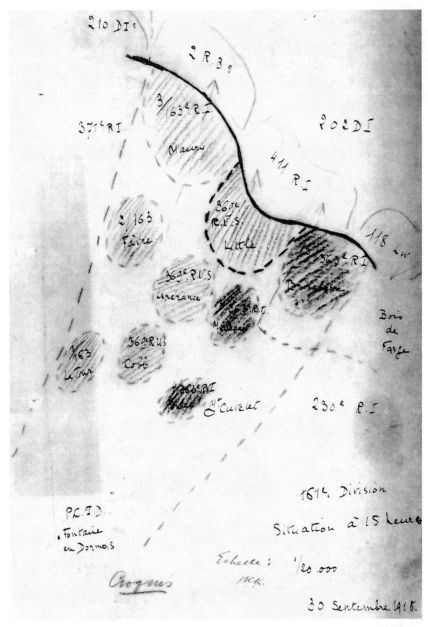

Map of French trench line at Séchault, 3:00 P.M. on September 30, 1918, with the 369th in the center of the line of 161st Division. Little's 1st Battalion is forward, with L'Esperance's 3rd in support and Cobb's 2nd Battalion in reserve (Cobb had already died in the assault). (Courtesy NARA, RG 165, Box 116)

93RD
DIVISION
(US)

369TH
INFANTRY
REGIMENT
(15TH REG-NYG)
(COLORED)

IN MEMORY
1918
MEUSE-ARGONNE
OFFENSIVE

RIPONT
MONT - CUVELET
SECHAULT
26 SEP - 1 OCT

Monument erected at Séchault in 1997 after a long struggle for approval and funding. (Courtesy Brig. Gen. Stephen R. Seiter)

Hartmannswillerkopf, known by the French as Vieil Armand (Old Armand), in the Vosges Mountains, the site of the Regiment's last battle and a highly contested observation post above the Rhine Valley. (Courtesy Guido Radig)

Plaque at the Vieil Armand Museum recognizing the contribution of the 369th Regiment to the defense of this strategic site. (Courtesy Jeffrey T. Sammons)

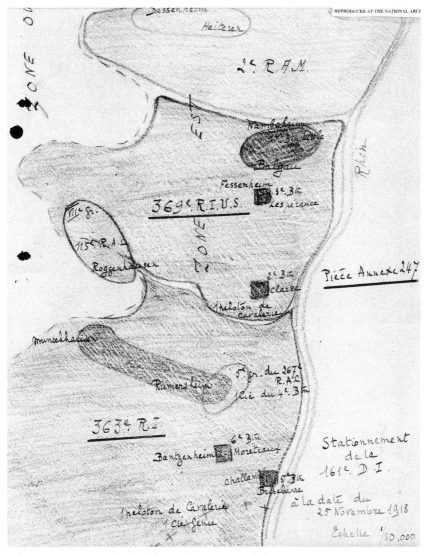

Map of Alsace showing the 369th Regiment at the Rhine River, Little's 1st Battalion to the north, L'Esperance's 3rd Battalion in the center, and Clark's 2nd Battalion to the south. (Courtesy NARA, RG 165, Box 116)

"The First to the Rhine," by S. J. Woolf, depicting the 369th as it led the 161st French Infantry Division (Lebouc) to Blodelsheim-on-Rhine between Mulhouse and Colmar on the morning of November 18, 1918. (Courtesy NARA)

Col. William Hayward in France in 1918 with men proudly wearing the Croix de Guerre. (© Bettmann/Corbis)

French general Collardet pinning the Croix de Guerre on Maj. Hamilton Fish; others receiving the honor are Maj. Lorillard Spencer to Fish's left and Lt. Col. Charles W. Fillmore to his right. The ladies are Mrs. B. S. Holden and Mrs. Charles Dean, mothers of two fallen soldiers, and the widow of Captain Cobb. Sgt. William Butler wearing a Distinguished Service Cross and Sgt. Valasta George of New York City by way of Barbados are next in line. Not shown is Colonel Hayward, who was made a knight of the Legion of Honor. (NARA, Signal Corps 95861)

The original caption of this February 12, 1919, photo reads: "World War I Hero Sergeant Henry Johnson: Sgt Henry Johnson of the 369th was awarded the Croix de Guerre for bravery during an outnumbered battle with German soldiers." (© Bettmann/Corbis)

Parade up Fifth Avenue to Harlem on February 17, 1919, in the French formation of sixteen abreast. (© Bettmann/Corbis)

The original caption reads: "Men from the 369th Infantry are served chicken dinner at the 71st Regiment Armory after the parade." (© Bettmann/Corbis)

Wounded veteran and well-dressed citizens of all ages view the parade.
(© Bettmann / Corbis)

A 1930 photo of the Fifth Avenue, or 369th, Armory. The structure features an art
deco–style administration building designed by Van Wart and Wein from 1930 to
1933 and a medieval-inspired drill shed designed by Tachau and Vought from 1920
to 1924. (Getty Images)

Brig. Gen. Benjamin O. Davis, Sr., shortly after his promotion and departure as the Regiment's first black commander in 1940. (© Bettmann/Corbis)

Col. Chauncey Hooper succeeded Davis as commander of the 369th Coastal Artillery in 1940 and would lead the unit in Hawaii. (© Bettmann/Corbis)

# IN FLANDERS FIELDS

*(With apologies to John McCrae.)*

In Flanders fields where poppies blow,
Beneath the crosses, row on row,
We blacks an endless vigil keep—
Yea, we, tho dead, can never sleep—
Ingratitude has made it so.

Why are we here? Why did we go
From loving homes, that need us so?
Was it for naught we gave our lives,
    On Flanders fields?

Ye blacks who live, to you we throw
The torch; be yours to face the foe
At home; and ever hold it high,
Fight for the things for which we die,
That we may sleep, where poppies grow.
        In Flanders fields.

                —Andrea Razafkeriefo.

© WILLIAM M KELLY Publisher

Andrea Razafkeriefo's (aka Andy Razaf) 1920s riff on John McRae's iconic "In Flanders Fields" (1915). Note the National Guard designations for the 369th (15th NYNG) and the 370th (8th Illinois), respectively.

William A. Rogers rendering of the "Battle of Henry Johnson," first published in the *New York Herald* in May 1919 as "Two First Class Americans" and republished in the *Chicago Defender* as "Two Real Americans."

# 9

## "The Battle of Henry Johnson" and Neadom Roberts

### The Night Two Ordinary Men Became War Heroes and Race Symbols

As of mid-May, the 369th had gradually assumed the defense of subsector US as part of the French 16th Division.[1] Following common French military practice, two battalions held the first line and a third stood in reserve. The three battalions rotated through the two frontline positions and the reserve.[2]

Subsector US extended for "a front of four kilometers, largely of marsh and thickly wooded swamp in the lowlands of the Aisne and Tourbe [Rivers]" northwest of St. Menehould. Two battalions of three rifle companies and one machine-gun company each occupied the front of the subsector, with the third battalion in reserve at Maffrecourt. The position's front-line and support positions consisted of hastily constructed and lightly fortified breastworks in the swampy ground. On tiny islands of higher ground stood stronger redoubts of earthen breastworks, surrounded by barbed wire and covered with overhead wood and earthen shelters to protect the men from shell splinters. Groups of four privates and an NCO armed with rifles, grenades, and French Chauchat automatic rifles occupied the small enclosed redoubts, which were located at distances ranging from fifty to more than 200 yards.

The left flank of the position ended in an open marsh spanning the Tourbe River and its tributaries, and consequently it could be reinforced, evacuated, or supplied only from the center of the line to its right and not from the rear. German advance posts lay some 200 to 300 yards distant, across a no-man's-land dotted with abandoned breastworks, shelters, and barbed wire entanglements that enabled the Germans to approach very near the left flank of the American position under cover.

Here, on this boggy ground, two African American soldiers would perform such heroic military deeds that their importance transcended time and place in the ensuing complex impact on ideas of black citizenship, race, and nation in the United States.

The 1st Battalion had spent its initial ten-day tour in the frontline trenches in the Montplaisir section, part of it with a French battalion, so the men knew the terrain. The first night of this second tour, the battalion observation posts, extended beyond the front trench line into no-man's-land, took fire from snipers *behind* them, between the observers and the American front lines. The next day, the 1st Battalion found and destroyed several dugouts at weak points in the line where enemy snipers had infiltrated. It then set ambushes at the points of infiltration to catch the Germans and take prisoners. The first night thereafter, no one came, so the battalion moved its ambushes to other positions.[3]

Very early in the morning of May 15, the Germans came through unguarded positions. Infiltrating 150 yards through the American lines, the German patrol split into two squads, one approaching the American position from the right, the other from the rear of the post of Combat Group 29. A corporal and four men manned Post 29, an observation point for Combat Group 28, a strongpoint some 60 yards away that was manned by a lieutenant and a half platoon.

At Post 29, the corporal and two men slept while two privates—Henry Johnson of Albany, New York, and Neadom Roberts of Trenton, New Jersey—stood guard. Exactly what happened next, like the specifics of most war stories and heroic deeds, cannot be determined with absolute certainty. No soldiers witnessed the encounter that ensued, and the official report of Capt. Arthur Little's reconstruction of the encounter, based on the testimony of Johnson and Roberts and his investigation of the scene of the struggle, has not been found. What does remain is Little's narrative of the "battle" in his book, which the following account presents—without the more fantastic and sensational verbal exchanges that embellished it.[4]

Roberts heard noise from his side of the post and moved stealthily to alert Johnson. Both men listened intently for further sound from the darkness. The noise—perhaps the sound of cutters on barbed wire—recurred. Both heard it, fired a flare, and shouted, "Corporal of the Guard." A shower of grenades descended, wounding both Roberts and Johnson and sealing the other three men in the dugout. The enemy patrol had breached the wire and was moving rapidly toward them in the dark. Roberts, too badly wounded to rise, threw grenades in the direction of the onrushing enemy. Johnson, his Lebel rifle at the ready, rose to meet the Germans. He emptied his three-shot clip into the first soldier. A second German, armed with a Luger automatic pistol, vaulted over his falling comrade toward Johnson. The small, lithe Johnson, wielding the Lebel by the barrel like a club, smashed him in the head with the rifle butt, knocking the German to the ground.

His second opponent felled, Johnson saw two Germans carrying Roberts away by the shoulders and feet toward their lines. At that, Johnson drew his bolo knife and leaped onto the German holding Roberts's upper body. He landed on the German's shoulders, knees first, and plunged the bolo downward, cutting powerfully through the man's round, gray-and-red cap. The 9-inch blade of the 3-pound knife sank to the hilt through the top of the German's head. He crumpled to the ground. Johnson landed on his feet, knife in hand, and wheeled about. The German he had hit with his rifle had regained his feet by that point and was rushing toward him. The Luger's bullets smashed into Johnson, knocking him to his hands and knees. The German closed. But he moved too close, as Johnson, still on his knees, came up under the German's guard and gutted him with the bolo knife.

The disemboweling of their comrade proved too much for the remaining Germans, who seized their dead and wounded and fled, pursued by a barrage of grenades from a badly wounded Johnson. The relief party from Combat Group 28, led by Lt. Richardson Pratt, arrived after the Germans departed, just as Johnson fainted. Like an automaton, he had been yelling for the corporal of the guard throughout the fight. Those were the last words from his lips to the lieutenant.

At 3:30 A.M., Sgt. Maj. Chauncey Hooper entered the cabin of 1st Battalion commander, Capt. Little, and reported that a fight had occurred. Two seriously wounded and probably dying soldiers lay on the small flatcar of their rail line, as a mule pulled it to the aid station to meet an ambulance. Little put on his rubber boots and his trench coat over his pajamas and ran to the aid station.

Roberts and Johnson, who had each received a cup of rum from the captain who was present, had regained consciousness. They were coherent and talkative despite the severity of their wounds. Little, aware that this was the Regiment's first encounter and his men its first casualties, took notes in his notebook as they spoke. He feared the men would die, but Johnson urged him not to worry, saying this was not the first time he had been shot. Whether the remark was factual, Johnson's bravado, or the product of Little's occasional penchant for both drama and racial humor remains uncertain. It is only one of countless quotable, memorable, and racially inflected statements attributed to Johnson, many of which Little recounted.

Later that day, after an ambulance had taken Johnson and Roberts away, Little cross-examined all witnesses and traced the Germans' circuitous retreat a half mile to where they had crossed a river. At the opening in the wire, Little's investigative party found hanging "a terrible mass of flesh and blood" and cloth, as well as the blown-open pulp of a first aid packet. One of Johnson's grenades had claimed a victim, and thick, sticky blood filled a hole the "size and shape of a five gallon punch bowl" in the chalky clay of the ground. It took more than a week for the soil to absorb the blood.

The Americans easily tracked the Germans' retreat from the trail of abandoned equipment and the pools of blood and bloody bandages. The Germans had left some forty potato-masher, or stick, grenades; three Lugers; seven wire cutters; and three caps, including one with a slit 2.5 inches wide through its crown and brown hair glued to the inner lining with dried blood. They found the marks of two stretchers outside the wire. Little knew that usually one of every four men in an enemy patrol carried heavy, long-arm wire clippers. This knowledge, coupled with the fact that the Germans had managed to carry off their wounded and dead and that Johnson had certainly killed four of them, led Little to conclude that the enemy patrol comprised "a minimum" of twenty-four soldiers. By 10:30 A.M., the captain had finished his investigation and dictated his official report, recommending Johnson and Roberts for decorations for valor. He sent the bloody German cap as a trophy to the division commander, General Le Gallais.

Shortly after, Colonel Hayward arrived with three civilian visitors: reporters Irvin Cobb, Martin Green of the *Evening World,* and Lincoln Eyre of the *New York World.* The black soldiers did not welcome Cobb, a southern humorist whose writings ridiculed black speech and black people. They commented that he had some nerve showing up there after "having written and said so many damaging things about our people." The noncommissioned officers turned their backs and avoided him.[5]

Cobb inquired if *"les enfants perdus"* (the lost infants) had had any interesting experiences. When Captain Little answered noncommittally that "things" had been generally "dull and quiet," Green asked if they had had any "fights." "Why yes," replied Little," we did have a little fight this morning. . . . A couple of our boys had a real pitched battle, for a few minutes. They did very well, too. I've just finished the report. I'm trying to get them the *Croix de Guerre.* Would you care to read it?"[6]

The enthralled correspondents read the report avidly and then insisted upon visiting the site of the encounter. Little warned them about snipers, advice they contemptuously dismissed. The heat, however, nearly finished the reporters, who required four rest periods to complete their tour. Enjoying every moment of it, Little insisted that they view the "grenade-blown punch bowl filled with blood."[7]

Later, at lunch, Cobb inquired about the extent of Johnson's special training in trench fighting. Little replied that the Regiment had undergone about three weeks of training in theory and one week in fact. Cobb deemed Johnson's exploit truly remarkable and the 369th "the finest [American regiment at the front] he had seen." That night after dinner, Sergeant Sissle and Sergeant Mikell decided that the band would serenade Cobb with "plantation melodies," to leave the white southerner with a favorable musical impression of his visit. In an article in the *Saturday Evening Post,* Cobb concluded that the band was the best one that he had heard anywhere in Europe during the war.[8] The men of the 369th and their bravery and discipline had greatly impressed Cobb, who later expressed his concern about the inadequacy of their combat training; perhaps, he mused, that was because Americans were accustomed to viewing black soldiers as laborers. A few days after the exploit, the front page of the *New York World* carried Lincoln Eyre's article "The Battle of Henry Johnson." The New York evening papers and then the Associated Press disseminated the news around the country.[9]

Divisional Order no. 697, issued by General Le Gallais on May 16, cited the soldiers of the 369th US Regiment of Infantry in the following manner:

1st: Johnson, Henry, No. 103348, soldier in the said command: doing double night sentry duty, was attacked by a group of a dozen Germans and put one out of the fight by gunshot and seriously wounded two with a knife. In spite of having received three wounds by revolver shots and grenades at the start of the action, went to the help of his wounded comrade who was being carried away by the enemy and continued the strife until the rout of the Germans. Gave a magnificent example of courage and energy.

2nd: Roberts, Needham, No. 103369, soldier in the said command: doing double night sentry duty was attacked and seriously wounded in the leg by a group of Germans; continued the strife by throwing grenades, in spite of having fallen to the ground, until the enemy was put to rout. Good and brave soldier.

The General requested that the citation for soldier Johnson be changed to the citation of the Order of the Army.[10]

The final request meant that Johnson would receive the Croix de Guerre with Gold Palm Leaf, the highest award, and Roberts the Croix de Guerre with Silver Star, the divisional award that ranked behind the Army Cross and then the Army Corps Cross. Johnson would receive his Croix much later, in October, as AEF HQ controlled not only the awarding of American medals to American troops but French (and British) medals as well, and it acted with all deliberate delay in granting medals to the 369th and other units detached from the AEF.

Lt. Col. M. A. W. Shockley of AEF General Staff visited the 369th to observe its training on May 15 and proceeded to investigate Johnson and Robert's encounter.[11] Shockley's concerns initially focused on the absence of any evidence that the Americans patrolled the area between fortified bunkers at night or during the daytime. His account of the two men's struggle consisted of two sentences, vague and short, noting that they encountered "some enemies" and that one of them "was said to have [used]" his bolo and rifle in a hand-to-hand fight. The corporal and two men in the shelter could give "little information," it was noted, and Shockley did not interview Johnson and Roberts, who had been sent to a French hospital in Bar-le-Duc.

Shockley noted the absence of firsthand information on the German raiding party, in terms of its numbers and casualties. He did cite the deduction of some twenty men, including an NCO, based on the equipment left behind, and he acknowledged two German casualties on the basis of the bloody, pierced cap and the blood, clothing, and gauze fragments remaining from the grenade explosion. However, he dismissed the intelligence officer's account of Johnson's stabbing the German in the stomach, based on his cursory examination of the bolo knife a day after the incident: how and why, he did not explain. In his summary *Comments,* Shockley stated that the assault had been "a carefully prepared raid" to capture prisoners or confirm the American presence and that the two lookouts' "activity and resistance" had prevented the taking of prisoners. The encounter "increase[d] the vigilance and confidence of the 369th Infantry." Nonetheless, he concluded negatively that the "very difficult" position required "a particularly well organized system of security" for which the Regiment's instructors had not trained them.

Shockley's official report of May 17, based on his investigation, was thus far shorter, more vague, more negative, and less informative than Little's detailed account, which included the statements of Johnson and Roberts. Furthermore, it was neither as specific nor as full of praise as the French assessment that culminated in the awarding of the Croix de Guerre. However, the French citation for Johnson's Croix cited an attack by only "a group of a dozen Germans."[12] Shockley's report dismissed the gutting of the third German and ignored the serious and near-fatal nature of Johnson's and Roberts's wounds, which would invalid both men from active duty. The soldiers required weeks of hospitalization—a fact confirmed by black YMCA worker Heyward E. Caldwell, who reported that the two men had not been released from the hospital as of June 24. Even official discharge records listed both men as "severely wounded in action."[13] Finally, Shockley's negative assessment of the Regiment's security training and his judgment of its failure to patrol the front overshadowed any accomplishments of the two soldiers and failed to do justice to their exploits.

Lewis Shaw wrote to his mother on May 20, stating that he was certain she would "read big headlines in the American papers about the wonderful fight one of our patrols put up." He elaborated in his next letter, written on July 5: "From all accounts we are the most famous and unusual regiment in the U.S. Army. Our men have improved a thousand percent and have a pride and esprit de corps entirely equal to their reputation abroad. Two of them drove off about twenty Boche in an advance post the other day and received the highest French decorations. It made every man in the regiment tingle for the same chance."[14]

When Lt. John Castles wrote to his mother about Johnson's exploit, he recounted that "one of our men, in 'C' Company" had received the "Croix de Guerre with the palm leaf for messing up 4 Boche with a bolo knife. They attacked his post about 20 strong & though he got 4 bullet wounds attacked the whole bunch & they beat it. He has been recommended also for the new U.S. war cross. As far as the K.O. [commanding officer] is concerned the war is won by the above feat."[15] Castles's characterization omitted entirely the role played by Neadom Roberts in the encounter, but, his sarcasm notwithstanding, his letter reflects the importance that Colonel Hayward attached to Henry Johnson's heroic effort.

On May 16, 1918, the day after Johnson and Roberts's encounter with the German raiding party, the AEF commander, Gen. John J. Pershing, released his first "official communiqué" from his headquarters via Secretary of War Newton Baker. Pershing was conforming to the established practice of his fellow Entente commanders, Douglas Haig of Great Britain and Philipppe Pétain of France, whose official communiqués kept civilians at home abreast of their armies' and soldiers' achievements at the front. Pershing's second official communiqué to the press, written on May 19 and released on May 20 in the United States, indicates that Shockley's report influenced his public pronouncements less than the more favorable assessments from Little and the French. Pershing understood the pressing need to appease black people's concerns about the treatment of their soldiers, since they were aware of the 369th's deployment in the French army, as well as the need to give good news to all regarding the war effort. He announced:

> Reports in hand show a notable instance of bravery and devotion shown by two soldiers of an American colored regiment operating in a French sector. Before daylight on May 15, Private Henry Johnson and Private Roberts, while on sentry duty at some distance from one another, were attacked by a German raiding party, estimated at twenty men, who advanced in two groups, attacking at once from flank and rear.
>
> Both men fought bravely in hand-to-hand encounters, one resorting to the use of a bolo knife after his rifle jammed and further fighting with the bayonet and butt became impossible. There is evidence that at least one, and probably a second, German was severely cut. A third is known to have been shot.
>
> Attention is drawn to the fact that the colored sentries were first attacked and continued fighting after receiving wounds, and despite the use of grenades by a superior force. They should be given credit for preventing, by their bravery, the capture of any of our men. Three of our men were wounded, two by grenades.
>
> All are recovering, and the wounds in two cases are slight.[16]

Pershing thus praised the men and their heroic feat, but "credit given" did not include American honors or timely approval of the French recommendations for the Croix de Guerre. Pershing did not mention Roberts's first name, thus contributing to his diminution, and he indicated that only one soldier suffered serious wounds when in fact both Johnson and Roberts were seriously wounded. The third soldier he mentioned was one of the men enclosed in the bunker. Nonetheless, with this validation from the AEF commander, news of the exploits of Henry Johnson and Neadom Roberts spread quickly in the AEF. On May 24, 1918, the first and second pages of the army newspaper, *Stars and Stripes,* carried this headline under "Guerre" (War): NEGRO UNIT IN TRENCHES. GREAT BOAST IS THAT THEY DON'T NEED LAMPBLACK FOR PATROL WORK. READY HELPER IN BILLETS. DARK SKINNED FOES OF "BUSH GERMANS" HAVE WON FRIENDS IN MANY FRENCH TOWNS.

The lengthy article began, "Two strapping American negroes have been awarded the *Croix de Guerre* with palm for valor in France." Although describing either the small, slender Johnson or Roberts as "strapping" required a great stretch of imagination, the article continued to note that "the porter from the New York Central station in Albany" and the "elevator boy for a

New York apartment house"—Johnson was actually an illiterate manual laborer in Albany and Roberts lived in Trenton, New Jersey—had done "fearful damage" to a "startled raiding party of 24 Germans whom they caught in the act and, all unaided, put to flight." The article located "the two dusky heroes" in a French hospital, "neither permanently the worse for wear," "chuckling gleefully over the great adventure and telling great tales to their admiring circle."[17]

The men's decoration, *Stars and Stripes* continued, "let one of the darkest cats out of the A.E.F. bag," a "secret . . . so well-kept that only a few of the all-wise at G.H.Q. had even a suspicion"—a "black American unit had been part and parcel of the French Army." Now, with the secret out, the army paper reported that French commanders and the French people spoke "in praise of the *soldats noirs de l'Amérique*." Then, *Stars and Stripes* praised the black American soldiers, albeit with obligatory minstrel references:

> They know what it was like to go over the top, to drop into the German trenches under barrage and emerge with prisoners, to scour No Man's Land every night even up to the Boche wire.
> There is nothing about No Man's Land they don't know, and it is their favorite joke and their great pride that unlike the white patrols, they do not have to make-up their tell-tale faces with lamp black before venturing on these excursions.[18]

The article then described with great gusto "What They Did," modifying the combat ever so slightly. In the *Stars and Stripes* version, Johnson "opened the burly German's skull and cut a hole in his side" with his bolo, "a long and tapering weapon, as sinister as a razor." When shot, Johnson did not stab the onrushing German but picked up a stray grenade and threw it at the invaders, putting them to flight. In the hospital, a grinning Johnson reportedly commented about the result, "My lan'. I reckon dey had to tote dat Bush German home to his fambly all wrapped up in a newspaper."

*Stars and Stripes* then reported that the encounter had entered "the songs and legends of the outfit," which now chose the bolo as "the weapon of weapons." As they sharpened their blades, men "crooned . . . a negro chant with so much of Africa in it" with the refrain "Bush Germans, Bush Germans, wese gwine-a git you yet!" The article noted that even though nearly all Yanks preferred the name *Bush* to *Boche* as a "term of reproach" for the Germans, the Negroes said *Bush Germans*.[19]

The article announced that the black soldiers had further impressed both the French authorities and the French people because they had cleaned up the towns that housed them. Women who initially panicked at the impending arrival of black Americans, according to *Stars and Stripes,* "will miss them when they go." One could often see "a great grinning American black ambling up a French street" carrying a French woman's load or helping with the gardening or housework. Their American commander expressed pride in the combat record of his "chillun," the paper said, who after undergoing less preparation for combat on French soil than other American troops still had yet to lose a prisoner to the Germans.

According to the article, the men "boasted all previous occupations from Baptist clergymen . . . to Corporal Smith of South Carolina," whose sergeant major had recommended him to repair the headquarters safe because he was a "burglar." They also boasted the tallest doughboy in France, a sergeant 6'7" tall whose size 14 double E shoes were "the despair of the Q.M. [Quartermaster]." The article concluded that the "Johnson-Roberts scrap" was now "the topic of the day in St. Menehould" and that the French general commanding the sector reported to his superior, "The American report is too modest. As a result of oral information furnished to me, it appears that the blacks were extremely brave. This little combat does honor to the Americans."[20]

The all too familiar use of dialect and minstrel/coon imagery and humor, including references to razors, blackening agents, large feet, and white women, so typical of the era, added an air of levity to and thereby diminished what was a brutal combat. *Stars and Stripes* nonetheless expressed admiration for and praise of the African American soldiers for their valor in the front lines and their docile, nonthreatening, and helpful conduct in the rear. Even as Colonel Hayward was busy distinguishing his men from Africans, *Stars and Stripes* likened them to African warriors who chanted as they sharpened their bolo knives. Yet, these ferocious warriors of African descent became children, or "chillun," in their behavior with French women. Later, white senior officers of the African American 92nd Division would stereotypically demean their African American soldiers as cowardly rapists who posed no danger to the Germans. *Stars and Stripes* stereotyped them as docile black "children" with French women who became dashing, slashing heroes in combat. The men's liaisons with French women were in fact certainly not as innocent as the depiction in *Stars and Stripes,* which reflected instead the comfort zone of white soldiers who could find in their perception of black men's relationships with white women no middle ground between the innocuous child and the threatening rapist.

The *Stars and Stripes* of May 31, 1918, carried an article entitled "Our Own 'Soldats Noirs' [Black Soldiers]," referring to French African soldiers, that quoted the French citations given to Johnson and Roberts and stated that the news of their Croix de Guerre awards had caused "jubilation" in "many a shanty back home." The article continued:

> Any one who knew American history, any one who had pondered the records of the Civil War and the Spanish American War, could have predicted that the American blacks would fight the new battles with all the fierceness and dash and exaltation of the old.
>
> Now the slaves of a century ago are defending their American citizenship on a larger battlefield. Now is their first chance to show themselves before the whole world as good and brave soldiers, all.

No matter the racial stereotypes and humor—including the reference to "many a shanty," which invoked an antebellum idyll and ignored the urban home of the Regiment's troops—the *Stars and Stripes* article's high praise of black soldiers' past exploits highlighted the absurdity of the American army's racist reluctance to train African Americans as combat soldiers. In any case, the 15th/369th had now made a lasting impression on many a white soldier, as evidenced by the remarks of 1st Sgt. John G. Mansfield of the 51st Pioneer Infantry, who commented on the diversity of Chinese, Negroes, and Indians in the army in a letter home on December 21, 1918: "[The] coons of New York have shown up well in battle. That old 15th N.Y. Inf that we looked at and smiled when they left the Albany armory have been in battle and the Jerrys had to hustle. Some of them didn't but they are there yet."[21]

In early June 1918, some three weeks after Johnson and Roberts's encounter with the Germans, when the 1st Battalion rotated from the trenches for a week's rest at Maffrecourt, Captain Little visited his two men in the hospital. Little asked Johnson how he had become so skilled with a bolo knife and whether he had ever fought with a knife before. Johnson became hysterical with laughter at the ridiculous question, and patients across the entire ward, Americans and French alike, reportedly laughed with him.

Little's story appears apocryphal. His very question suggested the gap between the sheltered existence of the rich white officer and the hardscrabble life of the poor black enlisted man, an economic and social gulf widened by race in the United States to an unbridgeable chasm. Yet, Little himself knew better, for he was certainly aware of the black man's reputation as an expert with knife or straight razor. Although Little's memoirs proved him to be a good officer concerned with the welfare of his men, he succumbed to a paternalistic voyeurism and occasional tendency to bend the truth for the sake of a good anecdote.

Neadom Roberts, whose side and hip bone had been split by a German bayonet and whose right elbow had been shattered by a German explosive bullet,[22] would return home for further hospitalization and discharge. Henry Johnson, after at least a month and a half in the hospital and three months away from the Regiment, managed to return to the 369th. By all rights, he too should have been sent home for discharge. French doctors had removed most of the bones in one of his feet, forcing him to walk in a manner that Little described as "slap-foot." A silver tube replaced the shattered shinbone of one leg. He suffered from other, lesser wounds, but he somehow convinced the French hospital staff to return him to his unit.[23]

Colonel Hayward and Captain Little, inspired by affection, admiration, and ultimately gratitude for the fame that Johnson's exploit had gained the Regiment, decided to retain him at headquarters. Hayward likened Johnson to Gen. George Armstrong Custer's horse—a dehumanizing metaphor—which the 7th Cavalry had kept at its headquarters to show off to company. Henry Johnson, promoted to sergeant, now became, in Little's words, "one of the great pets of the Regiment," a "sweet, unassuming boy" who, somewhat paradoxically, "never let anyone else forget" his award. Johnson had every right to be proud: his exploit had proved that he was a man as defined by the very arbiters of manhood—white military officers. To Little, however, he remained a boy, an indication of how difficult it was to change long-held stereotypes and prejudices, regardless of the magnitude of the achievement and despite Little's goodwill.

Meanwhile, the men of the 369th, largely unaware of the tidal wave of euphoria and pride their comrades had stirred, went about their daily routines as battalions rotated in and out of the trenches. They then rotated into reserve, but constantly on the move, behind the French in case of a German breakthrough. When the Germans began their offensive toward Paris on May 27, the front soon came alive in the 369th's sector, as it supported a French attack on June 6. But when the Germans counterattacked, the French commander shouted for the men of the Regiment to retreat, in the midst of the German barrage. An agitated Colonel Hayward, sans helmet, supposedly retorted, "My men never retire. They go forward, or they die!"[24]

Hayward's reply did not garner the fame of a similar exhortation uttered by another American soldier the same day. On June 6, the US Marines attacked Belleau Wood as the AEF sought to blunt the German offensive in the region around Château-Thierry. The marines—urged on by the immortal words of two-time Medal of Honor recipient Gunnery Sgt. Dan Daly, "Come on, you sons of bitches! Do you want to live forever?"—charged across the poppy fields and into the woods in waves, shoulder to shoulder. German machine gunners mowed them down, and the marines gained only a foothold on the edge of the woods. The mile of woods would not be captured until the end of the month, during which time army units replaced the marines while they recovered from the initial assault to take the area with artillery support. The marines had a 50 percent casualty rate, making Belleau Wood the costliest battle in marine history until the assault on the Pacific island of Tarawa in November 1943. Much like the 369th had benefited from the presence of news reporters on the scene after Johnson and Roberts's fight, the marines reaped a tremendous publicity coup because one of the best and best-liked reporters, Floyd Gibbons of the *Chicago Tribune,* actually entered Belleau Wood with them after filing a story *before* the attack. Army infantrymen condemned the presence of a "press agent" with the marines as a violation of "military etiquette."[25] But press coverage would do much to make the reputations of Henry Johnson, Neadom Roberts, and the 369th as well as the US Marines.

The 369th remained in the line until July 4. On June 12, the Germans had staged a strong raid on Montplaisir, which artillery and machine-gun fire repulsed with no American fatalities. Sgt. Bob Collins of the 3rd Battalion Machine Gun Company was awarded the Croix de Guerre for the role he played in repelling the German raid on Montplaisir with his guns, and his commanding officer, Lewis Shaw, received the congratulations of Colonel Hayward and promotion to captain in early July.[26]

Meanwhile, Lt. Jim Europe had been gassed and evacuated, and on his return, he was relegated to Physical Class B status, which prohibited front-line service.[27] Sgt. Noble Sissle located Europe among rows of suffering soldiers on cots in the gas ward of a little French army hospital 5 miles to the rear of Maffrecourt. He reported:

Some of them in places where their eyes were, were just large, bleeding scabs; others, their mouths were just one mass of sores; others had their hands up, and there were terrible burns beneath their arms, where the gas had attacked the moisture there. . . . Others, their nose had been burned so terribly that they could only breathe through their mouths and the sound of them gasping for breath resembled the sound of the croak of frogs that your hear at night passing down the country-road.[28]

Sissle was relieved to find a coughing Europe eager to describe his first draft of a future jazz piece entitled "In No Man's Land," which he had conceived during the gas bombardment. After rhythmically and dramatically describing all the dangers of a patrol, the song concluded, "Ain't life great out in No Man's Land."[29]

On July 4, the French 9th Cuirassiers relieved the 369th, which proceeded to the rear at Maffrecourt and then on for reassembly and reassignment. The entire front of the 16th Division had remained calm during the 369th's service, with only a few major assaults.[30] The 369th's strength from May through August varied, as follows:

May 21, 72 officers, 2,320 men
May 28, 82 officers, 2,721 men
June 4, 80 officers, 2,927 men
June 26, 71 officers, 2,948 men
July 3, 68 officers, 2,892 men
July 17, 52 officers, 2,816 men
July 31, 55 officers, 2,494 men
August 14, 79 officers, 2,920 men[31]

Over a period of some three months, the numbers of enlisted men in the Regiment had increased by nearly 25 percent, the number of officers by less than 10 percent. The Regiment was laboring under a dire shortage of commissioned officers, which would continue for the rest of the war.

The African American soldiers of the 369th Regiment had successfully completed their introduction to the trench warfare of the western front. Their early combat experience compared favorably to that of the 1st Division, AEF, the all-white "Big Red One" of World War I and World War II fame, which had arrived in France in 1917. Two weeks after the division entered the line, the Germans welcomed its men with a raid on the night of November 2–3, 1917. A German artillery barrage first isolated a platoon of the 16th Infantry Regiment. Then, German infantry rushed them using grenades, pistols, trench knives, and bayonets, capturing eleven American soldiers and leaving behind the bodies of three more, one with his throat cut. These three were "the first Americans killed in combat in an American unit in the First World War."[32] The German raiding party that attempted this on a smaller scale with the 369th on May 15, 1918, encountered Henry Johnson and Neadom Roberts, who turned the tables on the Germans. A French observer found the 1st Division's soldiers were solid, alert, and willing to fight, although at night, their nervousness and lack of fire discipline prompted them to shoot at anything. In the rear, the American soldiers demonstrated little discipline and no hygiene in camp, where drunken soldiers fired revolvers randomly into the air.[33] In comparison to the 1st Division in 1917, the 369th Regiment had acquitted itself well at the front and in the rear during its first five months with the French in 1918.

Back in New York in March 1918, however, rumors about white officers' abuse of black soldiers and about German torture of black prisoners of war had "tremendously upset" Harlemites. Two hundred mutilated black soldiers, with no eyes or arms, allegedly lay in Base Hospital No. 1 in the Bronx. Persistent rumors placed James Reese Europe in a Long Island hospital, "having lost his sight on the firing line in France," whereas Napoleon Bonaparte Marshall was said to be dead, his body mutilated.[34] The Germans had supposedly returned the prisoners to American lines, whence the US Army shipped them home in secret. Of course, at that time, the only black combat regiment in France was the 369th in the Argonne,[35] and the 369th lost no prisoners to the Germans, nor did its white officers abuse their men.

The circulation of such rumors would recur, an indication both of a general tendency toward rumor in the absence of concrete information and specifically of black mistrust of the segregationist government and army, although the rumors of white officers' mistreatment of black soldiers would be more than justified in the case of the 92nd Division AEF. In the New York press, the Committee of Public Information even denied the existence of discrimination in the army—a totally absurd claim—but in regard to the treatment of black and white prisoners of war and the presence of maimed black soldiers at Base Hospital No. 1,[36] the disclaimers were accurate.

Walter Loving, the first of two black agents in the Military Intelligence Bureau, organized a hospital tour for prominent Harlemites in mid-April so they could talk to the few black soldiers undergoing treatment there. Despite this effort, the rumors persisted. In June, a white agent considered the nightly open-air speeches of Marcus Garvey a possible source of the rumors, but he lacked hard evidence.[37] Most white officials attributed such rumors to the presence of German agents among the black populace. Loving suspected a systematic, highly organized, and well-funded propaganda campaign directed at Harlem, and he feared the situation could become volatile. He reported that women with men serving in France were receiving telephone messages and fake telegrams announcing the death or wounding of their loved ones.[38]

Loving considered Harlem to be a hotbed of dissidence and "the fountain head of all radical propaganda among Negroes." Young Socialists such as A. Phillip Randolph and Chandler Owen attracted his attention for their "radical publication," the *Messenger*. Moreover, their organization, the National Association for the Promotion of Labor Unionism among Negroes, was under investigation by the state of New York for "radicalism" and association with socialists and trade union leaders. The list of suspects included Cyril Briggs and Hubert Harrison, publishers of the *Crusader* and *Negro Voice,* respectively. Even *The Crisis* and the black YMCA came under Loving's scrutiny, for the government suspected *The Crisis* of possible pro-German leanings and the YMCA of aiding the publication's activities as its distributor.[39]

Even soapbox orators such as C. C. Payne, a poor and barely educated veteran of the 10th Cavalry and a part-time Pullman porter, aroused Loving's attention when, on the corner of 134th Street and Lenox Avenue on May 30, 1918, he declared that "America has no right to go abroad to help fight to settle differences over there before she has first settled her differences here with us"; he also threatened to make things right in Harlem if given "a rifle and 150 rounds of ammunition." Loving cautioned Payne against promoting violence and detected a direct relationship between German gains on the western front and "anti-American" activity in Harlem.[40]

In this atmosphere of mutual mistrust between Harlem and the US government, news of the exploits of Henry Johnson and Neadom Roberts exploded on the front pages of the New York papers. On May 20, Pershing's communiqué cited Johnson and Roberts, but war correspondents with the commercial press had already broken the story at home on May 19, the very day Pershing wrote his communiqué.[41] AEF HQ had lost control of the master narrative to the reporters on the scene in France.

On Sunday, May 19, the front page of the paper founded by Joseph Pulitzer in 1883, the *World,* carried Lincoln Eyre's article TWO N.Y. DARKIES WHIP 24 GERMANS. KILL OR WOUND HALF OF THEM WITH RIFLE, KNIFE AND BOMB— WIN FRENCH WAR CROSS. Eyre's references to "a unit composed mainly of New Yorkers," and to "their commander—an ex-Public Service Commissioner"—revealed that the 15th New York National Guard was in action, its morale was "splendid," and "their relations with the French soldiers and civilians . . . all that could be desired."[42] On Monday, May 20, 1918, the *World*'s lead headline trumpeted TWO NEW YORK NEGRO SOLDIERS FOIL GERMAN ASSAULT. The lengthy two-page article, which antedated the article in *Stars and Stripes* by four days, appeared under the extensive subheadlines THOUGH WOUNDED, TWO NEGROES ROUT GERMAN RAIDERS. HENRY JOHNSON AND NEEDHAM ROBERTS WIN FRENCH WAR CROSSES FOR GALLANTRY IN PUTTING TO FLIGHT 24 OF ENEMY. REGIMENT AIDS FRENCH ON FRONT WEST OF VERDUN. GOES INTO LINE AFTER ONLY THREE WEEKS' TRAINING—WORLD MAN GETS FIRST NEWS OF COLORED MEN IN ACTION.

The new headline at least elevated "Darkies" to "Negroes." Eyre cited the Old 15th New York as "the first colored American Army unit holding a sector on the French front" and proclaimed that the "glorious exploit" of the "dusky warriors" ensured that "the names of Johnson and Roberts would stand out forever on the roll of honor of their race." Colonel Hayward commended them for their "valor and intelligence." The first African Americans to fight in Europe "for the democratic ideals that set them free," these "chocolate soldiers" served "temporarily" "as part of the French Army" in "splendid isolation" from the rest of the American army. Only a very few individuals at AEF Headquarters knew of their presence in the front lines, and it had taken Eyre two days to locate the Regiment, so deeply "encased in the French Army" was it.

Eyre recounted the "most remarkable" story, of volunteers who *went into the trenches with less training on French soil than any of our other troops have had.*" They had served well and suffered few casualties in raids and under shellfire, but censorship prevented further the disclosure of details in order to keep "the Germans very much in the dark about the darkies." The "coffee creams," as French soldiers allegedly called their African American comrades, of the "chocolate front" required no lampblack for night raids, as their white counterparts did, and they had proved themselves capable of holding the front. The mule-drawn flatcar that had carried the wounded Johnson and Roberts to the rear, Eyre noted, was called by "the darkies" the "59th Street crosstown." Like his military counterparts at *Stars and Stripes,* Eyre could not resist injecting racial humor into his article.

After citing Hayward's affection for his "boys" and his "children," whom visiting French generals had liked so much that "I thought they were going to kiss them," Eyre relayed Hayward's graphic recounting of the struggle, which even claimed that the German Johnson stabbed in the stomach "shrieked in perfectly good American: "'Wow! the blank of a blank's got me!' as he fell dead." The men's officers were "well known in the social and business world of New York," Eyre noted, naming their Lt. Richardson Pratt "of the Brooklyn millionaire family." He reported the French general's comment that the American report of the "affair" was "too modest," as the men were "exceedingly brave" and had "done honor to the Americans." The men's fellow soldiers took pride in the feat and the honor it had brought to the unit, and they resolved to emulate Johnson and Roberts, and Eyre mentioned one little "ebony" chap who was sharpening his bolo knife on a chunk of tombstone, crooning to himself "Bush Germans, we're going to get you yet!"[43]

Both the black and the white press understood the significance of Pershing's communiqué of May 20 as an authenticating device, and they placed it side by side with journalistic accounts of the incident. A poster by F. G.

Renesch, titled "Our Colored Heroes," reproduced section B of Pershing's communiqué in full and forever linked the men and their feat with the AEF commander.[44]

A front-page special to the *World* on May 21 featured an interview with Mrs. Henry Johnson, conducted in Albany the previous day, under the title KAISER'S EARS NEXT, SAYS MRS. JOHNSON. The former Georgia N. Jackson from South Carolina proudly declared: "I just knew that Bill . . . if he ever got the chance he'd wade right into those baby killers of the Kaiser. . . . If those French doctors get Bill up on his feet again he'll never stop until he cuts the Kaiser's ears off! Bill ain't big, or anything like that—but boy, he can go some!" Unless Mrs. Johnson was Henry's mother, the preceding account may have been fabricated because Johnson's wife, if he ever really had one, was not named Georgia, nor was she from South Carolina. This woman's tough talk about taking on "baby killers" and cutting "the Kaiser's ears off" reinforced the perception of the aggressive, urbanized black female and assumed familiarity with and acceptance of anti-German propaganda at the same time that it promoted the image of the black man as "cut'n happy."[45] The reference to Henry Johnson as "Bill"—perhaps a nickname—also raises questions, as in all of his military records, Johnson used only "Henry," without any initial. His birth records cannot be located, and without the names of parents, census records help little. His very name, as many other aspects of Henry Johnson's life, reveals just how elusive a figure he was and still is.

The news reports on Johnson and Roberts obscured their real identities and made them mere vessels for the agendas of writers and publicists to fill. As a result, the lives of these two individuals literally disappeared in a welter of myth. In this process, Neadom Roberts would be diminished in two respects: his role in the episode would shrink, and few would ever know even the basic facts of his life.

Neadom Roberts, born on April 28, 1901, was the fifth and last child of Norman and Emma (Wilson) Roberts of 33 Wilson Street, Trenton, New Jersey. His father worked as a janitor at the local bank, and his mother washed clothes to support the family.[46] The claim that Norman Roberts pastored a church in Mount Holly, New Jersey, remains unconfirmed, although a "minister" on Sunday might well have held a menial job during the week.

Roberts's unusual first name literally caused problems at birth, as Leedom appears on the original certificate and remained there until Roberts himself changed it to Neadom. He had twice attempted and failed to join the navy in 1916 because he was underage, and he had gone to New York on the pretext of visiting his older brothers to join the 15th. At the time of his enlistment in the 15th on March 30, 1917, he had not reached the age of sixteen, let alone the nineteen years and eleven months that he claimed. The famous encounter with the Germans occurred when he was barely seventeen years old. The young Roberts, whose friends called him Bob, worked either as a bellboy at the Windsor Hotel in Trenton or as a stockboy at a local pharmacy when he enlisted.[47]

Until Neadom Roberts returned stateside, much of the coverage regarding him personally as well as his role in the raid came from his hometown newspaper, the *Trenton Times,* which ran the story on May 21 under the headline TRENTON NEGRO WINS WAR CROSS, accompanied by a photo of a boyish-looking Roberts in civilian clothes. The article gave top billing to its native son and noted that "Roberts with Henry Johnson, also colored, fought 20 Huns in a raiding party to a standstill and through their bravery saved from possible capture many of their comrades."[48] In 1933, Roberts published his own account, in which he shot three Germans, killed or wounded many others with grenades, stabbed two with his bayonet before he went down, and needed no help from Johnson. His account proves rather problematic, however, because he claimed to have fired a five-round clip when the Lebel rifle's clip held only three. Further, he described Johnson as splitting the German soldier's "helmet" and skull with his knife, when in fact the Germans wore no helmets but only soft caps. Finally, he claimed to have been decorated with the Distinguished Service Cross, which only Johnson would receive, half a century later.[49]

On May 21, 1918, an article in the *World* proclaimed NEGRO HEROES WIN ACCLAIM OF CITY. Of the 15th Regiment, Gen. Ferdinand Foch said, "They are very strong and stout-hearted and very rash." The article referred to a letter from Colonel Hayward to Frederick R. Moore, editor of the *New York Age,* describing the regimental commander's pride in his "clean, brave men, fearing nothing, daring everything." Hayward continued, "The friends of the regiment ought to rejoice that we are up here with the splendid French, where bravery, hardihood, character, and not a man's color count." Moore, citing how proud African Americans were of Johnson and Roberts and of the Old 15th, wishfully contemplated, "Maybe the conduct of these two men will result in doing away with the color line that seems to be drawn in some places in this war."

Moore seized the occasion to raise the subject of African American nurses:

There are many people who do not know that we have colored nurses who are ready to go to the front and minister to the wounded. We

[African Americans] have contributed liberally to the American Red Cross Fund. We draw no color line. Our nurses are no longer content to stay here, and they should receive some consideration when they ask to be sent to the front.

We don't want a black Red Cross, but we do want a universal Red Cross with every vestige of the old anti-colored prejudices wiped out and with nothing else required of its workers but ability, respectability and character.[50]

Like other members of the black press, Moore was seizing the opportunity that the valor of Johnson and Roberts presented to challenge the gendered color line in the United States. Unfortunately, despite the best efforts of black men and women (including Ada Thoms, a registered nurse at New York's Lincoln Hospital), the Army Nurse Corps and the Red Cross concluded that black women did not possess the educational, personal, and moral qualifications to join their ranks. Black women therefore found themselves relegated to auxiliary canteen services. Although the Red Cross eventually certified 1,800 black women as nurses, the army refused to accept any of them into the Nurse Corps until November 1918, when the influenza epidemic overwhelmed existing personnel. Then, the army decided that black women could treat even white soldiers, and it assigned eighteen black nurses to two integrated camps in the United States.[51]

Racist practices, even the most vicious, applied equally to black women and black men. Ironically, the same front pages of the *World* that presented the deed of Henry Johnson and Neadom Roberts also announced WOMAN IS LYNCHED BY MOB IN GEORGIA. VALDOSTA, GA. MAY 19.[52] In a land where white mobs lynched black men, women, and children with impunity, African Americans would hope in vain for racial equality.

Other New York newspapers carried the news, if less extensively, about Johnson and Roberts. The *Evening Post,* the paper of Oswald Garrison Villard, under a front-page headline on May 20 announcing General Pershing's communiqué, recounted the exploit of the two soldiers. The next day, May 21, the same paper proclaimed Pershing's "special pleasure to report the heroism of two negro soldiers, representing the American Army and their race." Their "honorable citation ought to help make head way against prejudice respecting men of their color in America, and cause the treating of negro criminals, or suspected criminals, as if they were wild beasts, to appear the fiendish thing that it is." The article continued: "That negroes make good soldiers and will fight as patriotically for their country as any white man, is no recent discovery." After referring to "their valor and devotion in our Civil War," the *Evening Post* had no doubt that Negro soldiers in France would further add to "that roster of their heroes."[53]

The paper could suggest that such heroism ought to counter American race prejudice and that it brought to mind the past feats of black American soldiers, but how quickly such feats disappeared from the memory—both individual and institutional—of white America in peacetime. Unfortunately, although these exploits might prove the black man to be just as good a soldier as the white, to white commentators African American heroes remained the heroes of African Americans and not of all Americans. At least the *Post* refrained from employing racial humor.

Yet, on May 22, the *Evening Post* published an apocryphal interview with "Mr. Henry Johnson (colored), of somewhere northwest of Toul," whom General Pershing had "reprimanded" for "trying to monopolize the war." In "disposing of a dozen Germans," Johnson allegedly excused himself for merely doing his duty in the style and words "of the late William Wordsworth."[54] The article mocked Johnson by using such elevated language and referring to Wordsworth, in contrast to white reporters' usual resort to constant references to color and use of dialect to belittle African American soldiers, some of whom were in fact well educated.

The May 23 front page of editor T. Thomas Fortune's African American paper, the *New York Age,* also carried a major article on Johnson and Roberts, which included a most articulate letter from Sgt. William Shepard of the 369th to his minister, Dr. William P. Hayes, of Mount Olivet Baptist Church, on April 16, 1918. Shepard likened the nightly bombardments of the big guns to a "fourth of July celebration," and he wrote that on the previous night, "our boys went over the top and captured three of the Huns and didn't lose a man." They were doing their duty to establish a record that would make everyone proud, and they would appreciate all prayers on their behalf.[55]

The *Sun* of May 21 and 22, 1918, contained two short articles, the first entitled PERSHING PRAISES BRAVE NEGROES, the second THE COLORED TROOPS FOUGHT NOBLY, in the words of the French general. The second article concluded, "How must the shade of ROBERT GOULD SHAW rejoice," thereby recalling the exploits of the 54th Massachusetts in the Civil War.[56]

Even the *New York Times,* which had not generally shown sympathy for the black regimental cause, announced BRAVERY OF NEGROES TOLD BY PERSHING. A later editorial entitled PRIVATES BILL AND NEEDHAM stated that "it seems but the other day that the proposal to organize the negro regiment was received with tepid enthusiasm." The *Times* extolled the exploits and record of the 24th Regiment in the war in Cuba and contemplated "the old story, the gallantry and stanchness of our negro soldiers when the country calls in the hour of her need. New York may well be proud of the 369th Infantry, which was the old 15th."[57] Such effusive praise must have been music to African American ears. How quickly—and momentarily—in the flush of the glory of the two soldiers' deeds had doubts about the effectiveness of African American men as soldiers disappeared, to be replaced by contemplation of their unmitigated loyalty and steadfastness as soldiers throughout American history. Yet, even in this laudatory article, the *Times* could not avoid stereotypical references to razors and bolo knives, and it saw something "demoniac" about Johnson and Roberts, suggesting that "the Germans will have to find as apt a name for the American negro fighters as they had given to the kilted Scots, whom they called 'The Ladies from Hell.'"[58] Perhaps the *Times*'s reference to "demoniac" and "Ladies from Hell" birthed the popular moniker of "Harlem Hellfighters" for the 369th.

In a separate article, the *Age* briefly mentioned the deaths of two mothers of soldiers in the 369th—Mrs. Eunice Streadwick, whose end had been "hastened" by her grief over the death of her son Howard at age twenty to tuberculosis in France, and Mrs. Clara Jackson, mother of Sgt. Edward Jackson. African American papers such as the *Age* regarded war as a largely male affair and consequently only sparingly covered women's issues. What few articles appeared often tended to perpetuate stereotypes about female roles, in this instance the grieving mother whose death was precipitated by learning her young son had died only two months after joining the Regiment.[59]

Yet another brief article in the *Age* that day mentioned the fund-raising efforts of the Circle for Negro War Relief, one of many such organizations that black women founded and ran. Service-oriented black women, according to historian Nikki Brown, "took a more localized approach to understanding the Great War in Europe." These women considered themselves indispensable agents in facilitating "a cultural transformation of the nation," and they often put "the plight of black families and black women ahead of international considerations."[60] The participation of the circle in preparing and distributing pamphlets titled "The Negro Soldiers' Valorous Part in America's Wars" did indicate the women's concern and identification with so-called men's issues and roles.[61]

The treatment that black families received from white agencies such as the American Red Cross made the work of the Circle for Negro War Relief and the Women's Auxiliary of the Fifteenth New York National Guard all the more necessary. Although the government attached a significant proportion of soldiers' monthly pay for the support of relatives at home, the checks often did not reach needy dependents in a timely fashion; in other cases, the amounts of the checks, starting at $15 per month for a wife, proved insufficient.[62] The Red Cross frequently provided relief to needy families, but it was as interested in policing morality and loyalty as in rendering services, and it had a notorious history of racial discrimination in its hiring practices.[63] Consequently, its relief workers did not reflect the diversity of clients and often lacked the sensitivity to serve people unlike themselves effectively.

The Red Cross's response to the plight of Mrs. Leander Willetts provides an interesting case in point. Pvt. Leander Willetts had joined the 15th in May 1917 at age twenty-two, leaving behind a young wife in Oyster Bay, Long Island. On January 10, 1918, Mrs. Willetts wrote the State Council of Defense that her husband had told her to expect a check from the government every month, but she had received neither a check nor further word from her spouse. Mrs. Willetts, who was unemployed and lived with her parents, urgently appealed for information on why she had not received the payment due her. The Council of Defense forwarded the matter to the Red Cross, which concluded that Mrs. Willett did not need assistance, partially because she had recently received a $30 payment from the Bureau of War Risk Insurance. Furthermore, Alexander M. Wilson, director of civilian relief of the Atlantic Division of the American Red Cross, judged that "she is without dependents, is a large, strong, young, colored woman without much inclination to care for herself." To the Red Cross, she therefore did not qualify as a member of the "deserving poor."[64]

Such news did not reach the press, as the black and white newspapers alike focused on the sensational and the heroic, which invariably meant the masculine. Characteristically, the press in Albany, New York, trumpeted news of the hometown hero Henry Johnson and his proud and dutiful wife. ALBANY NEGRO FIGHTS WITH GREAT HEROISM, announced the front page of the *Times Union* of May 20. The following day, another front-page article, with Henry Johnson's photograph, feature Johnson's "wife": "Mrs. Johnson Sends Wire to Hero Husband—Wife of Pershing Winner of Bravery Medal Happy and Proud of Him—'Dear Henry—I am so very proud of you, and I want you to come back to me.'—Your Dear Little Wife." Edna Johnson, "a heart proud little colored girl," had sent her "valiant husband" that message after receiving the news of his exploit. On September 17, 1917, Henry Johnson, a twenty-five-year-old native of Winston Salem, North Carolina, and a fifteen-year resident of Albany, had married his next-door neighbor. Mrs. Johnson lavishly praised "her husband—her man," who had "ENLISTED" and sent her "the best part of his pay," and she added that when he returned on the train, "there'll be Edna . . . waiting for 'her man.'"[65] However, no marriage certificate confirms their union, and Albany city directories from 1916 to 1921 list no Edna Johnson.

A second article in the *Times Union* declared, "The colored man is 'a fighting man,'" "formidable in battle," particularly in a "hand-to-hand fight," and it added that Albany would welcome "our Henry" upon his return. The article also noted "other heroes of the colored race," this time "in the industrial struggle," specifically an American team of riveters, "foreman and all . . . colored men," had bested an English team to become "the world's champion riveters."[66] In an article next to its major piece on Johnson and Roberts, the *New York Age* of May 23 explained that Negro riveters working at Sparrows Point, Maryland, in the Bethlehem Steel Corporation had broken the world's record for driving rivets. As the *Age* remarked, "This is the way the Negro is demonstrating his patriotism at home while his brothers in black in the army are showing it in France."[67]

The front page of the *Times Union* of Thursday, May 23, 1918, carried a cartoon from the *New York World* showing a stereotypical grinning Negro face in a US helmet superimposed on a French War Cross, with the caption "Henry Johnson, Albany's Colored Hero, wins 'The French War Cross' and the 'Golden Palm,' War's Highest Honors." Yet, after the obligatory humorous accounts of black life and the assertion that Johnson "knew his place," the article recalled the valor of the "Negro Fighting Man," mentioning, among others, Crispus Attucks, the black sailors with Perry on Lake Erie, Peter Carey at Bunker Hill and William Carney at Fort Wagner, the 24th and 25th Infantry Regiments in Cuba and in the Philippines, and the 10th Cavalry Regiment at Carrizal in Mexico. It emphasized in capital letters that THE NEGRO IN THE PROFESSION OF ARMS HAS NEVER HAD A TRAITOR IN HIS RANKS AND HAS NEVER HAD A BLOT OF COWARDICE UPON HIS SPOTLESS ARMY ESCUTCHEON. The article concluded that the American people had to recognize the most recent valor of Johnson and Roberts "in a manner worthy of the nation": "To resolve that so long as negro fighters face the enemy and thereafter so long as the Republic they have helped to defend endures, throughout the length and breadth of the United States, law, public condemnation and swift punishment for the guilty shall combine to make the lynching of a negro an abhorred and obsolete crime."[68] Here, a white newspaper used the heroism of Johnson and Roberts as a means to condemn lynching and exhort Americans to cease such despicable deeds.

The frenzy of press coverage in May still echoed occasionally during the following month. The *New York Age,* as a weekly, assembled reports about Johnson and Roberts from other papers. Page two of the *Age* on June 1 featured a sampling of articles about the two men's exploits in local and regional newspapers, including the *Bridgeport Telegram*, the *Albany Knickerbocker*, the *New York Evening Telegram*, the *New York Evening World*, and the *Brooklyn Standard Union*. The last stands out for its embrace of Roberts and Johnson as Brooklynites, heroes who "are citizens of this community." Their enlistment in the Brooklyn Battalion seems to have been the sole residency requirement, and according to the paper, the heroism of the two soldiers proved black capability and loyalty while dispelling any "suspicion that this race is anything less than 100 percent American."

The *Age*'s story about the pair, written by William Roberts, the elder of Neadom's two brothers, claimed that the Boy Scouts provided the impetus and training that led both men to volunteer to serve the nation after the US declaration of war on April 6, 1917. The story was too good to be true. A more likely cause for Johnson's interest was the active recruiting efforts in Albany by Lt. Col. Lorillard Spencer, then military secretary to Governor Whitman.[69] Neadom Roberts had already joined the Regiment in March, and no evidence exists to confirm his membership in the segregated Boy Scouts.[70]

On June 15, the *New York Times* recounted the praise of Henry Johnson upon the occasion of a speech by Secretary of the Navy Josephus Daniels in Albany on June 14. In introducing Daniels, former governor Glynn noted that Johnson had been born in North Carolina, close to Daniels's home. For his part, Daniels, who was urging fair treatment for German Americans, mentioned Henry Johnson in his speech and "paid high tribute to the colored people of the South," whose loyalty "had never been in doubt."[71] Of course, the same could not be said for northern blacks, whom white southerners feared "did not know their place."[72]

Two weeks later, the *New York Times* reported that more than 700 guests attended a meeting honoring Johnson and Roberts organized by the Woman's Auxiliary of the Old 15th Infantry; it was held at the Harlem Casino at 116th Street and Lenox Avenue. Celebrities who sent letters of regret included Theodore Roosevelt; Governors Charles Whitman and Walter Edge of New York and New Jersey, respectively; and Mayor James Watt of Albany. Colonel Roosevelt's letter to Susan Elizabeth Frazier, president of the Woman's Auxiliary, recalled his service with men of this "heroic type" in the 9th and 10th Cavalries in Cuba. A silk flag for the auxiliary accompanied his letter. Speeches by Edna Johnson and Neadom Roberts's father, identified as the Reverend Norman Roberts of Mt. Holly, New Jersey, elicited the "highest points" of audience enthusiasm.[73] Historian Chad Williams highlights the services of the Women's Auxiliary of the New York 15th National Guard, which had been the Women's Loyal Union, New York's oldest black women's club, until it changed its name on May 2, 1917.[74]

The day before the grand meeting, concern about the activities of German spies in the African American community reached the highest level of the army. On June 14, Gen. Peyton March, army chief of staff in Washington, wrote to AEF command:

> Stories, probably invented by German agents, have been widely circulated among colored people in this country to effect that colored soldiers in France are always placed in most dangerous positions and sacrificed to save white soldiers; that when wounded they are left on ground to die without medical attention; that other forms of discrimination are practiced against them; and that the Germans, if victorious, have promised to set aside a portion of this country where the colored people could rule themselves.[75]

March desired a "clear, specific, and emphatic" statement from Pershing denying such stories and presenting actual conditions, suitable for publication.

Pershing's answer arrived on June 19. He labeled the stories about placing black soldiers in the most dangerous positions and leaving them out to die "absolutely false" and pointed out that only the 369th Regiment had incurred casualties in combat—three dead from wounds and two severely wounded. Otherwise, twenty men had died from disease. Such low losses demonstrated that their positions had not yet become so dangerous and that "their physical condition is excellent." A recent inspection tour by officers of the Training Section of the AEF indicated "a comparatively high degree of training and efficiency among these troops." Their training was identical to that given other American troops serving with the French army, with preliminary service in quiet sectors before entering heavy combat. Pershing's closing paragraph provided telling evidence of the impact of Johnson and Roberts's exploit on African American troops, on the AEF High Command's perception of these men, and on their value in the propaganda war at home:

> Exploits of 2 colored infantrymen [Johnson and Roberts] some weeks ago in repelling a much larger German patrol killing and wounding several Germans and winning Croix de Guerre by their gallantry has [sic] roused fine spirit of emulation throughout colored troops all of whom are looking forward to more active service. Only regret expressed by colored troops is that they are not given more dangerous work to do. They are especially amused at the most dangerous positions and all are desirous of having more active service than has been

permitted them thus far. I can not commend too highly the spirit shown among the colored combat troops who exhibit fine capacity for quick training and eagerness for the most dangerous work.[76]

This exchange between Pershing and March concluded a discussion in early June about the use of "the large number of negroes being received from the draft." March proposed to employ them primarily as labor and pioneer battalions and to use the remainder in the 92nd Division as infantry regiments for the French, who offered "to train and use all colored regiments of infantry we can supply." In a cable dated June 8, Pershing agreed on all points, except to recommend "that their [the Negro troops'] training and use by the French not be considered."[77]

Yet, on June 26, Pershing informed March, "Present plans contemplate grouping the 4 colored regiments of 93rd Division into a complete division," including an artillery brigade, with "white officers in field grades and in the field artillery as battery commanders."[78] On July 6, March refused Pershing's recommendation.[79] The success of Johnson and Roberts in particular and the 369th in general would not change the US Army's plans to relegate most black soldiers to labor or pioneer battalions in the AEF. Pershing had calculatedly published the exploits of the black soldiers to assuage black concerns, but AEF HQ remained determined to limit black participation in combat to the greatest extent possible, undoubtedly for fear of the threat that these men might pose upon their return to domestic peace in a racist society. Trumpeting of African Americans' wartime exploits likely heightened such apprehensions on the part of many white Americans, particularly southerners. If white Americans did not minimize or deny the wartime competency of black combatants, they would have to address the fundamental inequality between the races upon which the United States was built. Although William Pickens, then a professor at Morgan State University, credited the men with destroying "forever the myth of Teutonic omnipotence," the valor of Henry Johnson and Neadom Roberts could not shake the foundation of white supremacy in America.[80]

In the meantime, Johnson and Roberts had appeared in the pages of the June 22 edition of the *Chicago Defender,* perhaps the leading African American newspaper of the day.[81] The front page carried the "first picture of the boys" of Col. William Hayward's "Hell Hounds (as the Germans call them)." Each time the 15th/369th acquired a descriptive name in the press, it invariably referred to or included the word *Hell.* The alliteration of Harlem Hellfighters, which so many authors have since used, proved irresistible. In fact, the soldiers still referred to themselves as the "Old 15th" or occasionally, in jest, as "the 15th Heavy Foot," which evoked memories of earlier times when infantry and cavalry regiments bore either light or heavy armor and weapons.

Under the headline COL. HAYWARD PENS LETTER TO PRIVATE JOHNSON'S WIFE, page three of the *Defender* carried in full a lengthy letter from Colonel Hayward to Edna Johnson. Hayward described Johnson as "at all times a good soldier and a good boy of fine morale and upright character," who had evinced further traits "of fine courage and fighting ability." After expressing regret at Johnson's serious wounds, wounds that any soldier would have been proud to receive, Hayward recounted the story of "our boys at grips with the terrible foe in a desperate hand to hand encounter in which the enemy outnumbered them ten to one." Captured German prisoners had earlier confessed that their officers had told them how easy it would be to "combat and capture" the black Americans. Instead, they had run afoul of Johnson and Roberts.

Hayward now claimed the German patrol leader that Johnson disemboweled had "exclaimed in American English, without a trace of accent, 'Oh, the son of a [bitch] got me.'" In other contemporary accounts, the German's last words appear as "Oh, the little black son of a bitch has killed me." Hayward thought the perfect English proved that the patrol leader had been a traitorous German American who had planned to use his command of English to fool the Americans—an indirect warning about the dangers of enemies at home. After detailing the encounter, Hayward concluded his letter with the news that the "great General Gouraud" had given him one hundred francs ($20) for the family of the "first of my soldiers wounded in a fight under heroic circumstances." He had sent half in American money to Mrs. Johnson and half to the family of Neadom Roberts, and he assured Edna Johnson that "you have made a splendid contribution to the cause of liberty by giving your husband to your country." Mrs. Johnson presented the letter to officials of the Albany Red Cross chapter.

The editorial page of the *Defender* carried a stark and graphic cartoon by W. A. Rodgers, first published in the white *New York Herald,* of Johnson and Roberts's feat, entitled TWO REAL AMERICANS, a significant change from the original title, TWO FIRST CLASS AMERICANS. In the cartoon, with the bodies of dead German soldiers slumped on the ground around him and another German with his rifle raised to fire, a dark and powerful, almost bestial Johnson, his sleeves rolled to the elbow, grimly glowers straight ahead, towering over the field of dead; his right hand is gripping a bloody knife, his left hand is on the shoulder of a muscular Roberts slumped to his knees, his head bowed though the rifle is still in hand. The dripping knife, its exaggerated blade well over a foot long, and the hulking Johnson, a brute who bore no resemblance to the small and wiry private, were, like the entire cartoon, symbolic. From one perspective, the black beast had been unleashed, with frightful implications. Yet, from another, the portrayal of a grim, avenging "real American," on this occasion a black man, exuded the power often displayed in cartoons and posters of fighting men. Both interpretations reflected the ambivalence of white America toward its new heroes. Henry Johnson had become the first African American hero of the Great War, to his Regiment, to the AEF command, and to the American public at home. "The battle of Henry Johnson" had truly seized the imagination of observers in the United States and had become the touchstone of valor for black soldiers during World War I as well as currency for securing the rightful recognition of blacks as authentic rather than "first class" Americans.

The publication of Irvin Cobb's book *The Glory of the Coming* later in 1918 confirmed the impact of the 369th. In a chapter entitled "Young Black Joe," Cobb first noted the contrast between that unit and a regiment of draftees from the South that he had previously visited. The men of the 15th, claimed Cobb,

> were apt to be mulattoes or to have light-brown complexions instead of clear black; they were sophisticated and town-wise in their bearing; . . . They were soldiers who wore their uniforms with a smartened pride; who were jaunty and alert and prompt in their movements; and who expressed, as some did vocally in my hearing, and all did by their attitude, a sincere and heartfelt inclination to get a whack at the foe with the shortest possible delay.[82]

They convinced Cobb that their performance in the war would transform the meaning of the word *nigger* that "hereafter n-i-g-g-e-r will merely be another way of spelling the word American."[83] Cobb's musings on the meaning of *nigger* notwithstanding, Henry Johnson would be the first private in the AEF to win a golden palm with his Croix de Guerre, and his and Neadom Roberts's exploit proved "that the colour of a man's skin has nothing to do with the colour of his soul."[84] In the following chapter, "Let's Go," Cobb rhapsodized about the nighttime performance of Sissle and the band—thorough indications that the 15th had worked its magic on the southerner.[85]

Prior to the exploits of Johnson and Roberts, the 369th had gained recognition for its justly famous jazz band, made up of James Reese Europe's talented musicians. Many observers consequently misperceived the Regiment as an appendage of its band. White Americans could accept African Americans as musicians but had denied black Americans the recognition they merited as soldiers. The little laborer from Albany, New York, and the youth from Trenton, New Jersey, had pulled aside this veil of denial and demonstrated anew, in the Great War, the black man in the role of soldier-hero. The 369th now became known as a fierce fighting regiment with a superb band.

Yet, the heroic deeds of the Regiment at the front threatened to become lost in the political struggle at home for the hearts and minds of black Americans. At the very moment that Pershing had written his cablegram to the army chief of staff, Peyton March, on June 19, 1918, the so-called editors' conference in Washington, DC, was meeting. Joel Spingarn and Emmett J. Scott had approached George Creel, head of the Committee on Public Information, with a plan to "bring about a more conservative policy among Negro editors" in order to mold public opinion.[86] With publishers Robert S. Abbott of the *Chicago Defender*, Robert L. Vann of the *Pittsburgh Courier*, and Fred Moore of the *New York Age*, as well as staunch government critics such as Ralph Tyler and William H. Brooks, former chaplain of the 15th, in attendance, Spingarn viewed the meeting as the opportunity to forge an alliance of competing black factions "mobilized in support of the country."[87]

Major Loving of the MIB, however, regarded the conference as an unmitigated disaster that stirred up the very "sleeping volcano" of radicalism that Spingarn sought to quell. William Monroe Trotter had scheduled the meeting of his National Colored Liberty Congress well in advance of the government-backed conference. Trotter proceeded to use his organization to condemn the editors' conference as a bold power play designed to thwart the plans of his "radical conference" and "to compromise race issues." In other words, the conference, "a hand picked star chamber affair," sold out the interests of blacks. With Ida B. Wells-Barnett, Hubert Harrison, and other radical voices, the Liberty Congress generated far more publicity for its proceedings and "outgeneraled the leader of the editors' conference . . . as the one most representative of popular feelings." Loving concluded that "the conference of Negro editors could not have served them [radicals] better if they had planned it themselves."[88]

Adding fuel to the fire, the July issue of *The Crisis* featured W. E. B. Du Bois's editorial "Close Ranks," in which the former bitter opponent of President Wilson and his government's policies now urged blacks not to allow their grievances to interfere with their first duty of fighting the war "with every ounce of blood and treasure."[89] The NAACP disclosed that the army had tendered Du Bois a commission to serve along with Spingarn in the intelligence branch. The news provoked outrage across the black political spectrum, including local branches of the NAACP as well as its national board. The consensus of African American opinion concluded that Du Bois would be censoring black publications, "making his apparent betrayal of the faith complete." Loving called the move a "boomerang" and urged his superiors to deny Du Bois a commission, leaving the latter to continue as editor of *The Crisis* and ride out "the storm of popular resentment." Heeding Loving's advice, the army withdrew its offer to Du Bois and removed Spingarn from MIB, which left Loving as the major authority on race in the bureau.[90]

This blatant governmental attempt to manipulate black leadership and undermine a free black press sought to weaken the trust of the black masses in their representatives. Yet, even under increasing surveillance and pressure, black Americans would continue to question the moral authority of a government that allegedly fought to make the world safe for democracy abroad while denying the same to its largest racial minority at home.

The 369th Regiment's war on the western front thus occurred within a larger struggle for the equal rights of African Americans at home in the United States. The accounts of Henry Johnson and Neadom Roberts's repulse of a German raiding party came as a shock and surprise to the AEF rank and file and to the American people. The "darkest cat," in the words of *Stars and Stripes,* was indeed "out of the AEF bag"—a black American regiment was fighting heroically in the French army. Its impact on the American consciousness buoyed African American spirits and hopes that such wartime service would demonstrate the equality of blacks and whites to all and would serve to diminish white persecution and unequal treatment of black Americans at home. Sadly, the disarray among African American leaders over support of the war effort and the concentration of Major Loving in the MIB on suppressing black radicalism rather than buoying black patriotism attenuated the impact of the soldiers' achievements. White Americans, by contrast, viewed the black soldiers' accomplishment, however remarkable, through a lens of racist stereotypes, disparaging humor, and their ultimate fear of the threat posed by combat-hardened and armed black men to the domestic status quo. At AEF Headquarters, Pershing responded to the dilemma by sending no more African American regiments to the French and by assigning black soldiers to labor duties in the AEF. At home, white Americans relegated these truly American heroes to the status of *African American* heroes and would ultimately resort to massive violence to keep them "in their place."

# 10

## A Midsummer's Nightmare

*Race Swirls above the 369th, May–August 1918*

AEF Headquarters had placed the black regiments with the French army for an indefinite period and reserved the option to regroup them in an American division. Meanwhile, it retained responsibility for promotion, discipline, and administration in these units, whereas the French determined their tactical use.[1] French prime minister André Tardieu observed to the French War Ministry that the 93rd Provisional Division had made such a favorable impression that he wanted to ask Pershing about the possibility of securing developing black units (for example, the 92nd Division) under the same conditions.[2] Of course, Pershing had already decided that the French would receive no more black units.

Furthermore, as early as May, the AEF, in collusion with some French commanders, was implementing a policy to impose all-white officer cadres on the black regiments of the 93rd Division, despite the fact that an AEF memorandum in May 1918 warned that all-white officer cadres commanding black regiments could "effect a direct injury to the spirit and the moral[e] of the colored troops by causing them to believe that they are not considered worthy of promotion to commissioned grades . . . whatever their merits may be."[3] AEF HQ could not control how the French used black soldiers, but through its control of personnel, it could determine the racial composition of the regimental officer corps, which, as the memorandum indicates, it desired to make all white. The 369th offered a particularly tempting target, as black captains and lieutenants commanded white commissioned officers in direct violation of the AEF dictum that no black soldier should ever command a white one, regardless of rank.

These racial policies had already begun to affect the 369th in late May. Henry Plummer Cheatham—born in 1892, the son of former congressman H. P. Cheatham of Oxford, North Carolina—had enlisted in the army after attending public schools in Washington, DC, and Shaw University in Raleigh, North Carolina. He attained the rank of regimental sergeant major in the 24th Infantry in the Philippines, then returned to live in New York, where, after America's entry into the world war, he joined the 15th New York as a private.[4] On May 30, Cheatham wrote to his father observing that his usefulness to the 369th was finished for two reasons. He had attained and already outgrown his rank of sergeant, but, he noted, "my Regimental Commander [Col. Hayward] has repeatedly acknowledged my thorough capabilities, and has stated to others and to me that I am highly deserving [of] a commission. But he has also stated that nothing could be done for me *here* because it is not considered to make any more colored officers in this regiment."[5] Cheatham observed that one of his good friends, Battalion Sgt. Maj. Benedict W. Cheesman, "a man and soldier without reproach," found himself in the same predicament. Because of the "policy" preventing black advancement, the 369th had recently filled an authorized increase in officers with twenty-nine young white reservists, prompting an exasperated Cheatham to comment, "It is to laugh!"[6]

Cheatham knew that the AEF was returning men to the States as instructors and, further, that general orders authorized the assignment of qualified noncommissioned officers to officer training schools or even appointments as officers directly from the ranks. He referred to a "certain colored colonel" who had recently made forty such appointments, which could have pertained only to the 370th Regiment at that time. Cheatham requested that his father write or even visit Emmett Scott and enlist the influence of North Carolinian Josephus Daniels, secretary of the navy, as Cheesman and he would willingly return to use their training and frontline service to whip a Negro draft regiment into shape or to serve with another unit already at the front.[7]

Henry Cheatham's subsequent career illustrates the experience of those noncommissioned officers stymied in the ranks of the 369th. In late June, Cheatham was reassigned to the 370th Regiment as a second lieutenant, where he was cited on several occasions for bravery under fire. In recognition of his outstanding leadership of his men under heavy fire at Champagne and Soissons, when he was severely gassed and suffered numerous shrapnel wounds from which he never fully recovered, the French government decorated him with the Croix de Guerre on December 8, 1918. As of December, Cheatham had risen to become acting adjutant of the

370th. After the Armistice, he returned to earn a law degree with honors from Temple University Law School in Philadelphia in 1925, graduating as vice president of his class. After fifteen years of successful practice, he succumbed to illnesses directly traceable to his wounds in France.[8] Cheatham's observations and achievements indicated that AEF policy was robbing the 369th of experienced and capable black commissioned officers and black senior noncommissioned officers in favor of inserting inexperienced white officers into the Regiment. African American soldiers in the 92nd Division in World War II would complain that its white division command appointed inexperienced white officers to company command positions that black officers had earned in combat, an indication that nothing had changed in a quarter century.

By the end of June, the AEF HQ policy of *blanchissage* (whitening) was in full swing, with inspections of the 370th, 371st, and 372nd Regiments in early July by AEF HQ liaison officers to the French army. On July 9, the liaison officer, Ordnance, Maj. Charles Bryan, and Col. Thomas A. Roberts of the AEF HQ General Staff submitted two damning reports on the readiness of the 372nd.[9] Bryan reported that the regiment's white commanding officer, Col. Glendie B. Young, "did not consult with his subordinates, who in turn lacked confidence in him,"[10] and that many of the regiment's black officers were "entirely unfit and incapable of leadership," making it necessary for white officers to monitor them "to see that they perform their duty and carry out instructions." The regiment, they asserted, was "completely demoralized and . . . totally unfit to sustain an attack; . . . [and] should be sent to the rear and reorganized and officered by white officers."[11]

Colonel Roberts, who had come "at the specific request" of the regiment's division commander, French general Mariano Goybet, added that "both white and colored officers were uncertain of their chief."[12] Goybet's 157th "Red Hand" Infantry Division, which had gained fame in the defense of Verdun, was due to receive the 371st and 372nd Regiments to fill its depleted ranks. Goybet, who considered Colonel Young "not a soldier," contemplated commanding the 372nd himself in case of a German attack, so he and Roberts recommended a change of command as soon as possible.[13] Roberts observed that "the whole outfit has a bad look—entirely different from either of the others." He had found that Col. Perry Miles's 371st Regiment "is in line and looks pretty good." Roberts had seen the reserve of the 370th (the former 8th Illinois), which had all black officers, and reported, "The colonel has some good ideas, his officers are a well educated lot and look well; they are confident they will do well and I hope they will—I want a little more time on them." Within two days, Roberts would "temporarily" replace the 370th's commander, Col. Franklin A. Denison, the "relief occasioned by sickness."[14]

When Colonel Roberts phoned Col. Fox Conner on Pershing's staff at 9:30 P.M. on July 9 to report negatively on the 372nd and positively on the 371st and what he had seen of the 370th, Conner appended to Roberts's message the following handwritten note to the AEF chief of staff: "It appears these negro regiments are all in bad condition."[15] Conner had received one further report earlier on July 9, from Capt. Paul Mills, liaison officer at 4th French Army headquarters, who reported that the 369th "appears to be in bad shape." Colonel Hayward was in the hospital, and the Regiment had only one major and half its complement of officers. Two officers had complained to Mills, and twenty-seven had applied to leave the Regiment. The French censors had intercepted letters indicating "bad" conditions and "poor" discipline, including one from an officer of the 369th to a general in the United States claiming that "all discipline and morale had gone to the winds." The chief of staff of the French 4th Army, Grant reported, had told him that "the non-commissioned officers appear to exercise no command over the men."[16] Fox Conner had thus concluded that "all" the Negro regiments were in bad condition, when the reports in fact indicated that only half of them were, the 369th and the 372nd.

Yet, Mills's report on the 369th, however damning, appears to have been dated because by July 5, the Regiment had received orders to occupy new positions and was advancing into the midst of French preparations to defend against a German offensive. If the Regiment were actually in such abysmal condition, its next month would have been disastrous. At the beginning of July, the French anticipated another major German offensive aimed at shattering British and French resistance on the western front. Gen. Erich Ludendorff, German chief quartermaster general and the mastermind of the German High Command, had been staging major attacks against French and British forces since March. These opportunistic attacks lacked strategic focus and in fact squandered valuable German troops, yet each German offensive seriously tested the Entente forces' very will to resist.

On July 7, Gen. Henri Gouraud, commander of the French 4th Army, warned his French and American soldiers to prepare for an impending general attack, which he would oppose with a defense in depth. The "first position" comprised an advanced line of observation posts and then a line of resistance beyond the range of enemy mortars, which would disrupt and then retreat before a general German attack while French artillery pounded the positions. The "intermediate position"—the main line of resistance— comprised two to four parallel lines of trenches and strongholds, which would protect the artillery batteries, maintain the integrity of the lines, and hold the enemy "blow for blow" (*coute que coute*).[17] There, the French army would turn the tide and stage its own offensive.[18]

The 369th Regiment received orders to occupy new positions and advanced into the midst of French preparations to strengthen sector defenses in front of it on July 5. A number of the Regiment's officers returned that day from leave in Paris,[19] and they rejoined their men as the Regiment moved to augment and support the French general Georges Lebouc's 161st Infantry Division. Ultimately, they would relieve the division's 4th Moroccan Regiment as an integral part of the 161st.[20] On July 14, Americans and French soldiers celebrated Bastille Day with champagne: every four soldiers and every two line officers shared a bottle, and field officers could drink as much as they desired.[21]

The Germans attacked on the night of July 14, but Gouraud, alerted with precise intelligence about the time of the German bombardment, disrupted the advance of German assault troops with a preemptive barrage, and both sides traded artillery fire for the rest of the night.[22] German shellfire caught the 369th as it was moving to positions in the intermediate trench line, and a combination of shrapnel and gas shells killed six men, wounded five, and gassed six in K Company, 3rd Battalion, Horace Pippin's unit.[23] In fact, German shellfire had struck Pippin's platoon just as it reached a road after running and crawling through thick, slippery mud in the rain. The barrage left the bodies of the men, including a friend of Pippin's, strewn about. Then, confronting a field "a life [alive] with shells," Pippin observed the fall of shot and, with three men in tow, bolted across the field, going to ground once to rest. When they reached the soldiers in their designated trench, he marveled that they had survived.[24]

On July 15, the Regiment moved 3 miles west under artillery fire to take new positions, as the French 4th Army held the second line all along a 50-mile front. Gouraud ordered his army to drive the Germans immediately from what little ground they had seized. On the front of the 369th's division, the 161st, the Germans had taken four French positions before the town of Minaucourt and around the Butte du Mesnil (Mesnil Hill), a sector the French appropriately named *Calvaire* (Calvary). As the 161st Division troops moved to the counterattack, the 369th fell in behind them. A regiment of the famous French Chasseurs Alpins—elite mountain troops nicknamed "the Blue Devils"—and a Moroccan regiment flanked the 369th to the left and right, respectively, prompting Captain Little's comment that the 369th was "traveling in fast company."[25]

For the next eight days, from July 15 to July 23, the 369th advanced under shellfire behind attacking units of the 161st, which ultimately captured the Butte du Mesnil and 209 German prisoners at the cost of 22 officers and 768 men killed, wounded, or missing. The French had turned the tide against the Germans, and the Entente assumed the offensive for the rest of the war. Yet, the German army in retreat proved a tenacious foe that would exact a heavy toll of French, British, and American soldiers for every foot of ground seized.[26]

On July 18, Capt. Ham Fish commented on the strain of staying up all night for ten days, and he noted that the German "deluge" of shells had killed three of his men, wounded five, and gassed four badly: "It was a terrible ordeal and the men stood it well. The shellfire was awful and I don't understand why our losses were not heavier." Continuous heavy German shelling hindered the delivery of food supplies.[27] Fish's exhaustion stemmed not just from lack of sleep but also from a touch of Spanish influenza—the worldwide flu epidemic had begun—which had felled two of his lieutenants ten days earlier. On July 23, Fish wrote his aunt, "War is fiendish."[28] By the end of July, he would leave the 369th to undergo further training in the rear as a line officer.

The 369th jointly occupied with French units a sector of line 1,250 yards in length between the Butte du Mesnil and La Main de Massige. The French 163rd and 215th Regiments defended its flanks. The American battalion commanders—Major Little (promoted July 17) of the 1st Battalion, Captain Cobb of the 2nd, and Major Spencer of the 3rd—assumed command posts that Colonel Hayward named "New York, Brooklyn, and Harlem," respectively. C Company of 1st Battalion (Little) lost two dead and six wounded moving to its positions on July 20–21, and then the next day and night, it lost two men to gas when the Germans drenched the communications trenches with gas shells about 6:00 P.M. To maintain discipline, some of the officers removed their masks to give orders. One of the two black captains in the 369th, Charles Fillmore, demonstrated "fine" leadership and set an "inspiriting" example as "with marked calmness and courage and persistency [he] moved among the troops" to form them into groups to move forward and relieve the French.[29] At Little's recommendation, Fillmore later received the Croix de Guerre.

Fillmore had played a significant role in the very creation of the Regiment and had carried on resolutely even after a cablegram in mid-February informed him that his wife had died over three weeks before.[30] However, Little dismissed Fillmore's belief that "he and all colored officers were the victims of racial prejudice, in every development that did not operate to their advancement or personal satisfaction."[31] A week later, when the orders from AEF HQ arrived transferring all the 369th's black officers, Fillmore departed, in Little's opinion, with "bitterness in his heart." Half a year later, as the Regiment was preparing to leave Le Mans for home, Fillmore would visit Little to learn that the captain had indeed recommended him for the Croix and to shake Little's hand.[32]

By dawn on July 23, the 369th had assumed control of Calvaire, with one battalion in the front line, another in the intermediate line, and the third in support in the rear. No-man's-land between German and American trenches varied from 15 yards to a half mile in length. German sniper fire from trenches that ran at angles to the American line took a steady toll of US soldiers. The Germans also "sniped" with artillery, as German artillery observers had registered the trench line and would call for a battery to drop a shell on positions where they spotted movement. The 15-cm shells were called "Jack Johnsons,"[33] after the black former heavyweight boxing champion, because they exploded in a black puff of smoke and left craters 25 feet across. The troops remained in dugouts during the day, with the exception of runners carrying messages or soldiers on Kitchen Patrol (KP), who had to bring food to the front lines three times a day at risk to their lives.

The French command was particularly concerned about preventing losses to German mustard gas.[34] They believed that the English gas masks they supplied the black troops did not fit the African American soldiers securely because the nose clips holding the masks in place could not accommodate the broader, flatter noses of the black troops, so the French promptly ordered three thousand American M2 masks for the 369th,[35] which also failed to protect the black soldiers adequately. Inexplicably, the question of French supply of gas masks for their own colonial soldiers never arose. The inadequate fit of available gas masks to perceived black facial features, which were in fact very diverse, would remain an unresolved issue.[36]

From July 24 until August 18, official communiqués from the 369th's sector invariably read "calm," which was a relative term because day and night soldiers reinforced their positions under harassing shellfire and patrols, ordered out nightly by the Regiment, clashed constantly with the Germans, all the while taking light but steady casualties.[37] After the 2nd Battalion, under Captain Cobb, replaced Little's 1st Battalion in the front lines on the night of July 30, the Germans disrupted the following day with harassing artillery fire and strafing runs made by low-flying aircraft. That night, German assault teams also attacked three of the 369th's frontline posts from close range. The Americans repulsed all three of the patrols, at the cost of eight Americans wounded and the death of Lt. Arch Worsham, who had joined the Regiment only two days earlier.[38]

Even reserve trenches 5 miles behind the lines were not safe. On August 1, the men of 1st Battalion were lounging in reserve, sunning themselves and picking lice, or "cooties," the bane of World War I infantrymen, from their clothes. For fear of attracting German shellfire, only four men at a time gathered in the open to bathe and wash their clothes at the public fountain in the village. Suddenly, some half a dozen shells fell right into the center of the town, the first terribly wounding the four bathing soldiers. Everyone took cover after the first shell, and within a half hour, everything continued as before. Hardened soldiers regarded such incidents as routine.[39]

Early in August, the French 4th Army command ordered the troops to prepare for a German offensive,[40] yet "calm" reigned through early August, disrupted only by sporadic shellfire, aerial activity, and exchanges of machine-gun fire and grenades. On August 10–11, two German raids accompanied by violent shelling caught the Americans by surprise, killing two and wounding seven men. A week later, early in the morning of August 18, after a five-minute bombardment that severed the German point of attack from the American lines, a German raiding party came from two sides, flanking four American outposts. They captured 1st Lt. Gorman Jones and four of his men, dragged them from the trench, and began to shove them toward the German lines through no-man's-land.[41] The raiders and their prisoners passed within 50 yards of an advance post where Sgt. William Butler and two privates crouched. Jones called to Butler, "Don't fire, Butler!" Butler replied, "Not yet, sir, but soon." The Germans, startled by the exchange, wheeled toward Butler's voice. Jones and his four men seized the moment to bolt from the trench, and Jones cried to Butler, "Let 'em have it!" Butler leaped from his shallow trench, Chauchat automatic rifle in hand, shouting and firing as he rushed the Germans. He killed four of the enemy soldiers and enabled Jones and his men to escape. As the rest of the Germans fled, Butler pursued them through the artillery barrage all the way to their own lines, throwing hand grenades into their dugouts, and "rambling all over the sector in search of grey-green prey, returning to the combat post when he was completely exhausted."

Lieutenant Jones, though wounded by a shell, regained the American lines with his men. He received the Croix de Guerre, as did the company commander, Capt. John O. Outwater, who heard groans from no-man's-land and crawled out to find the German patrol leader, a Lieutenant Sauer, mortally wounded, his arm torn off by Butler's bullets. Outwater carried

Sauer in and interrogated him in German before he died. Lewis Shaw wrote his mother that "the Boche fear the black Americans and raided us every night and sometimes twice to watch us." Although Shaw emphasized Outwater's bravery, he commented about Butler's assault, "It altogether was a fine ending of a most disagreeable month of shell fire and gave the men much heart to really kill a few of the bastards after standing under their shells for so long."[42]

Sgt. William Butler was awarded the Distinguished Service Cross and the Croix de Guerre for his bravery. In an article headlined 15TH REGIMENT SOLDIER ROUTS TWENTY GERMANS in the *New York Evening World,* Lincoln Eyre observed that Butler's exploit rivaled that of Johnson and Roberts. Yet, Butler, according to Eyre, took his deed in stride, commenting simply, "Guess I just ran amuck."[43] The native of Salisbury, Maryland, became the darling of the state's black press. The *Baltimore Afro-American* boasted: "Trenton, New Jersey, may have her Needham Roberts, but it takes Salisbury, Maryland, to produce a William Butler. Roberts had his comrade, Henry Johnson, to help him in repulsing a raiding party of Germans, but Butler took care of a German lieutenant and squad of Boches all by himself."[44] Butler had further rescued an officer in his display of "extraordinary heroism" near Maison de Champagne, France, that morning. The next night, after 130 days in the lines, the 369th rotated to the rear for rest.

The 369th, particularly Sgt. William Butler, had acquitted itself well at the front once again, where days and nights of hard labor reinforcing positions under shelling, sniping, and strafing were interspersed with vicious nighttime combat on patrols or raids, all of which took a steady toll of soldiers' lives even when *"calme"* reigned on the western front. This juxtaposition between calm and the daily deaths of thousands of men on both sides became the theme of Erich Maria Remarque's classic novel of 1929, *"Im Westen nichts neues"—All Quiet on the Western Front—*which in its movie version won the Academy Award for Best Picture in 1930. The 369th's successful stint at the front proved that the disarray reported by Captain Mills was no indication of the Regiment's combat readiness. The Regiment had long suffered from a shortage of commissioned officers, and the number allegedly leaving likely comprised the Ivy Leaguers dissatisfied with Hayward and black noncommissioned officers seeking advancement they could not attain within the Regiment. All morale and discipline "appeared" to have "gone to the winds" and noncoms "appeared" to exercise no discipline over their men, but appearances were clearly quite deceiving.

The frontline success of the 369th was in fact irrelevant to the concerted effort from AEF HQ and certain French commanders to "whiten" the commissioned officer ranks of the 93rd Division. Yet, Gen. Mariano Francisco Julio Goybet and his superior, General Auguste Édouard Hirschauer, were reluctant to condemn their prospective black charges as quickly as the American officers had. Hirschauer considered Bryan's "severe" conclusions premature and believed any definitive judgments awaited the test of fire,[45] and Goybet was certain that the 372nd's new commander, professional soldier Col. Herschel Tupes, would improve the regiment. Goybet averred that it remained to be seen how the black soldiers would perform under prolonged bombardment.[46]

Goybet did believe that the white American officer had more authority and a graver sense of his responsibilities and was thus more suited to command than his black counterpart. White American officers should not be subordinate to a black officer, Goybet affirmed, and he recommended that all captains should be white, except for rare exceptions justified by conduct under fire.[47] With good training, he concluded, black regiments would make excellent units for attack but not for defense because during ordinary trench life, black soldiers could escape the surveillance of their officers and resume their habits of laziness and carelessness, which rapid military training had not entirely eliminated. He granted that the black American regiments desired to excel, but the elimination of black company commanders would solve the problematic mixture of American white and black officers.[48] After claiming it was too early to judge black regiments, Goybet's a priori assessments of African Americans as lazy and careless—an echo of his white American counterparts' assertions—led him to conclude that black Americans should be used as offensive units just like black Africans.

Early in August, Goybet assented to Col. Hershel Tupes's request to replace all black officers with white officers in the 372nd, as the inability of white and black American officers to be comrades and the refusal of white officers to serve under black officers would result in conflict or malaise that would diminish the troops' value in combat. Goybet's decision meant that the African American soldiers of the 372nd, like African colonial soldiers, required white commissioned officers.[49] French officers would offend the sensibilities of white officers if they treated black officers cordially, and French officers lacked the tact to respect such nuances, but all the problems would disappear if the 372nd had exclusively white officers like the 371st Regiment did. Goybet concluded that good black officers—he himself knew several— would serve best in regiments with a black cadre such as the 370th (the former 8th Illinois), in which only the colonel was now white.[50] Goybet had thus made white American attitudes the determining factor in the composition of the officer corps of the French army's Negro regiments.

Later, on August 24, Colonel Tupes justified replacing "colored" with white officers in the 372nd Regiment to AEF commander Pershing. Tupes referred to an earlier letter from Goybet to Pershing on the same subject, dated August 21. He noted the natural continuations of "racial distinctions in civilian life" in the military, distinctions that presented "a formidable barrier to the existence of that feeling of comradeship which is an essential to mutual confidence and esprit de corps." Tupes then accused colored officers of a "characteristic tendency . . . to neglect the welfare of their men and to perform their duties in a perfunctory manner" and found them "lacking in initiative." "Defects" of this type demanded such "constant supervision and attention to petty details" from their superior officers and battalion commanders that they distracted the latter from "their wider duties, with harmful results." Tupes consequently recommended that no colored officers be sent to his regiment, that colored officers removed by efficiency boards be promptly replaced by white officers of the same grade or of lower grades if necessary, and that any remaining colored officers be transferred to labor units or replacement units for other colored combat organizations.[51]

Goybet's concern about French tactlessness recalled General Le Gallais's communiqué in April as the 369th entered the front lines, albeit with an ironic twist. Le Gallais's worries about French tactlessness focused on treating the black soldiers of the 369th as "good comrades." Goybet, by contrast, wanted to ensure that his French officers did not offend white American officers; the sensibilities of the black officers and men did not matter to him. His concern about black soldiers relapsing into their old "habits of carelessness and laziness" racialized the contrasting lifestyles between the rigidly disciplined life of the military and the less structured life of the civilian. Goybet and white American officers conflated negative civilian characteristics with the stereotypical traits they traditionally ascribed to black people.

Goybet's contention regarding the white officer's "graver sense of responsibility" reflects purely his subjective perception. The system of repression and discrimination produced the enhanced authority of the white officers even as it devalued black leadership of black soldiers, and this phenomenon obtained whether Frenchmen commanded colonial soldiers or white Americans commanded black American soldiers. Race, not individual ability, wielded authority. Goybet, however, did not share one white American prejudice toward black soldiers: he believed that they would make fine assault troops with good training and would not relegate them to labor duties exclusively. Here, Goybet reflected French sentiment about African soldiers. Apparently, Goybet believed black American soldiers might come from a "civilized" society but they still retained the warrior qualities of their African ancestors. Of course, the French designation as assault troops, which African regiments and a few French divisions shared, meant that these soldiers led every attack. They became, in a sense, the ultimate cannon fodder. Furthermore, by 1918, French prime minister Georges Clemenceau and some of the French commanders of African colonial troops believed that France had shed enough blood and preferred to shed the blood of Africans instead of Frenchmen.[52]

Goybet's and Tupes's assessments explain why the officer cadres of the 369th, 371st, and 372nd Regiments became all white, whereas the 370th Regiment (8th Illinois) remained all black except for its regimental command. Although the 369th did not serve together with the other three regiments, by August 1, black officers at or above the rank of lieutenant who had sailed to France with the Regiment—Captains Charles W. Fillmore and Napoleon Bonaparte Marshall, First Lieutenants George C. Lacy and D. Lincoln Reid—had been transferred from the 369th to either the 370th Regiment or the 92nd Division AEF. James Reese Europe also received reassignment orders, but he first went to Paris for several weeks of much-needed rest and recovery at the end of July.[53] On August 1, Noble Sissle and ten other sergeants of the 369th went to AEF officer training school, after which he joined the 370th Regiment as a lieutenant; there, he encountered some fifteen other former noncoms from the 369th. The 369th now had an all-white cadre of line and regimental officers, despite the fact that white lieutenants had earlier served under the two black captains.[54] A displeased Hayward judged that "our colored officers—did good work" in the July fighting and believed that capable "colored" officers should command "colored" troops.[55]

No one had consulted Colonel Hayward or Generals Le Gallais and Lebouc, under whom the 369th had served. Instead, General Goybet and Colonel Tupes held sway at the level of the division and regiment in the French and American armies. Hayward complained that the AEF consulted Tupes and not him, but AEF HQ naturally preferred the judgment of a professional to that of a National Guard officer. Furthermore, Goybet's 157th Division had two African American regiments, so the AEF turned to him. Tupes displayed the bigoted attitudes toward blacks typical of white professional officers, but Hayward was racially progressive.

The French and American army commands' discussions of policy toward African American soldiers led to the circulation on August 7, 1918, of a memorandum "On the Subject of Black American Troops," written by Col. Louis Linard, chief of the French military mission and military attaché at AEF HQ.[56] Linard's memorandum deserves citation in its entirety, as it was certainly the single most important document concerning the French and American armies' policies toward African American soldiers during the war. It also achieved much notoriety in France after the war:

I. It is important that French officers selected to command black American troops or to live in contact with them, have an exact notion of the situation of Negroes in the United States. The considerations discussed in the following note thus should be communicated to them and widely disseminated. The French military authorities must even inform the French populations of the camps of colored American troops about this subject through the civilian authorities.

II. The American point of view on the "Negro question" can appear debatable to many French minds. But it is not up to us French to discuss what some label a "prejudice." American opinion is unanimous on the black question and admits no discussion.

The elevated number of Negroes in the United States (about 15 million) created for the white race of the republic a danger of degeneration if an inexorable separation was not established between Blacks and Whites.

As this danger does not exist for the French race, the French public is accustomed to treating the "black" familiarly and being very indulgent towards him.

This indulgence and familiarity profoundly wound the Americans. They consider it an attack on their national dogmas. They fear that French contact will only inspire in black Americans pretensions that they consider intolerable.

It is indispensable that every effort be made to avoid profoundly alienating American opinion. Although a citizen of the United States, the colored man is considered by the white American as an inferior being with whom one can only have business or (domestic) service relations. They reproach him for a certain lack of intelligence, indiscretion, his lack of civic or professional conscience, his familiarity.

The Negro's vices are a constant danger for the American, who must severely repress them. For example, black American troops in France have occasioned as many complaints for attempted rape as the entire rest of the army although they have sent us as soldiers only an elite from the physical and moral point of view, as the rejections at enlistment were enormous.

Conclusion

I. It is necessary to avoid all excessive intimacy between French officers and black officers, with whom one can be correct and kind, but whom one cannot treat on equal footing with white American officers without wounding the latter profoundly. It is necessary not to eat with them and to avoid shaking their hand, and conversations or frequent contact outside of service.

II. It is necessary not to praise black American soldiers in an exaggerated manner, above all in front of Americans. Recognize their qualities and service, but in moderate terms conforming to strict reality.

III. Try to get the populations of the camps not to spoil the Negroes. Americans are indignant at all public intimacy of white women with the Blacks. They [white Americans] recently protested vehemently against a print in *la Vie Parisienne* entitled "child of the dessert" showing a woman in a private dining room with a Negro. Moreover, our experienced colonials profoundly regret the familiarities of white women with black men, and see in them a considerable loss of prestige of the white race. The military authorities cannot intervene directly in this question, but they can influence the population through the civil authorities.

Signed: Linard.[57]

The memorandum indicated the importance that Linard attached to respecting the racist sensitivities of white Americans in French army relationships with black American soldiers, a sentiment General Goybet reflected. The AEF was clearly determined to ensure that black Americans' experience in France did nothing to upset their position of inferiority in the United States. The historical record proves the assertions about rape and enlistment rejections were incorrect. Linard's reference to the cartoon of the African soldier in his fez and the double entendre about desert, whence he came, and dessert, which he was about to become for his French hostess, indicates the intolerance and total absence of a sense of humor on the part of white Americans about relationships between black men and white women.

The French government and public also did not condone such relationships in the case of their colonial troops, as they threatened the colonial hierarchy of racial supremacy, but the French government had tens of thousands of African troops serving at the front in France and colonial workers in French factories. The French government attempted to keep the workers in separate quarters and the African soldiers in separate camps away from the public, but it could not enforce total separation. Consequently, it tacitly accepted the fact of interracial liaisons and even allowed marriages between French women workers and colonial men.[58] Furthermore, black

Frenchmen and Senegalese living in the four communes, or urban regions, of Senegal enjoyed the rights of all Frenchmen and served in integrated "metropolitan" units—white French units—in the army. Black and white comrades went on leave together, and white soldiers respected their black superiors and followed their orders, under pain of punishment. Blaise Diagne, the brilliant representative of Senegal and the first black deputy in the French National Assembly during World War I, advocated for the recognition of equal rights for colonial soldiers as a result of their wartime service for France. Diagne, educated in France, had married a Frenchwoman.[59]

Race trumped rank in the US Army, as white soldiers refused to acknowledge the authority of a black soldier of superior rank, despite the fact that this was an organization where rank was supposed to reign. Segregation remained the law of the land, and custom and law dictated the superiority of white over black. The army had used the excuse of a medical condition to retire Col. Charles Young, its highest-ranking black officer at the outbreak of war, because a white junior officer had protested that he would find it insufferable to have to obey a colored officer. AEF HQ replaced Franklin A. Dennison, the black colonel of the 370th Regiment, because of illness and ordered him to report to AEF Headquarters.[60] The AEF command simply could not tolerate French acceptance of African American soldiers as equals and condone their consorting with French women because of the threat to the sexual mastery of white men over white and black women and thus white racial dominance. Even as the Americans exported their brand of racism, Europeans clung to their own racist assumptions, as Goybet's assertions demonstrated.

The French General Staff circulated Linard's memorandum to the region commandants in the zone of the armies, then on August 19 retracted it and prescribed its annulment.[61] The French desired to appease their American ally, but the sentiments Linard expressed in the document violated and contradicted the French government's public positions on its own colonial policy and treatment of its valuable colonial soldiers. In fact, when Blaise Diagne obtained a copy of the memorandum after the war, he was so incensed that he brought it before the French parliament, which officially condemned the memorandum. Yet, for the time being, the French had extricated themselves from a difficult position by making their army commanders aware of the importance of respecting white Americans' racial prejudice, while giving themselves plausible deniability or distance from the document.

Linard may actually have written the memorandum in an effort to forestall an AEF attempt to take African American soldiers away from the French army. On August 10, Brig. Gen. H. B. Fiske submitted a memorandum to the chief of staff, AEF,[62] stating that "after at least one month's service in quiet sectors at the front," the training of the 93rd Division "had progressed as far as it is likely to go while under French control, since about all their time outside of the trenches is spent in labor on rear positions." Fiske negatively portrayed the circumstances in the French army: "Supply and equipment under the French are not satisfactory; transportation is inadequate and of poor quality. Their organization is French. The quality of all these regiments appears to be deteriorating. It is believed that their permanent attachment to French organizations would in time create unfavorable comment at home on the ground that the treatment of black troops differed from that of white troops."[63] Fiske recommended withdrawal of the 93rd Division from the French army and its reorganization and training "to serve as pioneer regiments."[64] He based his damning assessment of conditions in the black regiments in the French army and their deteriorating morale on various reports, including Colonel Hayward's complaints about conditions in the 369th. Hayward observed that the Regiment had held sectors of the front longer than other American regiments without rest or additional training and that it suffered under the French from a constant shortage of horses and wagons. Most critically, Hayward asserted that the Regiment's morale deteriorated over the months of "trench drudgery continually exacted, the lack of opportunity for training, and the great influx of untrained and illiterate Negroes who came to the regiment from the southern states without any interest in the regiment and no pride in its reputation, and who but poorly could be assimilated." Hayward had repeatedly reported this condition in writing and in person, even to Pershing, as had every inspector who visited the Regiment.

Hayward believed that Fiske's memorandum reported "that the regiment, owing to its long tour without relief or training, was rapidly deteriorating, through no fault of its officers, and earnestly recommended that the condition be remedied."[65] He did not realize that Fiske's brief paragraph had stated none of these reasons or provisos, and he certainly would have opposed Fiske's recommendation to return the 93rd Division to the AEF as pioneer troops. Hayward appreciated the advantages of being attached to the French army, but his listing of issues affecting morale ignored the fact that "trench drudgery" was the norm for all infantry troops and that combat experience was more critical than further training. He most strongly resented the detachments of southern black draftees, who arrived 300 or 500 at a time, often just before offensives, untrained and without prior notice—a circumstance that had nothing to do with the French army but with the AEF's assignment of manpower. In fact, American conscripts in general, black and white, were poorly educated and arrived at the front inadequately trained.

Hayward intended his complaints to ameliorate conditions for the 369th within the French army, but Fiske used them to imply that the unit would enjoy better circumstances in the AEF, an absurd proposition in light of the AEF's racial attitudes and logistical problems. Any objections he might have voiced reflected AEF HQ's objection to the decent treatment of black soldiers in the French army. The treatment that black troops received in the French army was indeed different—and better—than what the AEF command planned for them in order to reinforce their acceptance of their subordinate position in American society.

On August 16, AEF HQ advised the French mission that it wanted the French army to arrange for the early relief of the black regiments of the 93rd Provisional Division and their return to US control. The memorandum presented several "compelling" reasons for this request. The troops of the 93rd allegedly desired to serve with other American troops as American units. Furthermore, the entire American people would insist that American troops, both white and black, serve as complete units in American divisions, corps, and armies. The regiments, now trained, had served with French units much longer than originally intended. Now, "their ultimate use is to be that of *pioneer troops* [emphasis added] of which just now we have urgent need." How soon could the French comply with this request?[66] AEF HQ had rediscovered the "lost infants" it now urgently needed for "engineering" and labor service behind the front to supply ammunition to the AEF 1st Army.[67]

Colonel Linard forwarded the request of AEF HQ immediately to the French High Command and called particular attention to the AEF decision to make the black regiments pioneers. Linard regretted that these units, which had completed training and demonstrated their capability as combat troops, would be lost to battle. He observed to French army commander Gen. Philippe Pétain that he had not sent a copy of this demand to the Allied commander in chief, Gen. Ferdinand Foch, but he requested its further transmission to the Generalissimo if appropriate.[68]

On August 20, AEF HQ reiterated its request for the return of at least one black regiment for ammunition supply duty.[69] That same day, Linard asked Foch to answer the American request for the regiments.[70] Foch wrote Pershing on August 26 that to return the 93rd Division would entail serious consequences for the French army, as two of its regiments formed part of fighting French infantry divisions and two more were destined for similar service. Their removal would necessitate the deletion of two French infantry divisions, which could not otherwise complete their ranks. Such modification of the French army would cause troublesome consequences compared to the "slight advantage" that the US Army would gain from using the black soldiers as labor troops.[71]

The Generalissimo had terminated AEF HQ's bid. The four regiments of the 93rd Provisional Division remained with the French army until the end of the war, the 369th until a month after the Armistice. The French army refused to surrender soldiers it had trained for combat just as Foch planned to continue his offensives against the German army. The AEF's request to turn battle-tested troops into laborers offended the army that had adopted these soldiers and prepared them to fight within its ranks. Within two weeks' time, Colonel Linard had gone from transmitting the US Army's racist demands concerning French treatment of African American soldiers to orchestrating opposition to the AEF's request for the return of the black soldiers.

In a lecture on the 369th at the Infantry School at Fort Benning, Georgia, on March 21, 1937, Maj. Joseph A. Cistero asserted: "Several times American GHQ had tried to have the Regiment returned to American control. General Gouraud, commanding the French Fourth Army, however, succeeded in retaining it because the Regiment had proven its efficiency as an organic unit of the French 161st Division replacing a French regiment."[72] Cistero's assertion that the AEF attempted several times to reclaim the 369th and his attribution of its retention in the French army to Gouraud seem correct, as the French High Command would surely have consulted one of its most prominent generals. Gouraud's staunch support of the 369th, combined with the determination of Linard and the French army command not to return seasoned combat veterans for the AEF to relegate to pioneer duties, sufficed to thwart the AEF's designs on the Regiment.

AEF HQ's reasons for the request were specious, with the exception of the likely need for laborers for ammunitions supply. If some officers and soldiers of the 369th hoped to return to the AEF, it was as combat soldiers, not as labor or pioneer troops. No available evidence supports the AEF claim that the American public insisted that all Americans, regardless of race, serve together in an American army; certainly, no outcry of white voices had arisen at the detachment of the 93rd Division from the AEF. By August, no one in the American command cared what the 369th had accomplished or what the other black regiments might achieve at the front. What concerned them was their fear that these soldiers would return to the United States with attitudes subversive of the contemporary racist order, and the way to avert this possibility was to secure their return to the AEF. Yet, for Colonel Linard to write the memorandum stipulating the AEF's desires about the treatment of black soldiers was one thing; to relinquish these capable troops to the AEF after the French had trained them for combat was quite another. Neither Linard nor the French generals would acquiesce in this matter.

Linard did move quickly to complete the segregation of the officer cadres in the regiments of the 93rd Division. On September 5, 1918, he advised French General Headquarters that he wanted to move black officers from regiments with integrated officer cadres into those with all-black officer cadres, the 370th Regiment, or perhaps to the 92nd Division AEF.[73] As late as October 25, the American liaison officer, Capt. Stuart Benson, voicing the views of the French commander of 10th Army, sought to replace even the African American officers of the predominantly black 370th Regiment (8th Illinois) with white officers as quickly as possible.[74] French general Eugène-Désité-Antoine Mittelhauser, commander of the French 36th Division, had recommended, according to a US military source, a gradual phasing out of black officers, starting at the field and staff levels. He reasoned that "if properly handled they [the soldiers of the 370th] would make a most valuable body of fighting men."[75] French general Rondeau, commander of the 59th Division, complained in late September that the black officers of the 370th were men of "pronounced inefficiency" and "vain strap- [stripe-] wearers (porte-galons) of no military knowledge and showing a lamentable lack of conscientiousness in their work."[76] Fortunately for racial peace in the regiment, the black officer cadre remained largely intact.

The 370th Regiment became the only regiment of the four that did not receive a regimental Croix de Guerre with Palm, although twenty-one soldiers of the 370th were awarded Distinguished Service Crosses and seventy-one the Croix de Guerre, and one of its companies, Company C, was given the Croix with Palm for conspicuous bravery. The record of awards to officers and men of the 370th indicates that as individuals, they were fine soldiers, but both French and American officers were convinced that black officers were not suited for command above the company level. Rondeau's negative assessment of the 370th's black officers led to the dissolution of the regiment as a separate frontline command and the dispersal of its battalions as its main fighting units attached to French regiments.[77]

The assault on black officers continued relentlessly and at the highest levels. Maj. Gen. Robert Lee Bullard, the commander of the 2nd Army, did all he could to remove black officers not only from the 92nd Division, which belonged to his 2nd Army, but also from the 93rd Division. On September

16, Bullard even informed AEF HQ that General Goybet urged that officer replacements for black troops come from among southern white officers. Clearly, Bullard was not content merely to make the lives of the black soldiers in the AEF miserable; he also sought to ensure that all black soldiers would have racist white southerners to command them. Most fascinating, he attributed his sentiments to General Goybet, who had previously expressed a desire to have white officers for his black troops but never specified white southerners.[78] Either Bullard simply placed his words in Goybet's mouth or the American regular army officers of the 371st and 372nd Regiments had convinced their French commander to adopt their mores to the extent that Bullard claimed Goybet understood black soldiers better than any white American officer.[79]

The subsequent career of Capt. Napoleon Bonaparte Marshall illustrates what could happen to African American commissioned officers who were transferred from the 369th to either the 370th or the 92nd Division. Marshall assumed command of Company A, 365th Regiment of the 92nd Division and even temporarily commanded the battalion when its major was ill. On the night of October 21, during the Meuse-Argonne offensive, the battalion commander suddenly appeared and ordered Marshall and forty-two men to raid a German machine-gun nest. Without prior notice and planning and with no hand grenades or wire cutters, they set off, the major ordering Marshall, as the patrol departed, to shoot any man who disobeyed an order. Marshall considered the undertaking "certain death, but orders are orders."[80]

As he feared, the patrol encountered intense German shell and machine-gun fire, but they lost only one man, a sergeant "cut in two by a shell while carelessly standing on top of the trenches." Unfortunately, Marshall tripped over some wire and fell, hitting his back on the rim of a shell hole, his head snapping back and hitting the ground. Dazed and paralyzed, his back nearly broken, his spinal cord sprained, and his back ligaments torn, Marshall survived only because his men carried him back. They had found the German machine-gun nest empty, but the flashes from the German artillery barrage enabled American artillery to locate and then destroy the enemy positions with counterbattery fire. The major, who congratulated them on their return, was killed two days later while reconnoitering in no-man's-land. Marshall was evacuated to the States and ultimately released from US Base Hospital No. 1 in the Bronx on May 16, 1919, but he could walk only by wearing a specially designed steel corset. The physician who discharged Marshall declared that he was 29 percent disabled, when the minimal limit for compensation was 30 percent. Despite such treatment from the US Army, Napoleon Bonaparte Marshall remained a staunch patriot.[81] His major was clearly a novice at trench warfare with far less experience than Marshall himself had, as would have been the case with most black officers and noncoms transferring from the 369th to the 370th or the 92nd, since the latter two units entered combat later than the 369th. The medical declaration that Marshall was short of the minimal limit for compensation for disability despite his obvious condition also seems representative of the experience of many black soldiers in both world wars.

The wartime experiences of the black regiments attached to the French army demonstrated that the French army was not devoid of racial prejudice. Comparisons between racial attitudes of Americans and French were relative. The experience of the 369th indicated that its white northern and elite officers treated black soldiers better than their US regular army peers, particularly southerners, and that it was preferable to be in the French army than in the American Expeditionary Forces. Yet, one should not be tempted to claim that the French held no prejudices against African Americans. Though some French generals, such as Le Gallais, Lebouc, and Gouraud, treated African American soldiers fairly, many others, such as Goybet, Mittelhauser, and Rondeau, drew their line of tolerance at African American commissioned officers and in fact saw little difference in capability between "primitive" West African colonial subjects and the urban blacks of New York City or Chicago. They concluded that black soldiers, in the crucible of war, would be useful only as assault troops and would not obey black officers, whom they did not trust to lead or punish them.[82] The 369th certainly gave the lie to both assertions, for it performed well during its extended tour in the trenches and its black officers, whether in the 369th or in other units later, led their men capably and the men obeyed them—even to the point, as in the case of Napoleon Marshall, of risking their lives to save their black commanders.

Now behind the lines for rest and refitting in August, the battalions of the 369th set about restoring the spit and polish necessary for a crack military organization. In the front lines, garrison manners were unnecessary, superfluous, and even dangerous; in the rear, the battalions now reintroduced the men to close-order drill, ceremonies, and parades. Regimental bands played an essential role in this process, as their music boosted morale when they played at ceremonies and parades. Lt. James Reese Europe returned after recuperating from the effects of gas to learn that AEF HQ had cancelled his reassignment to the 92nd Division; he remained in the 369th as a lieutenant. Good bands were so important to morale that AEF HQ had waived the rule proscribing officers from being band leaders solely in Europe's case, so he exchanged his official assignment as machine-gun officer for that of bandmaster of the 369th. Yet the 369th's famed band was not present to welcome the Regiment or to play for it during its time in the rear.

On August 9, two days after the Linard memorandum, AEF HQ informed the French military mission that it was assigning the band of the 369th to the American general in command of troops for temporary duty in Paris, where by order of General Pershing it would play for the Inter-allied Congress of Women (Conference of Allied Women, or Conference of Allied Women War Workers) on August 14–17. It would rejoin the Regiment on August 18. AEF HQ certainly appreciated the unique quality of the band.[83] Lt. James Reese Europe had imposed upon his friend Maj. Barclay Warburton, a member of Pershing's staff, to allow him to come as band-master—thus Europe's retention in the 369th as its lone black officer—and Hayward observed that the army command "seemed to think the band be-longed to the AEF and not to the 369th Infantry."[84]

The band played one concert in the Théâtre des Champs-Elysées to conclude the conference. The conference had included a garden party hosted by President and Mrs. Raymond Poincaré of France, an afternoon at the home of Mr. and Mrs. Theodore Roosevelt, Jr., and a banquet at the Palais D'Orsay. On the last night, the "final and crowning session of the Conference," the lights were low in the Elysées Theater. The audience included two African American women, Addie W. Hunton and Kathryn M. John-son, YWCA delegates to the conference. Hunton recalled that as the lights dimmed, someone commented that a "colored orchestra" sat in the pit. They rose to view Lieutenant Europe's head, though they could not see the rest of the band. As President Poincaré and his party entered their box, the band summoned the audience to its feet with "The Marseillaise." With Lord Derby, the British ambassador, presiding, the band announced each national organization with the appropriate anthem. In the women's words, the musicians "thrilled the house into rapturous applause."[85] Hunton later claimed that the band had "maintained the enthusiasm of that final meeting" as women of different nationalities crowded about to shake Eu-rope's hand at its conclusion.[86] After the audience had departed, the lights dimmed and the band played far into the night at the request of its "admir-ing friends," including the Roosevelts.[87]

The AEF insisted that Europe and his band remain in Paris to boost the morale of soldiers by playing in rest camps and hospitals. Colonel Hayward requested the return of the band on August 31 because it would help maintain regimental discipline and provide distraction for the men in camp at St. Ouen,[88] but he could secure the band's services only occasionally from

August to October, as it remained primarily in Paris. Noble Sissle believed that the band's performances enabled Europe "to render his greatest service to his government and regiment." Hayward agreed that it had "been the source of great solace and comfort" to the Regiment and to the hundreds of hospitals and rest camps it visited.[89]

The band played before troops of all the Entente countries. James Europe recalled, "Everywhere we gave a concert it was a riot."[90] In Paris, the band of the 369th gave a concert with the British Grenadiers' Band, the French Garde Républicaine Band, and the Royal Italian Band. The director and musicians of the band of the Garde Républicaine believed that Europe's men used special instruments until they examined them for themselves. While Europe acknowledged that the regimental band could not compare to these, the greatest military bands in the world, the 369th invariably drew crowds of as many as 50,000 people. He attributed it not to technical superiority, the novelty of a black band, better music, or European gratitude for the American presence but to "the jazz effects."[91]

By the fall of 1918, journalists who had witnessed the electrifying and highly publicized effect of African American military bands on European audiences applied the term *jazz* to the music. The French, including Gen. Philippe Pétain, loved "jazz music."[92] The Jazz Age began, in the final throes of the Great War, and the military bands of African American units, the 369th most prominent among them, introduced it to European audiences. AEF HQ had failed to retrieve the 369th and the other three regiments of the 93rd Division (Provisional), but it had appropriated the 369th's band to the benefit of all those fortunate enough to hear James Reese Europe and his men. In any case, the 369th was not destined to remain in the rear for long.

The Regiment integrated the replacement troops, numbering some 40 percent of battalion strength, who had arrived from the States with little or no training. Part of the daily training schedule consisted of intercompany baseball games. Perhaps most welcome of all, the men got daily hot-water showers and had their clothing sterilized to kill the lice and other denizens that shared their vestments, acquired during months in the trenches.[93]

During these times in cantonments in the rear areas, the soldiers turned to French civilians for extracurricular activities, as YMCA establishments existed only in the American zone of operation. The 369th did benefit from the Y's stationing of a few black males with combat units at the front, where "life is very spicy," wrote Heyward Caldwell in June 1918. Caldwell and his associate Franklin O. Nichols, the first black welfare worker to reach France, did "their best for the boys in every way." Caldwell proudly announced to his superiors in Paris that Nichols and he were with the 15th NY/369th Infantry, whose "boys were giving an honorable account of themselves at the front."[94] Not long after, Matthew W. Bullock replaced Nichols. A graduate of the Dartmouth College class of 1904, Bullock had starred in football and track. He attended Harvard Law School and paid his way by coaching at Massachusetts Agricultural College (now the University of Massachusetts) and Atlanta Baptist College (now Morehouse College). Many members of the Regiment knew his fame as an athlete and scholar.[95] The physical skills and mental toughness of a first-class athlete served him well in his duties, as "Bullock could be seen at all times making his way under tremendous shell fire that he might reach his men with necessary supplies." In addition to serving food and beverages and ministering to the recreational, spiritual, mental, and emotional needs of the men, Bullock and his colleagues also performed service normally associated with the Red Cross, such as giving first aid to the wounded.[96] Although YMCA facilities for black soldiers were wanting in size, comfort, supplies, programs, and staff, dedicated workers such as Nichols, Caldwell, and Bullock made up in commitment what the huts lacked materially.[97]

Black soldiers in the American zone did not feel welcome in YMCA establishments, which catered to white soldiers almost exclusively, posted signs that announced "no Negroes allowed," or limited hours when the facility would be available to black troops. The YMCA and military authorities shared the blame for such humiliating policies and practices.[98] When the Y opened a few separate facilities for black troops, white women staffed them and gave the most perfunctory service to the men "because their prejudices would not permit them to spend a social hour with a homesick colored boy, or even, to sew on a service stripe."[99] Only three African American women volunteers—Helen Curtis, Addie W. Hunton, and Kathryn M. Johnson—served in the YMCA in France before the Armistice. With only three black women among the 150,000 black troops, the fortunate few soldiers who saw them, let alone received their services, often burst into tears of joy and surprise.[100] Despite their wishes to serve the combat troops, Curtis, Hunton, and Johnson found themselves ministering to the needs of the pioneers, stevedores, and various labor units whose men faced stern discipline, cruel discrimination, "long hours of toil," and "scant recognition for service or hope of promotion." These men paid "their toll in death from accident, cold, and exposure," as well as overwork and enemy fire, which they could not return.[101]

Government and military officials supported the YMCA's activities as instruments of social control, which would inculcate values and promote good citizenship through civic, religious, health, and cognitive instruction. They also hoped the YMCA programs would reduce the likelihood of race friction. Although these very programs and policies might have unintended consequences by raising the level of soldiers' expectations through education or actually exacerbating racial tension by discrimination, neither the government nor the YMCA brooked real or perceived expressions of disloyalty, including those from women "suffused of the radical temper."[102]

On pass behind the lines, the men of the 369th visited village taverns (*estaminets*), where they could secure French wine. White American soldiers often complained that French villagers raised their prices and attempted to profit from them.[103] African American soldiers did not complain about such treatment, perhaps because being welcome in a white establishment was a pleasant change from their experiences in their own country, where this happened so seldom. Furthermore, the French villagers probably regarded them with a certain degree of curiosity. In so many villages, only the old, female, and young remained. White southerners feared contact between French women and African American soldiers, yet such contact proved unavoidable in these circumstances. Village women often washed the soldiers' clothes and ran the establishments they frequented on pass. Furthermore, every village had its individuals "of ill repute," so the admonitions and precautions the AEF preached against venereal disease proved useful.[104] Yet, the 369th in general spent little time in the rear, and this respite lasted only a week.

On the Regiment's second day in the rear, August 21, a singular event highlighted the often-ignored corollary of the 369th's loss of white and black officers—the suitability of their white replacements to serve in a regiment of black northerners. A second lieutenant named Emmett Cochran, a southerner and native Georgian who had lived in Montgomery, Alabama, before his training, had just arrived. Hayward was busy condemning the quality of enlisted draftees, many of them uneducated southern blacks, whom the Regiment received as replacements. In light of the Regiment's stateside experience with southern whites, the colonel might well have questioned the wisdom of assigning a southern officer to the ranks of the 369th. The following account renders the risks of such action abundantly clear.[105]

Behind the front at Camp les Maigneux, troops bought wine and even champagne in the neighboring villages, so on August 21, Maj. Lorillard Spencer, executive officer of the 369th, posted provost guards in the villages around the camp to corral drunken and disorderly soldiers. The guards ordered to the town of Dommartin-la-Planchette consisted of a five-man detail from F Company, reputedly the toughest unit in the Regiment. The five soldiers—Sgt. Thomas Emanuel, Cpl. Elmer Perry, Pvt. Charles James, Pvt. Roy Shiel, and Pvt. Walter Whittaker—were all veteran volunteers of the Old 15th, two of whom, Perry and James, had been with it from the start.[106] Perry and James carried pistols; Whittaker and Shiel unloaded rifles. Their orders were to stop any soldiers of the 369th who attempted to enter the village. They arrived in Dommartin late that morning, where Emanuel split the detail in two, sending Perry and James to one end of the village and Shiel and Whittaker to the other; he himself would circulate between them.

Shiel got a bottle of champagne from a French soldier, swilled most of it, became drunk and disorderly, and ended up under arrest in the judge advocate's office of Maj. Willis C. Knight. When Sergeant Emanuel arrived, Knight informed him that he had phoned the 369th to send another detail to relieve and arrest them. Emanuel ordered Whittaker to arrest Shiel and gave Shiel's rifle to Whittaker. Whittaker now carried two unloaded rifles, one slung over each shoulder, as they exited the office at 3:00 or 4:00 in the afternoon.

Knight exaggeratedly informed Major Spencer that Emanuel's entire guard detail was drunk and rioting, and Spencer ordered Lieutenant Cochran—the recently arrived junior lieutenant in M Company—to take a squad from F Company to Dommartin in a cart and use "every means" to arrest what "were probably pretty rough" men. He advised Cochran to go armed in case of trouble, so Cochran strapped on a .45 automatic.[107] Spencer then ordered the six soldiers accompanying Cochran to carry no firearms and to club any man who gave them trouble.

As the cart entered the village that evening, Sergeant Emanuel, recognizing F Company men, stepped into the road and raised his hand to stop the cart. Upon seeing the white officer, Emanuel dropped his hand, but Whittaker had already seized the horse's reins. Lieutenant Cochran yelled twice at Whittaker to let the horse go. When Whittaker failed to comply, Cochran leaped off the cart, drew and cocked his automatic, and confronted Whittaker. Whittaker placed one rifle on the ground, and as he stooped to put down the other in a crouching position while holding the rifle in both hands, Cochran shot him in the stomach at a range of 5 to 10 feet. In his book *Harlem's Hell Fighters,* author Stephen Harris inexplicably states, "As Whittaker crouched over—either to put the second unloaded rifle on the ground *or to take aim at Cochran* [emphasis added], the lieutenant shot him in the stomach."[108] Why would Whittaker have aimed an unloaded rifle at an officer confronting him with a loaded and cocked automatic?

The bullet exited Whittaker's back and fell into his pants. Whittaker somehow remained on his feet for four minutes and protested, "Lieutenant, you have shot me. You have shot a good man,"[109] and then he slumped to his knees and fell forward on his face. Cochran threatened to kill anyone who moved. He had his men load Whittaker in the cart and take him to a French aid station, where Whittaker later died. After the cart returned, Cochran, who had departed in the interim, came back with white soldiers and placed Emanuel's detail under arrest.

By the time a court-martial of white infantry officers convened to try Cochran for murder on September 23, 1918, at the headquarters of the 369th Infantry at Camp Rougon, France, the 369th was back in the front lines. Whittaker's black comrades described him as "intelligent," "a pretty quiet fellow," and "a very good fellow."[110] F Company's commander, Capt. John Holley Clark, Jr., whom Cochran's defense called as a witness, testified that Whittaker was not "quarrelsome," that he had "very little trouble with him," and that "his behavior was usually all right."[111]

Cochran's defense had to establish that he could have reasonably assumed he was in danger of being shot by Whittaker and consequently shot the private in self-defense.[112] Cochran testified on September 24 that F Company had the general reputation of being the most troublesome unit in the Regiment and that a sergeant might reprimand a soldier one day and be found shot the next morning.[113] Cochran, with Major Spencer's dire warning likely ringing in his ears, did not see Sergeant Emanuel raise his hand. Instead, he believed that the group of black men rushing toward his approaching cart "would go to extremes." He considered himself in "imminent" danger and described Whittaker as "very mad," "his face distorted with rage." When confronted with Whittaker, Cochran testified that "he had no time to say a word," other than repeating "Let go that horse," as "the man [Whittaker] was raising his rifle on me." He regarded Whittaker as "displaying an attitude more of an outlaw." If Whittaker started trouble, Cochran expected it from all of them, as he lacked confidence in the support of his own detail from F Company. "I had only myself to depend on," Cochran declared, "and being the only white soldier in the vicinity at the time, I was very careful to observe."[114] Cochran thus saw himself as a lone white man in the midst of hostile black men, not as an officer among soldiers, more than half of whom he commanded as a detail.

The military prosecutor, 1st Lt. Archibald King of the 161st Infantry, argued that the responsibility of an officer for enlisted men under his command became "all the greater" when the soldiers "are of another race, of a race which had not had the advantages of ours, against misuse of power."

The deceased, as a provost guard or sentry, had the power to stop the cart and the "authority to fire to kill." Cochran had violated army regulations in not respecting sentinels and in not challenging the private, and he had used unnecessary force in killing Whittaker while the latter was executing orders. The prosecutor considered Cochran's conduct "hasty and the homicide unnecessary, avoidable." Cochran would be subject to death or dismissal and imprisonment at hard labor if the court found him guilty of murder or manslaughter.[115]

The defense counsel, Major Knight of the provost marshal's office, retorted that Emanuel's detail had "violated their standing as sentries" and that Cochran could justifiably have expected that his own detail from this "troublesome company would sympathize with the provost guard." Cochran did not know that Whittaker's rifle was empty, and Cochran's prior service with white troops and his short time in the Regiment meant "that he knew nothing of the characteristics of these men, which everyone knows are considerably different from those of white troops, and especially a man from the South, . . . he understands more or less of the Negro character."[116] Knight's proclamation that a southerner understood "more or less" the "Negro character" yet Cochran knew "nothing" of the "characteristics" of these men was vague, contradictory, and racist.

Knight claimed that the Regiment's "men were very much out of hand when they came out of the trenches." He even recalled an incident one night when he was prepared to shoot two rowdy soldiers from the 369th in the street below his office window.[117] Knight's regimental commander in a neighboring village had complained to the 369th that three or four of its soldiers had confronted the commander's adjutant, "assuming threatening gestures toward him," in broad daylight. Finally, the colonel of a French regiment based in another nearby village had complained "that the men were firing pistols promiscuously around the streets in any direction." Knight concluded, "It is a well-known fact that the colored man is ordinarily rather uncertain when he is under the influence of liquor, and the action of Whittaker would reasonably indicate that his [Cochran's] information would be correct. I personally know that I would not care to be unarmed in the face of an armed Negro under the influence, and I would consider anything justifiable."[118] Once again, Knight's observations were both racist and irrelevant, as Whittaker was not drunk nor was Cochran unarmed.

Prosecutor King rebutted that the conduct of other members of the Regiment at other times and places, though regrettable, had nothing to do with the present case.[119] Yet he did not challenge Knight's barrage of racist allegations about "Negro character" and differences between black and white troops, perhaps an indication that all officers present accepted such prejudicial beliefs. In the end, the court found Cochran not guilty. A review of the verdict at the level of the adjutant general at AEF HQ, on October 28, 1918, approved the acquittal but acknowledged "that had this officer handled, in a different manner, the situation in which he found himself, extreme measures would not have been necessary." It concluded, "Lieut. Cochran will be released from arrest."

In some respects, the verdict was foreordained. To find a white commissioned officer guilty of the murder of a black enlisted man was unthinkable. A black man's word counted for naught against that of a white man stateside, and southern state laws even prevented black people from testifying against whites. What white southerners "knew" about African Americans consisted of the negative stereotypes and prejudices that they had formed to justify slavery and then violent post-emancipation repression. Southern whites and northern blacks formed a volatile mix, yet AEF replacement policy had sent Cochran, an inexperienced white officer, to a regiment of veteran black soldiers.

When Spencer ordered Cochran to bring back the culprits, Cochran went armed with two weapons—a loaded .45 automatic and prejudice against black men. None of the northern white officers in the Regiment ever expressed any fear of their black soldiers, including Captain Clark at the trial, and had Cochran processed the rumors about F Company rationally, he would have noted no risk to the lives of white officers. Unfortunately, Cochran's fear rendered him incapable of rational behavior. The unnecessary shooting resulted from his inept handling of the situation, as the review of the court-martial acknowledged.

The incident might have demonstrated to an unprejudiced mind the liability of having no African American commissioned officers in black regiments. Bigoted white officers constantly alleged that black soldiers would not acknowledge the leadership of black officers, yet black officers such as Napoleon Marshall, who had served as regimental provost marshal, and Charles Fillmore gave the lie to such claims. The racist diatribe of defense counsel Major Knight illustrated the double standard that the AEF's white officers applied to black and to white soldiers, whose behavior in fact could be equally, if not more, drunken, boisterous, and "uncertain" than their black counterparts. The fear of black soldiers expressed by Knight and Cochran reflected a more general white concern about the war's potential effect on black soldiers—that they would no longer unquestioningly obey white authority, however unreasonable. In any case, Cochran was freed on review in late October 1918, and he missed the rest of the war. He committed suicide twenty years later by shooting himself in the head in a hotel in Shreveport, Louisiana.[120]

Four days after the incident, on August 25, orders directed the Regiment to prepare to move at night by truck. On August 8, the French commander in chief, Gen. Philippe Pétain, had ordered the 369th placed at his disposition as of August 20. Once the Regiment had assembled in the rear of the 4th Army and was ready to depart, the French High Command would disclose the 369th's next assignment.[121]

At midnight on August 25–26, the soldiers of the 369th roared into the night in a convoy of some 150 canvas-covered trucks, or *camions,* driven by Singhalese (present day Sri Lankans). The French invariably used as drivers Indo-Chinese and other Southeast Asian men, all of whom were notorious for speeding and recklessness. The convoy split in four sections, one for each of the three battalions and a fourth for special units. The battalion commanders and their adjutants shared the touring cars of the "train master," or captain commanding each convoy section. The driver of the powerful touring car would roar ahead of the convoy section to stop at intersections so that the captain could direct the trucks and then count the number passing to be sure they had lost no one along the way. Then, the car would speed ahead to the next intersection. If a truck lost its way, the captain would halt the convoy until he located the missing vehicle; he then guided it back to his flock and continued.

The 369th rode southwest, away from the front, toward Chalons. After a night billeted east of Chalons, the Regiment's battalions marched south, part of the way on an ancient Roman road, to the excellent base camp at St. Ouen, where they encamped together as a regiment for the first time since mid-February. The men reunited with old friends and got acquainted with replacements; resumed training, athletics, and marksmanship practice; received promotions, new uniforms, and equipment; and attended religious services. Two new chaplains—Benjamin C. Robeson, the pastor of Harlem's Mother AME Zion and older brother of Paul Robeson, and Thomas W. Wallace—had reported for duty on the way to St. Ouen.[122] These African American pastors filled a void that had lasted a year, when the previous chaplain had failed his physical examination. They anticipated a month's respite from the front.

Rumors abounded of a future American offensive at St. Mihiel to reduce the German salient and ultimately to seize the fortress city of Metz. Some officers of the 369th believed that they might be returned to the AEF to participate in an American drive to victory,[123] and they anticipated at least a month's respite from the front. Capt. Lewis Shaw, however, had become convinced in mid-July that the 369th's war was already over. "Everyone here," he wrote his mother, "feels that the war is practically over. . . . I believe the Boche are nearly thru for the morale particularly of the prisoners we see is very low." Furthermore, he expected to "go south for the winter" by October 1 because the French sent their African troops to southern France to avoid the cold winters in northern France.[124] Early in September, Colonel Hayward confided in Shaw that "he would not be surprised if we saw no more fighting." The allies were driving the Germans back rapidly, and by the end of the 369th's anticipated rest period, the weather would be "too cold to send colored troops into the line." "We are all looking forward to a winter in southern France and an early peace."[125] Shaw correctly judged that the war would be over by the end of the year, but he and Hayward erred grievously in thinking that the 369th would depart for southern France by October. Hayward's expectations of a glorious rest in the sunny south of France remained wishful thinking. Pétain and the French army had other plans for their veteran regiment.

## The Big Push

*Offensives in Champagne/Meuse-Argonne
and the Capture of Séchault, September 7–October 4, 1918*

In the afternoon of September 7, a French motorcycle courier decelerated in front of 369th regimental headquarters in a cloud of dust, bringing orders for the unit to move out early the next morning. After a day's march of 20 miles, a truck convoy ferried the men back toward the front on the night of September 9.[1] Little did they know that they were about to participate in the climactic Franco-American battles of World War I, the contiguous French offensive in Champagne and the American offensive in the Meuse-Argonne.

The 369th relieved the French 215th Infantry Regiment of the 161st Division during the nights of September 10–12. Major Little's 1st Battalion entered the first line of trenches in subsector Beausejour—probably a French attempt at humor, via a corruption of the term *Beau Séjour* (beautiful sojourn)—which formed a horseshoe. The unit took control of the right side of a salient, and the French battalion on its left defended the left side of the parallel front lines. Little received a trench mortar unit and an additional machine-gun company for support.[2]

Little further requested that the departing French battalion commander's adjutant remain as adviser for twenty-four hours. That afternoon, the 1st Battalion received a warning to expect a German attack in the night. Little and the adjutant walked the subsector, assuring themselves of liaison with the French on their left and of Capt. Frederick Cobb's 2nd Battalion behind them in support. The night of September 12, the Germans planned to welcome the 369th in their traditional manner—with an attack.[3]

Just after 6:00 that evening, the Germans fired a mortar barrage of gas canisters into the American lines and then unleashed a violent hour-long series of continuous artillery barrages to cover their advancing troops, the approach trenches, and the rear of the American front to prevent any rein-forcement. The shock of an exploding shell knocked Little over, stunning him and cracking two of his ribs. The Americans repulsed the attack and riposted with a strong patrol, which took prisoners.[4]

When two "very large" German prisoners appeared at Little's battalion headquarters, where the major lay on his cot in pain, his chest tightly ban-daged, the grins on their faces initially panicked him into thinking that they were about to capture him. Then, a small soldier from D Company peered around his two captives, his rifle muzzle in the small of the back of one of the prisoners. A very relieved Little inquired about the fight.[5] The sol-dier reported that his patrol under 2nd Lt. Ernest McNish had successfully ambushed a German patrol and shot some, and as the other Germans ran away, they closed to take the rest prisoners. McNish had told the soldier to bring back five large German prisoners alone. Concerned with the odds and their size, the soldier confessed to Major Little that he decided "he'd better clean them out a bit."[6] Killing prisoners in cold or hot blood fre-quently occurred during the war, and in this case, the young soldier had calculatedly "thinned" their ranks.[7]

The next nights, through September 23, essentially remained quiet, with minor losses to artillery and machine-gun fire.[8] The 369th trained and moved munitions forward to stage its own major offensive, in the direction of the village of Séchault, as part of the simultaneous French and American offensives in the Champagne and the Meuse-Argonne. Colonel Hayward released the Regiment's prisoners—murderers, thieves, and the like—from the guardhouse to give them the opportunity to "wipe the slate clean" in the big push. Sgt. Hannibal L. "Spats" Davis, a company clerk at Major Little's 1st Battalion Headquarters, observed that "they were apparently de-termined to clean up the slate and everything else."[9] Gouraud's 4th Army, to which the 161st Division belonged, would support the attack of the AEF in the Argonne Forest to the Meuse River with one of its own divisions be-tween the Aisne River and Suippe, and the fronts of the French and Amer-ican armies would meet at Grandpré. Secrecy reigned to preserve every chance of rupturing the lines and exploiting the breakthrough.[10]

On September 25, the day before the offensive, Capt. John Holley Clark, commander of F Company, 2nd Battalion, confided in his diary, "It's only a few hours off now, and it's a little solemn and nervous for all we can do. . . . It's going to be a big thing and the Frenchmen tell us there may be little to bother us after our artillery gets through. But I'm of little faith when it comes to stories of Fritz's not having much to offer in the way of resistance. I expect lots, and we'll be lucky if we aren't bumped off."[11] Clark's expectations proved more accurate than the encouraging predictions of his French counterparts.

At 11:00 P.M. on September 25, French artillery began to bombard the German lines. The three battalions of the 369th began their march to the front by 6:30 P.M. and moved under cover of darkness to positions on the reverse slope of a ravine of pine trees, Le Ravin des Pins, a mile to the east of division headquarters in the town of Minaucourt. Fortified shelters offered some cover from German fire until time for the attack the next morning. Little's 1st Battalion, attached to the Division Headquarters, would fight under the direct orders of General Lebouc.[12] A giant traffic jam on the road to Minaucourt forced Little and his men to strike out cross-country for three hours to dodge trucks moving forward for the big push. From Minaucourt, they followed a trail to the ravine and arrived in position at 9:40 P.M., twenty minutes before their orders dictated. They shared the emplacement with batteries of the French field artillery, which opened fire an hour after they arrived.[13]

Cpl. Horace Pippin's *Composition Book* provides a rare account of the 3rd Battalion's attack from the enlisted man's perspective.[14] He knew something big was in the offing, as they remained in reserve with "Algerians." A steady rain drenched them as they pitched their pup tents and bedded down on wet hay. Rumors circulated among the officers that the 369th would return to the AEF to participate in a future American offensive to reduce the German salient at St. Mihiel and seize the fortress city of Metz. After some five days and nights of constant rain, during which German reconnaissance planes would fly overhead and occasionally fire at them, the rain stopped on the fifth night and the temperature dropped as they advanced into a dimly lit tunnel so crowded with troops that if you lay down to sleep, "some one would wolk on you."[15] There they stayed for two days. Then they stocked up with food and water, exited the tunnel at night with the stars shining brightly, and struck out for the main trench, German shells bursting in the fields and road ahead of them. They reached the main trench unscathed, and the French bombardment began. They would go over the top in the morning.

Spats Davis likened the noise of the bombardment to "being inside a huge iron barrel, totally enclosed, with a hundred thousand madmen beating on the outside with sledge hammers." The noise made "ordinary speech . . . impossible" and "rational thinking" nearly so. Nevertheless, the men, exhausted from marching with full packs and with nothing else to do, fell asleep.[16] Davis would serve as a runner during the battle, and his account provides another rare glimpse from the perspective of an enlisted man.

The next morning, September 26, at 5:25 A.M., the 161st Division went over the top on a front of some 2,000 yards between strongholds on two hills, the Butte du Mesnil and Mount Tetu, attacking north through the region of a farm, the Ferme des Maisons de Champagne. Their boundary with the neighboring attacking division, the 2nd Moroccan, lay through the town of Ripont. In the 161st Division, the 4th Moroccan Regiment spearheaded the attack, with the 3rd Battalion of the 369th under Maj. Lorillard Spencer in support in the second line.[17]

Despite a vigorous assault, the division made slow progress through the shattered terrain, and troops disappeared into fog and a cloud of dust that rendered observation impossible. As the companies fought their way forward, German resistance increased. Still, the American advance battalion seized its first objective at 7:25 A.M., and the Germans began to retreat in disorder. At 8:10 A.M. behind a rolling barrage, the infantry advanced toward its second objective, but German machine-gun nests took an increasing toll on the Americans as the fog lifted. The division took one further line of trenches by 10:35 A.M. but made no further progress because German airplanes ranging over the lines strafed anything that moved. While advancing, the Americans took 726 prisoners, including a German battalion commander and a General Staff divisional officer.[18]

During the attack, Major Spencer had noticed a gap forming between the attacking units of the 161st and the Moroccan division on its left flank. Without orders, he seized the initiative and launched his 3rd Battalion forward to close the gap. They seized the village of Ripont and advanced some 2.5 miles. The 161st Division commander, General Lebouc, highly praised Spencer's "most beautiful" initiative. The 3rd Battalion surprised a German battery of 77-mm cannon, killed the gun crews—Lebouc proclaimed with relish that "the blacks massacred the crews"—captured two cannon, and took thirty prisoners. Lebouc particularly commended such bravery from a regiment participating in a major attack for the first time, citing it as proof of the spirit that animated the officers and men of the 369th.[19]

The 3rd Battalion crossed the Dormoise River and fought its way through a swamp where the Germans had positioned machine-gun nests. Through the hail of bullets, Spencer led from the front at a walk until six bullets in the leg felled him in the swamp. Fortunately, 1st Lt. Samuel Shetlar, who had gone AWOL from the hospital where he was being treated for the flu in order to participate in the attack, managed under fire to get Spencer back to an aid station, a deed for which he was awarded the Distinguished Service Cross.[20]

Capt. Lewis Shaw, who had suffered with a temperature of 100 degrees for the two days before the attack, recalled later that "few of us expected to come out whole."[21] Shaw counted the 3rd Battalion officers who fell that first day:

> Larry [Maj. Lorillard P.] Spencer the big ass was hit the first day needlessly. Red [1st Lt. Edward A.] Walton was lucky in getting off with two leg wounds. [2nd Lt. John] Richards was wounded in the face but not seriously. [2nd Lt. John] McKensie was killed. I had to go on without officers but had Dave [Capt. and later Maj. David A. L'Esperance] and Cub [1st Lt. later Capt. Comerford McLoughlin] near me. Their bravery was inspiring. . . . It was terrible beyond description.[22]

Spencer had in fact, as Lebouc noted, taken the initiative and led from the front, demonstrating the élan that the French prized so highly. Only much later, in November after the war, would Walton recall to Shaw the latter's response to his wound. Walton had been on Shaw's right and Sergeant Alexander on his left, lying flat on their faces, elbows touching, when a "burst of machine gun fire put two bullets in Walton and five in the sergeant." Shaw, unscathed, asked Walton if he was hit. Upon Walton's reply of yes, Shaw said matter-of-factly, "Well goodbye, I'm going to get the sons of bitches," and then departed. Alexander, an older man, kept "calling on the Lord to have mercy on his sole" until Walton told him to shut up and that the Lord would. Shaw observed, "Sounds pretty heartless now after the battle for the poor fellow croaked and as Red says 'I didn't.'" Shaw considered "the old third battalion crowd were mostly fortunate."[23]

Shaw, with McLoughlin, assumed command of the entire battalion that afternoon until his senior, Capt. David L'Esperance, took over. Shaw and McLoughlin led the battalion through "an almost impassable swamp to shelter." Shaw had inhaled gas earlier while moving through the low places and found that he could not negotiate the swamp with a full pack under heavy fire, so he and some of his men crossed part of it on a foot bridge. The hail of bullets they attracted "almost cut the bridge in pieces around" Shaw, hitting his helmet and gas mask and shredding the clothes of the men behind him. McLoughlin and some of his soldiers waded through to the other side of the swamp, only for McLoughlin to wade back into the swamp in a vain attempt to rescue one of his best men. The soldier later died from his wounds, and Shaw both praised McLoughlin for a "most courageous and unselfish deed" and chastised him, calling it "entirely uncalled for in a company commander for a wounded man is so much clay in this game." Shaw had left 2nd Lt. John McKensie dead in the swamp.[24]

To Cpl. Horace Pippin of K Company, 3rd Battalion, the shells of the ferocious Allied barrage sounded like a "gush of air" as they passed over the American trenches. The barrage lifted, and in fog so thick they could see only 100 feet ahead, they went over the top. As they assaulted a hill that afternoon, cross fire from German machine guns nearly wiped out Pippin's platoon, leaving only four or five men with him in a shallow pit.[25] They had to cross the same swamp as McLoughlin and Shaw, as German fire enfiladed their position, bullets striking all around them, making it "shore death" to remain where they were. Yet, German machine gunners swept the swamp, and bursting German shells left holes so large "that you could get a teem of horses in the hole and bury them."[26] With dirt kicking into his face from bullets striking in front of him, Pippin and one of his men ran for the little bridge over the swamp as German gas and shrapnel shells exploded about them. Across that hurdle, they arrived at the bottom of a hill that had a German machine gunner on top of it. Pippin could not see the gunner, but he was determined to get the German, who he was convinced had "cleened out the first platoon." Keeping well down under the hill, Pippin, followed by his man, crept some 90 feet until he could see the gunner. Observing "Im a good shoot,"[27] Pippin shot him dead. That night, they reached the road that was their main objective. Allied artillery fire thinned out as the guns moved forward to new positions to support the continuing attack on the second morning.

Captain Cobb's 2nd Battalion occupied former German trenches close behind the assault forces and initially advanced so smoothly that Clark allowed his F Company men to nap at 2:00 that afternoon.[28] The 2nd Battalion came under heavy German shellfire later that day. After a dozen men died, Cobb moved to his right during the night to shelter behind a hill in order to prevent further losses. One of his machine-gun officers, Lt. Charles Dean, took his platoon and attempted to cut the enemy barbed wire to ambush the Germans. The Germans heard the noise and opened fire with their machine guns, killing the entire American platoon in the wire.[29]

As German prisoners streamed to the rear, the 1st Battalion moved forward to new positions behind the assaulting units. Major Little observed that one of his soldiers jeered at the Germans, "Well, what do you think of the Kaiser now?" A German officer replied, "God damn the Kaiser."[30] The 1st Battalion found itself advancing over trench lines and sectors that it had held two months before.

Spats Davis noticed the "brave," dead German soldiers of the rear guard, observing that the machine gunners were not chained to their guns, as some who sought to discredit German courage had claimed. Abandoned machine guns invariably had run out of ammunition, and the Americans found artillery and machine-gun crews and their equipment blown to bits by shells or American grenades. Davis stepped into something in the mud and kicking his foot free uncovered a "gruesome torso" disemboweled by a shell, its "torn face . . . leer[ing] up through its thin mask of mud."[31] Davis later took cover in a shell hole along with another soldier. When he rose to move on and called the soldier to follow but received no answer, Davis shook the man by the shoulder and "he collapsed and a great pool of blood came spilling out of his blouse." Davis surmised that the soldier had been hit as he dived into the hole and died without "murmur . . . or movement." "How thin is the line," mused Davis, "between the 'quick and the dead.'" Men fell before they ever fired a shot, and the farther they advanced, the more "organized, determined and deadly" enemy resistance became.[32]

While waiting in reserve, Davis would watch the sky, where as many as a hundred Allied airplanes patrolled the length of the battlefield at various altitudes, searching for German prey. Occasionally, he watched an aerial fight high in the heavens and marveled at the daring of aviators on both sides. Sometimes, the Allied planes would shoot down a German, but German airplanes seemed to tumble from the heavens out of control, only to recover just above the ground and regain their own lines.[33] German balloon-strafing aircraft set fire to Allied observation balloons in the absence of American planes and then escaped through a seemingly impenetrable hail of antiaircraft fire. On their way, they might strafe advancing American infantrymen, and the entire battalion seemed to fire at the German intruder to no effect. A soldier even threw a hand grenade at a low-flying plane only to have the grenade's descent scatter the men around him.[34] As the battalion rested and ate lunch on the side of a hill during the advance, someone saw a rabbit race across the field below. Some fifty men proceeded to "hunt" the rabbit, running about laughing and shouting. Davis mused that they seemed as if on leave, "instead of having a little fun while waiting their turn to go through the ranks of the tiring and diminishing assault wave, and themselves grow weary, and diminish."[35]

Early the next morning, September 27, Little's 1st Battalion reached the positions earlier occupied by Captain Cobb's 2nd Battalion, where they found a dozen dead bodies of 2nd Battalion men.[36] Once the dead "were laid out side by side, like so many sacks of oats," Davis wrote, "our Major Doctor [Maj. G. Franklin Shiels] . . . pointed them out to us as object lessons of 'what happens to damn fools who don't have sense enough to take advantage of cover during an attack.'" They found a number of "object lessons" along the road—some men crumpled and horribly mutilated, others without a scratch—everywhere a trap or hard fighting had occurred.[37] As Little's 1st Battalion approached, they watched the French artillery move their guns forward over the broken ground of trenches and dugouts, each artillery piece pulled by a team of four horses whipped on by cursing drivers, with three men pushing each wheel of the gun carriage through the sticky mud, over the bodies of dead men and horses.[38]

On September 27 in the 369th Regiment, Captain Cobb's move of the 2nd Battalion to the right during the night severed his communications with regimental headquarters, so the 2nd arrived late for its scheduled attack to advance beyond Ripont. Lebouc, annoyed at the delay, still launched his French and Moroccan regiments to the attack on the Americans' flanks. The 161st Division intended to cross the Dormoise River to the north shore. The Germans staged a fighting withdrawal, leaving strong rear guards and machine gunners that impeded French and American progress. The 369th's lead units managed to capture the village of Fontaine-en-Dormois, but the Germans' staunch resistance prevented them from further advance by that afternoon.[39]

Little's 1st Battalion, positioned on a hill south of the Dormoise, initially observed the attacks. Some of his men sat on the parapets to watch and cheer, until German shellfire and their officers reminded them that they were not watching a baseball game. They could see the French 163rd Regiment of their division and their own 3rd Battalion on the north side of the Dormoise climb a steep hill, sheltering them from German fire, and then, under German fire, deploy on to the plain deliberately and well aligned to the attack.[40] In the 3rd Battalion, Corporal Pippin observed that German airplanes had been after them "good and strong," but they had captured fourteen machine guns, 500 prisoners, and a town [Fontaine-en-Dormois]." Fortified by "corn willie" (corned beef hash) and "hired tack" (hardtack), they held the line for the artillery to advance to its positions for firing the next day as German machine guns ranged across their lines. German prisoners coming through their line toward the rear "were happy that they were out of it, for they knew that, they would see home a gan."[41]

Cobb's 2nd Battalion crossed the river in single file on footbridges. Shelling occasionally claimed a soldier, and the sight of men clumsily falling off the planks into the river amused some of his troops.[42] Clark and twenty men of F Company, 2nd Battalion crested a hill to observe German machine guns positioned on Bellevue Ridge and Bellevue Signal firing down at the rest of the battalion. Clark thought the gunners could not see them, only to learn otherwise as the German fire raked his line of men. They still advanced down the hill, losing men in the barbed wire, to take cover in shell holes. His men returned German machine-gun fire with rifle and automatic rifle fire, only to be hit every time they exposed a shoulder to take aim. Clark spotted Germans circling to his right, as a French officer ordered a retreat. Clark and his men ran back over the crest of the hill where they had begun, their dead and dying littering the ground while Clark assembled his remnants.[43] The acting adjutant, 1st Lt. Roger Whittlesey, later informed Little that "the 2nd Battalion was shot to hell."[44]

Little then sent two companies of his 1st Battalion and his machine-gun company to the left of Cobb's 2nd Battalion to cross the river on a stone bridge. Little crossed the narrow plank bridge with his headquarters group and another company. They met on the north side of the river in a cemetery, where they formed the third wave in the offensive, keeping Cobb's battalion to their right. Shell holes offered protection against the German shellfire, so their advance cost them only minimal casualties.[45]

On September 27, the 4th Army ordered the 161st Division to respond to the rapid advance of the AEF on the first day of the attack by energetically exploiting its own success and liaising with the AEF in the direction of Grandpré, more immediately toward Bellevue and the farms at Bussy and Petit Rosiers.[46]

Early in the morning of September 28, a dreary and rainy day, Cobb's 2nd Battalion and a French battalion attacked the ridge at Bellevue Signal, with a third French battalion in support. At 9:00 A.M., the Germans staged three successive counterattacks, the first against Cobb's 2nd Battalion in the center. Despite taking serious losses, the three battalions of the 161st repulsed all three ferocious assaults and doggedly took and held the hill. The wounded came streaming back to the 369th regimental aid station. Two surgeons, Major Shiels and 1st Lt. Keenan, handled some 300 to 400 American and French casualties.[47] Major Little sent Sergeant Spats Davis with nine men to establish liaison between regimental and 1st Battalion headquarters. Davis posted his men and was talking to the headquarters staff when a hard-boiled machine-gun sergeant from 2nd Battalion came around the hill, a machine-gun barrel in his hand. He was crying tears of "rage" and "anguish." As the lone able-bodied survivor among the twenty-plus men in his platoon, he had fired all the ammunition, taken the barrel, and come to headquarters to report and get aid for the wounded.[48] A medic, Pvt. 1st Cl. Charles Gantt,[49] who was assigned to the headquarters medical company, volunteered to accompany the sergeant back to his men with two stretcher-bearers. Just as they entered the dugout where the sergeant had left the wounded men, a German shell penetrated the dugout door, exploded inside, and killed them all.[50]

Little's 1st Battalion moved forward in support. His men spent the day seeking shelter in a few abandoned artillery battery positions or stretching canvas shelter tent halves over the narrow trenches. Little's battalion was running short of food, and the attacking battalions suffered even more severe shortages of supplies.[51] Spats Davis checked on the communications relay team he had established between regimental and 1st Battalion Headquarters. Shell holes filled with gaseous water offered the only shelter, and the men had to time their rushes during the pauses between German shell salvos. As Davis left one of his men on the run, the noise of a shell's "whistle" alerted him to the fact that a "stray," an "afterthought," was headed his way. As he dived for a hole, the shell blast hit him "like a sack of bricks."[52] The next thing he remembered, he was desperately clawing his way out of mud and muck, the black ooze of the valley's bog, as falling dirt and stones pelted him. His ears rang, and ooze covered him from head to foot. When he cleared his eyes, nose, mouth, and ears of grime, he saw his man peering over the edge of his own hole and grinning at him. Major Little observed that many soldiers thought Davis was a minister because he read the Bible and conducted religious ceremonies in the absence of the chaplain. The "few pertinent inspired remarks" that Davis uttered as he went on his way that day would have disabused them of that illusion.[53]

Davis returned to regimental headquarters, where he noted that all the men had devoured their rations and were scrounging for more food. One of the men found blood sausages and black bread in the pack of a dead German in the weeds. One end of the bread, Davis noted, was "a trifle soggy and off color," and he informed his comrade that it was probably due to blood. The soldier verified that observation, then cut off the soggy part and ate the bread and sausages nonetheless. He offered some to Davis, who politely declined, but then complained that the little hardtack he had took so much energy to chew that it left him hungrier when he was finished.[54]

The third day of the attack, K Company, 3rd Battalion took heavy casualties as it continued the attack. Corp. Elmer Earl of Goshen, New York, after running a gauntlet of bullets that riddled his clothes as he carried messages, tended to his wounded comrades. Fifty-eight men entered the swamp; eight emerged unscathed. Earl returned repeatedly to rescue them and would receive a Distinguished Service Cross for his valor.[55] The third day was Horace Pippin's last in combat. That morning, he and his "buddy" "got in with Co I," as K Company's losses had been so severe that he had difficulty locating its remnants. Pippin had long ago exhausted his rations. The men continued to advance slowly through hot and smoking shell holes, as the German line was strong and their artillery fire heavy. The Germans had placed machine guns in trees, bushes, houses—"any theing they could get a machine gun in. they had it there." Pippin surmised that "wimen as well as men" were firing the machine guns, since there were so many. "Snipers were thick all so."[56]

Pippin and his buddy cleaned out one machine-gun nest and went after another. From their shell hole, Pippin looked for another hole in order to get an angle on the German gunner, who was behind a rock where they could not see him. He ordered his buddy to go in one direction, while he went the other way at the same time. The gunner would have to concentrate on one or the other man; if the German shot one of them, the other would shoot the German.[57] Pippin darted for another hole, and just as he reached it, the German gunner shot him through the right shoulder and arm, clipping his neck. The force of the bullet knocked him into the shell hole, where he was plugging up his wounds when his buddy reached him to tell him that he had killed the gunner. The man did what he could for Pippin, who was lying on his back and could not stand up. Pippin shook hands with his friend who headed forward and never saw him again. Left with nothing to eat and only a little water in his canteen, Pippin could only lie helplessly as German shells sprayed pieces of shrapnel near him, while bullets from a German sniper clipped the edges of his hole.[58]

Pippin calculated that he was shot at 8:00 in the morning. Later that day, some French soldiers came by sweeping the area for Germans. One of them spied Pippin and stopped to speak to him, but before he could utter a word, a bullet passed through his head and he sank down on top of Pippin, who was too weak to move. At least Pippin could reach the Frenchman's water, bread, and even some coffee with his left hand. He then felt better, but he remained feeble. As night approached and rain began to fall, Pippin could neither get the blanket from his "Dead Comrad" nor move the Frenchman off him. As the water rose, he grew steadily weaker and finally fell unconscious.[59] Many a soldier drowned or never awoke in similar circumstances, but that night, two French soldiers found Pippin. As he awakened, they took him from the hole back some distance to leave him with other wounded. Through the night, every time Pippin fell asleep, the sound of French infantry moving forward to the attack awakened him. Near morning, French soldiers took Pippin to a doctor at an aid station in a dugout, where wounded men in worse shape than he surrounded him. He lay outside in the rain until German prisoners with a French officer maneuvered his stretcher down a hill to a road and an ambulance. They passed

French artillery arrayed hub to hub "all at work," and they shoved Pippin into an ambulance with five other wounded. German shells pursued the ambulance until it got out of range.[60]

When they arrived at the field hospital, Pippin, too weak to speak, could only point to his shirt where he had written "101127 Horace Pippin Co.K 369.INF," and then he lost consciousness again. He came to on the table, and they gave him "some dop[e] that put me a way for good."[61] When he regained consciousness, they took him to a hospital in Lyon. Horace Pippin's account ends there abruptly. His war was over, but his smashed shoulder and useless right arm meant that his peace would be a long time coming. Pippin had sketched some of his experiences at the front; the artist Horace Pippin did not know whether he might ever sketch or paint again.

Pippin's account reveals much about the nature of warfare in 1918 in particular and warfare in general. First, what often appears in historical accounts as a coherent offensive fragments into encounters of small groups and even individuals who sense little or no connection to the operation as a whole. In the case of 3rd Battalion, the officers were aware mainly of each other, and officers do not appear in Pippin's account. Pippin's men were following no officer when they took the initiative to cross the swamp and then attack the Germans; they were following Pippin, a proven leader, as their number steadily shrank. Pippin knew the risk when his friend and he split to flank the machine gun, and he took it, receiving a near-fatal wound in the process. He was fighting his own war, on his own initiative, and his account presents a graphic picture of how an offensive appeared to the lower ranks that were engaged. Pippin's account once again indicates the heroic nature of the decisions and deeds that battle calls upon capable infantrymen to make constantly—deeds that are so numerous and commonplace as to be assumed and consequently go unrecognized and unrewarded with medals. Many a soldier died in exactly the condition in which Pippin languished. Others lay for days in holes before corpsmen found them, and some badly wounded soldiers amazingly survived. Attacking soldiers continued to advance, leaving their wounded behind to manage the best they could. Pippin was fortunate that French soldiers found him twice, as he was too weak to call for help when conscious. Some soldiers expired calling in vain for help, and other badly wounded men simply wrapped themselves in their groundsheets or blankets, curled up, and expired alone, moaning or silent in their agony.

On the fourth day of the offensive, September 29, Little's 1st Battalion spearheaded the offensive. Shortly after 8:00 A.M., Little reported to regimental headquarters to receive the orders of the day. The three regiments of the 161st Division, with the 369th in the center, would attack the Belleville plateau, which Lebouc rather exaggeratedly described as a "mountain mass of three kilometers with abrupt peaks, multiple promontories, cut by a valley where the road runs through Séchault between two mountains." His division had to take this "veritable fortress" step by step.[62]

Early on the clear, cool morning of September 29, the men of Little's 1st Battalion ate their remaining rations, and the battalion and company officers passed their only two razors among themselves to shave. Little would later recall that every officer who shaved that morning survived the next two and a half days; everyone who did not would be either killed or severely wounded. While Little's memoirs portray these results as a curious coincidence,[63] they likely reflect the fact that the razors were passed around by rank, going from battalion to company officers. The latter, who bore the brunt of casualties in combat, probably chose not to risk cutting their throats with a dull razor before the attack.

Spats Davis observed that "going over the top" as a reserve posed even more difficulty than participating in the leading waves of an attack. The first waves did not have to endure the waiting, often under fire, while steadying the nerves and conserving rations. Worst of all, he considered, the second and third waves of attackers had to pass the wounded, dying, and dead men who were, or had been, friends and acquaintances, all the time aware that the same fate likely awaited them.[64] Davis asserted that every officer who wore a Sam Browne belt fell to German snipers. His own captain, "tart" old Scotsman Seth B. McClinton, wore a rumpled private's raincoat over his uniform and did not receive a scratch. When McClinton ordered his men to the attack as bullets and shells whistled and burst about them, he rose to his full height, his cane under his arm, and shouted over the din, "What in the blinkin' name of the hoppin,' bowlegged and blazin' bullfrogs of Behemoth do ye think we're havin' here? An ol' ladies' tea party? Come on, let's go." Davis added, "Or words to that effect. So we went."[65]

From its support position in the rear, Little's 1st Battalion moved nearly 2 miles to relieve the French battalion in possession of Bellevue's north face and crest. As soon as possible after the relief, they were to attack, descending the hill and crossing the plain bordered by Bussy Farm on the left and Mt. Cuvelet on the right. They would have to cover more than a half mile to storm and seize the town of Séchault. Having secured that town, they were then to advance another 2 miles, clearing the woods northeast of Séchault and taking Rosiers Farm, the final objective of their attack.[66] During the move to the front lines, Little's men experienced fire from German Whiz-Bangs, or 88-mm cannon, for the first time. Soldiers could hear the screeching arrival of shells fired from German 77-mm and 155-mm cannon during their arcing trajectory. The trajectory of the 88-mm, however, was so flat that it gave no advance warning, thus earning the name Whiz-Bang. Anyone located where it hit was, as the soldiers said, "a poor boy." Fortunately, the battalion suffered very few poor boys, losing fewer than ten casualties as it relieved French troops in daylight under heavy fire.[67]

At 2:30 P.M., the German cannon fired gas shells, while machine guns ranged along the line of the 369th. The 2nd Battalion under Capt. Frederick Cobb waited on the reverse slope of Bellevue Signal to support the 1st Battalion in the attack. Assuming skirmish formation under the cover offered by the 300-foot hill, Cobb's men found that German artillery had their range. Capt. John Holley Clark left the remnants of F Company to urge Cobb to advance before they were all killed, only to arrive at the battalion command post just in time to see a shell fragment tear off the back of Cobb's head. Clark placed Cobb's body in a position of repose, turned F Company command over to Lt. Oliver Parish, and assumed command of the 2nd Battalion. They advanced toward Séchault, through German shellfire so heavy that Clark wrote later, "I have never seen so terrifying a barrage, and I wonder how any of us got through. But the officers and men behaved splendidly."[68]

At 3:00 P.M. on September 29, Little's three companies went over the top at fifteen-minute intervals, starting from left to right. The units on the left descended the hill going north under cover of dense undergrowth and then wheeled to the right as officers and platoon sergeants deployed the men under fire on the open plain to advance in line to the northeast across the half mile of open terrain against the fortified town. The men captured German snipers and artillery observers, the latter positioned to direct fire on the advancing soldiers. Little followed with his liaison group.[69] The 1st Battalion advanced against the concentrated fire of German machine-gun nests positioned at the edge of the woods that dotted the plain. The men advanced by rushes and more often by crawling on their bellies or on hands and knees toward the town. In C Company, Pvt. Merritt Molson of Albany described the horror of the offensive in a letter to his mother: "I used to think that to go out on a raiding party was quite risky and daring but it is like eating pie alongside of going over in an attack, because the enemy are ready and looking for you." The open fields through which they ran toward German artillery and machine-gun fire seemed "to be a death trap." Although he wrote while recovering in a Paris hospital, Molson claimed to be one of the lucky ones because the "Huns tried to get him but did not succeed." They did, however, "leave a couple of marks" that he would always remember.[70]

C Company fought its way into Séchault and through the middle of the town, while D Company advanced on its right flank, the two forming a front a half mile in width. B Company remained entrenched on the left flank south of the town to offer reinforcement when necessary. With Davis at regimental headquarters, Little's liaison group had dwindled to one man, Cpl. William J. Cooper, who commandeered men to form a new liaison group.[71] As 1st Battalion troops fought their way through the village, they met small groups of Germans in hand-to-hand combat. These they killed remorselessly, leaving no German alive in Séchault. German machine-gun fire from hidden emplacements on the plain north of the town raked the streets. The Germans fired 77-mm cannon directly into the town at point-blank range.[72] A unit of the machine-gun company captured a German machine gun and turned it on the enemy, while C and D Company men captured a German 77-mm cannon as well as an ammunition and grenade dump. They would later capture another 77-mm cannon. Meanwhile, 1st Lt. George S. Robb flushed a machine-gun crew from a brick house on the northeast corner of town. Hit in his left side by a bullet, he applied his first aid packet and refused evacuation. D Company set up automatic rifle positions in the second story of the brick house to fire on German machine-gun nests on the plain north of town. They gave covering fire to the men of C and D Companies as they established a perimeter north of Séchault. Shrapnel wounded Lieutenant Robb in the arm; still, he refused evacuation.[73]

Just before 5:00 P.M., Little and his men spied a long line of black soldiers moving toward them across the plain. The remnants of John Holley Clark's 2nd Battalion, some 150 men, had arrived to support the 1st. They proceeded to clear the town of Germans. At 5:00 P.M., Little reported to the Regiment that they were cleaning machine-gun snipers out of the town slowly but surely and requested that his Headquarters Group (the lost liaison unit) be sent up to him when it was located. A German attack plane, flying so low that Little could see the facial features of one of the crewmen as he peered over the side of the plane, strafed the American lines, including the ditch where Little lay, from northwest to southeast. Later, some soldiers of the 372nd Regiment who had lost their way joined Little's troops.[74]

The village was in American hands by 5:30 P.M. Fifteen minutes later, C Company scouts reported an apparent German counterattack forming north of the town. Little left Clark and his men to conclude "mopping up" actions in the town with grenade and bayonet, and he ordered B Company and his remaining machine-gun sections and support platoons forward to meet any counterattack. Little assumed command of the remnants of the 2nd Battalion and parceled them out among his men. He established his Battalion Headquarters in the wreck of a stone house and planned to use another house 50 yards distant as a block house of last resistance if the Germans broke through. The counterattack never came, but had the Germans attacked, they would have confronted a town well defended by some twenty machine-gun positions to support the troops' emplacements around the north side of the town some 100 yards beyond the town limits.[75]

As Little's men seized the town, Lieutenant Colonel Pickering led the regimental headquarters group forward to a new position in a German dugout. As they rounded the hill that protected them from German observation, they came under a hail of German shell- and machine-gun fire. The party traveled in single file, Pickering leading the way. When they arrived in the trench leading to the dugout, Spats Davis noticed that he had lost some of his men and went back to try to find them. On the way, he passed a soldier kneeling on one knee, a rifle in one hand and papers in the other. Davis thought to himself, "That's a hell of a place to be trying to duck anything," and then he ran on. He failed to locate his men and on his return dash passed the kneeling soldier, who was dead.[76]

In Séchault, Little's 1st Battalion took "hideous and continuous" casualties that night, as enemy machine guns covered the town, making it dangerous for anyone to move except at a dead run. The circumstances distressed Major Little, who questioned his own abilities and lamented the loss of half his battalion. His adjutant, 1st Lt. Hayward Webb, reassured him before departing on detail for regimental headquarters. In the darkness of the command post, Little and some of his officers, with Corporal Cooper and his liaison unit, sat quietly. Robb, twice wounded, suffered in silence but swore he would be ready to fight the next morning.[77]

Having passed Webb's party heading in the other direction, Spats Davis and one of his runners, James "Jimmy" Beckton, arrived from regimental headquarters. In town, they ran by a temporary first aid post full of wounded and dying men as they headed for Major Little's darkened command post. Someone lit a candle so Little could read the message they carried from Colonel Hayward. The light attracted German machine-gun fire, and to the sound of bullets beating against the side of the stone house and whizzing through its windows, Little read his orders.[78]

Hayward ordered Little to hold Séchault for the night, with the French 363rd and 163rd Regiments on his left and right, respectively, some 440 yards to the rear. He also ordered Little to extend his forces to the left, to reestablish contact with the 363rd. Little blew out the candle. His scouts could find no French soldiers in their supposed positions, as the battalion was actually a mile in advance of the rest of the division alone on the open plain, nor did

Little have the men to lengthen his line toward the French. An officer advised him to withdraw from Séchault and fall back to the division because the position was suicidal and the men would desert. Little refused. The men overheard the discussion, and a sergeant reassured one of his privates that they were not going anywhere, since they had just arrived.[79]

Little replied via Davis and Beckton. He had received and understood the message but had lost too many men to execute the orders, so he respectfully suggested that he be allowed to consolidate his defensive position on the edge of town. Then, if the colonel ordered a barrage to destroy the machine-gun nests, his men could follow the barrage to contact the French on the left and perhaps establish combat groups in the direction of the French.[80] Davis and Beckton returned to regimental headquarters to recount Little's words verbatim to Hayward. Hayward requested a barrage from his French liaison officer, who telephoned the French artillery batteries, and meanwhile, Beckton returned to Little to instruct him to consolidate his position around the village until the barrage. Seven scattered shells whistled over, but the barrage never came. The 1st Battalion would hold in Séchault.[81]

Back at Little's battalion command post, Sergeant Major Marshall arrived in the dark with volunteers carrying eighty large, round loaves of French bread. The volunteers included Capt. Hamilton Fish, who had returned to visit the Regiment and had been observing the battle at regimental headquarters. The bread was the first food Little's men had had in eighteen hours, and they would receive nothing more for another thirty hours.[82] Little had given strict orders for his men not to open fire unless they could see the enemy in order not to give away their positions to the Germans. Despite constant German fire and flares, American fire discipline remained excellent throughout the night. Little did receive a visit from General Lebouc's aide-de-camp, who transmitted Lebouc's compliments and encouragement.[83] Shortly afterward, a party of soldiers approached the American lines from the northwest during the night. When they did not answer to a shouted "Halt," the Americans fired on them, killing one and wounding three men of a patrol from the French 163rd Infantry Regiment. An hour before dawn on September 30, a runner reported activity in the German lines. Officers alerted their men, one shouting, "All out for Custer's last stand!" Artillery shells rained on Séchault until noon, but no Germans came.[84]

Lebouc ordered the 161st Division to continue its advance at 7:00 A.M. on September 30 after an artillery barrage. That morning, the 163rd Regiment would lead, the 369th would follow 300 yards behind and to the right in the middle, and the 363rd would bring up the rear 440 yards behind the 369th on the right flank. At 7:00 A.M., Little detected no sign of French troops on either flank. Some three-quarters of an hour later, the 163rd moved by them, but then German shelling of Séchault delayed the advance of the 369th, placing them a little more than a half mile instead of 300 yards to the rear of the 163rd. The 163rd and B Company of the 369th on the left flank of the 369th encountered little resistance, but the 369th's C and D Companies in the center and right were taking casualties from machine-gun nests. It took until 10:00 A.M. to locate the nests, and a flanking movement from B Company drove more than twenty armed Germans out of shell holes.[85] About 1:00 P.M., they entered the woods in front of the Rosiers Farm, where they encountered determined resistance from machine gunners and snipers; the surrounding shrubbery was too low to cover the men's attempts to encircle the German positions. After two hours and only slight progress, Little ordered his men to withdraw from the wood and requested artillery fire to reduce what he estimated were a dozen machine-gun nests in concrete pillboxes.[86] Just as they withdrew, Little received a note from Lieutenant Robb. An enemy plane had spotted D Company's command post in a shell hole, and a few minutes later, a single shell had scored a direct hit, killing and wounding all the officers and some of the men. Robb, hit again, had remained until D Company withdrew, then he turned command over to the first sergeant and headed for an aid station.[87]

At 4:00 P.M., 3rd Battalion's commander, Captain L'Esperance, informed Little that the remnants of his command—7 officers and 137 men—stood ready to support him.[88] Capt. Lewis Shaw no longer remained among them. Shaw and his men had attacked under constant German fire since the start of the engagement, and after experiencing German treachery—probably ruses to surrender and then opening fire on the advancing Americans— Shaw's men "didn't bother to take many more prisoners." On September 28, German soldiers and machine gunners had caught L'Esperance, Mc-Loughlin, Shaw, and their men "in a hot place" until one of Shaw's machine guns manned by a "picked crew" "made it hot for the swine" and saved them. That night, Shaw inhaled gas while crawling to a forward position and was evacuated, leaving L'Esperance and Lt. Comerford "Cub" Mc-Loughlin, whom he commended for "personal tenacity and bulldog grit," "still going strong."[89] These remnants remained ready for action.

Little conferred with the remaining 1st and 2nd Battalion officers, and they decided that, although the men were ready to continue the fight, they were "'all in' physically." Little consequently wrote Hayward that either tanks or heavy artillery were required to destroy the pillboxes. The three battalions had a combined strength of some 20 officers and 537 men, who would obey orders to attack the woods but would remain in the woods, Little warned, and the "15 N.Y. will be a memory."[90]

At 4:15 P.M., a runner from Hayward assured Little of artillery support and ordered him to continue his advance. French artillery then fired only six rounds into the wood, and shortly after 5:30 P.M., another runner informed Little that the French 363rd Regiment would relieve the 369th and pass through its lines that night.[91] At 1:00 A.M. on October 1, the French 363rd Infantry Regiment relieved the 369th, whose men remained in the trenches with the French. The exhausted Americans promptly fell asleep. At 6:00 A.M., French artillery shelled the wood, and two hours later, the French advanced to take the wood and Rosiers Farm. The 369th finally received food at 7:00 A.M.[92]

In the afternoon of October 1, the division ordered the 369th to move back to the reverse slope of Bellevue Signal, where it regrouped. Colonel Hayward, displaying a foolhardy ardor that was typical of the time, claimed that a battalion of the remaining men and officers stood ready to return to its place in the line. Yet, Dr. Keenan, the frontline medic who had spent the entire time in Séchault, had collapsed from exhaustion and had to be carried out on a stretcher, to spend seven months in the hospital. Keenan, Lieutenant Colonel Pickering, Major Spencer, and three lieutenants were awarded the Distinguished Service Cross. Capt. Frederick Cobb and 2nd Lt. Charles Dean received the Croix de Guerre with Silver Star posthumously. Pickering and Capt. David L'Esperance would later receive the French Légion d'Honneur, reserved to reward the gallant actions of a few elite officers. The 369th rotated into reserve status.[93]

Right after the French attacked on October 1, Little inspected the wounded men in Captain Keenan's hospital in Séchault. A gas shell, fortunately not of a fatal variety, fell outside just after he arrived. He talked to Lieutenant Robb, whose hands and arms were swathed in bandages. Many years later, Robb would recall Little's words with pride, "Lieutenant, you are a man after my own heart, and you have enough guts for ten men."[94] George Robb, a Kansan who had done graduate work at Columbia University and taught in New York City and who had come to the Regiment as a replacement officer, had indeed conducted himself admirably. Seriously wounded by machine-gun fire in the initial assault and ordered to the rear, he continued to lead his platoon throughout the night and the next day, although wounded again the next morning. He assumed command of his company after he was wounded by the same shells that killed the other company officers and led his men forward, clearing machine-gun and sniper nests. Robb would spend a long time in the hospital, and he was unable to return home with the Regiment, which received erroneous reports that he succumbed to his wounds. Twenty-one-year-old 1st Lt. George S. Robb survived to receive the Medal of Honor for his exploits of September 29–30, 1918.[95]

Capt. Lewis Shaw remained in the hospital for nearly a month and considered himself lucky to escape with no aftereffects from the gas. In the bed next to him, 2nd Lt. Herbert W. "Bert" Maloney, his hip broken by a machine-gun bullet, was "crippled for life in greater or lesser degree." Shaw was soon on leave in the south of France, in Nice, where he socialized and played tennis with the "attractive society girls of Nice." He then recalled to his mother the death of "little Charlie Dean" and asked her to inquire about Dean's widowed mother, who was now "entirely alone."[96]

On October 4, John Holley Clark penned the following thoughts in his diary:

> Above all the horror of these days of battle, stands out my pride in my men and in their heroism. Where I bade them go they went, to their death too often, but with a heroic glad willingness that makes up for the rest. They were my men—the men I worked with and nursed and brought up as a father would his children, never knowing what glories they had undisclosed within them.[97]

Hamilton Fish had entered Staff Officers School on October 5 and then taken three days of leave to rejoin the 369th after hearing of the impending attack. Fish wrote his father on October 10 about the attack: "The offensive in which the regt took part surpassed my wildest imagination. Our losses especially among the officers were very heavy. Capt. Cobb who commanded the 2nd Bn was killed. . . . I am very glad now that I joined the regt and took part in the offensive. There is not much left of my company."[98] AEF HQ had wanted him to return to the 369th and assume command of a battalion, but Hayward had blocked that move. Fish continued, "I do not want to serve under H. [Hayward] a day longer than necessary." He termed it "awfully bad luck having joined the 369th," although he was fortunate to survive.[99] Fish concluded that he had participated "in the heaviest of the fighting. I had all kinds of luck having men killed all around me. I am not permitted to write details. Please do not publish any more of my letters."[100] Fish, who was officially visiting at regimental headquarters, had volunteered as an observer without rank for Sergeant Major Marshall's supply party to Major Little's 1st Battalion in Séchault on the night of September

29, a sortie that certainly placed him in "the thick of things," if not for long. Fish's visit to the Regiment and his letter to his father, taken together, indicate his palpable ambivalence toward the 369th. He certainly disliked his former commander, but his very visit to the Regiment and participation in the relief party demonstrated his attachment to K Company and the Regiment in their time of need. Whatever Fish claimed, his heart remained with the 369th, and he was awarded the Silver Star and the Croix de Guerre for his actions at Séchault.

On October 1, the 161st Division's commander, General Lebouc, informed his superior, Gen. Garnier Duplessix of 9th Army Corps, that he had ordered the 369th, which had suffered severe losses in its first difficult attack, to be relieved from the front line. As it regrouped south of Bellevue Signal, he had sent a staff officer to determine the morale and condition of the Regiment. In the unanimous judgment of his staff, the Regiment had conducted itself admirably under fire, and all units had displayed "splendid bravery." A General Staff officer confirmed that the capture of Séchault constituted a "veritable feat of arms."[101] Lebouc particularly cited Spencer's initiative in closing the yawning gap on the first day of the battle.

Such bravery in its first attack meant great losses, Lebouc noted, particularly among the white officers, of whom fewer than 18 remained. He estimated losses of 9 officers dead and 18 wounded and 150 men dead and 400 wounded. Lebouc deemed the losses of white officers "irreparable," as he could not replace the white section chiefs with black noncommissioned officers, although he had recently assigned 27 of the Regiment's best black noncoms to an officer training course, and Colonel Hayward considered the replacement of these losses indispensable to the Regiment's future offensive capability.[102] Both Lebouc and Hayward emphasized the critical loss of the 369th's white officers, but the Regiment had never had its full complement of officers to begin with, and the attack at Séchault had further diminished their ranks severely. AEF HQ's insistence on having only white commissioned officers and removing black officers during the summer had actually created an artificial shortage of commissioned officers in the African American regiments.

The white officers and black noncoms of the 369th had led well, and the black soldiers had certainly fought well, but previous assessments of regimental performance have ignored the critical factor enabling the 369th to function effectively in combat despite its shortage of commissioned officers—the African American noncoms. Capt. Lewis Shaw acknowledged the importance of the leadership of the noncommissioned officers: "Our colored boys have made a lasting name for themselves. They fought and won magnificently. My company kept going under its noncoms even after all officers were gone."[103] Cpl. Horace Pippin exemplified those determined noncommissioned officers.

Little commented that late in the attack, after losing so many officers, the men wanted to continue the fight, and Little's sergeant in Séchault reassured his private that they would not be retreating, as they had just arrived. The machine-gun sergeant whom Spats Davis encountered had continued the fight to the very end. While visiting the Regiment, Ham Fish noted the excellent performance and promotion of two of his former sergeants.[104] The attack of the 369th at Séchault demonstrated that African American soldiers had the capacity for leadership, and the attack had succeeded as well as it did because black noncommissioned officers carried on in the places of fallen white officers.

The black sergeants and corporals, like the white officers, paid for their leadership in blood. Indirect confirmation of the nature and importance of the black noncommissioned officer cadre of the 15th New York/369th derives from the 171 officers and men of the 369th buried in six major cemeteries of the American Battle Monuments Commission in France. The sergeants—Charles M. Alexander, Sims Belcher, Edward Harding, Oscar Jones, William G. Mills, William M. Van Durk—and corporals—Abraham Douglas, Norris Francis, Herbert Howard, Joshua Huff, Middleton Parker, Edwin Robinson, Lee Robinson, William Stephens, and Raymond White— all came from New York. Corporal Parker came from New Jersey.[105] The composition of the 369th had long since ceased to be solely New Yorkers, New Jerseyans, and Pennsylvanians with the incorporation of the drafts of African American soldiers from the South and the Midwest. The noncommissioned officer cadre, however, remained staunchly representative of the original 15th New York. A critical factor in unit performance resided in the strong esprit de corps, a sense of regimental pride, that the commissioned and noncommissioned officer cadre, both dominated by New Yorkers, had transmitted to the influx of black draftees.

General Lebouc's approval of twenty-seven noncommissioned officers of the Regiment for officer training school demonstrated his recognition of the capacity of the African American noncoms to assume commissioned officer rank and authority. Yet, contemporary observers invariably concentrated on the importance of white officers when the unstated and perhaps unacknowledged factor in the success of the attack actually lay in the ability of the black noncoms to carry on when officers fell. Neither Colonel Hayward nor General Lebouc had initiated the policy of having an all-white officer cadre in the black regiments serving with the French army. In fact,

Hayward had opposed the policy, as it meant that sergeants he sent for officers training became commissioned lieutenants in the 370th Regiment and the 92nd Division. Although forty-two black NCOs left, others remained, declaring "they would prefer to be sergeants in the 15th than lieutenants in other regiments."[106] AEF HQ's segregation of black commissioned officers operated to the detriment of the military efficiency of the 369th Regiment.

On October 3, the men of the 369th performed fatigue duty working on the roads to the front, where they were joined by the other two regiments of the 161st Division by October 5. On the evening of October 6, the French army relieved the 161st Division from participation in the offensive, and the remnants of the 369th marched back that night to Minaucourt, where the Regiment had begun the Meuse-Argonne offensive.[107]

In an account of the offensive from September 26 to October 6, written when the 161st Division withdrew to refit, Lebouc declared, "The capture of Séchault will remain a claim to fame of the 369th Infantry Regiment of the United States, which displayed there audacity, energy, and valor under the impetus of its officers who sacrificed without regard for themselves; the black soldiers worked wonders." Lebouc now had more reliable assessments of its losses, counting 9 officers killed and 25 wounded and some 200 men killed and 600 wounded.[108] The French regiments, the 163rd and 363rd, had demonstrated marvelous spirit and borne the brunt of the battle, Lebouc assessed, and in eleven days, the division had taken 7½ miles of formidably organized enemy territory that had remained unassailable for four years. The two French regiments had lost 38 officers and some 1,500 men; the 369th lost 34 officers and some 800 men.[109] The losses of men in the 369th were thus proportional to French losses, but regimental officer casualties were nearly twice those of the French.

Lebouc's casualty figures focused solely on the eleven days of the attack toward Séchault. Little's memoirs cited that during their tour of frontline duty, the offensive included, the 369th had lost nearly 1,300 men and 50 officers killed or wounded, which amounted to around 50 percent casualties.[110] Such monstrous losses truly rendered the 369th *hors de combat* (out of the fight). In an after-action report of November 2, the French General Staff informed the 369th that it had captured 169 prisoners, 6 77-mm cannon, and 45 machine guns during the offensive.[111]

Lebouc's proposal of a divisional citation for the 369th on November 3 included the Regiment's valiant comportment in repulsing several German raids and setting ambushes to take prisoners prior to the major offensive. Its participation in the attack in Champagne was marked by "courage" in its first major offensive, as it fought powerful enemy forces and captured the energetically defended village of Séchault at the cost of serious losses of officers and men.[112] In a follow-up memorandum to Gouraud at the 4th Army on November 4, Lebouc explained that, after a serious and lengthy examination, he was keeping his proposals of awards for the 369th to the AEF HQ to a strict minimum and consequently desired their acceptance. He deemed the officers' display of a "veritably remarkable control" and the loss of 33 of their complement of 45 worthy of reward. The 369th could not duplicate the accomplishments of his French regiments because of its relative lack of training and experience, but further training would make the 369th an excellent regiment, and he insisted upon its immediate recognition. AEF HQ had not responded to the proposals he had made immediately after the attack, an error that demanded rectification. A great spirit of sacrifice animated the officers of the 369th, but he knew that they were troubled about apparently being forgotten by AEF HQ, and he desired authorization to accord them the honor of a divisional citation because the 369th formed an organic part of his division.[113] General Lebouc consequently awarded the Regiment the Croix de Guerre with Palm.

Lebouc's concentration on the morale of the officers and not the men was not necessarily evidence of racism but rather an illustration of the class consciousness that pervaded European armies, which awarded separate medals to officers and enlisted men. Only the German army acknowledged the critical importance of NCOs, as it trained both noncommissioned and commissioned officers to assume command positions up to two ranks above their own. Class divided commissioned from noncommissioned officers, and the war eroded but did not erase that gap.

The French and American offensives in the Champagne and the Meuse-Argonne continued through October, but the exhausted French 161st Division and its American 369th Regiment did not return to the battle and rotated to a quieter sector of the front to refit and replenish their ranks. On October 7, 1918, the commander of the French 9th Army Corps, General Garnier Duplessix, issued the following order of the day:

> The 157th and 161st Divisions and the 2nd Moroccan Division are leaving the Army Corps.
> The General Commanding the 9th Army Corps presents his earnest and most hearty congratulations for the glorious success they have achieved through their wonderful spirit and indomitable tenacity. The General bows to the brave American Regiments who had wonderfully and heartily competed with their French comrades.

This is not the place to give an enumeration of the splendid deeds which have marked each of the days of our victorious progress. They are to be found written in the conquered soil, materialized through the trophies captured from the enemy and engraved in the heart of your Chief who bows deeply and salutes the troops.

Signed: Garnier Duplessix[114]

In early December 1918, Hamilton Fish met John Castles for lunch, and Castles subsequently revealed to his mother Fish's account of the battle: "Ham said it was horrible & the Regt. suffered big losses without accomplishing a thing & finally had to be taken out. . . . He said it was really awful." Castles concluded, "Don't say anything about what Ham told me as I would not like to be so quoted as I long ago washed my hands of that outfit."[115]

Was Castles exaggerating the negative aspects of his lunch conversation with Fish, or had Fish actually described Séchault in that manner? Any assertion that the Regiment had accomplished nothing was inaccurate. That the battle was "awful" and "horrible" describes the nature of battle in World War I, indeed in any war. Séchault was Fish's first and only experience of battle, and the horrors he witnessed in the town that night, where so many of his Regiment lay dead and dying in a bloody makeshift hospital, may well have blinded him to the very real advance the 369th had made. He already thought war was "fiendish," and he later became a pacifist, but he also remained a staunch supporter of the 369th for the rest of his life. Both Fish and Castles had departed the Regiment dissatisfied with its leadership, and Castles could never bring himself to admit that the men were truly capable soldiers. Fish, however, really was attached to the men of the Regiment, particularly those in his beloved K Company. The reluctance of both Fish and Castles to have their words published or quoted likely stemmed from the fact that disclosure of such information and opinions violated the stringent censorship of information from the front.

As Lebouc's assessment showed, the 369th had acquitted itself well. Just how well was attested by Pétain's assessment of the contiguous AEF offensive in the Meuse-Argonne sector. The French general considered conditions for the American attacks of September 26–28 very favorable, with feeble reaction from German infantry and practically no artillery response.[116] However, the American attack bogged down from inadequate command and liaison of infantry, artillery, and aviation, and the inexperienced American soldiers' lack of initiative, their tendency to bunch together, and their failure to entrench resulted in high casualties from German shellfire. Traffic jams clogged the roads behind the front because of the absence of a methodical organization of convoys, which delayed food supplies and relief intended for the exhausted troops. The American commanders simply ordered the capture of objectives at all costs, but without assuring continuity of effort or organizing supply services in the rear to bring forward adequate munitions and evacuate the wounded.[117]

The American offensive degenerated into combat waged by isolated units, which did not clear the Germans from the territory they took; as a result, enemy machine guns continued to fire at American troops *behind* the front for two days. On September 29, the American 35th Division retreated southeast of Exermont without good reason when it was met by what Pétain described as several artillery rounds and bursts of machine-gun fire. Pétain concluded that in its first attack on a distant objective, the AEF had proved incapable of accomplishing its mission.[118] The French commander in chief considered American soldiers excellent, and he suggested that they would have performed well with experienced French staff and command by bringing American divisions under French army corps.[119] Such an assessment sounds eerily similar to the contention that black soldiers required white officers.

One might dismiss Pétain's damning assessment as a prejudiced attempt to bring American divisions under French command. In fact, his judgments, if not his recommendation, coincided with American reports. The 35th Division after Exermont displayed what one inspecting officer termed "wretched discipline," as the men and their billets were unkempt and dirty.[120] An American general estimated that of some 850,000 American troops engaged in the Meuse-Argonne, roughly 100,000 were absent from their units.[121] Historian Richard S. Faulkner attributes the AEF's problems with performance and desertion to the rapid turnover of junior officers and its "poorly trained and rather dull non commissioned officers."[122] It would take until mid-October and the arrival of its experienced divisions from the successful American attack at St. Mihiel in mid-September for the AEF to demonstrate improved performance on the battlefield as the war drew to a close. All American units, whether the AEF, the black regiments in the French army, or the AEF II Corps of the 27th and 30th Divisions attached to the British army,[123] suffered high casualties because of their relative inexperience. Yet the casualties the other regiments of the French 161st Divisions suffered indicated that even as the war drew to a close, casualties on both sides remained high.

It was certainly clear in October 1918 that the 369th Regiment had captured and held Séchault. Yet the "fog of war" that observers often perceive during battle arose concerning that small French village eight years later, in a contest to control the memory of the battle in the United States. Battle monuments of past wars dot the European and American landscape, but visitors to these hallowed grounds remain unaware of the political infighting over contested space that often occurs prior to their construction. In spring 1927, the American Battle Monuments Commission completed a draft entitled "*Summary of Operations. 93rd Division (less 370th Infantry), in the Champagne. September 26–October 6, 1918.*"[124] In the offensive of the French 4th Army on the Mezieres-Sedan line, its 9th Corps assigned the 2nd Moroccan Division and the 161st Division, including the 369th Regiment, to spearhead the offensive and the 157th Division, including the 371st and 372nd Regiments to serve as corps reserve. The village of Séchault lay at one end of the corps's final objectives in its zone of advance. On September 29, at 2:45 P.M., the corps ordered the 161st Division to advance on the village, "with the 1st Battalion, 369th Infantry, leading the assault and followed by the 2nd Battalion in support and the 3rd Battalion in reserve."[125]

The draft continued:

> The 1st Battalion, 369th Infantry, launching its attack from the heights south of Séchault, captured the town after some severe house to house fighting and continued its advance to a line north and west of Séchault. . . . In this fighting a platoon of Company K, 372nd Infantry, was picked up by the 369th Infantry, they being the remainder of an unsuccessful attack on Séchault earlier in the day by the 372nd Infantry.[126]

The commission's summary of the capture of Séchault incorporated the 372nd Regiment because although the 369th's chronology ratified its capture of Séchault,[127] the 372nd's official narrative claimed that it had captured the village, despite the fact that it also acknowledged "more or less confusion" about the location of its battalions and the 157th Division's withdrawal of the 372nd for "reformation and reorganization" because of the regiment's heavy casualties.[128]

The circulation of this draft in September 1927 and the call for comments unleashed a barrage of correspondence from officers of the 369th and 372nd Regiments to the American Battle Monuments Commission. From the 369th, Maj. Arthur Little found it "difficult . . . to believe" that any regiment had attacked Séchault before the 369th.[129] Capt. John Holley Clark, whose 2nd Battalion's remnants had arrived in Séchault at 6:00 P.M. to be merged with Little's 1st Battalion, recalled, "During the time that I was in

Séchault I saw no soldier from any other American regiment but the 369th Infantry.[130] Seth B. McClinton, the captain commanding C Company, 1st Battalion, recalled that just prior to their assault on the village, Lt. Richardson Pratt, commanding C Company's assault group, "picked up a 2nd Lt. and 19 enlisted men of Co. K. 370 [372] Inf.," whom McClinton attached to his company.[131] Pratt himself only vaguely recalled that no more than six "colored soldiers, without an officer" joined his men on the "outskirts of the town," but he knew that the 369th captured the town.[132] Two more company commanders, Ralph M. Rowland of G Company, 2nd Battalion, and Comerford "Cub" McLoughlin of K Company, 3rd Battalion, answered the call for comments, and all the officers of the 369th agreed that their Regiment had captured the town.

Many of the officers of the 372nd Regiment remembered the capture of Séchault quite differently. Samuel M. Johnson, the major commanding 3rd Battalion, 372nd Regiment, claimed that the 1st Battalion of the 372nd captured Séchault, with his 3rd Battalion 500 yards behind, before noon on September 29, but then it had to withdraw because it had mistakenly marched in the wrong direction.[133] West A. Hamilton, an African American captain in the 372nd, recalled the regiment's "unsuccessful attack on Séchault,"[134] whereas C. S. Sumner, commander of L Company of the 372nd, asserted definitively that K and L Companies had captured Séchault early in the afternoon and then withdrew in the evening under German smoke and gas.[135] William T. McCann, commander of the 1st Battalion of the 372nd as of October 6, bitterly accused the 369th of having "a very good *press agent* [emphasis in the original]" and vehemently denied that the 369th had taken Séchault. He then claimed that the 1st Battalion, 372nd, captured the town "at least 24 hours before the 369th" and enclosed a map that he allegedly had received at that time from Col. Herschel Tupes, commander of the 372nd, confirming the seizure of these objectives.[136] Clark L. Dickson, an officer at regimental headquarters, also claimed that 372nd's 1st Battalion had captured Séchault "at least a mile in advance of neighboring units," but in light of heavy casualties and "the consequent confusion all units were withdrawn from Séchault." Dickson suggested the commission consult Colonel Tupes, the regiment's commander.[137]

Col. Herschel Tupes (ret.) termed the assertion that the 369th had captured Séchault "incorrect," as "elements of the 372nd Infantry . . . attacked Sechault" and "occupied the town."[138] Col. P. L. Miles, the former commander of the 371st Regiment, which had served with Tupes's 372nd in the French 157th Infantry Division, acknowledged only that the 372nd had advanced "unsuccessfully" on Séchault on the 29th."[139] Together during the war in their efforts to whiten the officer corps of the black regiments but in peace rather at odds in terms of Tupes's effort to rewrite the history of the capture of Séchault, the regular army colonels in any case forced the 369th to refight the battle of Séchault on paper.

Yet, help for the 369th came from an unlikely source. Herbert L. Allison, the lieutenant commanding K Company, 3rd Battalion of the 372nd, took the occasion of his company's reunion in Nashville, Tennessee, on Armistice Day 1927 to discuss the matter with his "surviving noncoms and privates." K Company had led the 3rd Battalion's advance on September 28 and lost all of its officers except Allison, who recalled that he and his remaining men saw Séchault off to their right. Believing that to be their battalion's objective, Allison and his men advanced "in skirmish formation" toward it, only to be greeted by heavy machine-gun fire. Pinned down, the men moved at dark to a crossroads just west of Séchault and dug in for the night of September 28, waiting for the enemy to attack them the next day. On September 29, the Germans attacked Allison's company in force, using a gas grenade "with rather telling effect." Just as the Germans began to flank them, Allison heard firing off to their right and saw American troops advancing on the town. "These troops," Allison continued, "proved to be of the 369th Infantry, and their timely appearance is all that saved us." Allison, suffering the effects of gas, escorted some German prisoners to the rear and left a Sergeant Collier in charge of the remnants of the 372nd's K Company, which joined the 369th in its seizure of Séchault. The survivors of the action had all authenticated his information.[140]

Capt. C. B. Cates of the American Battle Monuments Commission, blending the two claims as best he could, remained convinced that the 372nd detachments had "first entered the town, but they were badly disorganized and did not occupy the town. It is a settled question that the 369th did finish capturing and mopping up of the town in the afternoon of the 29th."[141] Allison's testimony had likely proved decisive in forcing Cates to acknowledge the role of the 369th in the face of the challenge from his regular army superiors, Colonels Tupes and Miles, and Cates credited the 369th with "finishing" the task started by the 372nd. Yet this compromise is absurd. If indeed the 372nd had seized the town earlier, and this seems highly unlikely, then the Germans had certainly reestablished solid defensive positions at Séchault in a remarkably short time. Furthermore, the 369th found no bodies of other American soldiers in front of or in the town, as would have been the case after a failed attack. The 372nd had managed partially to steal the thunder of the 369th in the conquest of Séchault *after* the war in the struggle over memory and memorialization.

At least the French army had credited, praised, and decorated their African American regiments for their achievements, which their officers could then debate to the American Battle Monuments Commission. The same could not be said for the AEF's treatment of the African American 92nd Division. Historian Robert H. Ferrell, a major authority on the Meuse-Argonne whose book *America's Deadliest Battle: Meuse-Argonne, 1918* reminds us that it was America's largest and deadliest battle,[142] has released the first full-length account of the 92nd, appropriately entitled *Unjustly Dishonored: An African American Division in World War I*.[143] Ferrell's work explains that the poor performance of part of one regiment early in the Meuse-Argonne led to characterizations of the 92nd as a failure, when in fact, as he proves, the 92nd did not fail and performed quite well militarily. Of course, the division's own commanders and AEF HQ were quick to condemn the 92nd and to blame its failure on the race of the 92nd's soldiers, yet when three white divisions retreated with their morale shattered, no one suggested that their poor performance proved that white soldiers could not withstand modern warfare. No better proof exists that the 369th Regiment was indeed fortunate to serve in the French army in 1918.

# 12

## War's End

*Final Campaign, First to the Rhine,*
*Occupation, and Hasty Departure*

Trucks convoyed the remnants of the 369th Regiment south during the night of October 8, where the three battalions billeted in separate villages southeast of Vitry-le-François. In balmy weather in French country villages, the officers and men bought fresh eggs, milk, and chickens.[1]

On October 9, Colonel Hayward sent a lengthy memorandum to the commander in chief AEF about the condition of the 369th. Although Hayward explained the purpose of his letter was not "excuse or complaint" but "better understanding . . . of existing conditions," its tone was one of angry protest. Hayward recalled that he had not been consulted about the earlier reorganizations—the removal of all black officers—of the Regiment required to conform to the later arriving regiments of the 93rd Division.[2] Although he had once pleaded with headquarters to fill the Regiment's ranks with the men on the docks of Brest, who clamored to join the unit when they could have been integrated and properly trained,[3] he now decried the arrival of detachments of several hundred illiterate southern black replacements "without previous notice . . . , some times equipped and some times not equipped, and never trained." Just prior to the battle of Champagne on July 15, the 369th had received 300 recruits, and the day before the Champagne offensive began on September 26, it received "six hundred untrained recruits," whom it obviously had no time to absorb before entering the battle.[4]

The Regiment never received commissioned officers with these detachments; in fact, he said, it had never enjoyed "anywhere near its quota of officers." It had only thirty-seven in

July, although the average complement should have been fifty to fifty-five officers, and the recent offensive had reduced it to fewer than twenty-five. Often, when he could anticipate a considerable gain in officers, fifteen to twenty of his own men would be "ordered away to school as instructors or students."[5]

What particularly galled Hayward was the AEF command's failure to award citations to the men of the 369th during its six months under fire. Officers and men had shown "conspicuous examples of bravery," which the French division commander, General Lebouc, and 4th Army commander, General Gouraud, desired to recognize when they cited their own men. The French generals had been writing to Headquarters AEF since May for permission to do so, to no avail and with no reply, although Pershing had cited two members of the Regiment (Henry Johnson and Neadom Roberts) in a communiqué to the American public. Repeatedly—after combat in June, after the battle of Champagne on July 15, and after combat in September—the officers and men of the 369th had to watch French soldiers receive their citations with "great ceremonies" while they themselves went unrecognized for similar achievements.[6]

Hayward had registered a telling point—the role that the AEF High Command's disregard of the 369th played in lowering regimental morale. Colonel Shockley's denigration of the feat of Johnson and Roberts was part of a larger and more corrosive AEF policy of failing to recognize the valor of the officers and men of the 369th. In fact, the French had cited Johnson and Roberts for their Croix de Guerre in May, but Johnson, who remained with the Regiment, had not yet been awarded his medal because the American High Command had failed to authorize the presentation of any medals, French or American, to the 369th. In light of this egregious and atrocious oversight, the unit's continued valor in combat became even more remarkable.

Hayward's other issues included the absence of leave areas for men of the Regiment despite application to military and YMCA authorities and the lack of stateside leave for a few enlisted men. AEF regimental commanders had been asked to recommend some of their captains to serve as instructors stateside. In Hayward's case, the personnel officer at AEF HQ had asked him to recommend Hamilton Fish and no one else.[7] General Headquarters's favoritism for the well-connected Fish and its infringement upon the prerogatives of Colonel Hayward could only have exacerbated the antagonism between the two officers of the 369th.

Finally, after pointing out that "a large percentage of the personnel of the Regiment conducted itself in the most heroic manner, standing the terrific losses inflicted without yielding," Hayward damned the conduct of many enlisted men in the recent offensive:

> To the disgrace of the regiment, the Negro Race and the American Army, . . . large numbers of enlisted men of this regiment conducted themselves in the most cowardly and disgraceful manner. They absented themselves without leave prior to each of the battles, stealing away in the night, throwing away their equipment, lurking and hiding in dugouts, and in some cases traveling many, many kilometres from the battlefield.[8]

These cases of men being absent without leave did not stem from any general panic, Hayward explained, and "the result was that practically all of the heavy casualties were suffered by the older and better men of the regiment, and of course, among the officers." He concluded:

> It is not believed that the remainder of the regiment can be made to attack again if the cowardly offenders escape punishment. Large numbers should be tried for misconduct in the face of the enemy. There should be wholesale executions following convictions. With all reward for bravery in the form of citations denied this regiment and no punishment for gross cowardice inflicted, the unit cannot be made a fighting unit.[9]

Hayward requested an immediate inspection by the inspector general, advice, and instructions.

Hayward's letter clearly targeted the recent draftees who had arrived just prior to the offensive, as he noted the heroic performance of the veteran soldiers—men who had borne the brunt of the assault and the casualties. In the immediate aftermath of the Séchault offensive, the colonel surveyed the severely depleted ranks of his Regiment and must have wondered how or if it could ever be restored to fighting condition. He angrily called for the heads of those deserters who threatened to undermine everything the Regiment had fought to achieve. Hayward considered them a blemish, a blot, on the escutcheon of the 15th, and he wanted them severely punished—or erased.

In his characterization of "the shirkers" as a disgrace to the Regiment, the army, and "the Negro Race," Hayward was obviously unaware of conditions in the AEF itself, where most draftees, black and white, arrived at frontline units untrained. Some 100,000 of 850,000 soldiers—obviously, the overwhelming majority of whom were white—went AWOL during the Meuse-Argonne offensive in October.[10] Moreover, condemning these draftees was much easier than attacking the individuals in charge or accepting personal responsibility for failures of training, command, control, and supply. In a moment of anger and wounded pride, the colonel had fallen prey to a tendency that was commonplace in the United States: the misdeeds of Negro individuals or groups invariably led to negative generalizations about the "Negro Race" on the part of whites. Many in the African American minority, under the microscope of the white authorities, feared the repercussions of such acts and also viewed them as a blot on the race. White Americans either did not acknowledge or did not punish comparable acts that whites committed, and if they did admit to them, they invariably blamed the deeds on individuals, never on their entire race. The appropriate color to blame here was green—that is, the inexperience of the draftees—irrespective of race.

Yet, Hayward explicitly and logically linked insistence on punishing offenders with the AEF's denial of citations to the Regiment: if bravery went unrecognized and cowardice unpunished, how could one expect to maintain the men's morale and willingness to fight and die? Hayward clearly despaired for the future of his Regiment. In his desperation, however, he had opened the Regiment to the machinations of the AEF command. Brigadier General Fiske's attempt in August to use the colonel's complaints in an effort to return the 369th to the AEF for labor duties demonstrated the readiness of the military politicos on the AEF staff to take Hayward's statements out of context and use them against the interests of the Regiment.

Col. M. A. W. Shockley and Lt. Col. E. Hunt arrived from GHQ AEF to inspect the 369th on October 15 and 16, and they submitted their report to Brigadier General Fiske on October 17.[11] They found that the replacements "varied in training" and were "low" in education and of "poor" mentality. Further, they said the men had arrived unequipped because the AEF expected the French to arm them. The Regiment, as reported, was short of officers, but in regard to insufficient equipment, the staff visitors found that the unit had taken poor care of its gear, which the men had thrown away or lost, prompting the French to furnish "old equipment in small quantities." The French had recently remedied the transport shortage.[12]

Shockley and Hunt concluded that the Regiment had not undergone sufficient disciplinary training to develop habits of obedience to orders in the enlisted men and leadership ability among noncommissioned officers and platoon leaders. Their inspection of October 15–16 showed a regiment that "appeared to be in the recruit stage in regard to basic training." The duo concurred with the regimental officers' judgment that the men needed a month of basic training and that they "lacked necessary intelligence and reliability" to develop an efficient liaison service. Where Hayward noted a decline in morale, Shockley and Hunt found that "morale has apparently not been built up and probably has decreased." They specifically found "no particular discontent in regiment" stemming from the delay in recognition for citations of bravery, the absence of leave areas, or the failure to send officers to the States.[13] Their report thus exonerated the AEF from any responsibility for the plight of the Regiment and actually placed any responsibility for the problems with draftees on the Regiment itself. As for their inability to detect any discontent about medals, French general Lebouc certainly disagreed vehemently with their contention in his comments on how the morale of officers and men had suffered from the AEF's failure to recognize them.[14]

In regard to "skulking" during the recent offensive, Shockley and Hunt found that of a complement of 2,700 men, a check after the offensive indicated some "600 absentees," of whom half remained "absent or missing." Men had failed to advance with their squads in the dusk and darkness; some claimed an inability to go on from gas or wounds; and in a few cases, officers and noncoms attempted to force men forward to no avail. They found shirkers equally divided between replacements and veterans and noted that the regimental officers had preferred no charges against anyone but had placed the 300 shirkers they had located in a separate provisional battalion in some disgrace and then returned them to their companies "without disgrace or change of status in their respective units."[15]

In this critical matter, Shockley and Hunt concluded that the "misconduct" stemmed from inadequate training to instill habits of obedience into recruits, "especially negroes of low mentality," coupled with a "lack of trained N.C.O.'s and officers of Regular Army experience." The Regiment needed to try men against whom it had "clear and substantial evidence of misconduct," Shockley and Hunt suggested, but they doubted the availability of evidence against "large numbers of absentees."[16] Notwithstanding the obligatory reference to "negroes of low mentality," their observations here seem reasonable, although the ill-timed arrival of a detachment of 600 replacements the day before the Séchault offensive, which they failed to mention, sheds interesting light on the reasons for inadequate training. Their conclusion that evidence would be hard to secure likely indicates their awareness of similar conditions throughout the AEF. Moreover, a group of American officers who visited various regiments to conduct courts-martial arrived at the 369th just prior to the battle and remained with it throughout the offensive. One of them, Maj. Joseph Cistero, later highly praised the 369th's conduct and observed that the courts had nothing significant to do.[17]

Then Shockley and Hunt moved beyond the inspection and Hayward's letter to their conclusion and recommendations. Although Hayward's letter, in their opinion, "implies that the French have not used the regiment well and that the regiment is discontented with service with the French," their report found that officers and men were "content" to serve with the French. The Regiment, however, "had been given more than its share of hard trench service without sufficient intervals for re-organization and training." They concluded that continuation of this circumstance would "cause greater deterioration than already exists." They consequently recommended that Hayward prefer charges against men if he had sufficient evidence and that "the regiment be withdrawn from French control and re-organized as a regiment of pioneer infantry."[18]

Shockley and Hunt had managed to twist Hayward's letter into a condemnation of the French army, not the AEF, and to return to the constant refrain of AEF Headquarters—return the Regiment to the AEF to serve as a labor battalion. Upon receipt of the colonels' report, Brigadier General Fiske quickly concluded that, for the most part, the regiments of the 93rd suffered from poor morale and discontent. Conditions would not improve as long as they remained with the French. Referring to the August request to return the "division" to the AEF, he recommended that "the matter be taken up directly with General Foch" and that regiments upon their return "be reorganized and trained to serve as pioneer regiments."[19] Despite the persistence that AEF HQ displayed in its efforts to secure the return of the black regiments, the latter would remain with the French army through the end of the war.

On October 10, the 161st Division received its orders to relieve the 1st Division in the region south of Vitry-le-François on the night of October 17–18. The 161st Divisional sector included the peak of Hartmannwillerskopf in the Vosges, which French and German elite mountain troops had bitterly contested early in the war before the scene of critical battles shifted to more northwesterly regions of the western front.

On October 13, the Regiment loaded men, mules, and vehicles on a train in the town of Chavannes for a two-day trip by rail. At a railroad station on the way, a white private by the name of Coughlan arrested four black soldiers who had left the first section of a train of replacements. When the second section of the train arrived, Coughlan attempted to place them on it, only to have a black sergeant stop him. Private Coughlan then ordered a white MP, Sgt. John B. Taylor, to arrest the black sergeant. When Taylor attempted to take the sergeant to the MP office, six or seven black soldiers brandishing pistols threatened him and forcibly took their sergeant from him. Taylor then noticed that the soldiers in the coaches were loading their rifles and pointing them at him threateningly. The black sergeant reboarded the train as it slowly left the station. From the last coach, the officer in charge of the train, Capt. T. Johnson of the 369th, inquired about the delay. When informed of the incident, he promised to take disciplinary action, which Col. F. W. Ralston of the office of the assistant provost marshal at AEF HQ said should be drastic.[20]

The incident and its account prove problematic. First, if a replacement train was involved, these men were likely fresh troops on the way to join the Regiment and not the 369th itself. The document presents no explanation of why the four soldiers left the first train or why the sergeant refused to let them on the second. The four soldiers whose arrest caused the incident were never named, nor was the sergeant. Finally, the absence of witnesses and the ability of the MPs to identify only the race of the men made it highly unlikely that the culprits would be brought to justice. The incident does, however, indicate a certain attitude on the part of the sergeant and his men. None of them felt obliged to obey the white military policeman who dared arrest their sergeant when they were in transit to the front, whereas the MPs enjoyed their privileged duty guarding a train station in the rear. Regimental insignia included the symbol of a rattlesnake with the slogan "Don't tread on me." Rigid adherence to rules might condemn the soldiers for disobedience; a more balanced perspective understands that most soldiers in the same circumstances would have responded the same way and that the military policeman had acted injudiciously. The captain likely pursued a perfunctory inquiry later because frontline soldiers in general held military police in low esteem.

After the train trip, the 369th transferred to trucks for the move into the Vosges Mountains to the Thur Valley in Alsace. Little, once again riding in the convoy commander's touring car, remarked on the beauty of the scenery. As they drove over mountains, which Little described as ranging from 4,500 to 6,000 feet, they could see the flat country of the Rhine Valley, the hills of the Black Forest in Germany beyond, and the peaks of the Alps in the background.[21] In the process of moving about, the 369th as of October 10 had left twelve coaches with all the men's packs at Valmy and now needed them back. General Lebouc's chief of staff, Colonel Hatton, drew Colonel Hayward's attention to the fact that no one had authorized the 369th to send packs to Valmy in the first place. Hayward had thus inconvenienced them by failing to conform to orders and then wasting gas and telephone messages in his attempt to remedy the situation. The French had not yet located the Americans' baggage, but Hatton politely insisted that Hayward conform to the French command's orders and not regard his unit as an autonomous regiment. Staff officer Hatton perceived deficiencies in the Regiment's attention to detail and orders in logistical matters behind the front.

As of October 17, Hatton did not believe that Hayward and his staff were ready to command a large sector, particularly one including Hartmannwiller. Consequently, he proposed to organize the sector into four subsectors, with a regimental colonel commanding each. During the time in the Vosges, Hayward needed to regain control of his Regiment, and Hatton intended to send different officers of the 369th regimental staff to spend several days with their French counterparts. The next day, Hatton received reports that soldiers of the 369th were buying provisions and bread in stores in Moosch and St. Amarin, explaining that they had no food. Some 369th soldiers had actually gotten lost and wandered into a different sector. Hatton insisted that Hayward verify the circumstances, which, if they were accurately reported, meant that the Regiment's supply service required better organization. The soldiers could not have wandered had the Regiment stationed sentinels at the entry to the camps in the various villages. Hatton insisted that the unit muster its men and punish absent ones severely, and he requested Hayward's report on the results of his inquiry.[22] In fact, Hatton's information was correct. On October 21, the divisional staff experienced difficulties communicating by telephone or telegraph with the 369th. Little's 1st Battalion lacked signals men and phones. Colonel Hatton obviously found the 369th and its commander, Colonel Hayward, rather deficient in discipline, order, and organization. The necessity of maintaining lines of communication and supply during the constant movement behind the front—the essential realm of logistics—was clearly beyond the capabilities of the 369th in its weakened condition after Séchault. It had excelled as a fighting unit, but now, its composition constantly in flux, time and the assistance of the French would be needed to restore its organizational efficiency.

As of October 19, the 161st Infantry Division had taken its positions in the Thur Valley, with the three battalions of the 369th located at St. Amarin, Moosch, Bitschwiller, Willers, and Thann, mountain towns about 4,000 feet above sea level. Little's 1st Battalion arrived without rations because of a confusion in orders, and during his unit's month in the Vosges, Little observed that the men never had enough food or blankets, although the mountain air restored the men's health and morale.[23]

During the 369th's month in the Vosges, the Germans invariably shelled the Regiment twice daily. Only one notable incident occurred, in the Collardelle sector, with Little's 1st Battalion in the front lines. At 5:00 A.M. on October 28, the Germans unleashed an hour-and-a-half barrage of shells and machine-gun fire down the length of the sector, ranging from the rear trenches to the front, but no German infantry emerged from the heavy fog enshrouding the valley in front of the American lines. The first rounds of the German barrage caused most of the casualties, which totaled sixteen, seven of whom died, including one lieutenant.[24]

On October 30, General Lebouc modified the prescribed occupation of the 161st's sector in the Thur Valley. His French regiments could not hold a first-line sector because of their inadequate numbers and depleted condition. The 369th, however, could hold a subsector of three command positions or posts; consequently, he proposed to place the 369th at the south end of the sector. As of October 30, the three battalions of the 369th occupied sector A, CP Bitschwiller. For service in the Thur Valley, the 369th received a Silver Band from the US Army, but less known is the honor accorded the Regiment by the French. In a letter to Arthur Little in 1936, John O. Outwater, who had served as an officer in the 369th, shared an astonishing discovery he had made on a recent business trip to Mulhouse and the Vosges during which he "took the time to explore Hartmannsweilerkopf, the most famous of all." There, he saw "the most imposing granite memorial with massive bronze doors flanked by caryatides leading to a crypt, on the walls of which were uniform bronze tablets commemorating regiments which had served there, and to my surprise in the top place of honour to the right was 369e RIUS." The prominence gave Outwater pause. Pride turned to uneasiness as he humbly remembered the Chasseur regiments and the Foreign Legion, which had lost as many as "5000 per regiment within a quarter-mile of the site." He found some solace in the spatial and artistic requirements of the plaque's placement, as "it was the only position which they could have given our regiment." Thus, he concluded with appropriate compassion and resignation that there was probably nothing "we can do about it."[25]

The 369th occupied the towns of Beronwiller, Wattwiller, and Uffohltz. As the war drew to a close in November, the unit saw little action. On November 2, Colonel Hatton responded to a request to designate battalions for firing courses by saying that he could designate none because all three of the 369th's battalions were in the line.[26] On November 5, a recently formed independent assault force of the 369th planned a surprise attack to capture German prisoners, but the assault never occurred.[27] On November 7, Hayward ordered patrols of the 369th to exercise caution in confirming an anticipated enemy withdrawal, although instructions from General Lebouc the next night concerned only defense against enemy raids.[28] On

November 9, a private of the 369th approached the French sergeant commanding a post near the juncture of the French and American lines and asked the sergeant to accompany him back to his American machine-gun post up the line, where a squad of some ten Americans under the command of an officer awaited. The French sergeant arrived to find a German soldier talking with the Americans, who had him covered with their weapons. The German distributed cigars and bread to the Americans, who then steered their benefactor to the rear. The French sergeant returned and reported to his superiors, who thought the German may have been "disoriented," despite the fact that he had requested an armistice. They ordered French soldiers to redouble their vigilance. The German was merely ensuring that he would not fall victim in the final days of the war.[29]

That same night, General Order no. 106 from General Lebouc advised the division that it was moving into Alsatian territory, where the population would receive it with open arms. The division's soldiers would have to give the impression of order and force to people accustomed to German rule. The French soldier would have to be a *beau soldat* (neat soldier) and carefully turned out. The 161st Division had to make an impressive entry into Alsace with bands playing, to give the impression that the troops returned as conquerors to their own "hearths."[30] That statement reflected the ambiguous position of Alsace and Lorraine, the "lost provinces" of France, after more than forty years of Germanization under German imperial and military rule.

The French army ordered the 161st Division to monitor and guard a sector along the Rhine. The 369th Regiment, supported by a platoon of French cavalry, now held the center of the division. On November 10, General Order no. 107 prescribed the monitoring of the German withdrawal and stated that French and American troops would advance upon the general's order only after patrols verified the withdrawal of the Germans. Then, troops in every subsector would advance, except for subsector A, occupied by the 369th, which would advance only after the French troops around them had done so.[31] Hayward issued an order to the 369th concerning "Flags of Truce," warning his men to avoid conversation with bearers of such flags and to treat them "with scrupulous propriety." They were to blindfold such interlopers to prevent the Germans' obtaining any information about their positions and shoot anyone who refused to obey their stipulations. Finally, the 369th was not to believe any rumors about an armistice; any announcement would come from headquarters.[32]

At 11:00 A.M. on November 11—the eleventh hour of the eleventh day of the eleventh month of 1918—the Armistice signaled the end of World War

I on the western front. The Germans had surrendered under the onslaught of the continuous Allied offensive, which the British and French armies primarily conducted with the significant assistance of the relatively inexperienced AEF. The towns of Alsace, like the cities in the West, celebrated that night, but the men of the 369th, like the great majority of soldiers, passed the night in relative silence, while their officers dined together and toasted the end of the war with champagne.[33]

Elsewhere in France, with the 77th Division, Hamilton Fish wrote his aunt on November 11 that he was glad the war was over. He firmly believed in a establishing a league of nations to eliminate war and armaments. American wealth needed to be spent "in improving the living conditions of our own people and in educating them to a higher standard of citizenship." Immediately after expressing such lofty sentiments, Fish expressed his regret that their "friend" Governor Whitman lost the recent election but added that he had "the consolation that a certain National Guard Colonel will not profit from his defeat."[34] His dislike of Colonel Hayward persisted.

With the end of hostilities, German soldiers and civilians began to fraternize with the soldiers of the 161st Division so enthusiastically that the men of the 369th occasionally had to hold them back firmly with rifles, bayonets fixed, at "Port Arms." Both French and African American soldiers fraternized with Germans, although it was officially forbidden. The American soldiers also fed the large numbers of released prisoners of war and refugees who passed through their lines on their way home. General Lebouc ordered patrols to prevent civilians and German soldiers from entering their lines and to arrest those who did. He insisted upon the strictest discipline and particularly desired that "promiscuous firing of rifles by our men" cease.[35]

Capt. Lewis Shaw returned to the 369th from recuperation and rest at this time. On November 12, Lebouc had awarded him the Légion d'Honneur "for his gallant conduct in the attack where he repeatedly lead [sic] his battalion against numerous machine gun nests sometimes fifty yards ahead of the battalion." General Lebouc had recognized Shaw as Major L'Esperance's machine-gun captain, and L'Esperance had emphasized to the general that one of Shaw's guns had saved the battalion from capture. Shaw acknowledged L'Esperance's "wonderful generosity," mentioned his major's tendency to "rather exaggerate everything," and attributed his second citation for the Croix de Guerre to L'Esperance's intervention with the general.[36] Clearly, L'Esperance, whose name indicates his French ancestry, had used his French language abilities to ingratiate himself with Lebouc, in this case to Shaw's advantage.

Shaw was quite pleased with his Croix de Guerre with two Silver Stars, noting that the Cross with Bronze Star denoted a regimental citation, with Silver Star a divisional citation, with Gold Star a corps citation, and with Palm Leaf an army citation. Back with Major L'Esperance and Captain McLaughlin, he considered them "a reunited and happy family well rid of Major Spencer whose wounds were serious enough to send him home." Captain Walton, his wounds healed, would return from the hospital soon.[37] All three of Shaw's comrades had earned promotions for their actions during the offensive, and L'Esperance awaited the outcome of his recommendation for the Légion d'Honneur. None of Spencer's subordinates had ever considered him a competent commander, and Shaw's remarks indicate their continued lack of respect for Spencer despite his grievous wounds.

At 4:30 A.M. on November 17, the men of the 369th departed sector Collardelle to march forward through the mountains to the Rhine River. The 1st Battalion lost one platoon, whose lieutenant had just joined the Regiment, but it reappeared some twelve hours later. When Major Little asked later what his officer's civilian occupation had been, the lieutenant answered that he had been a guide who conducted tours through Yellowstone Park.[38]

They passed through no-man's-land, then empty German trenches. The three separate battalions of the 369th joined in the town of Cernay, and they marched to their billets in separate towns of the region, led by the band. The evacuated towns where they stayed had suffered little damage. On the morning of November 18, the three battalions set out again and then joined in regimental formation to march to the town of Ensisheim, where they received a rousing reception from the inhabitants and passed in review before General Lebouc. Little contrasted the stiffness of American officers reviewing troops to Lebouc's cordial smiles and greetings to officers he knew.

From Ensisheim, the Regiment marched east to Blodelsheim, where the different battalions once again divided to proceed to different towns to establish their headquarters. The next day, November 19, town citizens deluged the battalion commanders with requests of the most mundane sort, from herding cattle to going to market in other towns. The Americans realized just how tyrannically the Germans had governed the people of Alsace. The commanders, in their official capacities as sole authority in their towns, consequently issued proclamations on November 20 that the occupation would be friendly. Former soldiers would have to register with the Americans, and no citizens could sell liquor to "the enlisted soldiers of this garrison (colored soldiers)."[39] Officers could drink all they wanted, but the soldiers were reined in tightly. Nonetheless, Melville Miller, a private during the war and raconteur extraordinaire after, recalled that the men "had a ball" during the occupation.[40]

Battalion commander David L'Esperance, according to Shaw, became "the dictator of the 500 inhabitants [in a village where everyone speaks German] and the many men of his command. The economic, civil and moral problems that we have to decide are most interesting." Shaw hardly knew his own company, "with so many new men & all new officers." He arrived in his billet a few hours after the German captain departed, to be greeted by his landlady, "a white haired French woman," with the statement that "she had waited 48 long years for us."[41]

That same day, November 20, at 10:30 A.M., Colonel Hayward ordered the battalions forward to the Rhine. They were to advance their outposts to the river, occupy towns, and cover the approaches to the Rhine. Spurred by the words *immediate execution,* they advanced to the Rhine. Upon receipt of the order to advance from Lebouc, Hayward and a party of officers rode to the banks of the great river, where Hayward made a speech and then descended the bank to drink a handful of water. He arrived at the Rhine at 10:30 A.M., the same time his order to advance arrived at his battalions. The colonel had ensured that he and his staff would arrive first.[42]

Among the group of American and French officers reaching the Rhine at 11:00 A.M., Capt. Lewis Shaw was proud to be "the first of the Allied armies to have this honor." Seeing the "beautiful blue stream," however, his mind turned to more serious thoughts:

> It makes me shiver to think what it would have cost in men to force a crossing in the face of the Germans. Thank heavens that is not necessary. . . . Since we began our peaceful advance thru most warlike and gruesome surroundings we have been very thankful that the armistice was signed first as it was. If it had not, we would have been fighting our way thru those miles of barb wire, trenches & machine guns as we did in September.[43]

Shaw's reflections contrasted greatly with the opinion of the AEF commander in chief, John Pershing, who desired to invade and finish Germany.[44] The Allied heads of state, including Woodrow Wilson, and their military commanders chose to sign the Armistice to avoid further bloodshed, and Shaw's observations indicate that American combat soldiers agreed.

The division commander, General Lebouc, had become a "warm personal friend [of L'Esperance] and calls on him every few days." That very evening, in Shaw's presence, "in walked the General and two very attractive

Red Cross nurses . . . making an informal call on Dave." The evening of November 21, Shaw reminisced with Colonel Hayward and Major L'Esperance about "the honors and comical episodes of the attack." The colonel "in fine spirits swears they will have us back home in a few months. I have great confidence in his ability to do it."[45]

The 369th Regiment occupied the towns of Blodelsheim, Fessenheim, Balgau, and Nambsheim and the west bank of the Rhine in the region of those towns. They passed nearly three weeks there uneventfully. Upon occasion, Sgt. Henry Johnson would stroll through Blodelsheim, wearing his Croix de Guerre with Palm jauntily pinned to his overseas cap. According to Major Little, an officer new to the Regiment spied the purple ribbon and, not knowing its bearer, called, "Halt, Sergeant! What is that thing you've got on your cap? And where did you get that *Croix de Guerre* anyway?" Johnson halted, cast a withering glance at the novice, saluted, and replied, "Sir, I guess you don't know who I am." "No, I don't," retorted the lieutenant, "who the hell are you?" "SIR, I'M HENRY JOHNSON!" the small sergeant concluded the exchange scornfully, turned about face, and walked away.[46]

On November 22, Lebouc wrote Hayward to compliment him for placing "the 'Black Watch' along the river." Lebouc commended the Regiment, "which, with little previous training, has fought with extreme bravery, . . . and as far as attitude and military discipline are concerned, . . . can compare with any of my French Regiments." From a French general, an American commander could receive no higher compliment. The letter informed Hayward that Lebouc was rewarding "officially the 369th R.I.U.S. with a collective citation in the orders of my Division."[47]

The Regiment passed a happy Thanksgiving in its comfortable surroundings. The officers dined particularly well on champagne and lamb and roast goose cooked by their own French chef. McLoughlin and Shaw, "now doing outpost duty on the Rhine," recalled that "just two years ago we were doing outpost duty on the Rio Grande. 'Join the army and see the world.'"[48] They were fortunate—they had lived to reminisce about and carried no physical scars from their experiences.

On December 8, the division transmitted AEF commander General Pershing's order to have the 369th ready to move to a port of embarkation for return to the United States. The French replied that they would place the 369th at the disposition of the US command on December 12, 1918, at 6:00 P.M. The Regiment departed its stations along the Rhine early on December 10, to march some 18 miles westward to new billets.

Early in the afternoon of December 13, the soldiers of the 161st French Division formed a hollow rectangle on the Plains of Munchhausen, about

10 miles north of Mulhouse. At the right side of the line on the north edge of the rectangle stood the 369th Regiment Infantry of the United States. All troops came to attention at the sound of trumpets, as from the west approached a dozen figures on horseback, riding at the gallop. In front, on a magnificent cream charger that was covered with a large crimson saddle cloth, rode General Lebouc, wearing a red cap adorned with gold bands of oak leaves, a horizon blue greatcoat, and crimson riding breeches. Lebouc entered the rectangle at the southwestern corner and made a galloping circuit of the troops, saluting and complimenting them as he passed. He then galloped to the center of the field and dismounted. The colors of all units to be decorated were ordered front and center.[49]

Hayward, Little, and the regimental executive officer, Lieutenant Colonel Pickering, bearing the regimental colors, stepped forward. General Lebouc read the following citation in French:

> Under command of Colonel Hayward, who, though injured, insisted on leading his regiment in the battle, of Lieutenant Colonel Pickering, admirably cool and brave, of Major Cobb (killed), of Major Spencer (grievously wounded), of Major Little, a true leader of men, the 369th R.I.U.S. engaging in an offensive for the first time in the drive of September, 1918, stormed powerful enemy positions energetically defended, took, after heavy fighting, the town of Séchault, captured prisoners and brought back six cannon and a great number of machine guns.[50]

General Lebouc pinned the Croix de Guerre to the peak of the colors and on each officer present, and he kissed them each upon the right and then the left cheek. After these presentations, the entire division, some 12,000 men including cavalry units and artillery, passed in review. On December 16, the full 161st Division moved to Ribeauville, where it would become part of the French Reserve Army before its own disbandment.

The swiftness of the orders to return the Regiment to the AEF and its impending date for withdrawal from the Alsace had to take both officers and men by surprise. None knew the secret maneuvering that had occurred to ensure that black soldiers had as little time as possible to interact with the French population, especially the women. Although the AEF was able to influence the actions of French officers, it had no such leverage with French civilians, especially when soldiers had far more time and opportunity to enjoy their surroundings and the inhabitants. On November 7, an official in the War Department had advised Secretary of War Newton D.

Baker to "get the colored troops out of France as soon as you can." Shortly after the Armistice, white officers of the 92nd Division alleged to a State Department official that "negro troops at Chateau-Thierry" had indulged in excesses and that drunken black soldiers had terrorized villagers, murdering and attempting rape. Although these were blatant lies, the diplomat urged the immediate return of all Negro troops to American shores before they discredited the United States. The American pressure was so strong that the French military mission at AEF HQ issued strict orders to limit contacts between black soldiers and French civilians, particularly females.[51]

The racist senior officers of the 92nd Division actively sought to discredit the performance of their black officers and troops. Gen. C. C. Ballou allegedly referred to his "rapist" division and his chief of staff, Col. Allen J. Greer, who was from Georgia, accused black officers in a letter to Tennessee senator Kenneth McKellar of cowardice, dishonesty, and inefficiency, being "dangerous to no one but themselves and women." Reports abounded that the men of the 92nd Division had committed twenty-six rapes, when in fact only seven of the unit's 12,000 men had been charged with rape, of whom two were convicted and one executed (AEF HQ had reversed one of the convictions).[52]

In the United States, Walter Loving, a black agent in the Military Intelligence Division, sought to prevent the undercurrent of racial friction from surfacing when black and white soldiers competed for French women, which could have caused "an American race war in France." Such encounters could prove catastrophic, Loving ventured, if French troops took the side of the black soldiers. Loving knew that some black soldiers were contemplating marriage to French women, which neither race at home would appreciate because black women would consider the soldiers potential spouses. For the good of the service and the "colored race," Loving advised discharging no black soldiers in France, preventing soldiers of different races from encountering one another in brothels, and shipping black troops home immediately.[53]

Thus, with overlapping motivations, government officials black and white insisted upon the rapid return of black soldiers from France. Neither Loving nor white civilian and military bureaucrats wanted black troops consorting with French women because of the problems that would cause upon their return to the States. The white officers of the 92nd Division further succeeded in discrediting their own black soldiers, an agenda Loving did not share. Loving's discussion of brothels was unusually candid given the AEF's insistence on abstinence, its indoctrination and campaigns against prostitution and venereal diseases, and its refusal of French offers of brothels, which were standard practice in European armies.

Furthermore, southern white supremacists informed Secretary Baker that they expected racial trouble. Black veterans would have aspirations that could only lead to bloodshed, as southern states had no intention of extending civil rights to their black residents. They insisted that the army prevent black soldiers from returning home in uniform or in groups and that the federal government and states cooperate in transforming black soldiers back into submissive civilians.[54] Clearly, no white Americans in power anticipated reforms to ease the injustices and discrimination against African Americans. They planned either surveillance or further repression to keep these Americans "in their place."

The day after General Lebouc's review, December 14, the Regiment rested in its town billets while Signal Corps cameramen from AEF HQ photographed the Regiment. Major Little received a complimentary autographed photo from General Lebouc. The morning of December 16, one of Lebouc's aides announced that the general would visit to pay his farewell respects that afternoon at 4:00. After a flurry of preparation, the general's limousine arrived to bugle flourishes and the company honor guard. Lebouc met the 1st Battalion's commissioned officers and assured them of his official respect and personal affection. They toasted "France and America, Allies and Friends!" The general again shook hands all around, then roared away in his limousine to the salute of the honor guard and the trumpeting of bugles. Little reentered his headquarters to find that the junior officers had made off with the rest of the champagne and the food.[55]

The next day, the 369th Regiment departed on foot to march by battalion in stages to the southwest for the next two to two and a half weeks, when the battalions entrained for the American camp at Le Mans. The troops trudged through rain, sleet, and snow, over mountains and through valleys, covering about 9 to 12 miles daily. The Regiment celebrated Christmas in the city of Belfort, opened presents from the Red Cross, and listened to music from Jim Europe's band, many men dancing with the civilian population. The battalions remained billeted in the suburbs of Belfort until New Year's, when they began to entrain for Le Mans, a process that continued over the next four days.

At Le Mans, the men deloused and reequipped, and the officers prepared embarkation lists. The troops lived in crowded quarters and walked around in the rain and mud, but they remained in high spirits—they were on their way home. The only annoyance they suffered involved compulsory attendance at lectures and musketry practice. The Regiment had endured these courses in the fall and winter of 1917 and had found them worthless in combat. The young American army instructor, the first they had seen during their time in France after 191 days under fire, had no combat experience.

On January 10, the Regiment departed Le Mans to arrive at Brest the next day. Major Little contemplated his cheerful soldiers, members of "a race which had suffered the wrongs of humanity for centuries," which some had classified "almost as one of the lower animal kingdoms, not quite as human beings, and which was "still suffering, and bound to suffer for a long time still to come, from prejudices in the hearts of white men." These men, despite such "worldly handicaps . . . , were going home as heroes!" Recruited and trained "in ridicule," sent to France "as a safe political solution of a volcanic political problem," and loaned to the French army "as another easy way out," the men had nonetheless "carried on." "Their triumphs in battle had been great; but their triumphs of orderliness, of cleanliness, of personal and civic decency, had been greater. . . . They had helped not only to win the war, but they had helped, too, in the long-drawn struggle still to be, for the betterment of conditions for their race."[56]

The train's arrival at Brest brought an abrupt halt to Little's grand musings and a sharp reminder that the African American soldiers had returned to the zone of the AEF, of the United States overseas. A few minutes after the Regiment detrained, a white MP split open the head of a 1st Battalion private who had dared to interrupt the MP's conversation to ask directions to the latrine. As the MPs started to carry the soldier away, Captain Mac-Clinton dispersed the gathering crowd of soldiers, only to have an MP captain address him insolently. Little arrived just in time to restrain an angry MacClinton and then to receive the same treatment from the MP. Little pulled rank on the MP, who then "let slip a line to the effect that they had been warned that our 'Niggers' were feeling their oats a bit and that instructions had been given to 'take it out of them quickly,' just as soon as they arrived, so as not to have any trouble later on." The police returned the private the next day, head swathed in bandages, without preferring charges against him.[57]

After supper that night, as the Regiment rested during its march toward camp, two mounted MPs passed without saluting Little and then returned a short time later to order him to stop a "disturbance" in the middle of his column. One MP, purposely and belligerently ignoring Little's rank, complained, "There's a lot of your 'niggers' yelling at us as we pass, 'Who won the war?'" Little retorted that his men were "well disciplined" and had "a right to speak," so if the MPs did not like what they heard, they should "make believe you don't hear it." At every stop during their train journey, the men of the 369th had called out, "Who won the war?" to every American unit they saw, and they answered their own question by chanting the name or nature of that unit. Everyone had greeted them good-naturedly, until now. Little continued, "You people in this town are the first people to act as if you didn't like our men. You two men are the first men in the whole army who have been unwilling to accept as a joke the call 'Who won the war?'" Little advised the MPs to be on their way. As they rode off, one threatened, "This will get you three months."[58] Of course, the MPs certainly knew that in their policing of the rear areas, they most definitely had not won the war.

During the three weeks it was at Brest, from January 11 to January 31, the Regiment received, every few hours of every day, "notice of petty fault-finding coupled with a threat of disciplinary action against the entire organization by placing its name at the bottom of the list for embarkation." Many men in the Regiment became sick with flu under the abysmal and unhealthy living and working conditions at Brest and Finistère. Chad Williams notes that the great numbers of soldiers overwhelmed the Brest embarkation center, whose social services and health conditions worsened, and the Red Cross and YMCA continued to segregate black soldiers in severely inadequate facilities.[59] According to Little, one black soldier wrote in his diary that at Brest, they "had struck something worse than the Germans," by which he meant "the front-dodging M.P.'s, the pampered pets of the war."[60] Capt. Lewis Shaw, in his last letter to his mother from France, wrote, "I have been thru more Hell in the last month than all the rest of my experience over here." After complaining about their 62-mile march from the Rhine to Belfort in terrible weather, he continued, "When we started to be re-Americanized they certainly did things to us which the censorship forbids my repeating." The authorities had led them to believe that they would ship for home over a month earlier. Now, he concluded, "I am O.K. physically but so low mentally as we all are at our treatment that I can't write a decent letter."[61] One can only imagine how the black soldiers must have felt, if the abusive treatment affected a white officer so negatively.

The MPs were delivering a warning. The savage harassment the military police meted out to the African American soldiers was meant to beat out of them any illusions about the treatment that they could expect back home in the United States. They returned as black soldiers to the reality of American life, a reality that African American soldiers who served in the AEF had never escaped. MPs treated black soldiers worse than their white counterparts, but the American military police in France earned a reputation for unmitigated brutality toward all soldiers. In France, stories circulated about their conduct in Brest, but even more were told in Paris, where the police relished cracking the skulls of and then beating and torturing American soldiers incarcerated in the AEF prison. After the war, inmates who recalled their treatment in Paris during the conflict nearly beat to death the military police officer in charge of the Paris garrison, who was imprisoned himself.[62]

The embarkation orders for the 369th finally arrived: Headquarters Company and 1st Battalion sailed on the SS *Stockholm* on January 31, Supply Company and 2nd Battalion on the SS *Regina* on February 1, and Machine Gun Company and 3rd Battalion on the SS *France* also on February 1. As they proceeded from camp to the docks, the men marched in silence to avoid any challenges or altercations. But as they boarded the tenders to take them to their ships, the chief of staff at the base asked for the musicians, and the 369th Regiment departed, as it had arrived, to the music of Jim Europe's vaunted band.[63]

The AEF allowed no black soldiers or units to participate in the Entente Victory Parade in Paris. Instead, black soldiers heard speeches from Robert Russa Moton of Tuskegee Institute, whom the army had sent to lecture them on the "modest and unassuming" attitudes necessary to appease white Americans. The AEF deployed the only black soldiers left in France, the labor battalions of the American Service of Supply, to rural areas, where they performed the gruesome and thankless task of clearing battlefields and reburying dead Americans in the war memorial cemeteries.[64] In January 1919, as the black combat regiments prepared to return to the United States, AEF's intelligence arm received reports that black officers of the 370th Regiment, the only unit with a black officer cadre, had formed a secret society for "the promotion of social equality" between colored and white after demobilization. The movement had enlisted members of the 369th and the 371st, while all camped at Brest awaiting transport home. Although G2 heard that the society would resist "white ascendancy," it could find no further evidence of the existence of such an organization. Brig. Gen. Dennis Nolan, chief of G2, warned the MID in mid-February, when the 93rd had already returned to the United States and the 92nd was on the way, about the probable existence of such an organization, despite the absence of evidence. The 92nd Division's G2 officer, Maj. F. P. Schoonmaker, could only determine that soldiers at the Le Mans camp had held a meeting on the "political, economical, educational betterment and co-ordination of the negro in the United States on the principles of Democracy as won the on the Battlefields of Europe."[65]

The AEF's concern about black postwar loyalty is fascinating. During the war, enemy aircraft had dropped leaflets encouraging black soldiers of the 92nd Division to desert, to no avail. Now, with the imminent return of black troops to the States, the MID planned to crack down on black troops. It particularly sought to prevent black soldiers from bringing home revolvers and automatic pistols, for fear of violence, social unrest, and race war.

The French Embassy and its military attaché in Washington, Gen. Louis Collardet, knew of such apprehensions and informed the French government of them. Collardet reported the concerns of white America about the potential dangers from black soldiers, while contrasting the treatment of black soldiers in France with that in the United States. His report of March 1919, issued on April 8, 1919, advised that returning black soldiers would probably support the Bolshevik Party, based on the reportage of A. Philip Randolph's socialist paper, the *Messenger*. Black soldiers, returning from France where social equality had eliminated nearly all barriers, resented the difference in the treatment they received in the United States. He further noted the presence of Japanese intrigues with African Americans and other peoples of color in an "International League of Darker Peoples." The Irish, Jews, and Germans were suspect as well.[66] Hysteria reigned in the United States.

Collardet was particularly concerned about white America's insistence on the importance of black soldiers' return to the South individually and not in uniform; in France, all soldiers returned home in uniform, proud of their service to their country.[67] The US Army, he felt, would deprive black soldiers alone of the proud return home in uniform that all veterans deserved because they would surely encounter hostility from southern whites. Collardet's memoranda heighten the sense that the American government had no concern for the effect on the black veteran that such discrimination would cause. His report of May 1919, sent on June 6, recounted a story about a "brawl" in which some 2,000 sailors killed two black men and wounded many others. He was not surprised that black people sought to organize and defend themselves. Strong religious ties prevented the success of Bolshevik efforts to recruit black adherents to their cause, but he noted the government seizure of the NAACP organ, the *Crisis,* under the pretext of stopping the journal's attacks on the government.

Collardet found it particularly egregious that Robert Russa Moton, the principal of Tuskegee, had felt obliged to defend black soldiers against charges of "failure," as the black regiments brigaded with the French had certainly proved their value. A black regiment of the Illinois Guard (the 370th) had returned with an entire battalion (actually a company) decorated with the Croix de Guerre, an achievement of which any regiment, without regard to race or nationality, could be proud. Furthermore, Collardet mused, the Negro American received too little credit for his part in making the supply service a success. Concerning the total record of the Negro as a soldier in France, he asserted there was no need for defense or anything other than "praise."[68]

On May 6, 1919, Maj. Walter Loving, a black agent with the MID, expressed his thorough outrage at the treatment of African American soldiers, particularly in the 92nd Division. Although Loving shared his superiors' assessment of the potential dangers that the returning black soldiers posed, he advised them in remarkable fashion that the situation was totally avoidable and brought on by the pronouncements, policies, and actions of the division's white officers. Loving considered that the quality of the white officers left much to be desired. Far too little attention had been paid to their incompetence, the assignment of Col. Allen J. Greer being "a conspicuous example of an unqualified man being placed in an important position." Loving vehemently condemned Greer, the chief of staff of the 92nd Division whose duty should have been "to work zealously for the efficiency, morale, and reputation of the division." Instead, his actions "on many occasions had the effect of undermining the morale of his own officers and men" and, in the process, negatively affected the honor and dignity of the War Department. Loving called in vain for a court-martial of Greer as the only way to prove to critics of the War Department that it was not shielding him from punishment. Moreover, he urged an investigation of the 92nd Division's performance because if it "was not a success," he believed the "fault rests with the division commander and his field officers and not with his men." Loving cited the performance of the black soldier in the regular army before the war as evidence for his conclusion.[69] His assessment of fault is reminiscent of Capt. Hamilton Fish's assessment of responsibility before the 369th entered combat—that if the Regiment did not perform well, it would be entirely the fault of the officers.

Loving continued to say that the "League for Democracy," about which military intelligence could find no information, was mainly composed of former officers and enlisted men of the 92nd Division, with headquarters in New York and branches in several large cities. "Social equality," often a euphemism for interracial social and ultimately sexual relations, was not the main goal of the organization. Its first objective was "to protest against the slandering of the Division by Colonel Greer," who could not have acted without the approval of the division commander, General Ballou. The leaders of the organization maintained that the latter's Circular no. 35, issued at

Camp Funston, served as ample evidence of his race prejudice. Even before a black audience after the war, Ballou spoke discouragingly about black officers and men of the division, leading one black newspaper to offer sarcastically, "There was nothing good about the 92nd Division except General Ballou and his white officers." Loving opined that Ballou's appointment to command an all-black division was just another example of the military's failed race policy.[70]

Although New York might have been the headquarters of the League for Democracy, the men of the 367th, and not the 369th, led it. Its field secretary was Osceola E. McKaine, formerly a first lieutenant in the 367th who was described by Walter Loving as "an able, aggressive young radical," assisted by the "highest type of officers and enlisted men" in the "pursuit of justice for the Negro." McKaine also edited the organization's publication the *Commoner*.[71] Nonetheless, the men of the 369th would face suspicion and fear, for right beneath the official welcome were reactionary forces intent on limiting the gains these soldiers hoped they had won for themselves and their people through their service.

As the works of noted historians Chad L. Williams and Robert H. Ferrell attest,[72] the black officers and men of the 92nd Division had ample reason to return home angered at their treatment by their very own commanding officers. The latter had relentlessly attacked their manhood, honor, courage, and intelligence and had done little to prepare the division for combat. Napoleon Marshall's experience with his major—who sent Marshall's large patrol out with no prior planning, practice, grenades, or wire cutters and with the sole instruction to shoot any man who turned back, a man who himself was killed two nights later while reconnoitering no-man's-land alone—exemplifies the inexperience and incompetence of some of the 92nd's white officers. In the course of combat, a number of the division's white junior officers came to respect their black comrades in arms, but the division's high command remained obdurate despite the number of decorations awarded to individual black soldiers. Maj. Walter Loving's willingness to lay the responsibility for the problems of the 92nd squarely on its commanding officers—General Ballou, Colonel Greer, and Col. George McMaster—stands out most conspicuously in this sad litany on injustice.[73] They were determined to discredit their own division on the basis of the race of its soldiers, although its performance in combat exceeded that of some white divisions.

In contrast, the men of the 369th enjoyed the firm support of their officers, for whom Hayward's belief in the elite nature of his Regiment and the quality of his African American volunteers set the standard. The officers held high expectations for their men and the Regiment, and the men measured up to them. The 369th was fortunate to serve in a French division, whose commander, supported by the high command of the French army, valued such a fine, if inexperienced, body of men and trained, led, and honored them accordingly. Whatever happened after, the officers and men could always recall with pride their decorated wartime service in the 369th Regiment. Certainly, that positive experience explains in part why the black officers and men of the 369th Regiment did not return to the United States with the rage in their hearts that many of their counterparts in the 92nd Division felt.

Walter Loving was correct in his assessment of responsibility, but his cogent analysis leads to a much larger point about the potentially radicalizing nature of the wartime experience of the African American soldier. The extent of the radicalization, depending upon the individual, stemmed not only from exposure to the more liberal values of the French in general and French women in particular about associating with African Americans but also from the treatment and attitudes that black soldiers confronted from the white commanders of their American units.

# 13

## "War Crossed Abroad and Double Crossed at Home"

### Triumphant Heroes, Objects of Ridicule, or Fearsome Trained Killers?

In January and February, after the departure of the 93rd Division for the United States, the French army suggested that it was high time for the black regiments to return their French matériel and (amazingly) animals. On January 1, 1919, the French War Ministry also asked its military mission at US Army Headquarters who would pay for the matériel that had been used by the black regiments, including the 369th. The French were willing to accept that part of the cost had been paid and the remainder charged to the Americans, whereas the Americans interpreted that it was time for the French to reimburse them for what they had paid. The French now required an accurate inventory of all the matériel, animals, and payments. The commander in chief of AEF answered on January 25 that the regiments of the 93rd Division had exchanged their French equipment for American while they were stationed at Le Mans preparing for debarkation.[1] His memorandum did not mention animals, but obviously, the troops of the 93rd had not taken French horses or livestock home with them in the ships; they had difficulty enough securing shipping space for the men, much less animals. What happened to the animals—which the 93rd probably returned with the matériel unless someone sold them along the way to farmers or cooks, since the French relished horsemeat—remains a mystery. Suffice it to say that a sometimes difficult and contentious wartime partnership between the French and American armies ended with their argument over even the trivial issue of payment for the 369th's horses.

The men of the 369th could not have cared less about the haggling over matériel and livestock and who owed what to whom.

They longed to escape the miserable and even deadly conditions in the seaport camps and return to loved ones and familiar surroundings. The voyage home of the 369th, absent the threat of submarines, proved relatively uneventful. Ten hours out of New York Harbor, Sgt. Maj. Francis Marshall of 1st Battalion Headquarters put his final comments on the battalion register: "The decoration of the flag with the French Croix de Guerre puts the Fighting 15th New York Infantry into the limelight as a bright star in the work of the great machine which forced the Kaiser to his knees and abdication, and helped make the world a safe place to live in. Don't forget our comrades who died for Uncle Sam."[2]

Fittingly, on Lincoln's birthday, February 12, and on Valentine's Day, February 14, the Old 15th returned to New York Harbor battalion by battalion. The Regiment was "very much disfigured but still in the ring," with 1,300 of the original 2,000 men and 21 of the 56 officers returning to the din of whistles, ringing bells, and loud cheers. The difference in numbers, Colonel Hayward inaccurately but dramatically reported, equaled "those who sleep on French and Belgian battlefields."[3] Although the survivors received an "exuberant and sincere welcome," they disappointed their well-wishers, who expected long, warm embraces and a spectacular parade. Instead, they got only brief and distant glimpses with each arrival, as the men were transferred by boat to Long Island City, where they boarded trains to Camp Upton for medical examination and demobilization.[4]

New Yorkers and their revered sons would have to wait for more intimate displays of affection and, perhaps, the big moment—the triumphant march up Fifth Avenue. In the meantime, the returning heroes received all the adulation and coverage they could possibly hope for in the city's press and in black papers throughout the nation. War stories abounded, some describing individual and collective exploits with customary exaggeration, vividness, and cool. Even the larger-than-life legend of Henry Johnson continued to grow. One paper reported that Johnson had slain thirty-four Germans with hand grenades, another that he had killed four and wounded thirty-two. Reporters attributed fantastic stories to Johnson himself, which included dialogue between him and a German officer who referred to him with the N word. Finally, others found the opportunity to share their moments of glory and become minor Henry Johnsons.[5] Pvt. William Scott of 19 East 134th Street told how he eliminated a German soldier with a bolo knife:

We stormed a trench and fifteen well armed Germans dashed out. One of them grappled with me. My gun slipped from my grasp and something hit me over the head. Down I went and the German jumped on me. We wrestled, and as I gained my feet again he jabbed his bayonet through the shoulder of my uniform. It did not cut me but it felt cold, and I thought it about time to end the argument. So I got my bolo knife. And believe me, when I got my strokes in there wasn't much of that German gentleman left.

Smith had a toothless mouth and a "severely wounded" notation in his service record to attest to his combat, if not the specifics of his story.[6]

In more restrained but no less dramatic fashion, others recounted the horrors of war, especially "going over the top" at Séchault. Their resolve rested not so much in measured cool but in unbounded faith. Samuel Deas of Brooklyn recalled that moment of truth when the captain interrupted the songs and storytelling with orders at 1:30 A.M.: "Boys we are going over." Warning his men regarding the dangers of being curious about weapons lying around, he gave them ten minutes to prepare themselves for the sure hell that was to follow. Deas recited the Twenty-Third Psalm, commonly attributed to the ultimate warrior, David, and "walked through the valley and shadow of death" fearing "no evil for Thou art with me." He and the others went over with blankets, rifles, and "plenty of ammunition of all kinds in bags strung across our shoulders": "At that moment the shells began to burst all around us and our comrades began to fall. You could hear their moans and groans. Words can't fully describe these awful moments. But those who were not killed or wounded went on and on, losing, yet gaining all the time." Deas was one of the lucky ones who survived the attack, only to be "horribly gassed" at the time the unit was relieved.[7]

Colonel Hayward found himself at the center of regimental lore as both subject and contributor. Sgt. John Jamison of 137 W. 141st Street told how Hayward led his men into fire and exposed himself during the offensive at Belleau Ridge, where a German counterattack created much heat for the Regiment. In this version of the oft-told tale, Hayward allegedly removed his colonel's insignia from his shoulders, grabbed "a rifle from a soldier, darted out ahead, and led us through a storm from German artillery." A French general ordered Hayward to retire only to have the colonel defiantly reply, "My men never retire. They go forward or they die." They went forward, and Hayward reportedly suffered a broken leg, landed in the hospital and returned to the front on crutches. His heroics reportedly earned him the nickname "Hell Man," although his men affectionately referred to him as "Old Bill, that fightn' white man." It was an appropriate response to the man who referred to them as "those scrapping black babies of mine."[8]

Hayward, realizing that a true hero always shared the glory, told the press that his men fought like tigers, never whimpered, and "cared less for shell fire than any white man that ever breathed." When asked what the Germans had to say of the black soldiers, he replied that he had seen a report during the occupation along the Rhine after the war that referred to these soldiers as *"Blutlistige Schwartze Manner"* (bloodthirsty black men). Contrary to his assertion that he saw the term in a report during the occupation, Hayward actually wrote in an official summary of January 7, 1919, that the phrase appeared in an enemy report of the raid led by Sgt. William Butler. According to Hayward, the report described Butler as an "enemy group in overwhelming number" whose *"blut lustige"* caused the abandoning of prisoners and the loss of eight men, including a Lieutenant Schmidt. Despite the ungrammatical rendering of the term, it stuck for obvious reasons. One newspaper imagined that the term fit because "the colored troops marched into battle laughing with a mirth that sent fear through Teuton veins." This characterization of blacks as gay and joyous killers is a traditional American representation of fear and dread projected onto an enemy. Even more telling is the *American's* somewhat pornographic rendering of the men as "easy striding," "lithe and loose-limbed," "flashy-toothed and somber-skinned," "efficient" killers. As for the French, Hayward said, "They judged men by their hearts and their valor over there and our men made good." Yet, the colonel not only commented on the men's valor and achievement under fire, he also spoke to their outstanding moral character, citing only six cases of drunkenness and only twenty disciplinary violations. In his mind, there was not "a braver or a cleaner lot of soldiers in the United States Army or any other army."[9]

Then there was the praise from the press, including a shockingly glowing account by the *New York Times* citing all the black combat troops for their display of "valor and invincible spirit" that they shared with the 1st and 2nd Regular Divisions, the 77th, 27th, 30th, and 28th. The *Times*, however, saved its greatest tribute for the Old 15th, which "had gone straight from a training camp near St. Nazaire to the battlefield." It even admitted that opposition to the Regiment's formation "now seems puerile." Postwar euphoria had changed the *Times*'s journalistic heart, and it affected its head as well. In a blatant disregard of facts, the editorial stated that "most of the regimental officers . . . were Negroes," which belied the old canard "that Negroes must be led by white men to stand the ordeal of fire and to advance steadily." The piece credited the 369th with stopping the Germans, which taught them to "class" the men of the 369th "with the dreaded French colonials from Africa." The *Times* relied on an account by Maj. David L'Esperance to lend substance to its claims: "The heaviest fighting was on Sept. 26 [Séchault], when we went into action with twenty officers and 700 men in our battalion [3rd] in the morning, and at the close we had seven officers and 150 men left. Our boys advanced steadily like seasoned veterans, and never lost a foot of ground they had taken or let a prisoner escape."[10] The *Age's* version of the major's account included the more fantastic claim that "the Germans became so frightened at the appearance of the Negro troops toward the finish that as soon as they saw them coming with the cold steel they would throw up their hands and yell 'Kamerad'?"[11]

Perhaps no one was more proud of the Regiment than the former governor, Charles S. Whitman. Never able or willing to accept the unit's federal designation or, as a seasoned politician, ever mindful of his audience, he still referred to it as the Old 15th. At a band concert in honor of the Regiment in early February, held at the 7th Regiment Armory, Whitman admitted that three years earlier, he "did not expect that you would go into the firing line, up to the front, and on to glorious, complete, and final victory." What impressed him more than their record as soldiers was that as men, "no soldiers acted better, not only at the front but on shipboard, in camps or villages or in the big cities. In all your dealings with other organizations, other nations and other races you did nothing that reflected [badly] on your conduct, dignity or manhood."[12]Although only a few officers of the Regiment attended the fete, Whitman still encouraged the men of the Old 15th to join the New 15th as a way of keeping the original organization alive. Hayward, Spencer, Little, L'Esperance, and Holley Clark, all in attendance, were sure to pass that message on to the men at Camp Upton, who anxiously awaited their grand moment and the opportunity to reunite with loved ones.[13]

Only two days before the parade, the men received one more magnificent signal of appreciation from their own community. The *Age*—which, with few exceptions, had stood steadfastly behind the Regiment from the beginning—delivered its finest tribute ever. It called the return of the Old 15th "a triumphal epoch in the history of the colored population of New York." The *Age* accepted charges that it paid too much attention to the 15th at the expense of other "colored regiments" but replied that "the Fifteenth was made up of the men from New York and its environs who volunteered for the defense of the nation." In the process, they "were transformed from ordinary everyday youths to regular soldiers . . . within the sight almost of their neighbors." Once the unit was overseas, the Regiment produced a record that aroused "the pride of all the home folks" and "entitles it to all the honors the home folks can heap upon it."[14]

But the *Age* did not limit the impact and identification of the 15th to New York: "Its record of achievement and endurance has not only won fame for the organization, but reflects everlasting credit on the race with which it is identified and the city whence it came."[15] Even then, the *Age* sold the Regiment short, for it was clearly a credit to America, if not the human race.

The men of the 369th looked forward to a victory parade in New York, certainly none more than Colonel Hayward. In the spring of 1917, according to Arthur Little, a photographer had annoyed the colonel by waving in his face a picture of men in a disorderly recruiting parade staged in Harlem. The photo had the desired effect, but it also provoked Hayward's determination to see that a magnificent, disciplined column of soldiers would return some day to march in their stead.[16] Early in the Regiment's tour in France, in February 1918, Hayward had reminisced with his senior officers about forming the Regiment. He recalled his bitterness and despair during August 1917. The 27th Division, from which the 15th New York had separated for guard duty in New York and New Jersey, had its farewell parade in New York before departing for Spartanburg. The 69th had also paraded through the city as it departed. Authorities denied Hayward's application for the 15th New York to participate in the parade, and the 42nd "Rainbow" Division had bluntly informed him that the rainbow did not contain the color black.[17]

An enraged Hayward swore that "even if they won't let us parade with them in going away, . . . we will have a parade when we come home that will be the greatest parade, in one sense, that New York has ever seen, and I swear to you that we won't let any division have us attached to them for that parade." Once all of the subordinates except Major Little left the meeting, Hayward pledged Little to the same oath in case he himself did not survive.[18]

Soon thereafter, Hayward learned that plans for a parade were in the works. He expressed pleasure at the intention but requested that the parade "be before our men are dispersed," in order to accommodate some of the replacements who lived far away. Revealing why his men felt such loyalty to him, he argued: "It wouldn't be just right to hold a parade without all of us." The prospect of marching in a victory parade in New York sufficed to keep all but the most incorrigible members of the Regiment in line. Since the Armistice, the officers had used the revocation of marching privileges as a disciplinary penalty. Very few men missed the parade.[19]

On February 17, 1919, the 15th New York Infantry Regiment, famed in France as the 369th US Infantry Regiment, prepared to march up Fifth Avenue. Special trains took the men from Camp Upton at dawn to Long Island City, where they crossed the East River on ferryboats. They marched by battalion in a column of squads, heading west on Thirty-Fifth Street to

Madison Avenue and down Madison Avenue until the head of the column stopped at Twenty-Third Street.

There, the men of the Regiment assumed a parade formation that they had learned from the French and that New York had never seen. According to Major Little's description of the process, the men formed a phalanx by company, in which equalized companies of sixteen squads each, four platoons of four squads each, marched in close line without interval—a solid mass of men that measured about 34 square feet. Sergeants marched two paces in front of their platoons, lieutenants three paces in front of the sergeants, and the captain five paces in front of the lieutenants.[20] Battalion commanders marched at the head of their battalions. The band of sixty brass and reed instruments, with a section of thirty trumpets and drums, led the procession and reportedly eschewed the "syncopated beat of ragtime" for martial music appropriate for a victory march. Automobiles bearing about 200 soldiers who were too wounded to march, including Sgt. Henry Johnson and Maj. Lorillard Spencer, brought up the rear.[21]

At 11:00 A.M., the word arrived that state and city officials were approaching the viewing stand at Sixtieth Street and Fifth Avenue. Colonel Hayward ordered, "Forward March!" The phalanx formation provided an impressive display of coordinated power as sixteen men abreast, a seemingly solid mass of African American soldiers, marched west along Twenty-Fifth Street and turned north up Fifth Avenue to the music of James Reese Europe's splendid band. Fittingly, Europe began the parade with the French "Marche du Regiment de Sambre et Meuse."[22]

The Regiment was the first of the units returning home to parade through the Victory Arch at Twenty-Fifth Street and one of the few ever to march up Fifth Avenue. Arthur Davis noted that when the enthusiastic crowd showered the marching soldiers with flowers and even when the "multimillionaire Union League Club at Fifth Avenue" threw coins and paper money from the clubhouse window to the people below, "not a single soldier moved a muscle to so much as glance at the gesture." Although the soldiers themselves were searching for relatives and friends, Davis recalled each "remained the stoic that he had become through having laid his life on the line, survived and had triumphed over ridicule, deception, ostracism, and belittlement."[23]

The men marched north past the reviewing stand, which accommodated Governor Smith, former governor Whitman, Acting Mayor Robert Moran, Emmett Scott, William Randolph Hearst, Rodman Wanamaker, and other luminaries. They proceeded to 110th Street and turned west to Lenox Avenue. Before the Regiment entered Harlem, Colonel Hayward halted the parade and modified the marching formation from the impersonal, massive phalanx to one of platoon front, with substantial distances between front and rear ranks so that the inhabitants of Harlem could recognize their soldiers. To the tune of "Here Comes My Daddy Now," the 369th ascended Lenox Avenue to 145th Street. Women rushed from the sidewalks to embrace their men, and for the final mile of the parade, Little estimated that every fourth soldier had a girl on his arm.[24]

Henry Johnson, the unquestioned star of the event, stood in his car the length of the parade, waving "with dignity" to the spectators, who numbered in the tens of thousands. Even Governor Smith, aldermen, and high-ranking military officials held Johnson in awe. One can only imagine how this once-obscure man felt as he heard adoring fans shout for 7 long miles: "O-oh, you wick-ed Hen-nery Johnson! You wick-ed ma-an!" "Oh, you Henry man, you are some Hun teaser." "There's the boy that made the Dutch be good!" "Oh you Black Death!" The last invocation was followed by condolences for the kaiser's men. And for all the adoration he received below Harlem, it was before the reviewing stand at 136th Street and Lenox Avenue that "he threw the population into hysterics." By parade's end, wreaths and ropes of roses garlanded the immortal sergeant.[25] It was his one glorious moment in the sun. Yet, the near-neglect of Neadom Roberts, his partner in triumph, should have signaled to Henry how fleeting and fickle fame could be.

At 145th Street, the Regiment turned east to the Lexington Avenue subway, which they took downtown to Thirty-Third Street. There, they marched to the armory of the 71st Regiment at Thirty-Fourth Street and Park Avenue. Sponsored by the New York Citizens' Committee, Delmonico's Restaurant catered a "sumptuous" luncheon at the armory, complete with "chicken consommé, bread and butter sandwiches, sweet bread patties, chicken salad, tongue sandwiches, ham sandwiches, Philadelphia ice cream, cake, apples, bananas, coffee, and cigarettes." Perhaps for the first time in their unit's history, the men of the 15th New York had gathered as one under a single roof.[26]

The general public could not enter the main floor with the diners, but the soldiers' parents and relatives filled the gallery. Arthur Davis wandered the gallery trying to locate his two brothers, Spats (Hannibal) and Ed, in the mass of soldiers dressed in olive drab below. His lady friend saw a sash lost by some official, boldly put it on, and entered the main floor, much to his resentment.

Davis outdid his friend when he located Spats. He yelled to his brother and vaulted over the balcony to the floor below, without gauging the height of the drop. Fortunately, he survived the plunge. After the two hugged, they went to find Arthur's other brother and friends in the 369th and spent, in his words, "a most wonderful day."[27]

The men of the 369th had earned and enjoyed their triumphal moment. Arthur Davis believed the "parade was the beginning of an era that would open many new doors of hope for the black man." Major Little's recollections of the parade also indicate that it was a high point in the lives of those who participated. Little claimed to have heard fewer than ten consecutive bars of music throughout the entire 7-mile march through the cheers, applause, and shouts of the crowds—also described by the press as continuous and deafening. He even concluded that on February 17, 1919, "New York City knew no color line." The masses that welcomed the 369th, he asserted, "greeted us that day from hearts filled with gratitude and with pride and with love, *because ours was a regiment of men, who had done the work of men* [emphasis in the original]."[28]

Later, Davis recalled taking his mother, his sister Anna, and her baby to greet the two brothers and the sister's husband at the armory. Sgt. Hannibal L. Davis was officer of the day, and the "soldier's soldier" greeted them "most cordially." They asked permission to see brother Ed and also Anna's husband, Adolph Lynch. Sergeant Davis replied, "Yes, you may, for exactly five minutes. Pvt. Ed Davis and Pvt. Adolph Lynch are in the lock-up."[29] Some of the men had clearly celebrated too heartily.

During the ten days after the parade, the Regiment disbanded at Camp Upton, as men underwent examinations and officers completed and signed service records, did final payrolls, lectured and delivered farewell speeches, and finally signed the discharge papers for every soldier. Replacement soldiers from the West and South returned in groups to the camps nearest their homes for discharge. Everyone was in a hurry to return to civilian life. By February 28, the officers had mustered the soldiers of the 369th Regiment out of the federal service.

Arthur Davis's and Arthur Little's sentiments suggest that the parade filled black and white men alike with hopes for the dawning of a new era. They were not alone. Colonel Hayward called the parade "magnificent," an event that left him without "adequate words to express my appreciation of the tremendous ovation the dear old town gave us." His only regret was that Generals Gouraud and Le Blanc, "those splendid French fighters, who taught us all we know could not have been here . . . to share with us our triumph."[30] The *Tribune* claimed that the "heartfelt and hearty reception" accorded "their black countrymen" showed that "racial lines" had been "for the time displaced." The only color that mattered was "red," like the "blood they shed in France." James Weldon Johnson viewed the reception given the men as "proof certain of the regiment's popularity and fame." So great was the occasion, he wondered how those who opposed giving blacks full citizenship rights could have watched the men "and not feel either shame or alarm." Perhaps as important to Johnson was the potential impact of the men on supporters of black equality, who he believed now had to be more "determined to aid them in their endeavor to obtain these rights." The *Tribune* agreed that these men had played "a great part in upholding a civilization they hope some day will also be completely theirs."[31]

Undoubtedly, the awe-inspiring spectacle of a regiment of African American soldiers marching through the center of Manhattan to the plaudits of black and white crowds instilled in all present, to some extent, the realization that they were participating in a unique event. Unfortunately, notions that New York knew no color line that day and that the parade opened a new era of hope for African Americans obscure a deeper, darker, and far more complicated reality.

Despite the unquestioned grandeur of the parade and all of the hoopla surrounding it, both then and in the historical record, a closer look reveals that all was not as it seemed to be. First, astute observers had to notice that only one black officer, James Reese Europe, marched. Only because of his unique status as a bandleader did he remain with the Regiment throughout the war. His placement alongside the band, in the uniform of a combat officer, and not in front symbolized his anomalous and awkward position. Also noticeable was the absence of Mayor John F. Hyland, who did not interrupt his Palm Beach vacation to attend the hastily arranged event. Moreover, the city fathers failed to proclaim an official holiday, although the board of education excused all "colored children" from school.[32] Even more astonishing is that only the persistence of some black citizens who sought and won the intervention of the influential Rocky Mountain Club of New York made the parade possible in the first place and then turned a potentially mediocre event into the grand spectacle that it became.[33]

At the beginning of February, parade organizers lacked proper authorization from the War Department for the men to march. Realizing that officials in Washington were unlikely to act favorably on their request, black citizens petitioned the influential Rocky Mountain Club. Founded by and composed largely of mining owners and engineers, the club had close ties to the War Department through its support of relief efforts in France and Belgium. Its membership included future US president Herbert Hoover, then chief of the Belgian Relief Fund. Accepting the delegation's argument that the War Department owed it to the men to afford the people of New

York the opportunity to give them the "welcome entitled for services rendered on the battlefields of France," the club acted upon its "patriotic duty to serve all American fighters" and wired Secretary of War Baker on February 11, urging him to issue orders that granted the men a "timely and fitting welcome." The club asked rhetorically: "'They marched down Fifth Avenue on their way to France. Why can't we let them march up Fifth Avenue on their way home?'"[34]

On February 13, Gen. Henry Jervey, director of operations in the War Department, responded that "part of the 369th Infantry has been authorized to parade in New York City." To the delegation, the authorization represented a slap in the face of Colonel Hayward, if not an outright betrayal of the men and the citizens of New York. Once again, organizers appealed to officials of the Rocky Mountain Club to intervene. Recognizing that the scale and significance of the parade would be greatly diminished should only the remaining 1,300 men of the Old 15th march, the delegation urged that all members of the 369th be included. On February 15, the club's secretary, Herbert Wall Seely, wrote Jervey: "Would it be possible to have instructions issued in order that the two thousand comrades of the old 15th in the 369th, all of whom have served our country be permitted to parade up Fifth Avenue with them?" Seeley ended the communication with a friendly reminder about the club's service to Jervey's old Sunset Division. On Sunday, February 16, only one day before the scheduled parade, the War Department authorized the entire 369th to participate. In the words of the club's secretary, only then were Colonel Hayward and his men assured that they would "march up Fifth Avenue on their way home to the plaudits of their fellow citizens of New York City."[35]

Not all blacks found the arrangement satisfactory. A parade with only the 369th struck one black newspaper as another example of Jim Crow and not an appropriate tribute. With the 27th Division scheduled for arrival shortly after the return of the 369th, the author bitterly complained that "every sane and just person will agree that it would have been more fitting, more stirring, and more democratic for New York to have had but ONE parade, with her dusky heroes in the line of march also." Calling it a "second hand" celebration, the editorial did concede that the "Hell-Fighters," with an unequaled record attested by "French history," had fulfilled the biblical prophecy: "The first shall be last and the last shall be first." Yet, biblical reward could not overcome the worldly injustice of a "Jim-Crow affair" in which "our Black heroes were 'war-crossed' in France and 'Double-crossed' in New York."[36]

One need not rely on such an extreme, if not isolated, example of discontent with the parade to find evidence that prejudice and tension abounded, not so much among the spectators as among those who influenced race relations and policed them. No doubt, the city's press, both black and white, consistently lauded the day's events. Reporters praised the Regiment's troops across the board for their service, courage, record, and bearing. The *Tribune* referred to the respect the men had engendered among the enemy, although "born of fear and bitter experience." Still, that same paper undermined the dignity of the event and its participants with stereotypical representations of "an old darky woman" and "dusky arms" encircling "brown necks" with "lips" meeting "lips in all the abandon of a race still in the childhood of its existence." Even a "Chickn' Dinner" merited mention in the lead. Where there was stereotype, dialect was soon to follow: "Dishyeah has be'n sho' some day," one soldier told another according to the *Tribune*.[37]

Unfortunately, the *Tribune* was far too representative, as paper after paper offered images of chicken bones picked clean, "fat pickaninnies," "bronze-hued damsels," hypersexual young women clinging to their men like an opposing "football team" on a "half back," and mammy types looking as though they "had just stepped out of an old Southern print" or "old slave days." The press treatment anticipated the script and imagery of *Stormy Weather*, as confirmed by one black reader's description of a paper's coverage as a "hopeless medley of fun, jokes, satire" as well as "hyperbolical statements of facts" and falsehoods.[38]

Even Henry Johnson took his share of racialist flak in the form of playful nicknames, such as "bronze baby," "black terror," and "black death."[39] The *World* took the color references to another level, however, in considering Johnson "about as black as any man in the outfit if not a trifle blacker." Even more, the *World* turned Johnson into a pampered and privileged pet, who, unlike the other soldiers, felt entitled to acknowledge the crowd. The paper clearly reveled in portraying a man who believed too much in his own self-importance, as he "bowed from the waist down with all of the grace of a French dancing master" and "grinned from ear to ear and . . . waived his lilies . . . taking in (and liking) all the tributes that were offered him."[40] The *Tribune* even made light of his accomplishments, reducing them to a humorous scorecard:

KILLED

With rifle shots ....................................................2

With butt of rifle................................................ 1

Scared to death................................................ 1

  Total................................................................4

INJURED

  Knocked down with rifle butt (until it broke) ..... 12

  Stabbed with bolo knife ....................................... 10

  Knocked out with grenades ..................................8

  Kicked and cussed out .........................................2

    Total................................................................. 32

The scorecard's putative source, Pvt. George Jackson, concluded: "An, do you know, that boy was just gettin' fightin' mad when it was all over."[41]

The *American* went even further and introduced or invented "Buck" Manley, a comic figure straight out of coon imagery, to undercut Henry Johnson even more. A supposed buddy of Johnson's, Manley followed Johnson for the entire parade, serving as his personal press agent and employing call and response all along the way:

> *That bird Johnson slew forty Prussians with a rifle.*
> *That guy did away with sixty Huns with a machine gun.*
> *That hound Johnson slew ninety fritzes with hand grenades.*
> *That mastiff Johnson crumbled a clean hundred boches with a cannon.*
> *That hellish hell cat dispensed with 135 Kraut eaters.*

And when a "Harlem hero worshipper" asked what Johnson used, Buck exclaimed, "He done it with a razor! Ain't he the great bird?" When Buck repeated the claim and called Johnson "some bird," a voice from the din responded, "Some razor!" By the end of the parade, Buck had credited Johnson with "an even 150" kills. According to the *American,* one spectator observed that had the parade lasted any longer, Buck would have claimed that "Johnson killed the entire German army single-handed."[42] In a stark display of the awesome might of cultural hegemony, the very stereotype (coon) that the Regiment's record should have erased instead gained renewed strength by insidiously undermining that which negated its validity.

In a letter to the *Age,* F. Wilcom-Elleger responded angrily to the representation of a "type and class" that "is fast dying out." He pointed out that black people wanted "to be regarded seriously, and not taken as a joke." Not every black soldier went "crazy over a Chicken dinner," nor was every person in Harlem "excitable and hilarious, with uncontrollable emotions." Wilcom-Elleger, an ardent protector of the "race's" reputation and proponent of "uplift," went to great lengths to demonstrate the respectability and refinement of blacks in the Regiment and the nation:

Now it is a fact that a very large percentage of the young colored troops went from some of the houses of the best colored families in the country, many of them very well educated, and hailing from some of the best schools, Sunday schools, churches and other organizations in the country, influenced greatly by home and other social ties and obligations, and their influence went a long way in moulding the conduct of those not so well equipped. "Evil communications corrupt good manners" it is said, "and it can be equally applied that good morals influence and check bad manners."[43]

This emphasis on respectability shared by many black leaders would not bode well for the future of Henry Johnson or others like him, who became the victims of acculturation models for black progress. In such a construction, class and behavior, not race, determined worthiness. Unfortunately, the strategy backfired, as many whites used the condemnation by black elites of their own less fortunate brothers and sisters to malign the race regardless of accomplishment, morals, or material standing.[44]

The *World*, unlike any other newspaper, even made fun of the parading men and questioned their status as decorated heroes, in stark contrast to Arthur Davis's recollection of the men's absolute discipline. Note the following description of a brief halt at 86th Street: "If it were for rest purposes apparently the 'Hell Fighters' didn't need it. For they were mighty active in scrambling for dimes and quarters tossed from an apartment house. They might be heroes, and 171 of them might wear the Cross of War, but they had no highfalutin' notions about scorning the stuff without which craps cannot be shot and they grabbed it."[45]

Not only did New York's white press employ a heavy hand in racist stereotyping, it also seemed uneasy with the apparent lack of prejudice in the streets. Even in the process of praising the men, it obsessed about their color, calling them "dark-skinned warriors," "swarthy men," "ebony warriors," and "dusky marchers," thus reinforcing the racial markers and distinctions the parade reportedly erased. Likewise, the white press undermined the discipline and control it attributed to the men with constant references to their weaponry, expertise, and record as "blood thirsty black men." Reminders of police "checking" the chaotic crowd's actions contrasted with praise for the discipline of the men and suggested a fine line existed between order and chaos: "While there was bedlam on both sides of the street, there was the most complete discipline among the soldiers. Every eye continued to face directly in front" to the "rhythmic clump, clump of hobnails on asphalt." These men were at once impressive and ominous, marching with "helmet as in battle array, bayonets bristling, shoulders squared, heads up and moving with snappy cadence their feet striking in a martial step that sounded on the pave like the tearing of cloth."[46] The uneasiness is palpable in these representations, which implicitly expressed concern that such discipline could possibly challenge rather than uphold the status quo.

Perceptions of the threat also manifested themselves in distorted descriptions of the Regiment as a collection of looming, dreadful giants: "On average the regiment is made up of big men. With their overcoats, trench hats, and bayonet-tipped guns the impression of their bigness was heightened, and whole platoons seemed to be made up of men of 7 feet or over. Most of them grim visaged from force of habit when marching or at attention, and the helmet chin straps added a hardening touch, so New York got a pretty fair idea of how they impressed the Germans."[47]

It is easy to read into these descriptions concern with the transformation of "elevator boys," "waiters," "Pullman porters," "shipping clerks," and "apartment house janitors" into "bemedalled veterans," many of whom spoke French as overt evidence of their threatening cosmopolitanism. Those who wondered whether these men would ever accept the place they had occupied before had to view the spectacle with alarm, as James Weldon Johnson had predicted. Yet, this fixation on the external seemed a nervous response to unknowable internal changes. What they feared most was that the greatest benefit of the war to these men "was their revolutionary appreciation of social values" and a possible commitment "to act as an imperishable leaven on the mass of those who are still in mental bondage." These were men "trained in the use of arms, taught to walk erectly," and conditioned to value themselves "in proportion." Stooping would not come easily.[48]

The difference in coverage of the parades of the 369th Regiment and the 27th Division is startling. There, one clearly sees how the press naturalized whiteness and made it normative. As such, whiteness deserved no particular attention and elicited no lasting fear. Even reports of unruly, stampeding, out-of-control crowds among the more than 3 million people provoked no sense of alarm in the press's coverage. Whereas the press scrutinized the intense and hearty demonstrations of blacks, especially in Harlem, it naturalized such behavior in its reporting on the white parade. The *Herald* referred to the spectators as "a good natured kindly crowd impressed with the solemnity of the occasion." Even "joyous shouts for the returning heroes" were "tempered with a note of sadness and a tear for those who made the supreme sacrifice and will return no more."[49]

Also missing was the suggestive language and voyeuristic gaze cast at black women. A reference to "Salvation Army lassies" distributing doughnuts came the closest to risqué reportage. The disparate treatment of almost identical incidents reveals how the men of the 369th were disparaged: "At 59th Street guests of the Savoy and Netherlands [Hotels] showered dimes and other coins down into the thoroughfare when a lot of wounded sailors were gathered there. There was an immediate scramble for the coins and some 'Smart Alecks' began throwing down buttons. 'Cheap Skates' the sailors called them and said they were 'skins.'"[50]

To the press, the parade honoring the 27th Division symbolized the "might of the nation." "Millions" cheered the 27th in what the *Evening World* called the "greatest demonstration ever held in the country." It was simply "a day of glory" and "a day of memorial," celebrating sons both living and dead "who gave their utmost for the imperishable cause of freedom and right triumphant."[51]

Not only did the coverage differ, the event itself indicated that the critic who condemned the separate parade as a Jim Crow affair had a valid argument. This time, Mayor Hyland attended, and moreover, he led the organizing of the parade, which unlike that for the 369th featured extensive planning and considerable public and private resources. The names behind the event speak to its standing and meaning. Rodman Wanamaker headed the Mayor's Committee and was supported by William Randolph Hearst, among many other wealthy and powerful New Yorkers. The event cost over $750,000, an expense shared equally by the city and private sources. Some 5,000 uniformed police and 500 detectives ensured order and safety among the more than 2 million spectators and 27,000 soldiers. Even more, the US Military Academy at West Point sent 600 cadets as an honor guard. Secretary of War Newton Baker afforded the cadets this rare honor and privilege "because he believed the sight of the returning veterans would give the future officers of the army an unusual inspiration." The Boy Scouts had served as the honor guard at the parade of the 369th.[52]

As for entertainment, the Mayor's Committee arranged for the soldiers of the 27th Division to attend any one of seventeen Broadway shows. Following their parade, the men of the 369th enjoyed a night of boxing, singing, and vaudeville acts. The treatment of the officers of the 27th Division only exaggerated the disparities. The Biltmore Hotel served as the division's headquarters. Further, the Mayor's Committee hosted a gala dinner for General O'Ryan and his officers at the Waldorf-Astoria. O'Ryan received a giant American flag as a gift and Mrs. O'Ryan a "love-knot pin set with rubies, sapphires, and diamonds."[53]

While the parade of the 369th might have made for a glorious day for the men and the community, signs were everywhere that hope for a new era might be misplaced. In 1918, during the middle of the war, at least seventy-eight African Americans had been lynched. The end of the war would only see race relations worsen. The military itself would set a terrible example. With the crisis of war behind them, those in the regular army who always believed that the creation of black combat soldiers and officers was a monumental blunder by the War Department now had a free hand to undo the wrong they believed had been done. The backlash began in Europe, as military officials prevented black American soldiers from participating in the glorious victory parade down the Champs-Elysées.[54]

This injustice led to subsequent charges that the War Department insisted that no African American soldiers be depicted in the heroic French frieze known as the *Panthéon de la Guerre*—in its original form, a 402-foot-long and 45-foot-high panoramic covering 18,090 square feet. Although rather obscurely positioned and unidentified in the original painting, two black soldiers do appear together. Research in the late 1950s revealed they are Henry Johnson and Neadom Roberts, despite the lack of resemblance to the men. A third black, Capt. Clarence Sumner Janifer, a surgeon and recipient of the Croix de Guerre, was added sometime between 1918 and 1927, perhaps, in order to represent African American officers in as safe a manner as possible.[55]

The inclusion of blacks in this work of art says far more about the French authorities and people than about their American counterparts. W. E. B. Du Bois saw the signs all too clearly and knew that the hopes for a new day were misplaced. If rights were to be won and lives protected, they would have to be gained through struggle. In "Returning Soldiers," both a call to "the fighting spirit of the race" and an attempt at personal redemption, Du Bois clung to his earlier patriotism but challenged blacks to fight internal threats with the same vigor: "But by the God of heaven, we are cowards and jackasses if now that the war is over we do not marshal every ounce of our brain and brawn to fight a sterner, longer, more unbending battle against the forces of hell in our own land." The soldiers had returned "from fighting" and "returned fighting."[56]

Unfortunately, the war contributed to extreme "religious and racial intolerance, political and judicial heavy-handedness and moralistic excess." Increased xenophobia, hostility toward labor, and economic hardships quickly translated into racial scapegoating, and black Americans across the nation found themselves under siege, from Longview, Texas, to Washington, DC. By the end of 1919, some two dozen race riots had erupted across the nation, accompanied by rampant lynchings and a new Ku Klux Klan.

Yet, the war and its manifold ramifications had changed blacks. In Chicago, where the largest and most deadly riot of the bloody year occurred, blacks not only defended themselves but also took the battle to whites. Black leaders worried that a "New Negro," more determined, assertive, and fearless, would pursue direct confrontation and risk annihilation. Whatever the tactical differences, most blacks had been influenced, if not transformed, by a war allegedly waged in the name of democracy and self-determination. That concept of the war, combined with the achievements of black soldiers and the anticolonial struggles of Africans, inspired some otherwise passive and unorganized blacks into organized political action and challenges to white supremacy until "the nation's white establishment" employed all the authority it could muster to quash such a threat.[57]

The postwar experience of the Old 15th/369th, its men, and the community from which it emerged speaks in both unique and representative ways to developments in African American life after the war. Unlike the officers and men of the 367th and even the 8th Illinois, the soldiers of the 369th never seemed to have played much of a role in the so-called radical organizations and causes to which many others belonged. The Lincoln Legion, for example, which was dedicated to improving the plight of the black soldier and correcting General Bullard's slander of black officers long after the war, was led by John Marshall of the 8th Illinois (370th during the war), and no names of former officers of the 15th/369th appear on lists of its officers or executive committee.[58]

Although the Regiment's attachment to the French might appear to have been the logical cause for the lack of involvement, that reason falls away somewhat because the 8th Illinois also had fought with the French, albeit under somewhat different and less favorable circumstances. What seems to matter more is that the 15th/369th had a largely white officer cadre respectful of and respected by its men. By the end of the war, only one black officer remained with the Regiment, and only five had gone with the Regiment to Europe in the first place. The fact that these men remained with the unit as long as they did speaks to their mind-set. Willing to accept a subordinate role and having grown accustomed to it, these men had been conditioned to integration and were less inclined to seek a more racially exclusive existence. Some of them committed themselves to the postwar survival of the Regiment and the fight for a black commander.

# 14

## Your Services Are No Longer Needed

### The War Department's Postwar Decimation and Denigration of Black Soldiers and the 369th's Fight for Survival and Recognition

The difficulty in obtaining War Department authorization for the parade and the press's disparaging coverage of the event clearly suggested that serious troubles awaited black soldiers and their military organizations. Among the first actions taken by the War Department after the Armistice were the demobilization and the disbanding of the black redesignated federalized National Guard regiments, including the 369th and 370th. As of February 28, 1919, the famed 369th Regiment US Infantry was no more. With such a tone set at the top, one is not surprised to learn that reports streamed into the NAACP headquarters about the mistreatment of black soldiers at Veterans Administration hospitals and about the harassment and physical assault of veterans by white citizens and law enforcement officials. Complaints even alleged that the American Legion, the proposed national organization of all who had served in the war, was not open to black soldiers and veterans. Worse, the NAACP reported that nine black soldiers had been lynched in 1919.[1] By the summer of that year, the nation erupted in a series of racial conflagrations in which the legacy of the war and its effects on blacks, especially males, would figure prominently. Unfortunately, the best efforts of the Pan-African Congress had come to naught. Sensing the potential for danger, the congress had hoped to capitalize on the lofty rhetoric, avowed principles, and stated aims on which the war had been justified and conducted by passing a resolution for presentation at the Versailles Peace Conference "proposing that the allied and associate Powers establish an international code for the protection of Negroes."[2] As many blacks would learn, the only protection they could count on would be that which they mustered.

Just how pervasive and institutionalized the fear of and hostility toward the black soldiers were came through in a deplorable essay by Hugh Wiley in the *Saturday Evening Post*. On March 8, within a month of the triumphant march of the 369th, "The Four-Leaved Wildcat" featured a fictitious but stereotypical character named Vitus Marsden, who lived by the motto: "I don't bother work; work don't bother me. Ise fo' times as happy as a buh-humblebee." As the story goes, this carefree, illiterate, and verbally chal-lenged clotheshorse, aptly named Wildcat, would rather support his sar-torial habit by gambling than working. Shortly after finding a four-leaved clover in a rare and brief moment of work, Wildcat learns that he has been drafted and must report for duty with a labor battalion. True to form and as his luck would have it, he manages to avoid work and does little more than sleep and eat while in training camp. Upon arrival in France, he is sent behind the front and placed in charge of a team of mules. One night, under heavy bombardment, the mules and Wildcat take off, not stopping until "the light of dawn dispelled the terror of the night." Wildcat unknow-ingly had entered "no man's land," which strikes him as misused farmland with its telltale barbed wire. He finds a saber and proclaims its value as a ceremonial article for a parade after the war. While flashing the sword, he encounters a group of surrendering German soldiers and mistakes them for "lost white folks" and offers them safe journey on his mules. Upon re-turning to French lines with thirty-seven prisoners, he is lauded as a hero and awarded the Croix de Guerre. Declared AWOL by the Americans, he faces a court-martial until the commanding officer reads the French reports and then awards Wildcat the Distinguished Service Cross, to which Mars-den remarks, "Looks a lot like a fo-leafed cloveh."[3]

Alice Dunbar-Nelson considered the piece a "pitiful travesty" and unwor-thy of comment except that it was the "the most dangerous and insidious propaganda against the Negro," designed "to minimize his achievements in France." She went on to cite the unfairness to the race in representing black men as "crap-shooters, ignorant of the commonest decencies of life." Even more galling to her was the "sneering slur on the gallant deed of Needham and Roberts (Henry Johnson and Neadom Roberts) in Flanders [actually, it was Montplaisir]." The war's most famous and significant act of black heroism and courage had been reduced to a tale of dumb luck, which Dunbar-Nelson considered "a slap at the entire race." What concerned her most was that the *Post* had been "one of our friends." Citing Irvin Cobb's "splendid tribute" to the black soldier in France, she at once expressed her appreciation for the publication's past record and urged the magazine's editor, George Horace Lorimer, to refuse to publish any more stories like Wiley's.[4] Far more than protests such as Dunbar-Nelson's, however, would be needed to stem the flow of racist vitriol and its physical manifestations.

Fortunately, the political and racial climate in New York appeared more respectful. Although the slurs of a Wiley might be hurtful, they would not prove fatal for the 369th. The record they had established might be easily overlooked and denigrated by those outside New York, but it had been too widely publicized from within to be reversed. Even more, the presence of the 15th New York Guard during and after the war afforded some men of the 369th the potential at least for continued or renewed association with a military organization. On the surface, New York authorities gave every indication after the parade that they would try their best to accommodate the men in ways that they deserved in light of their able performance under fire. Since the state had taken so much credit for the outcome, it was now obligated to find a permanent place for the men in its own National Guard. At a reception held in honor of the Regiment on February 23, 1919, only days after the parade, former governor Whitman admitted that "he never realized the standard he had presented would be later carried to the front in war and on to victory." He applauded these soldiers' bravery, fearlessness, and loyalty and the way in which they had acquitted themselves as men and "vindicated the confidence of the people of the State." Holding them up as examples of the highest morals and character, the former governor claimed that in all their dealings across national and racial lines, they had committed no act that reflected badly "on the character, dignity, and manhood of your regiment." Expressing the fears that pervaded city, state, and nation, Whitman, according to the *Times,* urged the members of the Regiment to continue to demonstrate their mettle by fighting for good citizenship and law and order at home.[5] Perhaps he should have given the French credit for treating the men as men and eliciting from them what they had given. The lack of radical political activism on the part of the 15th after the war suggested that the just treatment accorded them by foreigners did not "spoil" these men but engendered their respect and gratitude. Finding a permanent military organization for them would go a long way toward preserving that goodwill and channeling their training, experience, and loyalty constructively.

In this Republican-dominated affair with its lingering residue of xenophobia, Charles W. Anderson spoke to the unquestioned loyalty of blacks who knew "no other country and love no other flag." Apparently without a tinge of self-consciousness, Anderson linked the fight against the Germans to one against prejudice. The Reverend William Brooks—chaplain of the Old 15th New York National Guard and now its offshoot, the 15th New York Guard—spoke more forcefully and less ambiguously about what the men fought for and deserved in return: "If the colored men had been found to be worthy of wearing the same uniform as the white man he surely was entitled to equal treatment as a citizen."[6]

At a more practical level, the acting mayor, Robert L. Moran, promised to use his influence as a city official and member of the Armory Board to obtain a proper home for the soldiers. He assured them that the entire city sympathized with the efforts of the Regiment to secure suitable facilities.[7] The question was what regiment and under what auspices, considering the fact that the 369th no longer existed and the New 15th was still only a home guard despite the fact that many returning veterans had joined it. One year later, notwithstanding the lofty promises, the Regiment, which still no longer existed officially, was no closer to having a permanent home. The delay prompted Alderman Charles H. Roberts of the Twenty-Seventh District to petition the Armory Board for prompt and favorable action. In the absence of any progress, Roberts, joined by members of the Board of Aldermen as well as former commander William Hayward, Col. William Jay Schieffelin, and numerous members of the New 15th, met publicly with the Armory Board and made their case. Hayward argued for the morale benefits to the men and the support of the community that such a facility would bring. The current commander, Colonel Schieffelin, offered more details about the lack of space for equipment and drills and seconded Hayward's assessment of the potential benefits to the Regiment and the people of Harlem. The leaders and supporters of the armory movement had a powerful friend on the Armory Board in Alderman Fiorello La Guardia, the future congressman and New York mayor. On June 22, 1922, the New York City Board of Estimate appropriated $350,000 for the drill shed and opened bids for the armory's construction. The total cost was estimated at $750,000. In early February 1922, Mayor John F. Hylan signed the contracts, and construction began shortly thereafter.[8]

Regrettably but all too predictably, the policies and actions of the national government clearly revealed that it did not share Brooks's view and had no intention of altering the status quo. Without its support, the Regiment could not regain its federal recognition. The proposed facility appeared to be a home in search of a regiment. Much has been made of individual and collective attacks by citizens and local authorities upon black veterans and civilians alike after the war. Yet, few have commented upon how the nation's highest offices and officials contributed to an atmosphere that made such assaults expected and virtually acceptable. From the segregation they encountered aboard returning ships to their exclusion from hostess houses at one of the major demobilization and discharge centers, Camp Upton in New York, black soldiers soon realized that their service had not improved their status or increased their rights. Now, however, their high expectations for change, based on their unquestioned sacrifice, certainly made such treatment far less tolerable than it might have been before.[9] The Great Migration had helped to create the climate for the emergence of the New Negro, and the war had produced its shock troops, characterized, according to the *Messenger,* by "stiffened back bone, dauntless manhood, defiant eye, steady hand, and a will of iron."[10]

Despite protests from soldiers, leading citizens, and the press against the treatment of the soldiers, the defaming of and onslaught against them only intensified as time passed. Col. Allen Greer, formerly the 92nd Division's chief of staff and author of the infamous defamatory letter of December 6, 1918,[11] sought policy changes regarding the future use and role of black soldiers in accordance with his devastatingly negative conclusions about their worth as combatants, let alone officers. From his new position on the staff of the adjutant general in Washington, a sure sign that he acted with the approval and direction of his superiors, Greer sent a circular letter to high-ranking officers and military officials requesting their "views on the policy to be adopted by our Country in the use of colored men in the Army." Any semblance of objectivity in the questionnaire itself was belied by the final question, which led the respondent to consider race from a "practical and actual standpoint" rather than "a theoretical one."[12]

How Greer identified his contacts cannot be determined from the available evidence, but he certainly knew that some of them shared his strongly held views on the subject. One such respondent was George H. McMaster, an infantry colonel who had served twelve years with the 24th Regiment and had prepared a critical report of his own in 1913 with the assistance of Gen. Robert Lee Bullard and Col. James A. Moss. The report described the difficulties of commanding black troops, and as McMaster put it, further developments, such as the Houston riots, "have seemed to justify my observations." His experience as an assistant inspector general of the 1st Army, followed by a brief stint as commander of the 365th Regiment, led him to the conclusion that blacks were "unfitted" to be combat soldiers except "in shock of short duration, under close supervision of and in immediate personal touch with white superiors."[13]

McMaster went on to state that blacks were least suited for the infantry and best suited as labor and pioneer troops. Needless to say, he considered the colored officer "a failure in modern warfare, a fact that cannot [be] cam-ouflaged by exceptions nor by the heroic exploits and sacrifices of individ-uals." In his twisted logic, the exception only proved the rule that "the col-ored officer shows little capacity for leadership, aggression, or originality." Predictably, McMaster repeated the old canard that under the "spiritual and terrific physical strain of the modern battlefield the colored soldier prefers the white man as his leader." Yet, his real aversion to blacks as officers, one privately embraced by so many others in and out of the military, concerned a "disturbing element bent upon social equality, and bent upon using this war as leverage to change conditions in America—the conditions affecting the races." Interestingly, after making this point, McMaster moved on to a discussion of rape allegations against black soldiers, the advances of these men toward Red Cross nurses, and black officers' demands that they be housed on a homeward-bound ship by rank and not race. For their insis-tence on respect for rank, McMaster had the officers arrested. The *Age* con-demned the action and characterized McMaster as a southerner of "the old school with all its old traditions."[14] Unfortunately, those ways were far too often national ways.

Another respondent, Brig. Gen. Malvern-Hill Barnum, disagreed with McMaster on virtually every point. He forcefully argued that blacks should be judged on actual performance and conditions and not on prejudice, and he even supported blacks as officers. Moreover, he opined that the "race question should not enter into the discussion except that the white race should help the colored race in every way possible." Strangely, the typed let-ter ends with a scripted afterthought, perhaps in the author's own hand, stat-ing that the "possible" should not include "social mixing."[15] On this point, Barnum might have shown that North and South alike seemingly agreed on the subject of French women and Red Cross nurses and black men. Barnum and McMaster had common understandings of the true meanings and real fears associated with "social equality" and "social mixing." The "whispering gallery" that Robert Russa Moton described as spreading false and malicious rumors about the propensity for rape among black soldiers could not be quieted, no matter how much evidence existed to the contrary.[16]

The *New York Age* saw these moves in Washington as evidence of a "con-spiracy to deprive the race of the rightful position it has earned as a fighting factor." Citing the combat records of the 24th and 25th Regiments, the 9th and 10th Cavalries, and the 92nd and 93rd Divisions as well as the artillery at Camp Lacoutine, the *Age* concluded that nothing short of a congressio-nal investigation and a reorganization of the military on the basis of a fair deal would do justice. In the meantime, it hoped for a black division, even as the army looked for ways of reducing or effectively eliminating the four existing black regiments.[17]

This absolute betrayal of trust stirred ordinary black citizens into action. One such concerned individual, Henry E. Baker of Washington, DC, took the matter directly to General Pershing and asked that he counter "the odium upon the record of the colored soldier" by making "some specific reference to the general character of the military service rendered by [them]" in the war. After all, Secretary of War Newton Baker had presented official records to challenge the discrediting of these men. Pershing could do even more in his official report on the war. Instead, he had his senior aide, Col. George Catlett Marshall, inform Henry Baker that "in his report he pays a tribute to all American troops and does not consider it appropriate to make special reference to any particular race."[18] This was undoubtedly a lesson not lost on the future army chief of staff, who would be expected to continue the racist traditions of his teachers and sponsors.

In this hostile climate, there seemed little cause to believe that the 369th would regain its status as a federally recognized National Guard unit, despite its long and distinguished service on the front, a contribution that the French—unlike the Americans—recognized, appreciated, and rewarded. Even the latter, however, quietly and reluctantly admitted the Regiment's outstanding and perhaps unprecedented combat service, when General Pershing officially acknowledged that the unit was entitled to four Silver Bands for its actions in the Champagne-Marne defensive, Aisne-Marne offensive, Meuse-Argonne offensive, and the Thur Sector, Vosges, campaign.[19] The Silver Band, attached to the pike of the standard, lists the names and dates of battles in which regiments or battalions have engaged. The term *battle* itself carried specific and grave meaning in the context of the Silver Band. According to the Department of Army regulations in 1917:

> Battles are important engagements between independent armies in their own theaters of war, in contradistinction to conflicts in which but a small portion of the opposing forces are actually engaged, the latter being called, according to their nature, affairs, combats, skirmishes, and the like. A battle has for its object the determination of important questions of policy or strategy; an engagement may be partial, yet if it tends to these ends, it is also entitled to the dignity of being termed a battle.[20]

Yet, after all it had accomplished and sacrificed during the war, the Regiment's orphan status was never more evident or more debilitating during postwar demobilization and reorganization. The unit had never been accepted as an organic part of the New York National Guard. In Europe, it became part of a division that existed only on paper. On the front, it served with and as part of the French army. When the war ended, so did the Old 15th and its federal successor, the 369th. The only 15th Regiment in existence after the war was the 15th New York Guard, which was strictly a state organization under the complete control of the governor and his military aides and totally without federal recognition, standing, or benefits. Even more, it could not as such ever see combat abroad. Without any other military organization to attach themselves to, many of the local veterans joined the state Guard. Most prominent among them was Charles Fillmore, who still clung to a dim hope of becoming the regiment's first black commanding officer.[21]

His superior, William Jay Schieffelin, had been appointed to the post on July 30, 1918, by Governor Whitman. Schieffelin represented the best and the worst of the old militia tradition, when the richest and most-connected dominated the officer ranks. His mother was the great-granddaughter of John Jay, the first chief justice of the Supreme Court. His father's family had settled in America before the Revolution. It counted the Vanderbilts among its kin as well. Schieffelin headed the family pharmaceutical business, W. H. Schieffelin and Company, which transformed itself into one of the largest liquor importers in the country. Although Schieffelin was a veteran of the 7th Regiment and served as regimental adjutant in the 12th New York during the Spanish-American War, what led to his appointment as colonel were his political connections, civic activism, and involvement in "Negro welfare." A staunch opponent of Tammany Hall, Schieffelin led the Citizens Union of New York and crusaded for good government. His involvement with Booker T. Washington and various black causes convinced Governor Whitman that Schieffelin, a friend if not a father figure, had the experience and the willingness to lead a black military unit while garnering the acceptance of those he would command.[22] The appointment demonstrated that no one, including the governor, would entrust the command of a black regiment to one of its own. Although the highest-ranking black officer at the time and the Old 15th's first black officer, Maj. Vertner Tandy, seemed to have accepted the appointment in stride, things changed when the original 15th returned from the war. Charles Fillmore, the man who many hoped would go away, received a promotion to lieutenant colonel and stood second in command.[23] Whether given as reward or appeasement, the new rank and high position would not ease his resentment at the continued slights to him and his race. Neither did they diminish his commitment to correcting these injustices. No matter what one might think of Fillmore or attribute to him, his years of dedicated and courageous service at home and abroad and the fact that he was awarded a Croix de Guerre certainly gave him every right to protest his subordinate role.

Despite the presence of Schieffelin at the head, the veterans of the Old 15th/369th made clear to authorities that they expected a regiment of blacks from top to bottom. Knowing the political stakes, Assemblyman Martin J. Healy of the 19th Manhattan District introduced a bill "creating a colored regiment of infantry in New York City to be officered by colored men." The measure provided that the adjutant general would organize and equip the regiment to become part of the National Guard. Moreover, any member of the regiment who served overseas would be eligible for a commission, irrespective of length of time in active service.[24] Such a proposal was bound to produce much opposition, especially within the National Guard at the state and federal level. Nonetheless, many returning veterans of the 369th positioned themselves for such an eventuality by joining the "home guard" (the 15th NYG). Among those to hold commissions in the New 15th were Captains George Lacy, D. Lincoln Reid, and Chauncey Hooper; First Lieutenants DeForest D. Johnson and Benedict Cheeseman; and Second Lieutenants Raymond B. Wright, Francis E. Mikell, and William W. Chisum.[25] After serving abroad with such distinction, neither Fillmore nor the men would be satisfied with anything less than federal recognition. But if the state National Guard leadership opposed black command, the War Department and the Congress had no desire to see black officers and men return to anything approaching the role they had played during the war. Even if the unit reconstituted as a combat regiment, it could not expect to integrate the sacrosanct division unit. Thus, not only would the regular army be subject to reorganization, so too would the National Guard and the US Army Reserves.

Military officials and officers held fast to the belief that the division, the central organizational military unit, had to remain racially pure. They considered it "the smallest, self-contained, homogeneous and complete fighting unit." As such, it was a small army in itself, with some 27,000 men. According to the experts, the war had proven that the division "must be our basic tactical unit for war operations." The men of a division not only fought together, they also lived, ate, slept, and often died together. Conventional wisdom held that the inclusion of blacks in these conditions would create friction and lack of cooperation and impair the efficiency of operations.[26]

No matter how much each war proved to the nation that the military was woefully underprepared to engage in modern combat and needed to organize and utilize available manpower more effectively, race almost always transcended military imperatives. Irrespective of the stated objectives, military victory against foreign foes never superseded the deep-set need to maintain the racial status quo at home. Even a reorganized regular army, National Guard, and US Army Reserves carefully measured military preparedness against racial order. With the four black regular army regiments under siege, the greatest opportunity for black service rested with the National Guard. All too aware of this prospect, the War Department formulated a plan that allowed for little, if any, meaningful role for blacks in the new National Guard.

The War Department maintained that the recent conflict had proven the United States should not organize more than sixteen (soon expanded to eighteen) divisions from voluntary enlistment in the National Guard. A fundamental principle of the National Defense Act of 1920 was the "localization of units."[27] To this end, the department divided the country into divisional districts. New York, Pennsylvania, Ohio, and Illinois individually represented a district. The other fourteen divisional areas would comprise from two to six (and possibly more) different states, contiguous to each other. No black regiment or battalion could be an organic part of any of these divisions, including those in New York and Illinois, the homes of the 369th (15th) and the 370th (8th), respectively. The department held that organizing a complete division entirely of blacks "would be manifestly impracticable" because "its elements would be scattered all over the [country]," to say nothing about the virtual improbability that "efficient organizations of the different arms could be organized."[28] The War Department pointed to the fate of the geographically diverse 42nd, better known as the Rainbow Division, as evidence of the fair application of the policy.[29]

Where, then, did such a scheme leave blacks? Even the War Department did not dare to eliminate them totally from consideration. Instead, they would be granted separate and unequal status as a corps unit attached to Corps Headquarters for the purposes of supporting the work of the divisions. These units would be classified as Pioneer Infantry, not technically combat forces. The Pioneer troops, not exclusively black, emerged during World War I to work under the direction of the Engineers to build roads, bridges, gun emplacements, and camps "within the sound of guns." One of their officers reportedly remarked that the Pioneers "did everything the Infantry was too proud to do, and the Engineers too lazy to do." They received standard infantry training in order to defend themselves, but few documented instances of Pioneers using their weapons exist.[30]

A. W. Lynch of the *Philadelphia American* was among many in the black community to question and condemn the plan. In response, the chief of the Militia Bureau, Maj. Gen. J. McI. Carter, assured the influential editor that "there is no derogation of dignity in assigning any man or body of men to a Pioneer Infantry regiment," for the "service is exactly as honorable and valuable as that of any other arm of the service." Even more disingenuously, Secretary of War Baker shortly thereafter described the Pioneers as essentially "standardized" Infantry companies and nothing like the "labor battalions or stevedore regiments of colored personnel which were organized during the World War." General Carter unconvincingly added that the absence of machine-gun companies mostly distinguished the Pioneers from the regular Infantry.[31]

W. E. B. Du Bois, perhaps reflective of his ambiguous role and ambivalent feelings during the war, timidly requested information from Secretary of War Baker in light of several reports that the department had reached a decision about "Negroes in the militia." Wanting to be sure of his facts, Du Bois asked what effect the decision would have on troops in the Massachusetts militia as well as the 8th Illinois and the 15th New York National Guard (in reality, no such entity existed at the time). Avoiding any specific reference, let alone an explicit answer, to Du Bois's questions about the future of the units in Massachusetts, Illinois, and New York, Baker elaborated on the department's official position and concluded that the decision had nothing to do with discrimination and everything to do with "military efficiency."[32]

Others, such as James C. Waters of Hyattsville, Maryland, a self-described "special agent" and attorney-at-law with the New York and Washington firm of Wilson and Waters, questioned why the black soldier could not be used as he had during the war—in all branches of service. He called the Pioneers "a sort of bastardized boot-black-scavenger outfit" that was "neither 'fish, flesh, nor good red herring.'" Waters asserted the arrangement did nothing but give "aid and comfort to the gutter snipes who believe in humiliating and lynching the colored man in spirit or in body."[33]

Lynch found the reasoning even more reprehensible than the act and conveyed the "feeling of utter disdain and loathing" it caused him. More important, he framed his response in terms of citizenship and the enjoyment of "equal rights of justice" denied blacks only. Instead of blaming blacks for racial friction, Lynch argued that "a depraved and unreasonable prejudice" caused the friction, which a just government should "endeavor to wipe out." Calling his people "the most loyal Americans to be found among all the races in this country," he demanded that they be "accorded the same consideration in the new National Guard as all other races" that have, through military service, upheld "the principles of democracy which your department would now refuse to us."[34]

Evidently, pressure from blacks and, more likely, governors and a few National Guard organizations resulted in a slightly relaxed policy on the part of the War Department. On October 19, 1920, the adjutant general of the army informed commanding generals in all corps areas that the organization of black National Guard combat units was primarily a matter of state interest. The stated policy of the War Department still precluded the incorporation of "such units into the 18 National Guard Divisions, but requests from States for separate allotments to cover a reasonable number of such units will be favorably considered." For now, they would remain separate organizations, but in time of war, they might be combined in a division, thereby "perpetuating one of the World War colored Divisions."[35]

The modified policy seemed only to confuse observers, who now believed there would be at least one black National Guard division. The NAACP claimed to have received information indicating that the War Department contemplated "taking the colored units of the Federalized National Guard from the states of New York, Illinois, Massachusetts, Ohio, and the District of Columbia and forming them into a separate division." On May 20, 1921, James Weldon Johnson, NAACP secretary, requested confirmation from the new secretary of war, John W. Weeks.[36] Weeks informed Johnson that the War Department "had no such plan in mind at the present." The department did intend to pursue its Pioneer plan and at the same time consider requests from "states for a small number of colored combat units," which "were to be classed as separate organizations until they may be expanded and combined into a division in an emergency."[37]

Though the NAACP seemed to take a wait-and-see approach to the matter, the founder of the St. Paul (Minnesota) Afro-American League and editor of the *Appeal*, J. Q. Adams, condemned the War Department's actions as "fundamentally wrong," "unconstitutional," and "undemocratic." Adams argued that these were intolerable problems that the war "'to make the world safe for democracy' should have righted." He then proceeded to expose the plan for its blatant injustice and hypocrisy in every conceivable respect. First, it took the "colored soldiers out of their proper places in the states" and made "them a segregated part of the federalized National Guard." Second, it denied "them their rights as citizens of their respective states" and forced "them into a special segregated status" unlike that applied to other groups of Americans, including "other colored races." Adams concluded that such a policy excluded blacks from full citizenship and placed upon them "the badge of a pariah caste."[38]

The US Army Reserves fell largely beneath the radar screen because the branch had no history. Moreover, the War Department left recruitment of these units entirely up to corps area commanders, who, "in accordance with local conditions," would determine whether recruits came from "the white or colored population." Secretary of War Weeks made the dim prospects for blacks unmistakably clear in telling DeHaven Hinkson that the commanders "will undoubtedly be guided by the well-known policy, which does not permit combining white and colored troops in the same organization." Weeks's advice to Hinkson and, by inference, to all blacks was that they "fulfill the functions assigned to them in a spirit of devoted and disinterested patriotism." Although committed to the use of the nation's manpower "without respect to creed or color," the War Department had reserved the right, based on careful "professional study" and "the lessons of the World War, to assign citizens to duties which they are most capable of performing and will best develop the object sought."[39] In other words, they could take it or leave it.

Recent revisionist scholarship praises Woodrow Wilson's successor, Warren G. Harding, for speaking out against racial intolerance in Birmingham, Alabama, and undoing some of Wilson's segregationist policies. But the policies of Harding's administration toward blacks and the military appear to be just as bad as his predecessor's, if not worse.[40] The chief of the Militia Bureau, Maj. Gen. George C. Rickards, in an internal memorandum, revealed the real attitude of the War Department in his rant that "the numerous agitators for the formation of colored combat troops" should be brought to Washington and given the reports of the officers who served with black troops under fire overseas. Rickards had no doubt that the reports would "clearly establish the fact that colored troops have not yet progressed far enough to conduct themselves with credit under the terrific fire of the modern battlefield." If such protests continued, he recommended release of the findings to the press.[41]

With the victory of Harding at the national level, New York Republicans succeeded in ousting Tammanyite Alfred E. Smith and recapturing the state house. Perhaps dedicated to continuing the good work of Governor Whitman along these lines and recognizing the political value inherent in doing so, Governor Nathan L. Miller possibly encouraged the state's National Guard leadership in its effort to seek federal recognition for the 15th NYG. On April 15, 1921, more than two years after Assemblyman Healey's bill, Maj. Gen. John F. O'Ryan, the division's commanding officer, wrote to the state's adjutant general, J. Leslie Kincaid, recommending that New York request a "separate allotment, which would permit the present 15th Infantry (NYG) to be offered for federal recognition as a combat unit." Consistent with section 3a of the National Defense Act of 1920, which provided for the preservation of names, numbers, and designations used during the war, the unit would "be designated 369th Regiment Infantry for inclusion in the 93rd Division" in the event of an emergency—meaning war.[42]

General O'Ryan, evidently encouraged by the performance and record of the unit in the war, justified his request in carefully coded language. He noted that the unit was "in the process of reorganization under competent and experienced officers." These officers were, according to O'Ryan, largely white, and under them, he argued, the Regiment had "great possibilities . . . for the attainment of efficiency as a dependable combat unit." Despite a loss of strength in command numbers as a result of a recent change in leadership, the command impressed O'Ryan with its discipline and "excellent morale." His reference to the Regiment's location in a "populous colored neighborhood" spoke to the possible political considerations in his request as well as those related to order and control. He noted that city officials had already taken steps to build a new armory and that other measures were in place to improve the "administration, supply, and welfare of the present command." O'Ryan predicted that federal recognition would favorably influence "the large colored element of the better class in this section" and lead to the volunteering of "qualified personnel" in sufficient numbers to permit recognition.[43] Yet out of true conviction, he did not waiver in his steadfast commitment to the belief that blacks were incapable of military command. Although O'Ryan mentioned no names, he had selected his man—Arthur W. Little, who had returned to active duty with the Regiment on April 14, 1920. With Little's return, any chance that Charles Fillmore had of leading the Regiment evaporated. By May 8, 1920, Fillmore entered the ranks of the reserve list and left the Regiment.[44] In fact, Little had replaced Schieffelin as commander on January 4, 1921, some three months prior to O'Ryan's official request.[45] The timing reveals that Little was part of the general's original effort to fill the Regiment with white officers. O'Ryan's mission was to ensure not only white command but also a majority white officer corps, and Little would help facilitate that end and in the process engender considerable hostility from Fillmore and significant others.

On April 19, 1921, by command of the governor, the office of the adjutant general of New York forwarded O'Ryan's approved request to the chief of the Militia Bureau, J. McI. Carter.[46] Four days later, Carter wrote to the director of the War Plans Division and recommended acceptance of the request because an identical one had been "authorized by the War Department for the State of Illinois." Yet even approval could not assure full recognition, which depended "upon appropriations" and "the discretion of the Militia Bureau." Approval came from the adjutant general of the army,

Harrison Hall, on May 7, 1921, with the stipulation that the Regiment "not be considered for assignment to the 27th or 44th Divisions." On May 11, Carter wrote Kincaid that the request had been approved.[47]

Word of federal recognition and redesignation of the Regiment reached the public on May 7, as the *Age* ran a front-page story indicating that the 15th NY was to become the 369th and part of the federalized National Guard. In an attempt to assuage the feelings of many in the Harlem community who cherished the original designation and who regretted its loss, the *Age* touted the practical and symbolic benefits of the arrangement, which included federal pay for drilling and training and the right to display the battles in which the 369th fought on the regimental standard respectively. It pointed out that the men would even be allowed to wear a silver star on the sleeve in recognition of the Croix de Guerre with Silver Star the Regiment had received from the French. The citation, according to the *Age,* would make the members of the Regiment "conspicuous wherever they go," for no other New York military unit had one. But the article made the common mistake of concluding that the 369th would immediately become part of the 93rd Division and an organic component of the army.[48] Such an arrangement was most unlikely in peacetime. Moreover, the 369th would wait for more than two and a half years for official federalization. Conveniently and perhaps strategically, the *Age* omitted any reference to leadership. Maybe that issue was put aside in the protracted struggle to attain federal recognition.

Little, for the most part, certainly did and said the right things publicly to convince people of his ability, sincerity, and fitness for the job as commander of the unit. First, he proposed to city authorities new temporary facilities for the Regiment at 56–58 West 130th Street, which would relieve space problems for the Manhattan battalions. Second, he recommended consolidating the Brooklyn battalion (2nd), thereby reducing excessive rental costs and facilitating better command and control and organizational unity. The city quickly approved the proposal, and the Regiment finally had premises that could accommodate the headquarters; a supply base; the medical, legal, and employment bureaus; and meeting places for the Women's Auxiliary, the Veteran Corps, and the American Legion. Even more appealing than the space was the use to which it was to be put. Both men and community needed services, and Little vowed to provide them for securing medals, pension money, vocational training, war risk insurance adjustments, medical treatment, and women's work. In mixed tones of concern, commitment, and arrogance, the new commander made clear that his mission was not about charity and should not be construed as such. Instead, these arrangements were designed to instill "a desire for service in the National Guard by way of enlistment" and to train men in such a way as to make the Regiment "an asset to the city and to the state, instead of a liability as it is today and has been for many months." Little's plans for the permanent facility were even grander and included a recreational center for young children, a gymnasium and bathing area, a dormitory with 600 bunks, a community laundry, and a cooperative store. To assist in his mission, Little appointed an old friend and veteran of the 15th, Lt. Col. George F. Hinton, as morale officer. [49]

While in this state of recognition limbo, the newly designated but unrecognized 369th attempted to behave as a unit deserving of full acceptance. By mid-March, Little had the Regiment parading through the streets of Harlem in its first public appearance under its new commander. The *Age* reported that the men made an exceptionally fine showing, since "all the dead wood has been dropped" and only duty-performing personnel remained. The Board of Alderman president, La Guardia, reviewed the parade as scores of cheering spectators lined the streets. Little had no shortage of ideas to impress supporters and persuade skeptics. Whenever possible, he reminded all concerned of the 369th's French connections and benefactors, even to the extent of playing to stereotypes. For example, he paraded black soldiers of the governor's military bodyguard before former premier René Viviani in April 1921. The men were resplendent in their special French Zouave-style uniforms designed by none other than the colonel himself. The brown headgear was that of an Alpine chasseur. The jacket was tight-fitting and horizon blue in color and contrasted with the red knickerbockers, completed by black gaiters and stockings. The premier expressed delight at the "great compliment" the uniform paid to France. Little hoped that it would help recruiting. A man of his times, he shared the widely held view that blacks liked fancy, even flashy, attire. To be fair, Little also seemed to care deeply about his men and their welfare, albeit in the spirit and form of noblesse oblige. He even made arrangements with the Park Avenue Hotel to employ the regimental band for afternoon and evening concerts for the purpose of keeping this important morale-boosting and recruitment instrument intact but also as a way of providing income to musicians suffering "unemployment problem(s)." [50]

In addition, Little made sure that the new 369th stayed in the public eye and at the highest levels. Only a month after the affair with Viviani, the French figured in another public ceremony for the Regiment as Consul General Gaston Liebert offered poppies in honor of the 369th at a wreath-laying ceremony attended by 10,000 spectators. Even Civil War heroes played their part in promoting the cause of recognition. On the same occasion, Gen.

Nelson Miles reviewed the troops and presented a regimental flag donated by Lafayette Post 240 of the Grand Army of the Republic (GAR) and the Union League Club. Miles reminded all there and beyond that the unit had "lost 383 killed and 246 wounded but not a single prisoner nor an inch of ground."[51] The Regiment's attempt to impress the local population and the federal government continued in time and space.

On October 31, 1922, Arthur Little sailed to France to officially recognize a group of French officers, among them Generals Gouraud, d'Oissel, Le Gallais, and Lebouc, with New York's Conspicuous Service Cross. In addition, Adjutant General Kincaid requested permission from the War Department to authorize Little to confer to them the Distinguished Service Cross. Evidently, permission was denied, as Little only decorated them with the state honor on February 18, 1922.[52] In what appeared to be a continuing effort to make its case for recognition and to show appreciation to the French, the 369th honored Gen. Henri Gouraud in New York on August 13, 1923. Marked by gala events, including parades and dinners, the general's visit generated enormous favorable publicity for the Regiment and undoubtedly helped its cause. At a reception attended by some 2,000 people, Gouraud praised the 369th for its conduct and bravery on the field of battle and especially for its display of valor in the capture of the town of Séchault.[53]

Amid these high-level testimonials, the Pennsylvania American Legion surprisingly protested to allow blacks full participation in the new National Guard and US Army Reserves as a constitutional right of "equality of opportunity and unrestrained participation in every phase of activity of the Government." Nevertheless, the War Department had yet to recognize the 369th and had done little to open the doors to wider black participation in combat units. Although O'Ryan ended his active service before the Regiment received federal recognition, he had laid the groundwork in the appointment of Little, who was committed to carrying out his plan for a return to a preponderance of white officers. On December 11, 1923, Arthur W. Little, as commanding officer of the 369th New York National Guard, wrote the new commander of the New York National Guard, Maj. Gen. Charles W. Berry, requesting that he officially ask the War Department for federalization. Little understood that the department would not federalize the unit until the construction of the armory's drill shed was finished, but he hoped that everything would be in place for federalization by the expected completion date of February 1, 1924. What he needed were the resources, both financial and material, to be "included in the 1924 camp of instruction schedules." The new Regiment had reached full strength in December 1923, and the men had financed their encampment during the summer without any federal support, although the state did provide food rations. Not surprisingly, morale declined, and many feared the Regiment might be disbanded as the War Department cited budgetary reductions for the delay. Of the black units promised recognition, the 369th remained the only one to lack federal authorization. Pressure from high-placed Republicans such as Frederick C. Hicks, chair of the Eastern Headquarters of the Republican National Committee—citing dissatisfaction among the ranks and, by extension, the larger community—seemed to have the desired effect. On December 19, 1923, the War Department authorized "immediate organization of 369th Infantry (Colored) N.Y.N.G."[54]

On September 6, 1924, the 369th departed for training at camp in Peekskill. The trip probably brought back fond memories to many. Yet the fact that the Regiment went alone also reminded the men of their continued exclusion from the 27th Division. Other regiments trained as brigades of two regiments, but the 369th belonged to no brigade and remained separate and apart.[55] Such was the price of its recognition. Blacks slowly but surely came to the sad realization that they had possessed more power to make demands before the war than they did after it. Although they might have hoped for more, they settled for the best they could get. Put in context, this acquiescence becomes more understandable in that the 369th was one of five "Colored Organizations in the National Guard" at the time, two of which were companies and the other a battalion. As such, the 369th counted itself among the exceptional and fortunate.[56]

In 1924, the architectural firm of Tachau and Vought completed work on the medieval-inspired drill shed, which had nine-over-nine double-hung sash windows with brick trim embellishing most window openings. The interior of the building featured three tiers of balconies on all four sides and had a seating capacity of 6,000 to 7,000. The men finally had a suitable space to drill, although the administrative section of the armory, by Van Wart and Wein, was not completed until 1933.[57] On May 17, 1924, General Berry officially accepted the space and assigned it to the "369th Infantry (Colored) for possession at once."[58]

All involved had to consider acquiring an armory a great victory for the Regiment and its supporters. Moreover, the building was to become the most impressive structure in Harlem and an invaluable community asset. Yet, this facility came largely through state and local political channels, which no doubt saw the wisdom in appealing to the constituents of Harlem and enlisting them as allies. Although blacks in New York were appreciative, they sought something more—national recognition of the role of the black soldier in the Great War. A national movement had begun to memorialize these race heroes of the day, and New Yorkers wished to join it by honoring their own.

The available evidence suggests that the earliest efforts to establish a monument to the 369th actually began with officers of the Regiment shortly after the war. These men had planned to raise funds privately to erect a memorial in honor of those killed in the offensive that started on September 26. However, in response to an inquiry from Maj. X. H. Price of the Battle Monuments Board, Hayward reported that, despite his visit to France for the purpose of selecting the proper spot, efforts had not progressed past the talking stage. Nonetheless, all agreed on "the spot where a monument to our regiment should be erected": Belleview Signal, the bluff at the end of Belleview Ridge, "overlooking Séchault and visible for many miles along the main road running north and south from Ville Sur Tourbe to Vouziers, and being the spot from which we launched our attack, as well as the location of the regimental P. C. for several bitter days of fighting."[59] Although Hayward did not mention the monuments to the 371st and 372nd, they must have been a factor in the desire of his former officers to erect a monument of their own. The funds for these monuments had been raised by the officers and men of the regiments before they left Europe, and the rules of the game on monument construction would change dramatically within a few years.[60] The correspondence between Price and Hayward might have seemed promising, but the reality was far less sanguine.

When Major Price wrote Hayward again on September 28, 1923, more than a year later, the Battle Monuments Board had become the American Battle Monuments Commission by an act of Congress on March 4, 1923. At the request of the War Department, President Warren G. Harding recommended its creation as the office to oversee the erection of "suitable memorials to commemorate the services of American forces in Europe, and to exercise such control as possible over the erection of those memorials." Ostensibly motivated by the quantity, quality, accuracy, locations, and maintenance of existing memorials, the commission became more of a gatekeeper than a facilitator, and the 369th would suffer as a result of that development and perhaps the commission's leadership. Appointed to the commission by President Harding and elected chairman by the other members, Gen. John J. Pershing had proven to be no friend of the Regiment or, for that matter, the black soldier.[61]

From that point, Congressman Hamilton Fish, representing the Twenty-Sixth District of New York in the US House of Representatives, championed the cause. The man who had taken considerable pleasure in the dashed electoral hopes of his former commander now became the point man for leading the political charge for a monument to the 369th. In the process, old resentments between the two would erupt again.

On May 26, 1924, Congressman Fish formally "suggested" that the Battle Monuments Commission "provide for the erection of a monument to the . . . 15 New York or 369th Infantry" in the town of Séchault, which it had captured on September 30, 1918. Fish based his request for a special monument on the fact that the Regiment had never truly been a part of an American division but instead served with the French army. He admitted that his strong feelings on the subject and the justice of it led him to lobby for his own appointment to the commission in order "to advance . . . a simple matter of recognition of the splendid service of this regiment." Fish added that such recognition would extend to all "colored soldiers who served in our Army."[62]

On July 9, Fish received a rather vague and ambiguous message from the chairman himself, John J. Pershing. After acknowledging receipt of the congressman's letter, Pershing reminded Fish that the commission was headed for Europe "in the near future to study the entire question of American memorials and cemeteries abroad," and he informed him that the subject of a memorial to the 369th was already on the calendar of business to be considered by the commission at that time. Pershing told Fish that he had forwarded his letter to the other members, but he did not reveal what he had attached to it. The middle paragraph of the attached memorandum stated: "The question of a monument to this particular regiment is, of course, an integral part of larger questions to be decided by the Commission while abroad. It may be said, however, that a monument to this regiment is included in the project, which was submitted to the Commission by the Secretary of War."[63] As would become clearer shortly, the commission found a way to deny a monument to the 369th, despite a proposed addition of $25,000 to the commission's appropriation expressly for that purpose.[64]

Neither the justifications of Fish nor the operations of the 369th could sway the commission away from its insistence on a "stopping place" to prevent strains on "economy and good taste" that could result from "too many monuments in Europe." Thus, the commission "fixed this 'stopping place'" at the level of the division, it "being the smallest complete unit complete with all fighting arms."[65] To be sure, other regiments would be adversely affected by this ruling, but as Fish angrily maintained in a letter to James Weldon Johnson, secretary of the NAACP, out "of the 25 monuments to be erected not one has been assigned to the colored soldiers."[66]

Even before receiving official notification from the commission about the so-called stopping place, Fish had begun to change tactics. He planned to propose an amendment to the Independent Officers Bill for an appropriation of $25,000 to erect a monument to the "colored soldiers at Séchault in France, which includes the 369th, 371st, and 372nd Regiments."[67] Shortly after the release of the commission's decision, he proposed legislation for a monument to the 93rd Division at Séchault despite the fact that the 370th did not participate in the battle. Nonetheless, he would argue later that failure to pass such legislation would mean that the "93rd Division, with its unquestioned record for gallantry and conspicuous service will be the only American Division out of more than thirty that participated in the fighting to go unrecorded on adequate and suitable monuments erected by the government."[68]

Touting the monument as "the best possible answer to the slanderous attack on the record of colored soldiers" by Gen. Robert Lee Bullard, the NAACP mobilized its forces in support of the legislation. Yet, the fact that the 370th had not participated in the taking of Séchault and, further, that the 93rd Division had never functioned as such gave opponents of the monument movement a clear basis for opposition, and it also gave pause to supporters of the 369th.

The NAACP and Fish would be hit from all directions in their attempts to erect a monument to the 93rd Division. First, an organization called the National Memorial Association, founded in 1916, had been seeking funding from the federal government for the erection of a national memorial building in the capital "to commemorate the deeds and valor of Negro soldiers and sailors" in all of the nation's wars. Its president, Ferdinand Lee, believed that such a memorial was equally as important as a memorial in France, if not more so. It already had two sponsors for legislation in Representative William R. Wood of Indiana and Senator William B. McKinley of Illinois.[69]

As Fish predicted, southerners in the House attempted to block the legislation through filibuster, but Republicans burst the stalling tactics to allow a vote, which went 227 to 116 in favor of the bill. The bigger test would be in the Senate, where southern Democrats had perfected the art of the filibuster. Yet, before fully engaging that battle, Fish reported to James Weldon Johnson that his old nemesis, Col. William Hayward, "is finding fault with my bill." Fish sarcastically remarked that perhaps "he would like a monument to himself."[70]

Fish sent a blistering response to Hayward, who he believed was going back on his word and betraying not only Fish but the men of the Regiment as well as the others who would be honored by a monument. Fish accepted Hayward's concerns about including the 370th but saw no way around the ruling of the Battle Monuments Commission to recognize no unit smaller than a division. He pointed out that "several divisions have monuments to their infantry when they did not have their artillery with them." He urged Hayward to consider the "solid support" of the bill by the colored people and probably ninety of the Regiment's former officers. Fish could not understand why Hayward now opposed a bill identical to the one he had supported two years before. Moreover, the monument would list the names of all four regiments, thus rendering absurd Hayward's assertion that it would be "contradictory, inconsistent or ridiculous." Then Fish appealed to Hayward's sense of racial justice with the following assertion: "The very fact that the solid Democratic membership from the South was against the bill should rally the white officers from the North to its support."[71] It was a classic example of playing the race card.

Despite a valiant effort to mobilize support for the legislation in the Senate, the billed did not survive opposition in the upper house. The passionate yet reasoned testimony of Emmett Scott and others did not prevail, nor did appeals from prominent black ministers, black organizations, and the black press across the nation. Ironically, the southern opposition hid behind the ruse of being against the bill because it furthered segregation. On June 23 before a meeting of the NAACP in Indianapolis, Fish made what appears to have been his last public attempt to push his bill. Surprisingly, he revealed to his audience that support for the bill among blacks had been disappointing. Once again, he fell back on the argument that passage of his bill was a refutation of Bullard. All that he and his supporters asked for was "that the unjust discrimination against the courage and war services of the Negro soldier be done away with and that a battle monument be erected in France which will be for all time an inspiration to loyalty, patriotism and heroism for all the colored people of America."[72] Fish had to have known that many in the government, including some from his own party and the North, feared the very result he intended. The government's actions clearly indicated that the last thing officials wanted to do was encourage blacks' participation in the military, especially as combatants and officers.

Although the Military Affairs Committee of the Senate reported favorably on the bill by a six-to-five vote on May 28, 1926, there is no evidence that the measure came to a vote before the whole body.[73] The death of the bill in the Senate effectively killed any future efforts to secure a separate monument for the 93rd Division. In one of the great ironies, the 93rd shares with three other American divisions the Sommepy Monument on the crest of Blanc Mount Ridge, 3 miles north of Sommepy in the Department of the Marne. The monument was dedicated in 1937, the work of Arthur Loomis Harmon of New York City. Carved on the exterior walls are the dedications, insignias, and names of the American divisions that served in the area. Inside the tower, visible through the grid of the bronze door, is a stone with a brief description of the American operations in the area.

The units honored there beside the 93rd are: the 2nd Division, the 36th Division (Texas), and the 42nd Division (Rainbow). The last, made up of units from across the country, had once refused to allow the 15th to be a part of it or to march in its parade. Now they are forever linked on Mont Blanc, a name with its own ironic implications. The inscriptions to the divisions make no mention of any regiments. The one for the 93rd reads: September 26 to October 6, 1918/Ripont/Séchault/Ardeuil/Trières Farm.[74] Instead of a monument truly honoring the men of the 93rd Division, it is a memorial to utter hypocrisy, proving that integration is not always a good thing. The effect, if not the intent, of including the 93rd was to mislead, deceive, and obscure.

Before the erection of the monument at Sommepy, some former officers of the 369th, including Charles Fillmore, William Hayward, and Arthur Little, attempted to persuade the city and local authorities to fund the building of a monument locally.[75] Nothing seems to have come of the effort. Not until 1997, in an effort led by then Lt. Col. Stephen R. Seiter, did the 369th Regiment get a monument in its honor. Even then, it had to pay for the construction and upkeep of the monument after convincing the American Battle Monuments Commission that the presence of monuments to the 371st and 372nd Regiments in the area of Séchault constituted a great disservice to the 369th.[76] It was a greater one than Lieutenant Colonel Seiter or the members of the 369th Monument Planning Committee probably knew. Yet, the commission clearly understood the role of the 369th at Séchault and the attempt of the 372nd to take undeserved credit for it.

# 15

## Winning the Battle and Losing the War
### The Renewed Fight for a Black Commander
### and the Disfiguring Transformations of the 369th

As badly as the supporters of the Regiment might have wanted a monument in Europe or the United States to honor their service and as much as they appreciated a new home, they seemingly wanted a black commander more than anything else. This concern was an issue from the Regiment's inception, and it remained one after the unit's reorganization and federal recognition. In fact, the Regiment had a new home, but it would not prove happy for long. On January 21, 1925, the *Amsterdam News* ran a cover story featuring the armory, which it called NEW HOME OF REGIMENT MADE FAMOUS BY COL. WILLIAM HAYWARD. In addition to a large photograph of the structure, the coverage included portraits of Hayward and Little as virtual keystones of the building. The homage to the men could not be mistaken. Credit was given when due. Yet, there was much more to the story, and the paper tried to convey the complexities of race and the Regiment through the dialogue between images and words and the complicated and competing meanings within both. The headline above the images read: PETITION ASKS NEGRO COLONEL FOR 369TH INFANTRY. The Equity Congress, in which Charles Fillmore had played such a prominent role, had begun circulating a petition to be presented to Governor Alfred E. Smith to "use his authority . . . to cause the Officers' personnel of the 369th Infantry, N.Y.N.G. to be all colored men." The petition maintained that the original intent of the 1913 law was for an "all colored regiment" and that both Governors Sulzer and Whitman had promised "colored officers." The Equity Congress submitted that if there had been a justification for the present policy and practice, it no longer existed because the war had changed everything. It quoted Colonel

Hayward, who saw no reason why the Regiment should not be officered by colored men because "the situation is entirely different today." He pointed to the men who served as commissioned officers during the war and also to the noncommissioned officers, whom he described as "men of intelligence and now fully qualified to be commissioned officers." The Equity Congress realized that instead of improving, the prospect of a black officer corps had diminished, as had the plight of the individual officer. At the time of its action, the congress had counted twenty-three black officers and thirty-five white officers. The congress was certain that the departure of so many black officers was not voluntary. Under William J. Schieffelin, the number of black officers in the 15th NYG had approached fifty-four, with only two white officers.[1]

To remedy the rapidly deteriorating situation, the Equity Congress requested that "our boys in the ranks be given an opportunity for commissions," that those who had been asked to resign against their will be allowed to return, and that current officers be promoted. The congress nominated Maj. William H. Jackson for colonel and commander and Maj. Frank R. Chisholm as second in command. Jackson's military service had begun in 1891 with Company L of the 6th Massachusetts Volunteers and Chisholm's with the same unit in 1898. Jackson quickly rose from the rank of private to first lieutenant and served in that rank in the Spanish-American War as part of 6th Massachusetts US Volunteers. Chisholm also performed duty with the 6th during the war as a private but quickly moved up the ranks, becoming a second lieutenant with the 48th Infantry US Volunteers in the Philippines, where Jackson was his captain. Chisholm entered officer training camp nearly sixteen years after his honorable discharge, earned the rank of first lieutenant, and served with the 367th from November 1, 1918, to April 1, 1919. During the war, Jackson joined the 15th NYG as a major. Chisholm rejoined his friend and mentor in the 15th in May 1919 as a captain and received a promotion to major on July 2, 1919.[2] Their military experience certainly recommended these men for higher rank and possibly command.

Needless to say, the naming of these soldiers in such a public document put them in a most uncomfortable position. Within days, they and the others on the list to be promoted protested against their names being used in such a way. As good soldiers and men, they insisted that the Equity Congress's action was neither good for the Regiment nor good for the community. Despite pledging their loyalty to Colonel Little, not one of the men named ever took command of the Regiment.[3]

At the same time, Lt. Col. Seth McClinton, who had been with the Regiment in its infancy, resigned. Naturally, rumors connected the resignation to "internal differences" within the Regiment. McClinton vehemently denied the suggestion and cited the irreconcilable conflict between the great power and responsibility of being second in command of the Regiment, on the one hand, and a court recorder, on the other, even though he proclaimed the 369th to be "dearer to me than anything else in the world." Whatever his reason(s) for leaving, McClinton was reportedly "beloved by the officers and men of the regiment."[4] No doubt his departure left a tremendous void with all kinds of implications for the future of the Regiment. The question of his replacement probably loomed larger than that of ultimate command.

The community was, at best, divided on the issue. A few believed that black soldiers would not respect a commander of their own color and clung to the "crabs-in-the-basket" mentality. Some said they opposed Jim Crow organizations of any kind but understood that compromise was necessary. This position showed the fine line that Harlemites walked between racial identity and civic equality. Where would an all-black regiment fit in a Harlem that some believed should "include all classes of people"?[5] The fear was that a demand for separation would lead to alienation and neglect from the political and business powers of the city, state, and nation, who would be far more inclined to protect the interests of those in the majority as well as those who had political clout through numbers or resources. An all-black Harlem might have neither.

Others stressed the practical implications of black leadership from both sides of the issue. Among those supporting the cause, one observer astutely commented that the armory was not only for military and athletic purposes but for social activities as well. In that context, white officers apparently had little to do with the men or black officers outside of official duties. The reasoning went that black officers would be more likely to interact with their men socially and therefore be a factor for social uplift.[6] On the other side, some submitted that a colonel had to have money and influence, which few blacks possessed. Financial considerations had always been a deterrent to black officers and remained a very pressing problem. Yet the changing character of the Guard from social club to serious military institution and the growth of a black urban elite reduced the severity of the economic barrier for a few at least.

The *Amsterdam News*, however, "*unequivocally*" favored "the commissioning of Negro officers *from the colonel down* [emphases in the original]." While professing no quarrel with Little or Hayward, the paper opined that their time had passed and hoped for the day when black officers would march at the head of white troops, just as white officers led blacks. It refused "to believe that Negroes of New York State are less qualified to have a regiment officered entirely by men of their own race than the State of Illinois." Indeed, the example of the 8th Illinois (now the 370th) always loomed large in the minds of New Yorkers and prevented claims to the city's unquestioned supremacy as the black capital. The paper, for instance, even devoted the entire cover page of a second news section to the 8th Illinois. The textual and photographic history of the regiment, with its long and distinguished record as well as its stunning armory, competent black leaders, and courageous fighting men, served as a reminder of the many similarities and the one stark difference between the two famed units. Tellingly, one unnamed leading citizen questioned why a black population of 150,000 could have a regiment officered entirely by their own kind and a city of 250,000 could not.[7] Many had wondered about the same question for a very long time. The answer, however, lay in power politics more than in racial enlightenment.

Whether pressured from above or acting on his own volition, Colonel Little did not pick the highest-ranking major, as apparently required by law, to replace McClinton. Instead, he chose Louis Jallade, a prominent architect, who received his first commission as a second lieutenant with the 12th Infantry NYNG in December 1916. He eventually rose to the rank of major in February 1920 and moved to the staff of the adjutant general in January 1922. One year later, he joined the 369th as a major. Some insiders alleged that Little consistently appointed and promoted "untrained and inefficient white officers over their Negro seniors." He supposedly promoted "buck" privates to lieutenant within weeks of their joining the Regiment. Even more, some alleged that he "desired all white officers for the 369th" and that "his promotions and commissions were headed that way."[8] Tellingly, one of the original black officers of the Old 15th, D. Lincoln Reid, blamed Little for the wholesale resignation of black officers to make room for white men of wealth and black sergeants from the home guard. Particularly galling to Reid was the treatment of Lt. Francis Eugene Mikell, bandleader, who had to resign when assigned to a role for which he had no training as an officer. Why Mikell was not assigned the rank of warrant officer under the provisions of the National Defense Act of 1920 is not clear. One can speculate reasonably that he would rather have resigned than accept demotion.[9]

On March 4, 1925, the Equity Congress held a mass meeting attended by 4,500 citizens. After the call to order by Speaker Charles H. Bailey and the invocation by the Reverend Doctor J. W. White, the meeting took a patriotic turn with a stirring rendition of the national anthem followed by a poem written and delivered by Jeannette Halley, "tracing the history of the Negro as a fighting man and patriot from the time of Crispus Attucks to the World War."[10] Yet, the man the crowd had turned out to see was former governor Sulzer, who had signed into law the bill authorizing the Regiment. As noted earlier, some had placed Sulzer "in the class of Abraham Lincoln and Charles Sumner for his manly act."[11]

Although the law stipulated that the state "shall organize and equip a colored regiment of infantry," nowhere did it specify that the unit had to be entirely black. Even more subject to interpretation and manipulation was the language pertaining to officers: "The officers of such regiment shall be commissioned by the governor subject to the provisions of this chapter in relation to eligibility and examination." The law did not make a clear-cut case for black officers in part, let alone all. What the Equity Congress and its supporters hoped for was proof of legislative intent. Former governor Sulzer had already indicated in an open letter to the *Amsterdam News* that he had stated publicly "that the officers of the regiment must be the same race as members of the regiment." After witnessing the vindicating experience of the men in the war, he hoped that the current efforts would be successful. Sulzer reinforced the notion of intention not just on his part but also on the part of the legislature. Alderman Martin J. Healey backed him up on that point. In the end, Sulzer urged the citizens to petition Governor Smith, his old nemesis. As posited in the earlier discussion of Sulzer, his support of the black officer movement seemed more motivated by the desire for personal rehabilitation and vindication than by altruism. Speaker Bailey ended the meeting by promising another gathering and claiming that although some black politicians opposed the effort, the vast majority of citizens and the entire Democratic and Republican organizations of Harlem favored the movement.[12]

Bailey surely understated the level of opposition to the campaign, for he ignored serious divisions within the Regiment. Although the officers listed on the petition denied having signed it, an even larger problem threatened the movement—the resentment of black officers by some noncoms. On receiving reports that noncommissioned officers had petitioned Governor Smith to disregard the demand for black leadership, the *Amsterdam News* wrote that if that was true "God help them." After all, it was these men, "more than anyone else, [who] should be interested in keeping the door of hope and opportunity [open] to themselves and members of their race."[13]

The *Amsterdam News* hoped that the fight would not become a personal battle against Arthur Little, but as it turned out, Little ended his service with the 369th on April 8, 1925. He gave no reason for his resignation. According to the *Amsterdam News*, he brought the result upon himself by the "wholesale appointment and promotion of untrained and inefficient white officers over their Negro seniors." Despite Little's questionable record and the considerable opposition to his command, not all blacks supported his departure, for as bad as he might have been in some respects, many believed that others could do far more harm to the Regiment, including disbanding it.[14] In fact, as soon as news of Little's departure became public, leading citizens of Harlem of all political persuasions circulated a petition asking Governor Smith to reject his resignation. They cited Little's "important work of making the regiment one of the best in the National Guard" as the reason for having him continue in his position. In spite of this effort, Little did not return. But the man he had appointed second in command, Louis E. Jallade, did not succeed him and remained with the Regiment only a year after Little's departure.[15] The deal that Little struck with O'Ryan, to replace black officers with whites, made recognition of the Regiment possible but also sealed his fate with the black community and even with some of his men.

Despite the relentless pressure of the Equity Congress and the black press, Major General Berry's promise to consider the request of petitioners to appoint a black commander came to naught, as no one in a position to effect such an end seemed ready to do so. Least supportive was Governor Smith. Not until May 1927 did Smith appoint a single black to office, when he named Henri W. Shields, a Democratic alderman and Catholic, to a temporary commission to investigate defects in the law of estates. Clearly, with national political aspirations first and foremost in his every move, Smith would not risk a southern strategy on the appointment of a black commander of a military regiment. With a long list of failures on racial matters, Smith, according to the *Amsterdam News,* had not simply "ben[t] the knee to the South, but [had] gone down on all fours."[16] As expected, another white man, Col. William A. Taylor, succeeded Little as commander of the 369th on April 10, only two days after the latter's resignation. A resident of Brooklyn and a member of the staff of the inspector general, Taylor had the proper connections but reportedly was "entirely unknown to blacks." A former resident of Troy, New York, and a member of the Old 2nd Regiment, Taylor had served through the Spanish-American War as a private and attended Army Service Schools at Fort Leavenworth in 1915 and 1917. He became a director of small-arms practice at Camp Wadsworth and served with the 106th NYNG in France before his transfer to the command of the Division of Trains and Motor Transport. His mandate with the 369th was to make it or break it, as if the men were animals to be tamed or destroyed.[17]

Taylor's appointment began tumultuously. The number of black officers was at or close to an all-time low. Some wondered skeptically what the new commander could and would offer the community and what inspiration he could "give the young men of the race." Soon, a series of rifts in the Regiment emerged and widened. One seemingly pitted those who had served overseas against those who had not. The men who had seen combat chafed at the promotion of inexperienced white officers over them. Yet, even that group could not agree on the source of the problem. Many blamed black officers who had not seen combat for blocking their promotion. As they saw the matter, their war service threatened these less experienced officers. Consequently, they feared that the appointment of a black commander, especially from within, would only damage their chances of promotion.[18] A year later, a group of men, seizing upon the recent resignation of Lieutenant Colonel Jallade, issued a circular fixing September 27 as the date of a meeting to demand that "if we are going to have a regiment, let it be a colored regiment from the Colonel down and let it be officered by commissioned officers who have seen service on the field of battle." Colonel Taylor doubted the strength of the dissent and claimed that the protest was confined to a few men "who believed their overseas service entitled them to commissions." He also noted that "the number of Negro commissioned officers" had increased by 50 percent since he took command. The men tested Taylor's commitment by demanding that he replace Jallade with a black officer.[19] Although Taylor made no immediate decision, he clearly had something and someone else in mind.

Rumors had circulated earlier that John G. Grimley, known as a "Negro-hating major," would replace Taylor as commander. If true, the *Amsterdam News* predicted that would cause the most serious crisis in the 369th's existence, including the resignation of black and white officers resulting in the demoralization of the Regiment and its possible "demolition." According to reports, Grimley had refused to send sick soldiers to the hospital at Camp Smith because of the presence of white nurses. He reportedly told the Regiment's only black major, William Herbert Jackson, "what he would do to him if he had him in the South." For his part, Jackson publicly denied that Grimley had ever said anything of the sort to him, and he defended Grimley's record on race personally and professionally, citing the respectful relations that existed between them and the fact that Columbia Hospital, with Grimley as chief administrator, admitted black patients. Had Grimley said these things, Jackson assured the *Amsterdam News* and its readers, both men could have not have coexisted in the same regiment. Furthermore, he resented a rumor going around that, if believed, questioned his manhood. Going further, Jackson argued that such a story "can serve no good purpose; only tends to disturb the minds of and affect the morale of the men of this regiment, and lend false and unfair impressions to honest and kindly disposed people of our group."[20]

Despite Jackson's assertions, the *Amsterdam News* stuck by its story and maintained that several sources verified the charge as true, even going so far as to argue that the comment might not have been made in Jackson's presence. Whether Jackson was being the good soldier, was simply unaware, or was genuinely forthright cannot be determined from the available evidence.[21] What is clear and will become even clearer is that the internal politics of the Regiment were complex and unpredictable and in no way determined entirely by race. One can also safely conclude that Grimley, if not the "most detested" officer in the Regiment, certainly had his fair share of enemies. Although the rumors of Taylor's assignment as temporary proved untrue, the commander seemingly positioned Grimley as his successor by recommending that he replace Jallade. The *Amsterdam News* characterized the appointment as probably "the most unfortunate occurrence since Taylor assumed command." The paper feared that all of the progress Taylor had made to elevate the Regiment "following the demoralized depth to which it sank under the command of Col. Arthur Little" would be undone. The act brought into question the fairness of Taylor and left little doubt "that the 369th Regiment is to continue to be the stepping stone of the ambitious white men who are willing to trample the aspirations of Negroes under foot to satisfy their selfish desires for place and power." Not all saw Grimley's promotion to lieutenant colonel as a bad thing, since it prevented his command of any unit. Only in the absence of the colonel would he assume command.[22]

Despite the appointment of Grimley, who as a medic had no line experience, to such a prominent and telling position, Taylor seemed to have overcome the initial skepticism and gained the respect of community, press, and his men. Looking beyond Taylor, the *Amsterdam News* attributed the absence of a black commander, in part, to apathy among the black officers themselves. In early September 1926, Taylor made history—and friends— by turning the Regiment over to Maj. William H. Jackson for drill and review at Camp Smith in the presence of some 2,000 spectators. The act seemed less a publicity stunt or deflective tactic than a reflection of the commitment Taylor had to doing better than his predecessors, even though he soon removed Jackson from battalion command and requested his resignation. More important to observers was that under Taylor's command, several black officers had received promotions and a few noncommissioned officers had joined the ranks of officers as a result of the officer training school he had instituted within and for the Regiment.[23] Even charges of using Regiment funds to host dinners to which no black officers received invitations did not seem to damage Taylor's reputation among blacks. In the end, what mattered was his delivery on promises. In November 1933, Taylor promoted Wilmer F. Lucas to major. The promotion gave the Regiment two black majors out of three. Taylor predicted that a third would come soon, making all of the battalion commanders black.[24]

Unfortunately, Taylor abruptly resigned before realizing his vision. Yet he had set a standard that could not be easily undone. In fact, many credited him for the development of the Regiment to its "advanced status as a national guard unit" with field marks that compared favorably and in some instances exceeded the best of the leading white units of the state. Already assistant adjutant general of the state and US property and disbursement officer, Taylor long had been rumored for promotion.[25] His connections undoubtedly redounded to the benefit of the 369th and answered the questions of the critics who had wondered what he might offer the community, especially its young men. Even more than providing material benefits, Taylor, by increasing the size of the officer pool and the executive responsibilities those officers held, had afforded them an opportunity to disprove the critics who argued that "discipline would be slip-shoddy under Negro command." In tribute to the respect it held for Taylor, the *Amsterdam News* solicited testimonials from officers and citizens in his honor and "[shook] his hands with regrets." The Regiment's former chaplain, Capt. Alex C. Garner, praised Taylor for his fairness and uncommon ability to empathize with "the other man" or to "lose himself in the common cause." In the end, Garner credited Taylor with giving confidence to the men, dignity to the office of commander, and cooperation to the community. The Regiment responded by giving Taylor 197 pieces of silver as "a token of appropriate appreciation for his services, symbolic of the high esteem and regard in which he is held."[26]

To his credit, Taylor responded candidly, and few expected anything less. He admitted that he took over the Regiment with more than a little skepticism about the value of maintaining the unit in Harlem. The enthusiasm of the men convinced him affirmatively. He decided immediately that "the regiment would not be used for any codfish aristocracy . . . merely out for titles." Training, not social position, would determine advancement, hence the extraordinary rate of promotion from within. Moreover, he determined to ignore outside committees and political influence in the decision making. Military imperatives would dictate the operation of the Regiment. Yet, Taylor understood that as commander, he knew what was best for the unit. When advised to eliminate the 2nd Battalion by military consultants, Taylor threatened to resign if he was not given a free hand "to complete a good job." The advisers relented, and Taylor, with the acknowledged help of his black officers, created a "crack" outfit.[27]

On December 8, 1933, as expected, the politically well-connected Grimley succeeded Taylor as commander of the 369th and received a promotion to colonel. Surprisingly, the *Amsterdam News* did not condemn the appointment. Instead, it reasoned that Grimley had been changed by his experience in the Regiment and that through close association with Taylor, he had gained "sympathies for [Taylor's] plans." One of the first acts during Grimley's command supported the optimism with which his appointment had been greeted. On January 5, 1934, Capt. Clinton J. Peterson received a promotion to major and assumed command of the 3rd Battalion. Thus, Taylor's promise about having blacks command the battalions had come true, and beyond that, the day when there would be a black leader of the entire Regiment seemed close at hand.[28] Unfortunately, this first act might have been the high-water mark of Grimley's tenure.

The riots of 1935, although sparked by an incident between a Harlem merchant and a black youth, had root causes in bad relations between the police and the community. More fundamental still were "discrimination in business and schools, overcrowding, unfair rents, and 'inadequate institutional care.'" As historian Cheryl Greenberg astutely concludes: "The riot was, essentially, the raw expression of anger taught by political organizations" such as the Citizens' League for Fair Play, whose decline after the "Don't Buy Where You Can't Work Campaign" left a vacuum for frustrated and resentful Harlem residents to fill. The disorder sounded a wake-up call to New York authorities, alerting them that conditions had convinced some blacks that violence was the only means to change. One of the results of the violence was that the pleas and demands of more moderate voices suddenly registered on those who had ignored them previously.[29]

The Regiment, long a symbol of black pride and frustration, figured importantly in the struggle to win the hearts and minds of a beleaguered and outraged population. Its value to the community was more than symbolic, as it employed local citizens, provided members and families with services, sponsored athletic teams, hosted various events, and gave a few young men an alternative to the streets. According to the *Age,* the 369th was "one of the most constructive forces in Harlem" in its role as a training school for the hundreds of black youth in whom it fixed "habits of regularity." On the economic front, the construction of the armory's administrative building brought much-needed employment opportunities to Harlem residents, despite the fact that work went only to those who gave kickbacks to the employer.[30]

Thus, the appointment of Colonel Grimley to the Riot Commission was both purposeful and consequential. His reported refusal to sign the commission's report apparently became a source of contention between him and the black community. Moreover, his relationship to a health system that seriously underserved black New Yorkers could not have helped his image.[31] Even before the Riot Commission action, Grimley allegedly ran afoul of subordinates by treating them "as if they were his personal employees" and by acting like "a dictator." Moreover, he selected a white Catholic priest as chaplain, and only the intervention of Governor Herbert H. Lehman resulted in the naming of the Reverend Benjamin C. Robeson, pastor of Mother AME Zion Church, as the chaplain. Other charges against him pertained to his refusal to allow the Women's Committee of *The Crisis* to meet at the armory for a speech by Eleanor Roosevelt and his denial of accommodations to black veterans during the legion convention even as white commanders opened their doors to white conventioneers.[32]

If these charges against Grimley were not sufficient to bring about his ouster, many others were. In early October 1937, Maj. Gen. William N. Haskell, the commanding officer of the New York National Guard, asked for Grimley's resignation. Grimley refused and forced Governor Lehman to appoint a board of high-ranking National Guard officers to examine the commander's professional qualifications. According to press reports, regular army instructors familiar with the Regiment concluded that Grimley knew little, if anything, about the handling of an infantry in the field. Further, his own majors allegedly testified that Grimley's leadership style had destroyed unit morale. Not willing to go down without a fight, Grimley hired as his counsel Brig. Gen. Louis W. Stotesbury, NYNG retired and former state adjutant general. He also sought the help of Postmaster General James F. Farley and Commissioner of Hospitals Dr. S. S. Goldwater. The work of the examination board lasted over four months, and after a series of field tests and written and oral exams were administered, the board declared Grimley unfit for command. This is to say nothing of Grimley's character issues. As deputy commissioner of health, he received a $6,000 salary from the city but lived on the premises of the armory, where he also parked his car. Reports surfaced that he might have had a drinking problem, as he apparently collapsed in his chair during the testimony of his former commander, William Taylor, and it took "quite a few glasses of water and whiskey to revive him."[33]

In addition to having friends in high places, Grimley still had considerable support within the black community. When he called a meeting of his friends "to stand behind him in the fight," they reportedly included Assemblyman Fred R. Moore, owner and publisher of the *New York Age*; Benjamin Robeson, regiment chaplain; and Maj. D. M. Moses. Moreover, many leading citizens, within and without Harlem, "memorialized the governor with telegrams and other messages" for and against the removal of Grimley. The *Amsterdam News* urged the governor to follow the recommendation of his board to avoid "an injury to the colonel or an injury to the regiment." It concluded that the 369th "must have a man at its head, who can stand up under any examination." On February 23, 1938, Governor Lehman decided that Grimley was not such a man and accepted the unanimous recommendation of the special examination board to discharge him as commanding officer. The Regiment's other white officer, Lt. Col. James M. Roche, soon requested a transfer to the reserve list, and Capt. Thornton H. Wood received a promotion to major and assignment with the medical detachment. In the meantime, with the active involvement of Governor Lehman, the War Department assigned Col. Benjamin O. Davis, Sr., to the 369th as an instructor.[34] These developments were signs of rapidly changing times.

Two days after Grimley's removal, Col. Joseph A. S. Mundy, chief of staff of the 27th Division, succeeded the discredited and unpopular commander. Mundy had been a member of the National Guard since 1901 and rose to the rank of captain in 1913. He served on the Mexican border and went to France with the 106th and earned a Silver Star. After demobilization, Mundy rejoined the National Guard as a major of ordnance. He became a lieutenant colonel with the assignment of adjutant general of the 27th Division in 1922 and had been chief of staff of the division since October 1929.[35] The question on the minds of those outside the loop was how long Mundy would stay and who would replace him. Many believed that the time for a black commander was now or never, but Mundy gave no hint that he was not there for the long haul.

In an exclusive interview with the *Amsterdam News,* he pledged his "thirty-seven years' experience in the army to make this regiment one of the most outstanding in the state." He also recognized the need to become close with his men and the Harlem community. In an editorial published on the same day as the exclusive interview, the *Amsterdam News* complimented the governor on "selecting a fine soldier and gentleman to lead Harlem's crack regiment," but it expressed the hope "that his command would be short." Although disfavoring a Jim Crow regiment, as it did segregated schools, the editorial considered the reality and concluded that a unit of blacks led by whites "is an insult to the past bravery of the old Fifteenth and the present spirit and intelligence of the Negro officers of the regiment." Then the editorial revived the anti-immigrant rhetoric of the World War I era, comparing the unquestioned loyalty and courage of blacks to that of newer Americans. The argument continued that blacks, despite their long history as Americans, "are shunted aside and placed in inferior positions in both the army and the navy; while first and second generation foreigners are placed in high positions of trust and honor." Ironically, the outcome could be explained in one word—*prejudice*.[36]

Mundy seemed ready and willing to follow through on his intention of becoming close with his men and the community when he "sold himself to a group of Harlemites" at a dinner for the community sponsored by the Regiment's officers. He used the opportunity to take credit for the promotion of Chauncey Hooper, whom he had known for twelve years, to lieutenant colonel. The revelation proved to the *Amsterdam News* that Mundy "is a genuine soldier, who runs his military outfit on merit." Not all, however, were pleased with the promotion of Hooper. Fred Moore of the *Age,* a staunch Republican who was still smarting from the ouster of Grimley, opposed the promotion of Hooper, a Democratic stalwart, and the appointment of Mundy, but he pledged to work with both men. Interestingly, the *Amsterdam News* remained confident that Mundy would use his considerable skills to prepare black officers to take his place and hoped that would happen very soon.[37]

The time had finally come when blacks believed that a black man would command their beloved Regiment. The question was not so much when as who. Rumors had been circulating that "a ranking Negro officer in the regular army may be brought to New York as an instructor of the Regiment and later named to the post of commanding officer." This time, the rumors proved absolutely correct. His career seemingly at a standstill, Col. Benjamin O. Davis, Sr., had become the beneficiary of the 369th's leadership problems and the relentless pressure to appoint a black as commander. Testing the waters, the army first assigned him to the Regiment as an instructor in early 1938. New York's progressive governor, Herbert Lehman, saw in this appointment the opportunity to bolster his political fortunes and act on his heartfelt commitment to racial justice, evidenced by his long and close association with the NAACP. Lehman quickly lobbied the army to have Davis become the Regiment's commander. On April 27, 1938, officials named the aging soldier as commander of the 369th. It was a win-win outcome for both Governor Lehman and the army. According to Davis biographer Marvin E. Fletcher, Lehman had found a man with impeccable military credentials and no political ties to the state. The War Department could cite Davis as an example of its fair treatment of black officers by giving him a position that suited his rank and length of service.[38] But the consequences for the black citizens of New York were less certain, considering their preference for having one of their own, a Harlemite, to lead their boys.

The Regiment finally had its first black leader after twenty-five years of off-and-on struggles. Yet, he too was an outsider with mostly regular army experience and virtually no association with the unit except for his brief stint as an instructor.[39] Davis was a native of Washington, DC, where he attended public schools. He entered the army during the Spanish-American War as a first lieutenant with the 8th US Volunteer Infantry on July 13, 1898, and served at Fort Thomas, Kentucky, and Camp George H. Thomas, Georgia. He mustered out on March 6, 1899, and returned to service as a private with Troop I on June 14, 1899; he rose to squadron sergeant major of the 9th Cavalry before his separation on May 18, 1901. By February 1901, he had qualified for a commission as a second lieutenant in the regular army by examination at Fort Leavenworth, Kansas, and he was accepted on May 19, 1901. He served with the 2nd Squadron, 10th Cavalry in Samar and Panay, Philippine Islands, during the so-called Insurrection of 1901–1902. Upon his return to the United States, he was stationed at Old Fort Wasaki, Wyoming, before moving to Wilberforce University and later Tuskegee Institute as a professor of military science and tactics, where many thought the army wasted his talents. Davis became a first lieutenant in 1905 but stayed in rank more than ten years. In addition to his service at Wilberforce and Tuskegee, he was military attaché to the American Legation in Liberia and served with the Mexican Border Patrol from 1912 to 1915. His movements and assignments virtually shadowed those of Charles Young. During the world war, Davis rose to the rank of lieutenant colonel but was assigned to Camp Stotsenberg in Pampanga, Philippines, where he had served as a captain and major before his promotion there. He returned to the States in 1920 and served a five-year tour as an instructor with the Ohio National Guard. The trajectory of Davis's career was just another stunning example of how the army steered black field officers away from assignments that would lead to command of white troops and give them rank over white officers, especially in combat operations. In 1930, Davis obtained his colonelcy, and between 1930 and 1933, he accompanied six parties of black Gold Star Mothers on their pilgrimages to the cemeteries of Europe.[40]

Yet, for all his brilliance and accomplishments, Davis was an outsider not only to the Regiment but also to the community. Nonetheless, according to Fletcher, much of the black press embraced him. One of the stark differences between National Guard and regular army soldiers was the fact that the former were first and foremost members of the civilian community. Their social, economic, and political lives were carried on outside the military. Members of the regular army, by contrast, belonged to a totally different community of full-time soldiers whose first allegiance was to their military service. Benjamin O. Davis, Sr., was *in* Harlem but not *of* it. His mission was to apply regular army standards to his officers and men. His initial speech to the Regiment made that very point: "I feel that we will be competent and capable to fulfill all the duties which our commander-in-chief may assign us." Regardless, the press and the community embraced Davis because he was an officer, a gentleman, and a Negro, who would improve "morale and efficiency" and give Harlemites "additional reason to be proud of her boys." Davis's coming-out occurred in the summer of 1938, during the Regiment's annual training encampment. There, some 25,000 spectators, including public officials such as Governor Lehman as well as Albert Einstein and other notables, witnessed "the ceremony at which Davis officially took command of the Regiment."[41]

Soon, Davis and his wife, Sadie, became official residents of Harlem's Paul Lawrence Dunbar Apartments on Eighth Avenue and 150th Street, the first major nonprofit cooperative apartment complex specifically built for African Americans (1926–1928). Among its former occupants were the explorer Matthew Henson, the poet Countee Cullen, W. E. B. Du Bois, A. Phillip Randolph, Paul Robeson, and Bill "Bojangles" Robinson.[42] The Davises soon moved to more spacious accommodations on 162nd Street, which provided the colonel room to practice the piano and find some relief from his pressing professional and social schedule.[43] On a typical day, Davis could be expected to participate in official social functions by, for instance, giving a welcoming speech for Mayor La Guardia at Abyssinian Baptist Church, presiding over a military review, or holding a dinner dance in advance of troop exercises. With few exceptions, he went to the office during the day and returned to it in the evening for meetings and weekly drills. Davis led by example and did not hesitate to correct those who fell short of the model he represented. In a speech to his officers, he cited their failure to use military language in the issuance of commands or filing of reports. Even more important to him was respect for rank: "In the military service rank is everything." He understood that the basis of discipline was respect for superiors, and he knew that only came through conduct that commanded respect.[44]

If published reports accurately represent the response to Davis, it was extremely positive. As evidenced by the luminaries in attendance at his installation, he definitely added more prestige to a unit that was already the pride of Harlem. Frequent reminders of the Regiment's great history appeared in the press. These messages were directed not only to the community but also to the current members of the unit, who were expected to live up to and maintain its reputation. Moreover, these were reminders to the powers that be at the local, state, and national levels that the 369th deserved the best that authorities could offer to an unmistakable symbol of black discipline, courage, integrity, and leadership. Federal authorities were not impressed, however, and continued their onslaught against black soldiers and National Guardsmen even with, or perhaps because of, the prospect of war. Speculation ran rampant about the fate of the 369th, including continued training for the "eventuality of war" or deployment along the Mexican border or Panama Canal Zone.[45]

In April 1940, with World War II now raging in Europe, word leaked from the chief of the National Guard Bureau, Maj. Gen. John F. Williams, that the 369th as well as the 370th and some white infantry regiments were considered surplus. Although the men of the Regiment remained calm, considering the unofficial nature of the news and their roles as soldiers, others feared that the War Department would reduce the Regiment to a labor operation in the guise of Engineers or Pioneers. Then, the War Department heaped insult upon injury by issuing an order stipulating that the 369th "shall henceforth be officially designated as 'colored.'" Under the new organizational table, effective May 1, 1940, the Regiment became "the 369th Infantry (Rifle) Colored" to distinguish it from white units in the National Guard. The *Amsterdam News* expressed outrage at the racialized designation and decried it as part of continuing pattern of discrimination, segregation, and exclusion by the nation's armed forces against its most loyal citizens. It urged the government to scuttle its racist policies and practices or face the potential for "Fifth Columns," which "can grow faster in a nation which preaches Democracy for all but practices it for only a few."[46]

Fortunately, blacks and the Regiment had a strong ally in Albany. Fearing the worst, Governor Lehman renewed his request for permission from the War Department to convert some of the state's National Guard outfits, including the 369th, to antiaircraft units. The War Department had turned down his earlier request, ostensibly on the grounds that New York State could increase its National Guard strength but not add new units. The real reason for the denial was the unsuitability of the 369th for conversion. *Unsuitability* was simply a euphemism for "the necessity of using 'colored' officers" in such units. Yet, Lehman did not pull this feat off alone. His backing of Davis was already paying large dividends. Sensing a change in climate, Davis had taken up the issue in person with the army chief of staff, Gen. George C. Marshall, in April 1940. Davis warned that if the army decided in favor of conversion, it should include other New York units in the process. Otherwise, he cautioned War Department officials, the black community might perceive such a move as a diminution and marginalization of the

Regiment's potential combat role rather than as an opportunity for blacks to demonstrate a capacity for all kinds of service. Still, artillery training for black officers had been one of the most contentious, disappointing, and revealing episodes of the Fort Des Moines experience. Black soldiers had been set up to fail as artillery officers and would have that experience used against them. Nonetheless, Chief of Staff Marshall was convinced that Davis could do the job and thus gave the go-ahead.[47]

Davis might have worried too much. Circumstances favored a positive community reaction, for the threat of being denied a combat role in a wartime army made service in the artillery seem very attractive. It also represented a skilled-labor alternative to the image of the infantry grunt. Even the possibility of being assigned to coastal artillery did not signal a lesser role for the Regiment, since the concern among military and civilian officials about a foreign invasion of US shores loomed large in their plans for war and the nation's defense. An *Amsterdam News* editorial called Lehman's proposal "a splendid thing" because of New York City's vulnerability to attack and because of the opportunity it presented to blacks for combat service beyond foot soldiering. It could help remove beliefs that black soldiers "lacked sufficient education and technical knowledge to take over such a highly specialized field of military warfare." Under Davis's expert leadership and with the necessary resources, the conversion process proved successful and met with community and press approval.[48]

Davis had passed this important test with high marks, and many believed he deserved more than the command of a National Guard regiment. At sixty-three years of age, he had less than a year before mandatory retirement at his rank of colonel. The matter became a subject of public discussion and concern. The *Pittsburgh Courier,* forever associated with the Double V Campaign (Victory at Home and Victory Abroad), pressed for an all-black division to be commanded by Davis. Similar appeals came from staff and readers of the *Amsterdam News,* despite the uncertain impact of Davis's potential departure on the 369th.[49] Yet, when the promotions list appeared in late September 1940, Davis's name was not among the eighty-four new generals. Many believed that snub spelled the end of his chances to become the first black general. Letters of protest poured into Washington, demanding positive action. Still, despite his fine record, Davis was not without his detractors, including Robert Russa Moton and many white officers. The former had differences with Davis over the handling of the officer training program at Tuskegee; the latters' opposition requires no explanation. As the election date approached, anger in the black community grew in the face of discrimination in the defense industries, the military, and New Deal programs, to say nothing of the continuing problem of lynching and the refusal of the Senate and the president to support antilynching legislation. The Republicans seized on the Roosevelt administration's neglect of the black community and seemed poised to erode black support for the president's reelection. Roosevelt took the threat very seriously and on October 26, 1940, over Secretary of War Stimson's reluctance, approved the promotion of Davis to brigadier general (temporary). The nation finally had its first black general, and President Roosevelt got most of the credit for winning a five-day battle against his top generals, who reportedly opposed the promotion.[50]

The political calculus of the appointment could not have been made any clearer than by Secretary Stimson, who took credit for Davis's promotion and used it to defend the administration's poor record concerning blacks and the military. The same man who once claimed, as secretary of war under Taft, that there was no segregation in the military now told a group of young black protesters that he was "the first Secretary of War to have appointed a colored officer to be a Brigadier General" as well as the first to appoint a "colored person as civilian aide to the Secretary of War," Judge William Hastie. He then pointed to the unprecedented organization of an all-black pursuit squadron in Tuskegee, Alabama. Last, he assured the group that "the colored population will be represented by its proportionate representation in the Army."[51]

Characteristically, the distance between Stimson's public rhetoric and his private opinion was wide. Although Stimson often claimed that experience determined his views on blacks, they in fact were more a product of common racialist thinking that selectively considered objective reality to support preconceived notions. He clearly identified blacks with a lower order of human development. In a speech to veterans of World War I, he actually excluded African Americans from the races of civilized man by referring to the racial harmony among Americans as evidenced by the integration of the US Army and the senseless racial warfare among the same groups that threatened to destroy Europe. Stimson wanted posterity to believe that his World War I experience convinced him that Woodrow Wilson had made a mistake in submitting to the demands of blacks for combat troops led by black officers. In his mind, "the poor fellows made perfect fools of themselves" because "leadership is not imbeded in the negro race yet." He concluded that to make commissioned officers of such men "is only to work disaster" on officers and soldiers alike. He had no problem with blacks as foot soldiers if they were led by white officers. The number of black line officers certainly showed that Stimson's inner views determined a self-fulfilling prophecy that translated into actual policy. As late as 1939, Benjamin O. Davis, Sr., was one of only two line officers in the US Army. The other was his son, then 1st Lt. Benjamin O. Davis, Jr.[52] In addition, the senior Davis's command was of the all-black 4th Cavalry Brigade (9th and 10th Regiments) stationed at Fort Riley, Kansas, thus reinforcing the segregated army. Eventually, through Gen. George Marshall's design and urging, Davis became "an inspector and advisor in connection with matters pertaining to" black soldiers. In that role, according to some critics, he "followed the pattern cut out for him by the War Department," including echoing department sentiments about the lack of preparation and opportunity among blacks to be "leaders of combat troops in modern warfare."[53]

As for Hastie, his position seemed very similar to that held by Emmett J. Scott during World War I and represented little progress. Responding to intense pressure from blacks, President Roosevelt, through Associate Justice Felix Frankfurter, forced Hastie on Stimson. Even more, Hastie soon resigned in protest over what he perceived to be a lack of commitment to the fair treatment of black soldiers and his inability to bring about integration of the armed forces. Stimson remained committed to a segregated army and hoped "for Heaven's sake they won't mix the white and colored troops together in the same units for then we shall certainly have trouble."[54] Finally, black pilots had lobbied Congress for inclusion in the Civilian Pilot Program. Stimson had grave doubts about the efficiency and initiative of black pilots and even predicted disaster. Fortunately, the proponents found an ally in Senator Harry S Truman and gained access to the program. Their breakthrough helped to validate the capabilities of blacks as pilots and forced the War Department to act. However, the department established separate facilities for white and black fliers, and beyond that, the black pilots were trained to perform the most dangerous and demanding flying as pursuit pilots responsible for protecting transport planes and bombers. Even then, the War Department intended to train only 33 pilots for the 99th Pursuit Squadron, which was to consist of twenty-seven planes. Given that the army intended to train 30,000 pilots a year, blacks would represent just one-tenth of 1 percent of that annual total. As such, one important and knowledgeable observer, Roy Wilkins, predicted that they were more likely to learn how to fly than to learn how to fight.[55]

With Davis's promotion and reassignment, New York and War Department officials had a critical decision to make. Appointing a white officer to take Davis's place seemed out of the question, considering the precedent already set. The most likely candidate, Benjamin O. Davis, Jr., was only a captain and was tapped to lead the Tuskegee experiment. The most qualified internal candidate was Lt. Col. Chauncey M. Hooper, a member of the Old 15th and a war veteran with impeccable employment and public service credentials and deep political connections to the Democratic Party. After all these years, the powers that be finally chose one of the Regiment's own to take its helm. Clearly, state and federal officials had reacted to the enormous pressure applied locally and nationally to eliminate discrimination in the armed forces. The government responded by drafting a policy proposing black enlistment in proportion to the black population—but only in separate units. It also facilitated the training of black officers to handle the increased number of enlistees.[56]

Hooper had volunteered for service with the 15th Regiment on July 14, 1916, as a private. He quickly rose through the ranks and served as a battalion sergeant major before his transfer to the 367th after qualifying as a second lieutenant. Upon his discharge and return to New York, he joined the 15th New York Guard and was commissioned a first lieutenant on May 29, 1919, and promoted to captain on July 8, 1919. In 1921, he transferred to the state reserve list and returned to active status in 1926 with the 369th. He was promoted to major in 1931 and on March 18, 1938, received a promotion to lieutenant colonel and an order to report to the 369th as executive officer.[57]

Hooper's civilian existence was equally rooted in the institutions and activities of his community. Although a native of New Jersey, Hooper had been educated in New York public schools. In 1919, he earned a clerkship in the district attorney's office from a civil service list, and three years later, Judge John F. McIntyre appointed him as his private stenographer, a post that he continued to hold in 1927 under McIntyre's successor, Judge George L. Donnellan. In the meantime, Hooper had earned a law degree from Fordham University and was admitted to the bar in 1926.[58] A staunch Democrat and Tammany insider, he was no stranger to partisan politics. Indeed, his political connections no doubt contributed to his appointment as commander, but at the same time, they alienated some in the community. Hooper was elected as a delegate to the 1938 Constitutional Convention from the 19th Senatorial District and found himself supporting the losing candidate in a controversial Tammany Hall executive committee election.[59]

The unit Hooper now commanded bore little resemblance to that with which he had been associated for so long. As of August 30, 1940, the 369th Regimental Infantry United States was no more. The War Department had converted and redesignated it the 369th Coast Artillery. Upon its federalization on January 13, 1941, the Regiment was reunited with General Davis, whom the War Department assigned to direct its preliminary training.[60] That training period reminded many of the troubles that the Old 15th

Regiment had encountered in Spartanburg, South Carolina, and two New York camps—Mills and Upton. At Fort Ontario near Oswego, New York, reports of "marauding bands of white soldiers" engaged in a "reign of terror" circulated in the black press. Then, the arrest of a member of the 369th for an attempted break-in and loitering in white neighborhoods prompted the Regiment to boycott merchants in the town. Similar incidents occurred at other military camps around the country and severely eroded the morale of black troops. According to the *Amsterdam News,* the onrush of Hitlerism abroad could not be stopped "until we have first checked Hitlerism at home."[61] This was another kind of two-front war—one that the men of the 369th had recognized since serious talk of fighting Mussolini and Hitler had begun in 1938. In this context, veterans of World War I, especially, did not see any reason to risk their lives overseas unless "the government would give our folk a decent break on civil rights in the South."[62]

Certainly, the War Department had to weigh carefully the benefits of additional training against the dangers of race wars at home. Before the army would send the 369th overseas, however, it had more plans for the transformation of the Regiment. On December 12, 1943, it divided the 369th into much smaller units and split off other parts into separate and distinct battalions, including the 870th Antiaircraft Artillery Automatic Weapons Battalion and the 726th Antiaircraft Artillery Searchlight Battery.[63] Now, the 369th had become part of an elaborate army shell game. Antiaircraft artillery units were undoubtedly fighting units of high status and skill, and thus, the army seemed to be "showing good faith in the ability of the 369th and four other black combat units trained in 1941 for AAA [antiaircraft artillery] status." Yet, these units were in a special category of combat outfits. As William Hastie astutely recognized, the antiaircraft units could be given separate and possibly permanent defensive positions in a theater of operation. They could remain self-contained. In other words, the military employed blacks as combatants while carefully maintaining the racial integrity of regiments and divisions. After guarding the US coasts from Cape Cod to Southern California, the 369th Antiaircraft Artillery Gun Battalion did serve in the Pacific, and it earned a Silver Band for participation in the Ryukus (Okinawa) as part of the 10th Army. By challenging the segregationist policies and practices in Hawaii, the 369th had a profound effect on race relations on that American possession.[64]

As a fighting unit, the 369th had seen its best days in World War I, and so had the black man as a front-line infantry troop. World War II represented a very mixed experience for the African American soldier. In World War I, blacks had the 92nd Division and the four regiments of the 93rd

Provisional, but for most of World War II, only the 92nd existed, and it had to fight under the same rotten preconditions it had fought under in World War I. Although the infantry took a back seat to mechanized units in World War II, that was not necessarily a bad thing, as the 761st Tank Battalion, the 333rd Field Artillery Battalion, and the 969th Field Artillery Battalion distinguished themselves in support roles.[65] Additionally, black marine and naval shipboard ack-ack gun crews existed by the end of the war, not to mention the Tuskegee airmen and the soldiers of the so-called fifth platoons, black soldiers who volunteered and served successfully in white companies in Europe after the Bulge and Huertgen Forest battles drained white infantry reserves. The 93rd Division, however, came to the war late and dispersed and fought on secondary fronts to "mop up" Japanese soldiers in the Pacific.[66]

The 369th's role continued to change and its size continued to shrink as the unit experienced frequent shifts in designation, federal and state control, and type of service—from antiaircraft artillery to field artillery to howitzer battalion.[67] Yet, an even more drastic change loomed as the unit's days as an all-black outfit neared an end. During the war, Walter White pressed hard with state and federal officials to integrate the unit. Such an initiative could not have sat well with the men, who saw the Regiment as an exclusive club in which potential members had to be sponsored from within and were carefully screened for moral fitness and self-discipline. That process included visits to families and employers and required a willingness and ability to attend the summer camps. Once accepted, the men of the Regiment felt a mutual obligation to uphold each other and maintain the proud record of their organization and the people who supported and took pride in it. Failure reflected badly on friends, family, and community and, by extension, the race.[68]

Yet, postwar violence against blacks clearly indicated that segregation reinforced notions of superiority and inferiority and consequently created the climate for attacks against the racial other. As a result, black leaders pressed government officials for redress in the form of integration, even when it meant the transformation of successful institutions. On October 29, 1947, the President's Committee on Civil Rights issued its landmark report *To Secure These Rights,* which condemned segregation wherever it existed, including in the military. The accelerated push toward integration symbolized by Jackie Robinson's breaking of the so-called color barrier in sports in 1947 and President Truman's Executive Order no. 9981 integrating the armed services signaled the coming of the end of the all-black regiment.[69] The Supreme Court decision in *Brown v. Board of Education* in 1954 and subsequent civil rights acts made such institutions, in the minds of many, anomalous. Others saw the demise of all-black institutions as a loss of opportunity, but few dared to speak out in such terms. By the late sixties, the 369th had become 85 percent white, according to Maj. Gen. Nathaniel James, president of the unit's historical society and commander from 1980 to 1984. In fact, the 1968 decision to have the 369th march on Fifth Avenue rather than in Harlem reflected the impact of integration on the unit and the divide among blacks on the issue. On the one side, opponents argued that a march through Harlem "would provide an inspirational experience for children of that ghetto." On the other side, proponents maintained that limiting the parade to Harlem would be a step backward in the move toward integration and a missed opportunity "to acquaint both black and white with the progress of the black man in America." Even today, one can sense the regret and even resentment of the end of the all-black Pride of Harlem. According to Brig. Gen. Sam Phillips, a veteran of the 369th, the Regiment's racial makeup shifted dramatically during the Vietnam War when the National Guard became a safe haven from combat.[70]

On February 1, 1968, the Regiment suffered perhaps its biggest blow when it lost not only its designation as the 369th but also its status as a combat unit, becoming the 569th Transportation Battalion. Some have suggested that the move was made in response to widespread black opposition to the Vietnam War and the fear of having an armory full of armed combatants in the heart of New York City. The 569th spent just seven days in active federal service (March 24–30, 1970) before reverting to state control. On the surface, the reaction to the relegation and the name change seemed surprisingly mild. The men of the unit responded like soldiers to an order—"Follow it." Yet the muted public reaction showed just how far the 369th had fallen as an institutional reality and symbol for the people of Harlem. Although the armory was used to house homeless families in the 1960s, the relationship between the military and the black community had changed. Black people turned less toward the military as an institution of advancement as other avenues opened up. In 1967, the mayoral victories of Carl Stokes and Richard Hatcher in Cleveland, Ohio, and Gary, Indiana, respectively, were far more important than the 369th or black generals. Moreover, the war in Vietnam was immensely unpopular in many black circles, seen as another attack against people of color and a clear example of the link between militarism and imperialism. Besides, National Guard units would become more identified with police actions in quelling public disorder or the expression of black anger, resentment, and frustration. Though some might hope that black troops would handle such duty differently, others worried that they might simply follow orders regardless of the consequences. On February 1, 1968, the 369th Artillery Battalion was reorganized and redesignated the 569th Transportation Battalion and rendered less likely to see policing action.[71]

On March 1, 1974, the army reorganized and redesignated the unit as Headquarter and Headquarters Detachment, 369th Transportation Battalion. At least the Rattlers had their original federal designation back and the 369th Armory housed a unit of the same name once more. Interestingly, through all the changes, the tradition of black commanders started by Benjamin Davis in 1938 continued without interruption until 1995, when Stephen R. Seiter became the first white commander in fifty-seven years. Seiter, who played a major role in securing approval and funding for the Séchault monument, was succeeded by another white commander, Robert Cochran, in 1998. Irving F. Donaldson, a black man, succeeded Cochran in command of the 369th. The unit made history again when Col. Stephanie Dawson replaced Col. Kevin McKiernan as commander of the 369th Sustainment Brigade and became the first female brigade commander in New York National Guard history. Shortly thereafter, Colonel Dawson would make an even larger historical breakthrough as leader of the 53rd Troop Command, one of two major commands in the New York Army National Guard. In May 2012, she entered the New York Veterans Hall of Fame. Col. Reginald D. Sanders succeeded Dawson as commander.[72] The history and traditions of the 369th are continued by the 369th Historical Society, the 369th Veterans Association, and the 369th Women's Auxiliary.

This study has provided a detailed and thorough treatment of the Regiment's history, from the extended and difficult period leading to its formation through the great conflict of 1914–1918, in particular the years 1917–1918, the apogee of the 369th's existence. Yet its postwar and interwar experiences speak loud and clear to the continued disparagement, mistreatment, and betrayal of the black soldier. Furthermore, this history shows the continuing relevance of the military experience to the quest for black citizenship. Until the rise of the civil rights movement in the 1940s and 1950s and the subsequent rise in black electoral power, only the black church and the historically black college could rival the military as institutions for black advancement. Even then, no other institution could provide black men with the opportunity to demonstrate discipline, courage, skill, and leadership as the military could. Although shining in war has been largely a male thing, it sometimes redounded to the benefit of the black women who could produce and groom such men in addition to trying to play their part as best they could. In other respects, it reinforced their subordination or difference.

The story of the Regiment would be incomplete without an accounting of the post-Regiment lives of some of the leading men in this incredible drama—an important but largely elided or ignored subject, much of it cloaked in distortion and misinformation if not outright myth. For this tale of triumph and woe and mystery, the concluding chapter features the picaresque and sad adventure of Henry Johnson and the tortured life and tragic end of Neadom Roberts.

# Conclusion

## Henry Johnson and Neadom Roberts:
## Cautionary Tales

The black volunteers and draftees of the 15th/369th Regiment composed the vast majority of its members, who, under the orders of their officers, fought in combat and labored constantly in their trenches when they were not fighting. Most of them fought and lived or died in obscurity. For the fallen, their only memorial is a marble cross in one of the American cemeteries in France maintained by the American Battle Monuments Commission. Henry Johnson and Neadom Roberts, however, gained immediate and widespread fame because of their unique exploits and the providential circumstances that led to their recognition. Their fame and the myths that ultimately obscured their exploits as well as both men eventually destroyed them as individuals. Unlike their officers, both black and white, who possessed the family and educational background or social prominence to return to civilian life positioned to use their medals to their advantage, Johnson and Roberts had no skills. Their wounds had scarred and crippled them for life and, a consequence that is rarely factored in, left them in pain—in Roberts's case, a pain both physical and psychological because of his youth and the severity of his wounds. Johnson, the illiterate manual laborer, and Roberts, a drugstore delivery boy, returned to civilian life deprived of the one capacity that they had possessed before the war, their physical abilities. The fact that they were black men meant possibly that the US Army would minimize their disabilities in order to avoid paying them benefits. And as their fame dissipated, they would face a struggle to survive in civilian life, a struggle for which Henry Johnson was particularly ill equipped because of his illiteracy and poverty.

Henry Johnson has long symbolized the triumphs and tragedies of the 369th. When Toni Morrison fictionalized the plight of the veterans of the unit in *Jazz*, she obviously had Johnson in mind. Set in 1926, only seven years after the Armistice and in stark contrast to the unbridled jubilation on that unforgettable February day when the 369th made blacks so proud that their hearts "split in two," *Jazz* features characters who embody a bleak and dreary postwar existence—a world in which veterans still wore "their army-issue greatcoats, because nothing they can pay for is as sturdy or hides so well what they had boasted of in 1919." The legacy of their service was poverty and disfigurement, and external trappings revealed internal turmoil as memories simultaneously haunted and sustained.[1] That description almost solely applied to enlisted men because most officers had the social, educational, and economic wherewithal to fall back on their civilian occupations and roles, if not to capitalize on their military experience and honors.

Others were far more direct in their references to and even exploitation of Johnson. Among them was his battalion commander, Arthur Little, who understood Johnson's value as heroic/comedic/tragic figure. Little, in fact, began and ended his regimental history with Johnson. The frontispiece of his book features portraits of Johnson and Roberts along with their Croix de Guerre citations. The book ends with a dialect-spouting, eternally grateful Johnson, who walked miles to tell Major Little, "Yer made a man of me!" Only a few days before, an AWOL Johnson had reported to Little for possible punishment, and upon questioning, he revealed that a group of gentlemen had taken him "to a number of 5th Avenue clubs and hotels" and "entertained" him with food and drink and "rewarded" him with money. Johnson characterized the men as friends of regimental officers and said that to have resisted their kindness might have offended them and possibly jeopardized the Regiment's reputation. As proof that the episode took place, he pulled out a wad of money in excess of $600. As usual, the paternalistic Little forgave the childlike Johnson for his missteps. After all, Johnson had made a special trip in gratitude, and in the process, he taught Little "a lesson of peace, even as he had taught hundreds of his comrades a lesson of combat."[2]

In that last conversation with Johnson, Little asked the soldier not to forget him. The implication was that he himself would never forget Johnson. Yet, Little's 1936 publication did not go beyond Henry Johnson paying respects to his battalion commander. Although one can accept the possibility that the two men never met again, it is harder to believe that Little heard nothing about Johnson after that fond farewell. Thus, Little abandoned Henry Johnson the man and left us with the legend—his "homicidal king," as he fondly referred to the little sergeant.

Johnson's postwar existence reveals as much, if not more, about his significance than his brief but glorious career as a soldier. Unfortunately, Henry Johnson the man and his life story remain largely unknown and neglected. Even his real name is still a source of confusion. The woman publicly identified as his wife, Edna, referred to him as Bill. As a result, he is also known as William Henry Johnson, although his service record lists him simply as Henry Johnson. So does the headstone at Arlington National Cemetery, although William has been crossed out on the official documentation related to his interment. However, the name Henry Lincoln Johnson appears on the citation for the Distinguished Service Cross. These inconsistencies indicate the extent to which Henry Johnson remains a man of mystery and invention.

Most people cared not for Henry Johnson the person but for how his achievements and reputation might benefit them. One of the most egregious examples came from Kelly Miller, the distinguished Howard University scholar and writer who credited Neadom Roberts and Henry Johnson with establishing the "colored" officer training camp at Fort Des Moines.[3] In referring to their citation for gallantry (French, of course), Miller wrote: "Whether this citation arrived on May 19th, 1917, by design or by accident, it served the purpose of dissolving completely all opposition to the idea of training Negroes to halt the Hun. Immediately thereafter, the War Department created a training camp for educated Negroes at Fort Des Moines, Iowa." Of course, the deed for which these men were celebrated occurred one year *after* the establishment of the camp, and in fact, Johnson did not even join the Regiment until June 5, 1917. Few claims for Johnson's significance have been so clearly in error as Miller's, but many others verge on the hyperbolic and apocryphal. Both kinds, the erroneous and the exaggerated, have been extremely damaging to Johnson's reputation and the causes his legacy continues to serve.

Other contemporaries believed that the postwar Johnson had already outlived his usefulness. The aforementioned critic of the parade coverage made clear that "Buck" Manley, Henry Johnson's supposed friend, was no decent representative of the race and that, by association, neither was Johnson. Unfortunately, some members of the black elite valued proper pedigree and cultural refinement as much as, if not more than, heroic achievements. Ideally, they could accept the heroic only from the respectable. Thus, among the first to forget Henry Johnson the man were the very people for whom he had done the most. Time would only make matters worse.[4]

The most brazen mode of exploitation came in the form of impersonation, and Henry Johnson impostors wasted no time in cashing in on the war hero's fame. Even before the end of the war, men knew that they could profit from Henry. One such opportunist fooled admirers of Johnson in Brooklyn and Harlem before the soldier's friends ran him out of the public place and forced him into a hasty retreat for his personal safety.[5]

That man, standing "more than six feet tall" and of "decidedly ebony hue," shared only the latter physical feature with Johnson. What fooled his audience was his uniform, his command of details, and his facility with tough questions. When asked why he was not in Europe, he told his audience that he had been given a thirty-day furlough along with Neadom Roberts, who was in Trenton to see his parents. For those who questioned the absence of medals, the impostor claimed that they had been sent to Washington or had been stored for safekeeping. Reports maintained that his account was so vivid and compelling that he transported the audience to the trenches, where they imagined fighting the Boche themselves.

Among his victims was none other than the Reverend W. Spencer Carpenter, a veteran of the Spanish-American War and an ardent advocate for the black soldier. Although Carpenter had doubts about the man's authenticity, he had not dared to risk offending the real Henry Johnson in front of his congregants at the Bridge Street African Methodist Episcopal Church. Not content with the "bold bills" he had collected through his deception, the "fake hero" pressed his luck by seeking press coverage from the New York offices of the *Chicago Defender.*[6] The newspaper staff found holes in the man's story, but what proved to be his Waterloo was the attention he garnered by his visit. He seemed to have attracted some who knew Johnson and others who knew *him*. Revealed as Robert Davis, the man fled with the crowd and later with the police in hot pursuit.[7]

Davis, fifty-seven years old and a native of Nashville, Tennessee, was quickly apprehended and found guilty of petty larceny. At his sentencing, he pleaded for mercy as "an old soldier" who did not intend "to disgrace his uniform." A normally severe Judge Dyke, influenced by the pleas for leniency and forgiveness from the imposter's victims, gave the con artist a suspended sentence and ordered him to pay back those he had bilked at the church.[8]

Worse yet, members of Johnson's own Regiment were caught in a scheme of selling copies of his photographs in Albany. New York City photographer E. T. Welcome (aka Madame E. Toussaint Welcome) had hired these soldiers to impersonate Johnson and, possibly, Neadom Roberts. The scheme quickly collapsed because one of the impostors was six feet tall, whereas Johnson measured just five and one-half feet. Privates John Martin and Elder Griffin of New York City were arrested and jailed, and Welcome reportedly abandoned them. Johnson refused to press charges but blamed the photographer and vowed to "leave for New York tonight to look him up."[9] Of course, Johnson could not have imagined that a woman was party to such a scheme or that she was a proprietor of an art studio in Harlem and the self-proclaimed "'foremost female artist of the race.'"[10]

Henry Johnson and Neadom Roberts seem to have been a revenue stream for the Welcome enterprise. Not long after the famous incident involving Henry and Neadom, Toussaint Studios had produced "the one picture that should be on the walls of every colored home in America." Entitled "Our First Heroes in France," it featured engraved renderings of the two men in full uniform, with a "vivid scene of the battle itself." The cost of $.15 per print seemed a small price to pay for art that "encourages the old, inspires the young, and teaches the children that bravery knows no color."[11]

Madame Welcome's brother, James VanDerZee, also seems to have profited from the apparent fabrication of images of Johnson and Roberts together—and with much greater success and far more damage to the visual historical record. In Deborah Willis-Braithwaite's *VanDerZee: Photographer, 1886–1983*, the author identifies two sets of photographs as portraying Johnson and Roberts. The first, dated 1920, actually features rather tall and large men, which Johnson and Roberts were not. Even more, the color of both men is substantially lighter than that of Henry Johnson. Another photograph, dated 1916, supposedly features Johnson and Roberts in civilian clothes, the former captured in profile and literally festooned with medals of questionable authenticity and relevance. Recognizing the irreconcilable date, Willis-Braithwaite corrects it to 1932, corresponding with the timing of the portrait of Neadom Roberts, which appears to be authentic. Mark Whalan corrects the date of the photograph to around 1929 to reconcile it with Johnson's death that year. Neither Willis-Braithwaite nor Whalan questions the authenticity of the photographs, and Whalan takes great pains to interpret the photograph and read into Roberts's gaze at the medals the man posing as Johnson wears.[12] Furthermore, there is no resemblance between the real Johnson and Roberts and the two men in the 1920 photograph, and there is no individual portrait of the man posing as Johnson. Perhaps even VanDerZee understood the transparency of having someone who had died in 1929 pose for a photograph in 1932. The circumstances and purposes of these photographs might never be known, but what we do know is that VanDerZee's photography changed dramatically in the postwar period. According to Willis-Braithwaite, the attention shifted from the sitter to the desired effect created by "a variety of studio props and elaborate painted backdrops."[13] In this instance, perhaps the quest for artistic quality and symbolic meaning trumped reality.

As deceptive as it might have been, VanDerZee's apparent fabrication paled in comparison to the fraud committed in Johnson's name shortly after the war. On February 17, 1919, either unaware or dismissive of the Regiment's parade that same day, an impostor took the stage before a large gathering in St. Louis, even as the real war hero had just captivated his adoring fans in New York. Lester A. Walton reported that more than 10,000 "persons of both races" had packed the auditorium in St. Louis and that Mayor Henry W. Kiel and other dignitaries had attended. Then, after introductory speeches by the mayor in praise of black soldiers in general and Henry Johnson in particular, "the cheering throng," in an "atmosphere charged with patriotism," reportedly heard Lt. George L. Vaughan, a recent returnee from France, announce that the man with "the Napoleonic look" and "more regalia and medals than Pershing and Foch" could not possibly be the hero of "No Man's Land" because he was in New York.[14]

With no place to run or hide, the impostor, Albert Parker, not only gave himself up to authorities but also implicated the Reverend Benjamin G. Shaw in the hoax. According to Parker, Shaw had met him in a Mobile, Alabama, restaurant and offered him "a big batch of money" if he would pose as Johnson. Walton reported that the "irate citizens" would be "more disposed to hold the Rev. Dr. Shaw responsible for the disgraceful incident than the fake hero."[15] What few could have expected, however, is that the "real" Henry Johnson would create even greater controversy.

Reportedly, representatives of the largest booking agencies in New York City, who expected to profit from a speaking tour by the war hero, offered Johnson as much as $10,000 to sign with them. He declined them all, believing he could profit more by selecting his own manager and booking his own engagements, including some in vaudeville. With press hype about his feat growing with the passage of time and repeated telling, so did the demand for his services. There was even talk of an offer from Universal Studios for Henry to play himself on screen.[16]

The following account of an informal talk given by Johnson also reveals how both he and the press undermined his accomplishments through embellishment, distortion, and even fantasy. Some may have believed all that was said or written about him or else understood exaggeration for what it was, but others undoubtedly viewed such lapses in memory or judgment as a reason to question Johnson's very accomplishments. More became less, and Johnson's reputation suffered as a result. So, too, did Roberts's, for his role shrank with each telling.

Shortly after his return to a hero's welcome in his hometown, a tired and weary Johnson "reluctantly" agreed to attend a reception and "a big chicken dinner." Whether he addressed the crowd at this event is not clear, but an unnamed correspondent at the *Age* attributed the following account to Johnson:

> Roberts and I were in an outpost, and I posted Roberts at one side and myself at the other . . . so that if the Germans sent a patrol along we could take it in either flank. In a little while the lieutenant (French) came along and I told him I thought the Germans meant to come over, and he said to retreat back to the line. I said to him "Lieutenant, I'm an American, and I never retreat."[17]

Johnson's disregard of the French lieutenant's order is eerily similar to Hayward's equally defiant declaration that "my men never retire. They go forward or they die." Both are in the American tradition of justifiable disobedience of superiors—and they are also in the tradition of American mythology.

Johnson allegedly continued:

> About three-thirty, sure enough, along came two platoons, and as they rushed they knocked Roberts out with a shot through the right arm. They had two stretchers with them and they intended to get two of us, dead or alive. I threw out a box and a half of grenades, and then I fired 31 clips of 3 cartridges each from my rifle, French ammunition, but that did not stop them. Then I tried some of my American ammunition, and that jammed in my rifle.[18]

Inconsistencies plague this tale. In previous accounts, Roberts, though wounded, had thrown grenades at the Germans. But in this telling, he has been incapacitated early in the fray and reduced to helpless bystander. Moreover, the Germans' stretchers were intended for their own casualties, not the enemy troops. Germans commonly carried one stretcher for every twelve men; in fact, the number of stretchers had always been an important clue for determining the size of a raiding party. This new rendering bore no relation to that theory and logic.

Next comes the climactic, hand-to-hand phase of Johnson's story:

> By this time they had thrown Roberts on a stretcher and were starting with him, and I just pushed through that crowd with my rifle butt, and finally I broke my rifle on them, and then I had nothing but my good American bolo knife. Well, I fought and I got Roberts off the stretcher and stood over him, and I kept on fighting."

This description, sans stretcher, could have been scripted based on the famous Charles A. Rogers cartoon, depicted and described earlier in this volume.

The story grows even more unbelievable, but then, so do many accepted "truths" of American history. Unfortunately, the history of a devalued people has always faced a stricter realism test, and a reported (more likely invented) verbal joust and war of wills strained the limits of credulity:

> I had five gunshot wounds and two bayonet wounds, and worse than that a German captain slapped my face. "Leave here," he said. / "Leave where?" I asked him. / "Over the line." / "Not while I live."

In other accounts, the hand-to-hand encounter featured a German uttering in perfect English, "The black son of a bitch got me." The theme in this latest rendering was not so much German racism as German cowardice. In an unexpected dénouement, Johnson revealed:

> At last there seemed to be only one man left, and I grabbed him and he grabbed me. We hugged, me and him. "I don't want to fight," he cried. / "You must," I said, "or you wouldn't have come over here." / "Kamerad," next.

Johnson's story ended on a more factual and restrained note: "When relief came they accounted for twenty-four, some dead and some wounded, and I was bandaging up Roberts arm."[19]

How much, if any, of this account came from the mouth of Johnson cannot be known. Its prose seems well beyond his facility with words. For better or worse, however, it and many other accounts like it became his.

None of the preceding material fits with the description of Johnson that appeared in early press reports from Albany. If nothing else, Henry Johnson seemed modest and shy. According to the media, he did not consider himself to be a hero and had but one wish—to be left alone. When asked about his feat, Johnson reportedly replied: "I did it because it was my duty as a soldier. I did it for old Albany. That's what I went for." Even when he made an unexpected appearance before the Senate Judiciary Committee in Albany, he reportedly spoke few words and none selfishly. Instead, he urged the passage of the Baumes bill, which would have afforded veterans of World War I the same preferences and protections in civil service positions enjoyed by Spanish-American War veterans. Apparently uneasy in the role, Henry told the committee: "I don't know what to say. You all know all of us went over and that we did our bit. Only a few of us came back. What are you going to do for us? I hope that you will do something."[20]

Yet, the following story shows how difficult a subject Henry Johnson could be. Does it reveal that he might not have been as modest and unassuming as the *Albany Times Union* would have had its readers believe? Or is it another example of the press putting words into his mouth? While contributing to the feeding frenzy around Henry Johnson by running the *Sun*'s coverage of the parade in full, replete with the Buck Manley iteration of Johnson's exploits, the *Times Union* also published what appears to be another embellished, if not fabricated, episode in Johnson's combat record. The paper claimed that a star on Johnson's Croix de Guerre recognized his "initiative and leadership" in a completely different encounter than that on May 15, 1918, with Neadom Roberts. According to this account, Johnson had assumed command of his platoon after a seven-day battle for Snake Hill in the Argonne in which all officers were lost. He reportedly "conducted his men perfectly and under his command that platoon had a large part in the gallant final assault that captured this important position."[21]

Like the Buck Manley episode, the tale had the potential to render Johnson smaller through obvious exaggeration. Yet, the story cannot be read simplistically, as it raises far more questions than it answers. Were the details of his role provided by Johnson? There is no direct quoting, which prompts serious doubts about the source. Even the reference to Johnson's Croix de Guerre seems uninformed, for he was awarded one with gold palm; it was Roberts who received the Croix with Silver Star. Moreover, the name Snake Hill in the *Times Union* account is alien to France as a place and as a construct; on the surface, it appears more akin to a figment of someone's imagination. A close textual and contextual reading suggests, however, that Séchault, physically defended by a hill on which many soldiers of the 369th died, had been appropriated, through transfiguration and transliteration, as Snake Hill by the men known as the Rattlers. Thus, a name that seems invented from whole cloth probably had its basis in the verbal, visual, and experiential sensibilities of black soldiers. Though Johnson himself might have fueled the escalation of his role as he fought against rising expectations by contributing to his own legend with exaggerations to confirm and/or complement those supplied by others, evidence on this matter is not conclusive. Arthur Little claimed that Johnson had a flair for the dramatic and told a different story to each reporter he encountered. Yet, in a speech he would give later, Johnson assumed no such inflated role for himself in the conflict but instead "told how negroes captured Snake Hill after four hours of fighting."[22]

Despite his reported reluctance to seek attention and his apparent difficulties with words, Johnson remained a major attraction. Even his court appearances brought out hordes of fans and curiosity seekers and made him a celebrity with the court personnel, including judges.[23] Mention of his name alone was sure to boost attendance at any public event. On March 26, Johnson was poised to have what appeared to be one of the biggest moments of his life—a chance to share the stage with the regimental commander, Col. William Hayward, at the State Armory. Flyers announced in bold print: "Hear Our War Heroes," with Johnson's name prominently displayed just below that of Hayward, who as leader of "the colored troops in France will describe the battles where his brave men fought and died." Johnson, Albany's local hero, would "be there to tell how he killed the Germans," as if he had slain the whole army.[24]

Nonetheless, when the press advertised and reported on the event, it did not mention Johnson as a featured speaker; actually, it cast him in a supporting role. The event was to lend support to the Victory Loan and War Savings Stamp Campaigns, but it was undoubtedly influenced by a desire to promote Hayward as a gubernatorial candidate. The Albany press made clear who the star was, though it remained mum on the hidden agenda. According to the *Albany Argus*, "Hero Henry" led the greeting party and the entourage in the procession from the train station to the armory. Massive crowds cheered the local heroes and their commander. Hayward evidently spoke first and brought the war home to the audience in vivid detail and with intimate knowledge. He demonstrated a deep respect for the French, especially General Gouraud, and emphasized that the American notions that US troops showed the French what to do were wrong. "'The fact is,'" Hayward was said to claim, "'they showed us how to do it and we did it.'"[25]

The 10,000 in attendance at this event must have been sorely disappointed when Johnson, according to the *Argus,* said but a few words because he was "suffering from a head cold." Meanwhile, the *Times Union* reportedly let Johnson speak for himself, and a different story emerged: "'You've all heard what my Kunel had to say. All I got to say too I could not say as much as he said, but he told the same thing I was going to.'"[26] In his next speech, Johnson displayed no such reserve, which suggested that the "head cold" or case of "cold feet" that he had suffered on the stage with Hayward might have been caused by his astute awareness that he paled in comparison to the colonel as a public speaker and that distortion, embellishment, and/ or vitriol would not pass muster with his former commander nor please his hometown audience. If nothing else, his war experience had sharpened Johnson's ability to assess and navigate difficult situations.

Notwithstanding his shaky public appearances, Johnson still spurned offers from agents and contracted with groups in St. Louis to appear at the Coliseum on March 28 for $1,500. He left immediately after the event with Hayward—but not before receiving "a great send-off" from the mayor of Albany. Already offered less compensation than he expected, Johnson demanded payment in advance for the St. Louis event, considering what had happened to the $2,400 raised in his name earlier, and he refused to appear before the money had been handed to him.[27]

After keeping a senator, a congressman, the mayor, and other notables, as well as the large throng of 5,000, waiting, Johnson entered the Coliseum to great fanfare and anticipation. He approached the podium and, according to newspaper and intelligence reports, promptly offended most, if not all, whites in the audience by playing to the crowd and "openly" stating "that the white soldiers were cowards; that they retreated in the face of enemy fire; that the marines refused to fight in the same trenches with our men; and that the war was won by black soldiers." He also took on members of the white press, accusing them of rank opportunism in seeking photographs and stories from him now when they had avoided "No Man's Land" and ignored his deed at the time. Although the charges Johnson made grossly distorted his own experience with the white press, they certainly spoke to white reporters' general lack of interest in or honesty toward black combatants.[28]

If the account of the *St. Louis Republic* is accurate, Henry also revealed his humorous side by firing off a series of one-liners about racial injustice. First, he proclaimed that had he been a white man, he "would be the next governor of New York." The cheers of the crowd stirred his comic juices and led to even sharper social commentary about segregation and discrimination. "They may put the Negroes in the rear seats of cars here," he said, "but they did not make any discrimination in 'No Man's Land.' They sent the Negroes up ahead." He even went so far as to claim that one officer saw the war as a way of reducing the black population of Gotham by suggesting that the commander "'send the niggers to the front and there won't be so many around New York.'"[29]

That kind of humor was bad enough, as whites had been accustomed to blacks being the brunt of racial jokes, not the purveyors of them. What really aroused the ire of the audience members was when Johnson "nefariously" accused a "white lieutenant in charge of his platoon" of "cowardice while in action" because he would have abandoned his men had not Henry pulled a gun on him and forced him to stay.[30] The white soldiers and civilians in the audience reportedly "left the building in disgust" when "Johnson began to discredit the work of the white soldiers." An irate citizen of St. Louis warned Secretary of War Baker, with unintended irony, that Johnson's disparagement of white "manhood" would find "fertile" soil among "the weak and vaccilating [*sic*] brother(s) of his race."[31]

Although the War Department found Johnson's statements very offensive and threatening, it had no real authority to punish him. Its jurisdiction ended with Johnson's discharge in February.[32] Thus, reports that Johnson had been arrested on the technical charge of wearing a uniform after a prescribed time were not founded. Instead, the department hoped that civil authorities would consider arresting and prosecuting Johnson on charges of "inciting to riot." To this end, Capt. J. E. Cutler in the office of the director of military intelligence ordered Capt. T. S. Maffitt of the St. Louis office to investigate the incident. Maffitt reported that Johnson did make remarks that were likely "to stir up antagonism between the white and colored people," and these remarks "were particularly derogatory to the Marines." As a result, the marines took it upon themselves to bring Johnson to justice.

The day after the event, an unspecified number of marines paid a visit to the Grand Central Hotel in search of Johnson. The following is an excerpt from the official account of the meeting that ensued: "They were met at the door of subject's room by a man in civilian clothes, who stated that Johnson was not in at that time. It was later learned that this man was Johnson himself. Later in the day, the Marines returned and were unable to get into the hotel, but did talk to Johnson through a glass door. He was at that time dressed in Army uniform."[33]

"The first to fight"—the marines—decided that discretion was the better part of valor. Instead of apprehending Johnson themselves, "some 6 or 8 Marines then went to the office of the Department of Justice" to request the subject's arrest. The federal attorney was out, but an assistant called his superior for permission to arrest Johnson. When the Justice Department officials arrived the next day, they found no trace of Johnson and learned later that he had departed for Albany on Saturday night. The federal attorney was unavailable for comment. The assistant, William C. Sausele, informed Captain Maffitt that no further action had been taken in the matter.

The marines and the Department of Justice proved no match for the "Hero of No Man's Land." Like so many other stories about Johnson, the one that had him promising to retract his remarks in a formal statement in exchange for his freedom does not appear to be accurate. Instead of cowering under pressure, Johnson relied on his fierce reputation and considerable cunning to escape arrest and possible detention. It was one thing for the press to inflate his experience with the Germans but another to have him defeating the mighty marines and the Department of Justice.[34]

Not hesitating to condemn blacks who "shamed" the race, Maj. Walter Loving of the Military Intelligence Division judged Johnson to be "densely ignorant and . . . suffering from a severe case of 'swelled head.'" He recommended to the director of military intelligence that "the privilege extended to soldiers which allows them to wear uniforms for a reasonable length of time after being mustered out of the service, be immediately revoked in the case of Sgt. Henry Johnson."[35] Like so many others, Loving had seriously underestimated Johnson's resourcefulness and resolve.

At the same time, Johnson's apparent tactlessness and candor also eroded his support among those who had relied on the man's exploits to prove the valor of his race and others who had depended on his "stories" to sell newspapers. While harboring no doubts that Johnson was "the greatest individual hero produced by the whole American army" and without regard "to the verity of his statements," the *Age* had strong advice for him if he wanted to remain a hero—"stay off the lecture platform." Invoking the law of compensation, the *Age* opined that "gods seldom pour two or more elements of greatness into the same man." They certainly poured into Henry "the stuff that makes heroes," but "they failed to pour in any of the stuff that makes orators."[36]

The *Age* revealed deeper reasons for its advice as well. It did not want the real Johnson to be known, for he had greater value as a media illusion and construction. It argued that "heroes enhance their value through mystery and distance. Familiarity is to the hero what daylight is to theatrical scenery." After all, "not even Napoleon was hero to his valet." The final piece of advice the *Age* had to offer betrayed its true agenda. By suggesting that Johnson invite to Albany those who wanted to see him clearly, it showed that limiting Johnson's public impact weighed far more heavily than a fear that people would come to know him for what he was.[37] Henry had become another victim of the politics of respectability.

Neither the reaction of the *Age* nor Loving's characterization of Johnson as ignorant and arrogant captures the full significance of his seemingly foolish performance. Johnson probably understood that his career as a speaker would be short-lived. The fact that he thoughtfully ensured that $1,500 was in his hands before he entered the hall indicates that he knew and did not care that his intended words would cause trouble. Essentially, the poor and partially disabled veteran chose to say what he believed and pay the consequences. Was such behavior simply an act of destructive self-importance on the part of a man of limited intelligence, means, and vision? Or was Henry not just a war hero but also a race man, no matter how simple he might have appeared? Perhaps, as Chad Williams has demonstrated along with so many others, he did understand himself and his role in the larger context of the black soldier and the race.[38]

As the French intelligence reports indicated, whites barraged blacks with allegations about the cowardice and ineffectiveness of the black 92nd Division. The French military attaché even considered it unjust that Robert Moton of Tuskegee should have to defend black honor, especially in light of the fine service that the 93rd Division had rendered while attached to the French army. Black soldiers were angry about the treatment they had encountered while serving in the 92nd Division AEF, and they reacted strongly to Moton's speech prior to their return urging them to be "calm and unassuming." They damned General Ballou and his bigoted treatment of his African American troops—and justifiably so. They did not appreciate Moton's placatory advice, offered in lieu of their attendance at the Victory Parade in Paris. At a meeting in the "Colored Y.M.C.A." in Washington, DC, on March 14, 1919, Lt. Charles Shaw labeled Ballou "bereft of all decency" for sending the 368th Infantry forward without wire cutters and sufficient ammunition (a matter of record) and then volunteered, "I was born in the south and I am going back there to live. I am unable to tell you just what is going to happen, but I am going back there."[39]

As noted earlier, black veterans had returned home to race riots in American cities, suffered savage attacks by whites, and far too often found themselves the victims of lynching in the South. Johnson's words likely reflected the anger all this provoked, and they were not completely incorrect, though they were possibly exaggerations. The 369th, for example, had never retreated, but some white divisions, in particular the 35th Division AEF, had and with insufficient justification. Yet such failings did not reflect on the white race as did those of black units such as the 92nd Division, in which the poor performance of any segment or individual was attributed to racial failings.

In regard to the marines, Johnson's statement reflected the reality that the US Marine Corps was the most prejudiced service branch at the time. In fact, it totally excluded blacks from its ranks. Moreover, the marines had demonstrated a near-total disregard for black human life in their brutal treatment of the people of Haiti during their occupation of that country. This was not the action of rogue elements, for the hostility toward blacks, at home and abroad, by the Marine Corps was systemic. One leading officer even referred to Haitians as "miserable cockroaches." Because black

Americans shared a common ancestry with Haitians, both were believed to have inherited "a tendency to revert to savagery."[40]

Henry probably had firsthand experience in this matter. One black veteran of the 369th recalled years later in the film documentary *Men of Bronze* that every time soldiers of the 369th encountered marines behind the lines, the marines attacked them. The men fought back, and the encounters left dead on both sides.[41] The soldiers of the 369th had to fight for their lives not only in the front lines against the Germans but also in the rear against the marines. In light of such experiences, it probably was not far-fetched for Johnson to assert that the marines refused to serve in the trenches with black soldiers. They probably had.

As for Johnson's blanket assertions of white cowardice and black victory, they were incorrect—but no more incorrect or unjust than whites' blanket condemnations of the performance of African American soldiers during the war. Further, his assertions should be understood in the context of white denigration of and attacks on black Americans. A fine line often exists between courage and stupidity. Loving condemned Henry Johnson as "densely ignorant." From another perspective, Johnson's determination to tell his truth appears commendable and courageous in the atmosphere of 1919, just as courageous as his feat of valor to repel the Germans, protect his unit, and save his comrade in May 1918. And that seems to have been the way in which many in the audience took Henry's talk. After hearing mealy-mouthed ministers dwelling on "equanimity between the races," the crowd got what it wanted from Johnson, who "laid down a barrage that broke up all the thoughts and eloquence advanced by the other speakers."[42]

The price that Johnson paid for his words was probably greater than he could have imagined, in terms of both money and reputation. The man who had once been the toast of New York City, Albany, and even blacks nationwide apparently was abandoned. How far his star fell in so short a time is simply tragic. Before the end of the war, for instance, an Albany streetcar line had used Henry to promote war stamps, with large billboards atop their cars asking: "How many stamps did you lick today? Henry Johnson licked a dozen Germans!" Around the same time, Edna Johnson, Henry's wife, had been the guest of honor at a United Service Alliance reception held at the Albany County Courthouse—a rare, if not unprecedented, manner of recognition accorded a black person by that white organization.[43]

When Henry returned to Albany, a group known as the Henry Johnson Home Benefit Committee began a campaign to buy the local hero a house. How far that campaign went cannot be determined with certainty, but nearly a month after its inception, the fund totaled only $256. Another prominent Albany businessman gave Johnson a new uniform and got a photo opportunity and free advertising in return. Yet, it seems that Johnson could not find suitable employment, seemingly because the debilitating injuries suffered in combat prevented him from handling "Negro jobs." Even more, military discharge officers had declared him 0 percent disabled, in accordance with what appears to have been a systematic effort to keep the men of the Regiment below the 30 percent threshold for benefit eligibility.[44]

Thus, Henry apparently had to seek speaking engagements to make ends meet. In September 1919, the *Ohio State Monitor* reported that he had dropped in to the office to inform the staff "that he was the same Johnson that outfought a whole bunch of Germans, . . . capturing all he did not kill." The man purporting to be Johnson was short of stature and in uniform. Attached to his uniform were the Croix de Guerre and the Shoulder Cord of Honor awarded by the French, as well as a pin designating him as an expert rifleman. Johnson reportedly had arranged some appearances in Columbus, and the *Monitor* anticipated public interest in hearing "Johnson tell how he did it."[45] As will become evident, that visit was not without another specific purpose, and it tells much about the relationship between Johnson and Roberts.

Henry's last public appearance in New York was on an unspecified date in 1919, when Alderman Fred Moore invited him to aid in the Victory Loan drive. Johnson reportedly told of his war exploits to audiences on Wall Street and in Harlem. Thereafter, he seems to have wandered from city to city, never settling down.[46] Soon, he virtually disappeared from the public view and record. Henry's actions alone could not be blamed for this outcome, as he was also a victim of a systematic campaign by the government and the military, often aided and abetted by the press, to smear, denigrate, forget, dismiss, and deny the role of the black combat soldier in World War I.

A man whose name was invoked in unimaginable contexts and for all kinds of purposes only a few months before became largely forgotten overnight. When blacks, for example, were attacked by soldiers in Rockaway Beach, New York, the soldiers were said to have sought reinforcements, fearing that there might be "a Henry Johnson or Needham Roberts in the bunch." When the famous black orator Roscoe Conkling Simmons needed examples of black heroism, he invoked Henry and Neadom "above whom no hero of the struggle is to be placed." Indeed, Johnson and Roberts were the gold standard of heroism, and all subsequent acts would be compared to theirs. Lincoln Eyre likened William Butler's exploits, for which Butler earned the Distinguished Service Cross, to "the performance of Henry

Johnson and Needham Roberts." When blacks in Poughkeepsie, New York, celebrated the Fourth of July in 1918, they carried banners remembering the deeds of Crispus Attucks and Johnson and Roberts. The *Defender* had made a similar comparison in arguing that Attucks and the two heroes of the 369th were proof that no group of Americans was more willing to shed blood for the nation than blacks.[47]

On July 10, 1929, after little or no news on Johnson for almost ten years, the *Amsterdam News* reported Henry's death on page 1 under the headline TAPS SOUNDED FOR WM. H. JOHNSON, GREATEST OF WORLD WAR HEROES. The story, supplied by the Capital News Service, reported in a somber and restrained manner that Johnson had died on July 2 (it was actually July 1) "almost in poverty," was "buried with full military honors at Arlington National Cemetery," and was survived by his wife, Minnie. Though the story recounted Johnson's feat, along with Neadom Roberts's, it did not venture far beyond the official accounts.[48]

No cause of death was given by the paper, but official records indicate it was myocarditis, with acute cardiac dilatation as the contributing factor. In other words, Henry died of an enlarged heart, which could have been brought on by undue exertion; strong emotional excitement; or infectious diseases such as chronic bronchitis, tuberculosis, emphysema, and kindred pathologies.[49] Any of these might have been related to his war experience or the difficult life he lived after his service. The man who had shown so much heart in 1919 was laid low by its failure, brought on, perhaps, by the crushing pressure of fleeting fame without lasting reward.

Despite its restraint, the *Amsterdam News* report contained a seed of hyperbole that grew with subsequent tellings as the black press picked up the wire. Somehow, Henry's Croix de Guerre had multiplied into many medals "exhibited by the National Museum." When the *Chicago Defender* ran its version of the original release on July 20, Henry had "won almost every medal for bravery," totaling "nearly 100," including the Distinguished Service Cross.[50] In death, Henry's legend continued to grow, and accuracy could not compete with a good story.

Then, except for brief mention on special occasions, which will be discussed in the context of Neadom Roberts, Henry Johnson once again faded from public view and memory. Not until the 1970s did he begin to reappear. In 1972, John J. McEneny, an Albany official, commissioned a mural of Johnson for the city hall because he believed that Johnson had not received the credit he deserved. Painted by Gregory Green of Atlanta, the work of art won the Freedom Shrine award. Then, in 1976, the US Army bicentennial poster series featured a silhouette of Johnson uttering a version of the line attributed to him by Arthur Little, "Don't worry about me. I've been shot before." Evidently, the army believed the street-smart, tough-guy image would work with black youth, as it displayed the poster in African American communities.[51] Of course, the quote begs the questions of when, where, why, and how Henry had been shot before.

Johnson's adopted city finally honored him on Veterans Day 1991 as Mayor Thomas Whalen publicly acknowledged that proper recognition of one of the city's "finest heroes is long overdue." The city held a parade in his honor and named a major boulevard for him, and after years of fundraising, the Veterans Association of the 369th dedicated a granite monument to Johnson in Washington Park. On Memorial Day five years later, the Albany chapter of the Veterans Association, led by its historian, John Howe, completed the monument with a bronze bust of Johnson atop.[52]

The efforts of the Veterans Association of the 369th were beginning to pay off, but they had a higher award in mind for Johnson, namely, the Medal of Honor. As early as 1988, his supporters evidently convinced US senators Alphonse D'Amato and Daniel Patrick Moynihan to sponsor a bill for the relief of Henry Johnson by waiving "time limitations relating to the award of a Medal of Honor to a named individual for acts of heroism during World War I." Johnson was not eligible because he had not been recommended for such an honor within two years of his action.[53]

The chances for Johnson looked bleak, since no black soldier of World War I had been so honored until Freddie Stowers of South Carolina received the medal posthumously on April 24, 1991.[54] With that breakthrough, US representative Michael McNulty and fifteen cosponsors introduced a bill similar to that of the two senators from New York, on July 24, 1991. The effort was unsuccessful, as many others would be, despite the positive outcome in the Stowers matter. In that case, the commanding officer of the 371st had made the recommendation in a timely fashion, but the request had been "misplaced" until it was uncovered by Congressmen Joe DioGuardi and Mickey Leland. Thus, Stowers's review required no special legislation to circumvent the Pentagon's statute of limitations.[55]

A glimmer of hope had come on July 10, 1996, when President Bill Clinton awarded Johnson the Purple Heart. In January 1997, the Army Decorations Board, after a review of Johnson's case, found him unworthy of the Medal of Honor. Representative McNulty vowed to fight on "until justice prevails."[56]

By that time, New York governor George Pataki had taken up the cause. In 1996, with the premier of the History Channel film *Harlem Hellfighters*, Pataki authorized the adjutant general of New York to announce its showing and add that the state would do everything it could to obtain justice for Henry Johnson through suitable recognition. Henry once again had become a good and safe cause with which to be identified. The next year, the governor directed the Division of Military and Naval Affairs (DMNA) to submit a recommendation through military channels for awarding the Medal of Honor. In 1998 and again in 2000, he sent a separate letter to the secretary of the army urging the same.[57]

Senator Charles Schumer then joined the movement, and after two years of lobbying the Departments of Defense and the Army, victory seemed to be close at hand when Secretary of the Army Louis Caldera, in January 2001, recommended that Johnson receive the medal. In April, the chairman of the Joint Chiefs of Staff, Gen. Henry H. Shelton, refused to endorse Caldera's recommendation.[58] It was a sign of things to come from the new administration in Washington.

Schumer then called for civic action to pressure the Bush White House to support the award for Johnson. Western Union took up Schumer's call to businesses to become involved by distributing 9,000 calling cards to customers, "urging them to voice their support for giving the long overdue medal to Johnson."[59]

The movement received another unexpected boost when Brian J. Purnell, a research assistant who helped in preparing this book, found evidence indicating that Henry Johnson had received a full military funeral at Arlington National Cemetery in 1929. The finding reversed years of speculation about his final resting place, including his interment in a potters' field near the Albany Airport. Governor Pataki credited the "discovery" with giving "his story, which before was almost the stuff of legend, the tangible substance it had lacked for so many years." Maurice Thornton, then national vice president of the 369th Veterans Association and adjunct professor of African studies at Albany University, concluded that the fact that Johnson "was interred in this hallowed place of heroes, confirms that those responsible in 1929 were aware of his accomplishments on the battlefield, yet did not act to see that they were recognized with the appropriate military decoration."[60]

In response to the intense pressure from Schumer and others, the army employed a deflective strategy designed to defeat the movement by awarding Johnson its second-highest honor, the Distinguished Service Cross. The award ceremony took place on February 13, 2003, at the Hall of the Heroes in the Pentagon. Senator Schumer and Congressman McNulty joined the director of the Army National Guard, Lt. Gen. Roger Schultz, in presenting the DSC to Johnson's family.[61]

Although disappointed that the Pentagon still had not awarded Johnson the Medal of Honor, Schumer saw the awarding of the DSC not as a defeat but as a "significant step in our ongoing efforts to get him the Medal of Honor." McNulty applauded "the decision to recognize him [Johnson] with the Distinguished Service Cross," though he too maintained that Johnson deserved the Medal of Honor.[62] These political forces, formidable as they were, proved to be no match for the military establishment and the White House. The awarding of the DSC effectively sapped the energy of the Medal of Honor proponents by undermining the argument that Johnson has not been properly recognized by the military authorities. Moreover, all legislative efforts to bypass the statute of limitations have failed. The last attempt came in February 2005, when Representative McNulty sponsored a bill, without cosponsors, to exempt Henry Johnson from section 3744(b) of Title 10 of the US Code. McNulty left the House in 2009, and no exemptions to the legislation have been offered since.[63]

Instead of continuing to pursue the Medal of Honor for Johnson with their former vigor, Schumer and McNulty turned their attention to the civilian sector as a means to honor his service by promoting a bill naming the Albany postal facility the United States Postal Service Henry Johnson Annex. With the help of Congressmen Charles Rangel and Sweeney and Senator Hillary Clinton, both houses of Congress approved the legislation. President Bush signed it into law on December 21, 2004, thus giving Henry Johnson a prominence in his adopted city and state that was normally identified with high federal or state officials. Henry, who once stated that had he been white he could have been governor, had been elevated to a far higher symbolic position. It was another big step toward correcting the "injustices of the past," but McNulty said that he would "continue to work with Senator Schumer to go the final step and obtain the Congressional Medal of Honor."[64] On May 15, 2011, representing the month and day that Henry and Neadom made history, Senator Schumer submitted a recommendation for Henry to be considered again for the Medal of Honor. Much optimism surrounded this effort as the brief was based on a much larger body of evidence and the belief that Barack Obama's administration might provide a more favorable climate for success. As of March 27, 2013, Schumer and the Henry Johnson proponents were still waiting to hear from the secretary of the army, and Schumer called for an update on the status of the request and pressed for answers. As late as November that same year, no official answers had been made public.[65]

In the meantime, Henry Johnson's legacy will endure, via permanent reminders honoring his deeds, if not his life. A facility for troubled youth in South Kortright, Delaware County, New York, bears his name, and so does the recently opened Henry Johnson Charter School of Albany, which is dedicated to "building character" and "achieving excellence," in the image of its namesake.[66] One wonders if the truth of Johnson's illiteracy is known by those who found the man to be the appropriate symbol for a place of formal learning.

All of these reminders of Henry Johnson "are elements of the built environment that help (un)fix and represent social identities." Memorials are, in geographer Owen Dwyer's words, "among the preeminent places at which the dynamic relationships between that which is forgotten and remembered, between history and identity, are simultaneously confirmed and contested."[67] As such, they can safely speak to the injustices of the past while diverting attention from those of the present. In Henry's case, they honor a hero and victim but also ignore or obscure the multidimensional human being he was. Nobody cared to ask who he was and what he stood for when alive, and these memorials concretize that ultimate injustice.

In the eyes of the people of Trenton, New Jersey, Neadom Roberts was every bit the hero that Henry Johnson was. Early reports in the local press made him an equal partner in fending off the German raiding party and "possibly saving from capture many of their comrades." In addition, it reported that Roberts and Johnson shared the honor of being the first black soldiers wounded in battle.[68] An editorial in the same paper, one day later, saw the honors earned by these men as "an indirect tribute to their race." They had helped to "open the eyes of the world to their capacities" while stimulating "the growing spirit of liberalism and tolerance" in an increasingly democratic United States. Unfortunately, the paper, in its misjudging of both the present and the future America, assumed there was "no color line in valor."[69]

Roberts, after reportedly spending a month in a military hospital in France, was furloughed stateside and continued his recovery from a compound fracture to the right elbow and a fracture to his right little finger, both caused by bullets. In addition, he suffered from a bayonet wound to his side as well as the aftereffects of gas. He reported only stiffness in his side and finger and some forgetfulness from shock; otherwise, he said, he felt "as well as he ever did." Evidently, a military doctor largely agreed and declared him 8⅓ percent disabled at the time of discharge. On October 25, Roberts, on leave from a military hospital in Cape May, New Jersey, planned to visit his brother Norman in New York and then his family in Trenton.[70]

Excited about his return, Harlem had hoped to give Roberts a public reception but did not want to upstage his native Trenton by honoring its hero. New York could not resist, however, and did its part anyway. Charles Magill of the *Chicago Defender*'s New York office represented and contributed to the excitement generated by the return of Roberts by announcing that "our hero is here"—"the first member of the old Fifteenth Infantry to be wounded in action in France," who, along with Johnson, "held off 24 Germans" and "electrified America."[71] The community feted Roberts with a banquet hosted by Charles W. Anderson at the white-owned Dolphin restaurant in Harlem. Then, the manager of the Lafayette Theatre, simply known as Frenchy, arranged a box party at the theater for Roberts, where the hero accepted a signet ring, listened to poetry in his honor, and received cheers from the audience as he was introduced to the sound of "our national anthem."[72]

Neadom addressed the gathering, but press coverage hinted at an interest in Johnson's role because the newspaper stories had Roberts telling his audience that Henry had returned to the trenches and was still on the firing line. These were heady times for this young man, who some argued ominously should be promoted to captain for his exploits on the battlefield. The *Defender* wondered why "nearly every wounded white hero who returns" home invalided "has been promoted to a captaincy, majority, etc."—why not Roberts? It called on both the government and blacks to do the right thing in making this hero/our hero "what he should be."[73]

Before Roberts returned to Trenton, he was welcomed by a series of telegrams that, along with the treatment he was receiving, easily could have gone to his head. Mayor Frederick Donnelly of Trenton told him that for his glorious upholding of American traditions on the battlefield, his name "will have a cherished place in the remembrance of all patriotic Americans" long after the conflict ended. For that, Trenton saluted him. An officer in the clerk's office of the New Jersey Supreme Court promised Roberts that "the future holds sufficient good things in store to amply compensate you for all sacrifices you have made and for all pains you have suffered." This message would be most remembered for being honored in the breach. It was in many ways a cruel portent of promises unfulfilled. Even then, the tangible signs pointed toward disappointment, as Roberts had hoped to attend college but his "finances" were "not just what they might be."[74]

On November 6, 1918, Trenton saw to it that "no hero from any battlefield was more highly honored," as it recognized Roberts with a parade and grand reception. The press noted his modesty as he simply "smiled and bowed his head as the thousands along [the route] cheered" him as he rode in a convertible automobile. Later that night, hundreds had to be turned away from the testimonial reception at the Grand Theater, since "all wanted to get a look at the nineteen-year-old boy who slew a score of Germans and escaped with his life as he was about to be carried away a prisoner."[75]

Emmett Scott had been scheduled to give an address but sent a letter instead, ostensibly praising Roberts for having rendered "this signal service at a crucial moment." To put the young soldier's heroics in sharper relief, he called upon Irvin Cobb, as close to an eyewitness to Roberts's deed as any civilian. Cobb, who recently had addressed a "monster meeting" at Carnegie Hall in honor of the 15th New York National Guard, said "that the timely action of this fearless warrior, in risking his death that thousands of his fellow-countrymen might live, entitled him to a place in history beside the immortal Crispus Attucks, whose blood was the first to be shed in the revolutionary struggle" that helped to lay the foundation for "the grandest exponent of democracy in government that the world has ever seen."[76]

Scott graciously and tactically recognized the city and its officials for placing "a capstone upon Roberts's marvelous achievement that proves to him and to all of us that 'Republics are not ungrateful' to those who brave dangers for their preservation."[77] What Scott knew all too well was that Trenton's action was the exception in this regard. In fact, what he offered was less in praise of Roberts and more in the service of his superiors in Washington, who sought to appease blacks angry with the treatment black soldiers received from the government and the military. Once again, Roberts became something to be used and not so much honored.

Mayor Donnelly said that Sergeant Roberts, promoted two ranks for his heroics, had "put Trenton on the map of the world" as "the first colored American to be cited for bravery on the battlefield." In addition, the mayor presented Roberts with a considerable sum of money, which was supplemented by a collection at the dinner. Roberts refused an invitation to address the audience, a gesture that only added to the public perception of his modesty.[78] The fact of the matter was that age, not character, probably dictated his reticence. Instead of nineteen, he was only seventeen years old and would not turn eighteen until April 28.[79] Here was a boy who had gone to hell and back. In many ways, he seemed the perfect hero for those who wanted to use him for their purposes.

Roberts's return had, for a brief moment, elevated his role in the episode of May 15, 1918. There is normally room for only one hero, and as one "in the flesh," for now, Roberts occupied that spot; the name of Henry Johnson hardly appeared in connection with the deed in which he nearly always had played the lead. To show how much Roberts's actual presence on the home front meant to his standing, he, the hero-in-the-flesh, sat next to Theodore

Roosevelt at the event mentioned by Scott in which Irvin Cobb heaped such lavish praise on the "young man whose name will go down in the history of American valor on the field."[80]

Roberts's first public speech apparently took place on December 19 in Red Bank, New Jersey, at an event sponsored by "the colored auxiliary of Red Bank chapter of the American Red Cross" to recognize the service of the Red Cross around the world. Although Miss E. A. Knowles was president of the chapter, I. W. Parker chaired the meeting, and the Hon. A. A. Patterson, mayor of Red Bank, delivered the welcoming address. Once again, the women organized the event and the men took the lead.[81]

Neadom, described as the "plucky real life hero," approached the podium to the deafening cheers of the large assemblage. He then sketched his military experience "from enlistment to the day he was invalided home." He "thrilled" the audience "with his account of how he and Henry Johnson put a German raiding party to rout." The audience reportedly interrupted him with applause "upon every mention of the deeds of valor performed by Uncle Sam's colored soldiers." Roberts's speech, which seemingly avoided bitterness or accusation, made the evening "most successful."[82]

Just as he appeared to be gaining his sea legs as a speaker and adjusting to his newfound fame, Roberts was abruptly undercut by the return of the 369th and the darling of the press and public—Henry Johnson. As Arthur Little recalled:

> When the regiment had arrived in New York, the reporters made much of Johnson. They photographed him and they interviewed him. Johnson, always with an eye to the dramatic, told a new story of his fight to each new group of reporters. But it all went. In those days of excitement Sergeant Henry Johnson was not the only member of the regiment who yielded to the temptation to tell a good story.[83]

If Neadom Roberts participated in the parade, he certainly did not ride with Henry Johnson. The fact that Johnson commanded that stage alone symbolized the virtual disappearance of Roberts in the stories that his fellow soldier told and that were told about him. Even more, a rivalry seems to have developed between the two. Contrary to VanDerZee's contrived idealization of their relationship, the two men cannot be found appearing together in any photographs after the war. Moreover, Johnson and Roberts, in that order, apparently competed with each other for the role of hero in the public imagination and space.

When Johnson turned up at the offices of the *Ohio Monitor* in September 1919, he seems to have responded to an advertisement promoting a speech by Neadom Roberts in Memorial Hall on August 22, 1919. With a large picture of Roberts in full dress uniform with combat helmet, the circular read: "Coming! Coming! Sergeant Neadom Roberts: Our First Colored Hero of the Worlds War." The accompanying description elevated Roberts's role and stature even more, describing him as "the first American hero who, with Sergeant Henry Johnson, killed 36 Germans and captured scores of others."[84] Whether Roberts got his chance to "tell how he did it" cannot be determined, but Henry's subsequent appearance suggests that he wanted to make sure that the story would be heard from *his* perspective. All the while, Roberts probably seethed over the attention paid to Johnson and the diminution of his own role in what was arguably the defining moment of the American role in the war.

Though Henry had disappeared from public view, Roberts soon made news for the wrong reasons. His fading military glory and poor financial straits had pushed him to the brink. Perhaps even more crushing was the sensational crime committed by his oldest brother, Norman, who, in August 1923, killed his estranged wife (in front of their six-year-old daughter in a courthouse corridor) as she prepared to testify in divorce proceedings. A lengthy estrangement had come as a result of Norman's alleged involvement in bootlegging and her refusal to continue protecting him. Norman Roberts died at the hands of the police, fulfilling his death wish after a life of trying that had yielded nothing, as revealed in a letter to a friend. Less than a year later, Neadom reportedly attempted suicide by ingesting mercuric chloride. Prompt medical attention saved his life, but he required care for the mental health problems that had led him to this attempt. Sadly, the deep and invisible wounds to the psyche were the most neglected, denied, and difficult to treat.[85]

A year later, Roberts was arrested by federal marshals in New Orleans for impersonating an officer, an act of desperation and delusion. It seems he had internalized that which the *Chicago Defender* argued he deserved—a captaincy. His precarious mental state was revealed when, after being asked about the charges against him, he claimed not to know what they might be but would plead guilty to whatever was preferred. Roberts expressed concern for his family, which he could not support on the $50 he received from the government each month.[86]

In 1928, even more serious signs of Neadom's deteriorating mental health appeared as he was arrested for carnal abuse. According to one report, he was sentenced to fifteen months in jail. As a result of marital and legal difficulties, Neadom divorced his first wife and apparently remarried.[87] He then became a once-a-year hero, brought out for speeches and parades on Armistice Day.

With the passing of Johnson and the passage of time, the details of their historic encounter in the war had grown murkier, thus enabling Roberts and his mediators to place him in the forefront of the affair. A pamphlet of his, published in 1933, had him playing a much more active role not only in the events of May 14–15, 1918, but also, as we have seen, in earlier skirmishes as well. In this piece, he claimed to have earned the Distinguished Service Cross and numerous other honors.[88]

An interview with Roberts that appeared in the *New Jersey Herald News* on November 19, 1938, added some new twists to the tale, with him at the center of the action. As the story goes, Roberts and Johnson hurled Mills bombs at their attackers. Then, Roberts grabbed his rifle, which would not fire because dirt from the trench had gotten into it and caused it to jam. At that moment, four or five Germans entered the trench and forced Roberts to defend himself with a bayonet. He knocked one to the ground and ran his bayonet through another before a third German pushed his weapon through Roberts's side. He remembered that Johnson was "having a hot time at his end of the trench." Then Roberts tried "to stick" the downed German, who shot him in the elbow with an explosive bullet from a handgun. On his knees, Roberts killed the German who had shot him, and he and Johnson routed the rest of the Germans with "potato" bombs they found on their dead victims. Roberts then reported that Johnson, although suffering wounds to his legs and feet, tended his wounds until help arrived. He estimated that they had encountered forty Germans and killed twenty-eight.[89]

Arthur Little was absolutely correct in his assessment that Henry was not the only one inclined to tell a good story. Despite having been described as being from a prominent family, having all kinds of medals and honors, and once playing a leading part in New Jersey politics, Roberts now seemed to have nothing but time on his hands. Although not destitute, he was unemployed. He wanted nothing more than to have a job, and he believed that someone who saved the 369th from a potentially disastrous surprise attack deserved one.[90]

Yet, blackness trumped heroism in determining job opportunities, and the Depression only heightened the inequalities. In 1932, black New Jerseyans' unemployment rate exceeded that for whites by nearly 100 percent. They lost jobs faster than whites and stayed out of work longer. By 1937, the relief roles in New Jersey's eight largest cities revealed that blacks were three to six times more likely to be on the dole than whites. Further, black worker displacement by whites caused even greater hardships.[91] Neadom's war service seemed of little value in such an environment.

Roberts enjoyed a brief revival of fame after the declaration of war on December 7, 1941. As part of a massive effort to secure black support for and participation in the nascent conflict, a national advisory committee, working closely with the US Office of Education, created a series of radio programs entitled "Freedom's People" that dramatized black people's contributions to American life. The fourth installment of that series, scheduled to air on NBC's Red Network on December 21, treated the military and featured Henry Johnson and Neadom Roberts. Noble Sissle was also scheduled to talk about his dearly departed friend James Reese Europe. Once again, Roberts and Johnson and the 369th were called upon as symbols to rally the forces.[92]

For whatever reason, perhaps just to set the record straight or for financial considerations, Roberts applied for an official change of name on his birth certificate in 1945. Thus, the man officially recorded as Leedom but known mostly as Needham became Neadom as a matter of law. A family friend, Florence Kinney, attested to his identity.[93]

The name change likely signified that Neadom had brought some order to his life—but that order would be irreparably destroyed in the spring of 1949 when an eight-year-old girl in a Newark movie theater told another patron that Roberts was "bothering" her. The child's father summoned the theater manager, who called police. They took Roberts into custody and released him on a $1,000 bond.[94]

The incident proved devastating to Roberts and his second wife, Iola. With a job as a messenger or sound man for a radio station in New York, he had seemed to have found himself. Yet, there was deep trouble beneath the veneer of stability. According to Ruth Claggett, a good friend and neighbor, the incident in the theater caused the couple to brood. Then, the unimaginable happened. Claggett found Roberts and his wife hanging from a rafter in their basement. She discovered a note on the kitchen table penned by Iola Roberts, which read: "This is a very hard letter to write. Neadom and I are going together. It is the best way. He is innocent of any charges against him."[95] A double suicide, with an assist from Neadom, was not the solution that a stable, well-adjusted couple would choose.

Iola Roberts was thirty-nine and Neadom just six days shy of his forty-eighth birthday. The other hero of no-man's-land died unable to cope with the horror of war and the jarring ups and downs of its aftermath. The couple was buried in Newark's Fairmount Cemetery, with many veterans from New York and New Jersey in attendance.[96] Yet, Roberts went to his grave with nothing more than a Purple Heart from the US military and a typical military send-off with an honor guard, the playing of taps, and a flag-draped coffin; there was no army caisson in the funeral cortege. Even more, he would be trumped again by Henry Johnson, who was resting with other heroes in Arlington National Cemetery.[97]

From time to time, Roberts was remembered in nostalgic pieces published by the *Trenton Sunday Times-Advertiser* under the "Trenton in Bygone Days" column. Typically, they recited the episode that made him famous and characterized him as a "shy Negro boy." The articles were also typical in their inattention to facts and details, including the spelling of his name. One even perpetuated the falsehood that he had received the Distinguished Service Cross. Other than mentioning his parents and where he lived as a boy, the author of these articles cared nothing for the man but only the legend.[98] Not until Jon Blackwell's biographical essay in 1998 was there any treatment of Roberts as a very complex and troubled human being.[99] However, not even that attempt suggested the possible causal links between Neadom's postservice problems, on one hand, and his war experience and dark family history, on the other.

One must ask just one question to begin the process of understanding Neadom Roberts and the way he chose to depart this world. What is the meaning of life to someone who experiences his greatest triumph—in a desperate struggle for survival, in the service of country and his fellow man—at the age of sixteen? Yes, instant fame followed, but it proved to be not so much something that benefited him as something to be used by others. His fame did not facilitate the understanding of the hero as human being, and it did not provide him sufficient material reward. When Neadom cried out for help through his acts of desperation, no one listened because they neither knew nor cared for Neadom Roberts the person. Yet, that cry was not just for self; it represented the desperate plea of so many veterans, both black and white. If nothing else, Neadom's life and death should be an object lesson in how we care for our heroes, big and small. We do their memory no good whatsoever in glossing over their problems, for these men would not want what happened to them to befall those who come after. Henry told the truth and paid a large price. Neadom internalized his pain and suffered mightily. His final act was his last determined effort to regain control of a life that events and internal demons had overtaken.

On March 15, 2002, the Senate and General Assembly of New Jersey recognized Roberts with a joint legislative resolution. It was the state's way of remembering a native son "who served his country with honor and valor" and as "one of the first-ever African-Americans to receive the prestigious Croix de Guerre." The resolution does not mention that the award, which it refers to as "the highest military award at that time," came from the French. It rather aptly describes the episode of May 14–15 and proclaims that the "unparalleled bravery demonstrated by Needham Roberts in this fight for freedom and democracy . . . will never be forgotten."

Then, the resolution invokes Roberts's memory "as a testament to the pride and dedication of those men and women who serve in our armed forces." Thus, in its well-intentioned but subtly political honoring of Roberts, the document, as speech act, uses the man in ways that his mode and manner of death suggest he would have rejected. Though understandably avoiding the difficult circumstances of Roberts's life and death, the resolution not only denies the facts but also overcompensates for them by saluting him "as an individual of outstanding character and exceptional determination." This is what people want Roberts to be, not who he was, although they might have been right in unexpected and unintended ways in citing his "exceptional determination."

The resolution ends in a bizarre manner by paying "tribute to his meritorious acts of valor" and extending "best wishes for his continued success and happiness."[100] On the one hand, the authors of the resolution had neglected to revise a standard phrase obviously designed for the living. On the other, they distorted the lesson that Neadom Roberts's life and demise could teach—to take care of your heroes in life and understand and respect them as people. That effort would also include telling his story truthfully and spelling his name the way he insisted.

The sacrifice that Roberts made and the service that he gave his country should not go unrewarded. Johnson and he should not be honored so much for what they did but for what they meant and how they served so many so well for so many years.

# Epilogue

### *A Brief Look at the Postwar Careers and Lives of a Few Outstanding Black and White Officers and Men*

## James Reese Europe

According to the *New York Age,* when the 369th returned to New York, James Europe, along with William Hayward and Henry Johnson, was "more in the limelight than any other members of the regiment," and his band reportedly received "columns of space in the newspapers."[1] Yet Europe stands alone as the only member to have received book-length dedicated biographical treatment. That attention is as much for Europe's artistic contributions and fame before the war, his lasting musical legacy after the war, and the untimely and tragic circumstances of his death as it is for any role he played during the war.

The future seemed so bright for Europe and the band after the great victory parade. Well-known theatrical promoters realized the potential of the band and arranged to send it on a national tour. The first stop was the Manhattan Casino, with the beginning of the "jazz craze" and the crowning of Europe as the "jazz king."[2] After returning from a controversial and turbulent leg in the Midwest, the band performed its last concert with Europe at the helm on May 9, 1919, at Mechanics Hall in Boston. There, a disturbed drummer named Herbert Wright, one-half of the unrelated "Wright Twins," fatally stabbed the demanding Europe in a quarrel over perceived mistreatment.[3]

As a testament to his fame as well as the senseless and sensational manner of his death, Europe was front-page news not only in the nation's black press but also in the *New York Times,* which credited him with transforming a good military band into arguably the best in the world through studying French army bands, which were "incontestably superior to our own." The editorial saved its highest compliment for last: "Ragtime may be negro music, more alive than much other American music; and Europe was one of the Americans who was contributing most to its development."[4]

On May 13, thousands, black and white, paid their respects to Europe in one of the largest funerals ever held for a black person in the city. The Reverend William H. Brooks of the Old 15th and the 15th New York Guard delivered the eulogy. Among his white former superior officers in attendance were Hayward, L'Esperance, Fish, Hinton, and Clark. Ford Dabney directed the band, and officers of the 15th NYG, led by Charles W. Fillmore, served as honorary pallbearers.[5] In addition to being buried at Arlington National Cemetery, Europe was honored by having American Legion Post 5 in Washington, DC, bear his name since 1919, although few who belonged to the post in 2000 probably understood the significance attached to it.[6]

### Charles Ward Fillmore

There can be little doubt that without his unstinting devotion to the realization of a black regiment in the New York National Guard, there might not have been one in World War I. Fillmore's tireless efforts on behalf of the drive for a regiment and his refusal to surrender to the relentless stonewalling by politicians and the National Guard leadership in New York and Washington somehow managed to keep his beleaguered provisional regiment intact and available should a call come. Despite his desire to lead the regiment and the insults hurled from all sides against such an outcome, Fillmore never let personal ambition override his loyalty to the institution. When a white man, William Hayward, was named commander and received much of the credit for the formation of the Regiment, Fillmore accepted his role as captain and supported the enterprise. He won a medal for bravery while with the 369th—the Croix de Guerre. Like so many others, he received no American honors.[7] He only left the Regiment when he was reassigned to the 366th and 370th Regiments in the AEF purge of black officers from the 369th.[8]

When he returned to New York, his loyalty still lay with the 369th, and after its disbandment, he and a group of veterans established a temporary civic organization for the purpose of promoting the "social, beneficial, and civic protection of its members."[9] Fillmore also kept his military career active by joining the 15th New York Guard, in hopes of becoming its first black commander. After a promotion to lieutenant colonel, Fillmore stood next in line to lead the Regiment as it was at the threshold of regaining its federal recognition, but in May of 1920, he was moved to the reserve list, apparently forced out of active service as General O'Ryan maneuvered Arthur Little into command. Then, Fillmore continued the fight from the outside for a black commander, but he turned most of his boundless energy to politics and his job as an auditor in the office of the New York state secretary.[10]

Fillmore remained a loyal Republican and became the party's leader in the 19th Assembly District of New York County. For his successful efforts in sending Republicans from black districts to the state legislature, he was recognized by William J. Maier, chairman of the Republican State Committee of New York, in 1930. After two terms as leader, Fillmore retired because of failing health.[11]

Fillmore died on April 27, 1942, but not before seeing his dream of having a black commander at the helm of the Regiment fulfilled two times over. Chauncey Hooper, who had served with Fillmore in the Old 15th, the 369th, and the 15th NYG, ensured that the dedicated servant of the Regiment received a worthy final tribute by allowing his body to lie in state at the 369th Armory. Fittingly, Fillmore was buried in Arlington National Cemetery. In the end, none of the coverage of his death gave him credit for making the Old 15th possible.[12]

**Chauncey Hooper**

Although technically he was the second black to command the 369th, Hooper was in many ways the first. A native of New Jersey but schooled in New York, he was a true New Yorker. His long career with the 15th/369th and in public service as well as his activity in electoral politics attest to his membership in the community. He was the ultimate citizen-soldier.

Hooper led the unit during the very difficult times before, during, and after World War II. In addition to commanding a unit in transition from infantry to artillery, he also had to steer the men through the treacherous shoals of racial hostility, which confronted them virtually wherever and whenever they trained outside New York City. Even Hawaii, seemingly a place full of promise for harmonious race relations, was in reality a site where racial struggle became necessary. There, white soldiers and sailors had poisoned the minds of the territory's peoples against blacks, whom they had represented as bestial in appearance, behavior, and character. Even more, many of these servicemen refused to respect rank in Hawaii. Black soldiers insisted "that rank and not race, regulation and not custom" should determine relations among men of the military. Because of its World War I record, its status as a highly trained and skilled artillery unit, and its exposure to the most cosmopolitan environment in the United States, if not the world, the 369th led the charge against racism and toward a re-casting of the meaning of race in Hawaii."[13]

Hooper led his men through these internal struggles as well as an important battle in the Ryukus (Okinawa). After the war, he would see the Regiment through further reorganization as the 369th AAA Group, the 369th Signal Radar Maintenance Unit, and the 870th AAA Automatic Weapons Battalion. All were to be housed in the armory at Fifth Avenue and 142nd Street. In addition to the absorption of the 15th New York Guard, Hooper led an all-out recruiting campaign to ensure that his group reached the quota assigned to it.[14] This was all a continuation of the process by which the Regiment was destroyed in order to save it.

As testament to the high regard in which authorities held Hooper, when he reached the mandatory retirement age, fifty-five, as a commander of a combat unit in the New York National Guard, the commander of the NYNG assigned him to the state headquarters detachment. Thus, on June 1, 1950, Col. Chauncey Hooper left the Regiment that he had been associated with since 1916 as a private. He was replaced by Cato L. Baskerville, commander of the 771st Antiaircraft Automatic Weapons Battalion of Brooklyn.[15]

Hooper eventually became a general, ran for Manhattan Borough president, and lost in a tightly contested and highly contentious race in 1953. He retired from the National Guard on July 6, 1954, and died on December 31, 1966, at age seventy-six.

### Napoleon Bonaparte Marshall

Marshall was the first officer from the 15th/369th to return home. Technically, he was no longer a member of the Regiment because he had received a transfer to the 365th to become commander of Company A in July 1918. It was with that unit that Marshall suffered the injuries that sent him home in December. Nonetheless, his loyalty still lay with his Rattlers, who, he told the press, "were right after the Germans and kept after them." Harlem, he maintained, had done itself proud, as these black fighters with little training "went right into battle and made Germany's best troops feel pretty sick."[16]

Evidently, many of his former subordinates felt the same way about him. When a petition with 10,000 signatures was sent to Governor Smith in December 1920 seeking the appointment of a black man to command the 15th New York Guard, Marshall reportedly had the support of a majority of the 600 members of the Regiment, who were firm in their determination to have a black leader.[17]

Whether Marshall sought the position or desired future military service is not clear because he accepted President Harding's appointment of him as a legatee to Haiti, where he served from 1922 to 1928, only to become one of the staunchest critics of the occupation after he left that position. With the help of his wife, he institutionalized his support of Haitians and his opposition to the US occupation through the Save Haiti League.[18]

Haiti and his private law practice would become Marshall's life's work. He died on June 2, 1933, reportedly from injuries suffered in the war although he had also survived being hit by an automobile in New York after the war. Unlike many, Marshall understated his military record and exploits. He prided himself on preserving "the reticence of a veteran" and told his story rarely—once before a reunion of his Harvard class and again in a "cursory military autobiography." He was remembered fondly and respectfully by New Yorkers, who turned out to pay respects to him as his body lay in state at the 369th Armory. Fittingly, he received a hero's burial in Arlington National Cemetery.[19]

### Horace Pippin

Pippin was one of the Regiment's best noncommissioned officers and natural leaders as well as one of its great narrators, but he would speak most vividly about his experience through his art. During wartime, he filled notebooks with compelling sketches, but his greatest artistic achievements came later as a result of that experience coupled with endless practice to hone the skills he had shown from childhood. As he put it, the war had inspired his art because he could never forget the suffering and the sunsets that were seared into his mind, which allowed him to paint from these memories as though they were from yesterday.[20]

Born in West Chester, Pennsylvania, in 1888, Pippin spent his childhood in Goshen, New York, and dropped out of school at age fourteen to help support his domestic-worker mother. Before joining the 15th, Pippin had held a series of menial jobs. Fortunately, as a partially disabled veteran, he had an innate skill that turned him into one of the foremost self-trained American artists of the twentieth century. His paintings, according to art critic Stephen May, are characterized by "simplified forms, flattened perspectives, and an intuitive sense of color, composition and narrative," and as such, they combine "folk-art qualities with artistic sophistication." Remarkably, Pippin achieved all of this by wielding a paintbrush with his badly damaged right arm supported by his good left arm. "The End of the War" (c. 1930), his first major effort, reportedly took three years to complete and required 100 coats of paint. In 1937, N. C. Wyeth discovered one of Pippin's paintings and with the help of a Philadelphia art dealer was able to convince major museums to display his art. Before long, Pippin's patrons were famous actors John Garfield, Charles Laughton, and Edward G. Robinson. In addition to numerous military-related works, Pippin painted African American domestic life, stills, portraits, historical vignettes, and religious scenes. Yet, according to Karen Wilkin, his best renderings came from his experience and imagination.[21]

Despite his fame, Horace Pippin never became rich from his work. In fact, his wife continued to work as a laundress, not sure of how long his success would last. As it turned out, the man who used painting as therapy for his injured arm remained a success for the rest of his life and beyond. When he died in West Chester in 1946, Pippin was eulogized by the *New York Times* as the "most important Negro painter" to have appeared in America, an opinion that reflected a consensus about his place in American art and the significance of his achievement, according to historian Steve Conn. Even more, Conn argues that Pippin must be seen as connected to and engaged in the debates over the meaning of history taking place in the 1930s and 1940s, especially in relation to African American politics of the time.[22] A local historical marker in his memory seriously understates his significance:

HORACE PIPPIN

Born in West Chester in 1888, Pippin occupied this house
From 1920 until his death in 1946. A self-taught black artist,
he painted while living here such notable works as "Domino Players,"
"John Brown Going to His Hanging," and the "Holy Mountain" series.

## Noble Sissle

No former member of the Regiment could equal Noble Sissle in terms of visibility, longevity, and the fame brought by accomplishment. Although he was one of the Regiment's important narrators, his story was not centered on combat. He, like James Reese Europe, would be remembered for the incident in Spartanburg and, even more, for the band. Indeed, Sissle saw himself as responsible for carrying on the legacy of his great friend and mentor Europe. As the man who gave comfort to General Gourard by singing to him of Joan of Arc in French, Sissle honored the memory of the French, its outstanding general, his dear friend Jim Europe, and the Regiment by laying a wreath at the statue of the French martyr with a ribbon that read: "Reverently placed by Noble Sissle, who served with General Gourard's Fourth French Army, in memory of the songs he sang for his General. Jeanne d'Arc, La Victoire Est Pour Vous."[23]

Sissle was born in Indianapolis, Indiana, on July 10, 1889, to a Methodist minister father and a schoolteacher mother. As only dignified music was allowed in the home, he learned to play the organ and mandolin and to sing. He was an honor student in Cleveland and the only black member of the glee club, which he helped to organize. He toured with the Chautauqua Circuit and subsequently worked with orchestras at fine hotels before joining Europe's Fifteenth Band. After the war, Sissle collaborated with Eubie Blake on the all-black revue *Shuffle Along,* which featured the songs "I'm Just Wild about Harry," "Love Will Find a Way," and "You Were Meant for Me." They followed up that success with *The Chocolate Dandies* in 1925 and became international stars, performing for royalty and heads of state around the world.[24]

Sissle was the founder and first president of the Negro Actors Guild and a member of the American Society of Composer, Authors, and Publishers (ASCAP), which he joined in 1922. In the former role, he, among other things, supported and pushed for the representation of black performers at army bases and camps.[25] In the 1950s, his band was one of the most popular in the land, and he attracted large crowds to Billy Rose's Diamond Horseshoe nightclub in New York City. In 1950, Sissle succeeded the late Bill "Bojangles" Robinson as the unofficial mayor of Harlem, pledging to work for the improvement of interfaith business, civil, and welfare relations in Greater New York. Sissle also actively helped to keep the memory of the Regiment alive with his participation in government-sponsored radio programming and with a manuscript he wrote that was widely publicized but never published.[26]

In 1972, Sissle was among thirty outstanding black instrumentalists and singers to receive the Ellington Medal from Kingman Brewster, president of Yale University. Sissle's life was not without controversy, however, for he went through two public divorces and faced a charge of purchasing liquor illegally in Canada. Noble Sissle, characterized by ASCAP president Stanley Adams as a true gentleman whose talents have left permanent contributions to American music, died on December 18, 1975, and thousands paid their respects, including leading musical performers Billy Taylor, Honi Coles, Cab Calloway, and Eubie Blake, as well as Hamilton Fish. He was eighty-six.[27]

### William Hayward

Without question, Hayward returned from World War I a triumphant hero. He had earned the Legion of Honor and the Croix de Guerre with Silver Star from the French and shortly after his arrival stateside received a Distinguished Service Medal from General Pershing "for exceptionally meritorious and distinguished services."[28] The citation was small consolation for the difficult and trying circumstances that the AEF had forced upon

Hayward and his men, but it also vindicated him against his many detractors, including Hamilton Fish.

After the war, Hayward withdrew from the Regiment but advocated for the elevation of blacks to leadership positions in light of the "entirely different situation," meaning an ample supply of qualified men. However, he did pledge to support the erection of a monument to the 369th and the construction of an armory, the latter idea floated by the *Evening Sun*. Indeed, Hayward's last "official" act with the Regiment was to review the armory during its dedication ceremony. He was accompanied by, among others, Lorillard Spencer and Hamilton Fish, his old nemesis who was nonetheless an important political ally as a Republican member of Congress and a continued supporter of the Regiment.[29]

The tall, dark, and handsome man with big blue eyes, a dimple in his chin, and irresistible charm married a wealthy widow, Mae C. Plant, and started a legal practice with John Holley Clark and David L'Esperance, two former officers of the 15th/369th.[30] Then, on June 3, 1921, the US Senate confirmed Hayward as the US attorney for the Southern District of New York. The announcement came with the obligatory references to his leadership of the 15th/369th.[31]

Hayward would be mentioned in connection with political office for the next few years. In July 1921, rumors circulated that he would run for mayor. He avoided potential conflict of interest charges and disavowed any such intentions in a lengthy published statement.[32] Hayward, who had been the chairman of the State Republican Convention in 1920, remained active in politics and was a delegate to the Republican National Convention in 1924. One year later, his party considered him for the post of governor, but Theodore Roosevelt, Jr., received the nomination instead.[33]

Hayward left his position in 1925 to have more time to enjoy his newfound wealth. He became a big-game hunter and a patron of the Museum of Natural History as well as the city's zoos, which he provided with live polar bears. The former University of Nebraska baseball and football star also served as general counsel of the American Professional Football League, established in 1926.[34]

On October 13, 1944, Hayward succumbed to cancer after a long battle that had confined him to a wheelchair. More than 600 friends, business associates, officers, and members of the 369th attended his funeral service at St. Bartholomew's Church. Seventeen officers of the Regiment served as honorary pallbearers, and sixty members of the Old 15th formed a guard of honor for the flag-draped coffin. Hamilton Fish, putting aside old differences, was among the honorary pallbearers.[35]

Whatever one might think of Hayward's role and his overshadowing of Charles Fillmore as the most important figure in the Regiment's existence and subsequent success, there can be little doubt that he was, under the circumstances, the right white man for the job. He seemed to understand the psychology of the men of the Regiment and brought most of his officers around to his way of thinking. As such, he earned the loyalty and respect of his black subordinates, accomplishing "wonders" in the process.[36]

## Arthur West Little

Little, perhaps more than any other person, was responsible for the Regiment's postwar existence and its legacy. As an earlier discussion revealed, his contribution in both regards came at considerable cost to Little himself and to the Regiment. Little's appointment as commander assured that the Regiment would achieve federal recognition, but it also denied blacks the leadership they long had sought for the 369th. At the same time, many believed that Little saw to the virtual elimination of black officers. It was, no doubt, part of the deal he struck with his old friend and patron General O'Ryan, who facilitated Little's initial attachment to the Old 15th. As for a lasting legacy, his book *From Harlem to the Rhine* remained the only comprehensive book-length treatment of the 369th until Reid Badger's biography of James Reese Europe, *A Life in Ragtime* (1995), and Stephen Harris's *Harlem's Hell Fighters* (2003). Yet, as has been pointed out, Little's volume is marred by a paternalistic tone and littered with obligatory black dialect and darkey jokes.

No matter what one might think of Little's actions and words, there can be no question that he was intensely committed to the Regiment and its men. As evidence, in 1929 the sergeant major of his battalion, Francis S. Marshall, publicly attested that "for months" Little "had slept with us, had eaten with us, and had become one of us." The men were his children, and he accepted paternity. According to Marshall, the "boys had so much confidence" in his courage and "so much love for him that had he given the order to go anywhere, they would have followed him without blinking an eye." That confidence was born in recognition of Little's uncanny "knowledge of how to keep men from being killed."[37]

Little had returned home from the war as a highly decorated officer, receiving the Croix de Guerre with Palm and the Legion of Honor with Gilt and Silver Stars. In 1923, he received the Silver Star from his own nation for gallantry in action, as well as a Purple Heart. Little continued and strengthened his and the Regiment's ties with France and became a commander of the Order of Black Star. That relationship also seemed to have played a role in the eventual recognition of the 369th after the war. New York State awarded him the Conspicuous Service Medal.[38]

Little continued as chairman of the board of J. J. Little and Ives Company and remained active in Republican politics. He was considered as a candidate of the Fusion Party for mayor in 1929 but lost out to Fiorello La Guardia. In 1936, he unsuccessfully sought the nomination of the Republican Party for vice president. For ten years, Little was a member of the Business and Planning Department of the US Department of Commerce. In 1941, Mayor La Guardia named Little as his military aide to assist him in matters connected with the selective service, and Little served in that capacity without pay.[39]

Failing health caused him to relinquish his position after two months, and on July 18, 1943, he died. Little was a member of the National Farmers Union, the American Legion, the Veterans of Foreign Wars, and the Sons of the American Revolution. He had two sons—both soldiers—with his first wife. He outlived two other wives and married for a fourth time in 1941.[40]

By the time of his death in 1943, Little had become so identified with the Regiment that the *New York Times* credited him with not only championing "the rights of Negroes" but also commanding "the Fifteenth Infantry, later the 369th United States Infantry, of Negro troops in the first World War."[41] This news must have come as quite a shock to his still-living commander, William Hayward.

As a last gesture of allegiance to the Old 15th, Little's widow, Mary Sheldon Murphy Little, presented the regimental flag from World War I to the 15th Infantry New York Guard. Col. W. Woodruff Chisum, commander, accepted the memento. Mary also gave fifteen photographs of the 369th from their action overseas. The true successor to the Old 15th was serving in the Pacific. Chisum headed a group of caretakers, assigned to protect the armory and the community, until the real 369th returned.[42]

## Hamilton Fish

The term *maverick* has lost much of its meaning in recent years, but if anyone personified the term that was Hamilton Fish, who spoke truth to power as few ever have or might. Indeed, it was Fish's gift as a narrator that distinguished his role with the Regiment. As such, he shed rare and bright light on intramural politics, rivalries among officers, personal ambitions, and the everyday lives of white officers. His absolute disdain and disregard for the leadership of Hayward and his own personal ambition created in him extreme ambivalence toward the Regiment and a rather ambiguous relationship to it; he begged to leave yet could not stay away from it.

After the war, Fish won election to Congress and served twelve terms as a member of the US House of Representatives. His firm belief in free market capitalism and an embrace of pacifism eventually put him at odds with President Roosevelt and made him one of the most vehement opponents of his old friend FDR, since he opposed the New Deal and America's move toward war. Although he supported the war after Japan's attack on Pearl Harbor, he always maintained that FDR's nonneutral policies, especially toward Japan, had forced the nation into the conflict unnecessarily. On his hundredth birthday, Fish was asked about his relationship with FDR: he revealed that although he knew Roosevelt had hated him, he himself did not believe in hate but certainly did "despise" the president.[43] Fish also became a staunch anticommunist, which sometimes strained his relations with militant black organizations, even though he considered himself to be a true friend of blacks.

That friendship was most evident in Fish's enduring fight for the rights and recognition of black soldiers. In 1927, he led the ultimately unsuccessful fight for a monument to the 93rd Division, a measure that passed the House but died in the Senate. Before that, Fish had supported a monument to the 369th, only to have the goalpost moved by the Battle Monuments Commission when it decided to recognize no unit smaller than a division.[44] When Secretary of War Stimson effected the transformation of the 9th and 10th Cavalries into labor units, Fish challenged his authority to undo what Congress had done in 1866 without Congress's consent. Fish had done the same with other units converted from artillery to engineers. He had clearly exposed the War Department's efforts to eliminate or drastically limit black combatants overseas.[45] If Fish himself was not leading efforts to support black soldiers, his son carried on his work in support of House authorization of the 369th Veterans Association, to which his father became a charter member. In one of the last public pronouncements Fish made on behalf of the Regiment, he took local, state, and federal officials to task for the deplorable state of the armory, which was only a visible sign of the widespread neglect of the legacy of the 369th.[46]

Hamilton Fish died at age 102 in January 1991. He had been the last surviving officer of the 369th, white or black. Having that distinction over all others was a great source of pride for him, and he often began his letters to editors and officials with "as the last remaining white or black officer alive of the famous 369th Black infantry regiment of WWI." In the end, no better friend of the Regiment had ever lived. One partial explanation for his longevity might be the resurgence of conservatism in the 1980s, which gave him "enormous pleasure."[47] By that time, he already had lived a life far longer and richer than most.

## George Seanor Robb

Robb, the Regiment's only Medal of Honor recipient, was a white man and replacement officer. A native of Kansas with only limited ties to New York as a Columbia University graduate, Robb joined the Regiment in March 1918 and left it in October of the same year. Thus, his identification with the 369th was rather tenuous. Moreover, the fact that the man considered the Regiment's greatest hero, Henry Johnson, only recently earned the Distinguished Service Cross has created even further distance for Robb from the collective embrace of those who ostensibly protect and promote the Regiment's history and legacy. The French awards he earned also attest to his worthiness. They include the Legion of Honor, the Croix de Guerre, and the French Citation Certificate of Montenegrin Prince Danilo I. Consequently, Robb's heroic service cannot and should not be devalued; it should only be put in proper perspective, as we have tried to do in this volume.[48]

After the war, Robb returned to Kansas and entered the real estate business until President Harding appointed him postmaster of Salina, Kansas, in 1923. He held that position until he went to Topeka as the state auditor in 1935, having filled a vacancy created by the death of his predecessor. He won election to the office in 1936 and ran successfully every two years until his retirement at the age of seventy-two in 1960. Robb never talked much about the war, remained humble according to all accounts, and once told a reporter: "I don't consider the Medal of Honor as something that makes me better than some guy on the street. He might deserve the medal more than me." As further evidence of his reputed modesty, Robb even turned down an invitation to receive the medal at Fort Riley. Instead, the army took the event to Robb in his adopted home of Salina, where 15,000 spectators reportedly watched as he became the only Kansan from World I to receive the nation's highest military honor. Robb described the event as a "regular picnic" and enjoyed its informality.[49] A less generous assessment might be that he was not so modest after all and understood where the ceremony would make the biggest impact.

Despite his short stay with the Regiment, Robb had "a host of pleasant memories" and "many sad ones," the latter related to thoughts "of the many fine officers we left over there," especially those he "knew intimately." All of which, he concluded, made "the romance of that really glorious experience" fade "in a hurry." The officers of the Regiment did not forget Robb either. Arthur Little not only wrote about Robb but also tried to visit him, only to find that he was busy on the campaign trail. Hayward did have "a delightful visit with him" and treated Robb like "a long lost son." The only former officer he remained in frequent contact with was John Dunlap of Hutchinson, Kansas, with whom he "held a Council of War" at each meeting.[50]

Robb went on to live a very successful and honorable life. He had two daughters and a reputation as an honest, competent, and loyal servant to the people of Kansas and to his dear old Republican Party. Already suffering from a failing heart and blood clots in the lung, George Robb fell and broke his hip on April 3, 1972, and died shortly thereafter at the age of eighty-four. He was buried in Gypsum Hill Cemetery in Salina.[51]

### Lewis Edward Shaw

A very revealing postwar story emerges around one of the Regiment's most important narrators, Lewis Shaw, and shows that association with the Regiment, no matter one's social standing, could do harm to a military career. That became clear when Shaw applied in 1921 for a commission as major in the newly established US Reserve Corps.[52] As a highly decorated captain with the 369th and with a recommendation from Hayward to a majority, Shaw, a totally dedicated soldier, must have believed his application's chances for approval were good. No response from Washington can be found, but one from the adjutant general of New York State ordered him to report to the commanding officer of Squadron A, Cavalry, New York National Guard as a second lieutenant, effective April 27, 1921. Despite his wartime service and record and a prior history with Squadron A, with which he had served on the Mexican border from July 13, 1916, to December 15, 1916, Shaw had to start his new military career from the very bottom of the officer ranks. If not punishment for having served with the 369th, the action seemed at least a dismissal and disregard of prior service. Shaw accepted his demotion but tragically and ironically died on the way home from officers' training in 1926. He had risen to the rank of first lieutenant.[53]

### David L'Esperance

Shaw's was not the only kind of dismissal that former officers of the 369th suffered. One of the most revealing and intriguing instances involved former Lt. Col. David L'Esperance. After reading Arthur Little's book and ranking it "way out in front" of other books on World War I, Robert P. Holliday of San Francisco wrote Little and asked about "a man named L'Esperance, bearing the title of Colonel," who had made his acquaintance. Despite the fact that L'Esperance was an attorney, Holliday thought that "he was more or less of a four-flusher" with questionable honesty and ethics. Even L'Esperance's appointment to the Los Angeles district attorney's office did not convince this skeptic. His appearance and manner—he was "tall, thin, emaciated looking" and had a "slow drawl"—did not enhance his standing with Holliday, and L'Esperance's identification with the 369th must have heightened Holliday's doubts. The former newspaper publisher asked Little to clear up the matter, and if it was resolved in the affirmative, he pledged "to look [L'Esperance] up the next time I am in Los Angeles and apologize to him." Little's book, for all its faults, had rescued a fellow officer who literally wore his war experience and identification with the French and, by extension, with black soldiers on his sleeve.[54]

## Lorillard Spencer

Spencer, another officer with questionable leadership skills and a blueblood pedigree, returned from war a hero. Although never gaining the respect of junior white officers, Spencer was severely wounded in action and received the Distinguished Service Cross, the Croix de Guerre, and the French Legion of Honor with Gilt and Silver Stars. Mustered out of the service as a lieutenant colonel in August 1917 for failing the professional examination, he received a second chance as a major, probably because of his political connections, and commanded a battalion honorably and bravely, proving himself worthy in the crucible of battle.[55]

Shortly after his return home, Spencer pursued an interest in aviation and became president of Wittemann Aircraft Corporation in 1921 before heading the Atlantic Aircraft Corporation, which became the General Aviation Corporation. He also headed the Fokker Aircraft Corporation in 1927 and 1928. His prewar business expertise and extensive connections positioned him as one of the biggest financial backers of commercial aviation. Spencer never lost touch with his military roots and became a member of the Legion of Valor of the Army and Navy and in August 1924 was elected its national junior vice commander.[56]

Spencer died on June 9, 1939, following complications from a stroke suffered five years earlier. He was fifty-five and was survived by his second wife, four children, and mother. His mother established a trophy in his honor to be awarded annually by the National Council of the Boy Scouts for the region "showing the greatest progress" in making scouting available. She also established a companion cup for the Philippines, where she spent more than twenty-five years aiding the Moros on Sulu Peninsula.[57] It was a fitting tribute to the life of a man with service in his blood.

# APPENDIX
Deaths in the 369th Infantry during Service with the 93rd Division, AEF

## Officers

| Name | Rank | Cause of Death | Date of Death |
| --- | --- | --- | --- |
| Cobb, Frederick W. | Capt | KIA | 9/29/18 |
| Bucher, Elmer E. | 1st Lt | KIA | 10/28/18 |
| Dean, Charles S. | 1st Lt | KIA | 9/27/18 |
| Longshore, Furman B. | 1st Lt | D or OC | 1/30/19 |
| Seibel, George F. | 1st Lt | KIA | 11/11/18 |
| Vogel, William L. | 1st Lt | D or OC | 2/25/19 |
| Clendenen, Paul M. | 2nd Lt | KIA | 9/12/18 |
| Holden, Ernest H. | 2nd Lt | KIA | 11/18 or 9/30/18 |
| Leland, William F. | 2nd Lt | DOW | 9/29/18 |
| McKenzie, John J. | 2nd Lt | KIA | 9/27/18 |
| McNish, Ernest A. | 2nd Lt | KIA | 9/29/18 |
| Murphy, Walter H. | 2nd Lt | D or OC | 10/13/18 |
| Sargent, Harold J. | 2nd Lt | KIA | 11/11/18 |
| Worsham, Arch Dixon | 2nd Lt | KIA | 7/31/18 |

## Enlisted Men

| Name | Rank | Cause of Death | Date of Death |
| --- | --- | --- | --- |
| Alexander, Charles M. | Mec | KIA | 9/28/18 |
| Alladice, George | Pvt | KIA | 7/23/18 |
| Allen, Frank | Pvt | KIA | 9/26/18 |
| Allen, Wallace | Pvt | D or OC | 2/14/19 |
| Anderson, Houston | Pvt | KIA | 9/30/18 |
| Anderson, James | Pvt | D or OC | 1/18/18 |
| Anderson, James A. | Pvt | KIA | 9/27/18 |
| Anderson, John | Pvt | KIA | 10/1/18 |
| Anderson, Lake | Pvt | KIA | 10/28/18 |
| Anderson, Reed Thomas | Pvt | KIA | 9/26/18 |
| Andrews, Alfred | Pvt 1st Cl | KIA | 9/26/18 |
| Axxon, James | Pvt | DOW | 5/17/18 |
| Baker, Roy | Pvt | D or OC | 6/28/18 |
| Barron, Melver W. | Sgt | D or OC | 10/16/18 |
| Baskerville, Hillard | Pvt | KIA | 9/29/18 |
| Battle, Fletcher | Pvt | KIA | 7/15/18 |
| Baylor, Lewis M. | Pvt | D or OC | 9/30/18 |
| Belcher, Sims | Sgt | KIA | 9/27/18 |
| Bell, Edward | Pvt | DOW | 9/29/18 |

| Name | Rank | Cause of Death | Date of Death |
|------|------|----------------|---------------|
| Bell, James | Pvt | D or OC | 12/22/18 |
| Bell, Theodore R. | Pvt | KIA | 9/26/18 |
| Betha, John | Pvt | KIA | 9/30/18 |
| Black, Henry G. | Pvt | KIA | 10/2/18 |
| Black, Isaac | Pvt | D or OC | 1/13/19 |
| Bowe, Lester | Pvt | KIA | 9/27/18 |
| Boyd, Bun | Pvt 1st Cl | KIA | 9/26/18 |
| Brooks, Dorrance | Pvt 1st Cl | KIA | 9/28/18 |
| Brown, George T. | Pvt | DOW | 10/20/18 |
| Brown, Thomas W. | Pvt | KIA | 7/31/18 |
| Brunson, Frank | Pvt | D or OC | 1/3/19 |
| Bryant, Lewis Grover | Pvt | DOW | 9/28/18 |
| Bryant, Rossie | Pvt | DOW | 9/28/18 |
| Burman, Cleveland | Pvt | DOW | 9/26/18 |
| Burnett, Thomas L. | Pvt | DOW | 11/6/18 |
| Campbell, William W. | Pvt | KIA | 9/26/18 |
| Chandle, Arthur | Pvt | KIA | 10/1/18 |
| Chapman, Otto | Pvt | DOW | 9/30/18 |
| Chester, Willie D. | Pvt | D or OC | 3/25/19 |
| Chinn, Russell | Pvt | KIA | 9/26/18 |
| Clay, Walter | Pvt | KIA | 9/28/18 |
| Cloxon, Chris | Pvt | D or OC | 9/28/18 |
| Cook, Adolphus | Pvt | KIA | 10/1/18 |
| Cooper, Will | Pvt | KIA | 9/30/18 |
| Cousin, Robert | Pvt | KIA | 9/26/18 |
| Covington, Dorsey | Pvt | D or OC | 1/6/18 |
| Crews, Crawford | Pvt | KIA | 10/1/18 |
| Cruse, James J. | Pvt | DOW | 10/14/18 |
| Curry, Charlie | Pvt | DOW | 8/11/18 |
| Dancey, James A. | Mess Sgt | D or OC | 8/1/18 |
| Dancy, John | Pvt | D or OC | 11/15/18 |
| Davis, Eugene | Pvt | D or OC | 7/26/18 |
| Davis, George P. | Pvt | KIA | 9/28/18 |
| Davis, Powell | Sgt | D or OC | 5/11/18 |
| Dempsey, Frederick | Pvt | KIA | 9/26/18 |
| Desselle, Hilton | Pvt | KIA | 9/12/18 |
| Dixon, Walter | Pvt | DOW | 10/15/18 |
| Dodin, James | Pvt | D or OC | 6/1/18 |
| Douglas, Abraham | Corp | KIA | 9/26/18 |
| Douglass, Henry | Corp | DOW | 9/30/18 |
| Drumgold, James | Pvt | DOW | 10/7/18 |
| Duckett, Sylvester | Pvt | KIA | 10/1/18 |
| Emby, Edward | Pvt | D or OC | 12/19/18 |
| Emmerson, Jesse | Pvt | DOW | 10/1/18 |

| Name | Rank | Cause of Death | Date of Death |
|------|------|----------------|---------------|
| Evans, Henry | Pvt | KIA | 10/2/18 |
| Evans, Joseph | Pvt | D or OC | 1/1/19 |
| Farrow, Thomas | Pvt | DOW | 10/2/18 |
| Fennell, Jenkins | Pvt | KIA | 8/11/18 |
| Fields, John | Pvt | D or OC | 2/19/19 |
| Flanders, Felix | Pvt | DOW | 11/20/18 |
| Fleury, Oscar | Pvt | D or OC | 3/30/18 |
| Flood, William | Pvt | D or OC | 10/24/18 |
| Ford, James | Pvt | KIA | 9/26/18 |
| Ford, Robert | Mec | KIA | 9/29/18 |
| Forrest, Howard T. | Pvt | DOW | 9/23/18 |
| Francis, Norris | Corp | DOW | 10/29/18 |
| Franklin, Jesse | Pvt | DOW | 10/2/18 |
| Frazier, George H. | Pvt | KIA | 9/26/18 |
| Freeman, Joseph | Pvt | KIA | 7/15/18 |
| Frye, Eliza | Pvt | D or OC | 9/28/18 |
| Fulcher, Joseph | Pvt | KIA | 9/26/18 |
| Gantt, Charles | Pvt 1st Cl | KIA | 9/27/18 |
| German, William | Pvt | KIA | 9/26/18 |
| Geter, Arthur | Pvt | DOW | 9/28/18 |
| Gibbs, Burnett | Pvt | KIA | 8/11/18 |
| Gibson, Howard | Pvt | KIA | 9/26/18 |
| Gibson, Linzy | Pvt | D or OC | 11/20/18 |
| Gilder, Leon | Pvt | D or OC | 7/15/18 |
| Givens, Wholen | Pvt | KIA | 9/29/18 |
| Grant, Stanford M. | Pvt | D or OC | 4/3/18 |
| Grays, Hercules | Pvt | D or OC | 7/11/18 |
| Green, Benjamin F. | Sgt | KIA | 9/26/18 |
| Green, David | Pvt | KIA | 9/26/18 |
| Grier, Henry | Pvt | D or OC | 7/11/18 |
| Hamilton, James | Pvt | KIA | 9/26/18 |
| Harding, Edward | Sgt | DOW | 5/26/18 |
| Harrell, George | Pvt | DOW | 7/16/18 |
| Harris, Clark M. | Pvt | D or OC | 7/9/18 |
| Harris, Percy | Pvt | D or OC | 2/17/19 |
| Harris, Will | Pvt | KIA | 9/29/18 |
| Hartwell, Charlie | Pvt | KIA | 9/28/18 |
| Hauser, William | Pvt | KIA | 8/6/18 |
| Havens, Alonzo | Pvt | KIA | 10/1/18 |
| Hayes, John | Pvt | KIA | 10/1/18 |
| Hendricks, Roy | Pvt | KIA | 10/1/18 |
| Hicks, James E. | Pvt | KIA | 9/14/18 |
| Hinton, Will | Pvt | KIA | 9/26/18 |
| Holdman, Lyman | Sgt | KIA | 9/27/18 |

| Name | Rank | Cause of Death | Date of Death |
|------|------|----------------|---------------|
| Hollowell, Clennie | Pvt | KIA | 10/1/18 |
| Honaker, John | Pvt | KIA | 10/28/18 |
| Hopson, Arthur | Pvt | KIA | 10/1/18 |
| Howard, Herbert | Sgt | D or OC | 7/6/18 |
| Hubbard, Thomas | Pvt | D or OC | 12/17/18 |
| Hubert, Curtis | Pvt | KIA | 10/1/18 |
| Huff, Joshua J. | Corp | KIA | 8/14/18 |
| Hughett, Jim | Pvt | KIA | 9/26/18 |
| Hunter, Willie | Pvt | KIA | 9/26/18 |
| Hurley, George D. | Pvt | D or OC | 2/14/18 |
| Jackson, Ed | Pvt | KIA | 10/1/18 |
| Jackson, Emmanuel | Sgt | KIA | 10/2/18 |
| Jackson, Frederick | Pvt | KIA | 9/27/18 |
| Jackson, Harrison | Pvt | D or OC | 9/14/18 |
| Jackson, James | Pvt | D or OC | 12/27/18 |
| Jackson, Jesse | Pvt | DOW | 9/23/18 |
| Jackson, Leonard | Corp | KIA | 9/30/18 |
| Jackson, Thomas W. | Pvt | KIA | 9/28/18 |
| James, Oliver | Pvt | D or OC | 3/5/19 |
| Jenkins, Toney | Pvt | DOW | 9/28/18 |
| Jervis, Arthur | Pvt 1st Cl | DOW | 10/16/18 |
| Johnson, Champion | Pvt | D or OC | 2/3/19 |
| Johnson, George | Pvt 1st Cl | KIA | 9/26/18 |
| Johnson, James T. | Pvt | KIA | 9/26/18 |
| Johnson, Lee Grant | Pvt | KIA | 7/16/18 |
| Johnson, Solomon | Pvt | KIA | 10/2/18 |
| Johnson, Taylor | Pvt | KIA | 9/26/18 |
| Jones, John B. | Pvt | D or OC | 11/22/18 |
| Jones, Oscar A. | Sgt | KIA | 10/1/18 |
| Jones, Smithfield | Pvt | KIA | 9/26/18 |
| Judy, Morton | Pvt | DOW | 9/29/18 |
| Kennedy, Spencer | Pvt | KIA | 9/26/18 |
| Kennedy, William B. | Corp | D or OC | 4/3/18 |
| King, Joseph D. | Pvt | KIA | 10/1/18 |
| King, Perry E. | Pvt | KIA | 9/26/18 |
| Lawrence, Andrew | Pvt | D or OC | 3/3/19 |
| Lawrence, William | Pvt | DOW | 10/2/18 |
| Leonard, Howard B. | Sgt | D or OC | 2/4/18 |
| Link, Morris D. | Corp | KIA | 7/15/18 |
| Livingston, Loyd | Pvt | D or OC | 6/12/18 |
| Livis, Dave H. | Pvt | KIA | 10/28/18 |
| Luther, Ludlow | Pvt | KIA | 7/15/18 |
| Lynch, Adolph Henry | Sgt | KIA | 7/15/18 |
| McCaywood, Percy | Sgt | DOW | 8/9/18 |

| Name | Rank | Cause of Death | Date of Death |
|------|------|----------------|---------------|
| McCray, William | Corp | KIA | 9/12/18 |
| McGrew, Burrette | Pvt | KIA | 9/26/18 |
| McGriff, Harry | Pvt | KIA | 9/26/18 |
| McGriff, Leo | Corp | D or OC | 1/15/19 |
| McNeil, William | Pvt | KIA | 10/2/18 |
| Mallory, Blauvelt | Corp | D or OC | 12/15/18 |
| Martin, Conrad | Pvt | DOW | 10/6/18 |
| Mayo, Frank J. | Corp | DOW | 10/16/18 |
| Michael, Oliver | Pvt | KIA | 9/26/18 |
| Middleton, Parker | Corp | KIA | 9/26/18 |
| Miles, William | Corp | KIA | 9/12/18 |
| Mills, Alonzo | Mec | KIA | 9/30/18 |
| Mills, Benjamin J. | Pvt | D or OC | 10/1/18 |
| Mills, William G. | Corp | KIA | 10/2/18 |
| Minter, William | Corp | KIA | 9/26/18 |
| Minor, Theodore B. | Pvt | KIA | 9/26/18 |
| Moncrief, Joe | Pvt | DOW | 9/23/18 |
| Moon, Tarrance | Pvt | DOW | 8/23/18 |
| Moore, Monroe E. | Pvt | KIA | 7/20/18 |
| Moore, William | Pvt | KIA | 10/1/18 |
| Morgan, Eugene | Pvt | D or OC | 7/5/18 |
| Morris, Charles B. | Pvt | KIA | 9/27/18 |
| Morrison, Henry | Pvt | KIA | 10/1/18 |
| Murray, Roland | Pvt | KIA | 10/1/18 |
| Nash, Emmett | Pvt | KIA | 9/28/18 |
| Nash, William E. | Pvt | D or OC | 9/13/18 |
| Nelson, John | Pvt | KIA | 9/26/18 |
| Parish, Clemons | Pvt | D or OC | 10/3/18 |
| Parker, Harry | Pvt | D or OC | 5/29/18 |
| Parks, Charlie | Pvt | DOW | 9/28/18 |
| Parnell, Gilbert | Pvt | KIA | 9/26/18 |
| Payton, Henry | Corp | KIA | 9/28/18 |
| Peeples, Pernell | Pvt | D or OC | 10/12/18 |
| Perkins, Walter | Pvt 1st Cl | KIA | 9/30/18 |
| Perry, James | Corp | KIA | 9/26/18 |
| Pier, Joe | Pvt | KIA | 10/2/18 |
| Phifer, Monroe | Pvt | KIA | 9/26/18 |
| Powell, Williams | Pvt | KIA | 10/1/18 |
| Poyner, Luscius D. | Pvt | D or OC | 6/21/18 |
| Prioleau, Jacob | Pvt | DOW | 6/22/18 |
| Proctor, John | Pvt | D or OC | 1/24/18 |
| Reid, Leon Spencer | Pvt 1st Cl | D or OC | 11/15/18 |
| Reno, Frank | Pvt | KIA | 9/18/18 |
| Rhodes, Van | Corp | DOW | 10/11/18 |

| Name | Rank | Cause of Death | Date of Death |
|------|------|----------------|---------------|
| Richardson, Charlie E. | Pvt | D or OC | 7/12/18 |
| Robin, Eugene | Pvt | D or OC | 2/7/19 |
| Robinson, Eddie | Pvt | D or OC | 2/11/18 |
| Robinson, Edwin | Corp | D or OC | 12/3/18 |
| Robinson, George | Pvt | DOW | 8/1/18 |
| Robinson, Lee | Corp | DOW | 9/30/18 |
| Rollins, Lathan C. J. | Pvt | KIA | 10/2/18 |
| Rose, Buddie | Pvt | KIA | 10/2/18 |
| Saunders, Clemon | Pvt | DOW | 10/2/18 |
| Scott, Clarence | Corp | KIA | 9/26/18 |
| Scott, George | Pvt | DOW | 10/1/18 |
| Scott, Marshall | Pvt | KIA | 7/15/18 |
| Sealey, Leroy | Pvt | KIA | 9/28/18 |
| Shepard, William | Sup Sgt | KIA | 9/26/18 |
| Sheppard, James | Pvt | D or CO | 2/7/19 |
| Shorts, William | Corp | KIA | 11/1/18 |
| Smith, Henry J. | Pvt | KIA | 9/26/18 |
| Spears, Will | Pvt | D or CO | 12/3/18 |
| Spence, Lawrence | Pvt | KIA | 9/26/18 |
| Stephens, William | Corp | KIA | 6/25/18 |
| Stout, Ebin M. | Pvt | KIA | 9/28/18 |
| Stout, William L. | Pvt | KIA | 9/26/18 |
| Streadrick, Howard | Pvt | D or OC | 1/14/18 |
| Taylor, Camillus | Pvt | D or OC | 2/5/19 |
| Taylor, Lewis A. | Corp | DOW | 6/1/18 |
| Tate, Emerson | Pvt | DOW | 9/23/18 |
| Tebbs, Ulysses | Pvt | KIA | 9/29/18 |
| Terry, Arthur | Pvt | KIA | 6/5/18 |
| Thomas, Fagan, Jr. | Pvt | KIA | 9/30/18 |
| Thomas, Robert H. | Pvt | DOW | 10/1/18 |
| Thomas, William | Pvt | KIA | 9/28/18 |
| Thompson, Ernest M. | Pvt | DOW | 9/27/18 |
| Thompson, Henry | Pvt | DOW | 9/27/18 |
| Thompson, Julius | Pvt | DOW | 10/12/18 |
| Thompson, William F. | Pvt | KIA | 9/28/18 |
| Tinson, Jacob | Cook | KIA | 7/16/18 |
| Tyler, John | Pvt | KIA | 9/27/18 |
| Valentine, Earl A. | Pvt | D or OC | 2/4/19 |
| Van Dunk, William H. | Corp | KIA | 9/28/18 |
| Walker, Eldridge | Pvt | D or OC | 7/31/18 |
| Walker, Frank | Pvt | DOW | 9/30/18 |
| Walker, George | Pvt | DOW | 10/15/18 |
| Walker, Moses | Pvt | KIA | 9/28/18 |
| Waller, Edward | Cook | D or OC | 2/3/19 |

| Name | Rank | Cause of Death | Date of Death |
|------|------|----------------|---------------|
| Waltney, Hugh G. | Pvt | DOW | 10/10/18 |
| Ward, Dick | Pvt | KIA | 9/27/18 |
| Ward, Nelson | Pvt | D or OC | 8/16/18 |
| Watt, Conrad | Pvt | KIA | 10/1/18 |
| Weaver, Dee | Pvt | DOW | 10/2/18 |
| White, Raymond | Corp | KIA | 9/12/18 |
| Whittaker, Walter | Pvt | DOW | 8/21/18 |
| Wilkins, Frank A. | Pvt | KIA | 9/27/18 |
| Williams, Harry P. | Sgt | DOW | 10/7/18 |
| Williams, Walter F. | Pvt | D or OC | 2/20/19 |
| Williamson, Arbie W. | Pvt | KIA | 10/7/18 |
| Wilson, Howard | Pvt | D or OC | 2/7/19 |
| Wilson, John | Pvt | KIA | 9/26/18 |
| Winston, Charlie | Pvt | D or OC | 5/21/18 |
| Woods, Richard | Pvt | D or OC | 4/10/18 |
| Young, Nathaniel | Pvt | D or OC | 9/19/18 |
| Zellis, Ellis | Pvt | KIA | Unknown (*Deceased not found in any other record as connected to 369th*) |

KIA: killed in action
DOW: died of wounds
D or OC: disease or other causes

This list is based on the casualty report of the Adjutant General's Office, RG 407, NARA, and supplemented or revised by lists generated by the American Battle Monuments Commission, which also provides places of burial. Afterwar abstracts were used as well.

The 93rd Division only existed on paper and never functioned as an organic combat unit. Those who died in the 369th did so largely as members of the 16th and 161st Divisions of France's 4th Army.

The following acronyms are used in the notes and bibliography.

| | |
|---|---|
| AAA | American Archives of Art |
| ABMC | American Battle Monuments Commission |
| BLCU | Butler Library, Columbia University, New York, NY |
| BLYU | Beineke Library, Yale University, New Haven, CT |
| COS | chief of staff |
| COSPF | chief of staff personnel files |
| DUMC | Duke University Manuscript Collection, Durham, NC |
| EM | Etat-Major |
| GHQ | general headquarters |
| GPO | Government Printing Office |
| GQG | Grand Quartier Général (General Headquarters) |
| GQG N&NE | Grand Quartier Général Nord et Nord Est |
| H.R. | House of Representatives |
| HM | His Majesty |
| HQ | Headquarters |
| HQ AEF | Headquarters, Allied Expeditionary Forces |
| JAG | Judge Advocate General |
| KLCU | Carl A. Kroch Library, Cornell University, Ithaca, NY |
| LOC | Library of Congress, Washington, DC |
| LOCMD | Library of Congress Manuscript Division |
| MIB | Military Intelligence Branch |
| MOH | Medal of Honor |
| MS | manuscript |
| MSRC | Moorland-Spingarn Research Collection, Howard University, Washington, DC |
| NAACP | National Association for the Advancement of Colored People |
| NARA | National Archives and Records Administration, College Park, MD |
| NGB | National Guard Bureau |
| NYG | New York Guard |
| NYHS | New York Historical Society, New York, NY |
| NYMA | New York Municipal Archive, New York, NY |
| NYNG | New York National Guard |
| NYPL | New York Public Library, New York, NY |
| NYS | New York State |
| NYSA | New York State Archives, New York State Library, Albany, NY |
| NYSLMC | New York State Library Manuscript Collection, Albany, NY |

| | |
|---|---|
| NYSMM | New York State Military Museum, Saratoga Springs, NY |
| OFCS | Office of Family and Children Services |
| RG | Record Group |
| SC | Schomburg Center, New York Public Library, New York, NY |
| SCRBC | Schomburg Center for Research in Black Culture, New York Public Library, New York, NY |
| SHAT | Service Historique de l'Armée de Terre, Vincennes, France |
| SI | Smithsonian Institute |
| SLYU | Sterling Library, Yale University, New Haven, CT |
| USEM | United States État-Major |
| USMA | US Military Academy (West Point), West Point, NY |
| USMAL | US Military Academy Library, West Point, NY |
| USMC | US Marine Corps |
| WD | War Department |
| WO | War Office (Britain) |
| YMCA | Young Men's Christian Association |

NOTES

### Introduction

1. This spelling of Roberts's name is one of many versions that appear in newspaper accounts and even official documents. The problem literally began at the time of his birth when the "return of birth" (birth certificate) listed him as Leedom; the first census in which he appears (1905) listed him as Needom. See New Jersey State Archives, birth and census records, #6076 and #R163, New Jersey State Library, Trenton, NJ. The name is spelled Neadam in the abstracts of the 369th, Needom on the muster roll of the 15th NYNG, and Needham on the citation for the Croix de Guerre. See Abstracts of the 369th Regiment, Box 13, Roll 4, RG 13721–83, NYSA, and Muster Roll of the 15th NYNG, RG 13726–86, NYSA. Needham, an apparent francophone rendering, is by far the most common spelling. Yet, on February 21, 1945, Roberts officially corrected his name from Leedom to Neadom on his birth records. If he went to that kind of trouble to set the record straight, we should try to honor his choice. See New Jersey State Archives, corrected birth records #6076.

2. For Johnson's statement, see *New York Age,* March 1, 1919, p. 6. For Hayward's quote, see *New York Age,* February 8, 1919, p. 2. In this account, John Jamison, of 137 West 141st Street, a black soldier, told an *Age* reporter that Hayward removed "the insignia of his rank from his shoulders, and grabbing a rifle from a soldier, darted out ahead and led us through a storm from German artillery." When a French general ordered the unit to retire, Hayward reportedly replied that he did not understand the order. When the order was repeated, Hayward then uttered the famous words, and they went forward.

3. Adriane Lentz-Smith, *Freedom Struggles: African Americans and World War I* (Cambridge, MA: Harvard University Press, 2009), pp. 8–9. Violence and the capacity for violence, according to Lentz-Smith, offered African Americans one optional way to frame manhood. Black warriors were heroes who could offer hope that they would come home to defend and avenge the wrongs inflicted upon their persecuted and often terrorized sisters and brothers.

4. See http://www.nycroads.com/roads/harlem-river, accessed November 12, 2013.

5. In 1964, the 369th Veterans moved the parade from Harlem to Midtown in order to allow the people of Harlem "to have their day on Fifth Avenue too." See *New York Times,* May 25, 1964, p. 44. Organizers of the parade later criticized the Department of Defense for a lack of presence and support, especially compared to that which other so-called ethnic parades enjoyed. See *New York Times,* May 23, 1966, p. 43.

6. Toni Morrison, *Jazz* (New York: Alfred A. Knopf, 1992), p. 129.

7. Thomas Cripps, *Making Movies Black: The Hollywood Movie from World War II to the Civil Rights Era* (New York: Oxford University Press, 1993), p. 85.

8. Ibid., p. 85; *New York Age*, July 10, 1943, pp. 9–10, July 17, 1943, p. 1, July 24, 1913, p. 1, and August 7, 1943, p. 1; *Amsterdam News*, July 10, 1943, p. 5, July 24, 1943, p. 13, and August 7, 1943, pp. 1 and 4; *New York Age*, July 17, 1943, p. 6.

9. Daniel Kryder, *Divided Arsenal: Race and the American State during World War II* (New York: Cambridge University Press, 2001), pp. 148–149 and 176–177.

10. Donald Bogle, *Toms, Coons, Mulattoes, Mammies, and Bucks: An Interpretive History of Blacks in American Films,* 4th ed. (New York: Continuum, 2001), p. 131; Cripps, *Making Movies Black,* p. 83.

11. Cripps, *Making Movies Black,* p. 85; *New York Age,* July 10, 1943, p. 10; Leon H. Hardwick, "Negro Stereotypes on the Screen," *Hollywood Quarterly* 1, no. 2 (January 1946): 235.

12. This is our interpretation of *Stormy Weather* (20th Century Fox, 1943), directed by Andrew L. Stone and adapted to the screen by Hy Kraft, with writing credits to Jerry Horwin, Frederick J. Jackson, Ted Koehler, and Seymour B. Robinson.

13. Ibid. The mention of Europe in the past tense indicates ever so gently that he too had left the scene.

14. Ibid. David Levering Lewis, *When Harlem Was in Vogue* (New York: Oxford University Press, 1979), pp. 3–24.

15. Our interpretation of *Stormy Weather.* A close inspection of the drum also identifies the 15th as NYG (New York Guard), not NYNG (New York National Guard).

16. Ibid.

17. *Army Regulations,* "Wear and Appearance of Army Uniforms and Insignia," Ch. 29-4, p. 266, May 11, 2012, http://www.apd.army.mil/pdffiles/r670_1.pdf, accessed December 5, 2013. For the actual federal statute see Section 704, title 18 of US Codes (18 USC 704), http://www.law.cornell.edu/uscode/text/18/704, accessed December 5, 2013. *United States Code,* Title 18, chap. 33, sect. 704, August 3, 2005. Paragraph (a) provides for a fine or imprisonment for the unauthorized wearing of a medal. This rule would certainly apply to someone who did not receive the medal.

18. Cripps, *Making Movies Black,* pp. 80–86; Clayton R. Koppes and Gregory D. Black, "Blacks, Loyalty, and Motion Picture Propaganda in World War II," *Journal of American History* 73, no. 2 (September 1986): 383.

19. *Amsterdam News,* July 31, 1943, p. 13.

20. *New York Age,* August 7, 1943, p. 11.

21. *New York Age,* August 21, 1943, p. 10.

22. According to Leon H. Hardwick, the loudest protests against stereotypical treatments of blacks in film came from servicemen who had served overseas. They had "seen the astonishment of people in Asia, Africa, and Europe at discovering that the average American Negro soldier is a normally intelligent and self-assured individual." Contrary to *Stormy Weather*'s limiting of blacks largely to the realm of entertainment, the 1940 census listed 3,524 black physicians, 2,339 professors and college presidents, 1,052 lawyers and judges, 132,110 craftsmen and foremen in industry, and 6,801 trained nurses, to go along with 17,102 clergymen, 1,463 dentists, 63,697 schoolteachers, 1,231 electricians, 20,798 carpenters, 100,000 clerical workers,

1,210 real estate brokers, and 48,614 college students. Blacks also owned and operated 200 insurance companies and 6 banks. See Hardwick, "Negro Stereotypes,"
pp. 234–235.

23. Cripps, *Making Movies Black*, p. 96. In *Thank Your Lucky Stars*, a soldier played
by Willie Best marries a garishly dressed woman played by Hattie McDaniel. Koppes and Black, "Blacks, Loyalty," p. 403. Joe Louis in uniform made a brief and silent
appearance in the film, letting his fists do the talking while representing what the
well-dressed man in Harlem would wear—a military uniform.

24. Lena Horne and Richard Schickel, *Lena* (New York: Doubleday, 1965), pp.
163–165 and 174–177; Koppes and Black, "Blacks, Loyalty," p. 398; Denis Preston, *Jazz
Music*, October, 1943, quoted in Peter Noble, *The Negro in Films* (New York: Arno
Press, 1970), p. 205.

25. Bogle, *Toms, Coons*, p. 132.

26. Cripps, *Making Movies Black*, p. 85; Michael Rogin, *Blackface, White Noise: Jewish Immigrants in the Hollywood Melting Pot* (Berkeley: University of California Press,
1996), p. 5. Rogin maintains that "minstrelsy was the first and most popular form
of mass culture in the nineteenth-century United States. Blackface contributed to
the formation of a distinctive national identity in the age of slavery and presided
over melting-pot culture in the period of mass European immigration." Though
not the only distinctively American cultural form, it was a dominant practice that
infected others, including film. Rogin concedes as commonplace Hollywood's
importance "in giving people from diverse class, ethnic, and geographic origins a
common imagined community," but he nonetheless reveals something far more
complicated and sinister in the cinema's making of Americans—the power of the
medium "to make African Americans represent something besides themselves."
He names four films as critical to this process: *Uncle Tom's Cabin* (1903), *Birth of a
Nation* (1915), *The Jazz Singer* (1927), and *Gone with the Wind* (1939). Each contributed
to four transformative aspects in the history of American film—box office success,
critical recognition of revolutionary significance, formal innovations, and shifts in
the cinematic mode of production—that organized themselves around the surplus
symbolic value of blacks. See Rogin, *Blackface, White Noise*, pp. 14–15.

27. Cripps, *Making Movies Black*, p. 72.

28. *Amsterdam News*, July 31, 1943, p. 5. The *Amsterdam News* reported that *Stormy
Weather* was the first film in history to have a premier in Harlem and on Broadway
at the same time. See *Amsterdam News*, July 24, 1943, p. 17.

29. Cripps, *Making Movies Black*, p. 80.

30. Ibid., p. 107. Bert Williams is briefly referenced in the film but not in connection with the regiment. Gabe drops his name to impress antagonist Chick Bailey, played by Emmett "Babe" Wallace. Chick, light-skinned and straight-haired, is
clearly a black man who has let fame go to his head. He is put in his place by his
"business partner" and would–be lover, Selina, and the unpretentious striver Bill.
In some respects, Chick certainly could represent the pretentious and disrespected
absent black officer.

31. See http://www.defenselink.mil/news/jun2000, accessed November 12,
2013. Robinson's title as the "Mayor of Harlem" caused considerable resentment

among blacks, although many sought him out in times of trouble. See *New York Age,* August 7, 1943, p. 10.

32. See http://www.nycgovparks.org/sub_your_park/historical_signs/hs_historical_sign.php?id=8250, accessed November 12, 2013.

33. Paula J. Massood, *Black City Cinema: African American Urban Experiences in Film* (Philadelphia: Temple University Press, 2003), p. 39.

34. Cripps, *Making Movies Black,* p. 103.

35. Bogle, *Toms, Coons,* p. 132; Arthur L. Knight III, "Dis-integrating the Musical: African American Musical Performance and the American Musical Film, 1927–1959 (Ph.D. diss., University of Chicago, August 1998), p. 216.

36. Horne and Schickle, *Lena,* pp. 174–177.

37. Emmett J. Scott, *The American Negro in the World War* (Chicago: Homewood, 1919), reprinted as *Scott's Official History of the American Negro in the World War* (New York: Arno Press, 1969); Allison W. Sweeney, *History of the American Negro in the Great World War* (Chicago: Cuneo-Henneberry, 1919), reprinted in 1969 by Negro Universities Press; Madame Touissant Welcome, *A Pictorial History of the Negro in the Great War, 1917–1918* (New York: Touissant Pictorial, 1919); Charles Holston Williams, *Negro Soldiers in World War I: The Human Side* (New York: AMS Press, 1979), originally published in 1923.

38. Irvin S. Cobb, *The Glory of the Coming* (New York: Doran, 1918), p. 295. See note 50 below.

39. *New York Age,* May 29, 1920, p. 6.

40. Ibid.

41. Theodore Roosevelt, *Rank and File: True Stories of the Great War* (New York: Charles Scribner's Sons, 1928), pp. 91–116. Roosevelt's account, despite its flaws, is markedly more favorable than John J. Miles's *Singing Soldiers* (1927) and Charles E. Mack's *Two Black Crows of the AEF* (1928). According to John Trombold, the latter, a novel, treats the two main characters, Amos and Willie Crow, "as if every aspect of their lives were governed by the satirical conventions of a popular minstrel show." The former, a personal account of a white airplane pilot, depicts the minstrel shows and singing of African American soldiers. These representations could have influenced the writers of *Stormy Weather.* See Trombold, "The Minstrel Show Goes to the Great War: Zora Neale Hurston's Mass Cultural Other," *Melus* 24, no. 1 (Spring 1999): 85–107.

42. Reid Badger, *A Life in Ragtime: A Biography of James Reese Europe* (New York: Oxford University Press, 1995).

43. Noble Lee Sissle, "Memoirs of Lieutenant 'Jim' Europe," unpublished manuscript, 1942, NAACP Papers, Group 2, Boxes J 56 and J 70, LOCMD; Arthur P. Davis, *Here and There with the Rattlers* (Detroit, MI: Harlo, 1979).

44. *Men of Bronze: The Black American Heroes of World War I,* documentary film directed by William Miles, Men of Bronze, Inc., 1977; *Harlem Hellfighters,* documentary by George Merlis, Fisher/Merlis Television for the History Channel, 1997.

45. Charles Johnson, Jr., "Black Soldiers in the National Guard, 1877–1949" (Ph.D. diss., Howard University, 1976), published as *African American Soldiers in the National Guard: Recruitment and Deployment during Peacetime and War* (Westport, CT: Green-

wood Press, 1992); Stephen L. Harris, *Harlem's Hell Fighters: The African-American 369th Infantry in World War I* (Washington, DC: Brassey's, 2003).

46. *New York Age*, March 22, 1919, p. 4. Badger consistently refers to the band as the "Hellfighters" Band, thus helping to perpetuate a name for it that the men might have never really identified with or accepted. See index pp. 320–321 and photographs between pp. 150 and 151 in Badger, *Life in Ragtime*.

47. William Harris, *The Hellfighters of Harlem: African-American Soldiers Who Fought for the Right to Fight for Their Country* (New York: Carroll & Graf Publishers, 2002); Peter N. Nelson, *A More Unbending Battle: The Harlem Hellfighters' Struggle for Freedom in WWI and Equality at Home* (New York: Basic Civitas, 2009).

48. Richard Slotkin, *Lost Battalions: The Great War and the Crisis of American Nationality* (New York: Henry Holt, 2005).

49. Thomas Holt, "Marking: Race, Race-Making, and the Writing of History," *American Historical Review* 100, no. 1 (February 1995): 8.

50. Cobb, *Glory of the Coming*, pp. 306–307. According to Cobb, an officer in the 369th shared with him this letter from an eighteen-year-old soldier who was seemingly oblivious to the eye of the censor. We deleted Cobb's obligatory "Mammy" in the address.

51. Badger, *Life in Ragtime*, p. 142. Here and throughout the volume, readers will note that we have presented direct quotations without correction in most instances in order to preserve the tone of the speaker and to convey the flavor and/or attitudes of the time and circumstances that are at the center of this book. Accordingly, we have, for the most part, let stand odd spellings, atypical capitalizations, and ungrammatical constructions as well as the occasional slang or derogatory phrasing.

52. Margaret Randolph Higonnet, Jane Jenson, Sonya Michel, and Margaret Collins Weitz, eds., *Behind the Lines: Gender and the Two World Wars* (New Haven, CT: Yale University Press, 1987), p. 4, as quoted in Kathleen Kennedy, *Disloyal Mothers and Scurrilous Citizens: Women and Subversion during World War I* (Bloomington: Indiana University Press, 1999), p. xvii.

53. W. O. Waters to Arthur W. Little, August 14, 1936, "*From Harlem to the Rhine File*," NYSMM.

54. William Pickens, "The Negro in the Light of the Great War: Basis for the New Reconstruction," 3rd ed. (Baltimore, MD.: Daily Herald Print, 1919), pp. 1–3.

55. Mark Whalan, *The Great War and the Culture of the New Negro* (Gainesville: University Press of Florida, 2008); Lentz-Smith, *Freedom Struggles*; Chad L. Williams, *Torchbearers of Democracy: African American Soldiers in the World War I Era* (Chapel Hill: University of North Carolina Press, 2010); Nina Mjagkij, *Loyalty in Time of Trial: The African American Experience during World War I* (Lanham, MD: Rowman & Littlefield, 2011).

### Chapter 1. *"He HAS a Flag"*

1. Lt. Grote Hutcheson as quoted in Oswald Garrison Villard, "The Negro in the Regular Army," *Atlantic Monthly*, June 1903, p. 722.

2. Maj. Robert Lee Bullard, "The Negro as Volunteer: Some Characteristics," *Journal of the Military Service Institution of the United States* 29 (July 1901): 29–39.

3. Villard, "Negro," pp. 726–729.

4. Ibid. Capt. Matthew F. Steele, "The 'Color Line' in the Army," *North American Review* 183, no. 605 (December 1906): 1285–1286. Steele was born in Huntsville, Alabama, in 1861 and entered the US Military Academy in 1879. He was graduated in 1883 and missed overlapping with John Hanks Alexander (the second black graduate of West Point) by one year. He did, however, overlap with Bullard, who finished at the academy in 1885. Please note that Bullard's reference to the immateriality of race enlists a so-called Pickaninny Rhyme: "If I is er nigger, / Do it cut any figger?" See Bullard, "Negro as Volunteer," p. 29.

5. Benjamin Quarles, *The Negro in the American Revolution* (Chapel Hill: University of North Carolina Press, 1961), pp. 51–52; Daniel Ennis, "Poetry and the American Revolutionary Identity: The Case of Phillis Wheatley and John Paul Jones," *Studies in Eighteenth Century Culture* 31 (2002): 85–98; W. Spencer Carpenter, "The Negro Soldier's Contribution in the Wars of the United States," *African Methodist Episcopal Church Review* 29, no. 3 (January 1913): 217–218. A petition by Gannett for compensation after the war produced this response: "And whereas it further appears that the said Deborah Gannett exhibited an extraordinary instance of female heroism by discharging the duties of faithful, gallant soldier, and at the same time preserving the virtue and chastity of her sex unsuspected and unblemished, and was discharged from the service with a fair and honorable character." She received the sum of £34 for her services. See Carpenter, "Negro Soldier's Contribution," pp. 217–218.

6. Frederick Douglass, "Men of Color: To Arms! To Arms!," in *The Boisterous Sea of Liberty*, ed. David Brion Davis and Steven Mintz (New York: Oxford University Press, 2000), p. 488; Quoted in William S. McFeeley, *Frederick Douglass* (New York: W. W. Norton, 1991), p. 213. The War Department awarded seventeen Medals of Honor to black soldiers in the Civil War. See Carpenter, "Negro Soldier's Contribution," p. 222.

7. Steele, "'Color Line,'" p. 1285.

8. Benjamin Quarles, *The Negro in the Making of America* (New York: Simon & Schuster, 1996), pp. 209–211; James M. Guthrie, *Camp-Fires of the Afro-American, or The Colored Man as Patriot, Soldier, Sailor, and Hero in the Cause of Free America* (Philadelphia: Afro-American Publisher, 1899), reprinted by Johnson Printing in 1970; Mary Frances Berry and John W. Blassingame, *Long Memory: The Black Experience in America* (New York: Oxford University Press, 1982), pp. 308–310.

9. See "Presidio of San Francisco: Buffalo Soldiers," accessed October 20, 2013, http://www.nps.gov/archive/prsf/history/buffalo_soldiers/presidio_garrison.htm; Mitchell Yockelson, "'I Am Entitled to the Medal of Honor and I Want It': Theodore Roosevelt and His Quest for Glory," *Prologue Magazine* 30, no. 1 (Spring 1998), accessed November 12, 2013, http://www.archives.gov/publications/prologue/1998/spring/roosevelt; Frank N. Schubert, "Buffalo Soldiers at San Juan Hill," accessed October 13, 2013, http://www.history.army.mil?html?documents/wwspain/buffalos_sjh/sc.

10. Arthur E. Barbeau and Florette Henri, *The Unknown Soldiers: African-American Troops in World War I* (1974; repr., New York: Da Capo Press, 1996), p. xii.

11. Carpenter, "Negro Soldier's Contribution," pp. 215 and 223–224.

12. Ibid., p. 224.

13. Albon P. Mann, Jr., "Labor Competition and the New York Draft Riots of 1863," *Journal of Negro History* 36, no. 4 (October 1951): 375; Leslie M. Harris, *In the Shadow of Slavery: African Americans in New York City, 1626–1863* (Chicago: University of Chicago Press, 2003), pp. 279–288.

14. Johnson, "Black Soldiers in the National Guard," pp. 39–40.

15. Ibid., pp. 41–43.

16. Johnson, *African American Soldiers*, pp. 78–79.

17. *New York Times*, June 18, 1895, p. 4, June 23, 1895, p. 4, June 30, 1895, p. 4, September 14, 1895, p. 4, and September 19, 1895, p. 4.

18. *New York Times*, May 17, 1898, p. 3.

19. Ibid.

20. *New York Times*, June 22, 1898, p. 3.

21. *New York Times*, June 23, 1898, p. 2.

22. Ibid.

23. Ibid.

24. Ibid.

25. Ibid.

26. Gilbert Osofsky, *Harlem: The Making of a Ghetto—Negro New York, 1890–1930* (New York: Harper & Row, 1966), pp. 84–85; Irma Watkins-Owens, *Blood Relations: Caribbean Immigrants and the Harlem Community, 1900–1930* (Bloomington: Indiana University Press, 1996), pp. 1–3.

27. *New York Age*, May 11, 1911, p. 1. The National League for the Protection of Colored Women reported 20,000 blacks lived in Harlem in 1911. Their much narrower boundaries for Harlem extended from Eighth to Fifth Avenues and from 132nd to 137th Streets. Watkins-Owens, *Blood Relations*, pp. 3–9.

28. Badger, *Life in Ragtime*, pp. 140–141; A'Lelia Bundles, *On Her Own Ground: The Life and Times of Madam C. J. Walker* (New York: Scribner, 2001), p. 220.

29. Marcy Sarah Sacks, "'We Cry among the Skyscrapers': Black People in New York City, 1880–1915" (Ph.D. diss., University of California–Berkeley, 1999), pp. 4–5.

30. Ibid., p. 8.

31. George E. Haynes, "The Church and the Negro Spirit," *Survey Graphic* (March 1925): 695–709.

32. *New York Age*, July 18, 1907, p. 4.

33. Sacks, "'We Cry,'" pp. 85–89, quoted in *New York Age*, July 29, 1909, p. 1.

34. *New York Age*, April 21, 1910, p. 4.

35. *New York Age*, January 6, 1910, pp. 1 and 4. For extensive treatment of the power and pervasiveness of antiblack imagery, see Sacks, "'We Cry,'" chap. 2. Sacks does not, however, mention military organizations or service as a strategic counter to the problem. For a concise and compelling argument on the deep and lasting influence of minstrelsy and its evolving forms, see Holt, "Marking: Race, Race-Making," 1–20.

36. Mary Church Terrell, "The Disbanding of the Colored Soldiers," *Voice* 3, no. 12 (December 1906): 557.

37. Ibid.; Barbeau and Henri, *Unknown Soldiers,* p. xii; Joseph B. Foraker, "A Review of the Testimony in the Brownsville Investigation," *North American Review* 187, no. 4 (April 1908): 550–558.

38. *New York Age,* April 25, 1907, p. 1.

39. Ibid.

40. Barbeau and Henri, *Unknown Soldiers,* p. xxii.

41. Terrell, "Disbanding," p. 557. The gender implications of Brownsville also must have concerned Terrell.

42. *New York Age,* March 25, 1909, p. 4.

43. *New York Age,* August 12, 1909, p. 1.

44. *New York Age,* January 6, 1910, p. 4, and *New York Age,* January 27, 1910, p. 1.

45. Ibid.

46. Ibid.

47. *New York Age,* October 3, 1907, p. 1.

48. *New York Age,* August 15, 1907, p. 6.

49. *New York Age,* August 16, 1906, p. 1.

50. Johnson, *African American Soldiers,* pp. 41–42; Gabriel Hawkins, "The Eighth Infantry Goes to Cuba," *Newsletter of the Illinois State Military Museum* 2, no. 4 (Fall 1998): 1–2; Welcome, *Pictorial History,* pp. 40–41; Lineage Eighth Illinois Infantry, accessed October 20, 2013, http://www.il.ngb.army.mil.

51. Welcome, *Pictorial History,* p. 41.

52. Carpenter, "Negro Soldier's Contribution," p. 223; Johnson, *African American Soldiers,* p. 56.

53. *New York Sun,* December 1, 1910, p. 9, Spingarn Papers, Box 13, Folder 538, RG 95, MSRC. Technically, the "Appeal" was not officially sponsored by the NAACP. First, the organization was not officially incorporated as the National Association for the Advancement of Colored People until June 1911. Until that time, the organization was the National Negro Committee, created out of the National Negro Conference called in 1909. Du Bois used the letterhead of the National Negro Committee in issuing the document, and Washington interpreted the move as an indication that the signers wished to create the impression that the NAACP had sponsored the document. The *Sun* explicitly identified the "Appeal" with the NAACP. Even though Villard insisted that he had not been consulted, he admitted that he agreed with the document's sentiment. Nonetheless, he assured Washington that the organization was neither pro–Du Bois nor pro-Washington and sought his support. For a fuller description of the controversy, see Charles Flint Kellogg, *NAACP: A History of the National Association for the Advancement of Colored People* (Baltimore, MD: Johns Hopkins University Press, 1967), pp. 72–88; Elliot Rudwick, *W. E. B. Du Bois: The Voice of the Black Protest Movement* (Urbana: University of Illinois Press, 1982), pp. 134–137; and *The Booker T. Washington Papers, 1909–1911,* ed. Louis R. Harlan and Raymond W. Smock (Urbana-Champaign: University of Illinois Press, 1981), 10:422–425, for a facsimile of the letter.

54. *Booker T. Washington Papers,* 10:424–425.

55. Ibid.

## Chapter 2. "Positions of Honor and Trust"

1. *New York Age,* October 13, 1910, p. 4.

2. *New York Age,* May 8, 1909, p. 4, and October 13, 1910, p. 4.

3. Osofsky, *Harlem,* p. 160.

4. Charles E. Brown to Mayor Thomas F. Gilroy, July 5, 1894, Gilroy Papers, General Correspondence, Box 1450, Folder 120, NYMA.

5. Alfred Cowan to Mayor William L. Strong, August 27, 1896, Strong Papers, Box 90, Folder 314, NYMA; *New York World,* August 27, 1896 (article clipped by Cowan and attached to letter "Colored Democrats Roused").

6. Alfred C. Cowan (President of Colored Republican Association, NYS) to Mayor William L. Strong, August 27, 1896, Mayors Papers, General Correspondence of William Strong, Box 90, Folder 314, NYMA.

7. Richard B. Sherman, *The Republican Party and Black America: From McKinley to Hoover, 1896–1933* (Charlottesville: University of Virginia Press, 1973), pp. 20–21 and 48–51. Roosevelt received far too much blame from whites for his infamous dinner meeting with Booker T. Washington and far too much credit for it from blacks. His record shows that he was no true friend of black causes. In addition to his mishandling of Brownsville, Roosevelt had run afoul of elite blacks through his assertions that "the best class of Negroes were responsible for Negro crime." His embrace of Washington's restricted educational model as most appropriate for blacks also drew their ire. See W. E. B. Du Bois, "The President and the Soldiers," *Voice* 3, no. 12 (December 1919): 553.

8. Osofsky, *Harlem,* p. 160.

9. Gary Daynes, "United Colored Democracy," in *Organizing Black America: An Encyclopedia of African American Associations,* ed. Nina Mjagkij (New York: Garland Publishing, 2001), pp. 666–667; Durahn Taylor, "United Colored Democracy," in *Encyclopedia of African-American Culture and History,* vol. 5, ed. Jack Salman (New York: Simon & Schuster Macmillan, 1996), pp. 2707–2708. Not until 1911 did black leaders "irrespective of politics, race, color or creed assemble to pay tribute to a Negro Democrat." That Democrat was "Chief" Edward Lee, who just over ten years before had found himself an outcast "for allying himself with the local Democracy of New York City." *New York Age,* March 16, 1911, p. 1.

10. *New York Age,* March 30, 1905, p. 1; Johnson, *African American Soldiers,* pp. 10–11; Julie Saville, *The Work of Reconstruction: From Slave to Wage Laborer in South Carolina, 1860–1870* (New York: Cambridge University Press, 1994), pp. 143–149.

11. Osofsky, *Harlem,* pp. 161–162; Booker T. Washington, widely acknowledged and often resented for his role as "office-broker," took credit for the appointments of Anderson and Lewis to their lofty positions. To Anderson, Washington said that of all the people he had helped secure prominent, official positions, "you are practically the only one who has ever been able to help himself. The others lay completely down, and it is equal to carrying a load of lead." In return for such favors and confidence, Anderson fervently protected the interests and reputation of Washington. Letter from Washington to Anderson , February 26, 1911, in *Booker T. Washington Papers,* 10:596–597 and 8:189. *New York Age,* December 23, 1909, p. 4.

12. *New York Times,* April 28, 1942, p. 21; Charles Dick, Republican National Committee, to Fillmore, June 10, 1898, Fillmore File, accessed October 24, 2013, http://www.goantiques.com; Fillmore to Charles Hilles, July 7, 1911, Taft Papers, Reel 406, Series 6, File 816, LOCMD.

13. *New York Globe and Commercial Advertiser,* October 2, 1911, Taft Papers, Reel 406, Series 6, File 816, LOCMD.

14. Unidentified newspaper article in Taft Papers, Reel 406, Series 6, File 816, LOCMD; Letterhead of the Equity Congress, in Sulzer Papers, Box 16, RG 1147, Rare and Manuscript Collections, KLCU.

15. Washington to Anderson, April 7, 1910, *Booker T. Washington Papers,* 10:316.

16. Letterhead of Equity Congress, Fillmore to Adjutant General, June 5, 1913, Sulzer Papers, Box 16, RG 1147, Rare and Manuscript Collections, KLCU.

17. J. Frank Wheaton was born in Hagerstown, Maryland, on February 22, 1866. He was educated at Stover College, Howard University, and the University of Minnesota, where he was the first black graduate of its Law School. Wheaton served as a delegate to the Republican National Conventions of 1888, 1896, and 1900. After leaving Maryland for Minnesota in 1894, he became a clerk of the municipal court in Minneapolis from 1895 to 1899. In 1898, he became the first black to win election to the Minnesota House of Representatives. In 1901, he reportedly established the law firm of Wheaton and Curtis and successfully defended clients in a number of murder trials. He cofounded the Equity Congress. Wheaton ran unsuccessfully for the New York State Assembly in 1919 as a Democrat. See http://www.aaregistry.com and http://politicalgraveyard.com, accessed October 24, 2013. James C. Thomas was born in 1863 in Harrisburg, Texas, and reportedly worked his way to New York on a boat and found employment as a hotel steward. After graduating in 1897 from the Philadelphia Training School for Embalmers, he founded a prosperous funeral home in the Tenderloin district. Subsequently, he moved the business to Harlem's 134th Street, where it became the community's largest mortuary. He also invested in real estate and earned considerable wealth as the first president of the Afro-American Realty Company. See *Booker T. Washington Papers,* 10:75.

18. Anderson to Charles Hilles, May 5, 1911, and unidentified New York paper, May 6, 1911, both in Taft Papers, Reel 417, Series 6, File 1490, LOCMD; Joseph N. Kane, *Facts about the Presidents: A Compilation of Biographical and Historical Information,* 5th ed. (New York: H. W. Wilson, 1989), p. 162. Louis A. Culliver, Democratic chair of the New York State Assembly's Committee on Military Affairs, had introduced Wheaton and Tobias to Secretary of War Dickinson for the purpose of ascertaining if the US government would "approve of the organization of a Colored Regiment of Infantry as part of the National Guard, and indirectly a part of the National Army Reserve." The timing of Dickinson's resignation raises questions about his departure and the comments attributed to him about the regiment. See Culliver to Dickinson, April 24, 1911, NGB, General Correspondence, Series E 7, Box 97, File 24483, RG 168, NARA.

19. Jerry Cooper, *The Rise of the National Guard: The Evolution of the American Militia, 1865–1920* (Lincoln: University of Nebraska Press, 1997), p. 109.

20. Anderson to Hilles, May 5, 1911, Taft Papers, Reel 417, Series 6, File 1490, LOCMD. The editorial page of the *Age* of November 17 suggests that the Democrats had promised to support the regiment movement.

21. Lewis to Hilles, May 9, 1911, Taft Papers, Reel 417, Series 6, File 1490, LOCMD.

22. Anderson to Hilles, May 18, 1911, Taft Papers, Reel 417, Series 6, File 1490, LOCMD; *New York Age,* November 17, 1910, p. 4.

23. *The Consolidated Laws of the State of New York,* vol. 2 (Albany, NY: J. B. Lyon, 1909), p. 2340; Anderson to Hilles, May 18, 1911, Taft Papers, Reel 417, Series 6, File 1490, LOCMD; Robert F. Wesser, *A Response to Progressivism: The Democratic Party and New York Politics, 1902–1918* (New York: New York University Press, 1986), p. 236. In one of the few treatments of the regiment campaign, *The Crisis* independently supported Anderson's interpretation: "The United Colored Democracy of the State of New York has been organized for the coming campaign. They demand a colored regiment in the National Guard and also colored policemen and firemen." See "Along the Color Line," *The Crisis* 1, no. 1 (November 1910): 3. Scholars have completely ignored the importance of the regiment issue in city and state politics. They attribute Stimson's defeat almost solely to a Republican split along conservative and reform lines and the unwanted and resented intervention of Theodore Roosevelt in the election process.

24. Anderson to Hilles, May 18, 1911.

25. Johnson, *African American Soldiers,* pp. 79–80. We owe a tremendous debt of gratitude to Charles Johnson for the groundbreaking work he did in tracing the origins of the Old 15th. Nonetheless, for the most part, we did not rely on his account but instead followed the leads and consulted the primary sources his work uncovered in order to arrive at our own reading of those materials.

26. Anderson to Hilles, May 19, 1911, and *New York World,* May 19, 1911, both in Taft Papers, Reel 417, Series 6, File 1490, LOCMD; *New York Times,* February 8, 1911, p. 2, and April 19, 1911, p. 2. The *Times* reported on the Culliver bill and stated that the understanding was that Verbeck opposed such a measure and the War Department favored the idea.

27. Fillmore to Hilles, July 7, 1911, Taft Papers, Reel 406, Series 6, File 816, LOCMD.

28. Taft to Washington, March 21, 1911, Anderson to Taft, March 24, 1911, and Washington to Taft, undated, all in Taft Papers, Reel 368, Series 6, File 121, LOCMD; William H. Lewis to Charles D. Norton, September 27, 1910, Taft Papers, Reel 372, Series 6, File 190, LOCMD.

29. "The Election," editorial, *The Crisis* 1, no. 2 (December 1910): 20.

30. *New York Age,* June 9, 1910, p. 4, June 16, 1910, p. 4, and September 1, 1910, p. 4; Washington to Anderson, April 7, 1910, *Booker T. Washington Papers,* 10:316.

31. *The Crisis* 2, no. 3 (July 1911): 95; Fillmore to Hilles, July 7, 1911, Taft Papers, Reel 406, Series 6, File 816, LOCMD; *New York Age,* July 20, 1911, p. 1, and July 27, 1911, p. 1. For a more detailed description of this matter, see Harris, *Harlem's Hell Fighters,* pp. 14–17.

32. Fillmore to Hilles, July 12, 1911, Hilles to Franklin MacVeagh, July 15, 1911, Hilles Internal Memorandum, August 1, 1911, indicating that on July 29, Anderson

requested the transfer of Fillmore as storekeeper-gauger, and MacVeagh to Hilles, July 31, 1911, all in Taft Papers, Reel 406, Series 6, File 816, LOCMD; Anderson to Hilles, January 23, 1912, Taft Papers, Reel 417, Series 6, File 1490, LOCMD.

33. Charles W. Anderson to Henry L. Stimson, January 23, 1912, NGB, General Correspondence, Series E 7, Box 97, RG 168, NARA; *New York Times*, July 13, 1911, p. 8; Bill no. 157, January 18, 1912, NGB, General Correspondence, Series E 7, Box 97, RG 168, NARA.

34. *New York Age,* October 5, 1911, p. 1; *Consolidated Laws,* 3:2334; "Militia Act of 1792" and "Militia Act of 1862," in *Statutes at Large, Treaties, and Proclamations of the United States of America,* vol. 12, ed. George P. Sanger (Boston: Little, Brown, 1863), pp. 597–600.

35. *New York Globe and Commercial Advertiser,* October 2, 1911, in Taft Papers, Reel 406, Series 6, File 816, LOCMD.

36. *New York Age,* October 26, 1911, p. 1.

37. Charles Fillmore to Henry Stimson, October 8 and October 15, 1911, and Robert Shaw Oliver to Fillmore, October 26, 1911, all in NGB, General Correspondence, Series E 7, Box 97, File 28666, RG 168, NARA.

38. *New York Age,* November 16, 1911, p. 1.

39. Ibid.

40. *New York Age,* undated, and *New York Globe and Commercial Advertiser*, October 2, 1911, both in Taft Papers, Reel 406, Series 6, File 816, LOCMD; *New York Age*, November 10, 1910, p. 4, and November 16, 1911, p. 1. For a description of old militia as club, see William Verbeck, "The Employer's Duty to the Militia," *Militia Journal* 1, no. 2 (January-February 1913): 63.

41. *Amsterdam News*, November 18 and November 25, 1911, Taft Papers, Reel 406, Series 6, File 816, LOCMD.

42. Ibid.

43. *Cleveland Gazette*, July 24, 1897, p. 2, and January 15, 1898, p. 2.

44. *Cleveland Gazette*, April 30, 1898, p. 2, and August 21, 1897, p. 2. Foraker is reported to have said: "When I was governor, no one had to call twice for troops. When lynching is threatened, it is no time to make peace by telephone." See *Cleveland Gazette*, June 6, 1897, p. 3. Also see Harris, *Harlem's Hell Fighters,* pp. 10–14.

45. Harris, *Harlem's Hell Fighters,* p. 13; *Cleveland Advocate*, August 26, 1916, p. 1; Villard, "Negro in the Regular Army," p. 728.

46. Fillmore to Hilles, November 26, 1911, Taft Papers, Reel 406, Series 6, File 816, LOCMD.

47. "Colored Men Wanted," c. 1911 Recruitment Poster of First Colored Provisional Regiment of Infantry, accessed October 26, 2012, http://www.goantiques.com. The recruiting office address is listed as 343 W. 40th Street.

48. Oswald Garrison Villard, "The Negro as Soldier and Officer," *Nation*, August 1, 1901, p. 85, and Villard, "Negro in the Regular Army," p. 728.

49. James P. Finley, "Colonel Charles Young: Black Cavalryman, Huachuca Commander, and Early Intelligence Officer," *Huachuca Illustrated: A Magazine of the Fort Huachuca Museum* 1 (1993): 75.

50. In *Booker T. Washington Papers,* vol. 11, see Reed Paige Clark to Booker T. Washington, November 10, 1911, pp. 363–364, Washington to Clark, November 18, 1911, p. 370, and Washington to Charles Young, November 18, 1911, p. 370; Young to Washington, November 24, 1911, Charles Young Collection, 83-1, Ohio Historical Society online, accessed October 26, 2013, http://www.ohiohistory.org.cfm.

51. Young to Washington, November 24, 1911.

52. Brian G. Shellum, *Black Officer in a Buffalo Soldier Regiment: The Military Career of Charles Young* (Lincoln: University of Nebraska Press, 2010), pp. 219–220. Benjamin O. Davis also contracted the same disease while on assignment in Liberia in 1911.

53. Fillmore to Hilles, December 8, 1911, and Fillmore to Hilles, January 6, 1912, both in Taft Papers, Reel 406, Series 6, File 816, LOCMD.

54. Fillmore to R. O. Bailey, December 13, 1911, and *Amsterdam News,* November 25, 1911, both in Taft Papers, Reel 406, Series 6, File 816, LOCMD.

55. William Verbeck to Fillmore, January 19, 1912, NGB, General Correspondence, Series E 7, Box 97, RG 168, NARA; Anderson to Hilles, January 23, 1912, Taft Papers, Reel 417, Series 6, File 1490, LOCMD. Hilles's memorandum reported that a Fillmore letter to him on January 31, 1912, indicated Gen. Robert Shaw Oliver had long operated against his efforts to organize the regiment. That document could not be located, but a letter from Fillmore to Stimson on January 22, 1912, informed Stimson that if Verbeck's characterization were true, the national administration might do great harm to itself among blacks.

56. Anderson to Hilles, January 23, 1912; Henry L. Stimson to Charles W. Anderson, February 2, 1912, Taft Papers, Reel 406, Series 6, File 816, LOCMD.

57. Stimson to Anderson, February 2, 1912; Robert Shaw Oliver to Charles Fillmore, January 25, 1912, NGB, Series E 7, Box 97, RG 168, NARA. Brig. Gen. R. K. Evans was chief of the Division of Militia Affairs in the War Department.

58. Fillmore to Hilles, January 31, 1912, NGB, General Correspondence, Series E 7, Box 97, RG 168, NARA; Hilles to Stimson, January 31, 1912, and Fillmore to Hilles, February 20, 1912, both in Taft Papers, Reel 406, Series 6, File 816, LOCMD.

59. Unidentified newspaper article, Taft Papers, Reel 406, Series 6, File 816, LOCMD.

60. Ibid. Official records of the Equity Congress seem nonexistent. Newspaper reports on meetings attended by 200 people and a letter from the congress's secretary, James C. Thomas, Jr., to Governor William Sulzer on May 22, 1913, placed the membership at 1,500. See Sulzer Papers, Box 13, RG 1147, Rare and Manuscript Collections, KLCU.

61. Fillmore to Hilles, March 11, 1912, Taft Papers, Reel 406, Series 6, File 816, LOCMD.

62. Fillmore to Carmi Thompson, September 2, 1912, Taft Papers, Reel 406, Series 6, File 816, LOCMD. Wesser, *Response to Progressivism,* p. 326; *The Crisis,* October 1912, http://www.1912.history.ohio-state.edu/race/democrat, accessed December 7, 2013; Napoleon Bonaparte Marshall to William Sulzer, December 12, 1912, Sulzer Papers, Box 4, RG 1147, Rare and Manuscript Collections, KLCU. Napoleon B.

Marshall, with the support of James T. Lloyd, chairman of the Democratic Congressional Campaign Committee, traveled the country for over a year organizing local black Democratic Clubs into the National Colored Democratic League. The organization became an auxiliary to the Democratic Party.

63. Wesser, *Response to Progressivism*, p. 326.

64. R. E. Cabell (Commissioner of Internal Revenue) to Franklin MacVeagh, December 1, 1911, Taft Papers, Reel 406, Series 6, File 816, LOCMD; John Henry Adams, "Mr. Lewis gets his!," *The Crisis* 1, no. 6 (April 1911): 31.

65. Alexander Walters and Robert N. Wood, "Make Friends of Thine Enemies," *The Crisis* 4, no. 6 (October 1912): 306–307.

66. See http:// ehistory.osu.edu/osu/mmh/1912/race/WilsonApproach.cfm, accessed October 27, 2013.

67. *Booker T. Washington Papers*, 12:248 and 270. One of the few black officeholders to survive the purge was Robert H. Terrell, a municipal court judge in the District of Columbia. Despite attempts by segregationists to remove him, Terrell had established such a record of competence and honesty since his appointment by McKinley in 1901 that the Senate confirmed him over the opposition. *New York Age*, April 30, 1914, p. 1.

68. John Hope Franklin, *From Slavery to Freedom: A History of Negro Americans*, 5th ed. (New York: Alfred A. Knopf, 1980), pp. 324–325.

69. *New York Age*, January 23, 1913, p. 1.

70. Ibid.; *New York Times*, March 29, 1912, p. 3, and October 26, 1912, p. 1.

71. *New York Age*, May 5, 1913, p. 1, and January 23, 1913, p. 1.

72. Verbeck, "Employer's Duty," pp. 62–64. For a detailed look at the image of blacks in the press and popular culture, especially coon songs, which evolved from nineteenth-century minstrelsy and reflected the recent migration and urban conditions and race relations, see Sacks, "'We Cry,'" pp. 64–101.

73. Verbeck, "Employer's Duty," p. 67; *New York Age*, May 5, 1913, p. 1. This article stated that Fillmore had turned down an offer by Dix to have the unit be an artillery regiment, as an act of commitment to infantry. The letter to Hilles of January 31, 1912, however, clearly indicated that Fillmore would rather accept artillery over nothing at all.

74. *New York Times*, December 7, 1912, p. 6; *Detroit Free Press*, in *New York Age*, January 23, 1913, p. 4; *New York Age*, May 1, 1913, p. 4. Standish is believed to have held the first military commission in colonial America.

75. *Laws of New York, 1913*, chap. 265, sect. 40, p. 481; *New York Age*, June 22, 1916, p. 4; *The Crisis* 6, no. 2 (June 1913): 71; David Levering Lewis, *W. E. B. Du Bois: Biography of a Race, 1868–1919* (New York: Henry Holt, 1993), p. 490; Lewis, "Parallels and Divergences: Assimilationist Strategies of Afro-American and Jewish Elites from 1910 to the Early 1930s," in *Bridges and Boundaries: African Americans and American Jews*, ed. Jack Salzman (New York: George Braziller, 1992), p. 25. For a lengthy discussion of the Civil Rights Law of 1913, see Evan P. Schultz, "Group Rights, American Jews, and the Failure of Group Libel Laws, 1913–1952," *Brooklyn Law Review* 66, no. 71 (Spring 2000), Lexis-Nexis, pp. 7–8; *Butts v. Merchants & Miners Transportation Co.*, 230 U.S. 126, June 16, 1913.

76. *New York Age,* May 8, 1913, p. 1; *New York Sun,* in *New York Age,* July 10, 1913, p. 4.

77. *New York Age,* May 8, 1913, p. 1.

78. John A. Dix to William Sulzer, December 26, 1912, Charles G. Bennett to Sulzer, December 7, 1912, and Henry A. Gildersleeve to Sulzer, December 4, 1912, all in Sulzer Papers, Box 4, RG 1147, Rare and Manuscript Collections, KLCU; *New York Times,* October 5, 1912, p. 11, and January 2, 1913, p. 1. When Tammany pulled its support for Dix's bid for a second term and nominated Sulzer, almost by default, Dix fired O'Ryan as a way of getting back at Tammany.

79. Ladson & Langston (Real Estate and Insurance) to Sulzer, May 21, 1913, Rufus Lewis Perry (President of Hannibal Club) to Sulzer, May 7, 1913, J. H. McMullen to Sulzer, May 8, 1913, Eugene Kinckle Jones to Sulzer, May 7, 1913, and James C. Thomas, Jr., to Sulzer, May 22, 1913, all in Sulzer Papers, Box 13, RG 1147, Rare and Manuscript Collections, KLCU.

80. Thomas to Sulzer, May 22, 1913.

81. Oswald Garrison Villard to W. E. B. Du Bois , May 15, 1913, Charles Young Collection, 83-1, Ohio Historical Society online, accessed October 27, 2013, dbs. ohiohistory.org/africanam/mss/831.cfm.

82. W. E. B. Du Bois to Charles Young, June 17, 1913, Charles Young Collection, 83-1, Ohio Historical Society online, accessed October 27, 2013, dbs.ohiohistory. org/africanam/mss/831.cfm.

83. Robert N. Wood to Chester C. Platt, May 31, 1913, Sulzer Papers, Box 15, RG 1147, and Platt to Wood, June 2, 1913, Sulzer Papers, Box 16, RG 1147, both in Rare and Manuscript Collections, KLCU.

84. William Gaynor to Sulzer, June 2, 1917, Sulzer Papers, Box 16, RG 1147, Rare and Manuscript Collections, KLCU. The *Age* reported that members of the Equity Congress actually shuttled the legislation between Albany and New York and then back to Albany. Gaynor refers only to a messenger in his response to Sulzer. *New York Age,* June 5, 1913, p. 1.

85. Clarence Frank Birdseye, Robert Cushing Cumming, and Frank Bixby Gilbert, eds., *Annotated Consolidated Laws of the State of New York,* 2nd ed., vol. 5 (New York: Banks Law Publishing, 1918), chap. 41, sect. 183, pp. 5325–5326.

86. *Laws of New York,* chap. 793, sect. 40, in Sulzer Papers, Box 17, RG 1147, Rare and Manuscript Collections, KLCU.

87. *Consolidated Laws of the State of New York,* vol. 3, ed. Frederick E. Wadhams (Albany, NY: J.B. Lyon, 1909), sect. 30, p. 2350; John H. Delaney to Sulzer, June 2, 1913, Sulzer Papers, Box 16, RG 1147, Rare and Manuscript Collections, KLCU; *New York Age,* June 5, 1913, p. 1.

88. *New York Age,* June 5, 1913, p. 1; Sulzer to J. M. McMullen, June 9, 1913, Sulzer Papers, Box 16, RG 1147, Rare and Manuscript Collections, KLCU; *Laws of New York, 1913,* chap. 793, sect. 40, p. 2201.

### Chapter 3. "Second Only to . . . the Emancipation Proclamation"

1. *Albany Times Union,* June 3, 1913, p. 1; *Albany Argus,* June 4, 1913, p. 4.

2. *New York Sun,* reprinted in *New York Age,* June 12, 1913, p. 4, and June 5, 1913, p. 1.

3. *New York Age,* June 12, 1913, p. 1.

4. *New York Age,* June 12, 1913, p. 4. Accusations abounded that Booker T. Washington controlled and possibly owned black newspapers. It is a fact that one of Washington's closest associates, Emmett J. Scott, had a financial interest in the paper and that Charles Anderson and Washington communicated often about their dissatisfaction with Fred Moore, who had worked under Anderson. Both men believed that Moore was a Democrat under the influence of Chief Robert Lee and was betraying the Republican Party, especially in his condemnation of Taft. They also believed that he did not have the intellectual capacity to be editor and that the *Age* was sloppy and often out of touch with real news, especially locally, and was in danger of losing out to the upstart *Amsterdam News.* See *Booker T. Washington Papers,* 11:114 and 169–170, 10:304 and 558; Lewis, *W. E. B. Du Bois,* pp. 400 and 428–429.

5. *Albany Argus,* June 4, 1913, p. 4.

6. Charles W. Fillmore to Henry De Witt Hamilton, June 5, 1913, Sulzer Papers, Box 16, RG 1147, Rare and Manuscript Collections, KLCU.

7. Ibid.

8. W. E. B. Du Bois to Lindley L. Garrison, June 16, 1913, NGB, General Correspondence, Series E 7, Box 97, File 24483, RG 168, NARA.

9. W. E. B. Du Bois to Charles Young, June 17, 1913, Charles Young Collection, 83-1, accessed October 27, 2013, dbs.ohiohistory.org/africanam/mss/831.cfm.

10. Garrison to Du Bois, June 24, 1913, NGB, General Correspondence, Series E 7, Box 97, File 24483-A, RG 168, NARA.

11. Robert N. Wood to Sulzer, June 6, 1913, and James H. Anderson to Chester Platt, June 9, 1913, Sulzer Papers, Box 16, RG 1147, Rare and Manuscript Collections, KLCU.

12. Platt to editors of the *Guardian Monthly* (Birmingham, AL), the *Mississippi Odd Fellow* (Charleston, MS), *Peoples Christian Visitor* (LaGrange, GA), *Theological Institute* (Atlanta, GA), *Observer* (Wetumpka, AL), and the *Star* (Charleston, MS), June 27–30, 1913, Sulzer Papers, Box 16, RG 1147, Rare and Manuscript Collections, KLCU. See Barbara K. Henritze, *Bibliographic Checklist of African American Newspapers* (Baltimore, MD: Genealogical Publishing, 1995).

13. *Albany Argus,* June 8, 1913, p. 7; Office of Adjutant General (press release), June 10, 1913, Sulzer Papers, Box 16, RG 1147, Rare and Manuscript Collections, KLCU; *New York Times,* May 24, 1916, p. 9. In a letter dated June 10, 1913, W. D. Johnson, a publisher of a Kentucky newspaper and protégé of Booker T. Washington, referred to the Littman case as early as February 11.

14. Wesser, *Response to Progressivism,* pp. 101–102; Schultz, "Group Rights," pp. 7–8.

15. *New York Times,* June 26, 1913, p. 18, June 27, 1913, p. 5, June 28, 1913, p. 16, June 29, 1913, pt. 2, p. 9, and July 14, 1913, p. 3.

16. *New York Times,* July 14, 1913, p. 3.

17. *New York Times,* July 19, 1913, p. 6, and May 24, 1916, p. 9.

18. *New York Times,* May 26, 1916, p. 6.

19. *New York Times,* March 13, 1912, p. 4. The NYNG apparently rebuffed Jewish efforts to form a battalion in March 1912. The practice of discriminating against Jews

continued and came to a head in May 1916 when the Committee for the Protection of the Good Name of Immigrant Peoples formally complained to Governor Whitman. Whitman ordered an investigation by the adjutant general, who issued a statement that "such conditions would not be tolerated in the National Guard" and ordered a hearing on the matter. After four hearings with forty-nine witnesses, the governor directed that the scope of the investigation be broadened to include others who had met with such treatment. The investigation found evidence of discrimination but no "prevailing sentiment of prejudice." Nonetheless, the adjutant general issued General Order no. 36 on October 25, 1916, forbidding the rejection of an applicant "on account of his race or religion." See *Annual Report of the Adjutant-General of the State of New York for the Year 1916* (Albany, NY: J. B. Lyon, 1917), pp. 13–15. In a 1962 study, Isham G. Newton found that the number of blacks in National Guard units remained low "because of the existence of unwritten racially restrictive policies related to recruitment and acceptance of minority group applicants." See Newton, "The Negro and the National Guard," *Phylon* 23, no. 1 (Spring 1962): 22.

20. *New York Age*, July 3, 1913, p. 1.

21. Ibid.

22. Edward Howard, Assistant Adjutant General (NYS), to Charles Young, July 10, 1913, and August 5, 1913, Charles Young Collection, 83-1, Ohio Historical Society online, accessed October 27, 2013, dbs.ohiohistory.org/africanam/mss/831.cfm.

23. Villard to Young, August 2, 1913, Charles Young Collection, 83-1, Ohio Historical Society online, accessed October 27, 2013, dbs.ohiohistory.org/africanam/mss/831.cfm.

24. Wesser, *Response to Progressivism,* pp. 120–123.

25. Ibid.

26. Johnson, *African American Soldiers,* p. 81; Fillmore to Sulzer, August 25, 1913, and Chester C. Platt to Fillmore, August 26, 1913, both in Sulzer Papers, Box 21, RG 1147, Rare and Manuscript Collections, KLCU.

27. *Amsterdam News,* March 11, 1925, p. 9. Sulzer ran a vicious campaign for governor in 1914. His attacks on Glynn resulted in an easy victory for Whitman and the Republicans. Despite his claims of fairness, Sulzer accepted the endorsement of the American Party, which was anti-Catholic and nativist. See Wesser, *Response to Progressivism,* pp. 153–160.

28. Louis Stotesbury to Arthur W. Little, November 4, 1936, "*From Harlem to the Rhine* File," NYSMM.

29. *New York Age*, October 16, p. 1, and October 30, 1913, p. 1; Johnson, *African American Soldiers,* p. 80.

30. *New York Age*, October 30, 1913, p. 1.

31. Stotesbury to Little, November 4, 1936; *New York Age*, October 30, 1913, p. 1.

32. *New York Age*, December 18, 1913, p. 1.

33. *New York Age,* November 6, 1913, pp. 1–2, January 8, 1914, p. 1, and March 26, 1914, p. 1.

34. Louis A. Culliver to A. L. Mills, May 4, 1914, and Mills to Culliver, May 9, 1914, NGB, General Correspondence, Series E 7, File 24483, RG 168, NARA. Perhaps the nicknames of the 23rd and 28th Regiments, Tomahawks and Black Lions, respec-

tively, threw Culliver off. One can assume that he meant to cite the 24th and 25th Regiments in addition to the 10th Cavalry. If so, there is little evidence that men from these outfits comprised a significant percentage of the provisional regiment led by Fillmore.

35. *New York Age*, May 14, 1914, p. 1.

36. *New York Age*, July 2, 1914, p. 1.

37. *New York Age*, July 2, 1914, p. 1, and July 16, 1914, p. 2. Fillmore claimed that he changed the list but put it back to its original form after Carr had tampered with it.

38. Villard to Young, September 14, 1914, Charles Young Collection, 83-1, Ohio Historical Society online, accessed October 27, 2013, dbs.ohiohistory.org/africanam/mss/831.cfm.

39. *Annual Report of the Adjutant-General of the State of New York for the Year 1914* (Albany, NY: J. B. Lyon, 1916), p. 4.

40. Ibid.

41. Ibid.

42. *New York Age*, April 2, 1914, pp. 1 and 4, and April 16, 1914, p. 1; Sacks, "'We Cry,'" p. 86; James Weldon Johnson, *The Autobiography of an Ex-Colored Man* (1912), in *Three Negro Classics* (New York: Avon Books, 1995), p. 426.

43. *New York Age*, April 30, 1914, p. 4, and May 7, 1914, p. 4; *Chicago Defender*, March 14, 1914, p. 1; *New York Age*, March 30, 1916, p. 1, and April 23, 1914, p. 4. Of course, this was not the first and far from the last time that a group desperate for heroes, especially of the warrior kind, would claim anyone famous whose ancestry or provenance suggested an ambiguous racial identity. The list includes Agamemnon, Solomon, Hamilcar, and Hannibal, to name a few. That same article indicates that blacks are the most forgiving of people, for few others would have tolerated the treatment they suffered.

44. James Weldon Johnson, "Excess Patriotism," unpublished essay, 1911, pp. 1–3, James Weldon Johnson Papers, Box 58, Folders 200–201, BLYU. As testament to its prescience, the essay appeared in print four years later; see *New York Age*, May 20, 1915, p. 4.

45. *Chicago Defender*, March 14, 1914, p. 1. Japan was an ally of Great Britain at the time and demanded that Germany relinquish its Chinese leasehold and withdraw and/or intern its warships in the region. Americans reacted harshly to the Japanese ultimatum. *New York Age*, August 27, 1914, p. 4. Tyler, a former auditor for the Department of the Navy and one of the victims of the Wilson purge, continued to rail against government policies until he became an official war correspondent. Expediency necessitated adjustments on both sides. Emmett J. Scott to Charles W. Anderson, September 4, 1913, *Booker T. Washington Papers*, 12:270.

46. *New York Age*, August 6, 1914, p. 4.

47. *New York Age*, August 6, 1914, p. 4, August 13, 1914, p. 4, and August 27, 1914, p. 4. Blacks believed that France's prejudice toward blacks was less than that of Germany. The French acculturation model in Africa and the West Indies impressed blacks as more inclusive. Moreover, the experience of American blacks in France influenced this favorable impression. *New York Age*, September 3, 1914, p. 4; Susan Kerr Chandler, "'That Biting, Stinging Thing Which Ever Shadows Us':

African-American Social Workers in France during World War I," *Social Service Review* 69, no. 3 (September 1995): 501–502; Tyler Stovall, *Paris Noir: African Americans in the City of Light* (Boston: Houghton Mifflin, 1996), pp. 2–4.

48. *New York Age*, October 1, 1914, p. 1.

49. *New York Age*, October 8, 1914, p. 4, October 15, 1914, p. 4, and October 22, 1914, p. 4. The *Age* credited Charles Anderson for the appointment. The paper considered it one of the largest services to the community in his successful career. *New York Age*, December 23, 1909, p. 4.

50. Ibid.

51. *New York Age,* October 1, 1914, p. 4. Such a plan was floated after the war as officials struggled over the future of the black soldier in the regular army and the National Guard. *The Crisis* 2, no. 5 (March 1916): 240–242. The Pennsylvania legislature passed bills authorizing a black National Guard regiment, but Governor John Kinley Tener, a Republican, vetoed the proposed legislation. See *The Crisis* 6, no. 3 (July 1913): 119.

52. *New York Age*, October 22, 1914, p. 4, and October 29, 1914, p. 4.

53. *New York Age*, October 29, 1914, p. 4.

54. Sherman, *Republican Party,* pp. 119–121; *New York Age*, November 5, 1914, p. 1.

55. Sherman, *Republican Party*, pp. 119–121.

56. *New York Age*, November 5, 1914, pp. 1–4, and November 19, 1914, p. 1.

57. *New York Age*, December 3, 1914, p. 5, and November 5, 1914, p. 4.

58. *New York Age*, March 4, 1915, p. 4.

59. Ibid.

60. Louis Stotesbury to Gen. A. L. Mills, Chief, Militia Affairs, February 25, 1915, and Mills to Stotesbury, March 2, 1915, both in NGB, General Correspondence, Series E 7, Box 24483, RG 168, NARA.

61. *New York Age*, January 7, 1915, p. 1. The exclusion bill was defeated by an overwhelming margin in early January 1915. Only seventy-five votes, all Democratic, were cast in favor. *New York Age*, January 14, 1915, p. 4.

62. *New York Age*, March 25, 1915, p. 6, May 13, 1915, p. 4, and May 27, 1915, p. 1; Lewis, *W. E. B. Du Bois*, pp. 506–509.

63. Sacks, "'We Cry,'" p. 131; *New York Age*, September 23, 1915, p. 4.

64. *New York Age,* December 10, 1914, p. 1, October 14, 1915, p. 4, February 25, 1915, p. 4, and October 14, 1915, p. 4; Wesser, *Response to Progressivism*, p. 163.

65. See *The Crisis* 1, no. 1 (November 1910): 3; 2, no. 3 (July 1911): 95; 12, no. 4 (August 1916): 194; and 13, no. 1 (November 1916): 30.

66. *New York Age*, March 15, 1915, p. 4.

67. *New York Age*, February 10, 1916, pp. 1–2; Sacks, "'We Cry,'" p. 108.

68. *New York Age*, March 30, 1916, p. 1. Stotesbury's response to charges of discrimination by Jews was anything but admirable. He not only acknowledged the private club history of the NYNG and its strong legacy but also defended it. See *New York Times*, June 1, 1916, p. 6. Stotesbury's past involvement with the regiment question and his subsequent statements about Jews in the Guard did not inspire confidence in his motives or commitment. Besides, the presence of the one constant figure in all of this, General O'Ryan, raised the specter of an unseen hand in

the proposed "new" arrangement. Secret correspondence between O'Ryan and the chief of the Militia Bureau, William Mann, reveals O'Ryan's sinister role.

69. *New York Age*, March 30, 1916, p. 1; *New York Times*, May 3, 1916, p. 6; Birdseye, Cumming, and Gilbert, *Annotated Consolidated Laws*, sect. 241, p. 5354.

70. George C. Herring, Jr., "James Hay and the Preparedness Controversy, 1915–1916," *Journal of Southern History* 30, no. 4 (November 1964): 399–401.

71. Wesser, *Response to Progressivism*, p. 180; *New York Times*, May 2, 1916, p. 6, and May 24, 1916, p. 11.

72. *New York Times*, May 2, 1916, p. 6, and May 24, 1916, p. 11.

73. *New York Times*, May 26, 1916, p. 5.

74. *New York Times*, May 26, 1916, p. 5, and June 26, 1916, p. 5; Wesser, *Response to Progressivism*, p. 214. On May 9, 1916, President Wilson ordered out the organized militia units of Texas, Arizona, and New Mexico for federal service. Whitman must have known that an additional call involving New York could not be far away. On June 18, it came, "in view of the possibilities of further aggression upon the territory of the United States." *Annual Report of the Adjutant-General of the State of New York for the Year 1916* (Albany, NY: J. B. Lyon, 1917), p. 21; Stotesbury to Little, November 4, 1936. In fairness to Stotesbury, he did seek federal recognition for the regiment as early as September 1916 without O'Ryan's knowledge and with no apparent intention of reducing the number of black officers.

75. Harris, *Harlem's Hell Fighters*, p. 34; *Annual Report of the Adjutant-General of the State of New York for the Year 1916*, pp. 20–21.

76. *New York Times*, May 27, 1916, p. 10.

77. *New York Times*, June 18, 1916, p. 2, and June 22, p. 10; *New York Age*, June 1, 1916, p. 4.

78. *New York Times*, June 26, 1916, p. 5.

### Chapter 4. "Mulligan's Guards"

1. Judith Weisenfeld, *African-American Women and Christian Activism: New York's Black YWCA, 1905–1945* (Cambridge, MA: Harvard University Press, 1997), pp. 100–102.

2. Sacks, "'We Cry,'" pp. 109–110; *New York Age*, March 16, 1916, p. 1, and March 23, 1916, p. 1.

3. *New York Age*, March 16, 1916, p. 1, March 23, 1916, p. 1, and May 11, 1916, p. 1.

4. Davis, *Here and There*, pp. 18–20.

5. Arthur W. Little, *From Harlem to the Rhine: The Story of New York's Colored Volunteers* (New York: Covici Friede, 1936), pp. ix–x; *New York Times*, June 26, 1916, p. 5; *New York Age*, June 29, 1916, p. 1.

6. *New York Times*, October 14, 1944, p. 13; *New York Age*, June 29, 1916, p. 1.

7. Little, *From Harlem*, pp. ix–x; *New York Times*, October 14, 1944, p. 13.

8. Brooke Hayward, *Haywire* (New York: Alfred A. Knopf, 1977), p. 100.

9. Little, *From Harlem*, p. 111.

10. Ibid., p. 112. Hayward was not alone in the creation of the regiment, as Whitman appointed Lorillard Spencer of the 8th Coast Artillery and his military secretary to assist Hayward.

11. According to Arthur West Little, soon to be named a captain, the Brooklyn recruiting office had no medical personnel present and relied on Monson Morris, his old schoolmate, to determine the fitness of the volunteers. Little, *From Harlem,* pp. 2 and 113; *New York Age,* June 1, 1916, p. 1, and June 29, 1916, p. 1.

12. *New York Age,* June 29, 1916, p. 1.

13. Little, *From Harlem,* pp. 113–114; Abstracts of World War I Military Service, 1917–1919, RG B0808, NYSA.

14. National Guard Muster Rolls, 1878–1954, RG 13726–86, NYSA; Watkins-Owens, *Blood Relations,* p. 1. D. W. Ketcham to E. Theodore, April 27, 1918, General Correspondence, 1903–1919, Entry 296-Nm-84, 8142-128, RG 165, NARA. For a detailed discussion of the use of black British subjects in the British army, see File WO 32/4765, National Archives, Kew, Richmond, Surrey. Although a decision was reached late in the war to include black subjects in the regular British army, British officials strongly opposed the attachment of American blacks troops for purposes of training. See Peyton C. March, Chief of Staff, to Pershing, May 4, 1918, AEF General Correspondence, No. 1237-R, File 8.55, Entry 6, RG 120, NARA.

15. Little, *From Harlem,* p. 10. Ally's enlistment also raises interesting but unanswerable questions about race and the regiment. It might also suggest something about the expansive boundaries of the African diaspora.

16. Osofsky, *Harlem,* pp 28–29; Abstracts of World War I Military Service. According to Arthur Little, the Brooklyn headquarters was an old dilapidated dance-hall and beer garden at 191 Harrison Avenue. Little, *From Harlem,* p. 1.

17. *New York Age,* July 9, 1916, p. 1; Adjutant General New York (Louis Stotesbury) to Chief, Militia Bureau (William Mann), June 29, 1916, File 210.651/E-NY and File 325.4-E/NY, both in NGB, RG 168, NARA. Governor Whitman actually requested the services of Young and Capt. Benjamin O. Davis, an instructor in military science at Wilberforce University in Ohio. The Militia Bureau replied that "there is no authority for raising same regiment, and it is uniform policy of War Department to detail officers with their own arms of service." Young was promoted to lieutenant colonel on July 1 after being examined by Pershing and other officers while on the Mexican border. According to the press report, Young became the first black soldier to attain the rank of lieutenant colonel from field duty. *New York Age,* July 20, 1916, p. 1.

18. Little, *From Harlem,* p. 116.

19. William Hayward, *Mother's Sons of the Fighting "15th"* (New York: William Moseby, 1919), p. 6, Clipping File, 1925–1974, "World War I, 1914–1918," SC 005.880-2, SCRBC; Davis, *Here and There,* pp. 18–20.

20. *New York Age,* July 13, 1916, p. 1.

21. *Annual Report of the Adjutant-General of the State of New York for the Year 1916,* pp. 358–359; *Annual Report of the Adjutant-General of the State of New York for the Year 1917* (Albany, NY: J. B. Lyons, 1920), pp. 162–167; *New York Age,* July 20, 1916, p. 1.

22. *New York Age,* July 27, 1916, p. 1.

23. Ibid. Anderson seemed to harbor lingering doubts about Fillmore's loyalty to the Republican Party. In an early 1912 letter to Henry L. Stimson, Anderson referred to Fillmore as someone he believed to be a "republican." Anderson to Stimson, January 23, 1912, NGB, Series E 7, Box 97, RG 168, NARA.

24. *New York Age*, July 27, 1916, p. 1; Charles Anderson to Joel Spingarn, July 1, 1916, Spingarn Papers, Box 1, Folder 22, RG 95, MSRC.

25. Nicholas Biddle, MIB, NYC, to Col. Marlborough Churchill, Chief, MIB, July 22, 1918, Loving Papers, Series D, Military, Box 113-1, MSRC; *The Branch Bulletin*, March 1917, Spingarn Papers, Box 13, Folder 534, RG 95, MSRC.

26. Hayward to Spingarn, June 27, 1916, and July 5, 1916, both in Spingarn Papers, Box 5, Folder 205, RG 95, MSRC; N. B. Marshall to Sulzer, December 12, 1912, Sulzer Papers, Box 4, RG 1147, Rare and Manuscripts Collections, KLCU.

27. Gilchrist Stewart to Spingarn, July 31, 1916, Spingarn Papers, Box 10, Folder 427, RG 95, MSRC.

28. Lewis, *Du Bois*, pp. 520–521.

29. List of Attendees at Conference, Box 91-13, Folder 525, RG 95, MSRC.

30. Stewart to Spingarn, August 5, 1916, Spingarn Papers, Box 10, Folder 427, RG 95, MSRC; Hayward to Spingarn, August 10, 1916, Spingarn Papers, Box 5, Folder 205, RG 95, MSRC; "The Amenia Conference Programme," Spingarn Papers, Box 91–13, Folder 525, RG 95, MSRC; Hamilton Fish to Spingarn, May 7, 1917, Spingarn Papers, Box 5, Folder 155, RG 95, MSRC. Fish reported that regiment strength was 1,300 of 2,002: "Most of our men are recruited from New York and Brooklyn but we have accepted a few from Albany, Troy, Newburg, and Middletown, and will be glad to secure some more from any place along the River. The qualifications are 18 to 45 years of age and at least 125 lbs in weight. We want unmarried men but might possibly accept married men without dependants. We are desirous of making this the 'Crack' Regiment of the state and expect to be recruited to full strength within thirty days."

31. *New York Age*, August 10, 1916, p. 1; Little, *From Harlem*, p. 112; William Hayward, *Mother's Sons*, p. 5.

32. *New York Age,* August 3, 1916, p. 4, and August 10, 1916, p. 1; Samuel A. Duncan to Spingarn, August 9, 1916, Spingarn Papers, Box 4, Folder 144, RG 95, MSRC.

33. *New York Age,* August 3, 1916, p. 4, and August 10, 1916, p. 1.

34. Abraham Chew, *A Biography of Colonel Charles Young* (Washington, DC: R. I. Pendleton, 1923), p. 6, and *Dayton (Ohio) Journal Herald*, February 3, 1984, taken from the Internet article "Colonel Charles Young: Black Cavalryman, Huachuca Commander, and Early Intelligence Officer," accessed November 2, 2013, http://net.lib. byu.edu/~rdh7/wwi/comment/huachuca/HI1-19.htm?. W. N. Colson and A. B. Nutt called Hanks "servile." Cited by General Ballou as the model for any black candidate at the Colored Training Camp, Hanks, according to critics, "knew how to stay in his place." See Lt. W. N. Colson and Lt. A. B. Nutt, "The Failure of the Ninety-Second Division," *Messenger*, September 1919, Riot Number, p. 23.

35. *New York Age,* July 20, 1916, p. 4.

36. Ibid.

37. Ibid.; Maj. C. A. Bach, "Leadership," unpublished essay, Fort Sheridan Training Camp, November 24, 1917, p. 1, Sneed Papers, Military History Institute, Carlisle, PA. Emmett J. Scott, *Scott's Official History of the American Negro in the World War* (Chicago: Homewood, 1919), pp. 82–84; Michael David Perlman, "To Make Democracy Safe for the World: A Social History of the Origins, Development and Af-

termath of the World War I Military Preparedness Movement in America" (Ph.D. diss., University of Illinois, 1978), p. 15.

38. Butler R. Wilson to R. J. Randolph, September 28, 1916, Box 12, Folder 498, RG 95, MSRC; Lewis, *When Harlem Was in Vogue*, pp. 180–181 and 282.

39. *New York Age*, September 28, 1916, p. 1; "The Negro as a Soldier and a Sailor," Remarks of Murray Hulbert of New York, September 6, 1916, *Congressional Record* (Washington, DC: Government Printing Office, 1916), pp. 1–4

40. *New York Age*, September 28, 1916, p. 1; Maj. Gregg Benefiel, "A Treatise on the Proper Execution of Guard Mount in Garrison or in the Field," 1999, accessed November 11, 2013, http://www.19thalabama.org/onguard.doc.

41. *New York Age*, October 5, 1916, p. 1.

42. Ibid.

43. Ibid.

44. *New York Times*, October 2, 1916, p. 22; Little, *From Harlem*, p. 117.

45. Ibid.

46. Little, *From Harlem*, pp. 10 and 115; Col. G. W. McIver, Acting Chief, Militia Bureau, to Lt. Col A. P. Buffington, Senior Instructor-Inspector, October 3, 1916, NGB, File 325.4-E-NY, RG 168, NARA. The chief asked for a confidential report "on the subject matter of the attached newspaper article as to the regiment, armory, uniforms, and arms." For a very different rendering of this episode, see Harris, *Harlem's Hell Fighters*, pp. 67–69. Relying in part on Little's account, Harris has Hayward contributing to the comedy. He also uses Williams's own rendering to add to the levity.

47. The Adjutant General to Chief of the Militia Bureau, September 18, 1916, and Militia Bureau to the Adjutant General of New York, October 3, 1916, both in NGB, File 325.4-E-NY, RG 168, NARA.

48. A. B. Cosey, S. Banks, T. Motley to Secretary of War, October 9, 1916, Murray Hulbert to TAG [The Adjutant General], October 19, 1916, William M. Cruikshank, Adjutant General, U.S., to C. A. Hughes, National Colored Democratic League, November 3, 1916, Charles S. Whitman to Newton D. Baker, November 27, 1916, and Baker to Whitman, December 1, 1916, all in NGB, File 325.4-E-NY, RG 168, NARA.

49. Little, *From Harlem*, p. 10; *Evening Globe*, October 2, 1916, editorial page, reprinted in *New York Age*, October 5, 1916, p. 1; Jerry M. Cooper, "National Guard Reform, the Army, and the Spanish-American War: The View from Wisconsin," *Military Affairs* 42, no. 1 (February 1978): 21.

50. *New York Age*, October 12, 1916, p. 1.

51. Osofsky, *Harlem*, p. 137; *New York Age*, October 12, 1916, p. 1, and October 5, 1916, p. 4; Sacks, "'We Cry,'" p. 170; Birdseye, Cumming, and Gilbert, *Annotated Consolidated Laws*, p. 5340.

52. John Wesley Castles, "War Diary of John Wesley Castles, Jr.," June 18, 1917, USMAL; Little, *From Harlem*, p. 9; *New York Age*, November 16, 1916, p. 1; William Hayward to Captain Joseph L. Gilbreth, April 8, 1917, NGB, File 325.4-E-NY, RG 168, NARA.

53. *New York Age*, November 16, 1916, p. 1.

54. *New York Age*, November 23, 1916, p. 4.

55. Ibid.

56. Ibid.

57. Ibid.

58. Austin to Spingarn, January 24, 1917, Spingarn Papers, Box 1, Folder 31, RG 95, MSRC; Delancey Jay to Spingarn, December 22, 1916, Spingarn Papers, Box 6, Folder 236, RG 95, MSRC.

59. George J. Austin to Joel E. Spingarn, January 4, 1917, Spingarn Papers, Box 1, Folder 31, RG 95, MSRC.

60. Austin to Spingarn, January 24, 1917, Spingarn Papers, Box 1, Folder 31, RG 95, MSRC. Austin probably understood that Europe would not approve of his activities. Fillmore certainly would not have. General Leonard Wood to Spingarn, January 9, 1917, Spingarn Papers, Box 12, Folder 503, RG 95, MSRC; "Regulations and Information Concerning the Citizens' Training Camp," Bulletin no. 9, February 15, 1917, pp. 1–5, Spingarn Papers, Box 13, Folder 534, RG 95, MSRC; J. E. Spingarn, "Military Training Camp for Colored Men," February 15, 1917, Spingarn Papers, Box 13, Folder 534, RG 95, MSRC.

61. George W. Crawford to Spingarn, April 7, 1917, Spingarn Papers, Box 4, Folder 115, RG 95, MSRC; *New York News*, March 1917, editorial page, Spingarn Papers, Box 13, Folder 538, RG 95, MSRC; Lewis, *Du Bois,* pp. 527–529. Many blacks were very upset that Oswald Garrison Villard had supported Woodrow Wilson.

62. Charles Young to Harry Smith, March 23, 1917, Young Folder, RG 95, MSRC; Lewis, *Du Bois,* p. 531.

63. Spingarn to Mrs. M. C. Simpson, April 25, 1917, Spingarn Papers, Box 10, Folder 408, RG 95, MSRC.

64. Lewis, *Du Bois,* p. 531.

65. Ibid.; John Nail to Spingarn, February 27, 1917, and March 9, 1917, Spingarn Papers, Box 8, Folder 338, RG 95, MSRC.

66. *New York Age*, March 15, 1917, p. 4.

67. Fillmore to Spingarn, March 18, 1917, Spingarn Papers, Box 5, Folder 154, RG 95, MSRC.

68. *New York Age*, March 29, 1917, p. 4.

69. Ibid. Within a year, the British army began the recruitment of black British subjects in the United States.

70. *New York Age*, April 5, 1917, p. 1, and April 12, 1917, p. 1; *Chicago Defender*, April 7, 1917, p. 1.

71. *New York Age*, April 5, 1917, p. 1.

72. Col. T. A. Roberts, General Staff, to Personnel Officer (concerning Morris), May 27, 1918, Box 361, File 184, RG 120, NARA; Col. Glendie Young to Commanding Gen. AEF, June 23, 1918 (concerning Dayton), Box 361, GHO, File 11440-A71, RG 120, NARA; Hamilton Fish to Father, February 25, April 29, July 18, and October 10, 1918, Fish Papers, Box 11, Folder 26, NYSLMC; Lewis Shaw to Mumsie (C. H. Shaw), November 29, 1918, Shaw Papers, Manuscript Division, NYHS; *Annual Report of the Adjutant-General of the State of New York for 1917,* pp. 162–166.

73. *New York Age,* April 5, 1917, p. 1.

74. Byron Farwell, *Over There: The United States in the Great War, 1917–1918* (New York: W. W. Norton, 1999), pp. 31–35.

75. Ibid.; Jonathan Schell, "No More unto the Breach," *Harper's Magazine,* March 2003, pp. 36–38.

76. *New York Age,* May 13, 1915, p. 4, December 9, 1915, p. 1, and July 20, 1916, p. 4.

77. *New York Age,* February 15, 1917, p. 4; *Chicago Defender,* April 7, 1917, p. 1; *Baltimore Afro-American,* March 31, 1917, editorial page.

### Chapter 5. War and Expediency

1. Executive Committee of the Mayor's Committee on National Defense, "The Mobilization of the National Guard 1916: Its Economic and Military Aspects," New York, January 1917, pp. 10–12, File 149-11.4-65.4, RG 165, NARA. John F. O'Ryan to William A. Mann, February 9, 1917, Mann to O'Ryan, February 13, 1917, O'Ryan to Mann, March 22, 1917, and Mann to O'Ryan, March 23, 1917, all in NGB, File 325.4-E-NY, RG 168, NARA.

2. Mann to O'Ryan, March 23, 1917, O'Ryan to Mann, March 26, 1917, C. D. Rhinehart to William Hayward, April 6, 1917, John Purroy Mitchel to William Hayward, April 7, 1917, and Gilbreth to Mann, April 10, 1917, all in NGB, File 325.4-E-NY, RG 168, NARA.

3. Chief Militia Bureau to NY Adjutant General, April 25, 1917, and Newton D. Baker to Murray Hulbert (US Rep., NY), May 5, 1917, both in NGB, File 325.4-E-NY, RG 168, NARA. The letter from the Militia Bureau does not have Mann's signature, only a stamped signature of G. W. McIver, his assistant. The letter states that Mann had been directed by the secretary of war to inform the New York adjutant general of the recognition. Baker seems to have been working on old information. With the declaration of war only weeks before, he probably had more pressing matters on his mind.

4. *New York Age,* April 19, 1917, p. 1; Hayward, *Mother's Sons,* p. 4.

5. *New York Age,* April, 19, 1917, p. 1; Castles, "War Diary," June 6, 1917.

6. *New York Age,* April 19, 1917, p. 1.

7. Ibid.

8. *New York Age,* April 19, 1917, p. 1; official records indicate that Reid joined the Regiment on July 13, 1917. Abstracts of National Guard Service in World War I, 1917–1919, Roll 4, RG 13721–83, NYSA.

9. Johnson, *African American Soldiers,* pp. 82–83. See note 72.

10. Napoleon Bonaparte Marshall, *The Providential Armistice* (Washington, DC: Liberty League, 1930), p. 12.

11. *New York Age,* April 26, 1917, p. 1. The Fowler brothers were Bart (age 31), Benjamin (35), George (19), Howard (26), John (33), Richard (28), and Royal (21). All served overseas and survived the war. *New York Age,* September 20, 1917, p. 1; "Service Abstracts, 369th," Box 12, Volumes 38–39, NYSA.

12. Kennedy, *Disloyal Mothers,* pp. xii–xvii; Addie W. Hunton and Kathryn M. Johnson, *Two Colored Women with the American Expeditionary Forces* (New York: AMS Press, 1971), and Addie W. Hunton, *William Alphaeus Hunton: A Pioneer Prophet of Young Men* (New York: G. K. Hall, 1997), p. xviii; M. Cravath Simpson to

Joel Spingarn, April 19, 1917, Spingarn Papers, Box 10, Folder 408, RG 95, MSRC. Mrs. Cravath represented Suppression of Lynching, an organization under the umbrella of the Northeastern Federation of Women's Clubs organized in Boston in 1896. For a startling view on black women's attitudes, see discussion of letter from a "colored Wife and Mother" to James Weldon Johnson and the *New York Age* in Nikki Brown, "'Your Patriotism Is of the Purest Quality': African American Women and World War I" (Ph.D. diss., Yale University, 2002), pp. 26–30. Among other things, this anonymous writer maintained that black women would be without protection from predatory white men if black men joined the military and left their communities.

13. *New York Age,* April 26, 1917, p. 1; *Amsterdam News,* May 2, 1942, p. 1.

14. *New York Age,* May 17, 1917, p. 1.

15. *New York Age,* May 17, 1917, p. 1, and May 24, 1917, p. 2; Circular no. 95 by Order of Col. Hayward, November 7, 1917, Box 1, 293–13.6, RG 120, NARA; Emma Fox to Hayward, Box 1, 293-32.13, RG 120, NARA; *New York Age,* July 19, 1917, p. 1. The Neighborhood Whist Club of Brooklyn announced its intention to organize an auxiliary in that borough for the same purpose although Brooklyn already had representation on the committee in the person of Mrs. M. C. Lawton; Osofsky, *Harlem,* p. 36.

16. Sissle, "Memoirs," pp. 7–13 and 25–26. For a full and well-written account of Europe and the band as well as a fine history of the Regiment, see Badger, *Life in Ragtime.*

17. Sissle, "Memoirs," pp. 7, 9, 13–14, 17–14, 25, and 27; Muster Roll, 15th Regiment, NYSA.

18. *New York Age,* April 19, 1917, p. 1.

19. Ibid.; Sissle, "Memoirs," pp. 34–41; Badger, *Life in Ragtime,* pp. 142–146.

20. Sissle, "Memoirs," pp. 34–41; Badger, *Life in Ragtime,* pp. 142–146.

21. Badger, *Life in Ragtime,* p. 148.

22. *New York Age,* April 26, 1917, p. 1.

23. Spingarn to Major Halsted Dorey, March 31, 1917, Spingarn Papers, Box 4, Folder 133, RG 95, MSRC; *New York Age,* April 26, 1917, p. 1; "Military Training Camp for Colored Officers," press release, May 8, 1917, Spingarn Papers, Box 13, Folder 535, RG 95, MSRC.

24. "Training Camp Deferred," April 27, 1917, press release, Spingarn Papers, Box 13, Folder 536, RG 95, MSRC.

25. Spingarn to Major Allen Washington, April 17, 1917, Spingarn Papers, Box 11, Folder 475, RG 95, MSRC; "Training Camp Deferred"; Franklin, *From Slavery to Freedom,* p. 326; Wilberforce University and Tuskegee Institute had reservations about the training camp concept. Wilberforce already had a military science and cadet program. Robert Russa Moton reported to Spingarn that he would not distribute applications to students because a trustee had applied to the War Department to recruit a cavalry regiment of black troops and requested that Tuskegee supply both men and officers. William Joiner to Spingarn, April 9, 1917, Spingarn Papers, Box 6, Folder 244, RG 95, MSRC; Moton to Spingarn, April 16, 1917, Spingarn Papers, Box 8, Folder 333, RG 95, MSRC.

26. Ralph A. Hayes to Stephen M. Newman, May 12, 1917, Spingarn Papers, Box 5, Folder 200, RG 95, MSRC.

27. Barbeau and Henri, *Unknown Soldiers,* pp. 56–58.

28. Ibid., pp. 61–63.

29. *New York Age,* May 17, 1917, p. 1.

30. Ibid.; Barbeau and Henri, *Unknown Soldiers,* pp. 58–59. The War Department had no place for the men at the end of three months, and instead of paying them while the planning for the 92nd Division continued, it decided to extend the camp by one month. Sweeney, *History of the American Negro,* pp. 119–130. The nine men from the regiment who successfully completed training at Fort Des Moines were: Sgt. Maj. Robert Fearing, 1st Sgt. Archie McLee, Supply Sgt. Wilfrid Bazil, Sgt. Thomas J. Bullock, Sgt. Homer Butler, Cpl. Ira Aldridge, Cpl. George E. Brown, Pvt. Edward P. Rudd, and Pvt. William Gee.

31. Hayward, *Mother's Sons,* p. 3; Sissle, "Memoirs," pp. 55–61; Badger, *Life in Ragtime,* p. 149. For more on Sissle's derogation of Puerto Rican band members, see Badger, *Life in Ragtime,* p. 294n34, which nicely captures the role reversal in Sissle's characterizations of the Puerto Ricans; Little, *From Harlem,* pp. 9–10.

32. Farwell, *Over There,* p. 26.

33. Ibid., pp. 38–39.

34. Réquin EMA 40R to French War Ministry, July 21, 1917, 7N1717, SHAT.

35. Réquin 42R, July 31, 1918, 7N1717, SHAT.

36. Réquin 44R, August 11, 1917, 7N1717, SHAT.

37. Réquin, December 25, 1917, 7N1717, SHAT.

38. Russel F. Weigley, *History of the United States Army* (Bloomington: Indiana University Press, 1984), p. 386.

39. John S. D. Eisenhower, *Yanks: The Epic Story of the American Army in WWI* (New York: Free Press, 2001), p. 62; John H. Morrow, Jr., *The Great War: An Imperial History* (London: Routledge, 2004), pp. 76, 180, and 239.

40. Farwell, *Over There,* pp. 40–41.

41. Ibid., pp. 163.

42. Little, *From Harlem,* p. 357; Farwell, *Over There,* p. 96. The 26th Division came from New England. The 42nd included National Guard units from twenty-six states and the District of Columbia. Douglas MacArthur, then a major, compared the division's structure to that of a rainbow spanning the continent.

43. Farwell, *Over There,* pp. 95–96.

44. Ibid., p. 39.

45. Little, *From Harlem,* p. 8.

46. Ibid., p. 12; *New York Age,* May 17, 1917, p. 1.

47. *Chicago Defender,* June 16, 1917, p. 1; *New York Age,* May 24, 1917, p. 1, and June 7, 1917, p. 1.

48. *New York Age,* May 24, 1917, p. 1.

49. *New York Age,* May 17, 1917, p. 1, and May 24, 1917, p. 2. The quality and quantity of equipment and supplies in the National Guard units of the state could have been more the result of the unit's age and class makeup rather than its racial composition, although the two were interrelated.

50. Little, *From Harlem,* pp. 8 and x.

51. Walter Wilson, "Jim Crow in the A.E.F.," *New Republic,* August 26, 1936, p. 81. Wilson found the dialect to be "atrocious throughout."

52. Ibid., pp. 8 and 13; Howard Long, "Review of *From Harlem to the Rhine,*" *Journal of Negro History* 21, no. 4 (October 1936): 444–447. Only one of many letters criticizing Little for his use of dialect read: "I fear you have slightly exaggerated the 'broken' language used by your Negro troops." T. Edward Jones, MD, to Little, August 28, 1936, NYSMM. These letters were from people to whom the book had been sent, which undoubtedly tempered the expression of misgivings they might have had. Most found that the history of blacks in the military had been so damaging that Little's book would "go a long way to offset much of the misinformation that has already been broadcast"; W. G. Alexander to Little, June 15, 1936, NYSMM, *From Harlem to Rhine* file.

53. Sissle, "Memoirs," pp. 75–76.

54. *New York World,* June 17, 1917.

55. Ibid.

56. Ibid.; "Black History Month Pioneer Timeline," accessed November 2, 2013, http://www.ivyleaguesports.com/history/blackhistory/2005-06/harvard/time line; *New York Age,* May 24, 1917, p. 1; Tom W. Dillard, "Golden Prospects and Fraternal Amenities: Mifflin W. Gibbs' Arkansas Years," *Arkansas Historical Quarterly* 35 (Winter 1976): 332.

57. *New York Times,* June 10, 1939, p. 17, and October 25, 1940, p. 19; Harris, *Harlem's Hell Fighters,* pp. 85–86; Little, *From Harlem,* p. 3.

58. *New York Times,* December 21, 1919. The marriage took place on April 10, 1915, but the incident(s) occurred before the Regiment saw service in Europe. There is, however, a possibility that Winston's fellow officers were part of a scheme to secure a divorce for their friend. William Nelson of the New York University Law School has concluded that most acts of adultery were feigned because the circumstances were exactly identical, suggesting that an agreement was reached between the two parties and that the male would agree to accept blame for the illegal act. Whether that argument applies to this case cannot be determined on the evidence. No correspondence that we have found discusses the incident, nor does any even mention Eric Winston. Nelson also has indicated that the "life sentence" might have been very flexible because of the possibility of marrying in another state and New York's indifferent enforcement. Author's telephone conversation with William Nelson, March 10, 2004. For articles about Winston's squash prowess, see *New York Times,* February 5, 1915, p. 36, and February 7, 1915, p. 8. Kennedy had some issue of her own. She hit a workman on the Queensboro Bridge and failed to stop. Appearing in court in a hunting outfit, she admitted to failing to stop but argued that she did not believe that she had injured the victim, John F. McHugh. The man did require hospital treatment for contusions.

59. "Unpublished biographical sketch," Fish Papers, Box 111, Folder 4, NYSLMC.

60. Little, *From Harlem,* pp. 13–14; Hamilton Fish to Theodore Roosevelt, April 6, 1917, Fish Papers, Box 3, Folder 23, NYSLMC; Jon Guttman, "Regiment's Pride," *Military History,* October 1991, pp. 35–36.

61. *New York Times,* July 19, 1943, p. 15; *Brooklyn Daily Eagle,* June 26, 1934, p. 17; *Annual Report of the Adjutant-General of the State of New York for the Year 1917,* p. 163; Little, *From Harlem,* p. 1; Arthur W. Little to Edward House, October 30, 1916, House Papers, MS 466, Series 1, Volume 2, Box 70 A, Folder 2331, SLYU.

62. Little to House, February 8, 1917, June 15, 1917, and June 17, 1917, House Papers, MS 466, Series 1, Volume 2, Box 70 A, Folder 2332, SLYU.

63. House to Frank L. Polk, May 23, 1917, House Papers, Box 92, Folder 3164 SLYU; Newton Baker to House, May 27, 1917, House Papers, Box 9, Folder 267, SLYU; Arthur Little to House, June 6, 1917, House Papers, Box 70 A, Folder 2332, SLYU.

64. Little to House, June 15, 1917, House Papers, Box 70 A, Folder 2332, SLYU; House to Baker, June 18, 1917, House Papers, Box 9, Folder 267, SLYU.

65. *New York Age,* June 14, 1917, p. 1.

66. Ibid.

67. Ibid.

68. Program of June 22 event, Box 76, Gumby Collection, BLCU; *New York Age,* June 21, 1917, p. 1.

69. *New York Age,* June 21, 1917, p. 1; Lewis, *Du Bois,* p. 532.

70. *New York Age,* June 21, 1917, p. 1; Barbeau and Henri, *Unknown Soldiers,* pp. 66–68; Lewis, *Du Bois,* p. 533; Mark Ellis, *Race, War, and Surveillance: African Americans and the United States Government during World War I* (Bloomington: Indiana University Press, 2001), pp. 50–52.

71. Ellis, *Race, War, and Surveillance,* pp. 51–52; Barbeau and Henri, *Unknown Soldiers,* pp. 66–67.

72. Lewis, *Du Bois,* p. 534; *New York Age,* August 9, 1917, p. 1; *The Crisis* 15, no. 1 (November 1917): 33. Reprinted from a letter to the *Pittsburgh Courier;* Col. W. W. McCammon, Gen. Staff, WD, to Col. Gardner, War Department General and Special Staffs, COS Personnel Files, Entry 16, RG 165, NARA. The description of Young's assignment differs with that from the *New York Age,* which identifies a dispute over the officering of the unit as the reason for the War Department's refusal to authorize a black regiment in Ohio under Young's command.

73. *The Crisis,* 14, no. 6 (October 1917): 286.

74. Lewis, *Du Bois,* p. 532.

75. Ellis, *Race, War, and Surveillance,* p. 52; *New York Age,* June 28, 1917, p. 1; *The Crisis* 16, no. 1 (May 1918): 7; Benedict Crowell, Acting Secretary of War, to Philander C. Knox, U.S. Senate, September 28, 1918, WD General and Special Staffs, COSPF, Entry 16, RG 165, NARA. Young did leave Ohio on orders to report to the chief of staff in Washington on October 28 for "temporary duty." See Gen. Peyton C. March to Adjutant General, October 28, 1918, RG 165, NARA.

76. Gen. Peyton C. March to Jerome F. Donovan, May 10, 1919, WD General and Special Staffs, COS Personnel Files, Entry 16, RG 165, NARA; *The Crisis* 26, no. 3 (July 1923): 104–105. According to British law, Young's body could not be exhumed until a year had passed. His body was returned to the United States and interred at Arlington National Cemetery on June 1, 1923. The Young matter also raised questions about the future of the 15th and the confusing situation of the "Home

Guard" and the returning members of the redesignated 369th. The War Department interpreted the Defense Act of June 3, 1916, to mean that "no State has any right to maintain Militia other than the National Guard." It did admit, though, that courts were unlikely to uphold such an interpretation. In any event, the question came down to whether a retired army officer could serve with a state guard. The War Department concluded that the answer was yes. The 15th New York Guard remained a purely state organization after the war and integrated many of the returning soldiers into a "reconstituted guard."

77. Lewis, *Du Bois*, pp. 536–537; John Hope Franklin and Alfred A. Moss, Jr., *From Slavery to Freedom: A History of African Americans*, vol. 2, 7th ed. (New York: McGraw-Hill, 1994), pp. 342–345.

78. Lewis, *Du Bois*, p. 538; *New York Times*, July 16, 1917, p. 9; unidentified newspaper with Morris cartoon, Gumby Collection, Box 76, BLCU.

79. *New York Times*, July 16, 1917, p. 9.

80. *New York Age*, July 19, 1917, p. 1.

81. Lewis, *Du Bois*, p. 539.

82. Alessandra Lorini, *Rituals of Race: American Public Culture and the Search for Racial Democracy* (Charlottesville: University of Virginia Press, 1999), pp. 245–248.

83. "To the President and Congress of the United States," a petition from the committee of the Negro Silent Protest Parade, July 28, 1917, in the personal Madam Walker Family Collection of A'Lelia Bundles, Washington, DC, and the James Weldon Johnson Collection, MSS 58, Boxes 324–363, Folder 350, BLYU. Mrs. M. C. Lawton's name, misspelled as Layton, appears in the list of organizers of the parade in the *Washington Bee*, August 4, 1917, n.p., NAACP Papers, Group 1, Box C, File 432, LOCMD. Despite the wide coverage of the event, few papers name the two female members of the organizing committee. See Clippings File, NAACP Papers, Group 1, Box C, LOCMD.

84. Ellis, *Race, War, and Surveillance*, pp. 48–49. Queen, a teacher in the District of Columbia, had been sent by Howard University's Red Cross Auxiliary to investigate conditions in East St. Louis and to distribute funds to the needy. Queen reported on the "distemper" of blacks to her former mentor at Cornell University, Jeremiah W. Jenks, who was working for the war effort. Jenks passed on information to a friend in MIB, Maj. Herbert Parsons. Parsons met with Queen and found her eager to help the government improve black morale. See Ellis, *Race, War, and Surveillance*, p. 49.

85. *New York Times*, July 5, 1917, p. 9.

86. Ibid.; Joaquin was born in Charleston, South Carolina, and remained with the Regiment until his honorable discharge in 1919. He was severely wounded in the war and never rose above the rank of private. Neither Cox nor Isaac Brown appears to have been a member of the Regiment. The two men apparently came to the rescue of Joaquin or joined the fray when white citizens intervened. A review of regimental records failed to turn up either name.

87. Edward V. Howard to Louis Stotesbury, July 10, 1917, reprinted in *New York Age*, July 19, 1917, p. 1.

88. *New York Age*, July 19, 1917, p. 1.

89. Ibid.; *New York Age,* May 24, 1917, p. 1. Parks, a native of Kentucky and born March 24, 1882, rose through the ranks from private to captain. *Annual Report of the Adjutant-General of the State of New York for the Year 1916,* p. 359; Abstracts of the 369th Regiment, Box 13, Volumes 40–41, Roll 4, RG 13721-83, NYSA; Service Records of the 15th NYNG, NYSMM; Abstracts of the Fifteenth, Box 12, Volume 38, Roll 1, NYSA. Brooks was discharged per special order 186, Eastern Department. He died on May 20, 1923. Despite his age and the stricter standards, Brooks's dismissal does raise the possibility of a connection between his church's resolutions condemning the atrocities in East St. Louis and the War Department's findings.

90. *New York Age,* August 30, 1917, p. 1.

91. Castles, "War Diary," p. 4.

92. *New York Age,* August 30, 1917, p. 1. The band gained three new "crack" Puerto Rican musicians as well as three more players from the Jenkins Orphanage in Charleston, where Eugene Mikell had connections. One of these orphans was eighteen-year-old Herbert Wright, a drummer whom Europe featured, along with the others, on every program.

93. *New York Age,* August 30, 1917, p. 1.

94. Ibid.

95. *New York Times Magazine,* June 3, 1917, p. 12; Roosevelt, *Rank and File,* p. 97.

96. Little, *From Harlem,* p. 34.

97. Ibid., p. 36.

98. Ibid., p. 41.

99. *List and Directory: National Guard and Naval Militia, State of New York,* January 1, 1922, NYSMM; Roosevelt, *Rank and File,* p. 98.

100. Roosevelt, *Rank and File,* p. 98; *The Messenger* 1, no. 11 (November 1917): 31. "George" is the name by which most white male passengers addressed Pullman porters. It consequently came to be applied to any black man.

101. *New York Age,* August 23, 1917, p. 1; Final Muster Roll, 15th NYNG, July 15, 1917, to August 4, 1917, NYSA. Spencer failed the exam for lieutenant colonel, as noted in Regular Standing Order 196, 1917.

102. Newton D. Baker to Brigadier-General William E. Harvey, March 25, 1917, War Department Telegram, in Scott, *Scott's Official History,* pp. 35–37; Baker to Henry L. Stimson, March 23, 1917, House Papers, Box 9, Folder 267, SLYU.

103. Undated editorial from *Baltimore Afro-American,* in Scott, *Official History,* pp. 37–38.

104. General Order no. 44, State of New York, Adjutant General's Office, September 23, 1917, pp. 5–7, NYSMM.

105. Ibid.

106. *New York Times,* September 14, 1917, p. 3; *New York Age,* September 20, 1917, p. 1.

107. *New York Times,* September 14, 1917, p. 3; *New York Age,* September 20, 1917, p. 1. The *Age*'s characterization of the workers appears overdetermined by class and ethnic biases. It was as much an effort to demonstrate the fitness of the soldiers by contrasting them to "disreputable" white elements as it was a description of events.

108. *New York Times,* September 14, 1917, p. 3. There might have been more such incidents, but government censorship probably limited reporting.

109. Arthur W. Little to Col. Edward M. House, September 25, 1917, House Papers, Series 1, Box 70 A, Folder 2332, RG 466, SLYU.

## Chapter 6. Race War at Home or Combat Abroad?

1. Brig. Gen. Roy Hoffman to Chief, Historical Branch, War Plans Division, G. S., 293-11.4, RG 120, NARA.

2. *Annual Report of the Adjutant-General for the State of New York for the Years 1918–1919* (Albany, NY: J. B. Lyon, 1921), p. 23; Lee Kennett, "The Camp Wadsworth Affair," *South Atlantic Quarterly* 74, no. 2 (Spring 1975): 200–201.

3. *Spartanburg (SC) Journal*, August 1, 1917, p. 6.

4. *Spartanburg (SC) Journal*, August 20, 1917, p. 4.

5. Ibid.; Ellis, *Race, War, and Surveillance*, p. 9; Samuel J. Nicholls to Newton D. Baker, August 21, 1917, Nicholls to General William A. Mann, August 20, 1917, and Nicholls to Newton D. Baker, August 21, 1917, all in Nicholls Papers, Box 7, Perkins Library, DUMC.

6. Maj. Gen. Henry P. McCain to Commanding General, Camp Gordon, Atlanta, GA, October 8, 1917, NGB, General Correspondence, File 322.097 (370.01 Misc. Div.), RG 168, NARA; Memo. from Brig. Gen. Joseph E. Kuhn to W. D. Chief of Staff, July 31, 1917, General Correspondence 1903–1919, Entry 296-NM-84, File 8130-8142-12 (149), RG 165, NARA.

7. Gen. William A. Mann to Samuel J. Nicholls, August 21, 1917, Nicholls Papers, Box 7, Perkins Library, DUMC.

8. Barbeau and Henri, *Unknown Soldiers*, pp. 26–32; Berry and Blassingame, *Long Memory*, pp. 315–316.

9. Berry and Blassingame, *Long Memory*, pp. 315–316; Kennett, "Camp Wadsworth Affair," pp. 202–203; *Spartanburg (SC) Journal*, August 29, 1917, p. 4.

10. Kennett, "Camp Wadsworth Affair," 202–204.

11. Ibid.; *Spartansburg (SC) Journal*, August 30, 1917, p. 4; *Spartanburg (SC) Herald*, September 1, 1917, p. 4.

12. *Spartanburg (SC) Herald*, September 1, 1917, p. 4; *Spartanburg (SC) Journal*, September 4, 1917, p. 4.

13. Hamilton Fish to Franklin Roosevelt, October 4, 1917, Fish Papers, Box 11, Folder 11, NYSLMC.

14. Tasker Bliss to Franklin D. Roosevelt, October 11, 1917, and Bliss to Calder, October 8, 1917, Franklin D. Roosevelt Library, Hyde Park, NY.

15. Castles, "War Diary," p. 5.

16. *New York Age*, October 11, 1917, p. 1. (The *New York Age* attributed the "bar sinister" quote to the *New York Evening Sun*, October 9, 1917.)

17. *New York Age*, October 11, 1917, p. 1.

18. *Greenville (SC) Daily News*, September 25, 1917, p. 7.

19. Kennett, "Camp Wadsworth Affair," pp. 198–201; Little, *From Harlem*, pp. 28–32.

20. *New York Age*, October 18, 1917, p. 1.

21. *Brooklyn Daily Eagle*, October 12, 1917, p. 3.

22. John to Mother, Dad, and Brother, October 15, 1917, 369th Vets File, NYSMM.

23. Little, *From Harlem*, p. 56; *Brooklyn Daily Eagle*, October 15, 1917, p. 3, and October 18, 1917, p. 22.

24. Little, *From Harlem*, p. 57.

25. Sissle, "Memoirs," pp. 77–78.

26. Little, *From Harlem*, p. 57.

27. Sissle, "Memoirs," pp. 78–82; Little, *From Harlem*, p. 57.

28. John to Mother, Dad, and Brother, October 15, 1917.

29. *Wadsworth Gas Attack and the Rio Grande Rattler,* January 26, 1918, p. 15, March 9, 1918, pp. 2 and 9, March 16, 1918, p. 11, and March 30, 1918, p. 10; Alexander Starlight, *The Pictorial Record of the 27th Division* (New York: Harper & Brothers, 1919).

30. Little, *From Harlem*, pp. 59–61.

31. Ibid., pp. 61–62.

32. Ibid., pp. 60–62.

33. Ibid., p. 63.

34. Little, *From Harlem*, pp. 66–67; *Brooklyn Daily Eagle*, October 15, 1917, p. 3, and October 25, 1917, p. 2.

35. Little, *From Harlem*, pp. 66–68.

36. Ibid., pp. 67–70; Sissle, "Memoirs," pp. 78–83.

37. Little, *From Harlem*, pp. 68–69.

38. Sissle, "Memoirs," p. 81.

39. Ibid., p. 82; Little, *From Harlem*, p. 69.

40. Little, *From Harlem*, p. 69.

41. Castles, "War Diary," p. 5.

42. In Harris, *Harlem's Hell Fighters*, p. 130, taken from letter of Lt. Lewis E. Shaw to Mrs. C. H. Shaw, n.d., Shaw Papers, Manuscript Division, NYHS. We have been unable to find the original letter.

43. Little, *From Harlem*, pp. 69–71.

44. Scott, *Official History*, pp. 80–81; Sissle, "Memoirs," p. 77.

45. Scott, *Official History*, pp. 80–81.

46. Little, *From Harlem*, p. 71; Kennett, "Camp Wadsworth Affair," p. 208.

47. Hamilton Fish to Father, October 23, 1917, Fish Papers, Box 11, Folder 12, NYSLMC.

48. Ibid.

49. Sissle, "Memoirs," p. 84.

50. *Brooklyn Daily Eagle*, October 25, 1917, p. 2.

51. Sissle, "Memoirs," pp. 84–85. Interestingly, a website created in 2006, "Tent and Trench: Dedicated to the Memory of Camp Wadsworth," briefly mentions the 15th NYNG in an appendix listing nondivisional troops. According to the site, the 15th was just one among many units organized or stationed at Camp Wadsworth that were not a part of any division. They were sent overseas and attached to whichever American army or corps most needed them. Its listing of the 15th reads simply: "15th New York Infantry: African-American National Guard unit sent to train at Camp Wadsworth in October of 1917. Forced to leave due to rising racial tensions." Created by Jonathan Brooke and the Spartanburg County Historical Association, with support from the University of South Carolina, the site clearly is

intended to diminish if not deny one of the most important episodes in the history of the camp and what it reveals about race relations then and there. See http://schistory.net/campwadsworth/, accessed November 3, 2013.

52. Little, *From Harlem*, p. 75.

53. Mark Ellis, *Race, War, and Surveillance*, p. 86.

54. *Brooklyn Daily Eagle*, October 15, 1917, p. 3.

55. *Chicago Defender*, November 3, 1917, p. 1.

56. Ibid. For a discussion of John L. Sullivan and his challenges, see Elliot J. Gorn, *The Manly Art: Bare-Knuckle Prize Fighting in America* (Ithaca, NY: Cornell University Press, 1986), pp. 207–210.

57. *Brooklyn Daily Eagle*, October 30, 1917, p. 2. For a more detailed and complicated discussion of this incident, please see Slotkin, *Lost Battalions*, pp. 123–125. Whatever the facts of the matter, Slotkin concludes that the incident received enough publicity to convince the men that they had vindicated their manhood, boosting their morale and their sense of solidarity with their officers and each other.

58. *Chicago Defender*, November 3, 1917, p. 3.

59. Little, *From Harlem*, pp. 75–76.

60. Ibid., pp. 77–78.

61. Ellis, *Race, War, and Surveillance*, p. 86.

62. Castles, "War Diary," pp. 6–7.

63. Ellis, *Race, War, and Surveillance*, p. 86.

64. Little, *From Harlem*, pp. 80–82.

65. Castles, "War Diary," pp. 7–8.

66. Little, *From Harlem*, pp. 82–83.

67. Abstracts of the 369th Regiment, Box 13, Volumes 40–41, Roll 4, RG 13721-83, NYSA. The existence of Calcyetta or Calcyjetta, South Africa, or Basoutoland (now Lesotho) cannot be established. Zulus did and do inhabit Lesotho. Schita would later claim as a birthplace Natal, to which Zululand or Kwazulu belonged.

68. Harris, *Harlem's Hell Fighters*, p. 92. The article that Harris cites, October 25, 1917, p. 17, does not appear in the paper on that date and page. Since Schita joined the Regiment in August, the October date seems unlikely because the Regiment had just departed Spartanburg. In fact, a thorough search of the paper for the month of October reveals no such story.

69. *United States v. Valdo B. Schita*, Case no. 108885, General Court-Martial, no. 1320, Headquarters Eastern Department, November 27–December 17, 1917, Entry 15, pp. 192–194, RG 153 (Judge Advocate General), NARA.

70. Ibid., pp. 196–197.

71. Ibid., p. 198.

72. Attestation Paper, Canadian Over-seas Expeditionary Force, Valdo B. Schita, #931643, November 24, 1916, Accession 92–93/166, Box 8693-15, RG 150, National Archives of Canada; Particulars of Family of an Officer or Man Enlisted in C.E.F., December 11, 1916, Accession 92–93/166, Box 8693-15, RG 150, National Archives of Canada. This document was required of all men "warned for draft overseas." In the 1930 US census, his date of birth has been changed from the 1880s to 1864 or 1865, and his place of

birth is listed as Alabama. In the 1940 census, his birthplace is given as South Africa, and he also claims to have been widowed. Astonishingly, he also lists two years of college.

73. Ibid.

74. *United States v. Valdo B. Schita*, p. 199.

75. Medical History Sheet, February 12, 1917, Accession 92–93/166, Box 8693-15, RG 150, National Archives of Canada. Another medical card in the same file lists his rank as corporal and his age as twenty. No other evidence exists to confirm a promotion. Schita probably told medical personnel that he was a corporal.

76. Accession 92–93/166, Box 8693-15, RG 150, National Archives of Canada: Proceedings on Discharge, June 5, 1917; Last Pay Certificate, Canadian Contingent Expeditionary Force, June 26, 1917; and Casualty Form–Active Service, March 21, 1917.

77. *United States v. Valdo B. Schita*, p. 200.

78. Ibid., p. 199. Accession 92–93/166, Box 8693-15, RG 150, National Archives of Canada: Proceedings on Discharge, June 5, 1917; Last Pay Certificate, Canadian Contingent Expeditionary Force, June 26, 1917; and Casualty Form–Active Service, March 21, 1917.

79. *United States v. Valdo B. Schita*, pp. 106 and 116.

80. Ibid. Sergeant Green subsequently lost his stripes. Whether his demotion to private had anything to do with his relationship with Schita cannot be determined on the available evidence.

81. Ibid., p. 204.

82. Ibid., pp. 177–178.

83. Ibid., p. 205; Abstract Roll 1, Box 12, Volume 38, RG 13721-83, NYSA.

84. *United States v. Valdo B. Schita*, p. 205.

85. Ibid., pp. 221–225.

86. Ibid., pp. 98, 209, and 210.

87. Ibid., p. 55.

88. Ibid., pp. 54 and 93.

89. Ibid., pp. 63, 93, and 212.

90. Ibid., p. 141.

91. Ibid., pp. 111, 144, and 145.

92. Ibid., pp. 112 and 153. Private Fagan was interred at Cypress Hills National Cemetery, apparently without any family involvement. Sometime in December, the superintendent of the cemetery wrote that despite instructions on November 27 to open a grave for Fagan, the quartermaster general could not find Fagan on the record, thus delaying the process while revealing the haste in which the deceased had been recruited and processed. Even more, the authorities wrangled over the $50 submitted by the "Undertaker." Paragraph 167 of *Army Regulations* limited local interment to $35. The breakdown of expenses submitted by the funeral director comprised $30 for the coffin, $15 for "embalming, etc.," and $5 to transport the body from Camp Merritt to the funeral home. Since Fagan was not buried at Camp Merritt, the army ruled that the burial was not technically local and therefore not governed by the $35 cap. The matter was closed on December 27, 1917, ten days after the end of Schita's court-martial and only two days before the rendering of

the verdict and sentence. See Quartermaster General, Burial File Joseph Fagan, No. 518, Series 1942, RG 92, NARA.

93. Ibid., pp. 213–217.

94. Statement of the Accused, November 25, 1917, Camp Merritt, Entry 15, No. 108885, p. 3, RG 153 (Judge Advocate General), NARA.

95. *New York Times*, December 20, 1934, p. 1; *United States v. Valdo B. Schita*, pp. 246 and 249.

96. *United States v. Valdo B. Schita*, p. 258.

97. Ibid., pp. 259–263.

98. General Court Martial, No. 1320, December 29, 1917, Entry 15, Case No. 108885, RG 153, NARA.

99. *United States v. Valdo B. Schita*, pp. 268–270.

100. *Brooklyn Daily Eagle*, October 26, 1917, p. 2.

101. Ibid.

102. Little, *From Harlem,* pp. 80–83; *New York Age*, December 7, 1911, p. 1; Abstracts of the 15th NYNG/369th, Box 12, Volume 38, RG 13721-83, NYSA.

103. Prisoner File Card, Medical Center for Federal Prisoners, Springfield, MO, prisoner no. 1979-H, and "Medical Center for Federal Prisoners (Report, 1953)," Springfield, MO, p. 3, both in Bureau of Prisons Archives, Washington, DC; Misc. Form No. 25, Department of Justice, US Penitentiary, Atlanta, to Attorney General, August 21, 1939, pp. 5–6, in Brief of Appellee, *Schita v. King*, No. 12402, October 31, 1942, 8th Circuit Court of Appeals, Record of Transcripts and Briefs, RG 276, NARA Central Plains Region.

104. See Passenger Search, http://www.ellisisland.org, accessed December 10, 2013; http://translation.babylon.com/romanian/to-english/schita/ (accessed December 10, 2013); http://www.chabad.org/library/article_cdo/aid/222240/jewish/What-is-Shechita.htm (accessed December 10, 2013); and http://www.theyeshiva world.com/news/israel-news/39385/jerusalem-veterinary-services-preparing-for-kaporos.html (accessed December 10, 2013).

105. Prisoner File Card; *Schita v. King*, No. 12402, US Court of Appeals for the Eighth Circuit, 133 F. 2d 283, February 15,1943; *Schita v. Cox*, No. 12682, US Court of Appeals, Eighth Circuit, 139 F. 2d 971, January 21, 1944.

106. Little, *From Harlem,* pp. 84–85.

107. Ibid., pp. 87–92. Little identifies Lt. J. B. Streit as the company commander, but no record of him exists in the reports of the NYS adjutant general for 1917 or in the regimental abstracts. Also recounted in less detail in Fish, "At Sea with the U.S. Armed Forces," December 25, 1917, Fish Papers, Box 40, Folder 6, NYSLMC; Castles, "War Diary," December 20, 1917; Hayward, *Mother's Sons*, p. 6.

108. Fish, "At Sea with the U.S. Armed Forces."

109. Castles, "War Diary," p. 10.

110. Sissle, "Memoirs," pp. 96–100.

111. Castles, "War Diary," pp. 11–12.

112. Davis, *Here and There,* p. 42.

113. Sissle, "Memoirs," pp. 92–96.

114. Ibid., pp. 101–104.

115. Ibid., p. 101.

116. Ibid., p. 105; Castles, "War Diary," pp. 12–13.

117. Castles, "War Diary," pp. 13–14.

118. Fish to Franklin D. Roosevelt, January 1, 1918, Fish Papers, Box 11, Folder 14, NYSLMC.

119. Horace Pippin, "The Horace Pippin Notebooks," Reel 138, Horace Pippin Collection, AAA, SI. There is great uncertainty as to the actual date of Pippin's journals and their authorship. Only one seems likely to have been written during his time in France, and it lists Pippin as Harris Pippin, suggesting that he dictated it. It is also in the worst condition of the three notebooks and is incomplete. Another journal is dated October 4, 1920, and lists the author as Horace P. The printing differs from that in the other journal. The notebook with sketches is in cursive form and contains fewer spelling and grammatical errors. All, however, are reasonably consistent in their historical information. The notebook with sketches is titled "Autobiography of Horace Pippin," which would suggest that the author had achieved considerable fame at the time of writing and believed that people were interested in his life's story. The collection also contains a letter to "My Dear Friends" from Pippin, written while he resided on West Gay Street in West Chester, Pennsylvania. The letter "hit on some of the highlights" of his life, which would suggest that it dated from a time in which he had a large body of artwork and significant name recognition. Pippin achieved considerable fame as a so-called primitive or naive artist in the 1940s. For more information on his art and life, see Judith E. Stein, ed., *I Tell My Heart—The Art of Horace Pippin* (New York: Universe Publishing, 1993). Especially relevant to Pippin's military service is the essay "Scenes of War" by Judith Wilson in same volume. Also see Walter Kudlick, "African-American Soldier and Artist," *Stand To! The Journal of the Western Front Association*, no. 48 (January 1997).

120. William Slavens McNutt, *The Yanks Are Coming* (New York: Page, 1918), p. 189. *Colliers* dispatched McNutt to visit cantonments around the country. He reported a change in attitude among southern soldiers at two camps because they recognized the commitment of black soldiers. See Scott, *Scott's Official History*, p. 79. *The Yanks Are Coming* is an unmitigated piece of boosterism for the war. The book could have been authored by George Creel, as it turns every negative possibility into a positive result. McNutt wrote numerous books and enjoyed a successful postwar career as a screenwriter.

### Chapter 7. *"Over There"*

1. Réquin, Chef de Bataillon d'Infanterie Breveté, report, January 9, 1918, 7N1717, SHAT.

2. Sissle, "Memoirs," pp. 106–107.

3. Pippin's first comment comes from "Horace Pippin's Autobiography: First World War," p. 1. His further comments come from his "Composition Book," pp. 2–3. In the latter, Pippin's poor spelling and grammar are evident, and we have taken the liberty of rendering any quotes from it easily intelligible. Both sources, as well as a third set of "Notebooks," c. 1920, which we will also cite, are held in the Horace Pippin Collection, Papers of African American Artists, AAA, SI.

4. Little, *From Harlem,* p. 98.

5. Pippin, "Horace Pippin's Autobiography," p. 2, and "Composition Book," pp. 3–4.

6. Little, *From Harlem,* pp. 98–99, Castles, "War Diary," p. 14.

7. Castles, "War Diary," p. 15.

8. Fish to his father, January 13, 1918 [misdated 1917], Fish Papers, Box 40, Folder 4, NYSLMC; Fish to his father, January 23, 1918, Fish Papers, Box 11, Folder 16, NYS-LMC.

9. Sissle, "Memoirs," pp. 112–113; Pippin, "Horace Pippin's Autobiography," p. 3, and "Composition," p. 4.

10. Little, *From Harlem,* pp. 103–104.

11. Marshall, *Providential Armistice,* p. 4.

12. Fish to his father, January 23, 1918; Castles, "War Diary," p. 16.

13. L. E. Shaw to his mother, January 11, 1918 [misdated 1917], Shaw Papers, Manuscript Division, NYHS.

14. Castles, "War Diary," pp. 15–16.

15. Fish to his father, January 13, 1918.

16. Little, *From Harlem,* p. 105.

17. Ibid.

18. Fish to his father, January 23, 1918.

19. Castles, "War Diary," p. 16.

20. Ibid., pp. 16–19.

21. Fish to his father, February 19, 1918, Fish Papers, Box 11, Folder 17, NYSLMC.

22. Morrow, *Great War,* p. 237.

23. Little, *From Harlem,* pp. 100–101.

24. Quoted in Badger, *Life in Ragtime,* p. 164.

25. Little, *From Harlem,* pp. 100–101.

26. Roy Hoffman, Brig. Gen., to Chief, Historical Branch, War Plans Division, G.S., July 30, 1920, Historical Branch Doc. 293-11.4, Declassified DOD DIR5200 30, July 29, 2002, RG 120, NARA.

27. Cable from Pershing #P. 454, Subparagraph 1H, January 5, 1918, and Cable to Pershing #A. 553, Paragraph 1, December 22, 1917, War Department Historical Cable, History of the Subject Colored Soldiers, 7-12.5, RG 165, NARA.

28. Pétain, GQG N&NE, no. 11.318, January 11, 1918, Dossier 2, 6N141, SHAT.

29. Pétain, GQG N&NE, report on conversation between Pershing and Pétain, January 13, 1918, Dossier 2, 6N141, SHAT.

30. Commander in Chief (CIC) AEF to Chief, French Military Mission, January 15, 1918, 17N76, SHAT.

31. CIC AEF, January 16, 1918, addendum to prior message, 17N76, SHAT.

32. Ibid.

33. Hoffman to Chief, Historical Branch, War Plans Division.

34. Little, *From Harlem,* pp. 143–144 and 146.

35. Cable from Pershing #P. 543, Subparagraph 2C, January 26, 1918, RG 165, NARA.

36. Cable to Pershing #A. 726, Paragraph 4, February 2, 1918, RG 165, NARA.

37. Cable from Pershing #P. 591, Paragraph 8, February 11, 1918, RG 165, NARA.

38. Cable to Pershing #A. 800, Paragraph 3, February 16, 1918, RG 165, NARA.

39. Cable from Pershing #P. 626, Paragraph 4 and Subparagraph 4A, February 21, 1918, RG 165, NARA.

40. Cable to Pershing #A. 827, Paragraph 9, February 24, 1918, RG 165, NARA.

41. Eisenhower, *Yanks,* pp. 90–92 and 132–134.

42. Ibid., pp. 132–134.

43. Cable from Pershing #P. 693, Paragraph 3, March 7, 1918, RG 165, NARA.

44. Ibid.

45. Cable to Pershing #A. 906, Paragraph 8, March 13, 1918, and Cable from Pershing #P. 737, Subparagraph 4A, RG 165, NARA.

46. Cable from Pershing #P. 760, Subparagraph 1B, March 21, 1918, and Cable to Pershing #A. 990, Paragraph 1, March 26, 1918, RG 165, NARA.

47. Cable from Pershing #P. 720, Subparagraph 1B, March 12, 1918, RG 165, NARA.

48. Cable to Pershing #A. 932, March 16, 1918, Paragraph 4, RG 165, NARA.

49. Hoffman to Chief, Historical Branch, War Plans Division.

50. GQG N&NE, Nr 49570M, February 2, 1918, and Chief of Staff (COS) Harbord to Chief of French Military Mission, February 11, 1918, 17N76, SHAT.

51. Chef d'État-Major Dutilleul, February 12, 1918, 17N76, SHAT.

52. GQG ÉM 28078, February 25, 1918, HQ AEF, March 4, 1918, and GQG, March 6, 1918, USEM, March 10, 1918, 17N76, SHAT.

53. HQ AEF to French Military Mission, March 15, 1918, GQG, note, March 19, 1918, and GQG, note, April 1, 1918, 17N76, SHAT.

54. GQG ÉM 25083, March 23, 1918, 17N76, SHAT.

55. Cable to Pershing #A. 1237, May 3, 1918, and Cable from Pershing #P. 1074, Subparagraph 1C, May 8, 1918, RG 165, NARA.

56. Military Attaché, Washington, to War Office, March 9, 1918, T. 434, B. B. Cubitt, Assistant Secretary of War Office to the Secretary (R.3.), Ministry of National Service, June 7, 1918, referring to letter of Army Council to Secretary Ministry of National Service, March 26, 1918, 27/Gen. No./6806 (A.G.13.c.), and March 13, 1918, No. 27/Misc/2800 (A.G.13.c.), Cypher telegram to Lord Reading (Washington) from Foreign Office, June 21, 1918, No. 3825, referring to telegram No. 1832 of March 30, 1918, Gen. White to War Office, February 19, 1918, Ref. #W032 14765, The National Archives, Kew, Richmond, Surrey. A report by a British intelligence officer cited dissatisfaction among British subjects from island possessions near the United States drafted into the 367th Regiment. There was fear that these men might be a target of propagandists although no hard evidence had been found. See Capt. J. S. S. Richardson, R.C., Acting Intelligence Officer, "Special Report On: Negro Recruits, Subjects of Great Britain," December 20, 1917, War College Division, General Correspondence, Entry 296, File 10218-72, RG 165, NARA.

57. The following account of the band's exploits, unless otherwise noted, is based on Sissle, "Memoirs," pp. 114–129; quotes are from Winthrop Ames's letter to Sissle, February 10, 1920, in "Memoirs," pp. 125–126.

58. Badger, *Life in Ragtime,* p. 166.

59. Little, *From Harlem*, pp. 126–127.

60. Sissle, "Memoirs," p. 120.

61. Ibid.

62. Little, *From Harlem*, p. 129.

63. Ibid., p. 130.

64. Ibid., p. 132; A.P.O. 766, November 7, 1918, General Orders No. 31, in Scott, *Official History*, pp. 164–165.

65. Ames to Sissle, February 10, 1920, p. 128.

66. *Chicago Defender*, July 24, 1948, p. 15.

67. Marian Baldwin, *Canteening Overseas, 1917–1919* (New York: Macmillan, 1920), pp. 68–69 and 82.

68. Little, *From Harlem*, pp. 132–133. A YMCA worker, Marian Baldwin, found "the mammoth Casino" at Aix to be "the most splendid affair of its kind" with "marble pillars and wonderful frescoes and shiny hard-wood floors" and "generally flooded with sunshine" as it faced "a magnificent stretch of snow-capped mountains." The Casino could accommodate 3,000 and had a large theater, ballroom, a large reading and writing room, and gambling rooms. She described Chambéry's casino as much smaller (capacity of 300) but homier. See Baldwin, *Canteening Overseas*, pp. 66–67 and 72. For more information on leave areas and their segregation, see James Albert Sprenger and Franklin Spencer Edmonds, eds., *The Leave Areas of the American Expeditionary Forces, 1918–1919* (Philadelphia: John C. Winston, 1928), pp. 17–18.

69. Little, *From Harlem*, p. 137.

70. *Chicago Defender*, July 24, 1948, p. 15.

71. Little, *From Harlem*, p. 138.

72. Ibid., pp. 136 and 141.

73. Ibid., pp. 140–141.

74. Ibid., pp. 141–142.

75. Sissle, cited in Badger, *Life in Ragtime*, p. 134.

76. Marshall, *Providential Armistice*, p. 3.

77. Little, *From Harlem*, p. 146.

78. L. E. Shaw to Mrs. C. H. Shaw, March 9, 1918, Shaw Papers, Manuscript Division, NYHS.

79. William Hayward to Reginald Foster, March 18,1918, in Little, *From Harlem*, p. 146.

80. Ibid.

81. Col. William Hayward to Brig. Gen. Roy Hoffman, April 21, 1918, Box 7, File 333, RG 120, NARA.

82. John Wesley Castles to his mother, March 14, 30, and 31, 1918, Castles Papers, USMAL.

83. Hayward to Foster in Little, *From Harlem*, pp. 145–147.

84. H. B. Fiske to W. D. Connor, March 18, 1918, and W. D. Connor to H. B. Fiske, March 23, 1918, GHQ AEF, File 14996-B, RG 120, NARA.

85. Little, *From Harlem*, pp. 148–149.

86. Pippin, "Horace Pippin's Autobiography," p. 4.

87. Pippin, "Composition," pp. 4–7.

88. Little, *From Harlem*, p. 150. The mention of "General Le Gallais" at the outset of this paragraph reflects French military tradition, according to which last names only (without first names) are used for all but the most famous and highest-ranking officers.

89. Ibid., pp. 150–152.

90. Castles, "War Diary," p. 19.

91. Ibid., pp. 20–22. Hayward and Clark became law partners after the war. Thus, Castles might have exaggerated their differences.

92. Ibid., p. 22.

93. John Wesley Castles to his mother, April 4, 7, and 20, 1918, Castles Papers, USMAL.

94. L. E. Shaw to Mrs. C. H. Shaw, May 6, 1918, Shaw Papers, Manuscript Division, NYHS.

95. L. E. Shaw to Mrs. C. H. Shaw, April 10, 12, 21, 1918 (letter of the April 12 misdated 1917), Shaw Papers, Manuscript Division, NYHS.

96. L. E. Shaw to Mrs. C. H. Shaw, May 6, 1918.

97. Ibid.

98. Fish to his father, April 8, 1918, Fish Papers, Box 40, Folder 10, NYSLMC.

99. État-Major to HQ AEF, April 12, 1918, 17N76, SHAT.

100. HQ AEF 11440-W to French Military Mission, April 23, 1918, 17N76, SHAT.

101. Mission Militaire Française, Note sur les régiments noirs, April 14, 1918, 17N76, SHAT.

102. Chef de Bataillon Bonnolte, Rapport sur Entrainement du 369è Régiment, April 16, 1918, 17N76, SHAT.

103. Ibid.

104. Ibid.

105. Ian V. Hogg and John S. Weeks, *Military Small Arms of the 20th Century*, 7th ed. (Iola, WI: Krause, 2000), p. 317.

106. Ibid., pp. 314–316, 320–321, and 338–339.

107. Marshall, *Providential Armistice*, p. 5.

108. Chef de Bataillon Bonnolte, Rapport sur Entrainement.

109. Sissle, "Memoirs," p. 135.

110. L. E. Shaw to Mrs. C. H. Shaw, April 21, 1918, Shaw Papers, Manuscript Division, NYHS.

111. Fish to his father, April 8, 1918.

112. Williams, *Torchbearers*, pp. 106–119.

113. Robert B. Bruce, *A Fraternity of Arms: America and France in the Great War* (Lawrence: University Press of Kansas, 2003), pp. 128–131. See also Edward G. Lengel, *To Conquer Hell: The Meuse-Argonne, 1918, The Epic Battle That Ended the First World War* (New York: Henry Holt, 2008), pp. 27–28 and 34.

114. Mitchell A. Yockelson, *Borrowed Soldiers: Americans under British Command, 1918* (Norman: University of Oklahoma Press, 2008), p. 98.

115. Ibid., pp. 60–189.

116. See Williams, *Torchbearers*, pp. 86–88, 194–195, and 63–222. Also see Robert H. Ferrell, *Unjustly Dishonored: An African American Division in World War I* (Columbia: University of Missouri Press, 2011), pp. 1–106.

117. Slotkin, *Lost Battalions*, p. 136.

### Chapter 8. Trial by Fire

1. Gen. Le Gallais, CO French 16th DI, G-3, to Commanding General, French 8th Army Corps, No. 162/0, April 7, 1918, SHAT. For unknown reasons, the citation in French reads "369e R.I.U.S." when it should read "R.I.E.U." or, in full, "369eme Regiment d'Infanterie des États-Unis." Although "R.I.E.U." would be the correct abbreviation if the correspondents had adhered to use of the French language, the documents all read "R.I.U.S.," which is clearly an amalgamation of the French and English. In this situation, we must adhere to the documents, because to inject R.I.E.U., though linguistically correct, would be to inject a historical inaccuracy. Thus, we use "R.I.U.S." wherever it appears.

2. Gen. Le Gallais, CO French 16th DI, G-3, No. 175/0, April 7, 1918, SHAT.

3. Ibid.

4. Crispus Attucks, whom Sissle cites here among Negro "soldiers," is believed to have been a fugitive slave, the son of a black father and an Indian mother, who had become a sailor. One of a number of African Americans in a crowd that accosted a detachment of British soldiers in Boston on the evening of March 5, 1770, Attucks struck a soldier with a "large cordwood stick." The soldiers opened fire, killing Attucks and four others. Boston patriots proclaimed the forty-seven-year-old Attucks, who had led the crowd, the first martyr to British oppression at what became known as the Boston Massacre. Darlene Clark Hine, William C. Hine, and Stanley Harrold, *The African-American Odyssey* (Upper Saddle River, NJ: Prentice Hall, 2000), pp. 73–74.

5. Sissle, "Memoirs," pp. 136–140.

6. Ibid.

7. Pippin, "Composition," pp. 7–9.

8. Pippin, "Horace Pippin's Autobiography," pp. 4–5.

9. Pippin, "Composition," pp. 9–10, and "Horace Pippin's Autobiography," p. 5.

10. Little, *From Harlem*, pp. 165–166.

11. Pippin, "Composition," pp. 10–15.

12. Little, *From Harlem*, pp. 174–179.

13. Ibid.

14. Chef de Squadron Lobez to Chef, Mission Militaire Française, AEF, April 17, 1918, 17N76, SHAT.

15. Little, *From Harlem*, pp. 173–174.

16. Ibid., pp. 180–182.

17. Ibid.

18. Ibid., pp. 183—188.

19. Lieutenant Heineman, Information Officer, US 3rd Division, to French Military Mission, AEF, April 24, 1918, Doc. 70, 17N76, SHAT.

20. Ibid.

21. Ibid.

22. Little, *From Harlem*, pp. 189–190.

23. Marshall, *Providential Armistice*, p. 5.

24. Ibid.

25. Eisenhower, *Yanks*, pp. 259–260.

26. Capt. Hamilton Fish, Jr., letter to his father, April 29, 1918, Fish Papers, Box 11, Folder 19, NYSLMC.

27. Fish to his father, May 1, 1918, Fish Papers, Box 114, Folder 11, NYSLMC.

28. Ibid.

29. Fish to his father, May 15, 1918, Fish Papers, Box 11, Folder 21, NYSLMC.

30. Ibid.

31. Pippin, "Composition," pp. 16–18.

32. Pippin, "Horace Pippin's Autobiography," pp. 5–6.

33. Ibid.

34. Ibid., p. 7.

35. Ibid., p. 8.

36. Ibid.

37. L. E. Shaw to Mrs. C. H. Shaw, May 25 and July 5, 1918, Shaw Papers, Manuscript Division, NYHS.

38. Following account is in Sissle, "Memoirs," pp. 156–164.

39. Ibid.

40. Ibid.

41. Ibid.

42. Cited in Badger, *Life in Ragtime,* 179–180. Also available on the Internet at www.snowbiz.com/HWRepublican/HenryJohnson/haywardsletter.htm, accessed November 12, 2013.

43. Ibid.

44. Ibid.

45. This last opinion is confirmed in an article entitled "African Troops in France Are Fighters," *New York Age,* June 22, 1916, p. 1, based on correspondent Paul Ayres Rockwell's report of a letter from a white machine gunner from Brooklyn, Charlie Charles.

46. Castles, "War Diary," pp. 16–17, 20, 22, and 27. Castles to his mother, May 12, May 15, and June 8, 1918, and October 14, 1917, to August 28, 1920, Castles Papers, USMAL.

47. Cited in Lt. Gen. Walter S. Grant, GS, memorandum to ACS, G3, July 9, 1918, 193, File 590, RG 120, NARA.

48. Castles, "War Diary," pp. 23–25.

49. Ibid.

50. Ibid., pp. 25–26.

51. Castles to his mother, May 19, 1918, Castles Papers, USMAL.

52. Castles, "War Diary," pp. 27–30.

53. Ibid., pp. 31–32.

54. Ibid., pp. 32–34.

55. Ibid.

56. Cited in Robert A. Doughty, "More Than Numbers: Americans and the Revival of French Morale in the Great War," *Army History: The Professional Bulletin of the Army History,* no. 52 (Spring 2001): 1–11.

57. Ibid.

58. Capt. Alcan, French Military Mission at AEF, report of May 27, 1918, Doc. 104, 17N76, SHAT.

59. Col. A. T. Ovenshine, IG, memorandum for Inspector General, AEF, June 24, 1918, Box 361, 11440 A68, RG 120, NARA.

60. Davis, *Here and There,* p. 73.

61. Ibid., p. 52.

62. Castles to his mother, May 1, May 4, May 8, May 12, and June 18, 1918, Castles Papers, USMAL.

63. Castles to his mother, May 22 and May 25, 1918, Castles Papers, USMAL.

64. Pippin, "Horace Pippin's Autobiography," pp. 9–34.

65. Ibid.

66. Ibid., pp. 11–12.

67. Ibid.

68. Ibid., pp. 15–19.

69. Ibid.

70. Ibid.

71. Ibid., pp. 20–21.

72. Ibid., pp. 22–23.

73. Ibid., pp. 23–25.

74. Ibid., pp. 25–29.

75. These so-called Algerian troops may well have been Moroccan soldiers, as it is unclear whether Pippin distinguished between the two groups.

76. Pippin, "Horace Pippin's Autobiography," pp. 29–31.

77. Ibid., pp. 31–34.

78. Pippin, "Composition," pp. 19–36.

79. Ibid.

80. Ibid.

81. Ibid.

82. Ibid., pp. 36–50.

83. Ibid.

84. Ibid.

85. Ibid.

86. Pippin, "Notebooks," pp. 4–5.

87. Ibid., p. 5.

88. Ibid., pp. 5–7.

89. Ibid., pp. 7–10.

90. Ibid., pp. 13–14.

91. Ibid., pp. 10–12.

92. Ibid., pp. 12–13.

93. Ibid., p. 16.

94. Ibid.

95. Ibid., pp. 16–18.

96. Welcome, *Negro in the Great World War*, p. 54. The publisher was Madame E. Toussaint, who ran a photographic studio and publishing company in Harlem and claimed to be "the foremost female artist of the race."

97. Castles, "War Diary," pp. 83–89 and 101. The Tank Corps produced two Medal of Honor recipients. In both instances, the medal was awarded to men of Patton's brigade who performed life-saving acts. One of them, Cpl. Donald M. Call, was the driver of a tank that was hit by a 77-mm artillery shell as it advanced along a road on the first day of the Meuse-Argonne offensive. Call escaped from the burning vehicle through the driver's hatch and scrambled to the roadside. However, the tank's commander, 2nd Lt. John Castles, got stuck as he tried to climb out of the turret. Call ran back to the tank and plunged into the flames to rescue the trapped man. While doing so, he was hit and badly wounded by machine-gun fire, yet he was still able to drag Castles to the side of the road before the tank exploded. He then carried Castles more than a mile to safety. In addition to the Medal of Honor, Call received a battlefield commission for his exploit. He eventually retired from the army as a full colonel. See Dale E. Wilson, "American Armor in the First World War," Doughboy Center: The Story of the American Expeditionary Forces, http://www.worldwar1.com/dbc/tanks.htm, accessed December 13, 2013.

### Chapter 9. *"The Battle of Henry Johnson" and Neadom Roberts*

1. As alluded to in the title for this chapter, Arthur W. Little and other authors have referred to the encounter of May 15 as "The Battle of Henry Johnson," as if Johnson acted completely alone. We believe that Roberts deserves more credit than he has been accorded, starting with a renaming of the episode.

2. Lt. Col. M. A. W. Shockley, Memorandum for Asst. Chief of Staff, G-5, Subject: Report covering raid on Subsector occupied by 369th Infantry, May 15, 1918, GH AEF, May 17, 1918, File 590, RG 120, NARA.

3. Ibid.

4. The following account is based on Little, *From Harlem*, pp. 192–201.

5. Badger, *Life in Ragtime*, p. 184.

6. Little, *From Harlem*, p. 199.

7. Ibid., p. 200.

8. Badger, *Life in Ragtime*, pp. 184–185.

9. Little, *From Harlem*, p. 201.

10. Ibid., p. 369.

11. The following account is from Shockley's Memorandum for Assistant Chief of Staff, May 17, 1918, File 590, RG 120, NARA. Shockley's report in the NARA does not include the intelligence officer's report, which could be critical in reconstructing the encounter and reconciling the markedly different accounts of Little and Shockley.

12. Little, *From Harlem*, p. 369.

13. H. E. Caldwell to William J. Faulkner, June 24, 1918, Colored Work Dept. Records, Letters, 1918–1919, Box 2, YMCA Archives, University of Minnesota, Minneapolis. Despite noting the seriousness of Johnson's and Roberts's wounds, medical

examiners declared Johnson 0 percent disabled and Roberts 8⅓ percent disabled; see Abstracts of the 369th Regiment. The "science" of determining disability was subjective, and in light of the medical examiners' minimization of Capt. Napoleon Marshall's crippling wounds, one must contemplate whether the military demonstrated a penchant for minimizing the extent of black soldiers' disability. One must further question whether the examiners treated all soldiers accordingly, in an attempt to keep as many soldiers as possible below the 30 percent threshold of disability that would afford them benefits.

14. Shaw Papers, Manuscript Division, NYHS.

15. Castles to his mother, May 22, 1918, Castles Papers, USMAL.

16. *New York Times,* May 21, 1918, p. 6. Pershing's omission of Roberts's first name might have served to privilege Johnson. The *Times* supplemented Pershing's report and identified the Regiment and its location by citing unofficial dispatches from France, which "indicate the two negro soldiers who fought so gallantly against twenty Germans are members of the regiment recruited in this State and commanded by William Hayward. . . . Of the two men, Johnson came originally from Albany and Roberts from Trenton. . . . The encounter . . . is said to have taken place on the front west of Verdun, in the region north of St. Menehould."

17. Ibid.

18. Ibid.

19. Ibid.

20. Ibid.

21. John G. Mansfield to "Dearest Tess," December 21, 1918, File AA.2001.0051, NYSMM. Whether this letter refers to the Johnson and Roberts encounter is not clear. Although it specifically refers to Albany, by December 21 the 369th had taken Séchault, William Butler had been awarded the Distinguished Service Cross, and the whole Regiment had received the Croix de Guerre.

22. Neadom Roberts, "Brief Adventures of the First American Soldiers Decorated in the World War as Told by Neadom Roberts," February 10, 1933, p. 6.

23. Little, *From Harlem,* pp. 363–364.

24. Cited in Badger, *Life in Ragtime,* pp. 186–187.

25. Eisenhower, *Yanks,* pp. 144–148.

26. L. E. Shaw to Mrs. C. H. Shaw, July 18 and August 6, 1918, and Shaw to Adj. Gen., March 29, 1921, Shaw Papers, Manuscript Division, NYHS.

27. Badger, *Life in Ragtime,* p. 187.

28. Sissle, "Memoirs," p. 168. German gas could have even worse effects. The *Brooklyn Daily Eagle* reported in October 1917 that a "new German gas eats lining of lungs completely away," in addition to causing the "skin to peel off, leaving great raw blotches." The chemicals included chlorine gas, prussic acid, and something unknown that produced "the very faint odor of onions and mustard." That unknown agent was mustard gas, also called sulfur mustard and "Yperite." *Brooklyn Daily Eagle,* October 31, 1917, p. 4.

29. Ibid., p. 170.

30. 16th DI, *Journal de Marches et Operations,* 26N297, SHAT.

31. Documents 97, 106, 119, 130, 138, 142, 151, 162, 17N76, SHAT.

32. Eisenhower, *Yanks*, pp. 82–83.

33. Col. Hirschauer report on 1st D.I.U.S., November 24, 1917, Dossier 2, 6N141, SHAT.

34. Maj. Walter Loving to Col. Nicholas Biddle, MIB, NY, September 5, 1918, Loving Papers, Series D, M.I., Box 113-1, MSRC.

35. Ellis, *Race, War, and Surveillance*, pp. 81–82.

36. *New York Age*, March 16, 1918, p. 1, and April 20, 1918, p. 1.

37. Ellis, *Race, War, and Surveillance*, p. 82. Loving actually invited representatives from New York's black newspapers, the 15th New York Guard, and the New York Attorneys Association. On April 15, he attended the Interdenominational Ministers' Meeting and discussed the matter with the black ministers from Manhattan and Brooklyn. At the close of his address to the group, he received "their hearty support" and "a vote of thanks" for bringing the matter to their attention. The clergymen agreed to mention the subject at services the following Sunday. Loving further supplied them with copies of favorable newspaper articles for distribution. He also indicated that he would select one or two individuals to lecture to different clubs. He would prescribe the purpose of the lecture and exercise final editorial control. See Maj. W. H. Loving to Maj. Nicholas Biddle, April 9, 1918, and Loving to Chief, Military Intelligence Branch, April 16, 1918, in Loving Papers, Series D., M.I., Box 113-1, MSRC.

38. Loving to Chief, MIB, June 10, 1918, and Loving to Col. Nicholas Biddle, MIB, NY, September 5, 1918, Loving Papers, Series D, M.I., Box 113-1, MSRC.

39. Loving to Director of Military Intelligence, "Final Report on Negro Subversion," August 6, 1919, pp. 8–9, and Loving to Chief, MIB, May 30, 1918, both in Loving Papers, Series D, M.I., Box 113-1, MSRC. Loving requested that the ultraloyal Joel Spingarn as chairman of the board and a major in the army be contacted "before any further action is taken."

40. Loving to Maj. Nicholas Biddle, June 1, 1918, Loving Papers, Series D, M.I., Box 113-1, MSRC.

41. "Pershing Issues His First Report," *New York World*, May 17, 1918, pp. 1 and 8.

42. Lincoln Eyre, "Two N.Y. Darkies Whip 24 Germans," *New York World*, May 19, 1918, p. 1.

43. Lincoln Eyre, "Two N.Y. Negro Soldiers Foil German Assault," *New York World*, May 20, 1918, pp. 1 and 3.

44. *New York Evening Post*, May 20, 1918, p. 1; *New York Age*, May 25, 1918, p. 1; *New York Times*, May 21, 1918, p. 6; *New York Sun*, May 21, 1918, p. 2; F. G. Renesch of Chicago, collection, BLYU.

45. See Marcy S. Sacks, *Before Harlem: The Black Experience in New York City before World War I* (Philadelphia: University of Pennsylvania Press, 2006), pp. 72–106, on racism toward and stereotypes of black people.

46. State of New Jersey, "Return of Birth," #6076, and New Jersey State Census 1905, Mercer County, 13th Ward, Sheet 15, both in New Jersey State Archives, Trenton, NJ.

47. Corrected Birth Certificate, February 21, 1945, #6076, New Jersey State Archives, Trenton, NJ; *Trenton Evening Times,* May 21, 1918, n.p.; *New York Age,* June 1, 1918, p. 2.

48. *Trenton Evening Times,* May 21, 1918, n.p.

49. Roberts, "Brief Adventures," February 10, 1933, pp. 6–7.

50. "Negro Heroes Win Acclaim of City," *New York World,* May 21, 1918, p. 2.

51. Darlene Clark Hine, *Black Women in White: Racial Conflict and Cooperation in the Nursing Profession* (Bloomington: Indiana University Press, 1989), pp. 101–103. *Chicago Defender,* August 24, 1918, p. 1, and November 2, 1918, p. 1; also see http://www.buffalosoldiersresearchmuseum.org/research/women.htm, accessed December 13, 2013, and Scott, *Official History,* pp. 377–379.

52. *New York World,* May 20, 1918, p. 1.

53. *New York Evening Post,* May 21, 1918, p. 10.

54. *New York Evening Post,* May 22, 1918, p. 10.

55. *New York Age,* May 23, 1918, pp. 1–2.

56. *New York Sun,* May 21, 1918, p. 2, and May 22, 1918, p. 6.

57. *New York Times,* May 21, 1918, p. 6, and May 22, 1918, p. 12.

58. *New York Times,* May 22, 1918, p. 12.

59. Ibid., p. 2.

60. Nikki L. M. Brown, "'Your Patriotism,'" pp. 24, 30–31. The Circle for Negro War Relief, Inc., was a national organization with over fifty units in twenty-five states, headquartered in New York City. Caroline Bond was the first executive secretary of the organization, which raised funds and made clothing for the needy. The circle continued its activities as late as 1922. For more information on this organization, see the Johnson Papers, Box 27, Folder 35, BLYU.

61. *New York Age,* April 16, 1918, p. 2.

62. Military and Naval Insurance Form 1A, A4234, Box 1, File 9, NYSA. The schedule of family allowances was: wife, $15.00; wife and one child, $25.00; wife and two children, $32.50; and $5.00 for every child beyond two. Children and other relatives received allowances if no wife existed.

63. Scott, *Official History* , p. 377.

64. Abstracts of the 369th Regiment; Mrs. Leander Willetts to Dear Sir, January 10, 1918, and Alexander Wilson to F. E. Foster, February 5, 1918, both in Box 1, File 12, RG A4234, NYSA. For loyalty issues, see Box 1, File 3, RG A4234, NYSA. Even literacy seemed to play a role in the delivery of services. On January 25, 1918, an unidentified source wrote Alexander Wilson: "Some of these appeals are very difficult to translate in to plain English, but we will make copies of the latters [sic] as clear as possible for your agencies." The letter in question came from Mrs. Hallie Strothers of 157 or 159 West 133rd Street. Edward and John Strothers served in the 15th, and both listed Harlem addresses, although not the same as given here. See Box 1, File 12, RG A4234, NYSA, and Abstracts of the 369th Regiment.

65. *Albany Times Union,* May 20, 1918, p. 1, and May 21, 1918, p. 1.

66. *Albany Times Union,* May 22, 1918, p. 4.

67. *New York Age,* May 23, 1918, p. 1.

68. *Albany Times Union,* May 23, 1918, p. 14.

69. *Albany Evening Journal*, April 14, 1917, p. 1.

70. Telephone call from Stephen Price, archivist, National Scouting Museum, Irving, TX, to Jeffrey Sammons, July 10, 2003.

71. *New York Times*, June 15, 1918, p. 9.

72. Ibid.

73. *New York Times*, June 28, 1918, p. 8.

74. Williams, *Torchbearers*, p. 100.

75. Cable #1523 to Pershing for Nolan from March, June 14, 1918, Cable History, 7-12.5, RG 165, NARA.

76. Cable #1335 from Pershing for March, June 19, 1918, Cable History, 7-12.5, RG 165, NARA.

77. Cable #1265 from Pershing to March, June 8, 1918, Cable #1275, from Pershing to March, June 9, 1918, Cable #1447 to Pershing, June 3, 1918, and Cable #1501 to Pershing, June 11, 1918, all in Cable History, 7-12.5, RG 165, NARA.

78. Cable #1370 from Pershing, June 26, 1918, Cable History, 7-12.5, RG 165, NARA.

79. Cable #1675 to Pershing, July 6, 1918, Cable History, 7-12.5, RG 165, NARA.

80. Pickens, "Negro in Light of the Great War," p. 3.

81. *Chicago Defender* 13, no. 25 (June 22, 1918), p. 3.

82. Cobb, *Glory of the Coming*, pp. 294–295.

83. Ibid., p. 295.

84. Ibid., p. 296.

85. Ibid., pp. 299–307.

86. Emmett J. Scott and Maj. Joel Spingarn to George Creel, June 5, 1918, Intelligence Reports Index, #154, File 10218, MID, Box 62, 1-322, part 1, RG 165, NARA; Loving to Nicholas Biddle, MIB, NYC, July 22, 1918, Loving Papers, Series D, M.I., Box 113-1, MSRC.

87. Lewis, *Du Bois*, p. 554; Scott, *American Negro in the World War*, photo insert after p. 176, photo and caption of selected attendees.

88. Loving to Biddle, July 22, 1918, Loving Papers, Series D, M.I., Box 113-1, MSRC.

89. W. E. B. Du Bois, "Close Ranks," *The Crisis* 16 (July 1918): 111.

90. Loving to Biddle, July 22, 1918, Loving Papers, Series D, M.I., Box 113-1, MSRC; Lewis, *Du Bois*, p. 560.

### Chapter 10. A Midsummer's Nightmare

1. GQG memorandum, May 27, 1918, Doc. 113, 17N76, SHAT.

2. Présidence du Conseil André Tardieu no. 11028 M.O. to Ministère de Guerre, Doc. 124, 17N76, SHAT.

3. Memorandum for Chief of Staff, First Section General Staff, from Col. James A. Logan, Jr., A.C. of S., G-1, RG 120, Entry 11440-A.50, NARA. Logan wrote that the memorandum was the idea of Major Gibson and editorialized that Logan understood the problematics of the matter, pointing to a possible solution. Gibson had made visits to the black regiments in the 93rd Division and gathered this information firsthand. What is more remarkable is his argument that the removal of

black officers "was not in keeping with the wishes of a large portion of the American people and with the principles of our Government." Unfortunately, far too few in either the government of the United States or its military shared his views. See also Chief of Staff AEF to French Military Mission, April 12, 1918, Box 361, File 11440-T, RG 120, NARA.

4. Obituary, Henry P. Cheatham, Cheatham Papers, SCRBC.

5. Henry P. Cheatham to Hon. H. P. Cheatham, May 30, 1918, Cheatham Papers, SCRBC.

6. Ibid.

7. Ibid.

8. Henry Cheatham to brother Charles Cheatham, June 28, 1918, Cheatham Papers, SCRBC; General Orders No. 19 and 4785, HQ, 370th U.S. Inf., AEF, December 9, 1918; Obituary, Henry P. Cheatham, Cheatham Papers, SCRBC.

9. Maj. Charles S. Bryan to C.O., 2d French Army and Liaison Officer, GHQ AEF, July 9, 1918, Col. T. A. Roberts to Col. Leroy Eltinge, July 9, 1918, telephone message from Col. Roberts to Col. Fox Conner, 9:30 P.M., July 9, 1918, Box 361, File 11440-A 79, RG 120, NARA.

10. Bryan to C.O., 2d French Army and Liaison Officer, July 9, 1918.

11. Ibid.

12. Roberts to Eltinge, July 9, 1918; telephone message from Roberts to Conner, July 9, 1918.

13. Ibid.

14. Ibid.

15. Ibid.

16. Lt. Col. Walter S. Grant, General Staff, memorandum on "Discipline of the 369th Infantry, Colored," July 9, 1918, Box 361, File 11440-A 79, RG 120, NARA.

17. 4e armée, No. 4.17213, August 3, 1918, 24N2729, SHAT.

18. Little, *From Harlem*, pp. 217–223.

19. L. E. Shaw to Mrs. C. H. Shaw, July 5, 1918, Shaw Papers, Manuscript Division, NYHS.

20. The documentation for trench warfare in July and August in this chapter, except where noted, comes from two sets of daily reports in the French Army Archives. The first are the division reports, the *Sorties,* 161e Division Infantérie, EM 3e Bureau, of Gen. LeBouc's 161st French Infantry Division. The second are the daily regimental reports, or *Comptes-rendus,* by Lt. Col. W. A. Pickering, executive officer, 369th R.I.U.S., to the Division, 24N2729-31, SHAT.

21. Little, *From Harlem*, p. 222.

22. Ibid., p. 223.

23. See note 56. Lieutenant Colonel Pickering's operations report of the events of the night of July 14–15, 1918, also appears in File 293-452, RG 120, NARA.

24. Pippin, "Horace Pippin's Autobiography," pp. 42–44.

25. Little, *From Harlem*, p. 226.

26. Morrow, *Great War,* p. 254.

27. Hamilton Fish to Father, July 18, 1918, Fish Papers, Box 11, Folder 26, NYS-LMC.

28. Hamilton Fish to Tanta, July 23, 1918, Fish Papers, Box 16, Folder 9, NYS-LMC.

29. Little, *From Harlem*, pp. 239–240.

30. Castles to his mother, February 19, 1918, Castles Papers, USMAL.

31. Little, *From Harlem*, pp. 239–240.

32. Ibid., p. 240.

33. Ibid.

34. John Keegan, *The First World War* (New York: Alfred A. Knopf, 1999), p. 358. Roger Chickering and Stig Förster, *Great War, Total War: Combat and Mobilization on the Western Front, 1914–1918* (Cambridge: Cambridge University Press, 2000), p. 104. John Mosier, *The Myth of the Great War: A New Military History of World War I* (New York: HarperCollins), pp. 282–283.

35. On gas masks for the 369th, see *Comptes-rendus* for nights of July 22–23 and August 9–10, 1918; 161e D.I., EM 3e Bureau, 24N2729, SHAT.

36. Brig. Gen. George Van Horn Moseley to Commander and Chief of the French Mission, October 9, 1918, File 11440-A 157, RG 120, NARA. Moseley wrote: "In view of the difficulty, arising out of their facial formation, which negro troops find in wearing American box respirators, we desire to have these troops supplied with the French A.R.S. gas mask." In November, Moseley reported that the French would supply replacement troops with the same H-2 masks that the labor battalions used. See Moseley to GHQ, AEF, 4th Sec., A.G., November 9, 1918, File 11440-A 202, RG 120, NARA.

37. Little, *From Harlem*, pp. 242–243.

38. On the fate of the patrol and the two privates, see Lt. Col. W. A. Pickering, *Comptes-rendus*, July 31–August 1, 1918, 24N2731, SHAT. Little, *From Harlem*, pp. 247–250.

39. Little, *From Harlem*, pp. 244–245.

40. Daily Report, September 18, 1918, Doc. 240, 24N2730, SHAT.

41. *Sorties*, August 17–18, 1918, 24N2729, SHAT.

42. L. E. Shaw to Mrs. C. H. Shaw, September 2, 1918, Shaw Papers, Manuscript Division, NYHS.

43. 15TH REGIMENT SOLDIER ROUTS TWENTY GERMANS. SERGEANT WM. BUTLER RESCUES HIS LIEUTENANT AND FOUR MEN THE GERMANS HAD CAPTURED. BRAVERY WINS FRENCH WAR CROSS, headline of article in *Chicago Defender* 13, no. 35 (August 31, 1918): 1. See also Badger, *Life in Ragtime*, pp. 189, 304n47.

44. Quoted in Scott, *Official History*, pp. 211–212. Because of Roberts's early return to the States, he received considerable newspaper coverage and many requests to speak publicly about his experience. His role in the encounter diminished greatly with Henry Johnson's return as a hero in a highly decorated unit of a triumphant army. White America's tendency to have room for only one black hero at a time also hastened Roberts's decline as a heroic figure.

45. Général de Division Hirschauer, No. 2.79413 to G.Q.G., July 27, 1917, Doc. 148, 17N76, SHAT.

46. Général Goybet, CO 157th D.I., No. 507/3-S to Général, CO 13th Corps d'Armée, Doc. 149, 17N76, SHAT.

47. Ibid. In the 369th, black captains Fillmore and Marshall had commanded white lieutenants.

48. Ibid.

49. Gen. Goybet, No. 616/3-S, memorandum on 372nd Rgt., Doc. 181, 17N76, SHAT.

50. Ibid.

51. Herschel Tupes, Colonel, 372nd Inf., to the Commanding General, American E.F., Subj.: "Replacement of Colored Officers by White Officers," August 24, 1918, Box 361, RG 120, NARA.

52. Joe Lunn, *Memoirs of the Maelstrom: A Senegalese Oral History of the First World War* (Portsmouth, NH: Heinemann, 1999), pp. 139–140.

53. Badger, *Life in Ragtime,* pp. 190–191. According to Colonel Hayward, two of the officers requested transfer. See *New York Age,* December 28, 1918, p.1.

54. Sissle, "Memoirs," pp. 184–185.

55. Quoted in Badger, *Life in Ragtime,* 190n3.

56. Author John Morrow's translation document cited in Gilles Bernard and Pierre Besnard, "Les Combattants Noirs Américains de la Première Guerre Mondiale, 1917–1918," *Militaria,* no. 118 (May 1995): 13.

57. Ibid.

58. Tyler Stovall, "The Color Line behind the Lines: Racial Violence in France during the Great War," *American Historical Review* 103, no. 3 (June 1998): 737–769.

59. Lunn, *Memoirs of the Maelstrom,* pp. 103–186.

60. Barbeau and Henri, *Unknown Soldiers,* p. 122.

61. Blaise Diagne (commissariat générale de troupes coloniaux) to Ministère de la Guerre, November 16, 1918, 6N97, SHAT.

62. H. B. Fiske, Brig. Gen., G.S., "Memorandum for the Chief of Staff. Subject: Regiments of the 93d Division," August 10, 1918, G3, GHQ AEF, File 8.55, RG 120, NARA.

63. Ibid.

64. Ibid.

65. Commanding Officer, 369th Infantry USA to C-in-C, GHQ AEF, on "Condition of regiment and request for advice and instructions," September 11, 1918, G3 GHQ AEF, File 8.55, RG 120, NARA.

66. C. in C. AEF (MacAndrew), No. 11440-A 117, to French Mission, August 16, 1918, Doc. 163, 17N76, SHAT.

67. Col. Fox Conner to Chief of French Military Mission, August 20, 1918, File 8.55, RG 120, NARA.

68. Col. Linard, EM No. 9530/3I, to GQG, Doc. 164, 17N76, SHAT.

69. HQ AEF Col. Fox Conner, August 20, 1918, Doc. 169, 17N76, SHAT.

70. Col. Linard to Généralissimo Ferdinand Foch, August 20, 1918, Doc. 170, 17N76, SHAT.

71. Foch, No. 3315, to Pershing, 193, File 590, RG 120, NARA.

72. Talk by Maj. Joseph A. Cistero, "Operations of the 369th Infantry in the Champagne with the French Fourth Army, September 26 to October 1, 1918,"

Regular Course 1936–1937, The Infantry School, Fort Benning, GA, Watts Papers, SCRBC.

73. Col. Linard to GQG, September 5, 1918, Doc. 185, 17N76, SHAT.

74. Liaison Officer to Chief Liaison Officer, subject "Requirements of 370th Regiment U.S. Inf.," October 25, 1918, G3, GHQ AEF, File 8.55, RG 120, NARA.

75. Colonel A. T. Ovenshine, I. G., to Inspector General, A.E.F., July 20, 1918, 11440-A 95, Box 361, RG 120, NARA.

76. Translation of Memorandum from Le General Rondeau, Reorganization of 370th R.I.U.S., September 30, 1918, RG 120, File 11440-A156, NARA.

77. 93d Division, "Summary of Operations in the World War," prepared by the American Battle Monuments Commission (Washington, DC: Government Printing Office, 1944), p. 26. Memorandum from Eltinge to Col. Boyd, October 5, 1918, and unfinished letter from Roberts to Eltinge, September 30, 1918, both in File 11440-A 156, RG 120, NARA.

78. Maj. Gen. Bullard to AEF HQ, September 16, 1918, File 293-3201, RG 120, NARA.

79. Maj. Gen. R. L. Bullard, U.S.A., to A. C. of S., G-1, GHQ AEF, September 16, 1918, File 11440-A 146, RG 120, NARA.

80. Marshall, *Providential Armistice,* pp. 6–11.

81. Ibid. Marshall died June 7, 1933, in the Veterans Hospital in the Bronx at the age of fifty-seven. See *New York Times,* June 8, 1933, p. 19.

82. Gen. Vincendon, Commanding 59th Division, to Commanding General, 30th C.A., September 25, 1918, and Opinion of Gen. Commanding 30th C.A., September 26, 1918, File 11440-A 156, RG 120, NARA.

83. HQ AEF to French Military Mission, August 9, 1918, Doc. 154, 17N76, SHAT; GQG N&NE EM 3e Bureau no. 17786 (17986), August 11, 1918, 16N1698, SHAT.

84. Badger, *Life in Ragtime,* p. 191.

85. Hunton and Johnson, *Two Colored Women,* p. 220.

86. Badger, *Life in Ragtime,* p. 192.

87. Hunton and Johnson, *Two Colored Women,* p. 220.

88. Doc. 179, 17N76, SHAT; HQ 372nd Infantry to Commanding General, 93rd Provisional Division, January 24, 1918, File 322.5, Box 7, RG 120, NARA. General Hoffman believed that the presence of almost any kind of band was essential to the morale of black troops.

89. Quoted in Badger, *Life in Ragtime,* pp. 192–193.

90. Quoted in ibid., p. 193.

91. Quoted in ibid., p. 194.

92. Ibid., pp. 194–195.

93. Little, *From Harlem,* p. 252.

94. H. E. Caldwell to Mr. Faulkner, June 24, 1918, Colored Work Dept. Records, Letters, 1918–1919, Box 2, YMCA Archives, University of Minnesota, Minneapolis.

95. "Black Greens," Student Forum, Dartmouth College Library, http://www.ivyleaguesports.com/history/blackhistory/2005-06/dartmouth/timeline, accessed November 12, 2013, and http://raunerlibrary.blogspot.com/2011_05_15_archive.html, accessed December 13, 2013.

96. Hunton and Johnson, *Two Colored Women*, pp. 25–26. Matthew W. Bullock to Dr. J. E. Moorland, August 10, 1918, Colored Work Dept. Records, Box 2, YMCA Archives, University of Minnesota, Minneapolis.

97. "The Report of the Committee on Colored Work of the Sub-committee Appointed to Investigate the Charges against Dr. Moorland," YMCA Archives, University of Minnesota, Minneapolis. The army's Military Intelligence Division charged Dr. Jesse Moorland, who had appointed Mrs. Curtis in his capacity as senior secretary of the Colored Work Department, with disloyalty "as evidenced by his sympathy with people thought to be seditious and by his appointment to war service of those suffused of the radical temper." In a time when guilt by association ran rampant, this incident reveals the tenuous hold that African Americans had on their employment, reputations, and even freedom. The government demanded complete and utter loyalty and had countless informants spying on them.

98. Hunton and Johnson, *Two Colored Women*, pp. 25–29. Hunton and Johnson held the YMCA secretaries and not the association's leadership responsible for the discrimination. By the end of the YMCA's operations related to the war, the organization had a total of 97 African Americans in the field, 19 females and 78 males.

99. Ibid., p. 38.

100. Ibid., pp. 156–157.

101. Ibid., pp. 96–100.

102. Nina Mjagkij, *Light in the Darkness: African Americans and the YMCA, 1852–1946* (Lexington: University Press of Kentucky, 1994), pp. 86–100. The quote is from the report cited previously. Curtis was removed for straying beyond the narrow limits on thought, word, or deed set for aid workers, which could easily be used to malign all of them.

103. Gary Mead, *The Doughboys: America and the First World War* (Woodstock, NY: Overlook Press, 2000), pp. 151 and 402–405.

104. Ibid., pp. 201–204.

105. Record of Trial by General Court Martial of 2nd Lt. Emmett Cochran, 369th Infantry, November 29, 1918, 108, RG 153, Court Martial Files, 22983 (Cochran), NARA.

106. James had joined the Regiment on July 21, 1916, and Perry on July 28. The rest joined in 1917: Whittaker on June 8, Shiel on July 17, and Emmanuel on August 4. See Abstracts of the 369th Regiment.

107. Record of Trial by General Court Martial of 2nd Lt. Emmett Cochran, pp. 92–95.

108. Harris, *Harlem's Hell Fighters*, p. 236.

109. Record of Trial by General Court Martial of 2nd Lt. Emmett Cochran, pp. 10, 19, and 28.

110. Ibid., pp. 13–14, 50–51, and 82.

111. Ibid., pp. 97–98.

112. Ibid., pp. 84–85.

113. Ibid., pp. 103–116, for Cochran's following testimony.

114. Ibid.

115. Ibid., pp. 116–128, for the prosecutor's statement.

116. Ibid., pp. 228–235, for the defense's statement.

117. Ibid.

118. Ibid.

119. Ibid., p. 142.

120. Harris, *Harlem's Hell Fighters*, p. 237.

121. Pétain, GQG N&NE, EM 3e Bureau no. 17708 (12534), August 8, 1918, 16N1698, SHAT.

122. Paul Robeson Collection Index, SCRBC.

123. Little, *From Harlem*, p. 253.

124. Shaw's observations in this and following paragraphs appear in the following letters: L. E. Shaw to Mrs. C. H. Shaw, July 18, August 6, and September 2, 1918, Shaw Papers, Manuscript Division, NYHS.

125. Ibid.

### Chapter 11. The Big Push

1. Little, *From Harlem*, p. 257.

2. Ibid., p. 259.

3. Ibid., pp. 260–261.

4. *Compte-rendu*, 161è DI, September 12–13, 1918, 24N2730, SHAT; Little, *From Harlem*, pp. 261–265.

5. Little, *From Harlem*, pp. 266–267.

6. Ibid., p. 267.

7. *Compte-rendu*, September 12–13, 1918; Little, *From Harlem*, p. 267.

8. *Comptes-rendus*, 161è DI, September 14–15 to September 22–23, 1918, 24N2730, SHAT.

9. Davis, *Here and There*, p. 66.

10. *Compte-rendu*, 161è DI, September 18, 1918, 24N2731, SHAT.

11. Quoted in Harris, *Harlem's Hell Fighters*, p. 241.

12. Little, *From Harlem*, pp. 268–269.

13. Ibid.

14. Pippin's account of the Séchault offensive, which here is segmented according to day, is in Pippin, "Composition," pp. 45–59.

15. Ibid., p. 46.

16. Davis, *Here and There*, pp. 54–55.

17. *Compte-rendu*, 161è DI, September 25–26, 1918, 24N2730, SHAT.

18. Ibid.; Little, *From Harlem*, p. 270.

19. Gen. Lebouc to Gen. Cmdnt 9è corps d'armée, October 1, 1918, 24N2731, SHAT; Lebouc, account of September 26–October 6, 1918, 24N2732, SHAT.

20. Col. Wm. Hayward, HQ, 369th U.S. Infantry, account of regiment's service, January 7, 1919, p. 8, File 293-11.4, declassified 7/30/02, RG 120, NARA; L. E. Shaw to Mrs. C. N. Shaw, October 4, 1918, Shaw Papers, Manuscript Division, NYHS.

21. L. E. Shaw to Mrs. C. N. Shaw, October 4, 1918.

22. Ibid.

23. L. E. Shaw to Mrs. C. N. Shaw, November 29, 1918, Shaw Papers, Manuscript Division, NYHS.

24. L. E. Shaw to Mrs. C. N. Shaw, October 9, 1918, Shaw Papers, Manuscript Division, NYHS.

25. Pippin, "Composition," p. 49.

26. Ibid.

27. Both quotes in the paragraph are in Pippin, "Composition," p. 50.

28. Harris, *Harlem's Hell Fighters*, p. 244.

29. Ibid.; Little, *From Harlem*, pp. 271–272 and 310–311.

30. Little, *From Harlem*, p. 270.

31. Davis, *Here and There*, p. 66.

32. Ibid., pp. 56–59.

33. Ibid., pp. 60–63.

34. Ibid.

35. Ibid., p. 63.

36. Little, *From Harlem*, p. 271.

37. Davis, *Here and There*, p. 64.

38. Little, *From Harlem*, p. 271.

39. Gen. Lebouc, account of September 26–October 6, 1918. *Compte-rendu*, 161è DI, September 26–27, 1918, 24 N 2730, SHAT.

40. Little, *From Harlem*, pp. 272–274.

41. Quotes in the paragraph are in Pippin, "Composition," p. 51.

42. Ibid., p. 274.

43. Harris, *Harlem's Hell Fighters*, pp. 250–251.

44. Little, *From Harlem*, p. 275.

45. Ibid., pp. 273–274.

46. *Compte-rendu*, 161è DI, operations order, September 27, 1918, 24N2731, SHAT.

47. *Compte-rendu*, 161è DI, September 27–28, 1918, 24N2730, SHAT; Little, *From Harlem*, pp. 275–278; Col. Hayward, HQ, 369th U.S. Infantry, account of regiment's service, January 7, 1919, p. 9, File 293-11.4, declassified 7/30/02, RG 120, NARA.

48. Davis, *Here and There*, pp. 64–65.

49. Davis erroneously referred to Gantt, which he spelled Gant, as a sergeant. For correct information, see Abstracts of the 15th NYNG/369th R.I.U.S., #13721-83, Roll 2, Box 12, Volumes 38–39, NYSA.

50. Davis, *Here and There*, pp. 64–65.

51. Little, *From Harlem*, p. 277.

52. Davis, *Here and There*, pp. 67–68.

53. Ibid., pp. 67–68, dedication by Major Little.

54. Ibid., pp. 69–70.

55. Harris, *Harlem's Hell Fighters*, pp. 247–249.

56. Quotes in the paragraph are in Pippin, "Composition," pp. 51–52.

57. Ibid., pp. 52–59.

58. Ibid.

59. Ibid.

60. Ibid.

61. Quote is in ibid., p. 59 (actually p. 57 but misnumbered).

62. Lebouc, account of September 26–October 6, 1918.

63. Little, *From Harlem,* p. 278.

64. Davis, *Here and There,* pp. 63–64.

65. Ibid., pp. 71–73.

66. Little, *From Harlem,* pp. 280–281.

67. Ibid., p. 282.

68. Described and quoted in Harris, *Harlem's Hell Fighters,* p. 253.

69. Little, *From Harlem,* pp. 282–283.

70. Unidentified newspaper article dated December 18, 1918, in Abstracts of the 369th.

71. Little, *From Harlem,* pp. 284–285.

72. État-Major, 161è DI, *Compte-rendu,* October 1–2, 1918, 24N2730, SHAT.

73. Little, *From Harlem,* p. 286.

74. Ibid., p. 287.

75. Ibid., pp. 288–289.

76. Davis, *Here and There,* pp. 74–75.

77. Little, *From Harlem,* pp. 293–294.

78. Davis, *Here and There,* pp. 75–77.

79. Little, *From Harlem,* pp. 291–293.

80. Davis, *Here and There,* pp. 75–77.

81. Ibid.

82. Little, *From Harlem,* p. 294.

83. Ibid., pp. 295–296.

84. Ibid., pp. 296–297.

85. Ibid., pp. 298–301.

86. Ibid., pp. 302–304.

87. Ibid., p. 304.

88. Ibid., p. 305.

89. L. E. Shaw to Mrs. C. N. Shaw, October 9, 1918.

90. Little, *From Harlem,* pp. 305–306.

91. Ibid., p. 307.

92. Ibid., p. 308.

93. Ibid., pp. 308–311.

94. George Robb to Arthur Little, November 27, 1936, *"From Harlem to the Rhine File,"* NYSMM.

95. Ibid.

96. L. E. Shaw to Mrs. C. N. Shaw, October 31, 1918, Shaw Papers, Manuscript Division, NYHS.

97. Quoted in Harris, *Harlem's Hell Fighters,* p. 259.

98. Fish to his father, September 8, 1918, Box 16, Folder 10, Fish Papers, NYSLMC; Fish to his father, October 10, 1918, Box 16, Folder 11, Fish Papers, NYSLMC.

99. Fish to his father, October 10, 1918.

100. Ibid.

101. Gen. Lebouc, *Compte-rendu,* October 1–2, 1918, 24N2730, SHAT; Gen. Lebouc to Gen. Cmdnt 9è corps d'armée, October 1, 1918, 24N2731, SHAT.

102. Lebouc, *Compte-rendu,* October 1–2, 1918; Lebouc to Gen. Cmdnt 9è corps d'armée, October 1, 1918.

103. L. E. Shaw to Mrs. C. H. Shaw, October 4, 1918.

104. Fish to his father, September 8, 1918, and October 10, 1918.

105. List of dead acquired from American Battle Monuments Commission, Office at the American Cemetery, Romagne, France.

106. Davis, *Here and There,* xiii.

107. Little, *From Harlem,* p. 311.

108. Lebouc, account of September 26–October 6, 1918.

109. Ibid.

110. Little, *From Harlem,* p. 257.

111. État-Major, *Compte-rendu,* November 2, 1918, 24N2733, SHAT.

112. Gen. Lebouc, account of November 3, 1918, 24N2732, SHAT.

113. Gen. Lebouc to CG, 4è armée, November 4, 1918, 24N2732, SHAT.

114. Etat-Major, 9è corps d'armée, 3è Bureau, No. 255, October 7, 1918, RG 120, NARA.

115. Castles to his mother, December 8, 1918, Castles Papers, USMAL.

116. Summary of Pétain report on US operations between Meuse and Champagne, September 26–30, 1918, Dossier 1, 6N141, SHAT.

117. Ibid.

118. Ibid.

119. Ibid.

120. Eisenhower, *Yank,* pp. 259–260.

121. Ibid., p. 258.

122. Richard S. Faulkner, "Disappearing Doughboys: The American Expeditionary Forces' Straggler Crisis in the Meuse-Argonne," *Army History,* no. 83 (Spring 2012): 6–25. See also Faulkner's book *The School of Hard Knocks: Combat Leadership in the American Expeditionary Forces* (College Station: Texas A&M University Press, 2012).

123. Yockelson, *Borrowed Soldiers,* p. 220.

124. American Battle Monuments Commission (ABMC), *Summary of Operations,* March 29, 1927, p. 3, 719.3-A/DO, Box 259, RG117, NARA.

125. Ibid.

126. ABMC, *Summary of Operations.*

127. Excerpt from "Memorandum on Chronology and Statistics," Headquarters Division, NYG, July 1, 1920, File 719.3-A/DO, Box 259, RG 117, NARA.

128. Narrative of Action in Field of 372 US Infantry in Champagne, September 26–October 7th, 1918, and October 26, 1918, File 719.3-A/DO, Box 259, RG 117, NARA.

129. Arthur W. Little to ABMC, Washington, DC, September 20, 1927, 719.3-A/DO, Box 259, RG 117, NARA.

130. John Holly Clark to ABMC, September 21, 1927, and April 19, 1928, 719.3-A/DO, Box 259, RG 117, NARA.

131. Seth B. McClinton, Lt. Col. Inf. Res., to ABMC, October 20, 1927, 719.3-A/DO, Box 259, RG 117, NARA.

132. Richardson Pratt to Capt. C. B. Cates, USMC, April 20, 1928, 719.3-A/DO, Box 259, RG 117, NARA.

133. Maj. S. M. Johnson to ABMC, October 19, 1927, 719.3-A/DO, Box 259, RG 117, NARA.

134. West A. Hamilton to ABMC, October 26, 1927, 719.3-A/DO, Box 259, RG 117, NARA. Hamilton was a member of the 1st Separate Battalion from Washington, DC, the black unit that President Wilson called out to guard the White House. For more on Hamilton, see http://si-siris.blogspot.com/2013/01/col-west-hamilton-soldier-at-heart.htm, accessed November 7, 2013.

135. C. S. Sumner to ABMC, October 31, 1927, 719.3-A/DO, Box 259, RG 117, NARA.

136. Wm. T. McCon to ABMC, November 6, 1927, 719.3-A/DO, Box 259, RG 117, NARA.

137. Clark L. Dickson to ABMC, October 3, 1927, 719.3-A/DO, Box 259, RG 117, NARA.

138. Hershel Tupes to ABMC, January 6, 1928, 719.3-A/DO, Box 259, RG 117, NARA.

139. Capt. C. B. Gates's (ABMC) summary of claims of P. L. Miles, Col., 2nd Infantry Commanding, to ABMC, February 7, 1928, 719.3-A/DO, Box 259, RG 117, NARA.

140. Herbert L. Allison to ABMC, November 6 and 22, 1927, 719.3-A/DO, Box 259, RG 117, NARA.

141. C. B. Cates note on Col. Herschel Tupes's claims, undated but considered in final check, September 25, 1930, 719.3-A/DO, Box 259, RG 119, NARA.

142. Robert H. Ferrell, *America's Deadliest Battle: Meuse-Argonne, 1918* (Lawrence: University Press of Kansas, 2007), p. 148.

143. Ferrell, *Unjustly Dishonored,* pp. 1–106.

### Chapter 12. War's End

1. Little, *From Harlem,* p. 313.

2. Commanding Officer, 369th Inf. USA, to C-in-C, GHQ AEF, on "Condition of regiment and request for advice and instructions," October 9, 1918, G3, GHQ AEF, File 8.55, RG 120, NARA.

3. Col. William Hayward to Commander-in-Chief, or Chief of Staff, AEF, March 23, 1918, File 11440-M, Box 361, RG 120, NARA.

4. Ibid., p. 1.

5. Ibid., pp. 1–2.

6. Ibid., p. 2.

7. Ibid., p. 3.

8. Ibid.

9. Ibid., pp. 3–4.

10. Eisenhower, *Yanks,* p. 258.

11. Memorandum for Asst. Chief of Staff, G-5, subject "Condition of 369th Infantry," October 17, 1918, G3, GHQ AEF, File 8.55, RG 120, NARA.

12. Ibid., pp. 1–2.

13. Ibid., pp. 3–4.

14. Gen. Lebouc to CG, 4è armée, November 4, 1918, 24N2732, SHAT.

15. Memorandum for Asst. Chief of Staff, October 17, 1918, pp. 4–5.

16. Ibid., p. 5.

17. Cistero, "Operations of the 369th Infantry," p. 3.

18. Memorandum for Asst. Chief of Staff, October 17, 1918, pp. 5–6.

19. Memorandum for the Chief of Staff, Subject "Regiments 93d Division," October 17, 1918, G3, GHQ AEF, File 8.55, RG 120, NARA.

20. GH AEF, Office APM, October 14, 1918, 11440–A 163, RG 120, NARA.

21. Upon reading Little's account, another officer called him to task about his apparent exaggeration of the height of these mountains; see H. M. Landon to Little, July 14, 1936, *"From Harlem to the Rhine* File," NYSMM. In reality, Little was not too far off. The tallest of the Vosges Mountains is Grand Ballon at 1,424 meters, or 4,671 feet. Of course, the mountains are measured against sea level, and thus, those rising from locations at sea level appear far more impressive in relation to the surroundings. Vieil Armand, or Hartmannswillerkopf, is 956 meters, or 3,136 feet, high. See Haute-Alsace, "Guide Touristique, Soultz et Environs 2004" (Upper Alsace Tourism Brochure), pp. 16–17, accessed November 5, 2013, http://www.haute-alsacetourisme.com/en/brochures/.

22. Col. Hatton to Gen. Lebouc, October 17, 1918; État-Major 161é DI, October 18, 1918, 24N2733, SHAT.

23. Little, *From Harlem*, pp. 314–316.

24. Ibid., pp. 316–318; CO, 1st BN, 369th R.I.U.S., Report of Attack on Collardelle, October 28, 1918, 24N2733, SHAT; William Hayward to Adjutant General of the Army, June 23, 1920, p. 12, File 293-11.4, Historical Branch, NARA. (Written on the stationery of "Hayward, Clark, & Goldmark," it reveals that John Holley Clark, Jr., and David A. L'Esperance, Jr., officers of the 369th during the war, had rejoined their colonel in civilian life.)

25. John O. Outwater to Arthur W. Little, Esq., September 4, 1936, *"From Harlem to the Rhine* File," NYSMM. The plaque reads: (top line) REGIMENTS D'INFANTERIE; (second line) 369eme DES ETATS-UNIS; (third line) TERRITORIAUX 43eme 55eme 57eme 98eme; (fourth line) AMBULANCE 1/70; (fifth line) COMPAGNES DE TRAVAILLEURS. During the course of the war, Outwater reached the rank of captain in Company L of the 3rd Battalion. In addition to the humility and sensitivity that some of the officers showed, many also had fine senses of humor, which sometimes emerged in friendly barbs concerning internal rivalries. After thanking Little for the copy of the book, Outwater pointed to some errors, one of which he used to cleverly criticize Little's centering of the 1st Battalion: "I always thought that it was the 3rd Battalion and not the 1st that won the war." He then went on to correct Little about the misnaming of Yperite as "Hyporite" and for shortchanging him on medals. In addition to the Croix de Guerre, Outwater claimed to have earned the Légion d'Honneur. The official abstracts credit him with the Croix de Guerre with Silver and Bronze Stars. See Abstracts of the 15th NYNG/369th R.I.U.S.

26. Col. Hatton, November 2, 1918, 24N2733, SHAT.

27. "Attack Plans," November 5, 1918, 24N2733, SHAT.

28. Doc. No. 409, 293-32-13, RG 120, NARA.

29. French sergeant's report, November 9, 1918, 24N2733, SHAT.

30. Gen. Lebouc, Gen. Order 106, November 9, 1918, 24N2733, SHAT.

31. Gen. Lebouc, Gen. Order 107, November 10, 1918, 24N2733, SHAT; CO, 1sr BN, 369th R.I.U.S., report of attack on Collardelle, October 28, 1918.

32. "Flags of Truce," Hayward Doc. #10-11-1, November 10, 1918, 293-32-13, RG 120, NARA.

33. Little, *From Harlem*, p. 322.

34. Hamilton Fish to Tanta, November 11, 1918, Fish Papers, Box 40, Folder 11, NYSLMC.

35. HQ 369th U.S. Infantry, "Entry of Civilians and Prisoners into Our Lines," Doc. 12-11-4, 293-32-13, RG 120, NARA.

36. L. E. Shaw to Mrs. C. N. Shaw, November 16, 1918, Shaw Papers, Manuscript Division, NYHS.

37. Ibid.

38. Little, *From Harlem*, p. 327.

39. Ibid., p. 332.

40. *Men of Bronze.*

41. L. E. Shaw to Mrs. C. N. Shaw, November 21, 1918, Shaw Papers, Manuscript Division, NYHS.

42. Little, *From Harlem*, pp. 334–335.

43. L. E. Shaw to Mrs. C. N. Shaw, November 21, 1918.

44. Chickering and Förster, *Great War,* pp. 343–344.

45. L. E. Shaw to Mrs. C. N. Shaw, November 21, 1918.

46. Little, *From Harlem*, pp. 364–365.

47. Ibid., pp. 335–336.

48. L. E. Shaw to Mrs. C. N. Shaw, November 21, 1918.

49. Little, *From Harlem*, pp. 338–339.

50. Ibid., p. 340.

51. Ellis, *Race, War, and Surveillance*, p. 204.

52. Ibid., pp. 204–205.

53. Ibid., pp. 205–206.

54. Ibid., pp. 207–208.

55. Little, *From Harlem*, pp. 341–343.

56. Ibid., p. 350.

57. Ibid., pp. 351–353.

58. Ibid.

59. Williams, *Torchbearers*, pp. 195–196.

60. Ibid., pp. 351–354.

61. Lewis Shaw to Mother, January 27, 1919, Shaw Papers, Manuscript Division, NYHS.

62. Jennifer D. Keene, *Doughboys, the Great War, and the Remaking of America* (Baltimore, MD: Johns Hopkins University Press, 2001), pp. 72 and 152–153.

63. Little, *From Harlem*, pp. 355–356.

64. Ellis, *Race, War, and Surveillance*, pp. 208–209.

65. Ibid., p. 211.

66. Gen. Collardet no. 233, April 8, 1919, 7N1717, SHAT.

67. Military Attaché no. 62r, December 5, 1918, Collardet note, April 9, 1919, 7N1717, SHAT.

68. Gen. Collardet no. 343R, June 6, 1919, 7N1717, SHAT.

69. Major W. H. Loving to Director of Military Intelligence, May 6, 1919, Loving Papers, 113-1, Series D, M.I., MSRC.

70. Ibid.

71. Major W. H. Loving to Director of Military Intelligence, "Final Report on Negro Subversion," August 6, 1919, Loving Papers, 113-1, Series D, M.I., MSRC.

72. Williams, *Torchbearers*, pp. 106–195; Ferrell, *Unjustly Dishonored*, pp. 1–106.

73. On McMaster, who has often escaped notice, see Ferrell, *Unjustly Dishonored*, pp. 95–97; Williams, *Torchbearers*, p. 195.

### Chapter 13. "War Crossed Abroad and Double Crossed at Home"

1. Ministére de Guerre to Mission Militaire, AEF HQ, January 1, 1919; C in C AEF, January 25, 1919, 17N26, SHAT.

2. Davis, *Here and There*, pp. 46–47.

3. *New York Age*, February 15, 1919, p. 1; *New York Times*, February 13, 1919, p. 6. Hayward's statement was not entirely accurate, as many commissioned and non-commissioned officers, both black and white, received transfers to other regiments. Even Hayward admitted to numerous deaths in port resulting from disease. One afflicted soldier died en route. The *Age* reported that some 1,300 of the original 2,000 men returned. See *New York Age*, February 15, 1919, p. 1. The official casualty list names 14 officers and 266 men of the 369th who died during service with the 93rd Division. See Casualty Lists, Adjutant General's Office, RG 407, NARA. Another list, called a Standard Report, gives the names of 115 men from New York who died during the war. It includes no officers.

4. *New York Age*, February 15, 1919, p. 1; *New York Times*, February 13, 1919, p. 6.

5. *Baltimore Afro-American*, February 14, 1919, p. 1; *New York Times*, February 13, 1919, p. 6; *New York American*, February 13, 1919, p. 3.

6. *New York Age*, February 8, 1919, p. 1; Abstracts of the 369th Regiment. Private Scott of Companies A and D was one of fifteen wounded soldiers who returned early.

7. *New York Age*, February 8, 1919, p. 2. The service record lists Deas as a resident of Brooklyn by way of Charleston, South Carolina. The *Age,* on the basis of special dispatch from Rutherford, New Jersey, lists him as a resident of that city. Abstracts of the 369th Regiment.

8. *New York Age*, February 8, 1919, p. 2; Hayward, *Mother's Sons*, p. 12. There is some confusion about the nature of Hayward's injury. Little reported that he had a bad foot in Spartanburg. The *Age* report has him suffering a wound to his ankle in the charge. An editor's note in *Mother's Sons* reports a broken leg. Hayward was gassed in a later incident. Whether he received the wound chevron for the leg injury or the gassing cannot be determined from available sources. The *New York*

*World* referred to the exchange of racialized nicknames between colonel and troops as "fifty-fifty"; see *New York World*, February 18, 1919, pp. 1 and 3.

9. *Baltimore Afro-American*, February 14, 1919, p. 1; *New York Times*, February 13, 1919, p. 6. The proper term would be *blutdurstig*. *Lustige* would have sexual connotations and is normally associated with lechery. There is also a beastly quality associated with the term *blutdurstig*. The *New York Times* repeated the word *blutlistige* in a report on the parade and reported that one could tell by the appearance of the men why the Germans called them bloodthirsty black men. See Lewis, *When Harlem Was in Vogue*, p. 4; *New York Times*, February 22, 1919, pp. 1 and 6; Hayward Report of January 7, 1919, p. 5, AEF, File 293-11.4, RG 120, NARA; *New York American*, February 13, 1919, p. 3. Then, Hayward's *Mother's Son*, obviously under the influence of an imaginative editor, embellished the term even more and applied it directly to the men of the 369th and a particular style of fighting: "This characteristic—fighting to the death rather than giving themselves up—won for the men of the Old 15th the German title of '*blutlistige schwartzmaenner*.'" Knowledge of the nickname alone, according to Hayward, made the men "believe that no German could ever lick them—and no Germans ever did." We think this clear example of embellishment and invention actually reveals a profound truth about nicknames. They are often falsely credited to enemies for the purpose of building up the objects while tearing down their supposed creators. Although this particular name came too late to have that effect in the war, others such as "hell fighters," "hell hounds," "black devils," or "black watch" probably came from "friendly" sources in the name of the enemy for the reasons stated previously. We have found no hard evidence that the Germans or the French applied these names to black soldiers.

10. *New York Times*, February 12, 1919, p. 12. The *Times* also praised the record of the 370th (8th Illinois) and the 367th, which was based in New York and was part of the 92nd Division.

11. *New York Age*, February 15, 1919, p. 1.

12. OLD 15TH HONORED FOR WAR PROWESS, headline on an unidentified and undated newspaper article in Gumby Collection, R 76, BLCU. For a corroborating account of Governor Whitman's comments, see *New York Times*, February 24, 1919, p. 3.

13. Ibid.

14. *New York Age*, February 15, 1919, p. 4.

15. Ibid.

16. Little, *From Harlem*, pp. 358–359.

17. Ibid., p. 124.

18. Ibid.

19. *New York American*, February 13, 1919, p. 3; Little, *From Harlem*, pp. 357–358.

20. Little, *From Harlem*, pp. 359–360.

21. *New York American*, February 14, 1919, p. 3. Little, *From Harlem*, pp. 359–362. For the most detailed and nuanced account of the parade, see Reid Badger, "Pride without Prejudice: The Day New York 'Drew No Color Line,'" *Prospects: An Annual of American Cultural Studies* 16 (1991): 405–420. Badger raises questions about the kind of music played that day and suggests that even before the band reached Harlem, spectators heard the distinctive sounds of jazz music.

22. Little, *From Harlem*, pp. 357–336; Badger, "Pride without Prejudice," p. 412.

23. Davis, *Here and There*, pp. 83–84.

24. Little, *From Harlem*, p. 362.

25. Ibid., p. 365; *New York Herald*, February 18, 1919, pp. 1 and 6; *New York Tribune*, February 18, 1919, p. 8; *New York Times*, February 22, 1919, pp. 1 and 6; *New York World*, February 18, 1919, pp. 1 and 3.

26. Little, *From Harlem*, p. 360; *New York American*, February 15, 1919, p. 8.

27. Davis, *Here and There*, p. 83.

28. Ibid., pp. 84–83; Little, *From Harlem*, pp. 360–361.

29. Davis, *Here and There*, p. 84.

30. *New York Herald*, February 18, 1919, pp. 1 and 6.

31. *New York Tribune*, February 18, 1919, pp. 1 and 8; *New York Age*, February 22, 1919, p. 4; *New York Tribune*, February 18, 1919, editorial page.

32. Badger, "Pride without Prejudice," p. 413; Lewis, *When Harlem Was in Vogue*, p. 4. Numerous newspaper reports cited Europe's poor health as the main reason why he did not lead the band, fearing that he would not hold up. The *New York Times*, February 22, 1919, pp. 1 and 6, stated that he appeared at the head of the band, despite a reported bout with pneumonia. In "Pride without Prejudice," Badger does not mention Europe's illness at all.

33. *New York Age*, February 22, 1919, p. 8.

34. Ibid.; George I. Gay, with H. H. Fisher, *Public Relations of the Commission for Relief in Belgium, Documents* (Stanford, CA: Stanford University Press, 1929), accessed November 8, 2013, http://net.lib.byu.edu/estu/wwi/comment/CRB/CRB1-1.htm#1. Other members of the club included Bulkeley Wells, a retired brigadier general in the Colorado National Guard and president of Western Colorado Power Company and the First National Bank of Telluride as well as the managing director of sixteen metal-mining properties from Oklahoma to Alaska, and William Boyce Thompson, mining promoter extraordinaire and sometime business partner of the Guggenheims, J. P. Morgan, and Bernard Baruch. See http://www.localsofcolorado.com/tag/bulkeley-wells/, dated March 8, 2013, but accessed November 8, 2013, and John D'Agnillo, "William Boyce Thompson: An Enduring Legacy in Yonkers," accessed November 8, 2013, www.yonkershistory.org/8_2_2.html.

35. *New York Age*, February 22, 1919, p. 8.

36. JIM-CROW PARADES, headline of an unidentified, undated newspaper editorial in Gumby Collection, "Negro as Soldier" file, R 76, BLCU. This editorial seems to be in direct response to one written by James Weldon Johnson, in which he boasts that the Regiment is the first to have an official parade upon its return from France as well as the first to march under the Victory Arch at Madison Square. Johnson even writes: "There is a line somewhere in the Bible which says that the last shall be first. This prophecy has come true so many times and in so many ways for us as a race that we ought to have faith that it will finally be completely fulfilled." See *New York Age*, February 22, 1919, p. 4.

37. *New York Tribune*, February 18, 1919, pp. 1 and 8.

38. *New York Times*, February 22, 1919, pp. 1 and 6; *New York World*, February 18,

1919, p. 1; *New York Herald*, February 18, 1919, pp. 1 and 6; *New York Tribune*, February 18, 1919, p. 8; *New York Age*, March 22, 1919, p. 4.

39. *New York Times*, February 22, 1919, pp. 1 and 6; *New York Herald*, February 18, 1919, p. 1.

40. *New York World*, February 18, 1919, pp. 1 and 3.

41. *New York Tribune*, February 18, 1919, p. 8.

42. *New York American*, February 18, 1919, pp. 1, 4, and 5.

43. *New York Age*, March 22, 1919, p. 4.

44. Kevin Gaines, *Uplifting the Race: Black Leadership, Politics, and Culture in the Twentieth Century* (Chapel Hill: University of North Carolina Press, 1996), pp. xiv–xv.

45. *New York World*, February18, 1919, pp. 1 and 3.

46. *New York Tribune*, February 18, 1919, p. 8; *New York American*, February 18, 1919, pp. 1, 4, and 5.

47. *New York Times*, February 22, 1919, pp. 1 and 6.

48. *New York Herald*, February18, 1919, pp. 1 and 6; *New York Age*, February 15, 1919, p. 1; William N. Colson, "The Immediate Function of the Negro Veteran," *Messenger*, November 1919, pp. 19–20. Colson was a lieutenant in the 367th Regiment and wrote extensively on military affairs for the *Messenger*. See also "A Court Martial Tragedy," *Messenger*, October 1919, p. 23.

49. *New York Herald*, March 26, 1919, editorial page.

50. *New York Evening World*, March 25, 1919, p. 4.

51. *New York Tribune*, March 25, 1919, p. 12.

52. *New York Sun*, March 25, 1919, pp. 1 and 5; *New York Times*, March 25, 1919, p. 5. For the parade of the 369th, G. J. Koch Company, Inc., bid $74,000 for a contract to build grandstands and hang decorations. See *New York American*, February 14, 1919, p. 3; *New York American*, February 15, 1919, p. 8.

53. *New York Sun*, March 25, 1919, pp. 1 and 5; *New York Times*, March 25, 1919, p. 5; *New York American*, February 15, 1919, p. 8.

54. Lewis, *When Harlem Was in Vogue*, pp. 14–15.

55. An entire building at the Chicago World's Exposition was dedicated to and housed the painting. After that, a Baltimore restaurateur, William Henry Haussner, purchased the work and displayed pieces of it at his establishment. In 1959, he donated the central panels to the Kansas City Liberty Memorial Association for display at its museum. See Carter B. Horsley, "The Haussner's Restaurant Collection: 19th Century European and American Paintings," accessed November 8, 2013, http://www.thecityreview.com/f99shaus.html, auction date of November 2, 1999. Daniel MacMorris reduced and restored the painting to a 45-foot-long artwork to fit into the museum. A numbered key of subjects in silhouette identifies the flag-bearing Johnson and Roberts as numbers 6 and 31 in panel F, respectively, and Janifer as number 15 in panel E. From what source MacMorris found or gathered this identifying information is unknown. See Daniel MacMorris Papers, Liberty Memorial Museum, Kansas City, MO. None of the official publications we consulted lists any of the black soldiers by name, but neither is Sgt. Alvin York listed; he appears as number 14 in panel F. For the most authoritative treatment of this

subject, see Mark Levitch, *Panthéon de la Guerre* (Columbia: University of Missouri Press, 2006), pp. 95–96. For more on Janifer, see Geraldine R. Hutner, "Crossing the Color Barrier in New Jersey," *New Jersey Medicine* 91, no. 8 (August 1994): 527–531.

56. Du Bois, "Returning Soldiers," *The Crisis* 18 (May 1919): 13.

57. Lewis, *When Harlem Was in Vogue*, pp. 16–24; Steven A. Reich, "Soldiers of Democracy: Black Texans and the Fight for Citizenship," *Journal of American History* 82, no. 4 (March 1996): 1481–1482.

58. Chas. P. Howard, national adjutant, to NAACP News Service, June 27, 1925, NAACP Papers, Military Group 1, Gen. Adm., C-375, October–December 1926, LOCMD. His office was in Des Moines, Iowa, and the first national convention was held in 1925 in Chicago.

### Chapter 14. Your Services Are No Longer Needed

1. 369th Lineage and Honors, Department of the Army, NYSMM; NAACP Papers, Group 1, Box C-374, Adm. File, Gen., December 1919, Misc., LOCMD.

2. The *New York Age* of March 1, 1919, was a special issue dedicated to events surrounding the war. Much of the coverage included examples of injustice toward black soldiers and grievances blacks leveled in response. Black doctors wrote to protest their exclusion from the profession in the field and at base hospitals at home. They cited the denial of opportunity to black nurses and rejected the lame explanations of Secretary of War Baker for a policy that was simply racist. Veterans also complained about their mistreatment aboard ships returning home.

3. Hugh Wiley, "The Four-Leaved Wildcat," *Saturday Evening Post*, March 8, 1919, pp. 9–11, 45–46, and 49.

4. Alice Dunbar-Nelson to George Horace Lorimer, March 7, 1919, NAACP Papers, Group 1, Box C-374, Adm. File, Gen., March 1919, LOCMD.

5. Ibid.

6. *New York Times*, February 24, 1919, p. 3.

7. Ibid.

8. *New York Age,* February 21, 1920, p. 1, and May 22, 1920, p. 1; *New York Times,* June 23, 1922, p. 23; *New York Age,* February 11, 1922, p. 1.

9. *Amsterdam News*, February 28, 1923, p. 1; *New York Age*, February 11, 1922, p. 1.

10. "If We Must Die," editorial, *Messenger*, September 1919, Riot Number, p. 4. In May 1918, the *Chicago Defender* had already detected the change, stating that when the boys returned, "they [would] be filled with new ideas." Foremost among them was the realization that they were men, a fact they had been made to forget in the United States but not abroad. See "When Our Boys Come Back," *Chicago Defender,* May 18, 1918, p. 16.

11. Col. Allen J. Greer to Senator Kenneth D. McKellar, December 6, 1918, Box 704, File 322.97, RG 407, NARA.

12. Brigadier-General Malvern-Hill Barnum, Chief, American Section, PAC, to Adjutant General, GHQ AEF, April 20, 1919, File 11440, A-239, RG 120, NARA. The questionnaire instructs and asks the following: "a) The fitness of the colored man as a combat soldier. b) For what particular service is he best suited, considering one or more of the following classifications: infantry, cavalry, artillery, engineers,

pioneer, labor troops, etc. c) Please give a candid expression of opinion concerning the colored officer, his capacity, qualifications, and results obtained with him, so far as you can, with your recommendation as to whether or not they should be used. d) The question of race feeling must be considered from the practical and actual standpoint, instead of a theoretical one."

13. Col. George H. McMaster to Col. Allen J. Greer, April 28, 1919, p. 1, File 11440-A 239, RG 120, NARA.

14. Ibid., pp. 2–3. McMaster proudly admitted that he brought 112 officers up on charges for making such demands. For reaction to this incident, see *New York Age*, March 1, 1919, p. 1.

15. Barnum to Greer, April 19, 1919, File 11440-A 239, RG 120, NARA.

16. Robert Russa Moton, *Finding a Way Out: An Autobiography* (1920; repr., New York: Negro Universities Press, 1969), pp. 251–265.

17. *New York Age*, May 19, 1919, p. 1. See note 18.

18. Henry E. Baker to Gen. John J. Pershing, November 19, 1919, and George C. Marshall to Henry E. Baker, November 25, 1919, both in File 11440-A 244, RG 120, NARA. Even more alarming, some two and a half years later Pershing's deputy chief of staff, Maj. Gen. James G. Harbord, was seeking ways to reduce the four regiments of black troops. He maintained that with the reduction in size of the army, keeping these regiments intact was an absurdity, which, carried to its "logical extreme," would result in "an exclusively colored army." His solution was to reduce one or more of the regiments to inactive status, holding "that the regiment still exists but that the enlisted portion of it is withheld for a time, being subject to replacement at any time" with the officers carrying "on their assignment to such an inactive regiment." See Harbord to J. A. Hull, Acting Judge Advocate General, March 1, 1922, Box 704, File 322.97, RG 407, NARA. In a fascinating document on the actual and legislative history of black military service during and since the Civil War, Hull responded favorably to Harbord's suggestion. See Hull to Harbord, March 15, 1922, Box 704, File 322.97, RG 407, NARA.

19. Report prepared by C. W. Moffett, 1st Lieut., Inf., Historical Branch, October 30, 1919, File 293-11-4, RG 120, NARA. The four silver bands were three more than the 370th received and one more than the 371st and 372nd. The Department of the Army Lineage and Honors report for the 369th lists the four campaigns with slightly different participation credits: "Champagne-Marne, Meuse-Argonne, Champagne 1918, and Alsace 1918." It also cites the regimental French Croix de Guerre with Silver Star and the streamer embroidered "Meuse-Argonne." See records of the 369th Regiment at NYSMM, 369th Regiment File, NYSMM.

20. *War Department, Army Regulations*, 1917 (Washington, DC: Government Printing Office, 1917) p. 65, Ref Div, NARA; Lineage and Honors, Headquarters and Headquarters Detachment 369th Transportation Battalion, 369th Regiment File, NYSMM.

21. *Annual Report of the Adjutant-General for the State of New York for the Year 1919* (Albany, NY: J. B. Lyon, 1921), p. 295.

22. Ibid. If one were to rely solely on the inaccurate 1919 report of the adjutant general, then the picture would have looked even worse. In it, William J. Schief-

felin, Jr., some twenty years Fillmore's junior, is listed as colonel. Schieffelin had begun his military service as a private in October 1914 in the National Guard. He attained the rank of second lieutenant in June 1916 and was promoted to first lieutenant in October before receiving an honorable discharge on April 3, 1917. The record has him receiving his colonelcy on July 31, 1918. A mysterious gap in the record of service between April 3, 1917, and July 30, 1918, suggests a problem with the information. Furthermore, Schieffelin's obituary lists no affiliation with the 15th and has him serving overseas as a captain with the 12th Field Artillery during the war. The *Official Army Register* for 1918 lists Schieffelin as a "Captain (temp)" with the Field Artillery, US Army as of July 25, 1918. The *Official Army Register* for 1920 lists him among the casualties with the Field Artillery as of December 16, 1918, which means that he was in federal service at the time the *Report of the Adjutant-General* lists him as a colonel in the 15th NYG. Further evidence of the error appears in his father's obituary, which cites the father, not him, as the commander of the 15th, having received the appointment from Whitman. See *Official Army Register* (Washington, DC: Government Printing Office), December 1, 1918, p. 895, and January 1, 1920, p. 1078. *New York Times*, May 3, 1985, p. D23, and May 1, 1955, p. 88. Charles W. Fillmore to Friend and Comrade, April 3, 1920, accessed November 8, 2013, http://www.goantiques.com/search/images.jsp?id=4048. In this call to arms, Fillmore, a Republican operative, supports the candidacy of John J. Lyons for secretary of state of New York. Fillmore cites Lyons's efforts on behalf of the black citizens of the state in persuading the secretary of war not to disband the 369th without "a proper reception"—meaning a parade. Lyons, according to Fillmore, prepared and read the complimentary resolutions in honor of the Regiment at the parade.

23. *Annual Report of the Adjutant-General*, p. 295.

24. *New York Age*, March 1, 1919, p. 1.

25. *Annual Report of the Adjutant-General*, pp. 295–298.

26. Maj. Gen. J. McI. Carter, Chief, Militia Bureau, to A. W. Lynch, Editor, *Philadelphia American*, May 6, 1920, NGB, General Correspondence, File 322.097, RG 168, NARA.

27. John W. Weeks to Dr. De Haven Hinkson, October 21, 1921, NAACP Papers, Mil. Gen., C-375, 1924, January–December, LOCMD.

28. Ibid. In the end, the number of National Guard divisions totaled eighteen, rather than sixteen.

29. Weeks to Hinkson, October 21, 1921.

30. Ibid., p. 2; Mark G. McLaughlin, "'Little Louis and Big Bertha,' Doughboy Center: The Story of the American Expeditionary Forces," accessed November 8, 2013, http://www.worldwar1.com/dbc/lraab.htm.

31. "'Little Louis and Big Bertha,' Doughboy Center: The Story of the American Expeditionary Forces"; Secretary of War Newton D. Baker to W. E. B. Du Bois, May 17, 1920, NGB, General Correspondence, File 322.097, RG 168, NARA. The reference to machine-gun companies is in a letter from J. McI. Carter to Brig. Gen. Milton A. Reckord, Adjutant General of Maryland, May 7, 1920, NGB, General Correspondence, File 322.097, RG 168, NARA.

32. Newton D. Baker to W. E. B. Du Bois, May 17, 1920. Unsatisfied with Baker's response to Du Bois, NAACP's president, Moorfield Storey, sought clarification on the meaning of a Pioneer and wondered whether Pioneers had ever existed before, what they did, and whether whites would be included. See Storey to Baker, July 8, 1930, NGB, General Correspondence, File 322.097, RG 168, NARA.

33. James C. Waters, Jr., to Chief, Militia Bureau, May 29, 1920, NGB, General Correspondence, File 322.097, RG 168, NARA.

34. A. W. Lynch to Major General J. McI. Carter, May 22, 1920, NGB, General Correspondence, File 322.097 PA, RG 168, NARA.

35. Adjutant General of the Army to Commanding Generals All Corp Areas, October 19, 1920, NGB, General Correspondence, File 322.097, RG 168, NARA.

36. James Weldon Johnson to John W. Weeks, May 20, 1921, NGB, General Correspondence, File 322.097, RG 168, NARA.

37. John W. Weeks to James Weldon Johnson, May 31, 1921, NGB, General Correspondence, File 322.097, RG 168, NARA.

38. J. Q. Adams to Honorable Secretary of War, May 14, 1921, and John W. Weeks to J. Q. Adams, May 27, 1921, both in NGB, General Correspondence, File 322.097, RG 168, NARA; Adams to Weeks, June 28, 1921, NGB, General Correspondence, File 322.097 MN, RG 168, NARA. According to David Vassar Taylor, the *Appeal* "defended the race against malicious propaganda, accorded recognition for individual achievement, and spoke out about proscriptive legislation on national and state levels, while waging a militant local battle for civil rights." See Taylor, *African Americans in Minnesota* (Minneapolis: Minnesota Historical Society Press, 2002), p. 24. Taylor also provides information on Adams's organizational initiatives to combat Jim Crow locally and nationally.

39. John W. Weeks to J. Q. Adams, May 27, 1921. Hinkson was post commander of the George T. Cornish Post 292 of the American Legion, based in Philadelphia. See NAACP Papers, Mil., Group 1, LOCMD.

40. David Levering Lewis, *W. E. B. Du Bois: The Fight for Equality and the American Century, 1919–1963* (New York: Henry Holt, 2000), pp. 70–71; Robert E. Hauser, "'The Georgia Experiment': President Warren G. Harding's Attempt to Reorganize the Republican Party in Georgia," *Georgia Historical Quarterly* 62, no. 4 (Winter, 1978): 288–303.

41. Maj. Gen. George C. Rickards to Major Page, NGB, General Correspondence, File 322.097, RG 168, NARA.

42. Maj. Gen. John F. O'Ryan, Commanding General, to J. Leslie Kincaid, Adjutant General of the State, April 15, 1921, NGB, General Correspondence, File 322.097 NY, RG 168, NARA.

43. Ibid. There is a possibility that O'Ryan either exaggerated the numbers of white officers to make his case with Washington or facilitated an infusion of whites between 1919 and 1921. The *Annual Report of the Adjutant-General* after 1919 no longer lists names of officers, although the 1919 report indicates that a large number of the officers in the 15th were black. A systematic review of all the officers in the Regiment in 1921 is difficult if not impossible to conduct. By the end of 1920, the 15th

NYG numbered 579 men and officers, far short of the 1,200 needed for regimental strength. See *Annual Report of Adjutant-General of the State of New York for the Year 1920* (Albany, N.Y.: J. B. Lyon, 1923), pp. 34–35.

44. Service Record, Arthur West Little, and Service Record, Charles Ward Fillmore, both in 369th Regiment officer records, NYSMM.

45. *New York Times*, January 5, 1921, p. 2.

46. Edward J. Westcott, Asst. Attorney General, NY, to Chief, Militia Bureau, April 19, 1921, NGB, General Correspondence, File 322.097 NY, RG 168, NARA.

47. J. McI. Carter to Dir. of War Plans Division, April 23, 1921; Harrison Hall, Adjutant General, to J. McI. Carter, May 7, 1921; J. McI. Carter to Adjutant General New York, May 11, 1921, NGB, General Correspondence, File 322.097 NY, RG 168, NARA.

48. *New York Age*, May 7, 1921, p. 1.

49. *New York Age*, March 26, 1921, p. 1.

50. *New York Times*, June 22, 1922, p. 8. The *New York Age,* March 26, 1921, p. 1, indicated that Lt. Frederick W. Simpson led the band in March 1921. He was leader of the 15th NYG band during the war, according to the *Annual Report of the Adjutant-General* for 1918–1919, p. 298. On June 22, 1922, the *Times* (p. 8) reported that Eugene Mikell was the bandleader. Mikell returned to the Regiment on May 29, 1919, according to *Annual Report of the Adjutant-General* (p. 299).

51. *New York Times*, April 12, 1921, p. 18, and May 22, 1921, p. 16.

52. *New York Times*, November 1, 1922, p. 14, and February 19, 1923, p. 17.

53. *New York Times*, August 14, 1923, p. 30. The Regiment also kept in the public eye through boxing and wrestling tournaments, basketball games, and eventually track meets, in which it gained its greatest athletic success. See *New York Age*, February 19, 1921, p. 6, March 19, 1921, p. 6, and September 10, 1921, p. 6; *Pittsburgh Courier*, November 11, 1925, n.p.

54. Arthur Little to Commanding General N.Y. National Guard, December 11, 1923, and Maj. H. A. Finch, Asst. Chief, M.B. to A.G. of New York, December 19, 1923, both in NGB, General Correspondence, File 325.4-E NY, RG 168, NARA. Maj. Gen. John Francis O'Ryan entered the reserve list on May 22, 1923, to return to his law practice and real estate business. He left the service officially on August 21, 1928. In 1933, he briefly held the position of New York City police commissioner, and he was active in New York state and city politics for most of his remaining years. See General Orders no. 6, January 30, 1961, State of New York, Executive Department, Division of Military and Naval Affairs, NYSMM.

55. *New York Times*, September 7, 1924, p. 21, and September 21, 1924, p. E3.

56. Maj. Gen. George C. Rickards, Chief, Militia Bureau, to Eugene F. Gordon, April 10, 1923, NGB, General Correspondence, File 322.097 MA, RG 168, NARA.

57. "New York State Armory History," http://dmna.ny.gov/a_history/nyc5history.htm, accessed December 13, 2013.

58. *New York Times*, May 18, 1924, p. S6.

59. W. Hayward to Major X. H. Price, Corps of Engineers, Executive Officer, Battle Monuments Board, January 16, 1922, Box, File 619.3, RG 117, NARA.

60. J. B. Pate, Colonel U.S. Army, retired, Secretary-Treasurer, Assn. of Officers 371st Infantry WWI, to Chairman, American Battle Monuments Commission, July 2, 1937, and X. H. Price Memorandum for the Files, October 23, 1937, both in Box 30, File 619.3, RG 117, NARA.

61. X. H. Price to William Hayward, September 28, 1923, Box 30, File 619.3, RG 117, NARA; Statement by Major X. H. Price, Sec. ABMC, Concerning H. J. Resolution 178, March 23, 1935, pp. 1–2, RG 117, File 619.3.316, NARA. Also see the brochure *American Memorials and Overseas Military Cemeteries* (Arlington, VA: American Battle Monuments Commission, 2002), p. 2.

62. Hamilton Fish to the Battle Monuments Commission, May 26, 1924, Box 30, File 619.3, RG 117, NARA.

63. John J. Pershing to Hamilton Fish, June 9, 1924, and Pershing Memorandum for Commission, June 9, 1924, Box 30, File 619.3, RG 117, NARA.

64. X. H. Price to William R. Wood, Chairman, Subcommittee on Appropriations, January 17, 1925, Box 30, File 619.3, RG 117, NARA.

65. Ibid.

66. Hamilton Fish to James Weldon Johnson, January 13, 1925, NAACP Papers, Mil., Group 1, Gen. Adm., C-375, File 1925, January-May, LOCMD.

67. Ibid.

68. "Negro Soldier Monument," Press Service of the NAACP Release, April 2, 1926, and "NAACP Endorses Fish Bill," March 12, 1926, both in NAACP Papers, Mil., Group 1, Gen. Adm., C-375, January–December 1926, LOCMD.

69. Ferdinand D. Lee to James Weldon Johnson, April 12, 1926, NAACP Papers, Mil., Group 1, Gen. Adm., C-375, October–December 1926, LOCMD.

70. Hamilton Fish to James Weldon Johnson, April 30, 1926, NAACP Papers, Mil., Group 1, Gen. Adm., C-375, October–December 1926, LOCMD.

71. Hamilton Fish to Colonel William Hayward, April 30, 1926, NAACP Papers, Mil., Group 1, Gen. Adm., C-375, October–December 1926, LOCMD.

72. "Congressman Hamilton Fish Praises Heroism of Negro Troops," Press Service of the NAACP Release, June 24, 1926, Gumby Collection R 75, BLCU; Hamilton Fish, Jr., to James Weldon Johnson, April 30, 1926.

73. "Fish Memorial Bill Reported," Press Service of the NAACP Release, May 29, 1926, NAACP Papers, Mil., Group 1, Gen. Adm., C-375, January–December 1926, LOCMD.

74. See http://perso.orange.fr/champagne1418/circuit/circuitsouain/blancmont/blancmont.htm, accessed November 8, 2013; *Meuse-Argonne American Cemetery and Memorial* (Arlington, VA: American Battle Monuments Commission, 1998), pp. 23–24.

75. *Amsterdam News*, November 7, 1928, p. 9, and February 20, 1929, p. 2.

76. Lt. Col. Stephen R. Seiter, Commander, 369th Corps Support Battalion, to Col. Frederick C. Badger, Dir. of Engineering and Maintenance, ABMC, February 20, 1996, Seiter to Brig. Gen. James S. Dickey, Dir., ABMC (European Region), March 23, 1997, Seiter to Col. Dale F. Means, Dir. of Engineering and Maintenance, ABMC, May 6, 1997, and Means to Seiter, May 22, 1997, all from the personal papers of Stephen R. Seiter. The original members of the 369th Monument Initiative

Planning Committee were: Bruce Boeglin, pres., Federation of French War Veterans; Col. Roger Cestac, pres., American Society of Le Souvenir, Inc.; Monsieur Patrick Gautrat, consul general of France; Maj. Gen. and Mrs. Nathaniel James, pres., 369th Historical Society, William Miles, pres., Miles Educational Film Productions; Lt. Col. and Mrs. Stephen R. Seiter, cmdr., 369th Corps Support Battalion; and Col. Michel Somnolet, pres., French Reserve Officers Association.

### Chapter 15. Winning the Battle and Losing the War

1. *Amsterdam News*, January 21, 1925, p. 1.

2. Ibid.; *Annual Report of the Adjutant-General for the State of New York for 1918–1919*, p. 295; Anthony Powell, *Black Participation in the Spanish American War*, http://www.spanamwar.com/AfroAmericans.htm, accessed December 14, 2013; John K. Mahon and Romana Danysh, *Infantry Part 1: Regular Army*, Army Lineage Series (Washington, DC: Office of Chief of Military History, 1971), p. 36, http://www.history.army.mil/books/Lineage/in/infantry.htm, accessed December 14, 2013.

3. The other officers named were: Captains D. Lincoln Reid, Charles O. Steedman, L. F. Nearon, and George A. Brown, and Lieutenants Deforest D. Johnson, William W. Chisum, Holmer Butler, and Rufus A. Atkins.

4. *Amsterdam News*, January 21, 1925, p. 3.

5. Ibid.; *New York Age*, February 21, 1920, p. 4.

6. *Amsterdam News*, January 28, 1925, sect. 1, p. 1.

7. Ibid., pp. 1 and 4. The article on the 8th Illinois appears on page 1 of the second news section.

8. *New York National Guardsman*, April 1925, p. 28; *Amsterdam News*, March 3, 1926, sect. 1, p. 1.

9. *Amsterdam News*, June 3, 1925, p. 9; National Defense Act of 1920, sect. 4A, p. 761. Mikell's grade during the war was simply that of bandleader. By contrast, Europe, because of his commission in the machine-gun company, was an anomaly. This provision in the 1920 act might have been a response to Europe and black bandleaders specifically, if not to the more general problem. A warrant officer received the same pay and benefits as a second lieutenant but ranked just below him.

10. *Amsterdam News*, March 11, 1925, p. 9.

11. Nick Chiles to Chester C. Platte, July 8, 1913, Sulzer Papers, Box 19, RG 1147, Rare and Manuscripts Collections, KLCU. Chiles was editor of the *Topeka Plaindealer*. Robert N. Wood, president of the United Colored Democracy, expressed a similar view in a letter to Sulzer on June 12, 1913, Sulzer Papers, Box 16, RG 1147, Rare and Manuscripts Collections, KLCU.

12. The movement also had the support of Alderman Martin Healey.

13. *Amsterdam News*, March 11, 1925, p. 16.

14. *Pittsburgh Courier*, April 11, 1925, p. 1; Service Record of Arthur W. Little, NYSMM; *Amsterdam News*, March 3, 1926, p. 1.

15. *Pittsburgh Courier*, April 11, 1925, p. 1; *New York Herald Tribune*, August 24, 1926, n.p.; *Amsterdam News*, July 27, 1926, p. 2.

16. *Amsterdam News*, May 11, 1927, p. 24, and June 27, 1928, p. 16. Specific charges of malfeasance against blacks included: his failure to appoint a black commander

of the 369th, refusal to look into the Wills-Dempsey fight, his veto of the court bill because it "threatened" to make the election of a black to the municipal court bench possible, and his failure to appoint blacks to public office.

17. *New York Times*, April 11, 1925, p. 10; *New York National Guardsman*, May 1925, p. 19; *Amsterdam News*, March 3, 1926, p. 1, April 8, 1925, p. 16, and April 15, 1925, p. 1.

18. *Amsterdam News*, July 8, 1925, p. 16.

19. *New York Herald Tribune*, August 24, 1926, n.p.

20. *Amsterdam News*, March 3, 1926, p. 1, March 10, 1926, p. 3, and March 17, 1926, p. 17.

21. *Amsterdam News*, March 3, 1926, p. 1; William H. Jackson was promoted to major on October 14, 1918. See *Annual Report of the Adjutant General for the Year 1919* (Albany, NY: J. B. Lyon, 1921), p. 295.

22. *Amsterdam News*, April 6, 1927, pp. 1–2, and April 13, 1927, p. 24.

23. *Amsterdam News*, March 10, 1926, p. 16, September 15, 1926, p. 1, and January 19, 1927, p. 1. Taylor instituted the intraunit system of promotion and elimination, which at the time of his departure left the unit with only five white officers. See *Amsterdam News*, December 13, 1933, pp. 1–2.

24. *Amsterdam News*, March 29, 1933, p. 14. A correction followed in the next issue of the paper as a result of information from Capt. Wilmer F. Lucas, regimental adjutant, that Taylor had not used Officer Association funds to support the dinner. The fact remained that the dinners did not include black officers. See *Amsterdam News*, April 5, 1933, p. 1, and November 22, 1933, p. 3, for the promotion of Lucas by Taylor to major. Being a good soldier certainly meant something in this instance.

25. *New York Age*, November 25, 1933, p. 1, and December 16, 1933, p. 1.

26. *Amsterdam News*, December 13, 1933, pp. 1–2 and 6, December 27, 1933, p. 2, January 3, 1934, p. 1, and January 10, 1934, p. 3.

27. *New York Age*, January 5, 1934, p. 2.

28. Ibid.

29. Cheryl Lynn Greenberg, *"Or Does It Explode?": Black Harlem in the Great Depression* (New York: Oxford University Press, 1991), pp. 3–6.

30. *New York Age*, November 2, 1935, p. 11, and July 8, 1933, p. 1. Twenty-one black bricklayers and mechanics won a $2,800 verdict after a two-year legal battle against C and W Construction Company for being forced to work below union scale. Court testimony included evidence of racketeering in labor unions.

31. *New York Age*, March 27, 1937, p. 6, and July 24, 1937, p. 6. Mayor La Guardia's refusal to release the report and accept its findings on employment discrimination and inadequate health care remained a source of tension and resentment among Harlemites for years after the riot.

32. *Amsterdam News*, October 9, 1937, p. 1, and February 5, 1938, p. 1.

33. *Amsterdam News*, October 9, 1937, p. 1, November 13, 1937, p. 23, and February 5, 1938, p. 1.

34. *Amsterdam News*, February 19, 1938, p. 12; *New York Times*, October 15, 1937, p. 16, and February 24, 1938, p. 42. Grimley soon resigned from his position with the hospitals commission and took on the role of deputy commissioner of health with

responsibility for the World's Fair. See *Amsterdam News,* March 12, 1938, p. 1, and March 19, 1938, p. 2. Wood was a well-known Harlem physician. He graduated from Dartmouth College, where he was a ski-jumping champion. He was the first black graduate of New York University Medical School and the first black to attend the Army War College at Carlisle, Pennsylvania, where he completed a special course for medical officers that qualified him to command hospital units and centers. See *Amsterdam News,* November 27, 1937, p. 24.

35. *New York Times,* February 26, 1938, p. 17; *New York National Guardsman,* April 1938, p. 21. Mundy also received the Conspicuous Service Cross of the state of New York and was graduated from the Army School of the Line in France and the Command and General Staff School at Fort Leavenworth, Kansas.

36. *Amsterdam News,* March 5, 1938, pp. 1–2 and 12.

37. Ibid., March 26, 1938, pp. 12 and 20.

38. Marvin E. Fletcher, *America's First Black General: Benjamin O. Davis, Sr., 1880–1970* (Lawrence: University Press of Kansas, 1989), pp. 80–81.

39. *New York Times,* April 28, 1938, p. 14.

40. *New York National Guardsman,* October 1938, p. 9.

41. Fletcher, *America's First Black General,* p. 81; *Amsterdam News,* May 7, 1938, p. 12, and September 17, 1938, p. 2.

42. See http://www.vernonjohns.org/tca1001/vjharlem.html, accessed November 12, 2013.

43. Ibid.; also see http://www.nyc-architecture.com/HAR/HAR-History.htm, accessed November 12, 2013.

44. Fletcher, *America's First Black General,* p. 82.

45. *Amsterdam News,* September 11, 1937, p. 2, October 2, 1937, p. 2, March 26, 1938, p. 20, June 4, 1938, p. 20, September 17, 1938, p. 2, March 11, 1939, p. 8, September 16, 1939, p. 10, November 11, 1939, p. 5, November 18, 1939, pp. 1–2, and December 2, 1939, p. 2.

46. *Amsterdam News,* April 13, 1940, p. 2, May 18, 1940, p. 6, and June 1, 1940, p. 8.

47. Fletcher, *America's First Black General,* pp. 82–83; George V. Strong, Brigadier General, Assistant Chief of Staff to Chief of Staff, "Conversion of National Guard Units," January 1940, Incl. 4, Tab A, Gen., File 324.5, RG 407, NARA. Actually, blacks in New Jersey led by veterans of World War I had been pressing state authorities for the formation of black artillery units as early as 1928. They recognized that their call would reinforce segregation in the short run, but the long-term goal was to have black men "admitted to branches other than infantry." See *Amsterdam News,* January 25, 1928, p. 13.

48. *Amsterdam News,* June 22, 1940, p. 10, and August 17, 1940, p. 1; Fletcher, *America's First Black General,* pp. 82–83. In August 1940, Davis appointed a white, regular army instructor, Lt. Col. Robert D. Brown, as an adviser to the regiment. The *Amsterdam News* praised him for giving the soldiers the "highest type of training in modern warfare tactics and the use of modern equipment." The appointment possibly demonstrated one of Davis's strengths—knowing what he did not know. See *Amsterdam News,* November 9, 1940, p. 23.

49. *Amsterdam News,* February 3, 1940, p. 7, and October 19, 1940, p. 12.

50. Fletcher, *America's First Black General,* pp. 83–85; *Amsterdam News,* November 2, 1940, p. 16.

51. *New York Times,* October 26, 1940, p. 4, January 14, 1941, p. 12, and February 11, 1941, p. 11.

52. Berry and Blassingame, *Long Memory,* pp. 318–324.

53. G. C. Marshall to General Benjamin O. Davis, June 5, 1941, and Davis to Marshall, June 6, 1941, JAG 210.14, Records of Judge Advocate, General Correspondence, Entry 302, File 210.14, RG 153, NARA; *New York Age,* April 25, 1942, p. 6.

54. Henry L. Stimson Diaries, HM 51, Reel 6, Volume 31: 71–72, October 2, 1940, SLYU.

55. Stimson Diaries, HM 51, Reel 6, Vol. 30: 200, September 27, 1940; see http ://history.acusd.edu/gen/WW2Timeline/Tuskegee.html. Roy Wilkins, "Watchtower," *Amsterdam News,* April 5, 1941, p. 16.

56. *New York National Guardsman,* May 1938, p. 14; *New York Times,* March 20, 1938, p. 46.

57. *New York National Guardsman,* May 1938, p. 14.

58. *New York Times,* November 9, 1940, p. 7.

59. *New York Times,* October 6, 1939, p. 22.

60. *New York Times,* January 14, 1941, p. 9.

61. *Amsterdam News,* September 13, 1941, p. 16, and September 27, 1941, pp. 1 and 3.

62. *Amsterdam News,* September 17, 1938, p. 2.

63. Lineage and Honors, Headquarters and Headquarters Detachment, 369th Transportation Battalion, Department of the Army, NYSMM.

64. Beth Bailey and David Farber, *First Strange Place: The Alchemy of Race and Sex in World War II Hawaii* (New York: Free Press, 1993), pp. 140–144.

65. Richard Anderson, "The United States Army in World War II: Manpower, Replacements, and the Segregated Army," Military History Online.com, 2000, http://www.militaryhistoryonline.com/wwii/usarmy/manpower.aspx, accessed December 15, 2013.

66. See http://www.pentagon.mil/news/Jan1997/n01151997_9701154.html.

67. Lineage and Honors, Headquarters and Headquarters Detachment, 369th Transportation Battalion, Department of the Army, New York State Military Museum, Saratoga Springs, N.Y.

68. Bailey and Farber, *First Strange Place,* pp. 143–145.

69. Franklin and Moss, *From Slavery to Freedom,* pp. 462–463.

70. Author's telephone interview with Nathaniel James, August 15, 2005; *Amsterdam News,* May 18, 1968, p. 43; *New York Times,* June 25, 2003, sect. B, p. 1.

71. *Amsterdam News,* November 11, 1967, p. 1; Lineage and Honors, Headquarters and Headquarters Detachment, 369th Transportation Battalion, Department of the Army, New York State Military Museum, Saratoga Springs, N.Y.; Martha Biondi, *To Stand and Fight: The Struggle for Civil Rights in Postwar New York City* (Cambridge, MA: Harvard University Press, 2003), pp. 272–287.

72. List of commanding officers provided by Brig. Gen. Stephen R. Seiter, August 23, 2003, and updated. Racial identification provided by Maj. General Nathan-

iel James, via telephone conversation, August 12, 2005. Here is the full list: William Hayward, 1916–1919; Arthur W. Little, 1921–1925; William A. Taylor, 1925–1933; John G. Grimley, 1933–1938; Joseph A. S. Mundy, 1938; Benjamin O. Davis, Sr., 1938–1940; Chauncey W. Hooper, 1940–1950; Cato Baskerville, 1950–1956; Otho C. Van Excel, 1956–1958; John Y. Woodruff, 1958–1966; George A. Jones, 1966–1970; Louis Duckett, 1970–1976; John S. Cox, 1976–1980; Nathaniel James, 1980–1984; John C. Fong, 1984–1987; Thomas Jenkins, 1987–1990; Frederick G. Pinto, 1990; Francis W. Kairson, Jr., 1990–1993; Anthony L. Spencer, 1993–1995; Stephen R. Seiter, 1995–1998; Robert Cochran, 1998–2003; Irving F. Donaldson, 2003–2006; Kevin McKiernan, 2006–2008; Stephanie E. Dawson, 2008–2010. Colonel Dawson had thirty-two years of service in the US Army and National Guard before retiring in 2011. In 2001, she was appointed executive officer for the 369th Corps Support Battalion during its 9/11 operations and served as a commander of the 27th Rear Area Operations Center based in Kuwait; she led the first NYNG units to deploy in support of Operation Iraqi Freedom in 2003. Colonel Dawson has received the Legion of Merit, Bronze Star, and Meritorious Service Medal, among many others. She also earned a master's degree in strategic studies from the US Army War College. See *New York State Division of Military and Naval Affairs News*, Media Advisory Index, November 13, 2008, and http://www.nysenate.gov/story/5222012-veterans-hall-fame-colonel-stephanie-e-dawson, accessed November 12, 2013. A sustainment brigade provides command and control for combat service and combat service support units, enabling combat units to fight by providing fuel, ammunition, medical supplies, repair parts, and medical and other services.

### Conclusion

1. Morrison, *Jazz*, pp. 9–10 and 129.

2. Little, *From Harlem*, pp. 365–368.

3. *New York Times*, February 14, 2003, p. B8; see Abstracts of the 369th Regiment and Muster Rolls of the 15th NG/369th, NYSA; *New York World*, May 21, 1918, p. 1; William N. Colson, "Shoddyism Called History," *Messenger*, November 1919, p. 24.

4. *New York Age*, March 22, 1919, p. 4.

5. *New York Age*, July 13, 1918, p. 1.

6. Ibid.; *Chicago Defender*, July 13, 1918, p. 5.

7. *Chicago Defender*, July 20, 1918, p. 5.

8. *Chicago Defender*, August 10, 1918, p. 4, and August 17, 1918, p. 4.

9. *Albany Times Union*, February 28, 1919, p. 1.

10. Margaret D. Andrews, "Photography: The Art and Science," Yale–New Haven Teachers Institute, vol. 4, 1993, accessed November 4, 2013, http://teachers.yale.edu/curriculum/search/viewer.php?id=new_haven_93.04.01_u&skin=h. Toussaint was born Jennie Louise Van Der Zee on January 10, 1885, in Lenox, Massachusetts. Her parents were maid and butler to Ulysses S. Grant. She is the sister of James VanDerZee.

11. *Chicago Defender*, June 29, 1918, p. 4, and July 13, 1918, p. 11.

12. Deborah Willis-Braithwaite and Rodger C. Birt, *VanDerZee: Photographer, 1886–1983* (New York: Harry N. Abrams, 1993), pp. 83, 142, and 143; Whalan, *Great War*, pp. 227–230. For photographs of William Butler and Valasta George, see p. 259.

13. Willis-Braithwaite and Birt, *VanDerZee*, pp. 42–43.

14. *Albany Times Union*, February 28, 1919, p. 1.

15. *Albany Argus*, March 2, 1919, p. 3. The reports on this incident are not consistent. An *Argus* article stated that the impostor still maintained his name was Henry Johnson. Thus, Shaw seemed to be a victim of the scheme as well. Shaw supposedly reported to the *Argus* that he knew of no request of Johnson for the funds and that the money had been returned to churches involved in organizing the event. He told the *Argus* correspondent that he wanted the real Johnson, with whom the turnout—and receipts—would be even greater.

16. *Albany Times Union*, February 28, 1919, p 11.

17. *New York Age,* March 1, 1919, p. 6.

18. Ibid.

19. Ibid.

20. *Albany Times Union*, February 18, 1919, p. 1, and March 6, 1919, p. 12. The *New York Times* also reported on the event and quoted Johnson as saying, "Take care of the boys who did their bit." The *Times* article then distorted Johnson's actions, crediting him with "capturing forty-three." See *New York Times*, March 6, 1919, p. 7.

21. *Albany Times Union*, February 18, 1919, p. 2.

22. *St. Louis Republic*, March 29, 1919, p. 2; Little, *From Harlem*, p. 365. A less tenable interpretation of the Snake Hill story is that Johnson read the press clippings and later made the story part of his own.

23. *Albany Times Union*, February 28, 1919, p. 1.

24. Advertising bill from the files of John Howe, private collector, Albany, NY.

25. *Albany Times Union*, March 21, 1919, p. 16, and March 26, 1919, p. 14; *Albany Argus*, March 27, 1919, pp. 1 and 2.

26. *Albany Argus*, March 27, 1919, pp. 1 and 2; *Knickerbocker Press*, March 27, 1919, pp. 1 and 7. Hayward surprisingly revealed that the men of the 369th and the "gallant Irish fighters" of the 69th fought side by side with the French 4th Army. Maybe this was a ploy to appeal to the Irish vote. Hayward is quoted as saying that the 69th and the Rainbow Division were part of the French 4th Army. This claim does seem to square with the facts. The paper also reported that at end of war, Hayward wrote Whitman: "We have the Boche beaten. Our army will never be smaller and his will never be larger than it is now."

27. Maj. W. H. Loving to Director Military Intelligence, April 6, 1919, Loving Collection, 113-1, Military Intelligence, MSRC.

28. *St. Louis Republic*, March 29, 1919, p. 2.

29. Ibid.

30. Ibid.; *Kansas City Journal*, March 3, 1919, n.p.; *Des Moines Register*, March 30, 1919, n.p., in MID Files, E. 65, 10218–323, RG 165, NARA.

31. Maj. W. H. Loving to Director Military Intelligence, April 6, 1919, Loving

Collection, 113-1, Military Intelligence, MSRC; Henry O'Hara to Newton D. Baker, March 29, 1919, MID Files, E. 65, 10218–323, RG 165, NARA.

32. K. C. Masteller for M. Churchill, Dir. M.I., to Henry O'Hara, April 10, 1919, and Capt. J. E. Cutler for Churchill to Capt. T. S. Maffitt, April 10, 1919, MID Files, E. 65, 10218–323, RG 165, NARA.

33. Maffitt to Cutler, April 15, 1919, MID Files, E 65, 10218–323, RG 165, NARA.

34. Ibid.

35. Loving to Director Military Intelligence, April 6, 1919.

36. *New York Age*, April 12, 1919, p. 4.

37. Ibid.

38. Williams, *Torchbearers,* pp. 320–324. Henry seems to have been ahead of his time, as he anticipated the response of many to the later attacks by General Bullard on the character, intelligence, and worthiness of blacks as soldiers and especially officers.

39. Maj. Walter H. Loving to Director of Military Intelligence, March 18, 1919, Loving Papers, MSRC.

40. Brenda Gayle Plummer, "The Afro-American Response to the Occupation of Haiti, 1915–1934," *Phylon* 43, no. 2 (2nd quarter 1982): 130.

41. *Men of Bronze.*

42. *St. Louis Republic*, March 29, 1919, p. 2. If the reporting is to be believed, Johnson did apparently engage in considerable hyperbole during his talk, claiming that he had been decorated by King George and President Poincare.

43. Victor J. DiSanto, "Henry Johnson's Paradox: A Soldier's Story," *Afro-Americans in New York Life and History* 21, no. 2 (July 1997): 11.

44. *New York Age*, February 15, 1919, p. 2; *Albany Argus*, March 7, 1919, p. 12, and March 2, 1919, p. 11; DiSanto, "Henry Johnson's Paradox," p. 13.

45. *Ohio State Monitor* 2, no. 13 (September 13, 1919), p. 3, accessed November 9, 2013, http://dbs.ohiohistory.org/africanam/page.cfm?ID=2719.

46. *New York Age*, July 13, 1929, p. 1.

47. *Chicago Defender*, August 31, 1918, p. 4, November 30, 1918, p. 7, August 31, 1918, p. 1, July 13, 1918, and June 1, 1918, p. 16.

48. *Amsterdam News*, July 10, 1929, p. 1.

49. Certificate of Death, #321676, July 3, 1919, District of Columbia, Health Department; Rolla L. Thomas, *The Eclectic Practice of Medicine* (Cincinnati, OH: Scudder Brothers, 1906), pp. 444–451. That death certificate lists Henry's age as thirty-nine, which does not match the information in his military records. His age at the time of enlistment was twenty-three; thus, Henry in 1929 could have been no more than thirty-five. His parents are listed as "unknown," and Winston-Salem, North Carolina, is the place of birth.

50. *Chicago Defender*, July 20, 1929, p. A1. Reports also appeared in the *Pittsburgh Courier*, July 13, 1919, p. 1, and the *New York Age*, July 13, 1929, p. 1. These undoubtedly constitute a small sample.

51. DiSanto, "Henry Johnson's Paradox," p. 14.

52. Ibid., p. 15.

53. S. 2649, "A Bill for the Relief of Henry Johnson," July 14, 1988, accessed November 9, 2013, https://www.govtrack.us/congress/bills/100/s2649.

54. *New York Times*, April 6, 1991, p. 6; H.R. 3017, "A Bill for the Relief of Henry Johnson," July 24, 1991, accessed November 9, 2013, http://thomas.loc.gov.

55. *New York Times*, April 6, 1991, p. 6.

56. DiSanto, "Henry Johnson's Paradox," p. 15.

57. "Governor Pataki's Efforts in Behalf of the Award of the Medal of Honor to Sergeant Henry Johnson," undated document from the files of John Howe and the Henry Johnson for Medal of Honor Committee, in possession of the authors (also available at http://www.snowbizz.com/HWRepublican/HenryJohnson/2-12-Pataki.htmdal of Honor, accessed November 10, 2013).

58. Press release, Senator Charles Schumer, May 21, 2001, accessed November 9, 2013, http://schumer.senate.gov.

59. Ibid.

60. "Governor Pataki Honors WWI Hero Sgt. Henry Johnson," press release, Governor George Pataki, January 10, 2002, Jonathan Sutherland, *African Americans at War: An Encyclopedia,* Volume 1 (Santa Barbara, CA: ABC-CLIO, 2004), pp. 234–236. Jeffrey T. Sammons is the author for whom Purnell conducted the research on Johnson. (Pataki's release is no longer available on the site listed here. However, his role is spelled out at http://ww2.dcmilitary.com/dcmilitary_archives/stories/011802/13160-1.shtml, accessed November 9, 2013.)

61. *New York Times*, February 14, 2003, p. B8.

62. Ibid.

63. "H. R. 569, "To Authorize the President to Award the Medal of Honor Posthumously to Henry Johnson for Acts of Valor during World War I," http://www.govtrack.us/congress, accessed November 9, 2013.

64. "McNulty, Schumer: Bill Naming Albany Postal Facility as 'Henry Johnson Annex,'" press release, Senator Charles Schumer, http://www.senate.gov/~schumer, accessed November 12, 2013; Statement on House and Senate Resolutions, White House, H. R. 480, December 21, 2004, https://www.govtrack.us/congress/bills/108/hr480, accessed December 15, 2013.

65. Sen. Charles E. Schumer, "Recommendation for the Medal of Honor Sergeant Henry Johnson," May 15, 2011 (report provided to Jeffrey Sammons on October 12, 2011, by Caroline Wekselbaum, constituent liaison, office of Senator Charles Schumer, NYC); "Schumer Calls for an Update on His Effort to Secure Medal of Honor for WWI Hero Sergeant Henry Johnson, Ahead of 95th Anniversary of Battle of Henry Johnson," accessed November 10, 2013, http://www.schumer.senate.gov/Newsroom/releases.cfm?&type=1. In 2011 and 2012, the Veterans' Affairs Committee of the New York State Senate memorialized Governor Andrew Cuomo to name May 14 "The Battle of Henry Johnson Day"; see NY Senate Open Legislation K501-2011 and K854-2011 at http://open.nysenate.gov/legislation/bill/K501-2011, accessed December 15, 2013, and http://open.nysenate.gov/legislation/bill/K854-2011, accessed December 15, 2013.

66. Alan G. Hevesi, Comptroller, to John A. Johnson, Commissioner, Office of

Children and Family Services [OCFS], May 8, 2003, Rensselaer, NY, accessed November 9, 2013, http://osc.state.ny.us/audits/allaudits/093003/093003-h/02f43.pdf; Henry Johnson Charter School, http://www.hjcslearn.org/henry-johnson.html, accessed November 9, 2013. The OCFS established the Sergeant Henry Johnson Youth Leadership Academy as an innovative, six-month residential program on the Outward Bound model that promotes education, physical fitness, and wilderness training. It is often described as a youth boot camp. See John A. Johnson to H. Carl McCall, State Comptroller, Albany, NY, Report 2001-D-5, pp. 4, 9, and 28, http://osc.state.ny.us/audits/allaudits/093002/01d5.pdf, accessed November 9, 2013.

67. Owen J. Dwyer, "Interpreting the Civil Rights Movement: Contradiction, Confirmation, and the Cultural Landscape," in *The Civil Rights Movement in American Memory*, ed. Renee C. Romano and Leigh Railford (Athens: University of Georgia Press, 2006), pp. 6 and 10.

68. *Trenton Evening Times*, May 21, 1918, n.p., in Needham Roberts's Files, Trentoniana Collection, Trenton Free Public Library, Trenton, NJ.

69. *Trenton Evening Times*, May 22, 1918, n.p., in Needham Roberts's Files, Trentoniana Collection, Trenton Free Public Library, Trenton, NJ.

70. *Cleveland Advocate*, November 9, 1918, p. 1.

71. *Chicago Defender*, November 9, 1918, p. 5.

72. *Chicago Defender*, November 2, 1918, p. 1, and November 9, 1918, p. 5.

73. *Chicago Defender*, November 9, 1918, p. 5.

74. Ibid.

75. *Trenton State Gazette*, November 7, 1918, p. 1. The *Gazette* reported that Scott had called Roberts "the pride of 12,000,000 negroes" and compared him to a hero of the Civil War. Scott made no reference to the Civil War and on the other matter actually wrote: "The inspiration that you offer him goes out and beyond him to the 12,000,000 American Negroes, each of whom will be heartened by the generous words and public spirited appreciation of patriotic duty nobly performed." Instead of offering praise for Roberts, the statement reinforced Scott's concerns with how blacks negatively perceived the treatment of black soldiers. The *New York Age* carried an abbreviated story of the event on November 16.

76. *Cleveland Advocate*, November 16, 1918, p. 7. The paper ran a copy of Scott's letter, which indicates how far and wide he wanted his message to circulate.

77. Ibid.

78. *Trenton State Gazette*, November 7, 1918, p. 1.

79. State of New Jersey, Return of Birth, #6076, Leedom Roberts, April 28, 1901, to Norman J. Roberts, 38, laborer, and Emma Wilson Roberts, 29, of 33 Wilson Street, Trenton, N.J. Neadom was the fifth of five children. New Jersey State Archives, Trenton.

80. *Chicago Defender*, November 9, 1918, p. 2; *New York Times*, October 31, 1918, p. 13. The meeting was sponsored by the Circle for Negro War Relief.

81. *New York Age*, December 28, 1919, p. 2.

82. Ibid.

83. Little, *From Harlem*, p. 365.

84. *Ohio Monitor*, August 8, 1919, p. 8.

85. *New York Age*, August 18, 1923, p. 1; *Chicago Defender*, August 18, 1923, p. 1, and April 11, 1925, p. 4.

86. *Chicago Defender,* April 11, 1925, p. 4, reported that his wife was named Elgie and resided at 1631 Whitty Street, Houston, Texas. The article does not mention a daughter, Juanita, reportedly born in 1919. See Jon Blackwell, "1918: They Fought Racism on Two Fronts," *Trentonian*, December 6, 1998, n.p., accessed November 9, 2013, http://www.capitalcentury.com/1918.html.

87. Blackwell, "1918: They Fought Racism."

88. *New Jersey Herald News*, November 19, 1938, p. 4.

89. Ibid.

90. Ibid.

91. Giles R. Wright, *Afro-Americans in New Jersey: A Short History* (Trenton: New Jersey Historical Commission, 1989), pp. 63–64.

92. *Chicago Defender*, December 20, 1941, p. 5. Paul Lawrence Dunbar also gave the pair some play in a lengthy article entitled "We Have Fought in All U.S. Wars; If You Doubt It Get Your History," *Chicago Defender*, July 4, 1942, p. 6.

93. Corrected birth certificate, February 21, 1945, #6076, New Jersey State Archives, Trenton, NJ.

94. *Newark News*, April 18, 1949, p. 13.

95. Ibid.; Death Certificate of Neadom Roberts, #13390, State Department of Health of New Jersey, State Bureau of Vital Statistics, Trenton, NJ. The newspaper article lists the spelling of Roberts's name in the suicide note as *Neadham*. One would think that his wife knew the correct spelling of his name and that the press changed it to comport with their records. In fact, the article lists the couple as Mr. and Mrs. Neadham Roberts and then changes the spelling in the death notice on April 20 to Neadom.

96. *Newark News*, April 18, 1949, p. 13, and April 20, 1949, n.p.; *Newark Star Ledger*, April 19, 1949, p. 13; *New York Age*, April 23, 1949, pp. 1 and 9; *Amsterdam News*, April 23, 1949, pp. 1 and 27.

97. *New York Age*, April 30, p. 11. According to the medical examiner, Harrison S. Martland, Neadom first placed a noose with a fixed knot around the neck of his wife and then placed a second noose with a loose knot around his own neck. The fixed knot could not have been tied or applied by his wife. Then, they kicked away the box upon which they stood.

98. *Trenton Sunday Times-Advertiser*, March 31, 1957, p. 71, and October 17, 1965, p. 33.

99. Blackwell, "1918: They Fought Racism."

100. State of New Jersey, Joint Legislative Resolution, honoring "the memory of Needham Roberts, pays tribute to his meritorious acts of valor, and extends best wishes for his continued success and happiness," by Senator Turner, Assemblyman Gusciora, and Assemblywoman Watson Coleman, Senate and General Assembly, State House, Trenton, NJ. Found in Needham Roberts's files at the Trentoniana Collection, Trenton Free Public Library, March 15, 2002.

### Epilogue

1. *New York Age,* May 17, 1919, pp. 1 and 6.

2. Ibid.

3. *New York Age,* May 17, 1919, pp. 1 and 6; *Chicago Defender,* June 28, 1919, p. 10.

4. *New York Times,* May 12, 1919, p. 12.

5. *New York Age,* May 17, 1919, p. 1.

6. Ibid.; *New York Times,* May 14, 1919, p. 17; Badger, *Life in Ragtime,* pp. 222–223.

7. *Amsterdam News,* May 2, 1942, p. 23.

8. *New York Times,* April 28, 1942, p. 21; *New York Age,* May 2, 1942, p. 1; *Amsterdam News,* May 2, 1942, p. 1.

9. *New York Age,* May 17, 1919, p. 6.

10. Service Record, Charles Ward Fillmore, NYSMM.

11. *Amsterdam News,* May 2, 1942, pp. 1 and 23; *New York Age,* April 5, 1930, p. 1.

12. *Amsterdam News,* May 2, 1942, pp. 1 and 23; *New York Age,* May 2, 1942, p. 1.

13. Beth Bailey, "The 'Double-V' Campaign in World War II Hawaii: African Americans, Racial Ideology, and Federal Power," *Journal of Social History* 26, no. 4 (Summer 1993): 3–4; *Chicago Defender,* June 17, 1944, p. 5.

14. *New York Times,* September 21, 1947, p. S8.

15. *Chicago Defender,* May 27, 1950, p. 5.

16. Marshall, *Providential Armistice,* p. 6; *New York Age,* December 14, 1918, p. 1.

17. *Chicago Defender,* December 18, 1920, p. 1, and November 26, 1921, p. 9; Brenda Gayle Plummer, *Rising Wind: Black Americans and U.S. Foreign Affairs, 1935–1960* (Chapel Hill: University of North Carolina Press, 1996), pp. 125–140.

18. Washington Conservatory of Music Collection, Finding Aid, p. 9, MSRC.

19. *New York Times,* June 8, 1933, p. 19; Marshall, *Providential Armistice,* pp. 11–12.

20. Stephen May, "Horace Pippin: World War I Veteran and Artist," http://www.historynet.com/horace-pippin-world-war-i-veteran-and-artist.htm, accessed December 15, 2013, originally published online June 12, 2006.

21. Karen Wilkin, "The Naïve & the Modern: Horace Pippin & Jacob Lawrence," *New Criterion,* 13, no. 7 (March 1995): 34. In Wilkin's view, there is no doubt Pippin does not belong in the pantheon of great modern artists, including Jacob Lawrence to whom he has been compared even in a joint retrospective. For a very different view, see Steve Conn, "The Politics of Painting: Horace Pippin the Historian," *American Studies* 38, no. 1 (Spring 1997): 24. Conn maintains that Pippin was much more interested in teaching through his art than Lawrence and had far less interest in Modernist experiments with form. His paintings were to give "lessons about justice, freedom, and humanity."

22. May, "Horace Pippin"; Conn, "Politics of Painting," 5–8. For historical marker, see http://explorepahistory.com/hmarker.php?markerId=1-A-1A0, accessed November 10, 2013.

23. *New York Times,* September 28, 1927, p. 6.

24. *Amsterdam News,* December 27, 1975, p. A1; *New York Times,* December 18, 1975, p. 48.

25. *Chicago Defender,* July 5, 1941, p. 21.

26. *New York Times*, December 18, 1975, p. 48; *Chicago Defender*, April 6, 1940, p. 21, and August 19, 1939, p. 1; *New York Age*, May 2, 1925, p. 1.

27. *New York Age*, May 2, 1925, p. 1, and August 19, 1939, p. 1; *New York Times*, December 18, 1975, p. 48; *Amsterdam News*, December 27, 1975, p. A1.

28. *New York Times*, April 14, 1919, p. 8, and April 28, 1919, p. 14.

29. *Amsterdam News*, December 16, 1925, p. 9; *New York Age*, February 22, 1919, p. 1; *Albany Times Union*, March 27, 1919, n.p.

30. Hayward, *Haywire,* p. 99. See this work for a fuller biographical treatment of Hayward and his son's dysfunctional family, which included fame, fortune, and unimaginable tragedy.

31. *New York Age*, July 10, 1920, p. 4, and June 11, 1921, p. 1.

32. *New York Age*, July 2, 1921, p. 1.

33. *New York Age*, July 21, 1921, p. 1.

34. *New York Times*, October 14, 1944, p. 13, and March 8, 1926, p. 1.

35. *New York Times*, October 14, 1944, p. 13; David Patrick Columbia, "New York Social Diary.com," April 12, 2001, accessed November 10, 2013, http://www.newyork socialdiary.com/; Hayward, *Haywire,* p. 106. The inside scoop on the funeral was that Hayward's widow had asked his son, Leland Hayward, to attend to the funeral arrangements. The son believed that his father would have wanted an austere and dignified affair befitting a military hero. Instead of the pine coffin he had in mind, however, his stepmother purchased a $6,000 bronze casket and, despite her enormous wealth, sent the bill to Leland (p. 107).

36. Unidentified clipping in Gumby Collection, BLCU; the article references the opinion of James Anderson, editor of the *Amsterdam News,* that Hayward was not responsible for the transfer of black officers and that the soldiers had nothing but the highest regard for him. Moreover, were he to run for state or national office, black New Yorkers would support him. The date of the article would be very close to the return of the 369th in February of 1919, as it references the mustering out of soldiers.

37. *New York Age*, February 23, 1929, p. 4.

38. *Brooklyn Daily Eagle*, July 1943, p. 7.

39. *Brooklyn Daily Eagle*, February 9, 1941, p. 8, and July 19, 1943, p. 7.

40. *New York Times*, July 19, 1943, p. 15.

41. Ibid.

42. *New York Times*, October 14, 1943, p. 23.

43. Ibid.

44. *Amsterdam News*, May 11, 1927, p. 2.

45. *Pittsburgh Courier*, April 8, 1944, p. 1; *Baltimore Afro-American,* March 4, 1944, p. 1.

46. *Amsterdam News*, November 19, 1983, p. 41; *Baltimore Afro-American,* February 7, 1987, p. 5; *Amsterdam News*, April 26, 1986, p. 12.

47. *New York Times*, January 20, 1991, online obituaries, http://www.nytimes.com/1991/01/20/obituaries/hamilton-fish-in-congress-24-years-dies-at-102.html, accessed December 15, 2013.

48. Ken Peterson, "Kansan Exceptional in Both War, Peace," *Topeka Daily Capitol*, May 19, 1971, n.p.; see http://www.snowbizz.com/HWRepublican/George_Robb/georgerobb.htm, accessed December 15, 2013.

49. See http://www.snowbizz.com/HWRepublican/George_Robb/georgerobb.htm; Nate Jenkins, "Salinan Won Congressional Medal of Honor for World War I Heroics," *Salina Journal*, May 28, 2000, n.p., see www.snowbizz.com/HWRepublican/George_Robb/pershings10, accessed November 10, 2013.

50. George Robb to Arthur W. Little, November 27, 1936, *"Harlem to the Rhine File,"* NYSMM.

51. *Salina Journal*, May 28, 2000, n.p.; "Kansas War Hero in WWI Dies," unidentified newspaper, pp. 1–2, George S. Robb File, NYSMM.

52. Lewis E. Shaw to Adjutant General United States Army, March 29, 1921, Shaw Collection, Manuscript Division, NYHS.

53. Special Orders no. 116, May 18, 1921, J. Leslie Kincaid, the Adjutant General, New York National Guard, and Content Note, both in Shaw Collection, Manuscript Division, NYHS; Officer Card, 369th Regiment, NYSMM.

54. Robert P. Holliday to Arthur W. Little, August 10, 1937, *"Harlem to Rhine* File," NYSMM.

55. Special Orders no. 196 (1917) and Officers Cards, NYSMM; Final Muster Roll, 15th NY Infantry, July 15, 1917 to August 4, 1917, B0814–85, NYSA.

56. *New York Times*, June 10, 1939, p. 17.

57. *New York Times*, October 25, 1940, p. 19.

## Primary Sources

### Archives, Manuscript Collections, and Government Records

Abstracts of World War I Military Service, 1917–1919. RG B0808. NYSA.

*Black British Subjects in British Army.* File WO 32/4765. (British) National Archives, Kew, Richmond, Surrey.

*Booker T. Washington Papers.* Edited by Louis R. Harlan and Raymond W. Smock. Champaign-Urbana: University of Illinois Press, 1972–1989.

Castles, John Wesley, Jr. Castles Papers and "War Diary of John Wesley Castles, Jr." USMAL.

Cheatham, Henry P. Cheatham Papers. SCRBC.

Colored Work Department Records. Letters, 1918–1919. YMCA Archives, University of Minnesota, Minneapolis, MN.

Fish, Hamilton. Fish Papers. NYSLMC.

*"From Harlem to the Rhine* File." NYSMM.

Gilroy, Thomas F. Gilroy Papers. General Correspondence, Box 1450, Folder 120, NYMA.

Gumby Collection. BLCU.

Henry Johnson for MOH Committee. John Howe private collection. Albany, NY.

House, Edward M. House Papers. MS 466, Series 1, Volume 2, Box 70 A, Folder 2331. SLYU.

Johnson, James Weldon. Johnson Papers. BLYU.

Loving, Walter. Loving Papers. Series D, Mil., Box 113-1. MSRC.

MacMorris, Daniel. MacMorris Papers. Liberty Memorial Museum, Kansas City, MO.

Medical Center for Federal Prisoners, Springfield, MO. In Bureau of Prisons Archives, Washington, DC.

NAACP Papers. Group 1, Box C-374, Adm. File, Gen., Dec. 1919, Misc. LOCMD.
——. Mil., Gen., Box C-375. LOCMD.

NARA–Central Plains Region. RG 276, 8th Circuit Court of Appeals, Record of Transcripts and Briefs, Kansas City, MO.

National Archives and Records Administration. RG 92, 117, 120, 153, 165, 168, 407, JAG 210.14. NARA.

National Archives of Canada. RG 150, Accession 92–93/166, Box 8693-15. http://www.collectionscanada.gc.ca/databases/cef/001042-100.01-e.php.

National Guard Muster Rolls, 1878–1954. RG 13726-86. NYSA.

Nicholls, Samuel J. Nicholls Papers. Perkins Library, DUMC.

Pippin, Horace. Pippin Collection. "Horace Pippin's Autobiography, First World War," "Composition Book," and "Notebooks, c. 1920." AAA, SI.

Robb, George. Robb File. NYSMM.

Roberts, Needham [Neadom]. Roberts Files. Trentoniana Collection, Trenton Free Public Library, Trenton, NJ.

Service Historique de l'Armée de Terre, Vincennes, France (SHAT). 6N141, 7N1717, 16N1698, 17N76, 24N2729–2733, 26N297, Nos. 162/0, 175/0.

Shaw, Lewis W. Shaw Papers. Manuscript Division, NYHS.

Spingarn, Joel. Spingarn Papers. RG 95, MSRC.

State Bureau of Vital Statistics. State Department of Health of New Jersey, Trenton, NJ.

Stimson, Henry L. Stimson Diaries. SLYU.

Strong, William L., Strong Papers. Box 90. NYMA.

Sulzer, William. Sulzer Papers. Box 16, RG 1147. KLCU.

Taft, William Howard. Taft Papers. Reels 368, 372, 406, and 417. LOCMD.

369th Lineage and Honors. Department of the Army. NYSMM.

Vital Records. District of Columbia Department of Health, Washington, DC.

Washington Conservatory of Music Collection. MSRC.

Watts, Faulkner. Watts Papers. SCRBC.

Young, Charles. Young Collection, Ohio Historical Society online. Papers, General Correspondence. http://dbs.ohiohistory.org/africanam/home.cfm.

**Newspapers and Periodicals**

*Albany Argus*
*Albany Times Union*
*Baltimore Afro-American*
*Bergen County (NJ) Record*
*Brooklyn Daily Eagle*
*Camp Wadsworth Gas Attack and Rio Grande Rattler* (27th Division), NYSMM
*Chicago Defender*
*Cleveland Advocate*
*Cleveland Gazette*
*The Crisis*
*Knickerbocker Press* (Albany)
*The Messenger*
*Newark News*
*New Jersey Herald News*
*New York Age*
*New York American*
*New York Amsterdam News*
*New York Evening Sun*
*New York Evening World*
*New York Herald*
*New York National Guardsman*
*New York Sun*
*New York Times*
*New York Tribune*

New York World
Pittsburgh Courier
Spartanburg (SC) Herald
Spartanburg (SC) Journal and Carolina Spartan
St. Louis Republic
Trenton Evening Times
Trentonian
Trenton State Gazette

## Government Publications and Legal Cases

*Annual Report of the Adjutant-General of the State of New York for the Year 1914 [1916,*
*1917, 1918–1919, and 1920].* Albany, NY: J. B. Lyon, 1916 [1917, 1920, 1921, and 1923].
NYSMM.

*Army Regulations.* Chap. 28, pp. 670–671, "Wear and Appearance of Army
Uniforms and Insignia," September 1, 1992, sect. 28-4d, "Unauthorized Wearing
of Medals." http://www.americal.org/awards/wearing.htm. *United States
Code,* Title 18, chap. 33, sect. 704, August 3, 2005.

Bach, C. A. "Leadership." Unpublished essay. Fort Sheridan Training Camp.
November 24, 1917. Sneed Papers. Military History Institute, Carlisle, PA.

Birdseye, Clarence Frank, Robert Cushing Cumming, and Frank Bixby Gilbert,
eds. *Annotated Consolidated Laws of the State of New York.* 2nd ed., vol. 5. New
York: Banks Law Publishing, 1918.

*Butts v. Merchants & Miners Transportation Co.,* 230 U.S. 126, June 16, 1913.

Gay, George I., with H. H. Fisher. *Public Relations of the Commission for Relief in
Belgium Documents.* Stanford, CA: Stanford University Press, 1929.

GPO, 1917. War Department, Army Regulations.. Reference Division, NARA.

H.R. 3017. "A Bill for the Relief of Henry Johnson." July 24, 1991. https://www.
govtrack.us/congress/bills/browse#text=henry+johnson&congress=102.

Hulbert, Murray. "The Negro as Soldier and a Sailor." Remarks, September 6, 1916.
*Congressional Record.* Washington, DC: Government Printing Office, 1916.

*List and Directory: National Guard and Naval Militia, State of New York.* January 1,
1922, NYSMM.

*New York State Division of Military and Naval Affairs News.* Media Advisory Index.
November 13, 2008.

S. 2649. "A Bill for the Relief of Henry Johnson." July 14, 1988. https://www.
govtrack.us/congress/bills/browse#text=henry+johnson&congress=100.

*Schita v. Cox,* No. 12682, US Court of Appeals, Eighth Circuit, 139 F. 2d 971, January
21, 1944.

*Schita v. King,* No. 12402, US Court of Appeals, Eighth Circuit, 133 F. 2d 283,
February 15, 1943.

Sprenger, James Albert, and Franklin Spencer Almonds, eds. *The Leave Areas of the
American Expeditionary Forces, 1918–1919.* Philadelphia: John C. Winston, 1928.

*Statutes at Large, Treaties, and Proclamations of the United States of America.* Vol. 12.
Boston, 1863.

*United States v. Valdo B. Schita*, Case No. 108885, General Court-Martial, No. 1320, Headquarters Eastern Department, November 27–December 17, 1917. RG 153, NARA.

Wadhams, Frederick E., ed. *The Consolidated Laws of the State of New York.* Vol. 2. Albany, NY: J. B. Lyon, 1909.


**Memoirs**

Baker, Newton D. *Why We Went to War.* New York: Harper & Brothers, 1936.

Davis, Arthur P. *Here and There with the Rattlers.* Detroit, MI: Harlo, 1979.

Hunton, Addie W. *William Alphaeus Hunton: A Pioneer Prophet of Young Men.* New York: G. K. Hall, 1997.

Hunton, Addie W., and Kathryn M. Johnson. *Two Colored Women with the American Expeditionary Forces.* New York: AMS Press, 1971 [1920].

Little, Arthur W. *From Harlem to the Rhine: The Story of New York's Colored Volunteers.* New York: Covici Friede, 1936.

Lunn, Joe. *Memoirs of the Maelstrom: A Senegalese Oral History of the First World War.* Portsmouth, NH: Heinemann, 1999.

Mangin, Charles. *La Force Noire.* Paris: Hachette, 1910.

March, Peyton C. *The Nation at War.* Garden City, NY: Doubleday, Doran, 1932.

Marshall, Napoleon Bonaparte. *The Providential Armistice.* Washington, DC: Liberty League, 1930.

Moton, Robert Russa. *Finding a Way Out: An Autobiography.* New York: Negro Universities Press, 1969 [1920].

Pershing, John J. *My Experiences in the Great War.* 2 vols. New York: Frederick A. Stokes, 1931.

Roberts, Neadom. "Brief Adventures of the First American Soldiers Decorated in the World War as Told by Neadom Roberts." February 10, 1933.

Sissle, Noble Lee. "Memoirs of Lieutenant 'Jim' Europe." Unpublished manuscript, 1942. NAACP Papers, Group 2, Boxes J 56 and J 70. LOCMD.


**Contemporary Articles and Works**

Bullard, Robert Lee. "The Negro as Volunteer: Some Characteristics." *Journal of the Military Service Institution of the United States* 29 (July 1901): 29–39.

Carpenter, W. Spencer. "The Negro Soldier's Contribution in the Wars of the United States." *African Methodist Episcopal Church Review* 29, no. 3 (January 1913): 215–224.

Cobb, Irvin S. *The Glory of the Coming.* New York: Doran, 1918.

Colson, William N. "The Immediate Function of the Negro Veteran." *The Messenger,* November 1919.

———. "Shoddyism Called History." *The Messenger,* November 1919.

Colson, W. N., and A. B. Nutt. "The Failure of the Ninety-Second Division." *The Messenger,* September 1919, pp. 80–83.

Du Bois, W. E. B. "The President and the Soldiers." *The Voice of the Negro* 3, no. 12 (December 1906): 552–553.

Foraker, Joseph B. "A Review of the Testimony in the Brownsville Investigation." *North American Review* 187, no. 4 (April 1908): 550–558.

Guthrie, James M. *Camp-Fires of the Afro-American, or The Colored Man as Patriot, Soldier, Sailor, and Hero in the Cause of Free America.* Philadelphia: Afro-American Publisher, 1899; reprinted by Johnson Printing, 1970.

Haynes, George E. "The Church and the Negro Spirit." *Survey Graphic* (March 1925): 695–709.

Hayward, William. *Mother's Sons of the Fighting "15th."* New York: William Moseby, 1919. Clipping File, 1925–1974, "World War I, 1914–1918," SC 005.880-2, SCRBC.

McNutt, William Slavens. *The Yanks Are Coming.* New York: Page, 1918.

Pickens, William. "The Negro in the Light of the Great War: Basis for the New Reconstruction." 3rd ed. Baltimore, MD: *Daily Herald Print,* 1919.

Scott, Emmett J. *The American Negro in the World War.* Chicago: Homewood, 1919; reprinted as *Scott's Official History of the American Negro in the World War,* by Arno Press, 1969.

Steele, Matthew F. "The 'Color Line" in the Army." *North American Review* 183, no. 605 (December 21, 1906): 1285–1288.

Sweeney, Allison W. *History of the American Negro in the Great World War.* Chicago: Cuneo-Henneberry, 1919; reprinted by Negro Universities Press, 1969.

Terrell, Mary Church. "The Disbanding of the Colored Soldiers." *The Voice of the Negro* 3, no. 12 (December 1906): 554–558.

Thomas, Rolla L. *The Eclectic Practice of Medicine.* Cincinnati, OH: Scudder Brothers, 1906.

Verbeck, William. "The Employer's Duty to the Militia." *Militia Journal* 1, no. 2 (January-February 1913): 60–74.

Villard, Oswald Garrison. "The Negro as Soldier and Officer." *Nation,* August 1, 1901, p. 85.

———. "The Negro in the Regular Army." *Atlantic Monthly,* June 1903, pp. 721–729.

Welcome, Madame Toussaint. *A Pictorial History of the Negro in the Great War, 1917–1918.* New York: Toussaint Pictorial, 1919.

Wiley, Hugh. "The Four-Leaved Wildcat." *Saturday Evening Post,* March 8, 1919.

### Secondary Sources

**Books and Articles**

Anderson, Richard. "The United States Army in World War II: Manpower, Replacements, and the Segregated Army." Military History Online.com, 2000, http://www.militaryhistoryonline.com/wwii/usarmy/manpower.aspx, accessed December 15, 2013.

Badger, Reid. *A Life in Ragtime: A Biography of James Reese Europe.* New York: Oxford University Press, 1995.

———. "Pride without Prejudice: The Day New York 'Drew No Color Line.'" *Prospects: An Annual of American Cultural Studies,* vol. 16, 1991, pp. 405–420.

Bailey, Beth, and David Farber. "The 'Double-V' Campaign in World War II

Hawaii: African Americans, Racial Ideology, and Federal Power." *Journal of Social History* 26, no. 4 (Summer 1993): 817–843.

———. *The First Strange Place: The Alchemy of Race and Sex in World War II Hawaii.* New York: Free Press, 1993.

Benefiel, Gregg. "A Treatise on the Proper Execution of Guard Mount in Garrison or in the Field," 1999. http://www.19thalabama.org/onguard.doc.

Bernard, Gilles, and Pierre Besnard. "Les Combattants Noirs Américains de la Première Guerre Mondiale, 1917–1918." *Militaria,* no. 118 (May 1995): 11–24.

Berry, Mary Frances, and John W. Blassingame. *Long Memory: The Black Experience in America.* New York: Oxford University Press, 1982.

Biondi, Martha. *To Stand and Fight: The Struggle for Civil Rights in Postwar New York City.* Cambridge, MA: Harvard University Press, 2003.

Blackwell, Jon. "1918: They Fought Racism on Two Fronts." *Trentonian,* December 6, 1998. http://www.capitalcentury.com/1918.html.

Bogle, Donald. *Toms, Coons, Mulattoes, Mammies, and Bucks: An Interpretive History of Blacks in American Films.* 4th ed. New York: Continuum, 2001.

Brown, Nikki. *Private Politics and Public Voices: Black Women's Activism from World War I to the New Deal.* Bloomington: Indiana University Press, 2006.

———. "'Your Patriotism Is of the Purest Quality': African American Women and World War I." Ph.D. diss., Yale University, 2002.

Bruce, Robert B. *A Fraternity of Arms: America and France in the Great War.* Lawrence: University Press of Kansas, 2003.

Bundles, A'Lelia. *On Her Own Ground: The Life and Times of Madam C. J. Walker.* New York: Scribner, 2001.

Chew, Abraham. *A Biography of Colonel Charles Young.* Washington, DC: R. I. Pendleton, 1923.

Chickering, Roger, and Stig Förster. *Great War, Total War: Combat and Mobilization on the Western Front, 1914–1918.* Cambridge: Cambridge University Press, 2000.

Cooper, Jerry M. "National Guard Reform, the Army, and the Spanish-American War: The View from Wisconsin." *Military Affairs* 42, no. 1 (February 1978): 20–23.

———. *The Rise of the National Guard: The Evolution of the American Militia, 1865–1920.* Lincoln: University of Nebraska Press, 1997.

Cripps, Thomas. *Making Movies Black: The Hollywood Movie from World War II to the Civil Rights Era.* New York: Oxford University Press, 1993.

Dalessandro, Robert J., and Gerald Torrence. *Willing Patriots: Men of Color in the First World War.* Altglen, PA: Schiffer Military History, 2009.

Daynes, Gary. "United Colored Democracy." In *Organizing Black America: An Encyclopedia of African American Associations,* edited by Nina Mjagkij. New York: Garland Publishing, 2001.

Dillard, Tom W. "Golden Prospects and Fraternal Amenities: Mifflin W. Gibbs' Arkansas Years." *Arkansas Historical Quarterly* 35 (Winter 1976): 307–333.

DiSanto, Victor J. "Henry Johnson's Paradox: A Soldier's Story." *Afro-Americans in New York Life and History* 21, no. 2 (July 1997): 7–18.

Doughty, Robert A. "More Than Numbers: Americans and the Revival of French

Morale in the Great War." *Army History: The Professional Bulletin of the Army History,* no. 52 (Spring 2001): 1–11.

———. *Pyrrhic Victory: French Strategy and Operations in the Great War.* Cambridge, MA: Belknap Press of Harvard University Press, 2008.

Dwyer, Owen J. "Interpreting the Civil Rights Movement: Contradiction, Confirmation, and the Cultural Landscape." In *The Civil Rights Movement in American Memory,* edited by Renee C. Romano and Leigh Railford. Athens: University of Georgia Press, 2006.

Eisenhower, John S. D. *Yanks: The Epic Story of the American Army in WWI.* New York: Free Press, 2001.

Ellis, Mark. *Race, War, and Surveillance: African Americans and the United States Government during World War.* Bloomington: Indiana University Press, 2001.

Daniel Ennis, "Poetry and the American Revolutionary Identity: The Case of Phillis Wheatley and John Paul Jones," *Studies in Eighteenth Century Culture* 31 (2002): 85–98.

Farwell, Byron. *Over There: The United States in the Great War, 1917–1918.* New York: W. W. Norton, 1999.

Faulkner, Richard S. "Disappearing Doughboys: The American Expeditionary Forces' Straggler Crisis in the Meuse-Argonne." *Army History,* no. 83 (Spring 2012): 6–25.

———. *The School of Hard Knocks: Combat Leadership in the American Expeditionary Forces.* College Station: Texas A&M University Press, 2012.

Ferrell, Robert H. *America's Deadliest Battle: Meuse-Argonne, 1918.* Lawrence: University Press of Kansas, 2007.

———. *Unjustly Dishonored: An African American Division in World War I.* Columbia: University of Missouri Press, 2011.

Finley, James P. "Colonel Charles Young: Black Cavalryman, Huachuca Commander, and Early Intelligence Officer." *Huachuca Illustrated: A Magazine of the Fort Huachuca Museum,* 1, 1999. http://net.lib.byu.edu/~rdh7/wwi/comment/huachuca/HI1-19.htm?.

Fletcher, Marvin E. *America's First Black General: Benjamin O. Davis, Sr., 1880–1970.* Lawrence: University Press of Kansas, 1989.

Franklin, John Hope, and Alfred A. Moss, Jr. *From Slavery to Freedom: A History of African Americans.* 7th ed., vol. 2. New York: McGraw-Hill, 1994.

Gaines, Kevin. *Uplifting the Race: Black Leadership, Politics, and Culture in the Twentieth Century.* Chapel Hill: University of North Carolina Press, 1996.

Gorn, Elliot, J. *The Manly Art: Bare-Knuckle Prize Fighting in America.* Ithaca, NY: Cornell University Press, 1986.

Greenberg, Cheryl Lynn. *"Or Does It Explode?": Black Harlem in the Great Depression.* New York: Oxford University Press, 1991.

Guttman, Jon. "Regiment's Pride." *Military History* 8 (October 1991): 34–41.

Hardwick, Leon H. "Negro Stereotypes on the Screen." *Hollywood Quarterly* 1, no. 2 (January 1946): 234–236.

*Harlem Hellfighters.* Fisher/Merlis Television. The History Channel. February 23, 1997.

Harris, Leslie M. *In the Shadow of Slavery: African Americans in New York City, 1626–1863*. Chicago: University of Chicago Press, 2003.

Harris, Stephen L. *Harlem's Hell Fighters: The African-American 369th Infantry in World War I*. Washington, DC: Brassey's, 2003.

Harris, William. *The Hellfighters of Harlem: African-American Soldiers Who Fought for the Right to Fight for Their Country*. New York: Carroll & Graf Publishers, 2002.

Hauser, Robert E. "'The Georgia Experiment': President Warren G. Harding's Attempt to Reorganize the Republican Party in Georgia." *Georgia Historical Quarterly* 62, no. 4 (Winter 1978): 288–303.

Hawkins, Gabriel. "The Eighth Infantry Goes to Cuba." *Newsletter of the Illinois State Military Museum* 2, no. 4 (Fall 1998): 1–2.

Hayward, Brooke. *Haywire*. New York: Alfred A. Knopf, 1977.

Henritze, Barbara K. *Bibliographic Checklist of African American Newspapers*. Baltimore, MD: Genealogical Publishing, 1995.

Herring, George C., Jr. "James Hay and the Preparedness Controversy, 1915–1916." *Journal of Southern History* 30, no. 4 (November 1964): 383–404.

Higonnet, Margaret Randolph, Jane Jenson, Sonya Michelle, and Margaret Collins Weitz, eds. *Behind the Lines: Gender and the Two World Wars*. New Haven, CT: Yale University Press, 1987.

Hine, Darlene Clark. *Black Women in White: Racial Conflict and Cooperation in the Nursing Profession*. Bloomington: Indiana University Press, 1989.

Hine, Darlene Clark, William C. Hine, and Stanley Harrold. *The African American Odyssey*. Upper Saddle River, NJ: Prentice Hall, 2000.

Hogg, Ian V., and John S. Weeks. *Military Small Arms of the 20th Century*. 7th ed. Iolam, WI: Krause, 2000.

Holt, Thomas. "Marking: Race, Race-Making, and the Writing of History." *American Historical Review* 100, no. 1 (February 1995): 1–20.

Horne, Lena, and Richard Schickel. *Lena*. New York: Doubleday, 1965.

Horsley, Carter B. "The Haussner's Restaurant Collection: 19th Century European and American Paintings." http://www.thecityreview.com/f99shaus.html.

Hutner, Geraldine R. "Crossing the Color Barrier in New Jersey." *New Jersey Medicine: The Journal of the Medical Society of New Jersey* 91, no. 8 (August 1994): 527–531.

Johnson, Charles, Jr. *African American Soldiers in the National Guard: Recruitment and Deployment during Peacetime and War*. Westport, CT: Greenwood Press, 1992.

———. "Black Soldiers in the National Guard, 1877–1949." Ph.D. diss., Howard University, 1976.

Johnson, James Weldon. *The Autobiography of an Ex-Colored Man* (1912). In *Three Negro Classics*. New York: Avon Books, 1995.

Kane, Joseph N. *Facts about the Presidents: A Compilation of Biographical and Historical Information* 5th ed. New York: H. W. Wilson, 1989.

Keegan, John. *The First World War*. New York: Alfred A. Knopf, 1999.

Keene, Jennifer D. *Doughboys, the Great War, and the Remaking of America*. Baltimore, MD: Johns Hopkins University Press, 2001.

Kellogg, Charles Flint. *NAACP: A History of the National Association for the Advancement of Colored People.* Baltimore, MD: Johns Hopkins University Press, 1973.

Kennedy, Kathleen. *Disloyal Mothers and Scurrilous Citizens: Women and Subversion during World War I.* Bloomington: Indiana University Press, 1999.

Kennett, Lee. "The Camp Wadsworth Affair." *South Atlantic Quarterly* 74, no. 2 (Spring 1975): 197–211.

Knight, Arthur L., III. "Dis-integrating the Musical: African American Musical Performance and the American Musical Film, 1927–1959." Ph.D. diss., University of Chicago, August 1998.

Koppes, Clayton R., and Gregory D. Black. "Blacks, Loyalty, and Motion Picture Propaganda in World War II." *Journal of American History* 73, no. 2 (September 1986): 383–406.

Kryder, Daniel. *Divided Arsenal: Race and the American State during World War II.* New York: Cambridge University Press, 2001.

Kudlick, Walter. "African-American Soldier and Artist." *Stand To! The Journal of the Western Front Association,* no. 48 (January 1997): 10–14.

Lengel, Edward G. *To Conquer Hell: The Meuse-Argonne, 1918—The Epic Battle That Ended the First World War.* New York: Henry Holt, 2008.

Lentz-Smith, Adriane. *Freedom Struggles: African Americans and World War I.* Cambridge, MA: Harvard University Press, 2009.

Levitch, Mark. *Panthéon de la Guerre.* Columbia: University of Missouri Press, 2006.

Lewis, David Levering. *W. E. B. Du Bois: Biography of a Race, 1868–1919.* New York: Henry Holt, 1993.

———. *W. E. B. Du Bois: The Fight for Equality and the American Century, 1919–1963.* New York: Henry Holt, 2000.

———. *When Harlem Was in Vogue.* New York: Oxford University Press, 1979.

Long, Howard. "Review of *From Harlem to the Rhine.*" *Journal of Negro History* 21, no. 4 (October 1936): 444–447.

Lorini, Alessandra. *Rituals of Race: American Public Culture and the Search for Racial Democracy.* Charlottesville: University of Virginia Press, 1999.

Mahon, John K., and Romana Danysh. *Infantry Part I: Regular Army,* Army Lineage Series, 1971. http://www.army.mil/cmh-pg/books/Lineage/in/infantry.htm.

Man, Albon P., Jr. "Labor Competition and the New York Draft Riots of 1863." *Journal of Negro History* 36, no. 4 (October 1951): 375–405.

Massood, Paula J. *Black City Cinema: African American Urban Experiences in Film.* Philadelphia: Temple University Press, 2003.

May, Stephen. "Horace Pippin: World War I Veteran and Artist." http://www.historynet.com/culture/african_american_history. Originally published in February 1998 issue of *Military History.*

Mead, Gary. *The Doughboys. America and the First World War.* Woodstock, NY: Overlook Press, 2000.

*Men of Bronze: The Black American Heroes of World War I.* Directed by William Miles. Men of Bronze, Inc. 1977. DVD. Direct Cinema Limited, 1996.

Mjagkij, Nina. *Light in the Darkness: African Americans and the YMCA, 1852–1946.* Lexington: University Press of Kentucky, 1994.

———. *Loyalty in Time of Trial: The African American Experience during World War I.* Lanham, MD: Rowman & Littlefield, 2011.

Morrison, Toni. *Jazz.* New York: Alfred A. Knopf, 1992.

Morrow, John H., Jr. *The Great War: An Imperial History.* London: Routledge, 2004.

Mosier, John. *The Myth of the Great War: A New Military History of World War I.* New York: HarperCollins, 2002.

Nelson, Peter. *A More Unbending Battle: The Harlem Hellfighters' Struggle for Freedom in WWI and Equality at Home.* New York: Basic Civitas, 2009.

Newton, Isham G. "The Negro and the National Guard." *Phylon* 23, no. 1 (1st quarter 1962): 18–28.

Noble, Peter. *The Negro in Films.* New York: Arno Press, 1970.

Osofsky, Gilbert. *Harlem: The Making of a Ghetto—Negro New York, 1890–1930.* New York: Harper & Row, 1966.

Perlman, Michael David. "To Make Democracy Safe for the World: A Social History of the Origins, Development and Aftermath of the World War I Military Preparedness Movement in America." Ph.D. diss., University of Illinois, 1978.

Plummer, Brenda Gayle. "The Afro-American Response to the Occupation of Haiti, 1915–1934." *Phylon* 43, no. 2 (2nd quarter 1982): 125–143.

Powell, Anthony. *Black Participation in the Spanish American War.* http://www.spanamwar.com/6thmasscol.htm.

Quarles, Benjamin. *The Negro in the Making of America.* New York: Simon & Schuster, 1996.

———. *The Negro in the Revolutionary War.* Chapel Hill: University of North Carolina Press, 1961.

Reich, Steven A. "Soldiers of Democracy: Black Texans and the Fight for Citizenship." *Journal of American History* 82, no. 4 (March 1996): 1478–1504.

Roberts, Frank E. *The American Foreign Legion: Black Soldiers of the 93d in World War I.* Annapolis, MD: Naval Institute Press, 2004.

Rogin, Michael. *Blackface, White Noise: Jewish Immigrants in the Hollywood Melting Pot.* Berkeley: University of California Press, 1996.

Roosevelt, Theodore, Jr. *Rank and File: True Stories of the Great War.* New York: Charles Scribner's.

Rudwick, Elliot. *W. E. B. Du Bois: The Voice of the Black Protest Movement.* Urbana: University of Illinois Press, 1982.

Sacks, Marcy Sarah. *Before Harlem: The Black Experience in New York City before World War I.* Philadelphia: University of Pennsylvania Press, 2006.

———. "'We Cry among the Skyscrapers': Black People in New York City, 1880–1915." Ph.D. diss., University of California–Berkeley, 1999.

Saville, Julie. *The Work of Reconstruction: From Slave to Wage Laborer in South Carolina, 1860–1870.* New York: Cambridge University Press, 1994.

Schell, Jonathan. "No More unto the Breach, Part 1." *Harper's Magazine,* March 2003, pp. 33–46.

———. "No More unto the Breach, Part 2." *Harper's Magazine,* April 2003, pp. 41–55.

Schultz, Evan P. "Group Rights, American Jews, and the Failure of Group Libel Laws, 1913–1952." *Brooklyn Law Review,* 66, no. 71 (Spring 2000), LexisNexis.

Sherman, Richard B. *The Republican Party and Black America: From McKinley to Hoover, 1896–1933.* Charlottesville: University of Virginia Press, 1973.

Shields, John C. *Phillis Wheatley and the Romantics.* Knoxville: University of Tennessee Press, 2010.

Slotkin, Richard. *Lost Battalions: The Great War and the Crisis of American Nationality.* New York: Henry Holt, 2005.

Stein, Judith E., ed. *I Tell My Heart—The Art of Horace Pippin.* New York: Universe Publishing, 1993.

*Stormy Weather.* Directed by Andrew Stone. 20th Century Fox, 1943. DVD. 20th Century Fox Home Entertainment, 2005.

Stovall, Tyler. "The Color Line behind the Lines: Racial Violence in France during the Great War." *American Historical Review* 103, no. 3 (June 1998): 737–769.

Sutherland, Jonathan. *African Americans at War: An Encyclopedia,* Volume 1 (Santa Barbara, CA: ABC-CLIO, 2004.

Taylor, David Vassar. *African Americans in Minnesota.* Minneapolis: Minnesota Historical Society Press, 2002.

Taylor, Durahn. "United Colored Democracy." In *Encyclopedia of African-American Culture and History,* vol. 5., edited by Jack Salzman, David L. Smith, and Cornel West. New York: Simon & Schuster Macmillan, 1996.

Trombold, John. "The Minstrel Show Goes to the Great War: Zora Neale Hurston's Mass Cultural Other." *Melus* 24, no. 1 (Spring 1999): 85–107.

Watkins-Owens, Irma. *Blood Relations: Caribbean Immigrants and the Harlem Community, 1900–1930.* Bloomington: Indiana University Press, 1996.

Weigley, Russel F. *History of the United States Army.* Bloomington: Indiana University Press, 1984.

Weisenfeld, Judith. *African-American Women and Christian Activism: New York's Black YWCA, 1905–1945.* Cambridge, MA: Harvard University Press, 1998.

Wesser, Robert F. *A Response to Progressivism: The Democratic Party and New York Politics, 1902–1918.* New York: New York University Press, 1986.

Whalan, Mark. *The Great War and the Culture of the New Negro.* Gainesville: University of Florida Press, 2008.

Wilkin, Karen. "The Naïve & the Modern: Horace Pippin & Jacob Lawrence." *New Criterion* 13, no. 7 (March 1995): 33.

Williams, Chad. *Torchbearers of Democracy: African American Soldiers in the World War I Era.* Chapel Hill: University of North Carolina Press, 2010.

Williams, Charles Holston. *Negro Soldiers in World War I: The Human Side.* New York: AMS Press, 1979 [1923].

Willis-Braithwaite, Deborah, and Rodger C. Birt. *VanDerZee: Photographer 1886–1983.* New York: Harry N. Abrams, 1993.

Wilson, Judith. "Scenes of War." In *I Tell My Heart—The Art of Horace Pippin,* edited by Judith E. Stein. New York: Universe Publishing, 1993.

Wilson, Walter. "Jim Crow in the A.E.F." *New Republic,* August 26, 1936, p. 81.

Wright, Giles R. *Afro-Americans in New Jersey: A Short History.* Trenton: New Jersey Historical Commission, 1989.

Yockelson, Mitchell A. *Borrowed Soldiers: Americans under British Command, 1918.* Norman: University of Oklahoma Press, 2008.

———. "'I Am Entitled to the Medal of Honor and I Want It': Theodore Roosevelt and His Quest for Glory." US National Archives and Records Administration (NARA). *Prologue Magazine* 30, no. 1 (Spring 1998), http://www .archives.gov/publications/prologue/1998/spring/roosevelt-and-medal-of-honor-1.html, accessed December 15, 2013.

## Websites

http://www.aaregistry.com, accessed November 12, 2013

http://www.defense.gov/specials/AfricanAm2003/honors.html, accessed November 12, 2013

http://www.defenselink.mil/news/jun2000, accessed November 12, 2013

http://www.ehistory.osu.edu/osu/mmh/1912/race/democrat.cfm, accessed November 12, 2013

http://www.8thinfantry.org/hist.html, accessed November 12, 2013

http://www.ellisisland.org, accessed November 12, 2013

http://www.explorepahistory.com/hmarker.php?markerId=1-A-1A0, accessed November 12, 2013

http://www.goantiques.com, accessed November 12, 2013

 http://www.govtrack.us, accessed November 12, 2013

http://www.ivyleaguesports.com/history/blackhistory/2005-06/dartmouth /timeline, accessed November 12, 2013

http://www.ivyleaguesports.com/history/blackhistory/2005-06/harvard /timeline, accessed November 12, 2013

http://www.nps.gov/prsf/historyculture/buffalo-soldiers.htm, accessed November 12, 2013

http://www.nyc-architecture.com/HAR/HAR-History.htm, accessed November 12, 2013

http://www.nycgovparks.org/sub_your_park/historical_signs/hs_historical _sign.php?id=8250, accessed November 12, 2013

http://www.nycroads.com/roads/harlem-river, accessed November 12, 2013

http://www.nysenate.gov/story/5222012-veterans-hall-fame-colonel-stephanie-e -dawson, accessed November 12, 2013, as an archive (no longer active website of Senator Huntley)

http://www.politicalgraveyard.com, accessed November 12, 2013

http://www.rootsweb.com, accessed November 12, 2013

http://schistory.net/campwadsworth, accessed December 15, 2013

http://www.senate.gov/~schumer, accessed November 12, 2013

http://www.snowbizz.com, accessed November 12, 2013

http://www.vernonjohns.org/tcal001/vjharlem.html, accessed November 12, 2013

http://www.yonkershistory.org, accessed November 12, 2013

*Note: italicized numbers indicate photos or illustrations located in gallery*

Abbott, Robert S., 294
Addams, Jane, 40
AEF. *See* American Expeditionary Forces (AEF)
the *Age.* See *New York Age*
Aisne-Marne offensive, 405
*Albany Argus,* 71, 73, 456, 577n15
*Albany Knickerbocker,* 288–289
*Albany Times Union,* 69, 287–288, 455, 456
Aldridge, Ira, 129–130, 527n30
Alexander, Charles M., 331, 348
Alexander, John Hanks, 103, 506n4
Allison, Herbert L., 355
*All Quiet on the Western Front* (Remarque), 304
Alsace campaign, 190, 211, *257*, 363, 366–367, 368, 567n19
American Battle Monuments Commission, 348, 353–354, 355–356, 417–419, 420–421, 447, 497
American Expeditionary Forces (AEF)
  and black officers, 233, 296, 298, 304–305, 324, 347–349
  black troops and overseas mobilization of, 132, 133–134, 185, 189, 191, 195–202, 207, 208, 214–215
  formation of, 201–202
  Henry Johnson and Neadom Roberts investigation by, 270–272
  and postwar black loyalty, 376–377
  and recognition of black soldiers, 358, 360, 361
  and return of black regiments to US control, 311–313
  and treatment of black soldiers, 291, 307, 312, 313–314, 324, 357, 376
  *See also* Pershing, John J.
American Red Cross, 283–284, 286–287, 319, 373, 375
*Amsterdam News.* See *New York Amsterdam News*
Anderson, Charles W.
  and black regiment campaign and recruitment, 46–48, 49, 50, 57–58, 100, 102, 106, 115, 511n23
  Booker T. Washington relations with, 45, 509n11, 516n4
  on Fillmore's loyalty to Republican Party, 521n23
  and McDougald appointment, 519n49
  and Neadom Roberts celebration, 468
  and reception honoring 369th Regiment, 401–402
  and Republican Party ties, 42, 44, 45, 46–48, 49, 100, 516n4
  and Woodrow Wilson's racist policies, 61
Anderson, James, 72–73, 583n36
Armory, 369th, 3, *261*
Army Nurse Corps, 284
Army Reserves, US, 407–408, 410–411, 415
Attucks, Crispus, 146, 219, 288, 425–426, 463, 469, 542n4
Austin, George J., 103–105, 110–111, 112, 524n60

Badger, Reid, 15, 16, 17, 126, 484, 505n46, 563n21, 564n32
Baker, Henry E., 405

Baker, Newton D., 19
  and Allied demands for American
    soldiers, 201–202
  and black soldiers in southern
    training camps, 157, 161, 165, 167
  and Charles Young removal, 142–143
  and combat duties of 15th/369th,
    198–199
  and federal recognition of 15th
    Regiment, 120, 525n3
  and Peyton March appointment,
    198–199
  and removal of black troops from
    France, 371–372, 373
  and 369th postwar status, 409
  369th reputation defended by, 405
  and training of 15th/369th, 127, 140,
    141
  and victory parade, 396
Ballou, Charles, 130, 372, 378–379, 460,
  522n34
Baltimore Afro-American, 118, 153, 304
Barbeau, Arthur, 129
Barnum, Malvern-Hill, 404
Barthman, Henry C., 74
Baskerville, Cato L., 479, 575–576n72
Baumes bill, 454–455
Beckton, James "Jimmy," 342, 343
Belcher, Sims, 348
Bell, Watson, 159
Belleau Wood, 242, 276–277
Berry, Charles W., 415, 416, 427
Besner, Eugene J., 153–154
Biddle, John, 197–198
The Birth of a Nation, 89, 146, 503n26
Black, Frank S., 28, 29, 70
black Democrats, 42–44, 49, 50, 52,
  75–76, 87
  See also Democratic Party; National
    Colored Democratic League
black manhood and masculinity
  black regiment campaign and, 17, 65,
    94, 110–111
  Camp Mills incident and, 534n57
  in films, 9

and Henry Johnson as hero, 276, 287
military and, 18–19, 24–25, 403
and Pancho Villa in the black press,
  83
and violence, 501n3
black militias, 19th Century, 27–28
black officer training, 19, 40, 114–115,
  129–130, 347, 348, 429, 438
black press
  Benjamin O. Davis in, 434, 435
  Brownsville incident in, 36
  and Democratic politics, 89
  government attempt to manipulate,
    294–295
  Henry Johnson and Neadom
    Roberts in, 264, 282, 283–284,
    291–292, 304, 450, 463, 468, 471
  New York racial issues in, 33–34
  Pancho Villa in, 83
  Séchault monument proposal in, 420
  southern training camps in, 169–170
  William Butler in, 304
  See also Chicago Defender; New York
    Age
black prisoners of war, German torture
  of, 279
black regiment campaign
  Charles Fillmore and, 3, 40, 44–46,
    49–55, 57–60, 62–63, 65, 70–71, 76,
    77–79, 80–81, 91, 93, 99, 100, 106,
    514n73
  and Charles Young as Regiment
    commander, 56–57, 66, 71–72, 103,
    111
  and Equity Congress, 50–54, 59, 70,
    75, 80, 84, 99–101
  in local and state politics, 18, 34,
    46–50, 52, 57–60, 62, 63, 70–71,
    85–87, 100, 510n18, 511n23
  manhood and masculinity in, 17, 65,
    94, 110–111
  NAACP and, 40, 41, 90, 100–101, 102,
    105, 113–114
  partisan politics in, 18, 28, 34, 44–50,
    52, 57–60, 62–63, 70–71, 74–76,

85–88, 92–93, 100, 416, 510n18,
511nn20, 23
racial politics in, 64, 80, 84, 85–86
and recruitment, 79–80, 115, 126, 142
in *The Crisis,* 50, 90, 511n23
and training camps, 40, 105, 113–114,
128–130, 132
War Department and, 52, 58–59,
63, 68, 78–79, 88, 91, 105–106, 109,
511n26
William Hayward and, 97, 99–102,
108, 110, 115, 120, 123, 124–125,
520n10
black soldiers, hostility toward, 274, 144,
162, 163–164, 178, 215, 377, 399–401,
460–461, 478
black veterans, 373, 377, 395, 399–400,
402–403, 406, 432, 442, 447–448,
460
Bliss, Tasker, 160, 198–199
Blunt, Hamilton Herman, 52
*"Blutlistige Schwartze Manner"*
(bloodthirsty black men), 384,
563n9
Bogle, Donald, 10
*Bridgeport Telegram,* 289–290
Briggs, Cyril, 280
British Army, black troops and, 174, 202,
521n14, 524n69
*Brooklyn Daily Eagle,* 162, 170, 173, 175,
546n28
*Brooklyn Standard Union,* 288–289
Brooks, William H., 31, 135, 145, 148–149,
150, 294, 402, 477, 531n89
Brown, Charles E., 42, 43
Brown, George W., 182
Brown, Isaac, 147, 530n86
Brown, J. W., 85
Brown, Nikki, 286
Brown, Robert D., 574n48
Brownsville (TX) incident, 26, 31, 34–36,
39, 50, 123, 509n7
*Brown v. Board of Education,* 443–444
Bryan, Charles, 298, 305
Bullard, Eugene, 229

Bullard, Robert Lee, 23, 314–315, 398,
403, 419, 420, 506n4, 578n38
Bushnell, Asa W., 54
Butler, William, 259, 303, 304, 384,
462–463, 546n21

Caldera, Louis, 465
Call, Donald M., 545n97
Calloway, Cab, 5, 13, 482
Camp Dix, 152, 154–155, 176, 177, 182
Camp Funston, 378–379
Camp Lacoutine, 404
Camp Logan, 157–158
Camp Merritt, 171–172, 182–183, 535–
536n92. *See also* Schita, Valdo B.
Camp Mills, 169–170, 441–442, 534n57
Camp Peekskill, 14, 130, 134–135, 136,
140, 149, 151, 416
Camp Smith, 428, 429
Camp Upton, 152, 154–155, 382, 385, 386,
389, 403, 441–442
Camp Wadsworth, 156–169, 182, 188,
206, 207, 441–442, 481, 533–534n51
*Camp Wadsworth Gas Attack and Rio
Grande Rattler,* 163
Camp Whitman, 146, 148–149, 151, 152
Canadian army recruitment of black
Americans, 110, 174, 175, 176
Caraway, Thaddeus Horatius, 105
Carmody, Thomas, 73, 78
Carpenter, W. Spencer, 26–27, 450
Carr, C. Franklin, 80–81, 518n37
Carr, James D., 31, 43–44
Carter, J. McI., 408–409, 412–413
Castles, John Wesley, Jr.
awards to, 242
en route to France, 185, 186–187
on front lines, 192, 193, 194, 208,
209–210, 215
on Hayward leadership, 121, 149, 172,
187, 215, 229, 230–231, 232, 233, 242
on Henry Johnson, 271
and Séchault capture, 229, 230–232,
233, 242, 351
on southern camps, 160, 166, 171, 172

casualties, 369th Regiment, 491–497, 562n3

Caulder, William Musgrave, 160

Cheatham, Henry P., 130, 137, 186, 297–298

Cheesman, Benedict W., 137, 297

Chicago (IL), 27, 37–38, 80, 89, 118, 397–398

*Chicago Defender,* 116, 118, 169–170, 264, 291–292, 450, 463, 468, 471

*Chicago Tribune,* 277

Chisholm Frank R., 423

Chisum, William W., 407, 572n3

Chisum, W. Woodruff, 485

Civil War, black soldiers in, 23, 24–25, 84, 93, 106, 219, 284–285, 506n6

Clark, John Holley, 257, 322, 324, 328–329, 332, 334–335, 340, 341, 346, 353–354

Clark, Reed Paige, 56

Clarke, Clarence, *251*

Cleveland, Grover, 42, 43

*Cleveland Gazette,* 54

Cobb, Frederick
    Croix de Guerre awarded posthumously to, *259,* 345, 371
    death of, 340, 346
    on front lines, 301, 302–303
    and Séchault capture, *254,* 327, 332, 333, 334–335, 340, 371
    *See also* 2nd Battalion, 369th Regiment

Cobb, Irvin, 14, 268, 269, 293, 302, 400–401, 469–470, 505n50

Cochran, Emmett, 320, 321–325

Cochran, Robert, 445

Collardet, Louis, *259,* 377–378

Collins, Bob, 277

Colson, William N., 522n34, 565n48

Conick, Charles, 137, 182

Conn, Steve, 481, 582n21

Conner, Fox, 299

Connor, W. D., 208

Cooper, William J., 341, 342

Cox, William H., 222, *253*

Cox, Vernon, 147, 530n86

Creel, George, 294, 537n120

Cripps, Thomas, 9, 10, 11

*The Crisis*
    black regiment campaign in, 50, 90, 113, 511n23
    Charles Young removal issue in, 143, 144
    government suspicions of, 280
    Taft and Republican Party in, 60
    W. E. B. Du Bois as editor of, 31, 71–72, 113, 294
    *See also* NAACP

Croker, Richard, 42, 43–44

Crumb, Leverett F., 134

the *Crusader,* 280

Culliver, Louis A., 510n18

Culliver bill, 50, 511n26

Curtis, Helen, 319, 554nn97, 102

D'Amato, Alphonse, 464

Daniels, Josephus, 289, 297

Davis, Arthur P., 99

Davis, Arthur W., 16, 387, 388–389, 394

Davis, Benjamin O., Jr., 440

Davis, Benjamin O., Sr.
    as first black general, 439
    blackwater fever contracted by, 513n52
    369th commemorative history presented to, *243*
    as 369th Regiment first black commander, 262, 434–436, 437–438, 441–442, 445, 574n48

Davis, Ed, 388, 389

Davis, Hannibal L. "Spats," 234, 328, 329–330, 333–334, 335, 339, 341, 342, 343, 348, 388–389

Davis, Henrietta Vinton, 46

Davis, Robert, 450

Davis, Sadie, 436

Dawson, Stephanie E., 445, 575–576n72

Dayton, Edwin, 116, 136, 137–138, 152, 170, 172, 185, 208

Dean, Charles, 332, 345, 346

Deas, Samuel, 383, 562n7
de Broit, Frank, 126–127
Democratic Party
  and black civil rights, 115
  and black dissatisfaction with
    Republican Party, 42–44, 60–61
  black press and, 89
  and black regiment campaign in
    New York politics, 18, 34, 46–50,
    52, 57–60, 62, 70–71, 85–87, 100,
    510n18, 511nn20, 23
  exclusion bill and, 519n61
  in 1910 midterm elections, 48–49
  in 1912 presidential election, 59–60
  and 1914 midterm elections, 85,
    86–87
  and 93rd Division monument
    proposal, 419–420
  See also black Democrats; Wilson,
    Woodrow
Desvarreux, Raymond, 251
Dick, Charles, 47
Dickinson, Jacob M., 47, 510n18
Dickson, Clark L., 354
DioGuardi, Joe, 464
disability status, determination of,
  545–546n130
Dix, John A., 47, 48–49, 51, 52, 57, 62,
  64–65, 514n73, 515n78
d'Oiselle, Helie, 222, 415
Donaldson, Irving F., 445, 575–576n72
Douglas, Abraham, 348
Douglass, Frederick, 24–25
draft riots of 1863, 27
Du Bois, W. E. B., 19
  and black regiment campaign and
    formation, 66, 81, 113
  and Charles Young support, 71–72,
    76, 144
  and criticism of Taft and Republican
    party, 50
  as Harlem resident, 436
  and "open letter" on race relations
    to European community, 39–40,
    508n53

and postwar call for racial justice,
  397
and Silent Protest Parade, 146–147
as The Crisis editor 31, 71–72, 113, 294,
  397
and Woodrow Wilson, 61, 294–295
Dunbar-Nelson, Alice, 124, 400–401
Duncan, Samuel A., 81
Duplessix, Garnier, 347, 350–351
Dwyer, Owen, 467

East St. Louis (IL), riots in, 19, 144–145,
  147, 157, 531n89
Equity Congress of Greater New York
  and black regiment campaign and
    formation, 50–54, 59, 70, 75–76,
    78–79, 80, 84, 99–101, 115, 510n17
  membership of, 46, 59, 513n60
  and partisan politics in black
    regiment campaign, 18, 46–50,
    58–59, 61–62, 64–65, 66, 67–68,
    75–76, 100, 515n84
  and postwar demand for black
    regiment commander, 422–423,
    425–426, 427
Emanuel, Thomas, 321, 322, 323
Europe, James Reese
  as 15th Regiment band leader, 16,
    126–127, 250, 373, 376, 476, 531n92,
    564n32
  New York Times on, 476–477, 564n32
  postwar life and death of, 476–477
  in prewar Harlem, 32
  in raid, 226
  in victory parade, 387, 390
  See also 15th New York Infantry Band
Executive Order 9981, Truman, 443
Eyre, Lincoln, 268, 269, 280–281, 304,
  462–463

Farley, James F., 432
Faulkner, Richard S., 352
federalization of 369th Regiment, 413,
  415–416, 441
Ferrell, Robert H., 356, 379

15th New York Guard (NYG), 10, 148, 153, 401–402, 406–407, 411, 423, 441, 477–479, 485, 499, 502n15, 530n76, 547n37

15th New York Infantry Band
  Egbert Thompson as former leader of, 106, 126
  in 15th Regiment recruitment efforts, 126, 142
  in films, 6–7, 12, 14, 16
  in France, 191, 193–194, 202–206, 215, 219, 316–318, 368, 373, 376
  in *Harlem Hell Fighters*, 16
  in *Life in Ragtime*, 126, 505n46
  in negotiations to send 15th Regiment to the front, 202–203, 214
  Noble Sissle in, 130, 149, 203, 204, 206, 294, 481, 527n31
  in postwar 369th, 414
  recruitment for, 126–127, 130, 527n31
  reputation of, 293–294
  and 369th en route to France, 185–186
  in victory parade, 387, 390, 563n21
  *See also* Europe, James Reese

15th New York National Guard
  and black women's support role, 124–125
  and color-bearers in prewar Harlem, 246
  and drilling in prewar Harlem, 247
  federalization of, 108, 115, 116, 120
  postwar status of, 401–402, 405–416, 422, 441–445, 477–478, 479, 529–530n76
  rattlesnake as symbol of, 2, *243*, 363
  in 369th victory celebration, 386–389
  *See also* black regiment campaign; US 369th Regiment (15th NYNG)

Fillmore, Charles Ward
  and AEF purge of black officers, 477
  as black 369th officer, 117, 136–137, 324
  and black regiment campaign, 3, 40, 44–46, 49–55, 57–60, 62–63, 65,
    70–71, 76, 77–79, 80–81, 91, 93, 99, 100, 106, 114, 514n73
  Croix de Guerre awarded to, *259*, 301–302, 406–407, 477
  in 9th Volunteer Infantry (Ohio), 45, 54–55
  and postwar demobilization and reorganization of 369th, 406–407, 412
  postwar life of, 412, 477–478
  Republican Party loyalty of, 45, 478, 521n23
  and victory parade, 568n22

Fillmore, Elizabeth, 124
Fillmore, Helen Mae, 124
films, African Americans in, 9–10, 89, 502n22, 503n23, 503n26. See also *Stormy Weather*

Fish, Hamilton "Ham," III, 19
  as anticommunist, 486
  awards to, 116–117, *259*, 346–347
  background of, 139
  and black regiment recruitment, 102, 123, 522n30
  as congressman, 117, 417–418, 483, 486
  en route to France, 184–185, 187
  on 15th/369th officers, 187, 193, 211
  on front lines, 224, 232, 301
  and Hayward leadership, 346, 358, 367, 482–483, 485
  in *Men of Bronze* documentary, 16
  and monument campaign, 417–419, 486
  postwar life of, 485–486
  and Séchault capture, 343, 346–347, 351
  and support for black soldiers, 211, 214, 215, 216, 224, 348, 378, 486
  at training camps, 159–160, 170, 171
  in training in France, 192, 193–194, 211, 214

Fiske, H. B., 208, 311–312, 360, 362
Fletcher, Marvin E., 434, 435
Flipper, Henry O., 103
Flower, Roswell, 42

Foch, Ferdinand, 283, 312–313, 362, 452
Foraker, Joseph B., 35, 54, 85, 512n44
Fort Des Moines, 128–130, 438, 439, 449, 527n30
Fortune, T. Thomas, 28, 285
Foster, Reginald L., 207
Francis, Norris, 348
Frazier, Susan Elizabeth, 124, 125, 289
French 2nd Moroccan Division, 330, 350–351, 353
French Fourth Army, 201, 222, 299–300, 303, 325, 328–329, 335, 353, 358, 497, 577n26. *See also* Gouraud, Henri
French 4th Moroccan Regiment, 300, 330
French 8th Army Corps, 201, 217, 222
French 9th Army Corps, 347, 350–351, 353
French 16th Infantry Division, 209, 217–222, 233, 265, 278, 497. *See also* Le Gallais (General)
French 157th Infantry Division, 197, 298, 307, 350–351, 353, 354–355
French 161st Division
    en route to Blodesheim-on-Rhine, 258
    and Séchault capture, 254, 327–330, 338–339, 343–344, 370–371
    in the Vosges, 362, 364–367
    369th attachment to, 300–301, 313, 327–336, 497
French 163rd Regiment, 301, 334, 342, 343–344, 349
French treatment of African American soldiers, 233, 312, 316, 401
*From Harlem to the Rhine* (Little), 14, 15, 20, 135–136, 484, 528n52, 560n25

Gannett, Deborah, 24, 506n5
Garrison, Lindley L., 71–72, 79
gas weaponry, 213, 224, 225–226, 234, 235, 236, 277, 300, 301, 302, 546n28, 551n36
Gaynor, William J., 34, 66, 67, 69–70, 515n84

General Militia Act of 1862: 28
George, Valasta, 259
Gibbons, Floyd, 277
Gibbs-Marshall, Harriet, 138
Gilbreth, Joseph L., 116, 120
Glynn, Martin H., 78, 81, 85, 86, 87, 122, 289, 517n27
Goldwater, S. S., 432
Gouraud, Henri, 222, 292, 299–300, 313, 316, 328, 350, 358, 389, 415, 456
Goybet, Mariano, 298, 305, 306–307, 309, 310, 314–315, 316
Great Migration, 403
Greenberg, Cheryl, 431
Greer, Allen J., 372, 378–379, 403
Griffin, D. W., 89
Grimley, John G., 428–429, 431–433, 434, 573–574n34

Haig, Douglas, 271
Hamilton, Henry De Witt, 63, 64–65, 69, 71, 72, 73, 76, 78, 80, 81–82, 91
Hamilton, West A., 354, 559n134
Harding, Edward, 348
Harding, Warren G., 158, 411, 417, 479–480, 487
Harjes, Herman, 209
Harlem
    and Bill "Bojangles" Robinson, 12, 482, 503–504n31
    black population of, 31–33, 37, 41–42, 89–91, 94–95, 97–98, 110, 507n27
    and black regiment campaign, 94–95, 97–98, 99–100, 110
    government mistrust of, 279–280
    and integration in 369th Regiment, 443–444
    in local and state politics, 41–42, 44, 89–90, 94–95, 99–100
    and Neadom Roberts, 467–468
    and postwar role of 369th Regiment, 424, 426, 430, 431, 433–434, 435–436, 444–445
    race riots in, 4, 5
    369th Armory in, 416

*Harlem's Hell Fighters* (Harris), 16, 321
Harmon, Arthur Loomis, 420
Harris, Stephen, 16–17, 173, 321, 484, 523n46
Harris, William, 16–17
Harrison, Hubert, 31–32, 280, 294
Hartmannswillerkopf monument, 256, 365, 560n21
Haskell, William N., 432
Hastie, William, 439, 440, 442
Hatton, Colonel, 363–364, 365
Hay, James, 47
Hayes, Rutherford B., 42
Haynes, George Edmund, 32
Hayward, Leland, 583n35
Hayward, William, 258
    and AEF report on 369th conditions, 357–361
    awards to, 370–371, 482–483
    background of, 95–96
    and black officers issue, 111–112, 121–122, 129–130, 347, 348–349, 357, 422–423
    and black regiment campaign and formation, 97, 99–102, 108, 110, 115, 120, 123, 124–125, 520n10
    defiant quote attributed to, 1, 383, 453, 501n2
    Edwin Dayton friction with, 172, 185
    and 15th/369th return from France, 379–380, 382
    and 15th Regiment and overseas troop mobilization, 148, 165, 167, 169, 170, 171, 172, 185
    and Fish monument legislation, 419–420
    on French treatment of black soldiers, 227–228
    on front lines, 219, 222–223, 227–232
    Hamilton Fish relations with, 346, 358, 367, 419–420, 482–483, 485
    and Henry Johnson and Neadom Roberts, 268, 271, 276, 281, 283, 291–292, 456

and lack of training for 369th replacements, 311–312, 320, 357, 359–360
    leadership of, 116, 120–121, 149, 187, 194, 210, 229–231, 232, 233, 242, 346, 358, 367, 346, 364, 482–483, 583n36
    and 93rd Division return to US control, 311–312
    postwar life of, 482–484, 541n91
    and regiment band, 126, 214, 242, 317–318
    and Séchault capture, 301, 311–312, 320–321, 328, 342–343, 344–345, 347
    and 369th Armory, 402, 422
    and support for 15th/369th soldiers, 16, 215, 216, 227–229, 232–233, 276, 277, 283, 307, 383–384
    in training camps, 130–131, 134, 140, 149–150, 161–162, 164–165, 166–167
    in training in France, 194, 202, 203, 207, 208, 209, 211, 214–215
    and victory parade, 386–388, 389, 390–391
    wounding of, 562n8
Healey, Martin J., 426, 572n12
Hearon, Charles, 159
Hearst, William Randolph, 387, 396
Heinemann (Lieutenant), 222–223, 232–233
Henri, Florette, 129
Henry, Nelson Herrick, 48, 49
Hicks, Frederick C., 416
Hilles, Charles D., 46–47, 48, 49, 50–51, 57–60, 87, 513n55
Hinkson, DeHaven, 411
Hinton, George, 116, 414, 477
Hirschauer, August Edouard, 305
Holliday, Presly, 111
Holliday, Robert P., 488–489
Holt, Thomas, 18
Hooper, Chauncey, 137, 168, 262, 267, 407, 434, 440–441, 478–479
Hoover, Herbert, 390
House, Edward M., 19, 133, 139–140, 141, 154–155

Houston (TX), riot in, 19, 35, 157–158
Howard, Edward V., 148
Howard, Herbert, 348
Howard University, 128–129
Howe, John, 464
Huff, Joshua, 348
Hunt, E., 360–362
Hunton, Addie W., 317, 319, 554n98
Hyland, John F., 390, 396

"In Flanders Fields," 263
integration of the armed forces, 439,
    440, 443

Jackson, Louis F., 71
Jackson, William H., 29, 423, 428–429,
    573n21
Jallade, Louis E., 425, 427, 428, 429
James, Nathaniel, 10, 444, 572n76,
    575n70
Janifer, Clarence Sumner, 397, 565n55
Jaxson, J. A., 52, 53
Jay, Delancey, 112
Jervey, Henry, 391
Jews, National Guard discrimination
    against, 73–75, 516–517n19,
    519–520n68
Joaquin, Lawrence, 147, 153–154, 163,
    530n86
Johnson, Charles, 16
Johnson, DeForest D., 407, 572n3
Johnson, Edna, 287–288, 289, 292, 449,
    461
Johnson, Henry, 248
    AEF investigation of battle of,
        270–272
    in AEF Stars and Stripes, 272–275, 295
    Albany Veterans Association
        monument to, 464
    awards to, 259, 269–271, 272–273,
        274–275, 358, 370, 455, 464
    and denigration of black soldiers,
        578n38
    embellishments in accounts of battle
        by, 452–455, 578n42

as "hero," 1–2, 250, 259, 276, 287,
    293–294, 456, 459, 551n44
imposters of, 450, 452, 577n15
in Little's regimental history, 275,
    448
Medal of Honor campaign on
    behalf of, 3, 464–466
and Panthéon de la Guerre, 397, 565n55
Pershing's praise of, 271–272, 280,
    281–282, 285, 290–291
postwar legacy and myths of, 19–20,
    447–449, 466–467
in the press, 1, 264, 269, 277, 280–282,
    283–286, 287–289, 291–293, 304, 382,
    392–394, 450, 454–455, 463, 468, 471,
    546n16, 577nn15, 20, 22
profits at expense of, 449–451, 452
and Toni Morrison's Jazz, 447–448
in victory parade, 387, 388, 392–394
wounding of, 276, 447
See also Roberts, Neadom
Johnson, Henry M., 28
Johnson, James Weldon
    on black Americans and loyalty, 118
    and black regiment campaign and
        formation, 85, 86, 115
    and Democratic Party rebuke, 85, 86
    as Harlem resident, 31
    and 93rd Division monument, 418,
        419
    on nationalism, 83–84
    and postwar reorganization of
        15th/369th, 410
    and Silent Protest Parade, 146–147
    on 369th parade, 390, 395, 564n36
Johnson, Kathryn M., 317, 319, 554n98
Johnson, Marshall, 222, 229–230
Johnson, Samuel M., 354
Johnson, William Henry. See Johnson,
    Henry
Jones, E. Montgomery, 124
Jones, Eugene Kinckle, 65
Jones, Gorman, 303
Jones, Oscar, 348
Jones, Samuel, 153–154

Kane, Thomas, 64, 70
Karney, T. Henry, 81
K Company (3rd Battalion). *See* 3rd
    Battalion (369th Regiment)
Kincaid, J. Leslie, 411, 413, 415
King, Archibald, 322–323
Kryder, Daniel, 5

Lacy, George, 117, 136–137, 186, 307
La Follette, Robert M., 59
La Guardia, Fiorello, 402, 414, 436, 485,
    573n31
Lebouc, Georges
    black officers and, 348–349
    fair treatment of African American
        soldiers by, 316
    New York Conspicuous Service
        Cross awarded to, 415
    and praise for 369th, 330, 331, 347,
        349–350, 351, 358, 361, 365, 367, 368,
        370, 371, 373, 368, 370, 371, 373
    *See also* French 161st Division
Lee, Edward E., 43–44, 509n9
Le Gallais (General), 209, 217–219, 222,
    223, 228, 233, 268, 269–270, 306,
    307, 316, 415
Lehman, Herbert H., 432, 433, 434, 436,
    437, 438
Leland, Mickey, 464
Lentz-Smith, Adriane, 21, 501n3
Leonard, Harry, 164
L'Esperance, David A.
    French Légion d'Honneur awarded
        to, 345, 368
    Lebouc friendship with, 369–370
    postwar life of, 483, 488–489
    and Séchault capture, 254, 331,
        344–345, 367, 384–385
    and victory parade, 385
Lewis, David Levering, 6, 63–64, 89,
    143, 145
Lewis, William H., 19, 47–48, 49, 54, 60,
    61, 509n11
Linard, Louis, 307–309, 310–311, 312,
    313–314, 315, 317

Little, Arthur W.
    awards to, 371, 484
    background of, 139–140
    and black regiment formation,
        521n11
    and desire for French combat
        service, 154–155
    on 15th Regiment and southerners,
        169–170
    on General Lebouc, 368
    on Henry Johnson and Neadom
        Roberts, 266, 267–269, 270, 271,
        277, 278, 370, 448, 455, 463–474,
        545n1
    postwar life of, 484–485
    as postwar 369th commander, 412,
        413–415, 426–427
    on Schita incident, 172–173, 182
    in 369th Armory, 422
    on 369th in France, 205–206, 209,
        560n21
    in training camps, 134, 135–136, 137,
        140, 149, 151, 161, 162, 164–165
    and victory parade, 386, 387, 388, 389
    and white officers, 138, 412, 415
    See also *From Harlem to the Rhine*
        (Little); 1st Battalion (369th
        Regiment)
Little, Mary Sheldon Murphy, 485
Littleton, Martin W., 180, 181
Littman, Samuel, 73–75, 516n13
Logan, James A., Jr., 549–550n3
Lorini, Alexandra, 146
Louis, Joe, 503n23
Loving, Walter, 279–280, 294, 295,
    372–373, 378–379, 380, 459, 461,
    547n37, 547n39
Lucas, Wilmer F., 430, 573n24
Lynch, A. W., 408–409
Lynch, Adolph, 389
Lyons, John J., 568n22

MacArthur, Douglas, 527n42
MacIntyre, R. F., 42
Mack, Charles E., 504n41

MacMorris, Daniel, 565n55
Magill, Charles, 468
Maloney, Herbert W. "Bert," 346
Mangin, Charles E. M., 36, 99, 191
Manley, "Buck," 393, 449, 455
Mann, William A., 119–120, 140, 157, 520n68, 525n3
Manning, Richard I., 159
March, Peyton, 199–200, 290–291, 294
Marshall, Francis S., 382, 484
Marshall, George C., 437, 440
Marshall, John R., 29, 38, 52–53
Marshall, Louis, 73
Marshall, Napoleon B.
    as black 15th/369th officer, 35, 117, 138, 192, 228
    and black regiment recruitment, 123
    and Brownsville court-martial, 35, 123
    at Camp Wadsworth, 162
    death of, 553n81
    and 15th/369th attachment to French Army, 207, 213, 228, 223–224
    in NAACP, 39–40
    and National Colored Democratic League, 513–514n62
    postwar life of, 479–480
    in prewar Harlem, 32
    and reassignment to 92nd Division, 307, 315, 379
    and Schita incident, 176–178, 180
    wounding of, 315–316, 546n13
Massood Paula, 12
McCann, William T., 354
McClinton, Seth, 423–424
McDougald, Cornelius W., 85, 519n49
McIntyre, John F., 441
McKaine, Osceola E., 379
McKay, Claude, 31
McKellar, Kenneth, 372
McKensie, John, 331, 332
McKiernan, Kevin, 445, 575–576n72
McKinley, William, 29–30, 43, 54, 514n67
McLee, Archie, 129–130, 527n30
McLaughlin, Hugh, 42

McLoughlin, Comerford "Cub," 210, 331–332, 344, 354, 368, 370
McMaster, George H., 379, 403–404, 567n14
McNish, Ernest, 328
McNulty, Michael, 464, 465, 466
McNutt, William Slavens, 188, 537n120
McPherson, Richard C., 81
Men of Bronze (documentary), 16, 461
the Messenger, 152, 279, 377, 403, 565n48
Metcalf, Walden S., 229–230
Meuse-Argonne offensive, 190, 315, 327, 328–329, 349–351, 352, 356, 360–361, 405, 567n19. See also Séchault, capture of
Mexico, US policy in, 61, 83, 84, 92, 93, 101–102, 105, 117, 133
Mikell, Francis Eugene, 127, 269, 407, 425, 570, 572n9
Miles, John J., 504n41
Miles, Nelson A., 84, 414–415
Miles, Perry, 298, 354, 355
Miles, William, 16, 17
Miller, Kelly, 128, 449
Miller, Melville, 16, 368–369
Miller, Nathan L., 411
Mills, A. L., 79, 80, 88, 169
Mills, Paul, 299, 304
Mills, William G., 348, 571–572n76
Mitchel, John Purroy, 89, 97, 109, 120, 159
Mitchell, Clark, 54
Mittelhauser, Eugène-Désité-Antoine, 314, 316
Mjagkij, Nina, 21
Moore, Frederick Randolph, 41–42, 50, 54, 115, 161, 283–284, 294, 432, 434, 516n4. See also New York Age
Moran, Robert L., 387, 402
Morris, Monson, 116, 152, 165, 166, 170, 193, 521n11
Morrison, Toni, 3, 447–448
Morton, Levi P., 28
Moses, D. M., 432
Moss, James A., 403

Moton, Robert Russa, 149, 376, 377–378, 404, 438, 460, 526n25
Moynihan, Daniel Patrick, 464
Mundy, Joseph A. S., 433–434, 574n35
Murphy, Charles, 48, 62

NAACP
  *Birth of a Nation* and, 89
  and black activism and civil rights, 5, 8–9, 39–40, 41, 72, 75
  black regiment campaign and, 40, 41, 90, 100–101, 102
  and black training camps issue, 40, 105, 113–114
  and Booker T. Washington Tuskegee Machine, 41, 56, 72
  and National Negro Committee, 508n53
  and 93rd Division monument, 418, 419
  and postwar reorganization of 15th/369th, 399, 410
  rise of, 19, 39–40, 41
Nail, John E., 90, 102, 113–114, 115, 146
Napier, James C., 47
Nash, Roy, 105, 128
National Association for the Advancement of Colored People. *See* NAACP
National Association for the Promotion of Labor Unionism among Negroes, 279–280
National Colored Democratic Convention (1892), 42
National Colored Democratic League, 60–61, 513–514n62
National Colored Liberty Congress, 294
National Defense Act of 1916: 108, 120, 529–530n76
National Defense Act of 1920: 408, 411–412, 425, 572n9
National League for the Protection of Colored Women, 507n27

National League on Urban Conditions Among Negroes, 65
National Memorial Association, 419
National Negro Committee, 508n53
National Security League, 92
*Negro Voice*, 280
Nelson, Dean, 51
Nelson, Peter, 16–17
Nelson, William, 528n58
*New Jersey Herald News*, 472
Newton, Isham G., 517n19
*New York Age*
  *Birth of a Nation* and, 89
  black regiment campaign and formation in, 48, 53, 62, 63, 70–71, 82, 86, 87, 90, 93, 97, 102, 103, 111, 114–116, 120–121, 129–130, 511n20
  on blacks in Chicago politics, 38
  black women in, 82–83, 286
  Canadian army recruitment of black soldiers in, 110
  on Charles Whitman and Republican Party, 85, 87, 89–90, 109
  Equity Congress in, 75, 515n84
  on 15th/369th postwar status and role, 413, 431
  15th Regiment tribute in, 385–386
  Henry Johnson and Neadom Roberts in, 1–2, 285, 288–289, 453, 459
  on McDougald appointment, 519n49
  on postwar racism toward black soldiers, 404–405
  and praise for black troops, 36–37
  race relations in, 33–34, 95
  and special issue on race and the war, 566n2
  and support for black civic organizations, 46, 90
  and William Hayward, 121–122
*New York Amsterdam News*
  black regiment campaign in, 50, 53–54

Henry Johnson in, 463
and postwar demand for black 369th
    commander, 424–425, 426, 427,
    428–429, 430, 431, 433–434
*Stormy Weather* in, 9, 503n28
on 369th Armory, 422
on 369th role in WWII, 437, 438, 442,
    574n48
*New York Evening Post*, 284
*New York Evening Sun*, 160, 483, 532n16
*New York Evening Telegram*, 288–289
*New York Evening World*, 268, 288–289,
    304, 396
*New York Herald*, 264, 292
New York State Colored Volunteers,
    28
*New York Sun*, 70, 285, 508n53
*New York Times*
    as antiblack, 107–108
    Bert Williams in, 107–109
    on black soldiers, 87
    on Culliver bill, 511n26
    on 15th/369th, 152, 384
    on Henry Johnson and Neadom
        Roberts, 285–286, 289, 577n20
    on James Europe, 476–477
    and overseas troop mobilization,
        29
    Pippin obituary in, 481
    369th victory parade in, 563n9
*New York Tribune*, 28
*New York World*, 33, 137, 268, 269, 288
nicknames, racialized, 392, 562–563n8,
    563n9

Oliver, Robert Shaw, 58, 513n55
O'Ryan, John F.
    at Camp Wadsworth, 159, 163
    Dix firing of, 64–65, 515n78
    and federal recognition of 369th,
        411–412, 415
    on Mexican border, 106
    in New York local and state politics,
        64–65, 515n78, 570n54

as New York National Guard
    commander, 78, 91, 92, 96, 116,
    159, 160, 163
and opposition to black officers, 66,
    91, 96, 119–120, 122, 140, 412, 415,
    427, 519–520n68, 569n43
and opposition to black regiment,
    62, 63, 64–65, 69, 78
Old 15th. *See* 15th New York National
    Guard
Osofsky, Gilbert, 42
Outwater, John O., 303–304, 365, 560n25
Ovenshine, A. T., 233
Ovington, Mary White, 40
Owens, Chandler, 152, 279

*Panthéon de la Guerre*, 397, 565n55
Parish, Oliver, 340
Parker, Albert, 452
Parks, Virgil H., 99, 117, 148, 531n89
Pataki, George, 464–465, 579n57, 60
Patton, George, 242, 545n97
Payton, Philip, Jr., 31, 81
Pershing, John J. "Black Jack"
    and black officers, 182, 296, 306
    and black troops in France, 195–202
    and commitment of troops to
        France, 133–134, 200–202
    and desire to invade Germany, 369
    and Henry Johnson and Neadom
        Roberts, 250, 271–272, 280, 281–282,
        284, 358, 546n16
    and leadership issues, 133, 546n16
    in *Stormy Weather*, 7
    in 10th Calvary, 95
    and 369th assignment to French,
        200–202, 207, 208, 214–215
    and 369th awards for service in
        France, 405, 482
    and 369th monument denial,
        417–418
Pétain, Philippe, 195, 196, 198, 214–215,
    271, 312, 318, 325, 326, 351, 352
Peterson, Clinton J., 431

Pickering, Woodell A., 172, 187, 342, 345, 371
Pioneer Infantry regiments, 408–409
Pippin, Horace
    as an artist, 188, 480–481, 537n119, 582n21
    on the front lines, 220–221, 224–226, 235–236, 237–242
    journals and notebooks of, 480, 537n119
    in New York Times, 481
    postwar life of, 480–481
    and Séchault capture, 329, 332, 334, 336–338, 347–348
    in training in France, 191–192, 209
Pittsburgh Courier, 294, 438, 578n50
Plattsburg officer training camp, 92, 104–105, 112–113, 128, 129, 139
Pocahontas (ship), 171, 178, 183, 184–188
Poincaré, Raymond, 317
Pollard, Lee A., 81, 91
post–World War I status, 15th/369th Regiment, 406–407, 411–412, 426–427, 441–442
Powell, Adam Clayton, 32, 85, 115
Pratt, Richardson, 138, 267, 281, 354
Preparedness Movement, military, 104–105, 139
President's Committee on Civil Rights, 443–444

Quigg, Lemuel Eli, 43

Randolph, A. Phillip, 105, 152, 279, 377, 436
Randolph, Richetta J., 105
rattlesnake as 369th Regiment symbol, 2, 243, 363
Reed, E. L., 52
Reid, Dennis Lincoln, 122, 136–137, 186, 228, 307, 407, 425
Reid, Daniel G., 126
Remarque, Erich Maria, 304

Republican Party
    and black civil rights, 43, 46, 50, 60, 61, 438–439
    black dissatisfaction with, 39, 42–44, 48–49, 50, 60–61
    and black officers, 426
    and black regiment campaign, 18, 28, 44–46, 47, 48–50, 57–60, 62, 70–71, 87, 92, 100, 416, 511n23
    in New York local and state politics, 43–46, 47–49, 59–60, 85, 86–87, 92, 100, 411
    and 93rd Division monument, 419
Réquin, Edouard, 131, 132
Revolutionary War, blacks during, 24
Rhinehart, C. D., 120, 181–182
Richards, John, 331
Rickards, George C., 411
Robb, George S., 341, 342, 344, 345–346, 487–488
Roberts, A. B., 91
Roberts, Charles H., 402
Roberts, Emma (Wilson), 282, 580n79
Roberts, Iola, 473–474
Roberts, Neadom, 248
    and AEF investigation of battle, 270–272, 295
    in AEF Stars and Stripes, 272–275, 295
    in books and films, 14–15, 448, 451
    Croix de Guerre awarded to, 455, 474–475
    and diminution of role in battle, 272, 470–471, 545n1, 551n44
    in Henry Johnson's account of battle, 453–454
    as hero, 467–470, 471, 472, 474–475, 551n44, 580n75
    as Leedom Roberts, 282, 473, 501n1
    New Jersey's honoring of, 474–475, 581n100
    in Panthéon de la Guerre, 397, 565n55
    Pershing's praise of, 271–272, 280, 281–282, 285, 290–291, 358

post-war life of, 446, 471–474
in the press, 1, 264, 269, 277, 280–282,
283–286, 287–289, 291–293, 304, 382,
392–394, 450, 454–455, 463, 468, 471,
472, 546n16, 577nn15, 20, 22
suicide of, 473–474, 581n95
in victory parade, 388
wounding of, 447, 467, 545–546n13
*See also* Johnson, Henry
Roberts, Thomas A., 298–299
Roberts, William, 289
Robeson, Benjamin, 325, 432–433
Robeson, Paul, 325, 436
Robinson, Edwin, 348
Robinson, Jackie, 443
Robinson, James W., 128
Robinson, Lee, 348
Robinson, William "Bojangles," 5, 6,
8–9, 10, 12, 436, 482, 503–504n31
Roche, James M., 433
Rocky Mountain Club, 390–391, 564n34
Rogin, Michael, 503n26
Rogers, William A., 264
Roosevelt, Eleanor, 432
Roosevelt, Franklin D., 160, 187,
438–439, 440, 486
Roosevelt, Theodore, 24, 26, 31, 35, 43,
87, 104, 133, 139, 145, 289, 469–470,
511n23
Roosevelt, Theodore, Jr., 15, 150, 317,
483, 504n41

Salant, Henry, 64
Sanders, Leon, 73
Sanders, Reginald D., 445
Sapp, William B., 36
*Saturday Evening Post,* 269, 400–401
Savage, Ezra P., 96
Schieffelin, William Jay, 402, 406, 407,
412, 423, 567–568n22
Schita, Valdo B., 173–181, 182–184, 247,
534nn67, 68, 535nn75, 92
Schoonmaker, F. P., 376
Schumer, Charles, 465–466

Scott, Emmett J., 13, 104, 153, 161,
167, 227, 294, 297, 387, 420, 440,
469–470, 516n4
Scott, William, 382–383
Séchault, capture of
American Battle Monuments
Commission and, 353–356, 418,
420–421
and casualties, 347, 349–350, 359
Gouraud praise for 369th and, 415
Hamilton Fish account of, 351
and Lebouc praise for 369th, 349–350,
371
monument recognizing, 3, 255, 417,
418–419, 421, 445
*New York Times* on, 384–385
strategy in, 254, 328
*See also* US 369th Regiment, 1st
Battalion; US 369th Regiment,
2nd Battalion; US 369th Regiment,
3rd Battalion
segregation
of black officers, 233, 298, 314,
347–349
in New York City, 34, 90–91
and postwar institutional change,
443–444
in Red Cross and YMCA, 375
training camps and, 112–113, 115
in US armed forces, 5, 58, 105,
127–128, 279, 437, 439–440, 443
Warren Harding and, 411
Woodrow Wilson policies of, 61, 82,
115–116, 411, 439
*See also* NAACP
Seiter, Stephen R., 421, 445
Shaw, Lewis E.
awards to, 367–368
on 15th/369th arrival and training
in France, 192–193, 207, 210–211,
213–214
on leadership of noncommissioned
officers, 347–348
on front lines, 226, 277, 304, 325–326

Shaw, Lewis E., *continued*
  postwar life of, 488
  and Séchault capture, 331–332, 344
  on 369th's advance to the Rhine, 369, 370
  wounding of, 345–346
Shelton, Henry H., 465
Shetlar, Samuel, 330–331
Shockley, M. A. W., 270–272, 358, 360–362, 545n11
Simmons, Roscoe Conkling, 462
Simpson, Frederick W., 570n50
Simpson, George W., 64
Simpson, M. Cravath, 124
Sissle, Noble
  on black and French soldier relations, 213
  Ellington Medal awarded to, 482
  en route to France, 185–186
  in 15th New York Regiment Band, 130, 149, 203, 204–205, 206–207, 294, 481, 527n31
  and James Europe, 125–126, 318, 473, 481
  postwar life of, 481–482
  in prewar Harlem, 32
  and Camp Wadsworth incident, 162–163, 165–166, 167, 168–169, 481
Slotkin, Richard, 17, 216, 534n57
Smith, Alfred E., 77, 144, 387, 388, 411, 422, 426, 427, 479
Sommepy Monument, 420–421
Spanish-American War, 23, 25–26, 28, 38, 44–45, 64, 133, 148, 211, 423, 454
Spartanburg camp. *See* Camp Wadsworth
*Spartanburg Journal,* 167
Spencer, Lorillard
  awards to, 116, 259, 345, 489
  and charges of incompetence, 116, 193, 368
  as 1st Battalion commander, 116, 135, 136, 138, 141–142, 152, 170
  on front lines, 301
  postwar life of, 489

and Séchault capture, 330–331, 345, 347, 371
at 369th monument dedication ceremony, 483
369th recruitment efforts of, 98, 99–100, 289
wounding of, 330–331, 368, 371, 387, 489
Spingarn, Joel, 19
  and black regiment and recruitment campaign, 100–102
  and government manipulation of black press, 294
  in Military Intelligence Branch, 40, 294–295
  as NAACP board chairman, 40, 100–101, 102, 113–114
  and training camps, 40, 105, 112–114, 127–128, 130, 526n25
*St. Louis Republic,* 457
*Stars and Stripes,* 272–275, 280–281, 295
Steele, Matthew, 24, 25, 506n4
Stephens, William, 348
Stewart, Gilchrist, 35, 101, 102, 114
Stewart, T. McCants, 29
Stimson, Henry L., 19, 47, 48–49, 57–59, 439–440, 486, 511n23, 513n55
Storey, Moorfield, 128, 569n32
*Stormy Weather* (film), 5–14, 16, 392, 503n28
Stotesbury, Louis, 77, 78–79, 88, 91, 97, 106, 108–109, 116, 119, 432, 519–520n68, 520n74
Stowers, Freddie, 464
Strong, William, 43
Sullivan, John L., 170
Sulzer, William
  and authorizing of black regiment, 70–71, 72–73, 77–78, 426
  and black officers, 69–70, 122, 422
  black regiment campaign and, 62, 64–68
  black voters and, 60
  gubernatorial campaign of, 60, 62, 64, 67–68, 515n78, 517n27

impeachment of, 76–77
and Jewish discrimination in
    National Guard, 73–74
in Tammany political machine, 65,
    76–77, 515n78

Taft, William Howard, 19, 35, 46–47, 48,
    50, 57, 58–59, 60, 61–62
Tammany Hall political machine
    black Democrats and, 42, 43–44, 50,
        62, 66, 87
    and Charles Whitman race, 87
    government reform and, 406, 411
    and William Sulzer, 65, 76–77,
        515n78
Tandy, Vertner, 32, 79, 97, 98, 99, 102,
    117, 148, 406
Tank Corps, 231, 242, 545n97
Tanner, John R., 38
Tardieu, André, 296
Taylor, David Vassar, 569n38
Taylor, John B., 362–363
Taylor, Thomas E., 150
Taylor, William A., 427–428, 429–431,
    432, 573nn23, 24
Tener, John Kinley, 519n51
Terrell, Mary Church, 35–36, 508n41
Terrell, Robert H., 514n67
Thomas, James C., 46–47, 65, 91, 115,
    510n17
Thomas, V. T., 70
Thompson, Clarence L., 252
Thompson, Egbert E., 106, 126
Thornton, Maurice, 465
369th Armory, 3, 402, 416
369th Historical Society, 3, 444, 445
369th Veterans Association, 3, 445, 464,
    465, 486, 501n5
Thurston, Nathaniel, 78
Tobias, D. E., 46–47, 510n18
training camps. See individual camps by
    name
Trenton State Gazette, 580n75
Trotter, William Monroe, 294
Tupes, Herschel, 305–306, 307, 354–355

Tuskegee Institute, 167, 174, 376, 435,
    438, 439, 440, 526n25
Tyler, Ralph, 84, 294, 518n45

US 1st Division, 133, 202, 242, 278–279,
    341, 362, 384
US 8th Illinois Infantry Regiment
    (370th)
    AEF suspicions of "secret society"
        within, 376
    band of, 126
    black officers in, 233, 298–299, 305,
        307, 314, 376
    and John Marshall, 29, 398
    in mobilization of overseas troops,
        195, 196, 198–199, 201
    New York Times praise for, 563n10
    and postwar status of black
        regiments, 408, 409
    reputation of, 38–39, 80, 115, 425
US 9th Calvary, 25, 36, 55, 87, 219, 289,
    404, 435, 486
US 9th Infantry Battalion. See 8th
    Illinois Infantry Regiment (370th)
US 9th Volunteer Infantry (Ohio), 45,
    54–55
US 10th Calvary
    as black regiment, 25, 34, 80, 86,
        102–103, 219, 288, 404
    at Carrizal, Mexico, 92, 102–103, 105,
        116, 288
    Charles Young as commander in, 86,
        98–99
    as labor unit, 486
    in New York Age, 87, 404
US 23rd Infantry Regiment, 80,
    517–518n34
US 26th (Yankee) Division, 133, 527n42
US 27th Division
    and attachment to British army, 202,
        215, 352
    at Camp Wadsworth, 160–161,
        163–164, 165, 167–169
    and disparities in officer treatment
        in, 396

US 27th Division, *continued*
  parade honoring, 395–396
  369th's exclusion from, 215, 416
  white officers of, 396
US 28th Infantry Regiment, 80,
    517–518n34
US 30th Division, 157, 202, 215, 352, 384
US 42nd (Rainbow) Division, 133–134,
    242, 386, 408, 421, 527n42
US 77th Infantry Division, 17, 229–230,
    367, 384
US 92nd Division
  allegations of poor performance of,
    403, 460
  and attachment to French army,
    198–199, 202
  maltreatment of black officers
    and troops in, 204, 216, 274, 279,
    356–357, 372, 378–379, 380, 460
  in the Meuse-Argonne, 356
  military race relations and, 376–377,
    379–380, 404–405
  removal of black officers from, 314
  white officers of, 216, 274, 279, 298,
    314–315, 348–349, 372–373, 378–379
  in World War II, 442–443
US 93rd Division (Provisional)
  in American Battle Monuments
    Commission report, 353–355
  as an "artificial construct," 197
  and attachment to French army,
    195–197, 199–202, 312–314, 460
  departure from France of, 381
  and proposed monument at
    Séchault, 418–420, 486
  regimental composition of, 196–197
  segregation of black officer corps of,
    233–234
  and Sommepy Monument, 420–421
  white officers in, 296, 304–305,
    549–550n3
  in World War II, 443
US 367th Infantry Regiment, 379, 398,
    423, 441, 539n56, 563n10, 565n48

US 369th Antiaircraft Artillery Gun
    Battalion, 442
US 369th Regiment, 1st Battalion
  in *From Harlem to the Rhine*, 15,
    560n25
  on front lines, 221–222, 223, 230, 266,
    301, 303
  Lebouc's compliments to, 373
  and monument controversy, 352–355
  at Séchault capture, 254, 327–328,
    329–330, 332–334, 335–336, 338–347,
    342–347, 352–355, 371
  in the Vosges, 364–365, 368
  withdrawal from France of, 373–374,
    376
  *See also* Little, Arthur W.
US 369th Regiment, 2nd Battalion, 254,
    257
  and departure from France, 376
  on front lines, 301, 302–303
  and Séchault capture, 327, 328, 332,
    333–336, 340, 346, 353–354
  in training, 152, 154, 159–160, 162, 170
US 369th Regiment, 3rd Battalion, 257
  Dayton as commander of, 116, 152,
    170, 172
  on front lines, 219, 220–221, 222, 223,
    224–227, 230–231, 233, 235, 300
  Hayward friction with, 172, 185
  K Company of, 168, 220–221,
    224–226, 238–239, 300, 332, 336–337,
    347, 351, 353, 354, 355
  return home of, 376
  and Séchault capture, 254, 329, 330–
    331, 332, 334, 336, 338, 344, 353–354
  Spencer as commander of, 185, 301,
    330–331
  in training, 152, 156, 159–160, 162
US 370th Infantry Regiment. *See* US 8th
    Illinois Infantry Regiment (370th)
US 371st Infantry Regiment
  and attachment to French 157th
    Division, 195–196, 197, 198, 199,
    201, 211–212, 298–299, 354–355

and Séchault monument, 417, 419, 421

white officers in, 233, 307

US 372nd Infantry Regiment

and AEF *blanchissage* (whitening) policy, 298, 306–307

AEF report on readiness of, 298–299

and attachment to French 157th Division, 195–196, 197, 198, 199, 201, 211–212, 298, 354–355

and Séchault monument, 417, 419, 421

US 969th Field Artillery Battalion (World War II), 443

Union League Club, 28, 106, 108, 387, 415

United Colored Democracy (UCD), 43–44, 49, 50, 66, 67, 70, 86, 87, 511n23

VanDerZee, James, 451–452, 470

Van Durk, William M., 348

Vann, Robert L., 294

venereal disease, 194–195, 214–215, 320, 372–373

Verbeck, William, 49, 57, 63, 65, 511n26, 513n55

victory parade, 369th, 260–261, 386–392, 395–397, 452

Vietnam War, 444

Villa, Pancho, 83, 91, 93, 103, 133

Villard, Oswald Garrison, 19, 23–24, 39–40, 55–56, 61, 66, 72, 76, 81, 146, 284, 508n53, 524n61

Wald, Lillian, 40

Walker, Madam C. J., 19, 31, 82–83, 146–147

Wallace, Thomas W., 325

Walters, Alexander, 60–61

Walton, Edward A., 176, 331, 368

Walton, Lester A., 14, 37, 89, 125, 452

Walton, Romulus Foster, 66

Wanamaker, Rodman, 387, 396

War Department, United States

and black regiment campaign, 52, 58–59, 63, 68, 78–79, 88, 91, 105–106, 109, 511n26

Charles Young and, 56–57, 71–72, 76, 81, 98–99, 142–144, 529n72

Defense Act interpretation by, 529–530n76

efficiency of, 189, 198–199

and federal recognition of 15th Regiment, 108–109, 116, 119–120, 121, 151–152, 525n3

military death sentences reviewed by, 158

and officer training camps, 128–129, 132, 527n30

and ordering of black troops out of France, 371–372

and postwar role and status of black officers and soldiers, 399, 407–412, 415, 437–438, 441–442

and 369th authorization to parade, 390–391, 399

and treatment of black combatants, 4, 105, 397, 486

*See also* Baker, Newton D.; Stimson, Henry L.

Washington, Booker T., 19, 39, 40, 41, 45, 47, 50, 56, 61, 72, 85, 102, 108, 181, 406, 516n4

Waters, James C., 409

Waters, W. O., 20

Webb, Hayward, 342

Wesley, Allen A., 39–40

Whalan, Mark, 21, 451

Whalen, Thomas, 464

Wheatley, Phillis, 24

Wheaton, J. Frank, 46–47, 52, 53, 510nn17, 18

White, Raymond, 348

White, Walter, 5, 443

Whitman, Charles S.

and black regiment campaign and formation, 44–45, 87–88, 90,

Whitman, Charles S., *continued*
92–93, 94, 98–99, 100, 101, 102, 109,
520n10, 521n17
black support for, 85, 109
and Charles Young, 98–99
and discrimination in National
Guard, 516–517n19
in elective politics, 87, 96, 367, 517n27
and federal recognition of 15th
Regiment, 106–107
and Mexico border conflict, 520n74
and support for Old 15th, 385
Wilcom-Elleger, F., 393–394
Wiley, Hugh, 400–401
Wilkin, Karen, 481, 582n21
Wilkin, Roy, 440
Willetts, Mrs. Leander, 287
Williams, Egbert "Bert," 14, 19, 32,
46, 107–109, 117, 125, 163–164, 244,
503n30
Williams, Chad L., 21, 214, 289, 375, 379,
460
Williams, Charles H., 13
Williams, Frederick, 16
Williams, John F., 437
Williams, John Sharp, 142–143
Williams, William J., 29
Williamson, Bill, 6, 7, 13
Willis-Braithwaite, Deborah, 451
Willis, Dorsie, 35
Wilson, Alexander, 287, 548n64
Wilson, Butler, 105
Wilson, Walter, 136
Wilson, William J., 28
Wilson, Woodrow
and AEF formation, 201–202
Armistice signed by, 369
and black combat troops and
officers, 439
and black regiments and troop
mobilization, 123, 124, 140
civil rights leaders' appeal to, 146–147
and 15th Regiment call to service,
148

and Houston violence, 158
and Mexico border conflict, 92–93,
520n74
and Pershing appointment, 133
racist policies of, 26, 60–62, 115–116,
122–123, 411
and US entry into WWI, 83, 117–118
W. E. B. De Bois and, 61, 294
War Council formed by, 189
Winston, Eric, 138–139, 528n58
Women's Auxiliary of the 15th/369th,
19, 124, 125, 135, 145–146, 286–287,
289, 413, 445
Wood, Leonard, 99, 104, 112–113, 128,
133, 139
Wood, Robert N., 49, 50, 66, 70, 72, 81,
572n11
Wood, Thornton H., 433
Wood, William R., 419
World War II, 4, 9, 278, 298, 437–438,
442–443

Yates, Ted, 9
YMCA, 90–91, 94, 95, 149–150, 202–203,
206, 280, 318, 319–320, 358, 375,
554nn98, 102
YWCA, 94, 317
Young, Charles
and black training camps issue, 113
death of, 144, 529n76
en route to West Africa, 245 (photo)
military service of, 54–56, 103, 521n17
as potential 15th Regiment
commander, 56–57, 66, 71–72, 103,
111
Villard as advocate for, 55, 56, 66
W. E. B. DuBois support for, 71–72,
76, 144
War Department handling of,
71–72, 76, 81, 98–99, 142–144, 310,
529nn72, 75
at West Point, 103–104